Praise for *Thomas Jefferson's Education*

"[Thomas Jefferson]'s main mission was planning for a university that would rival the great universities in the North . . . In *Thomas Jefferson's Education*, Alan Taylor . . . probes that ambitious mission in clear prose and with great insight and erudition. . . . Taylor is superb on the mistreatment of the enslaved who worked at the university." —Annette Gordon-Reed, *Atlantic*

"[Alan Taylor]'s focus is not so much on illuminating particular financial links between the university and slavery, or on documenting the indispensable contributions of African Americans to university life, although he does do both these things. The overarching purpose of his book is instead to demonstrate how the University of Virginia was from its very conception shaped and distorted by slavery, by the habits of mind and behavior slavery necessitated, by the social structures and values it yielded, by the moral compromises it required. . . . Taylor warns that Jefferson's misconceptions about education are not just history; they remain in important ways our own." —Drew Faust, *Washington Post*

"Mr. Taylor does a splendid job of documenting the sordid goings-on at William & Mary and the University of Virginia, establishing how saturated in slavery they both were." —Alan Pell Crawford, *Wall Street Journal*

"In *Thomas Jefferson's Education*, Alan Taylor . . . provides a richly detailed account of the origins of UVA. . . . Taylor presents a lively and informative analysis of the lived experience of undergraduates and professors in late 18th- and early 19th-century Virginia." —Glenn C. Altschuler, *Minneapolis Star Tribune*

"A Pulitzer prize–winning historian, Taylor explores the links between slavery and the founding of the University of Virginia. . . . Taylor shows how modern inequalities still undermine attempts to improve higher education."　　　—Michael T. Nietzel, *Forbes*

"No historian has more astutely investigated or more powerfully written about the early American republic than Alan Taylor. In *Thomas Jefferson's Education*, Taylor adds to his previous prize-winning studies of early American politics, expansion, and arts and letters, with an examination of the founders' vision of education, reckoning, at once, with its audacity and its timidity."
　　　—Jill Lepore, author of *These Truths:*
A History of the United States

"Alan Taylor's extraordinary new book illuminates the limits of republican reform in a society built on slavery. It is a major contribution to our understanding of Thomas Jefferson's career as an educational reformer and to the history of democratic self-government in Virginia."
　　　—Peter S. Onuf, Thomas Jefferson Foundation Professor
Emeritus of History, University of Virginia

"With characteristic eloquence, Alan Taylor chronicles the unlikely emergence of one of the most important experiments in American education: the University of Virginia. Caught between the promise of a new nation of freedom and the reality of a declining slave society, Thomas Jefferson and his allies forged an institution at once intellectually innovative and socially conservative. Taylor's rich, evocative book captures the surprising drama of that invention."
　　　—Edward L. Ayers, author of *The Thin Light of Freedom*

THOMAS JEFFERSON'S EDUCATION

ALAN TAYLOR

W. W. NORTON & COMPANY
Independent Publishers Since 1923

Frontispiece: Benjamin Tanner, engraving, University of Virginia, 1826 (Albert and
Shirley Small Special Collections Library, University of Virginia)

For information about permission to reproduce selections from this book, write to
Permissions, W. W. Norton & Company, Inc., 500 Fifth Avenue, New York, NY 10110

For information about special discounts for bulk purchases, please contact
W. W. Norton Special Sales at specialsales@wwnorton.com or 800-233-4830

Manufacturing by LSC Communications, Harrisonburg
Book design by Helene Berinsky
Production manager: Anna Oler

Library of Congress Cataloging-in-Publication Data

Names: Taylor, Alan, 1955– author.
Title: Thomas Jefferson's education / Alan Taylor.
Description: First edition. | New York : W. W. Norton & Company, [2019] |
Includes bibliographical references and index.
Identifiers: LCCN 2019014796 | ISBN 9780393652420 (hardcover)
Subjects: LCSH: Jefferson, Thomas, 1743–1826—Political and social views. |
Education, Higher—United States—History—19th century. |
University of Virginia—History. | Slavery—Virginia—History.
Classification: LCC E332.2 .T39 2019 | DDC 973.4/6092—dc23
LC record available at https://lccn.loc.gov/2019014796

ISBN 978-0-393-35857-5 pbk.

W. W. Norton & Company, Inc., 500 Fifth Avenue, New York, N.Y. 10110
www.wwnorton.com

W. W. Norton & Company Ltd., 15 Carlisle Street, London W1D 3BS

1 2 3 4 5 6 7 8 9 0

For Pablo, Ana,
Isabel, and Camila Ortiz

And in Memory of
Jan Lewis
and
Wilson Smith

*This institution will be based on the
illimitable freedom of the human mind.
For here we are not afraid to follow
truth wherever it may lead.*

—Thomas Jefferson, 1820

— —

Is this the fruits of your education, Sir?

—"A Slave," addressing Thomas Jefferson, 1808

CONTENTS

ILLUSTRATIONS AND MAPS

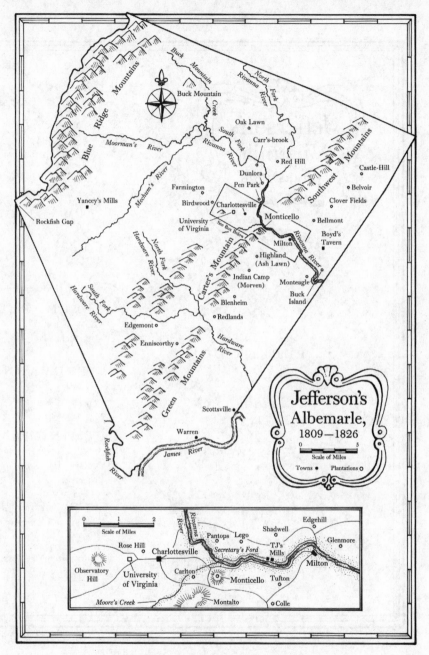

Jefferson's Albemarle, 1809–1826

(©Thomas Jefferson Foundation at Monticello)

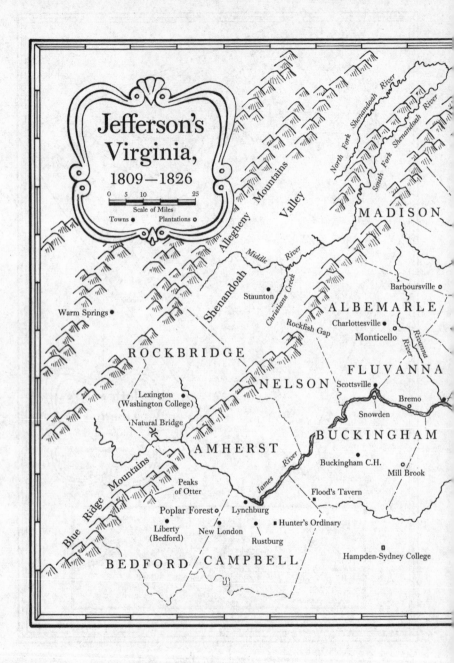

Jefferson's Virginia, 1809–1826 (©Thomas Jefferson Foundation at Monticello)

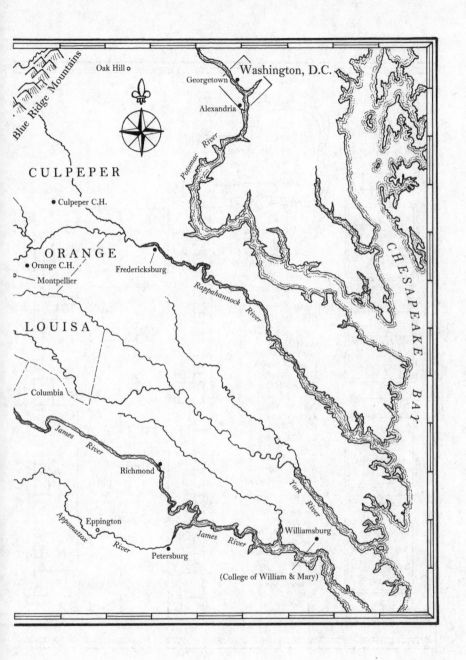

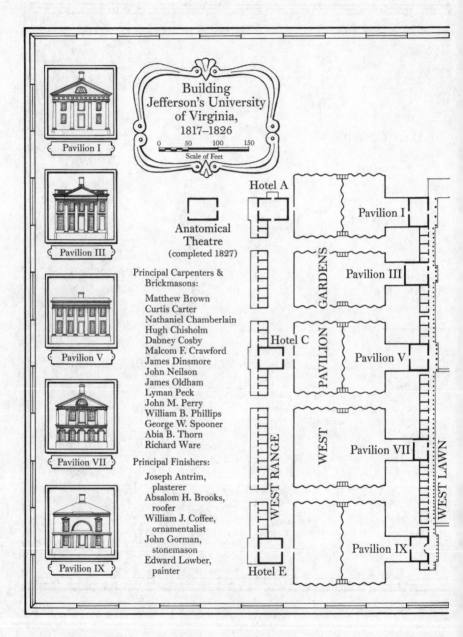

Building Jefferson's University of Virginia, 1817–1826

0   50   100   150
Scale of Feet

Anatomical Theatre
(completed 1827)

Principal Carpenters & Brickmasons:

Matthew Brown
Curtis Carter
Nathaniel Chamberlain
Hugh Chisholm
Dabney Cosby
Malcom F. Crawford
James Dinsmore
John Neilson
James Oldham
Lyman Peck
John M. Perry
William B. Phillips
George W. Spooner
Abia B. Thorn
Richard Ware

Principal Finishers:

Joseph Antrim, plasterer
Absalom H. Brooks, roofer
William J. Coffee, ornamentalist
John Gorman, stonemason
Edward Lowber, painter

Pavilion I
Pavilion III
Pavilion V
Pavilion VII
Pavilion IX

Hotel A
Hotel C
Hotel E

GARDENS
PAVILION
WEST
WEST RANGE
WEST LAWN

Pavilion I
Pavilion III
Pavilion V
Pavilion VII
Pavilion IX

Building Jefferson's University of Virginia, 1817–1826 (©Thomas Jefferson Foundation at Monticello)

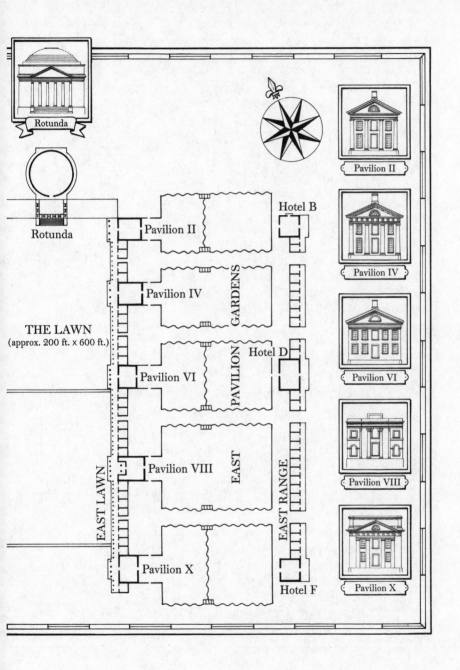

Rotunda

Rotunda

THE LAWN
(approx. 200 ft. × 600 ft.)

Pavilion II

Pavilion IV

Pavilion VI

Pavilion VIII

Pavilion X

Hotel B

Hotel D

Hotel F

EAST LAWN

PAVILION GARDENS

EAST

EAST RANGE

Pavilion II

Pavilion IV

Pavilion VI

Pavilion VIII

Pavilion X

THOMAS JEFFERSON'S
EDUCATION

INTRODUCTION

I N HIS OLDEST SURVIVING LETTER, written on June 14, 1760, Thomas Jefferson discussed his education. Jefferson lived on the family planta-tion, known as Shadwell or "the Mountain" (near where he would later build Monticello), in Albemarle County, Virginia. Aged seventeen, he sought permission from the executor of his father's estate to attend the College of William & Mary in Williamsburg: "In the first place as long as I stay at the Mountain the Loss of one fourth of my Time is inevitable, by Company's coming here and detaining me from School." He added, "By going to the College, I shall get a more universal Acquaintance, which may hereafter be serviceable to me."[1]

Thomas Jefferson, by Saint-Mémin, 1805 (Library of Congress)

Jefferson was an unusual young man: the first, and probably the last, who could plausibly pledge that he would party less if he went to college. While seeking distance from the gregarious sociability of wealthy planters, he also aspired to "universal Acquaintance," which meant building ties with sons from other prominent families. How he could make useful new friends while reducing sociability Jefferson did not explain.

Forty-eight years later, in a letter to his grandson, Jefferson credited education for saving him from "the society of horse racers, card players, [and] foxhunters." When he "recollect[ed] the various sorts of bad company with which I associated from time to time, I am astonished I did not turn off with some of them, & become as worthless to society as they were." Education enabled him to make the most of his privileged birth, large inheritance, and powerful friends by serving society rather than playing cards, racing horses, and hunting foxes. Jefferson had mixed feelings about his fellow Virginians, longing for their approval while hoping to reform their sons through improved education, just as he had transformed himself.[2]

In Jefferson's Virginia, most education was informal and took place in households, where parents taught sons and daughters how to make a living, usually by farming or housekeeping. This book deals instead with formal schooling, which was limited and sporadic for most Virginians, who acquired basic literacy from a few months in a crude, neighborhood school. Only the wealthiest families could afford further education: several years in the study of foreign and ancient languages and the new sciences at an academy and then college. In Jefferson's youth, the colony had only one college, while the postrevolutionary state had three until 1825, when Jefferson's University made four. Excluded from academies and colleges, females rarely even went to a primary school.

This book examines Jefferson's efforts to reform Virginia through education. Treating curriculum only in passing, I explore the social relationships of education: between professors, teachers, students, parents, and politicians. In this version, Jefferson's social context in Virginia looms even larger than his unique personality and career achievements. Slavery dominated that society, affecting everyone and every institution, including schools. Enslaved labor subsidized education for masters but complicated attempts to school common whites; limited female education; and blocked literacy for black Virginians. The profits of slavery also underwrote the planter hedonism that so troubled Jefferson as antithetical to self-discipline and study. The story told here was more tragic than heroic, as Jefferson's more noble aspirations became entangled in the inequalities of Virginia.

Often Jefferson serves as the inspirational prophet of schooling for all Americans, but he appears here constrained by politics and society in his own time. Never has a failed proposal received more acclaim than Jefferson's 1779 bill to educate all white children. That program faltered because Virginia's legislators preferred to keep taxes low rather than invest in schools and teachers. In 1805, a Richmond newspaper writer complained that the state would spend $50,000 annually on criminal prosecutions "and yet not give a single cent towards educating the poor": a skewed priority all too familiar today. Jefferson contributed to that failure by opting, in 1819, to secure state support for only the most elitist element of his vision: a university to educate the sons of wealthy planters, lawyers, and merchants. Never quite the egalitarian that we now wish him to be, Jefferson believed in elite rule; he just wanted to improve the planter class into a meritocracy through education. He made the University of Virginia his great legacy project, meant to train an improved generation of leaders for the state.[3]

Colonial Virginians rarely spoke of generations as distinct, for they favored continuities over time. The revolution, however, promoted a new sense of time and change, which induced leaders and educators to think of generations as real and powerful. The revolution created a republic in Virginia, but it seemed fragile as well as precious. The aging generation wanted to train young men to cherish and defend free government. In 1810, Jefferson explained, "The boys of the rising generation are to be the men of the next, and the sole guardians of the principles we deliver over to them."[4]

Unlike most of his elite peers, Jefferson also wanted the next generation to reform Virginia. By 1785, when only forty-three years old,

Jefferson announced that it was too late for him to transform society. Let younger men take up the challenge of democratizing the state constitution and emancipating the enslaved: "It is to them I look, to the rising generation, and not to the one now in power, for these great reformations." Students were supposed to accomplish what Jefferson and his generation could not, or would not, do. By building a university, Jefferson claimed to keep faith with his radical goals, even as he backed away from pushing them. But he made a desperate bet in counting on the sons of wealthy planters to liberalize Virginia. And he assigned to them a second, contradictory goal: to restore Virginia's primacy in the American Union of states. In the end, the next generation would focus on defending Virginia rather than on reforming their state.[5]

Claiming national preeminence, Virginians celebrated the superior size, population and wealth of their state. They also cited the brilliance and prominence of their great statesmen, who included Jefferson, Patrick Henry, James Madison, and George Washington. In the new Union, Virginians saw an opportunity to lead an "empire of liberty" as a projection of their power. During the early nineteenth century, however, they found their leadership challenged by northern states with dynamic economies and a moral critique of southern slavery. By creating a university in Virginia, Jefferson promised to defend state sovereignty in an increasingly contentious Union. But the revolution had changed Virginia in ways that increased the defiance of young men.[6]

During the revolution, Virginia's Patriots rejected an old regime that imagined society as properly organic and cohesive. Such a society arranged everyone in slots on a hierarchy dominated by an elite defined by superior wealth, education, manners, and connections. In that social order, common people deferred to gentlemen, who, in return, were supposed to protect the liberties and small properties of ordinary folk. Favoring social stability, that old regime distrusted social mobility from one class into another. Colonial Virginia also empowered a single Anglican Church that could tax and regulate everyone in a parish. But that church establishment had frayed during the 1760s and early 1770s, as dissenters grew in number and defiance.[7]

To rally broad support for a revolutionary war against British rule, Virginia's Patriots offered a new vision of society as a loose association of competitive individuals, each striving to get ahead. The great champion of individual rights was Jefferson, who insisted, "The rights of the whole can be no more than the sum of the rights of the individuals." When accused of promoting anarchy, Jefferson replied that truly free individuals formed social bonds naturally because of an instinct for benevolence and sociability. They needed no management by a privileged elite or an established church.[8]

In the name of individual rights, Patriots ditched the declining church establishment that had held society together in colonial Virginia. In the new republic, every free man could choose his church (or to attend no church) and elect his political leaders. No one would have to pay any tax to support a church. Virginia's Patriots took pride in separating church and state, destroying what had been the most expensive and powerful establishment in British America. Stripped of tax support and its lands, the Anglican Church withered in Virginia, as Presbyterians, Methodists, and Baptists surged in number, with no single denomination enjoying a majority or any privileged status. When challenged for failing to end slavery, Virginians replied that they had achieved something even greater by separating church and state.[9]

Individual choice meant burdens as well as opportunities, pitfalls down as well as ladders up, losers as well as winners in the race for property and power. In 1809, St. George Tucker, a judge and educator, declared: "If there was a period in the History of Man which demonstrated the necessity of a Man's being able to place his reliance on *Himself*, the last thirty years may be considered as furnishing the most awful and instructive Lessons upon that Head."[10]

Virginia's postrevolutionary society never developed the internal cohesion promised by Jefferson and other liberal theorists. Premised on equal opportunity, individualism provided weak bonds in a society as unequal as Virginia. Two-fifths of the inhabitants lived in slavery because of their race. Among free and white people, the male half denied political and property rights to women. Even among free, white men, a huge gap separated wealthy planters and lawyers from the many common people with a small farm or no land at all. A third of white men lacked enough property to qualify for the vote under Virginia's state constitution adopted in 1776. The old regime had celebrated such inequalities as a source of stability. But those inequalities seemed more ominous in a new society that was supposed to offer equal chances to get ahead. All men may have been created equal, but in Virginia they grew up unequal. Despite Jefferson's efforts, Virginia failed to endow the poor with free land or to establish a system of public schools that could have promoted social mobility by common people. Primary education cost enough to exclude most poor whites and all slaves, while higher education remained an elite monopoly.[11]

Individualism in an unequal society bred an aggressive new emphasis on honor among young gentlemen. By asserting honor, they claimed superiority over common whites, who allegedly were more crass, cowardly, and conniving. Young gentlemen defended honor so forcefully because they could no longer count on deference from common people in the new republican order. Above all, gentlemen claimed honor to display complete mastery over enslaved people. In their calculation, the true opposite of slavery was honor rather than freedom, for common whites were free but not honorable. Only gentlemen were both.[12]

Prickly about honor, young men troubled the academies and colleges of Virginia. They felt dishonored by rules that treated them as children instead of respecting them as gentlemen: as the future masters of slaves and their state. They even asserted a right to defend honor by dueling with one another. By doubling down on eating, drinking, and carousing, young men defied school rules and became the horse racers, card players, and foxhunters that Jefferson had disavowed. Above all, they refused to inform on one another when summoned before faculties or magistrates investigating misdeeds and disorder. Leading Virginians worried that a wayward new generation would fail to sustain their state's leadership in the Union.[13]

These turbulent young men created a troubling paradox for Jefferson. Only a new university could enlighten and discipline them to lead Virginia, but how could they become educated without sub-mitting to their professors? Their disorder threatened to ruin his new university meant to save them and their state. To resolve this paradox, Jefferson designed an integrated system of curriculum, rules, and build-ings meant to coax students toward self-improvement. The University expressed Jefferson's vision of an ideal society composed of liberated and cooperating individuals. But slavery skewed that University not least through the defiant honor of young masters.

Celebrating its bicentennial, the University of Virginia tends to extoll Jefferson as founder and seek a straight line from his precepts to modern strengths. But a historian wants to understand the very dif-ferent context of two hundred years ago, when Virginians created a university to defend a way of life that included slavery. Many twists and turns separate Jefferson's university from today's version, which has become far larger, more complex, and cosmopolitan. During the last sixty years, the University made new commitments to diversity and equal opportunity, including the overdue admission of women and African Americans. There is more to celebrate in what the University has become than in how it began. But we could benefit from cherished parts of Jefferson's legacy, including the pursuit of democracy, a devo-tion to rational inquiry, and a determination to pursue truth wherever it leads. If that pursuit leads us to conclude that he fell short, the burden is on us to do better.

Although set two hundred years ago in a slave society, this book tells a story with modern resonances. Our political leaders also praise educa-tion as essential to preserving freedom, but too few invest enough pub-lic money to fulfill their words. We also retain the Jeffersonian conceit of seeking reform on the cheap by redesigning education for the com-ing generation. Young people seem conveniently malleable if provided with proper instruction by suitable teachers. We just cannot agree on the means, as some reformers seek more testing while others favor more money for schools. We also clash on the ultimate goals of education: to remake students into consistent egalitarians, or rugged individualists. In fact, we cannot fully do either, for students are less moldable than we imagine. We can find a cautionary tale in Jefferson's failure to bend students to his reformed vision through a new university. Most of the students remained horse racers, card players, and foxhunters.[14]

Modern inequality impedes our efforts to reform education, and better schools, while necessary, are not sufficient to heal social divisions. True reform will have to advance on many fronts and with a sense of urgency—rather than repeat Jefferson's investment of all hope in the distant future and the elusive promise of a better-educated generation.

1

COLLEGE

L ATE IN LIFE, Thomas Jefferson recalled "the regular, annual riots & battles between the students of William & Mary, with the town boys, before the revolution, *quorum pars fui.*" The Latin translates as "of which I was a part." The colonial college's most spectacular riot erupted in July 1760 during his first year there. Some students gathered in the gallery of the Williamsburg church during services and spat and urinated on the townspeople below. Chased away, the students rallied at the College and returned to counterattack, led by two professors, who carried cutlasses and pistols. Anticipating that foray, the town's apprentices gathered in the main street, but broke and fled upon seeing the weapons. A witness

The College of William and Mary, c. 1740, appears on the top row, with the capitol and palace on the middle tier (Library of Congress)

reported that "the exulting Conquerers" returned to the College, where they drank "Bumbo and Madeira," shot off their pistols, and whipped some captive apprentices.[1]

The riot troubled Virginia's leading men because it enlisted their sons under professors from Britain. Colonial leaders feared that British influence might win over young Virginians, drawn by the allure of a cosmopolitan empire to reject the ways of their colonial parents. Peyton Randolph had a special reason to worry, for he was a preeminent politician attentive to his young cousin Jefferson. But the young man soon put his cousin's fears to rest. After the briefest flirtation with college rioting, Jefferson became the best and brightest of students. During the 1770s, he would help lead the colonial resistance to the British Empire and the church and state establishment in Virginia.

Virginia

Virginia embraced Chesapeake Bay: a vast, two-hundred-mile-long estuary replenished by the many rivers of a humid climate. On the expansive western shore, the Appomattox, James, York, Rappahannock, and Potomac Rivers framed peninsulas thrusting into the bay. Virginians distinguished between the low, relatively flat "Tidewater" region, located along the lower rivers, and the rolling hills of the "Piedmont" to the west. At the headwaters lay the mountainous Blue Ridge and, on its other side, the long and fertile Shenandoah Valley, which ran from northeast to southwest. Beyond the valley, westernmost Virginia featured heavily forested mountains.[2]

Tidewater's navigable rivers provided ships with many dispersed landings beside farms and plantations, a landscape that discouraged the development of commercial centers. Tidewater had only two: the capital at Williamsburg and the leading seaport, Norfolk, neither with populations over 3,000. Newer, more promising towns emerged along the Fall Line, the first rapids in the rivers, where the Piedmont met the Tidewater. Millers tapped the waterpower to grind wheat into flour, and merchants loaded boats with barrels of wheat or tobacco. These commercial centers included Petersburg on the Appomattox; Richmond on the James; Fredericksburg on the Rappahannock; and Alexandria on the Potomac.[3]

Virginia's searing summer heat and dense humidity shocked new-comers from cool and clammy Britain. Jonathan Boucher moaned that the heat "fevers the blood & sets all the animal Spirits in an uproar." He added, "Hence we think & act tumultuously & all in a flutter, & are Strangers to that cool Steadiness which you in England justly value yourselves upon." During prolonged midsummer droughts, a fierce sun withered crops and discouraged free people from working. Then a sud-den thunderstorm might smash the plants with wind and hail and fill the streams and rivers with torrents of rain, sweeping away riverside mills and crops. A planter complained of "this cursed climate" during summer: "After being scorched with a drought of nearly three months' continuance, we have been deluged for a fortnight past with tropical floods of water to the utter destruction of all that the drought had not ruined before."[4]

The robust nature both enthralled and sickened. In spring, the for-est blossomed with flowering plants and trees rich "with odoriferous perfumes." Summer brought abundant "fruits of exquisite relish and flavor," especially peaches. The woods resonated with singing birds, croaking frogs, and clacking cicadas. But, a planter lamented, "The air swarms with insects thirsting for the blood of man." Tidewater's mos-quitoes carried an endemic and debilitating malaria locally known as "ague and fever," which spiked in August and September.[5]

Colonists exploited the long growing season (about two hundred days) to cultivate tobacco for export to Britain. Virginians also raised pigs and corn for local consumption and kept peach orchards to make brandy. In the Piedmont, the farms and plantations grew more wheat and less tobacco, save in the southern portion, known as the Southside, between the James River to the north and the North Carolina bound-ary on the south. People and goods moved more easily along the rivers in boats than by wagons over land. The roads were rutted, stumpy, and clogged with mud—save in the droughts of midsummer.[6]

Virginia was a woody countryside pocketed with farms and

plantations. Wealthy planters built brick mansions of two or three stories on bluffs beside the rivers, and within they hung oil portraits of ancestors. Their compounds were small villages featuring wooden kitchens, smokehouses, barns, and workshops for enslaved artisans. Enslaved field hands dwelled in scattered "quarters" composed of log huts with stick-and-clay chimneys and earthen floors. White families of middling means lived in small log or plank cabins with stone chimneys and wooden floors. They lacked paint, inside or out. Instead of glass windows, most common houses had wooden shutters, open on nice days and closed in the cold and rain. A visitor reported, "Now & then a solitary farm house was to be seen, a narrow wood building, two stories high, with gable ends & a small portico over the central door. A cluster of small, miserable negro huts, a canoe & a brood of little negroes paddling in the mud completed the landscape." Jefferson added, "It is impossible to devise things more ugly, uncomfortable, and happily more perishable." Zigzag fences of wooden rails surrounded fields, while cattle and pigs roamed in the surrounding forest.[7]

To ease their rural isolation, genteel Virginians welcomed visitors, who could linger for a week or two of feasting, drinking, hunting, talking, singing, and laughing—particularly over Christmas. Boucher noted, "They are the most hospitable, generous People I ever saw. . . . And really they have the Art of Enjoying Life." Travelers marveled at the heaping meals of bacon, eggs, chicken, ham, and beef, bread and butter washed down with wine, brandy, tea, and coffee. Languid leisure as well as abundant food displayed freedom in a land of slavery and long, hot summers. Enslaved people mocked and envied the laziness of their master, likening him to the hog who "does not do anything except eat, drink and stroll about; he lies down when the fancy takes him; he lives like a *gentleman*."[8]

Rather than take pride in their work, Virginians boasted of their hospitality, praising their own generosity as superior to all others, particularly those frosty colonists dwelling to the north. When reminded of any fault in their character or society, Virginians insisted that their congeniality redeemed all. Called indolent, wasteful, boastful, and superficial—that mattered little to the Virginian proud of gregarious generosity as the consummate merit.[9]

Inequality prevailed in colonial Virginia. A traveler noted, "There is a greater distinction supported between the different classes of life here, than perhaps in any of the rest of the colonies." Wealthy and genteel planters dominated the more numerous common whites. A French visitor noted the many "miserable huts inhabited by whites, whose wan looks and ragged garments bespeak poverty." Common whites disdained education, Boucher explained, because they lived among illiterate slaves, for the white man "whilst he sees others who are still lower, he ceases to be ashamed of his deficiencies." Enslaved people comprised two-fifths of Virginia's inhabitants. Wielding clubs and whips, masters compelled field hands to work long, hard days in ragged clothes, with scant food, before retiring to sleep in crude cabins.[10]

Because of their inequalities, Virginians fussed over external appearances to display status and read that of others. Seeking the latest British fashions in clothing and furniture, the gentry ran up debts beyond what their crops could pay. A traveler received this apt advice: "Virginians are a very gentle, well-dressed people, & look p[er]haps, more at a Man's Outside than his Inside. . . . Pray go very Clean, neat & handsomely Dressed in Virginia."[11]

To consolidate wealth, genteel sons and daughters married into related families, turning the ruling gentry into an extended cousinage. Blands, Blairs, Burwells, Byrds, Carters, Corbins, Harrisons, Lees, Ludwells, Nelsons, Nicholases, Pages, and Randolphs led their counties as justices of the court, vestries of the church parish, officers of the militia, and representatives in a legislature, known as the House of Burgesses. Each patriarch owned thousands of acres and scores of slaves, but a few also dabbled in the law.[12]

The gentry relied on common whites to control enslaved people and fight Indians on the western frontier. At elections, commoners selected between ambitious gentlemen competing for seats in the legislature. Every county, no matter how populous or small, chose two representatives. Only a white man who owned a farm or shop could vote, for gender, poverty, or race disqualified most adults from civic rights. Women, children, slaves, indentured servants, free blacks, or white men without property seemed too dependent on others to exercise free choice. Even widows with land lacked the vote because the culture denigrated all females as unstable and untrustworthy.[13]

The preeminent gentlemen held lifetime appointments in the smaller house of the legislature—the Council—that advised the governor, managed patronage in the counties, and controlled grants of frontier lands. Often in the thousands of acres, those grants favored younger members and protégés of elite families in a process that extended their power westward and into the next generation.[14]

The gentry educated their sons to claim cultural and social superiority by mastering sacred, classical, and legal texts. Education in the Greek and Latin classics elevated a young man far above the common folk. Learning also improved diction, avoiding the drawling speech of commoners. Nathaniel Burwell declared that an uneducated young man was "unfit for any Gentleman's conversation & therefore a Scandalous person & a Shame to his Relations." Virginians measured learning as an ability to shine in conversation.[15]

Rather than support public schools for all, gentlemen hired tutors to board with them and teach their children and those of nearby friends. Few Virginians became tutors because that role smacked of dependence and required study, so planters imported them from the northern colonies or Britain. After a few years with a tutor, the boys (but not girls) could venture off to a boarding school kept by an Anglican clergyman.[16]

To cap an elite education, genteel sons went to college, usually the College of William & Mary or the College of New Jersey (the future Princeton). Some families could afford to send sons to a British university, which offered the finest learning and most polished manners in the empire. Richard Ambler shipped his boys to England to procure "such an Education as may set you above the common level & drudgery of Life." Ambler reminded them "that many Children capable of learning are condemned to the necessity of Labouring hard, for want of ability in their Parents to give them an Education. You cannot, therefore, sufficiently Adore the Divine Providence, who has placed your Parents above the lower Class and thereby enabled them to be at the expense of giving you such an Education which (if not now neglected by you) will preserve you in the same Class & Rank among mankind." [17]

Relishing the advantages of birth and higher education, Virginia gentlemen dreaded social mobility, lest it elevate commoners and reduce their own sons to the lower ranks. They defended an unequal social order with themselves at the top, common whites in the middle, and slaves on the bottom. Colonel Richard Bland explained, "Societies of men could not subsist unless there were a subordination of one to another, and that from the highest to the lowest degree. . . . That in this subordination, the department of slaves must be filled by some, or there would be a defect in the scale of order." [18]

Virginians struck outsiders as paradoxes prone to extremes. An English visitor concluded: "In short, take them all together, they form a strange combination of incongruous, contradictory qualities and principles directly opposite; the best and the worst, the most valuable and the most worthless, elegant accomplishments and savage brutality, being in many of them most unaccountably blended." This was Thomas Jefferson's Virginia. [19]

Inheritance

Birth entitled Jefferson to a privileged place in an unequal society. His father, Peter Jefferson, was an ambitious land surveyor and speculator who had grown wealthy by helping to extend planter society westward into the Piedmont during the 1730s. He settled in Albemarle County, on the red clay hills around the upper James River and its tributary, the Rivanna. These navigable rivers linked the county to Tidewater society and the transatlantic market with Britain. Eastern gentlemen hired Peter Jefferson to find and survey the best tracts of frontier land beside the rivers. Then they secured large grants from the royal governor and Council for themselves and Jefferson. The grantees brought in scores of slaves to work their core plantations and sold marginal plots to common farmers. A visitor to Albemarle County reported that the enslaved could "seldom get anything to eat than [a] bread made of corn. . . . They are very poorly clad, almost half naked." Albemarle was a land of opportunity for free folk because they exploited the labor of slaves just as their parents and grandparents did in the Tidewater.[20]

In Albemarle, Peter Jefferson acquired 7,200 acres and more than 60 slaves, who tended the house and cultivated corn and tobacco. His enslaved artisans worked as blacksmiths, carpenters, and boatmen. He erected a riverside mill to grind grain for his household and earn fees from common farmers. No raw frontiersman, Jefferson built a fine mansion named Shadwell, which he stuffed with fashionable furniture and British books. Shadwell replicated elite Tidewater ways designed for raising refined children and hosting genteel guests. His wealth and congeniality qualified him to become the county surveyor, commander of the local militia, a court justice, and parish vestryman. An active, able, and wealthy man, he represented Albemarle County in the House of Burgesses. Jefferson also benefited from a fortunate marriage, for his wife Jane came from the prestigious Randolph family and was the daughter of a wealthy merchant with London connections. Jefferson ranked in the top 1 percent of the county's property owners, with enslaved people making up three-quarters of the value of his estate.[21]

Born in 1743, Thomas Jefferson was the couple's second child but eldest son, and male privilege favored him over his older sister Jane. Slavery was literally in the mother's milk that nourished him. The prompt birth of another child a year after Thomas indicates that his mother Jane did not nurse him for long. Considering breast-feeding debilitating, a Virginia lady relied on an enslaved wet nurse, who had milk because of the recent birth of her own child. By nursing the master's son, she partially deprived her son or daughter.[22]

Jefferson grew up with the contrasts of a plantation, where masters ate huge meals, wore fine clothes, rode fast horses, slept in a grand house, entertained genteel guests, and commanded, bought, sold, and punished enslaved people, who could do none of those nice things.

Slaves prepared and served food, cleared and washed dishes, cleaned the house, tended at births, nursed children, repaired carriages, made clothing, shoed horses, and tended the garden. They also hoed, weeded, harvested, cured, packed, and shipped tobacco to market. The son of a master often became sexually active by exploiting an enslaved woman. More than some abstraction, slaves were familiar faces, who knew all too well those who owned them.[23]

In 1757, at age forty-nine, Peter Jefferson died, leaving Jane a widow responsible for eight living children. His will carefully distributed that property to preserve genteel standards for his children while differentiating among them to specify roles based on gender and age. Each daughter received £200 in money plus one house slave. Fourteen-year-old Thomas inherited most of the slaves and land, including the Shadwell estate. He also obtained key tokens of Peter's learning and authority: his desk, silver sword, books, mathematical instruments, and the estate's most valuable slave, a valet named Sawney. But until Thomas Jefferson turned twenty-one, four executors managed the property.[24]

In 1758, Jefferson went to the school kept by Reverend James Maury, an Anglican who held the parish near Shadwell and had delivered the funeral sermon for Peter Jefferson. Praising Maury as "a correct classical scholar," Jefferson declared, "I thank on my knees him who directed my early education for having put into my possession this rich source of delight." Jefferson cherished his school days and mates: "Reviewing the course of a long & sufficiently successful life, I find in no portion of it, happier moments than those were." In his last, ailing months of life, Jefferson wrote to a classmate, declaring that he would "welcome the hour which shall once more reassemble our ant[ient] class with its venerable head," James Maury. Jefferson did not often write about heaven, but he anticipated a school reunion there.[25]

Born in Ireland to a Protestant family of French origins, Maury came to Virginia as an infant with his parents. Educated at William & Mary, he settled in Albemarle, where he secured a large farm. Learned, energetic, and genial, Maury was a clear thinker, elegant writer, and eloquent speaker. Jefferson recalled that Maury lost his composure on just one subject: "I was at school with Mr. Maury during the years 1758 & 1759 and often heard him inveigh against the iniquity of the act of 1758 called the two-penny act." Passed by the House of Burgesses, that act threatened to degrade the social standing of parsons beneath that of the gentry.[26]

Parsons

Virginia's gentry were proud of living in the oldest, largest, richest, and most populous colony of British America. A fifth of the continent's British colonists and half of the enslaved people lived in Virginia, which a resident boasted was "the brightest gem in his Majesty's crown." Gentlemen delighted in British books, plays, and fashions, and they revered the king and his empire. After dining with a gentry family, an Englishman noted, "The first toasts which are given by the Master of the family, are the King; the Queen and royal family; the Governour and Virginia; a good price for Tobacco." To demonstrate that loyalty, the House of Burgesses committed men and money to fight the Indians and French on the western frontier.[27]

Thanks to their loyalty, power, and contributions, Virginia's gentry claimed a privileged position in the empire. They expected imperial support for their own vast claims to frontier lands that stretched west to the Mississippi and north to the Great Lakes. This projected empire included about 359,480 square miles, most of it still held by Indians and their allies, the French based in Canada and Louisiana. Determined to build an American empire within the global British Empire, Virginians wanted acceptance as partners with the aristocrats who governed in London. Because Lord Botetourt flattered that conception, he became the most popular of Virginia's royal governors. Botetourt imported a grand and gilded coach with a Latin motto on the side: *En dat Virginia quartam*, which translates as Virginia rules a quarter of the world. This vision of imperial grandeur meant, however, that Virginians bristled at any British interference in the management of their counties, slaves, and clergymen.[28]

Leading Virginians sustained the monarch's favored church, and they discouraged religious dissenters from rival denominations. In 1751, five parsons praised the "Glory of this Colony, which hitherto hath been remarkably happy for uniformity of Religion." The Church of England (or "Anglican Church") provided a bond of community in a colonial society in which people lived dispersed and usually pursued pleasure and profit. The church was "established": favored over competitors by law and supported with taxes. Virginia's leaders insisted that religious uniformity promoted a Christian morality deemed essential to law and order. Maury explained that church and government had "such a close & mutual Dependence & connection with each other, & reciprocally give & receive such Stability & Support to & from each other, that they must necessarily stand or fall together." Without such cohesion, gentry and clergy imagined society collapsing into a grim and violent anarchy of unrestrained self-assertion.[29]

The establishment was expensive. Each parish sustained a substantial brick church and provided the minister with a farm (known as a "glebe") and an annual salary, set by provincial law, at 16,000 pounds of tobacco, which the minister then sold for cash or credit. About half of the parishes also provided a few slaves to help work the glebe. At an average of thirty-five pounds of tobacco per taxpayer, the parish levy was twice as high as any other tax paid in a Virginia county.[30]

Virginia lacked a bishop, which invited the colony's gentry to fill the gap between king and parsons. In each parish, a dozen gentlemen served on the vestry, which administered the church and collected taxes to pay the parson's salary and maintain his glebe. As county magistrates, the gentry enforced laws requiring every free man, no matter his private beliefs, to attend church and pay the parish tax. No marriage in Virginia was legally valid unless performed, for a fee, by an Anglican parson, and the vestry provided poor relief for free whites.[31]

Learning pulled gentry and parsons together—and set both apart from the common folk, who were barely literate. But clergy and vestry contested the uncertain and uneasy boundary between their spheres of authority. A parson expected to correct the morality and guide the spirituality of the gentry, who set a tone for the rest of the community. Vestrymen, however, meant to control the parson as an employee, hiring and firing as they saw fit. Coveting status as gentlemen, parsons dreaded dependence on another man as demeaning and impoverishing. According to Maury, parsons wanted recognition as "Gentlemen, Christians, and Clergymen"—a revealing sequence of priority. Many parsons shared in the gentry vices, buying fine clothes, and drinking and gambling at cards and dice with the glee of vestrymen. Gentlemen often caroused at night with their parson, only to denounce his excesses once everyone sobered up in the morning. The gentry held the clergy to a double standard: to behave like gentlemen without their sins.[32]

Virginia had some spectacularly wicked parsons, including Reverend John Ramsay, who held the southern parish in Albemarle County. In 1767, the vestry denounced Ramsay for beating his wife, seducing a parishioner's spouse, and preaching while drunk with profane results. But we find only a handful of such cases among more than a hundred clergymen. As fair-minded people noted, most parsons were dutiful and moral men like James Maury. But Virginians loved to gossip, spreading and magnifying the scandals of a few through the colony to tar most parsons as lazy degenerates who lost the respect of their laity.[33]

The crisis came in 1755, when a prolonged drought reduced the tobacco crop, so prices tripled to 6 pence a pound. Instead of their usual pay in tobacco worth about £140, a parson stood to make £400. Planters, large and small, struggled to pay their tax in tobacco, but parsons relished the windfall income as their just desserts. They wanted to profit in tough times just as planters did when the market favored them, but the gentry held a trump card: control of the House of Burgesses. In 1755, that legislature passed the "Two-Penny Act," a law converting the tax from tobacco to money at an artificially low price of 2 pence per pound. Payment reverted to tobacco in the good harvests of 1756 and 1757, but the Burgesses passed another Two-Penny Act in 1758, when drought again curtailed the crop and inflated the price of tobacco. In 1755 and 1758, the governor approved both acts because he needed legislative support for his priority: raising money and men to fight the French.[34]

Parsons howled that their compensation shifted from tobacco to money and back again depending on which "shall happen to be the least profitable." Clergymen felt subordinated to the gentry, who governed the colony for their own benefit. "Our being deprived of the benefit of this rising market, will still keep us in debt & so in a dependent State, a thing much aimed at by the great men of this Country," ten parsons complained to the Bishop of London.[35]

Several intrepid parsons, including Maury, petitioned the Crown to reject the Two-Penny Act. Their leader was John Camm, the learned but acerbic professor of moral philosophy at William & Mary. Governor Francis Fauquier denounced Camm as "a Man of Abilities but a Turbulent Man who delights to live in a Flame." English-born and Cambridge-educated, Camm had risen from a middling family thanks to a scholarship. In late 1758, he returned to London to lobby the Crown on behalf of the parsons. In August 1759, the king's Privy Council vetoed the Two-Penny Act and impugned Fauquier for approving an unjust and irregular law.[36]

That ruling outraged Virginia's leaders, who felt insulted and exposed when denied their cherished pose as the king's most loyal subjects. In response, they developed a new constitutional position that defined the House of Burgesses as fully sovereign within Virginia, conceding authority to the empire only for external trade and war. The gentry denied that the Crown could intervene in social relations within Virginia—such as those between parsons and vestries. No longer able to shelter under the Crown's authority, the gentry recast their common constituents as sovereign within Virginia and treated the parsons as traitors to the colony.[37]

Both gentry and parsons claimed to defend liberty, which in Virginia always brought up its inversion, slavery. A young lawyer, Edmund Randolph, noted, "The system of slavery, howsoever baneful to virtue, begat a pride, which nourished a quick and acute sense of the rights of freemen." Parsons often interpreted this gentry pride as domineering. In a moment of frustration, one parson urged his patrons in England to "send no more of your young gentlemen into this wretched land of

Tyrants & Slaves." Camm mocked Colonel Richard Bland, a leading Burgess, for describing Virginia as a land of English liberty where "all Men are born free." Detecting hypocrisy, Camm asked, "Does the Colonel mean to affirm that Virginia is not an *English Government*, or that Negroes are not under it *born Slaves*, or that the said Slaves are not *Men*?" Had Bland forgotten "the *Aegyptian* Bondage of his own Slaves." Camm also owned slaves, but he never mistook Virginia for a land of liberty.[38]

Returning to Virginia with the Privy Council ruling in 1760, Camm called on Governor Fauquier at his palace in Williamsburg. In a rage, Fauquier confronted Camm in the lobby and ordered him to depart and never return. To complete the insult, Fauquier summoned his slaves. Pointing at Camm, the governor told them, "Look at this gentleman, look at him that you may know him again & if he ever attempt[s] to come hither do not suffer him to enter my gates." One of the other parsons noted the depth of "this last indignity, for it is the greatest affront that can be put upon a free man here to give orders concerning him to the slaves. It is what a white servant would not endure." By subjecting Camm to the authority of slaves, Fauquier declared the parson as no longer a proper white man. Another Virginian explained that Fauquier had marked out Camm as "a black Sheep."[39]

After the Privy Council ruling, the battle over the Two-Penny Act shifted into the courts of Virginia, where several parsons sought back pay from their vestries. The most celebrated case involved Maury. In November 1763 in Hanover County, judges ruled in his favor, but left determination of the damages to a jury. In that phase of the trial, a young, ambitious, and eloquent lawyer, Patrick Henry, defended the vestry by escalating the stakes. Henry denounced parsons as greedy "Enemies of the Community" for appealing to the distant king, who acted as a tyrant by annulling the Two-Penny Act. After just five minutes of deliberation, the jurors returned with an insulting award of a single penny for Maury, far short of his true loss of £288.[40]

Celebrated for his courtroom performance, Henry won election to the House of Burgesses, where he became a fiery critic of king and parliament. The other parsons also lost their cases, depriving them of any benefit from the Privy Council's ruling. Despite this legal nullification, the gentry had received a great scare from the ruling, which put them on high alert to resist all British measures to enhance imperial power. In particular, they resented new taxes levied on the colonists by Parliament during the 1760s.[41]

As gentry and parsons wrangled, they emboldened dissenting preachers to seek converts, challenging the ideal of religious uniformity. During the 1740s and 1750s, evangelical Presbyterians, known as New Lights, competed with the Church of Virginia. During the 1760s, an even fiercer challenge appeared with "Separate Baptists," who claimed a license from Jesus to preach wherever and however they wished. They compensated for their lack of schooling with emotional fervor. The Baptist itinerant preachers shocked Anglicans, who insisted that a minister required years of formal education and ordination by learned parsons.[42]

The itinerants offered a fiery and spontaneous style of extemporaneous preaching that appealed to common people. Practicing a more emotional and evangelical faith, dissenters denounced parsons as sinners devoid of divine grace; their soothing, droning, soulless words could only lull poor listeners to a hellish eternity. If few parsons were truly wicked, most seemed dull, for they read written sermons and appealed to reason. In sharp contrast, evangelical preaching was so pointed, personal, and emotional that listeners fell down twitching and speaking strange words. Evangelicals insisted that only complete submission could win salvation from the awesome power of God. They appealed to souls troubled by the world and longing for a heavenly respite after death. Preachers cultivated in listeners a painful despair until it ripened into an emotional release, known as the New Birth, a feeling of blissful union with God.[43]

Evangelicals demanded a strict new code of behavior, renouncing the worldly pleasures of Anglican gentry and parsons as soul-sapping distractions from the pursuit of eternal salvation. An Anglican teacher complained that dissenters were "destroying pleasure in the Country; for they encourage ardent Prayer, strong & constant faith, & an intire Banishment of Gaming, Dancing, & Sabbath-Day Diversions." Joining an evangelical church meant submitting to moral supervision by new brethren and sisters.[44]

Asserting the right of each soul to choose his or her own faith, evangelicals challenged the overlap of church, state, and society so dear to gentry and parsons. Itinerant ministers defied Virginia law, which demanded that they obtain a license and preach in no more than one county. Magistrates arrested, jailed, and fined preachers or encouraged common mobs to disrupt evangelical meetings, sometimes flogging or dunking preachers, to parody their baptisms. Relishing the role of martyrs, they converted punishment into performances of evangelical zeal by shaking off a jailing, dunking, or whipping to resume preaching. This persistence through pain won converts and spread doubts among the gentry about the wisdom of further persecution.[45]

Some parsons concluded that they needed a bishop in Virginia to resist inroads by dissenters. A resident bishop would save prospective clergymen from the high cost and many miseries of crossing the Atlantic for ordination in distant and expensive London. A bishop could purge the clergy of a few bad apples who tainted the rest. Fewer bad, old parsons and more good, new ones promised to roll back the rising tide of dissent. Proponents added that a bishop would reverse Virginia's drift away from British rule.[46]

But the proposed bishop outraged Burgesses, who defended their control over the clergy in Virginia. Many gentlemen questioned their uneasy partnership with parsons in propping up a tottering establishment. With religious uniformity declining, gentry sought a new way to manage society without a church establishment. The path forward lay with Thomas Jefferson, who proposed to make individual consent the basis for religious and political authority. He developed these radical ideas as a student at the College of William & Mary.[47]

Masters

In March 1760, on the cusp of his seventeenth birthday, Jefferson enrolled at the College in Williamsburg. He was tall and thin, with red hair and freckles. He disliked William & Mary's large, rambling main building that he described, along with the nearby insane asylum, as "rude, misshapen piles, which, but that they have roofs, would be taken for brick-kilns." A friend recalled that Jefferson developed a passion for building after buying a book on architecture "from an old drunken Cabinetmaker" who lived near the College gate. The friend marveled that this purchase later led Jefferson to design a sprawling university and "that immense pile of building on the top of Monticello."[48]

Located on a level plain, Williamsburg had a population of 1,800 and a main street one hundred feet wide, a mile long, and named for the Duke of Gloucester. At the east end of town, a brick Capitol housed the legislature. A royal coat of arms, featuring lion and unicorn, appeared over the front door. At the west end of the street, three brick buildings comprised the College. Midway along the street on the north side, a traveler came to Bruton Parish Church, where a parson preached from a lofty pulpit and the governor had an elevated pew with a canopy overhead. Across the street stood a brick magazine filled with gunpowder and weapons to arm free men in case of a slave revolt or French invasion. On the opposite side of a green lay the local courthouse. At the northern edge of the green stood the governor's elegant brick palace, topped with a wooden cupola. Artificially sustained by its status as the colonial capital, Williamsburg lacked any port or other geographic advantage and supported no manufacturing and little commerce. Most of the 250 private homes and shops were built of wood and painted white, giving the village a gleam.[49]

During the 1760s, the College of William & Mary was an intense microcosm of the larger clash of Virginia gentry with imperial authority. On this smaller stage, the conflict also pivoted on a constitutional controversy, in this case over the College's royal charter. That document failed to specify the boundary between the authority of faculty and the superintending Board of Visitors, composed of eighteen prominent men, including the colony's governor. The Visitors made governing statutes, dismissed defiant and deviant professors, and meddled in managing students and staff: housekeeper, gardener, bursar, and usher. The

Visitors treated the college as their property and the faculty as employees. In return, a professor denounced the Visitors as "ignorant & intemperate men totally unqualified for the important Trust of directing & governing" a college devoted to "propagating Religion & Learning."[50]

Born in England and educated at the universities of Cambridge and Oxford, the professors were ordained Anglican clergymen. They claimed life tenure and the power as "Masters" to govern the staff, design curriculum, award degrees and scholarships, and discipline students: "We presume to think that we are not the servants of the Visitors; we have a Charter to incorporate us into a regular Society." While accepting the Visitors as legislators who framed the institution's rules, professors claimed equal power as executives who applied the rules "without further Control from the Visitors." Professors appealed to the king, "as supreme Visitor of the College," to determine their dispute by defining the charter's terms. That appeal outraged Visitors as repeating the treachery of the parsons in protesting the Two-Penny Act.[51]

The six faculty included an overworked Master of the grammar school, who taught Greek and Latin to many adolescent students preparing to enter the College. By contrast, the underworked Master of the Indian school usually had only a couple of Natives to instruct—and soon enough those managed to escape. Few students worked with the two professors of divinity. Many more attended the two professors of philosophy, one specializing in rhetoric, logic, and ethics, and the other in physics, metaphysics, and mathematics. A professor usually doubled his income by serving as a parson in a nearby parish, where he performed Sunday services.[52]

The College's arrangement of space reinforced a hierarchy derived from Oxford and Cambridge. At meals in the dining hall, the Masters sat at an elevated table overlooking the lower tables for students. In each classroom, the presiding Master occupied a raised seat atop a pulpit. In chapel, the students sat on crude benches while honored guests filled the prime pews in front. At 3,000 volumes, the library was substantial for the time, but heavy on theology and light on contemporary science.[53]

Defined by a religious purpose, the student's day began with morning prayers in the chapel: at six in the summer and seven in winter.
After a round of classes, the day ended with readings in chapel from
the Anglican Book of Common Prayer. At nine in the evening, students
attended a roll call in the Common Room, before they retired to their
beds. Sunday offered a full Anglican service either in the chapel or in
nearby Bruton Parish Church. Every student had to learn the Anglican catechism in English and Latin. But the regimentation had scant
impact on young Virginians used to having their way. In a given year,
about seventy attended the grammar school, and fifty the College. Most
came for only a year or two to get a smattering of education, so almost
all left without a degree rather than meet the high standards enforced
by the Masters.[54]

Masters expected to enforce student discipline, including corporal
punishment, "without Respect of Persons." But the students came from
prestigious families with friends and relatives on the Board of Visitors. As the owners of slaves, Virginians expected to inflict rather than
receive blows. Young gentlemen resented submission to mastery by
English-born professors. The tutor Philip Fithian reported that, when
Robert Carter returned home from William & Mary, his sister Nancy
mocked him "with being often flogged . . . by the Masters in College."
This "so violently exasperated *Bob* that he struck her in his Rage."[55]

At the College, older students claimed immunity from punishment
and the power to beat grammar students and enslaved servants. In
1756, the faculty expelled Cole Digges and Matthew Hubard "not only
for their remarkable Idleness & bad Behaviour in general, but particularly for whipping the little Boys in the Grammar School." The Masters
also sacked Hubard's brother, James, who served as an usher, when he
interfered with the disciplinary hearing.[56]

Unfortunately for the faculty, Digges and the Hubards had friends
in high places. In 1757, the Visitors retaliated by firing the grammar
Master and forcing another professor to resign and return to England.
Then the Visitors demanded that the president and three remaining
professors reinstate James Hubard as an usher. The weak-willed and

alcoholic president, Thomas Dawson, agreed, for he kept his post by doing the Visitors' bidding. The other three professors refused, insisting that the Visitors lacked jurisdiction. In November, the Board sacked the defiant three. One promptly caved and won reinstatement, but two— John Camm and Richard Graham—went to England and petitioned the Privy Council for restoration to their positions.[57]

In 1758, three replacement professors arrived from Britain: Goronwy Owen, Jacob Rowe, and William Small. To the Visitors' dismay, Owen and Rowe defied the president and became notorious for public drinking and profanity. In July 1760, they led a student riot against the townspeople, which was the last straw. In August, the Visitors tried Rowe, who confessed to all charges save for insulting the president "whom he said he had not used ill, as he did not deserve any better Treatment." That did it. The board sacked Rowe and Owen, but their removal failed to subdue faculty resistance, because Camm and Graham returned in 1763 with a Privy Council order restoring them to the College.[58]

The key flashpoint remained the power to discipline students. A faculty supporter complained that Visitors relied on "private information of the Boys in the Grammar School," so that the professors were "more properly under the care of their Pupils than vice versa." Masters accused Visitors of inviting students "to enter into a Contest with us to try whether they have not a more powerful Influence with the Visitors than the President & Masters have." If so, the professors asked, "Would not their Authority & Government be at an End?"[59]

In April 1769, students rioted in the dining hall, making "uncommon Waste & Havock" to furniture, plates, and windows. Frustrated in an investigation, the Masters concluded "that the Youth of this College, some from a false Notion of Honour & others from Fear of being beaten & abused by the Delinquents" had vowed "to maintain a Falsehood [rather] than to utter any Evidence" against a fellow student. Here lay the roots of the student code of silence that would cause so much trouble at Virginia's colleges in the next generation.[60]

The faculty regarded Thomas Byrd as the ringleader. When confronted, Byrd denied the charge and demanded to know the names of those who had informed against him as "he would call them to Account . . . that he would knock them down." Then Byrd boldly confessed and defied the faculty to do anything about it, adding that he neglected his studies because "he had no Genius to be a scholar and . . . that his Father did not expect him to receive any Improvement at the College." His father, William Byrd III, was one of the colony's leaders and a Visitor. Rather than back down, the faculty "resolved that the said Thomas Byrd should submit to a Whipping in the grammar School." Young Byrd replied "that he would never submit to that Punishment and concluded with many violent & threatening Expressions against the President." When the elder Byrd showed up a day later, the faculty withdrew their sentence "out of regard to the Father." Instead, they expelled Thomas, which his family deemed less disgraceful than a whipping.[61]

The faculty retreat shifted the battlefront in favor of the students. No longer able to whip boys from elite families, professors faced student demands to command and strike slaves belonging to the College. At home, young gentlemen had learned that their honor demanded extracting submission from slaves at all times, so any saucy encounter required immediate punishment. Students acted as if they, and not the College, owned the help. William & Mary had about a dozen resident enslaved people, who cleaned rooms, built and repaired buildings, chopped and hauled firewood, tended the garden, cooked and served meals, cleaned and mended clothes, nursed sick students and, in any spare time, ran errands for the boys. At night, they slept on the floors of the kitchens, sheds, and shops where they worked by day. They did all the work that students disdained doing for themselves—and had to do it with a docile, ingratiating manner or risk blows. William & Mary also owned a 2,119-acre plantation on the Nottoway River, stocked with thirty slaves, who raised tobacco to support four scholarship students.[62]

In November 1769, John Byrd, younger brother to Thomas Byrd, entered the dining hall with a horsewhip in hand. He seized an enslaved boy. When the housekeeper protested, Byrd replied that "he would horsewhip her also." The College president intervened, but Byrd "made use of many oaths and indecent expressions which . . . showed a gross contempt of the President." Fearing another intervention by Visitor Byrd, the faculty settled for ordering John to "ask pardon of the President for the personal affront to him, and of the Society for . . . ill treatment of their Servant." As the mastery of the faculty shrank, that of the students grew.[63]

Visitors and Masters also clashed over educational philosophy. The Visitors favored lower academic standards and few examinations, lest rigor discourage their sons and evaluation empower the faculty. Given that most students would run plantations, Visitors wanted a practical curriculum that taught basic skills such as surveying rather than adhere to the traditional Cambridge-Oxford emphasis on philosophy and ancient languages. Claiming the power to allocate student scholarships, the Visitors favored family pedigree over academic diligence.[64]

Masters rejected the "undistinguishing Cheapness of Education," fearing that parents would encourage sons to "quit their Classical Reading & Exercises very early for the Sake of making a premature & superficial Progress in the Mathematics." Doubling down on the traditional model, professors wanted enhanced rigor, a longer period of study, and discretionary power to reward or punish students. Instruction should proceed in three measured stages: a thorough grounding in classics, then a mastery of natural and moral philosophy, and finally professional training in theology, law, or medicine. This program would stretch schooling into a student's early twenties, as in Britain.[65]

The wrangling sapped the College's reputation. Visitors spread scandalous stories of drunken and lazy faculty indulging raucous youth. Masters begged the Visitors (in vain) to "forbear [from] general & aggravated Harangues on the Irregularities of Youth & the Disorders of the College, which destroy its Reputation." Professors insisted that the Visitors caroused at least as much and undermined the college discipline by meddling. But the Visitors succeeded in spinning their version of the college's woes to other Virginians. As with gossip about parsons in general, tales of immoral faculty from England seemed more compelling than reiterating the familiar vices of local gentlemen.[66]

Manners

Jefferson praised Williamsburg as "the finest school of manners and morals that ever existed in America." Visiting the Capitol, Jefferson saw legislative leaders and learned legal and political procedures. His musical talent and precocious brilliance won attention from Governor Fauquier. An amateur musician, Fauquier befriended the College's most cosmopolitan professor, William Small, who brought along Jefferson to play violin in weekly concerts of chamber music. The governor also hosted frequent dinners attended by Small, Jefferson, and their mutual friend, the lawyer George Wythe. "At these dinners, I have heard more good sense, more rational & philosophical conversations than in all my life besides," Jefferson recalled.[67]

Teaching natural philosophy and mathematics, Small became Jefferson's cherished mentor: "To his enlightened & affectionate guidance of my studies while at College, I am indebted for everything." The first layman appointed to the faculty, Small taught with "an extraordinary conjunction of eloquence & logic" that, Jefferson concluded, had "fixed the destinies of my life."[68]

Small championed the Enlightenment, the eighteenth-century intellectual movement that challenged traditional beliefs and institutions, deeming them tainted by the superstition of priests and corrupted by rulers empowered by birth rather than ability. For Small, as for Jefferson, truth was progressive, emerging from new, careful, and rational inquiry and experimentation. Small and Jefferson called this inquiry "science," which for them embraced more than our current use of the term. Their science meant any systematic investigation that revealed new and fundamental truths: in history, law, linguistics, literature, and politics—as well as in the biological and physical sciences. Jefferson noted, "From his conversation I got my first views of the expansion of science & of the system of things in which we are placed."[69]

Jefferson was an exceptional student capable of studying fifteen hours a day, despite the pranks of peers, who broke into his room at night to overturn the table and dash off with some of his books. A friend marveled that Jefferson "could tear himself away from his dearest friends, to fly to his studies." He never received a degree at the college, but almost no one did during the 1760s. After two years of study with Small, Jefferson moved down the street to learn law with George Wythe. Erudite, polite, and kind, Wythe became another profound influence on Jefferson.[70]

Although raised an Anglican, Jefferson developed doubts about traditional Christianity, as Small and Wythe drew him toward "deism." Promoted by the Enlightenment, deism tested Christian scriptures against rational skepticism to eliminate the miraculous. Deists insisted that God had created a perfectly synchronized cosmos, comprehensible fully and only by reason. Thereafter, the creator did not interfere in the world, but instead allowed the laws of nature to unfold and maintain the universe. Rejecting the Trinity of orthodox Christianity, deists regarded Jesus as the most ethical and inspirational teacher of men—but just a man and not a dimension of God. Deists disdained traditional Christianity as distorted by selfish priests, who sought power over credulous minds. By exposing contradictions in the scriptures, deists promised to free people from superstition and tyranny. Conventional Christians, however, denounced deism as a heresy known as "Socinianism" or simply as "infidelity" to the true faith.[71]

A more conventional Virginian, Edmund Randolph, noted that Jefferson persuaded other young gentlemen to challenge religious orthodoxy: "When Mr. Jefferson first attracted notice, Christianity was directly denied in Virginia only by a few. He was an adept, however, in the ensnaring subtleties of deism; and gave it, among the rising generation, a philosophical patronage, which repudiates as falsehoods things unsusceptible of strict demonstration."[72]

Admitted to the Virginia bar in 1767, Jefferson often competed in the courts with Patrick Henry, his primary rival. They exhibited stark contrasts in personality, for Jefferson was a learned student of the law, while Henry lacked the discipline to read. Edmund Randolph recalled, "Mr. Jefferson drew copiously from the depths of the law, Mr. Henry from the recesses of the human heart." Never attending college, Henry had studied human nature as a barkeeper. With a touch of envy, Jefferson recalled Henry as blessed with a popular temperament: "His passion was fiddling, dancing & pleasantry. He excelled in the last and it attached everyone to him." Jefferson lacked flair in addressing jurors, while Henry came alive in a courtroom, playing to passions and prejudices. Jefferson resented that Henry got ahead with so little work, for it affirmed Virginians' conceit that native genius required little cultivation. Where Jefferson sought to transcend the company of foxhunters and cardplayers, Henry was the life of their party.[73]

Jefferson frequently returned from the court circuit to manage his Shadwell plantation. His first publication was a 1769 newspaper advertisement for a runaway, a shoemaker and carpenter named Sandy, thirty-five years old, short and stout and "something of a horse jockey; he is greatly addicted to drink, and when drunk is insolent and disorderly, in his conversation he swears much, and his behavior is artful and knavish." Sandy allegedly lacked the self-control that Jefferson cultivated in himself. Recovering Sandy, Jefferson sold him four years later.[74]

In January 1772, Jefferson married, at age twenty-eight, a young (twenty-three), charming, and propertied widow, Martha Wayles Skelton. Her former husband had been Jefferson's friend at the College. Her father was John Wayles, a leading lawyer, planter, and slave trader from Charles City County. Jefferson recalled Wayles as a consummate Virginian: lacking "eminence in the science of his profession" but "a most agreeable companion, full of pleasantry & good humor, and welcomed in every society." His welcome extended into the slave quarters, where Wayles took a mistress, Elizabeth Hemings, who bore him six children, including Sally Hemings. Wayles died in May 1773, leaving his "handsome fortune" to three free daughters and their husbands.

Martha's and Thomas's inherited assets included the Hemings family, who were skilled artisans and house servants. To secure those assets, Jefferson assumed a third of Wayles's debts owed to British merchants for consumer goods and imported slaves. In many and growing ways, Jefferson was indebted to slavery.[75]

Elected to the House of Burgesses in 1769, Jefferson embraced the Patriot cause, which challenged taxation by Parliament. Virginia's leaders felt vulnerable to increased British power because of their declining incomes and mounting debts. Six generations of erosion and tobacco cropping had depleted the Tidewater soil, reducing harvests and profits. The many new farms and plantations in the Piedmont and Southside glutted the overseas market with tobacco, depressing prices. Imperial trade regulations also compelled Virginians to export their crop only to Britain, where merchants reaped the profits of transshipment to continental Europe. Parliament also skewed the terms of trade in favor of Britain by banning the paper money issued by colonies to compensate for their shortage of gold and silver coin. Virginians blamed their economic woes on exploitation by British merchants. Jefferson complained that debts became "hereditary from father to son for many generations, so that the planters were a species of property annexed to certain mercantile houses in London."[76]

Planters defended their "independence," which was especially precious in an unequal society, where they saw the dependence of debt and slavery all around them. A visitor from Britain noted, "They are haughty and jealous of their liberties, impatient of restraint, and can scarcely bear the thought of being controuled by any superior power." Virginians opposed any new insertion of British power within their colony, their empire within the empire.[77]

Virginia's gentlemen sympathized with Boston's Patriots, who dumped taxed tea into their harbor. In 1774, Parliament punished Boston by shutting down the port and occupying it with military force. Britain also revoked the charter of Massachusetts to impose a more arbitrary colonial government. Dreading those ominous precedents, Virginia's elite sought to rally public support for the New

Englanders. In the House of Burgesses, Jefferson helped the cause by drafting a pious resolution for the clergy to read to their parishioners, recommending a solemn fast to show solidarity with suffering Boston. Setting aside his religious doubts, Jefferson understood the need, Edmund Randolph explained, "to electrify the people from the pulpit." Jefferson later boasted, "Our fast produced very considerable effect" as the people "came together in great multitudes." The message had to be powerful to persuade Virginians to cease eating from sunrise to sunset.[78]

The fast-day resolution enraged the royal governor, Lord Dunmore, who dissolved the House of Burgesses. The members simply moved up the street to meet in rump session at the Raleigh Tavern, where they created county committees to coordinate resistance to British taxes by enforcing a boycott on imports from the mother country. The committees became an alternative, Patriot frame of government that worked around the royal governor and his Council. Patriot mobs marginalized and punished the few Virginians who dared violate the boycott or speak against it. As a vivid warning to Loyalists, Patriots hung a bag of feathers over a barrel of tar on Duke of Gloucester Street. Helpless to suppress the Patriot committees and mobs, Dunmore hoped in vain that "the lower class of people" would "discover that they have been duped by the richer sort."[79]

Whip

In 1775, as Virginians approached revolution, the College students escalated their conflict with Masters over controlling enslaved servants. In May, eight students, including a future president of the United States, James Monroe, accused the College's housekeeper, Maria Digges, of entrusting "the Keys of the Store Room to the Slaves to which they have been seen to have free Ingress & Egress." Allegedly, she also barred the enslaved from performing errands for students. But they offered no credible evidence when the faculty investigated their complaints. The worst witness was Monroe, who testified "that he never read the Petition, & consequently could not undertake to prove a single Article."[80]

Digges did better in her own defense, blaming the trouble on James Innes, a grammar school usher with a fiery personality and huge body, so tall and wide that people thought him the largest person in Virginia. He also had a booming voice, keen wit, and strong mind. Entering the college in 1770, he excelled and secured a coveted Nottoway Plantation scholarship endowed by slave labor on the college plantation. Three years later, he won a degree, one of the precious few issued by the College, and the faculty appointed him as an usher. Rather than control his students, Innes rallied them for the Patriots and to the detriment of slaves.[81]

Rebuking Innes for his "warm and passionate Temper," the faculty denounced "his Beating & Punishing the Negroes of the College when he thinks them in fault, which has encouraged Students to do the same, and which tends to transfer the Command of the said Negroes from the President and Masters to the Ushers & Students." The faculty concluded "that the Students will best consult their own Interest, the credit of the College, and the Welfare of their Country by attending to their own peculiar Studies & Business, leaving the care and regulations of the Servants to the President and Professors."[82]

Instead of returning to his teaching duties, Innes recruited students for an armed company of "Williamsburg Volunteers" to challenge the royal governor. The Masters complained that the student volunteers gathered at a tavern during "unseasonable hours until some of them were drunk, which occasioned a midnight disturbance in the College." Returning to the college in the wee hours of May 17, the patriotic students harassed Professor Gwatkin, who had supported Digges and denounced Innes. The rioters beat on "Mr. Gwatkin's Door in so violent a manner" that he feared for his life. The student rioters included Walker Maury, a son of the late Reverend James Maury. The faculty compelled him to acknowledge "the Necessity of maintaining a due Subordination, a proper Obedience & Respect to my Superiours in a Collegiate Society." The professors defended a fading tradition at a time of revolution.[83]

Irritated by Innes and his volunteers, Lord Dunmore sent Royal Marines at night to seize gunpowder from the town's public magazine for transfer to a Royal Navy vessel in the nearby York River. Innes and an angry mob gathered at the palace gates to menace the governor and demand the powder back. Instead, Dunmore threatened to "declare Freedom to the Slaves and reduce the City of Williamsburg to Ashes." By seizing the gunpowder, Dunmore enhanced Patriot alarm, for without sufficient firepower, the planters might lose to rebel slaves.[84]

Innes's armed volunteers patrolled the Williamsburg streets and kept the governor cooped up in his palace. On the night of June 7–8, claiming to fear assassination by Innes, Dunmore escaped to a British warship. Innes's volunteers then broke into the palace and plundered it. Disgusted with "rebellious colonists and disorderly collegians," Professors Thomas Gwatkin and Samuel Henley joined Dunmore in flight from the revolution. The two professors left behind papers, books, and household furniture. To the victor went some of the spoils, for Jefferson scooped up the best of their collections for his library.[85]

Dunmore attempted a military comeback with black soldiers recruited from runaways who reached his warships and camp near Norfolk. By freeing and arming slaves, Dunmore outraged white Virginians, converting many waverers into Patriots. Jefferson noted that Dunmore had "raised our country into [a] perfect phrensy." But Dunmore lost his bid to reclaim Virginia. After suffering defeats and a smallpox epidemic that depleted his men, Dunmore gave up and sailed away in August 1776.[86]

Virginia's Patriots fought to preserve their liberty by maintaining slavery. Most regarded enslaved labor as an economic and social foundation for sustaining the freedom of white men. Indeed, the sale of slaves helped finance the revolution in Virginia. The Bland family sold forty slaves to buy imported gunpowder to replace that taken from the Williamsburg magazine by Dunmore. Patriots also confiscated his slaves and sold them. The push by students to control the College slaves paralleled efforts by their parents to oust their British rulers who threatened to compromise the slave system.[87]

Madison

In 1772, John Camm had become the College president. As war erupted in 1775, he defended old standards of hierarchy and order despite the revolutionary turmoil in the nearby streets of Williamsburg. For students, however, the excitement outside their windows made studying seem tedious and pointless. Vandalism surged, producing more broken windows, and some students brought firearms to their rooms. In September, Camm tried to ban students from leaving the college to visit town without a Master's permission. In defiance of that futile order, the revolution continued to flow into the College, where students and professors clashed over controlling the enslaved servants. In November, the faculty lamented "the run of ill treatment which has of late been bestowed by the Boys upon the Servants of the College both Male & Female and the contemptuous conduct of them towards the President & Professors."[88]

In May 1776, Virginia's Provincial Congress declared the colony a state independent from Britain, more than a month before the United States followed suit. Only one delegate, Robert Carter Nicholas, spoke against independence as premature. The conservative champion of tradition, including the church establishment, Nicholas felt threatened by revolutionary change. In the end, he went along with his peers, declaring "that he would rise or fall with his country," Virginia. The final vote was unanimous: the sort of elite solidarity cherished by the gentry.[89]

Filling the streets of Williamsburg, common people destroyed royal symbols that included the coat of arms over the entrance to the Capitol and the gilded coach left behind by the late and formerly beloved governor, Lord Botetourt. Edmund Randolph noted, "So irrational was the fury of some, that the noble statue, which public affection had erected to the memory of Lord Botetourt . . . was with difficulty saved from a midnight attack." Although spared destruction, the statue suffered much abuse, primarily from patriotic college students.[90]

At the College, the future belonged to James Madison, a cousin of the more famous statesman of that name. Raised in Augusta County, this

Madison was "a very clever Lad," who attended James Maury's school, where he met and befriended Jefferson. Madison briefly served as an assistant teacher at a prep school run by Reverend Jonathan Boucher, a fiery Loyalist who soon dismissed Madison as "pert and petulant." In 1770, Madison entered the College, and won a rare degree as an exceptional student. He then served as an usher in the grammar school while studying law with George Wythe. In 1773, Madison became the College's professor of natural philosophy and mathematics.[91]

A Patriot, Madison exploited the revolution to replace Camm as the College's president. Per the royal charter, William & Mary derived an income by commissioning the land surveyors of Virginia. On November 29, 1776, in a meeting of the faculty, Madison moved to cease dating these commissions from the regnal year of the king in favor of "the Date from the Birth of our Saviour." While the other three professors supported the change, Camm dissented. He acted not out of blind loyalty to the king but from a well-informed devotion to the College's royal charter. By adhering to the letter of that charter, he protected faculty autonomy from domination by Visitors and legislators. For more than thirty years, including two visits to England, Camm had defended that charter for the professors' benefit. In 1776, he saw Madison as an opportunist butchering the precious charter to serve himself and a revolution. But Madison had cleverly trapped Camm into taking a public position that tainted him as a Loyalist. The Visitors sacked Camm and appointed Madison as the new president. The coup resolved the long-standing power struggle between faculty and Visitors, with the latter winning in a rout. Thereafter, they controlled the faculty and could even meddle in the curriculum.[92]

Purging the College, the Visitors fired others cast as crypto-Loyalists, including the housekeeper, Maria Digges, who had clashed with James Innes. Early in the revolution, Innes recruited her impressionable younger brother Edward for his volunteers. But the two men fell out during the war, when Innes commandeered two cannon to discharge in Duke of Gloucester Street at the peak of a festive ball. By taking the cannon without permission, Innes irritated the state's governor, Patrick

Henry, who sent Captain Edward Digges with sixty soldiers to reclaim them. A witness recalled, "Innes stepped up to Captain Digges and, shaking his cane at him, swore that he would *cane him* if he did not depart instantly with his men!" Backing down, Digges marched his troops away "and the evening closed with great joy" and the firing of cannon. Disgraced by defeat, Digges lost his reason, becoming the babbling ward of his impoverished sister.[93]

After the war, Maria Digges sent a pathetic letter to Jefferson, whom she had known in Williamsburg during the 1760s. Begging for $100, she wrote, "Immagination cannot furnish Ideas Strong Enugh to Paint my Distrest Melancholy Situation. . . . I live in a Cottage that I feare, will Crush us." She supported her invalid brother, who was "in a Derainged State quite unable to Assist him Self." Digges concluded, "Wee have all Suffered by the late Revelution." Many had suffered, but not Innes, who rose to become Virginia's attorney general, or Jefferson, who succeeded Henry as governor of the new state.[94]

As governor during the late 1770s, Jefferson had tried to modernize and republicanize the College of William & Mary. He urged the legislature "to aid and improve that seminary, in which those who are to be the future guardians of the rights and liberties of their country may be endowed with science and virtue." Jefferson wanted legislators to revoke the royal charter and substitute its own to "render the institution publicly advantageous in proportion as it is publicly expensive." But the legislature balked at altering the charter and investing in the College, so Jefferson turned to the Board of Visitors to implement his plan. In December 1779, at a meeting chaired by Jefferson, the Board eliminated both divinity positions and the grammar school, substituting new professorships in anatomy and medicine, modern languages, and law. Jefferson made the College more secular and scientific.[95]

Although reformed, the College was nearly bankrupt. Most of its endowment derived from Britain, and the imperial government sequestered that property during the conflict. Desperate for money to wage war, the state legislature could not fill the gap. Indeed, legislators reassigned the College's income from taxes on exported tobacco and imported liquors. Madison mourned, "Since the Revolution, its former Resources have been almost annihilated." From a prewar annual income of £5,000 sterling, the College's revenues shrank to just £500 in 1780. In early 1781, the grim finances led Madison to consider reviving his legal career: "The Law is disagreeable—but Divinity & Philosophy . . . will starve a Man in these Times."[96]

To obtain cash, the College liquidated assets, beginning in 1777, with the sale of thirty slaves employed at the Nottoway Plantation. Madison also sold off half of the enslaved staff at the College, reducing the total to just five people, too few to clean rooms and serve meals. The short-handed College obliged students to board in town. When the revolution began, students tried to control the institution's slaves, but the war left few for them to bully.[97]

Deprived of endowment and starved of public funding, William & Mary depended on student tuition more than ever. But enrollment declined as young men went off to war or just stayed away to avoid exposure in Williamsburg to British attack. Skyrocketing inflation also undercut the value of tuition, until Madison converted it from the state's worthless paper money to pounds of tobacco. By 1780, it cost a student 1,000 pounds of tobacco annually per professor. The College could only afford to educate young men with lots of tobacco. Access to the College narrowed as costs soared and the faculty eliminated scholarships. In the name of republican austerity, William & Mary became more elitist, for only the sons of the rich could afford to attend. Such ironies do revolutions make.[98]

As compensation for higher costs, the faculty allowed greater lee-way to the students, who no longer had to pass an entrance exam to demonstrate proficiency in Greek and Latin. The collegians also could choose their classes, contrary to the tradition of a prescribed course of study. No other students in Europe or America had so much autonomy in designing (or neglecting) their studies.[99]

The changes scandalized Jedediah Morse, a New Englander used to more rigorous and religious standards. In 1786, Morse visited William & Mary to find just thirty students, who "attend or not as they please.

When the Lecture is delivered, the business of the day is done, both for Professor & the Student. They have no public Prayers, Morning nor Evening, no recitations, no public Speaking, no examinations to determine the proficiency of the Students, excepting when they receive their degrees, no attention to the dead languages." Students had plenty of time to spend "in the Tavern [or] at the Gaming table without control." Morse concluded: "Such, however incredible, is the State of William & Mary College."[100]

Madison, however, insisted that a republicanized William & Mary could regenerate Virginia's imperial power. In 1780, he exulted, "But surely it belongs to our Colleges & Universities to lay the Foundation from which the future glory of America shall arise." No longer charged with conserving a hierarchy, as in the colonial past, postrevolutionary colleges were supposed to build an idealized republic. In theory, a republic provided equal rights and favored individual merit rather than the privileges of birth or corporate entitlements. But promoting equality and opportunity was easier said than done in a society as unequal as that of Virginia.[101]

2

REVOLUTION

T HOMAS JEFFERSON DID NOT WANT to write the Declaration of
Independence for the United States. In the spring of 1776, as a
member of the Continental Congress, he favored independence but
thought that someone else could write the document, for Jefferson had

Bishop James Madison (1749–1812), by unknown
(Virginia Museum of History & Culture)

somewhere more important to be. By returning to Virginia, he could write a new constitution for the state, which he called his "country." Jefferson considered Virginia far more real and significant than the United States, which seemed weak and evanescent. He was a Virginian rather than an American, but there were precious few Americans in 1776. Almost everyone identified with a home state and regarded the United States as an awkward, wartime necessity that probably would not last.

Jefferson longed to define a republican government for Virginia: "In truth, it is the whole object of the present controversy." Passionate in his political philosophy, Jefferson feared letting this opportunity slip into the hands of other, lesser men. But Virginia's leaders rejected his pleas for permission to leave Congress and return to write the state's constitution.[1]

Unable to attend in person, Jefferson sent to the state convention a draft constitution that expressed his democratic vision. Jefferson proposed elected sheriffs; legislative representation proportioned by population; inheritance reforms to discourage concentrations of wealth and privilege; and allowing almost all white men to vote, by providing poor people with small farms taken from public lands. Jefferson also wanted to abolish the Anglican establishment by separating church and state. But his proposed constitution was dead on arrival, for it asked the delegates to sacrifice their county oligarchies. By the time Jefferson could slip away from Philadelphia, in mid-August, the delegates had adopted a conservative constitution that he despised for the rest of his life.[2]

In that constitution, counties elected the state legislators who formed two houses. The numerous and powerful House of Delegates replaced the colonial House of Burgesses, and a smaller, more exclusive, but less important State Senate succeeded the Council. The constitution shifted the regional balance of power away from Tidewater in favor of the Piedmont but did not similarly empower the far western counties. Each county, no matter how large or small, elected two men to the House of Delegates, a distribution that favored the older, smaller, and numerous eastern counties while denying proportional representation to the newer and larger counties west of the Blue Ridge.[3]

The Tidewater and Piedmont leaders made common cause on leg-islative representation, insisting that they needed greater power to protect their enslaved property. The constitution restricted the vote to white men who owned at least fifty acres of land or a town property of comparable value. The property requirement disenfranchised a third of Virginia's white men. Virginia's leaders did not trust poor whites in general, and westerners in particular, to understand and protect the slave system.[4]

The constitution weakened the governor and empowered the legisla-ture, particularly the House of Delegates. Virginia's governor could not veto legislation, and his decisions needed approval by a Council of State chosen by, and from, the legislators. The joint houses of the legislature met together at the end of each year to choose the governor, who could serve for no more than three years.[5]

The constitution included a Bill of Rights, which began with a sweep-ing philosophical premise: "that all men are by nature equally free and independent." This wording struck Robert Carter Nicholas as absurd and pernicious, a standing invitation to poor whites or enslaved blacks to wrest property and power away from their superiors. According to Edmund Randolph, the delegates answered Nicholas's concerns "with too great an indifference to futurity, and not without inconsistency, that with arms in our hands, asserting the general rights of man, we ought not to be too nice and too restricted in the delineation of them." In other words, during the Revolutionary War, Patriot leaders needed to inspire common white men to fight for them. The delegates also reassured Nicholas "that slaves, not being constituent members of our society, could never pretend to any benefit from such a maxim." The delegates founded a republic to benefit white men by excluding black people from political society.[6]

Although briefly shaken, slavery survived the war to become as important as ever in Virginia. Natural increase more than compensated for the 6,000 runaways who fled to the British during the war. When peace returned in 1783, the state had 236,000 enslaved people, up from 210,000 at the start. In 1790, nearly half of the nation's enslaved people lived in Virginia.[7]

Leading Patriots recognized the gap between their soaring ideals and the sordid practice of slavery. While fighting for liberty, St. George Tucker noted, "We were imposing upon our fellow men, who differ in complexion from us, a *slavery* ten thousand times more cruel than the utmost extremity of those grievances and oppressions, of which we complained. . . . Should we not have loosed their chains, and broken their fetters?" Patrick Henry regarded slavery "as repugnant to humanity as it is inconsistent with the bible, and destructive to liberty." But Henry never freed his slaves, citing "the general inconveniency of living here without them." Enslaved people comprised so much property in debt-ridden Virginia that emancipation would ruin many white men and their creditors.[8]

Revolution benefited the Piedmont at the expense of the Tidewater. The old gentry of the Tidewater were relatively reluctant Patriots while the Piedmont leaders, including Henry and Jefferson, aggressively pushed the revolution. In the process, they advanced themselves and their region. The new leaders proved more comfortable and adept at appealing for votes from common citizens, for Patriots had to mobilize farmers and artisans to fight the British and guard the enslaved.[9]

Tidewater bore the brunt of wartime raids and a postwar depression. Taking advantage of Tidewater's decline, in 1780 Piedmont's legislators moved the state capital out of Williamsburg and up the James River to Richmond. Legislators supposed that the inland location promised greater security from British coastal raids. After the war, many old estates collapsed from lawsuits, leaving the losers with the hollow pride of genteel poverty. Tidewater looked worn and depressed. Many old fields reverted to second-growth forests of stunted pines. A traveler described the farms as "miserably poor. Here and there a hovel and the inhabitants of them look half starved." John Randolph mourned the landscape of decay: "Nothing . . . can be more melancholy than the aspect of the whole country on tide-water,—dismantled country-seats, ruinous churches, fields forsaken, and grown up with mournful evergreens,—cedar and pine."[10]

The College stayed in Williamsburg, where it trained the next generation of political leaders. Eleven of the state's first seventeen governors attended William & Mary—as did thirteen of the twenty-four judges of the state supreme court. But the College was vulnerable to the ascendant power of the Piedmont, whose leaders regarded the Tidewater climate as unhealthy for their sons. In 1792, Edmund Randolph aptly predicted: "I suspect that the day is not very far off, when the remaining property [of William & Mary] will be transferred by some violent act of the legislature to the erection of a university, in the neighbourhood of Richmond. The influence of the lower country would avail nothing against such a project."[11]

Reform

Patriots challenged the colonial conception of society as a corporate body that could compel individual adherence to collective goals such as religious uniformity. They also rejected the traditional notion of society as held together by a hierarchy with a monarch at the top and gradations of inequality stretching downward through the gentry and middle class to laborers, servants, and slaves at the bottom. To dissolve the old corporate and hierarchical society, Jefferson insisted that society consisted of freely contracting and autonomous individuals, each with the same rights (except for enslaved people). Once truly freed from hierarchy and coercion, he argued, individuals would naturally cooperate because of their instinctual sociability. He explained, "I am among those who think well of the human character generally. I consider man as formed for society, and endowed by nature with those dispositions which fit him for society."[12]

Patriots claimed that merit triumphed when individuals could freely compete for property and political office. Deriding inherited advantages as artificial, they sought to substitute a more "natural" social order led by worthy men advanced by popular election. They believed that a just society had a "natural aristocracy" of talented men, who would emerge in each generation, empowered by accomplishments rather than inheritance. Although born into wealth, Jefferson considered himself a natural rather than an artificial aristocrat because, he asserted, of his efforts to serve common men.[13]

Patriot leaders persuaded common folk that the revolution would improve their prospects and status. Downplaying the inequality of property, Patriots promised a new equality of legal and political rights. The revolution enhanced opportunities for ambitious commoners by increasing the number of leadership positions as militia officers, county committeemen, and legislators. The Patriots cut the poll tax, the colony's most regressive levy on white men. By defending the slave system against Lord Dunmore's 1775 offer of freedom to runaways, Patriot leaders also appealed to small farmers, who owned or rented a slave or two, or who hoped someday to do so.[14]

During the revolution, Virginia's political leadership shifted from the old gentlemen planters to lawyers who often doubled as planters, such as Jefferson. Although a minority in the House of Delegates, lawyers shone as the best-educated and most experienced speakers. They held sway in a republican political culture, where oratory moved voters and backbenchers. Less polished legislators needed expert help in drafting laws. Starting in the 1790s, the elite also included more bankers, who financed campaigns, and newspaper editors, who persuaded voters to support their new rulers as champions of liberty in a slave state.[15]

Some leaders disliked the more competitive and contentious society of a republic. A scion of an elite family, John Randolph, felt nostalgic for colonial Virginia. Instead of "the Nelsons, and Pages, and Byrds, and Fairfaxes, living in their palaces, and driving their coaches and six," while sipping madeira and claret, postwar Virginia was run by "a knot of deputy sheriffs and hack attorneys, each with his cruet of whiskey before him, and [a] puddle of tobacco-spittle between his legs." Randolph predicted worse to come: "The old families of Virginia will form connections with low people, and sink into the mass of overseers' sons and daughters; and this is the ... inevitable conclusion to which Mr. Jefferson and his leveling system has brought us."[16]

A champion of inequality, Randolph derided Jefferson's philosophical introduction to the Declaration of Independence: "That all men

are born free and equal, I can never assent to, for the best of all reasons, because it is not true." Mocking Jefferson's radical rhetoric and
eccentric attire, Randolph declared, "We are governed by the old red
breeches of that Prince of Projectors, St. Thomas of Cantingbury." Eloquent at hyperbole, Randolph exaggerated Jefferson's power to democ-
ratize a society based on slavery.[17]

Church and State

During the hard-fought war, Virginia's Patriots needed support from
all quarters of the state, including the growing number of evangelicals.
In June 1776, to promote unity, the state's new Bill of Rights guaranteed
the "free exercise of religion, according to the dictates of conscience."
In a key step, Patriots redefined freedom of conscience as a natural and
inalienable right rather than a concession granted by the legislature.
Therefore, no magistrate could violate any man's conscience by forcing
him to attend or support another church.[18]

Taking Anglicans for granted, Patriot leaders sought evangelical
support for the war effort. In return for helping to recruit young men
for the Patriot army, dissenters demanded an end to the church establishment. Championing free choice by individuals, evangelicals posed
as the truest republicans. In Albemarle County, a Baptist elder preached
that "he knew of no difference between his patriotism and his religion."
Formerly seen as a threat to the social hierarchy of colonial Virginia,
evangelicals championed the new social order premised on equal rights
for free white men. In December 1776, the legislature suspended tax
support for Anglican ministers—and made that shift permanent three
years later. In return, the legislators promised to protect Anglican property, including glebes and churches, "in all time coming."[19]

To compensate for lost tax support, Anglican ministers relied on
subscriptions by vestrymen and other leading parishioners. But too
many subscribers failed to pay. As more laymen defected to evangelical
meetings or lapsed into irreligion, the remaining subscribers balked at
their growing burden to support a dying church. In 1783 one parson

wrote: "The revolution, however important in its effects, has been fatal to the Clergy of Virginia. From a fixed salary they are reduced to depend on a precarious subscription for bread." Ministers could count on little, he concluded, in a society where "every man [is] at liberty to contribute or not to the support of the Minister of his own persuasion as he judges best."[20]

In Albemarle County, the Anglican parson Charles Clay had given fiery sermons in support of revolution. "Cursed be he who keepeth back his sword from blood in this war," because, Clay explained, the "cause of liberty was the cause of God." Grateful for his Patriot politics, Jefferson arranged a subscription to replace the parson's tax-based salary. While Jefferson paid, most of his neighbors defaulted. Irritated, Clay suspended church services and sued the vestrymen, which soured them on his ministry. In 1784, Clay moved away to Bedford County and abandoned the clergy to turn politician: a far more promising career in the new republic. When he died, Clay's will mandated erecting "an immense heap of stones," twenty feet wide by twelve feet high, over his grave—as if he feared that former parishioners would steal his body as they had taken his income. The heap and grave now survive on a golf course.[21]

During the war, Anglican parsonages and churches suffered from vandalism by common Patriots who claimed to smite symbols of royal domination. When parsons retired or moved away, most parishes were too poor to replace them. As pulpits became empty, the outflow of parishioners to evangelical churches or rowdy taverns became a flood. Common folk preferred either more whiskey or the cheaper ministry of Baptist preachers, who made do with small contributions while tending their own small farms. Losing his parishioners, the Reverend Devereux Jarrett mourned: "When I now go to places where formerly some hundreds used to attend my sermons, I can scarcely get forty hearers."[22]

After the war, Anglicans tried to rebuild their battered church. In 1784, the Reverend David Griffith rallied Churchmen to petition the legislature for authority to reorganize as the Church of Virginia, free from British control. No longer Anglican, the church became Episcopalian. The Episcopal Church could only prosper, one parson predicted, if legislators again "thought public religion essential not only to the good order but to the very existence of government. . . . Otherwise, they cannot reasonably expect that religion will flourish in a country where its ministers are reduced to a state of beggary and contempt."[23]

Episcopalians subscribed to a Gresham's law of religion: that cheap preaching drove out the good. Who would devote expense and years to study theology without the prospect of secure financial support from a parish? Instead, people would favor cheap Baptist preachers, who believed, a critic lamented, that any "layman or mechanic, if he finds a motion within him from the spirit, may leap from the anvil or plough and in a few minutes" become a minister without "sitting a number of years in a college." Unless obliged to pay for learned ministers, ignorant people would prefer "the harangues of fanaticks" over "the most sensible discourses of sober-minded, rational men."[24]

Individual choice in religion appalled traditionalists as "wholly selfish and unsocial" because it denied a community's right to demand that everyone pay something for public worship. Episcopalians insisted that public morality was a public good, which required tax support for community worship. A leading Patriot, Richard Henry Lee, warned, "The experience of all times shows Religion to be the guardian of morals— and he must be a very inattentive observer in our Country, who does not see that avarice is accomplishing the destruction of religion, for want of a legal obligation to contribute something to its support." Without publicly funded religion, society allegedly would collapse into a vicious, selfish anarchy.[25]

Rather than revive their old establishment, Episcopalians sought legal incorporation and a general-assessment tax to support ministers of all denominations. Incorporation would secure the title of Episcopal vestries to church property and provide, through an annual convention, a governing body. This change would free the church from past laws regulating the church and from future intervention by legislators. A general assessment would tax every landholder but allow him to choose the church that should receive his payment, or he could designate his payment to support a school. The bill amended the voluntary principles of the new order by denying the most common choice made by Virginians: to support no church and no school.[26]

Entitled "Establishing a Provision for Teachers of the Christian Religion," the general assessment bill treated religion as educational, as meant to promote "a general diffusion of Christian *knowledge* . . . to correct the morals of men, restrain their vices, and preserve the peace of society." The bill implicitly favored college-educated clergymen— Episcopalians and Presbyterians—at the expense of unlettered Baptists and Methodists. Proponents insisted that Virginia needed "learned teachers who may be thereby enabled to devote their time and attention to the duty of instructing" common people. Finally, the bill designated "seminaries of learning," primarily conducted by Episcopalians and Presbyterians, as the default beneficiaries of the new tax.[27]

Baptists denounced Episcopal incorporation and general assessment as reuniting church and state, contrary to Virginia's Bill of Rights. Evangelicals regarded any relationship between church and state as mutually corrosive. A newspaper writer explained, "The Church and the State are two societies, and in their natures and designs, as different as Heaven and Earth, and to unite them in one, is greatly to injure, if not utterly to ruin, both together." Baptists insisted that ministers should answer only to their brethren and Jesus.[28]

With Episcopalians supporting, and Baptists opposing, a general assessment, Presbyterians became the swing element in the politics of religion. Disappointed by voluntary contributions, their clergymen found a general assessment tempting. In the fall of 1784, they tentatively endorsed the proposed tax.[29]

In the legislature, James Madison (of Orange County) opposed the general assessment bill championed by the formidable Patrick Henry. Playing for time, Madison went along with Episcopal incorporation, calculating that it would alarm Presbyterians into renewed distrust of Churchmen. Then he appealed to the legislators' cautious preference to postpone difficult decisions in favor of going home to consult their constituents. Rather than pass general assessment, they printed and circulated the bill for public consideration before adjourning. Legislative votes demonstrated strong support for assessment in the Tidewater, division in the Piedmont, and almost universal opposition in western Virginia. Jefferson applauded Madison's moves: "I am glad the Episcopalians have again shewn their teeth & fangs. The dissenters had almost forgotten them."[30]

As Madison expected, delay split the Presbyterians from the Episcopalians. "The mutual hatred of these sects has been much inflamed by the late act incorporating the [Episcopalians]. I am far from being sorry for it, as a coalition between them could alone endanger our religious rights." Presbyterian laity rebuked their clergy for flirting with Churchmen, denounced as "a set of Bungling, thick-skulled, fat-Bellied Disciples of Christ." During the summer of 1785, the clergy beat a hasty retreat, unanimously revoking support for general assessment.[31]

In August 1785, a leading Churchman, John Page, naïvely wrote to his old friend Thomas Jefferson for support. Appealing to his values of tolerance and gentility, Page insisted that only well-funded and well-educated ministers could defend rationality and inclusion against "bigoted and illiberal" evangelicals. In a reply, Jefferson characteristically avoided the controversy that divided them. Meanwhile, he wrote to Madison, early and often, to oppose assessment. More secular than Page, Jefferson counted on the free circulation of ideas outside of churches to fend off evangelical irrationality. He dismissed as counterproductive any effort by the state to favor particular churches as defenders of rationality. Jefferson overestimated the power of secularism and underestimated the evangelical drive to remake society.[32]

When the legislature reconvened in late 1785, the political tide had shifted thanks to the spring elections and the Presbyterian break with the Episcopalians. It also helped that Henry had left the legislature. Dreading his political clout, Jefferson assured Madison: "What we have to do, I think, is devo[u]tly to pray for his death." Madison had a better idea: to support Henry's election as governor, which elevated him into an honorable but impotent position. Madison also made the most of an unprecedented flood of petitions, which ran twelve-to-one against general assessment and Episcopal incorporation.[33]

Distaste for any new tax fed the unpopularity of assessment. Deeply in debt to British merchants, planters struggled to pay taxes during the mid-1780s, when a commercial depression decreased the demand for, and price of, tobacco. Already scarce, cash drained from the state to pay for imports. In 1785, the crops of tobacco and corn fell short, adding to planter woes. In 1784 and 1785, legislators delayed or reduced taxes to avoid massive defaults. A wry legislator declared, "We are all contending for popular applause & he is the cleverest fellow who bellows most against taxes" as "distressing the good citizens of the country, who are so dear to us all."[34]

The legislative supporters of assessment gave up, and Madison seized the initiative by reviving a "Statute for Religious Freedom" written by Jefferson in 1779 but postponed then. With a little tweaking to his deistical preamble, the statute passed (74 to 20) in January 1786. It banned state assistance to any church. The second shoe dropped a year later, in January 1787, when legislators repealed the act incorporating the Episcopal Church in Virginia. Repeal finally dissolved Virginia's long and special relationship with an established Church.[35]

A generational shift was manifest in the votes cast by Wilson Cary Nicholas against general assessment and Episcopal incorporation. A new representative from Albemarle County, Nicholas was the son of Robert Carter Nicholas, the pious champion of an established church before the revolution. The elder Nicholas died in 1780, and his worldly son became a political disciple of Jefferson. Nicholas's dismayed mother rebuked her son for "pulling down the Church," but there was worse yet to come for the Episcopal Church of Virginia.[36]

Glebes

The members of other denominations envied the church buildings and farm glebes retained by Episcopal ministers. Rivals cast that property as the ill-gotten gains of a corrupt establishment, which had duped and exploited the common people of colonial Virginia. Critics insisted that glebes corrupted Episcopal ministers and gave them an unfair advantage in competing for congregants. Rivals depicted the Episcopalian church as a new entity unjustly claiming the property of a shattered and discredited predecessor. In impassioned petitions to the legislature, Baptists recited colonial sufferings and dreaded an Episcopal revival. In 1790 they denounced the glebes as the bastard offspring of "the adulterous connection between Church and State, the impositions of king craft and priest craft." Bitter memories of past persecution endured in the politics of religion after the revolution.[37]

Episcopalians defended the glebes and churches as private property, which the state could not confiscate with any pretense to justice. Churchmen warned that all property lost security if legislators could seize land from an unpopular minority to please a new majority. Citing their sacrifices to sustain a united front during the revolution, Episcopalians recited the legislative pledge of 1776, reserving their church property "in all time coming." Denouncing the Baptists, Reverend David Griffith complained, "It would seem that nothing will satisfy these people but the entire destruction of the Episcopal Church." Former persecutors, Episcopalians now felt persecuted.[38]

In defending their glebes, Episcopalians suffered from the weak leadership of their new bishop (as of 1790): the other James Madison (the president of William & Mary), who had a knack for taking over dying institutions. Conciliatory and genteel, he lacked zeal for his church and avoided clashing with his secular friends in the legislature. A critic mocked him as a great contradiction: "a *Republican Bishop*" with "the head of an *Ass*, the feet of a *Bull*, and the tail of a *Monkey*."[39]

During the late 1780s and early 1790s, legislators defeated motions to confiscate the glebes but did so by dwindling margins. At last, in January 1798, the legislative dam gave way. By a 99-to-52 vote, the House of Delegates authorized counties to confiscate. In the final vote, Tidewater delegates defended the glebes, but their western and Piedmont peers united to take them. The state senate held out for another year before caving in January 1799. The law declared that all Anglican property had "devolved on the good people of this commonwealth on the dissolution of the British government here." In January

1802, legislators passed an act that authorized county overseers of the poor to sell all glebes not occupied by an Episcopal minister. A county could confiscate the remaining glebes once the incumbent ministers left or died. Rather than invest the proceeds in education, the counties reduced taxes.[40]

Defeated in the legislature, Episcopalians appealed to the courts to strike down the confiscatory laws as unconstitutional. In 1803, the key test case reached the state court of appeals. The plaintiffs cast the glebes as a private property retained by a church, which had continued from the colonial into the republican era. The defendants of confiscation countered that the revolution was a radical disjuncture that had vested the church's property in the republican state. The attorney general insisted "that all the rights which the church ever had, were overset by the *revolution* and nullified by the [state] *Bill of Rights*."[41]

The Episcopalian plaintiffs expected to win because the presiding justice, Edmund Pendleton, was a staunch defender of the church and private property. In an evenly divided court, Pendleton held the swing vote, but he was eighty-two years old and in failing health. The court scheduled the final ruling for October 26, 1803, but Pendleton failed to appear in court that morning. Calling at his room in the Swan Tavern, attendants found his dead body.[42]

His death left the court deadlocked 2 to 2, which sustained the lower court ruling in favor of confiscation. The public derived scant benefit from confiscations, for the county overseers of the poor included many selfish incompetents. Some pocketed the money, while others charged extortionate commissions for supervising the sales. Some counties lost the funds by investing them in unstable banks.[43]

Losing the glebes accelerated the decline of the Episcopal Church, as they had been a chief means to recruit and support clergymen. On the eve of the revolution, the church had ninety-five active parishes. That number declined to forty-five by 1785 and took a further dive to twenty-five by 1805. For want of interest and energy, the annual state convention met only twice in the fourteen years after 1797. During the 1810s, John Marshall was a Churchman from Richmond as well as the United States Chief Justice. When a young clergyman solicited a contribution, Marshall gave a little but added "that it was a hopeless undertaking, and that it was almost unkind to induce young Virginians to enter the Episcopal ministry, the Church being too far gone ever to be revived."[44]

Most of the old parish churches crumbled from neglect and vandalism. A traveler found many "with the windows broken, and doors dropping off the hinges, and lying open to the pigs and cattle wandering about the woods." In Isle of Wight County, people pulled down the church, to build a kitchen from the bricks, and reused the wooden pews as stalls for a stable—until lightning struck to burn the whole. The people swapped the church bell for a still to make brandy, which better suited the tastes of postrevolutionary Virginia.[45]

After the revolution, the parish church no longer drew together local communities. Instead, people divided into rival churches or belonged to none. Rather than attend church, most people spent their Sundays at taverns, barbecues, hunts, fishing, horse races, and plays. A pious visitor from New England noted, "Plays, horse-races & games are almost the sole objects of pursuit. . . . It seems to be the taste of the Virginian[s] to fix their churches as far as possible from town & their play houses in the center."[46]

Colonial Virginia had sustained the largest and best-funded church establishment in British America, but the revolution substituted the strictest separation of church and state in the new nation. By taking the glebes, Virginia went far beyond any other state that dissolved its church establishment. Maryland, South Carolina, New York, and the New England states abolished church-state ties but left religious property alone. At an average of about 300 acres, multiplied by 95 parishes, the Virginia confiscations exceeded 25,000 acres.[47]

The move against the church establishment decisively shifted public finance in Virginia. Prior to the revolution, the parish tax had been the greatest single tax levied on Virginians; its elimination cut the local tax burden by two-thirds. Poor relief suffered as the new county overseers spent less per capita than had the old vestries. After 1790, per capita taxes, paid by free men in Virginia, were only a third of those in Massachusetts. Compared to northern states, Virginia favored individual autonomy over community obligation. Jefferson had hoped that Virginians would reinvest their tax savings from disestablishment by funding a public system of education for white children. Instead, county elites decided to keep the money in their pockets and pose as champions of individual liberty.[48]

Religion made for strange bedfellows in politics. The push for disestablishment united secular leaders, including Jefferson, Madison (of Orange County), and Wilson Cary Nicholas, with evangelicals. The civic leaders championed a secular rationality at odds with the passionate supernatural faith of their pious allies. Secularists preferred a diversity of denominations, each a minority of the whole, as the best means to preserve free minds and government. To achieve that counterpoise of minorities, the political elite helped topple the church establishment without, they hoped, enabling any other denomination to grow into a new domination. Evangelicals and rationalists found common ground by emphasizing individual, free choice as the basis for society—within limits set by race and gender.[49]

In November 1824, the Marquis de Lafayette, a French veteran of the American Revolution, returned to Virginia to see Jefferson and Madison. Frustrated by the tenacity of slavery in a republic led by his old friends, Lafayette urged them to do more to hasten emancipation. At Madison's home, Montpelier, Lafayette broached the subject to his host and a gathering of slaveholding neighbors. According to Lafayette's secretary, they countered that Europe remained enslaved by "the religions of the state. The friends of Mr. Madison congratulated themselves that at least this species of slavery is unknown in the United States." The Virginians continued: "Religious liberty we possess in the full extent of its meaning. . . . Thanks to our new laws, worthy of the immortal legislators who were entrusted with framing them, no individual can be compelled to practice any religious worship, nor to frequent any place, nor to support any minister, of any religion whatever." The separation of church and state became Virginians' proudest accomplishment and their retort when accused of insufficiently cherishing freedom. They cast disestablishment as more than enough to win them a pass for clinging to slavery.[50]

Jefferson listed the Statute for Religious Freedom on his grave monument as one of his four greatest achievements, omitting such lesser achievements as presidency of the United States. In 1823, however, Jefferson expressed a surprising regret at the unanticipated damage inflicted on education by abolishing the church establishment: "Before the revol[utio]n a good grammar school was kept in almost every parish by it's incumbent . . . so that every man who could afford it had schools convenient for educating his sons. It is not so now and we have been and still are declining in character." In this remarkable concession, Jefferson admitted that education and character had regressed because of disestablishment. It might have been different if Virginia's legislators and county justices had adopted his system of public education, but they preferred to reduce taxes.[51]

By seeking a new university, Jefferson tried to heal the damage to genteel education wrought by disestablishment. To help finance that university, Jefferson secured the proceeds from selling the two confiscated glebes in Albemarle County, including one formerly held by his beloved teacher, James Maury. The University of Virginia would rise on the ruin of the church establishment.[52]

Union

Jefferson had served as Virginia's governor in early 1781, when British troops invaded the state and captured Richmond, brushing aside feeble militia resistance. Jefferson and state legislators fled westward while the victors looted and burned most of the town. In June, British cavalry swept into Charlottesville as Jefferson escaped on a fast horse: the culminating embarrassment of his unhappy governorship. The raiders drank his wine and took away twenty-three slaves, who sought freedom with the British.[53]

Rattled and disgusted, Jefferson abruptly resigned a week before his term expired, leaving the state without a governor during the invasion crisis. Prodded by his rival Patrick Henry, the legislature investigated Jefferson's conduct as governor. Although quickly vindicated, Jefferson felt betrayed by any criticism of his leadership, so he sulked in retirement at Monticello. In April 1782, his Albemarle neighbors elected him to the legislature, but Jefferson refused to serve. Older legislators chided him, citing the tradition that leading men owed public service to their constituents. As an individualist, Jefferson insisted that his own happiness trumped any duty to serve: "If we are made in some degree for others, yet in a greater [degree] are we made for ourselves." He had more "right in himself than one of his neighbors or all of them put together."[54]

In late 1782, the death of his beloved wife pushed a grieving Jefferson down from Monticello to seek distraction in public life, first as a delegate to Congress and then, in 1784, as the American minister to France: the preeminent diplomatic post for the Union. But Jefferson remained deeply pained by criticism of his wartime conduct as governor, including persistent charges of cowardice. He longed for a second chance to save Virginia from an external power and thereby vindicate his resolve and reputation.[55]

In October 1781, George Washington's Continental Army and French forces had rescued Virginia by trapping the British army of Lord Cornwallis at Yorktown. Taking credit for that great victory, Virginians forgot the exposure of their weakness by the British invasion. Indeed, they reverted to celebrating their power as the supreme state in North America. In 1783 at a dinner with Virginia gentry, a German visitor marveled: "The talk most of the time was of the great advantages which the Virginia state has over all other states in all the world and the nation of Virginia over all other nations." Virginians disdained the "poor New Englander who gains his bread in the sweat of his brow . . . or the Pennsylvanian, who drudges like a negro and takes butter and cheese to market." The best man in the world, they declared, was "the Gentleman of Virginia, for he alone has the finest horses, the finest dogs, the most negroes, the most land, speaks the best English, makes the most elegant bow, has the easy grace of a man of the world, and is a baron on his estates, which yield him everything."[56]

Rather than consolidate a unified American nation, Virginians wanted to preserve a loose confederation of essentially sovereign states. The wartime "Congress was an assemblage of different diplomatic corps, rather than a national senate," Edmund Randolph explained. And the different state delegations distrusted one another. In 1777, a disgusted Virginian in Congress assured Jefferson: "Rely on it, our Confederacy is not founded on Brotherly Love." In late 1783, Jefferson hoped that the end of the war would dissolve Congress: "The constant session of Congress cannot be necessary in time of peace, and their separation will destroy the strange idea of their being a permanent body." In the spring, Jefferson reconsidered when he rejoined Congress and found it nearly bankrupt for lack of state support.[57]

In 1783, Virginians welcomed the return of peace as a chance to rebuild ravaged farms and restock their worn-out wardrobes with British fashions. Virginians feared, however, renewed exposure to lawsuits by British merchants seeking to collect colonial debts, which had soared with interest added during the war years. During the mid-1780s, debt cases clogged Virginia's courts and drained the state's limited supply of money. Virginians denounced their British creditors as financial bloodsuckers preying on the wreckage left by rampaging redcoats. Appealing to those resentments, populist politicians proposed controversial measures: to inflate the economy with paper money and suspend collecting taxes and debts until the economy improved. In 1787, Mathew Maury of Albemarle County worried, "From the Distresses & the general Discontent of the People I take it for granted we are on the Eve of a Revolution."[58]

The weak Union contributed to Virginia's economic woes, for Congress lacked the clout and credibility to negotiate favorable commercial treaties with European empires. A Federalist party emerged in Virginia willing to limit state sovereignty by empowering a Union with enough unity and revenue to command respect overseas. Above all, Federalists worried that, if the confederation collapsed, the states would fight devastating wars over boundaries and trade. A Virginia lawyer predicted, "An independent Sovereignty in each state will directly & immediately produce scenes of blood amongst ourselves, & make us an easy prey to the first powerful foreign invader."[59]

In 1787 at Philadelphia, Washington and Madison attended the convention that drafted a new Federal Constitution. That constitution provided a stronger national government that could directly tax people in the states, regulate interstate trade, and deal with foreign nations from a position of strength. A Virginia merchant hailed the constitution as "the salvation of America. For at present there is hardly the semblance of Law or Government in any of the States, and for want of a Superintending Power over the whole, a dissolution [of the Union] seems to be impending."[60]

Many Virginians, however, distrusted the new federal government as too strong. After escaping from the centralizing power of the British Empire, Anti-Federalists worried that an American nation would threaten Virginia's cherished autonomy and grandeur. Edmund Randolph recalled, "To mention the surrender of one atom of sovereignty, as a contribution to a continental reservoir, was to awaken a serious alarm." An Anti-Federalist, Colonel William Grayson, harangued the people assembled at his county's courthouse. Holding out a snuffbox, Grayson bellowed, "Perhaps you may think it of Consequence that some other States have accepted of the new Constitution, [but] what are they? When compared to Virginia, they are no more than this snuff Box is to the Size of a Man."[61]

Virginia's Anti-Federalists dreaded a strong nation potentially dominated by northerners who did not own slaves. Warning that Congress could "lay such heavy taxes on slaves, as would amount to emancipation," Patrick Henry concluded, "This government is not a Virginian, but an American government." According to Henry, a true Virginian distrusted an American government. He added "that the other States cannot do without us, and therefore we can dictate to them what terms we please." Federalists suspected that Henry sought to split off the southern states for Virginia to control.[62]

Leading the Federalist response, Madison insisted that Virginia would dominate the stronger Union. He added that the Federal Constitution offered valuable new protections for southern slavery. Madison praised the three-fifths clause, which bolstered representation for the slave states, and the fugitive-slave clause, which required northern states to help recover runaway southern slaves. He also emphasized that the federal military could help suppress slave revolts.[63]

In June 1788, Virginia's ratification convention met in Richmond and seemed evenly split, with, as one witness put it, "Half of the Crew hosting sail for the land of Energy—and the other looking with a longing aspect on the Shore of Liberty." Witnesses feared violence between the two crews. A Virginian warned an absent brother, "You never saw your Country Men so much agitated, not even at the time of Cornwallis's Invasion, every Man warm for or against the measure & nothing but debate and altercation in all companies." Henry led the debate for the Anti-Federalists, and Madison countered for the Federalists. On June 25, the delegates narrowly ratified the Federal Constitution. A witness recorded, "The scene was truly awful & solemn."[64]

Away in Paris as the American minister, Jefferson missed the ratification struggle. He felt deeply conflicted about the new constitution. On the one hand, he cherished the Union as the only alternative to civil wars between the states. On the other hand, he disliked the powerful new presidency and the lack (until 1791) of a federal Bill of Rights. Jefferson favored a loose Union in which every state enjoyed fundamental equality. With none subject to domination by a majority, all would adhere in common sentiments of mutual support. He believed that such a consensual union would generate a deep allegiance, making it far stronger than a centralized government with coercive power. But Federalists disdained Jefferson's vision as naïve.[65]

At the start of Washington's presidency, wary Virginians took heart from his appointment of Jefferson as secretary of state and reliance on Madison as the administration's legislative leader. In 1791, however, both soured on the growing power of the secretary of the treasury, Alexander Hamilton, who sought to consolidate a national government with a powerful military, a central bank, and robust taxes. Jefferson and Madison organized an opposition party, the "Republicans," who denounced Hamilton as a corrupt aristocrat bent on subverting republicanism to erect a British-style monarchy, with Washington as his supposed stooge.[66]

Noting New England's strong support for the Federalists, most Virginians perceived the Union as distorted to serve northern interests. John Tyler denounced the "dirty efforts . . . made by these Northern cattle to reduce the consequence of Virginia. Every circumstance of human Life (both civil and political) proves how unfit the States were for such a Union as ours." In 1794, most Virginians denounced the federal treaty negotiated by John Jay with the British, for that treaty increased their exposure to lawsuits by overseas creditors.[67]

Republicans feared that the federal government could deploy patronage to build support in Virginia, perpetuating the division of 1787–1788. While Republicans controlled the heart of Virginia—the Southside and Piedmont—Federalists were competitive along the state's margins: the Eastern Shore, Tidewater, Northern Neck, and west of the Blue Ridge. Seeking to restore unity, Republicans denounced Federalists as latter-day Tories, who allegedly betrayed Virginia's true and proper solidarity. Republicans cherished such unity as essential to control enslaved people.[68]

In 1797, a New England Federalist, John Adams, succeeded Washington as president. A year later, Adams and the Federalist Congress exploited diplomatic tensions with France to rally voters for war. Federalists enlarged the army and navy, raised taxes, and adopted restrictions on immigration and dissent known as "the Alien and Sedition Acts." Federalists hoped to discredit their Republican critics as treacherous supporters of French subversives. Highlighting Jefferson's unorthodox religious views, Federalists cast him as an atheist bent on destroying Christianity.[69]

Republicans denounced the Federalists as crypto-aristocrats undermining free speech and republicanism. In 1798, Jefferson and Madison drafted provocative resolutions adopted by the Kentucky and Virginia legislatures. The resolutions insisted that the states had created the

Union as a consensual compact and concluded that any state legislature could determine the constitutionality of federal laws. They even implied that an offended state could nullify execution of a federal law within its bounds. Equating "the Spirit of 1798" with that of 1776, Virginia's Republicans led a pivotal struggle meant to save republican government from Federalism. At last, Jefferson had his cherished chance to rescue Virginia, proving his courage and vindicating his character besmirched by the wartime crisis of 1781.[70]

In the pivotal national election of 1800, Republicans captured both houses of Congress and elected Jefferson as president and his running mate, Aaron Burr of New York, as vice president. Because Jefferson and Burr finished tied in the Electoral College returns, however, the lame-duck Federalist Congress tried to make trouble by pushing Burr for the presidency. For a suspenseful week in early February 1801, the House of Representatives deadlocked, while both parties threatened civil war.[71]

Balloons

In Williamsburg, almost all students and most townspeople supported Jefferson in the election. Every morning, they gathered at the Raleigh Tavern, anxiously awaiting the stage from Richmond with news about the political crisis. One student, Joseph C. Cabell, noted, "I have never in my life seen the public mind so perfectly alarmed." At last, in late February, thrilling news arrived that Jefferson had prevailed in Congress, winning the presidency. Another student, Joseph S. Watson, reported, "I think our joy almost bordered on madness." Mustering in front of the College, students formed a column led by a band of musicians and a flag-bearer and, in Cabell's words, "marched with triumphant joy down the main street." When they reached St. George Tucker's house, he invited them in to drink wine and toast the new president. Resuming their parade, the students headed to the crumbling old Capitol, "where we shouted a number of republican sentiments" and then to the ruins of the royal governor's palace. "Here we planted our colours &, to the sound of the drum, *shouted* . . . 'May the banner of

liberty thus forever wave triumphantly over the ruins of Despotism.'"
Then, in a novel move for students, they "retired in the most perfect
tranquility to our respective lodgings."[72]

During the next evening, students invited inhabitants to join them in
another parade, in which they stopped in front of every "house of a confirmed aristocrat," meaning a Federalist, to yell "Huzza for Jefferson."
A few days later, the students hosted a ball at the Raleigh Tavern, and
invited the locals, including "several of the Professors & a number of
ex-aristocrats." The inhabitants returned the favor with their own ball,
inviting all the students. Watson exulted, "Except the declaration and
establishment of American Independence, perhaps the annals of Modern History cannot record a circumstance more truly glorious, or more
fortunate not only for America, but for mankind in general."[73]

The triumph inspired students to build a hot-air balloon. Made
of cloth, and only about ten feet in diameter, their balloon was too
small to carry a person. Still the flight promised a novel spectacle in
Williamsburg. Townspeople and students gathered at the courthouse
green to watch the first attempt. Alas, Watson reported, the balloon
"tilted, took fire, and our hopes were blasted. This, which happened in
the presence of a pretty numerous concourse, was a little mortifying
to young philosophers." A few days later, the students tried again, but
produced a second burning failure to the laughter of inhabitants and
chagrin of the builders.

The students staked their hopes on a third try, building a bigger balloon, sixteen feet in diameter and powered by "spirits of Wine, which
gives a greater heat with less flame" than the turpentine of the first
attempts. They paraded to the courthouse green on a beautiful spring
day, shortly before sunset. Almost everyone in town assembled to watch.
While the students shouted in triumph, the balloon slowly rose two
hundred yards into the sky and floated away to the northwest. Cabell
thought it "one of the most beautiful objects I ever beheld." The fire
beneath it "resembled a planet emerging behind the moon in eclipse. At
last nothing but the blaze was visible & it twinkled like a star as it gradually descended beneath a bank of clouds." The joyful students spent

the evening dancing at Tucker's house. The flight seemed symbolic and powerful because the students had ornamented the balloon with sixteen blue stars, one for each state in the Union, which so recently had escaped the perils of civil war.[74]

Republicans exulted in their victory in 1800 as a revolution matching in importance that of 1776. They repealed the Alien and Sedition Acts, rolled back national taxes, and radically shrank the federal government, including the military. Halting the Federalist drive to build a powerful national government, the Republicans favored a decentralized Union that entrusted to the states all responsibilities but foreign affairs, customs collection, a bare-bones military, and postal service. Republicans insisted that a minimal and cheap government would inspire a passionate popularity that no monarchy could match.[75]

In Virginia, Republicans purged Federalists from state offices and the boards of publicly chartered banks. Solidarity restored to Virginia, Republican leaders vowed to keep it that way, deploying the fear of a Federalist revival as the great bogeyman of politics. Every contested election renewed the crusade to save the republic from supposed aristocrats and monarchists, but contested elections became ever fewer in Virginia. Between 1801 and 1820, half of the races lacked any competition, and voter turnout declined to less than a quarter of free white men. While professing their devotion to democracy, Virginia Republicans created a one-party regime. Except on the state's eastern and western margins, only a professed Republican could win elective office in Virginia. In most of the state, to cast an opponent as a Federalist was his political kiss of death.[76]

A Republican clique based in Richmond managed patronage and elections to block any Federalist resurgence. Known as the "Richmond Junto," this informal group of lawyers, bankers, and judges pivoted around Virginia's primary newspaper, the *Richmond Enquirer*, and its talented editor, Thomas Ritchie. That newspaper defined political orthodoxy, and the rest of the Junto enforced it. That orthodoxy included a relentless defense of the separation of church and state and a deep suspicion of political change. They defended the state constitution from reformers in western Virginia and from nationalists in the federal government, both seen as crypto-Federalists. By casting disestablishment and the "revolution of 1800" over the Federalists as paramount defenses of freedom, Virginia's Republicans balked at reforms, including emancipation of the enslaved.[77]

During the 1810s, Jefferson would seek the Junto's support by pitching a university as the means to improve the state's political leaders. Then that new generation could both defend Virginia against renewed Federalism based in the north *and* make his reforms proposed but postponed during the revolution. He did not recognize that his first goal worked against the second.

3
HONOR

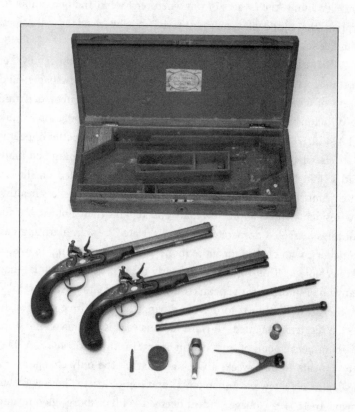

WILLIAMSBURG SUFFERED SEVERELY from the war, enduring occupation by a succession of American, British, and French troops (allied to the Americans). Each army commandeered the public buildings—including the College—to serve as barracks and hospitals.

John Randolph's dueling pistols (Virginia Museum of History & Culture)

Armed, bored, hungry, cold, and irritated with their officers, soldiers soiled and smashed the structures assigned to them. By war's end, the governor's palace and the home of the College president had gone up in flames, and the main College building was a shambles. In Williamsburg, a traveler found "the ravages of war wherever I went, and one cannot be surprised that the people, who were preyed upon by friends as well as foes, should be soured by their losses."[1]

Williamsburg withered into a backwater village after the removal of the state government to Richmond in 1780. The local newspapers and dozens of shopkeepers and artisans followed the government, deflating the Williamsburg economy. From 1,880 in 1775, the population shrank to 1,424 in 1782. Young men and women left to pursue better opportunities elsewhere. Because older people stayed, Williamsburg had more deaths than births. The letters of aging residents dwelled on illness, which contributed to the belief that the place had become less healthy. Few residents could afford to repair and repaint their homes. Vacant buildings attracted desperate people dislocated by war, alarming city councilors, who begged for more money to pay for policing. In 1782 a traveler noted, "This Town was formerly the Capital of Virginia—had many fine Buildings & the people were gay. But its Glory is departed!"[2]

The town continued to decline during the next three decades. In 1793, a resident lamented, "A third tedious year is now revolving since the commencement of my confinement in this Prison. . . . A Day here appears to be a week; a week a Month." The only changes were the deaths of "a few old Inhabitants" and some rickety "houses Blown down." In 1804, a College student deemed Williamsburg "gloomy and melancholy. . . . Many of the houses have tumbled down, and others are daily crumbling into ruins." Another dubbed it "the mouldering City."[3]

The town government was too broke to repair public buildings or assist the many poor people. In 1791 a visiting preacher reported that the "old Capital . . . was a mere desolation, & used at pleasure by the beasts that went at large in the streets." In 1793, the city corporation tore down the eastern half of the Capitol to sell bricks and beams to fund repairs to the other half. In April 1796, a sick and aging barber greeted the arriving stage bearing a traveler. Afflicted with "a bedridden mother, a crazy wife, and half a dozen children dying of the smallpox," the barber displayed a certificate authorizing him to beg because the city lacked funds for poor relief.[4]

Although decaying, Williamsburg sustained a dozen genteel families of fine manners and generous hospitality. Hosting teas, dinner parties, and balls, they relished witty banter, poetry readings, and after-dinner songs accompanied by a daughter or wife on the piano. They invited one another and students who had proper letters of introduction. A new student found the people "extremely gay and extravagant. There have been not less than four balls, since I came to town, & there will be another this week. To one, who has spent his life in Louisa [County], where a ball is almost a phenomenon, this must appear the height of extravagance." Despite their fraying means, the old families tried to maintain colonial standards of lavish hospitality, for which they remained famed throughout Virginia.[5]

At balls and parties, the students courted young women who came to stay with relatives or attend a nearby boarding school. Potential marriages preoccupied everyone as they danced, flirted, talked, and promenaded through town, while watching inhabitants gossiped. Joseph C. Cabell noted, "The students . . . are held in a state of dreadful, pleasing captivity by women." When he left college and returned home to Albemarle County, another student missed "that Gaiety and Mirth which Williamsburg affords. . . . Believe me, I did not know my attachment to Williamsburg till the time had arrived when I was to bid Adieu."[6]

Williamsburg retained "The Public Hospital for Persons of Insane and Disordered Minds," which people usually called simply "Bedlam" or "the Mad-House." In 1766, Governor Fauquier had proposed an asylum for "a poor unhappy set of People who are deprived of their Senses and wander about the Country, terrifying the Rest of their Fellow Creatures." Completed in 1773, the two-story Mad-House had twenty-four rooms within stout brick walls and barred windows. On the eve of the revolution, Robert Carter Nicholas considered the new institution timely: "for the Reception of Lunaticks & other unhappy objects of insane Minds, which it is to be feared will Multiply too fast in this Country." When the state government departed, leaving College and Bedlam behind, wits declared that that old city offered a haven for "the lazy and the crazy." Dismayed by the shabby inhabitants, a preacher reported that the asylum was "desolate, but whether because none are insane or all are equally mad, it might, perhaps, be difficult to tell."[7]

After the war, two elderly sisters and widows planned a move to Williamsburg, but they wanted a dwelling away from "the Mad house" lest "the Cries of the Mad people will increase our Melancholy." They worried too much, for James Madison, the president of the asylum as well as of William & Mary, insisted that he had calmed those cries. In the spirit of the Enlightenment, Madison experimented in behavioral modification. He constructed a "cold bath . . . to plunge the patients of the hospital, especially such as are attended with paroxysms of fury and violence, until they shall be fit subjects for the resuscitative process." Madison explained: "The patient is carried blindfold to the bath; the chain in which he is fixed is raised by pullies over the bath, and by a weight attached to it, he is carried suddenly to the bottom, about six feet; then quickly drawn up." He submerged patients "just sufficient to occasion a temporary suspension of respiration; but it is surprising to see what calmness, what complacency, the experiment produces immediately, even in the most violent." Madison repeated this treatment two or three times per patient per session and felt vindicated by the results: "The alarm or fright which is experienced, appears to be highly beneficial. A threat from the keeper of submersion to one who has undergone the operation will instantly quiet the most unruly." But the asylum could neither contain nor cure all of the madness loose in Williamsburg.[8]

Randolph

John Randolph came from Virginia's most prestigious family, which contributed to his prickly personality. Randolph recalled his boyish self as "the most thin-skinned, sensitive little creature in the universe." A classmate described him as "the most beautiful boy in Virginia. . . . His face was as smooth and delicate as that of Adonis." Proud of his lineage and quick mind, Randolph disliked study or any teacher's authority. The classmate added, "Randolph was [so] very idle at school that he was flogged regularly every Monday morning and two or three times during the week."[9]

In 1775, Randolph's father died and, four years later, his mother, Frances Bland Randolph, married a learned lawyer, St. George Tucker. As stepfather, Tucker became responsible for educating John, who was six in 1779 and his older brothers Theodorick (eight), and Richard (ten). In 1782, Tucker sent the Randolph boys away to a boarding school in Orange County, where the schoolmaster was Walker Maury, the son of Jefferson's teacher, the Reverend James Maury. Tucker had befriended Maury when they were classmates at the College of William & Mary shortly before the revolution. In October 1782, Maury assured Tucker that the Randolph boys were "orderly & governable and possess good capacities." John Randolph remembered it differently: "I was tyrannized over and tortured by the most peevish and ill-tempered of pedagogues, Walker Maury. This wretch excruciated me body and soul." An old-school disciplinarian, Maury meant to control the next generation.[10]

In 1783, Maury relocated his school and the Randolph boys to Williamsburg at the invitation of Tucker and other friends. They placed the school in the old capitol building, abandoned by the legislature with the move to Richmond. Maury paid for repairs by charging admission for plays, which he staged with his students as actors. With the help of four ushers, Maury taught French, Latin, Greek, math and science. For want of quality competition, the school grew rapidly to over a hundred students, becoming the largest in the state, but Maury struggled to manage so many boys.[11]

After the revolution, teachers faced contradictory expectations from genteel parents. They wanted enough discipline to keep boys studying rather than lapsing into dissipated indolence. But they also protected their sons from physical punishment, which seemed more degrading after the revolution than before. Maury decided to err on the side of rigor. Assured that "the credit of the school will depend on the disci-

pline, I shall minutely attend to," Maury promised "to curb every irregularity" and to have "perfect command over the school."[12]

Maury's authority rankled the Randolphs, who considered themselves the finest and first family in Virginia, the masters of slaves rather
than the subjects of discipline. In August 1786, the great blowup at
school involved John's even wilder brother Theodorick, then aged fifteen. Maury reported, "He has for some time past been assuming the
[manners of a] fine gentleman very fast and of consequence [has become]
very inattentive to his studies." One morning, Theodorick appeared
dressed to the nines, powder in his hair, and wearing a huge ring.
When Maury mocked the ring, Theodorick took offense, in Maury's
words, "with much impertinence. I slapped his chops for it." When the
boy responded "with additional insolence. I repeated the blow." Then,
Maury added, "I gave him several boxes on the ear & there the matter was to have rested"—except that the boy ran away from school and
enlisted support from his relatives.[13]

According to his uncle, when Theodorick returned to Williamsburg,
"Mr. Maury made a violent attack, which our young Gentleman repelled
with such address that a defeat of the Master would have ensued had he
not called in his usher" to rescue him. The uncle's pride in the boy's self-
defense did not bode well for Maury's coercive power over genteel boys.
According to Maury's version, Theodorick returned "with such an air
of consequence & importance that I could not . . . pardon him; besides,
I never do forgive an offence of this kind."[14]

All three Randolphs bolted from the school, shouting defiance back
at Maury. Seeking support from Tucker, Maury explained, "I never
wished to see insolence blended with a fine dress. . . . I console myself
with a full conviction that I have done my duty." Tucker, however,
sided with the boys; delayed paying money owed for their tuition; and
refused even to answer Maury's letters. "If I have forfeited your friendship, surely, I was entitled to the common civility of an answer to one,
at least, of my several letters," Maury begged. The schoolmaster never
expected Tucker to "despise & cruelly treat the man who so long rubbed
with him the chain of mutual friendship." Unable to sustain his school

in Williamsburg without Tucker's support, Maury moved to Norfolk, where he became an Episcopal clergyman: further evidence that he was out of touch with the new order in Virginia. In October 1788, at the age of thirty-six, Maury died of yellow fever.[15]

By striking Theodorick Randolph for displaying pride and gentility, Maury had crossed a new line that he did not know existed. Clinging to old standards in a new republic, Maury tried to restore the mastery over students that he associated with the colonial era and his own father. By siding with his stepsons, Tucker registered a shift in genteel families toward nurturing, rather than curbing, the will of adolescent boys. What Maury considered insolence, Tucker regarded as an appropriate pride that the Randolphs would need to lead their state.

In 1787, Tucker sent the three boys north to school, first to Princeton and then to Columbia. At neither college did they develop self-discipline. John recalled Theodorick: "Of all things in the world, he detested most a book. Devoted to pleasure and fun, he not only set me a bad example but (with his dissolute companions) absolutely prevented me from reading. Often have they forced the door of my study and tossed the books over the floor; sometimes out of the window." Haunting taverns instead of classrooms, Theodorick ruined his health, ran out of money, and had to go home. John soon followed, after a desultory sojourn studying law with his cousin Edmund Randolph in Philadelphia.[16]

In July 1792, in Williamsburg, John Randolph suffered a nearly fatal and life-altering bout of scarlet fever. The crisis arrested his physical development, leaving his body slight and boyish. He recognized his "delicacy or effeminacy of complexion that but for a spice of the devil in my temper would have consigned me to the distaff or the needle." Overcompensating for his lack of masculinity, he sought to intimidate with his sharp tongue, and if that failed, he resorted to dueling pistols.[17]

In the fall of 1792, Randolph recovered enough to enter William & Mary, the last stop in his unstable education. He did not last long. Excessively proud of his superior diction, he insulted another student, Robert B. Taylor, for mispronouncing a word. Taylor demanded an apology, which Randolph refused, leading to a duel. On February 6, 1793, they assembled, each with a second, at dawn in a field on the outskirts of town. Randolph proved the better shot, putting a bullet "in the right side of the right Buttock," where it lodged too close to Taylor's spine for removal, and so it remained for the rest of his life. Having demonstrated courage to mutual satisfaction, the two young men reconciled and bonded. Fifteen years later, Randolph declared of Taylor: "He is a noble-hearted fellow, and I love him."[18]

Duels

In 1793, the Randolph-Taylor confrontation caused a sensation because duels were relatively new in Virginia. Often mistaken for a traditional legacy from a distant past, dueling was a new fashion in Virginia, emerging during the revolution. In the colonial era, a duel had seemed

Robert Barraud Taylor (1774–1834),
by Cephas Thompson
(Virginia Museum of History & Culture)

John Randolph (1773–1833)
(Library of Congress)

absurd, foreign, and an impious insult to God. Contending gentlemen relied on lawsuits or, if in a drunken passion, sudden blows with fists, knives, or sword. In 1767, when Arthur Lee challenged James Mercer to a duel in Williamsburg, the *Virginia Gazette* ridiculed Lee's affectation of "the Principle of Honor" as superior to "that antiquated thing, Religion." The newspaper mocked Lee for promoting a future where "the laws of honor will take place, and flourish on the ruin of all other laws." Lee had learned about dueling as a student at Eton, a prestigious school in England, where the sons of aristocrats prevailed.[19]

If Lee acted prematurely in his 1767 challenge, he was a prophet of honor in his own land, for dueling proliferated, paradoxically, during the revolution against British rule. Duels emerged among the officers of the Continental Army, who came together as strangers from diverse states and mixed social backgrounds. Often distrusting one another, they fiercely competed for military rank and social prestige, struggling to set a hierarchy in their new profession. Growing thin skins, they asserted their "honor," an aristocratic concept that combined personal integrity, genteel manners, and a willingness to die or kill rather than swallow any slight. Dueling became a perverse means for insecure American officers to claim that they had as much honor as their British rivals. Social climbing, and a fear of falling, drove the new practice.[20]

Returning to their home states, officers disseminated notions of personal honor and practices of dueling. That culture thrived in revolutionary Virginia, which was becoming a more contentious society. With the collapse of the Anglican Church as the common culture of gentlemen, notions of personal honor filled the vacuum and reinforced the emerging individualism. While freed from the moral restraints of a publicly shared religion, young gentlemen felt newly pressured to compete with one another to lead their state. In the new republic, frequent elections increased fiery words between contending gentlemen, and some sought redress through arms. The revolution rendered social place more uncertain thanks to new inheritance laws, more elections, and increased social mobility, both up and down.[21]

Young men defended their honor against rivals for prestige and power. But dueling also created perverse bonds, as with the friendship that Randolph and Taylor formed after shooting at each other. Another vivid example involved the next generation. Their friend and classmate Littleton Waller Tazewell became, along with Taylor, one of the top two lawyers in Norfolk. Tazewell's son and Taylor's son attended the new University of Virginia, where they quarreled and agreed to duel when home in Norfolk. Their alarmed fathers intervened, inducing magistrates to bind the boys to keep the peace. Instead, they carefully cooperated to slip out of town at dawn in a shared carriage, heading south across the nearby state line into North Carolina. Honor promoted an aggressive and prickly individualism, but in the formalized rituals of the duel, young men practiced a striking, but potentially fatal, mutuality.

Noting the boys' absence, parents guessed their deadly purpose and destination. A relative noted, "Both families sent out carriages, beds, & physicians for the relief of as they then presumed dead or wounded Sons." On the outskirts of Norfolk, the county sheriff spotted the two boys driving south. Knowing of their hatred, the sheriff guessed that this surprising cooperation meant that they were going to shoot one another. The sheriff "overtook them on the battle ground just after they had measured their distance (ten paces) arrested & brought them over the Virginia line. . . . What a happy escape, 5 minutes more & one or both might have been launched into eternity."[22]

A gentleman only challenged a peer, never an inferior, for whom a simple beating with a cane would do. Because the principles and seconds in a duel accepted one another as having honor to defend, dueling defined the line between commonality and gentility. As it became too vulgar for gentlemen to brawl with one another, they resorted to the studied formalities of challenge and duel or apology. Their black eyes diminished as shooting increased. Most duels ended in reconciliations after both missed or one suffered a flesh wound.[23]

Mastery over slaves reinforced honor culture in the South. Gentry taught sons that honor won respect and advancement in an unequal society led by the masters of slaves. Gentry defined their freedom and honor as complete because they denied both to enslaved people. Young men had to learn how to command slaves, lead families, and impress common whites. Gentry did so by defending their honor against any insult, however slight. Anyone who tamely swallowed an insult behaved like a slave and forfeited the respect of gentlemen. Masters liked to believe that the enslaved chose their lot because they allegedly were too cowardly to risk death by resistance. Per this conceit, masters insisted that they had to risk death to demonstrate their freedom. By treating sons indulgently, fathers encouraged them to become assertive, willing to submit only to the honor code of their genteel peers.[24]

The defense of honor played out before the collective audience of other gentlemen, who judged each performance. Young men dueled because they feared censure as cowards. An English traveler concluded, "The barbarous baseness and cruelty of public opinion dooms a young man, when challenged, to fight." Honor required men to care too deeply for the opinions of other gentlemen trapped in the same cultural web. Honor was intensely social as well as personal. No one could have honor without being honored by others as a member of their club. Duelists often appealed to public opinion, as a sort of jury, for their seconds spread rival accounts meant to shame the other party for violating the proper rules. Failing to display proper courage could disqualify a gentleman from public office in the eyes of common voters, who did not duel but expected their leaders to do so. Thomas Mann Randolph felt he had to duel to avoid public shame, which he described as the "painful sensation produced by the scorn or contempt of others, whether real or imaginary."[25]

Duels appalled Thomas Jefferson, who avoided them by practicing scrupulous good manners and by avoiding contradicting another gentleman to his face. Because other Virginians lacked such self-control, Jefferson wanted stricter laws to suppress dueling. In one of his reform bills from 1779, he proposed a draconian solution: "Whosoever committeth murder by way of duel, shall suffer death by hanging; and if he were the challenger, his body, after death, shall be gibbeted," which meant displayed to rot in an elevated cage as a grim example to deter others. A treatment reserved for the vilest criminals, gibbeting was far too much for Virginia's gentlemen to consider for their dueling sons. The legislature quietly rejected Jefferson's proposal.[26]

Jefferson had contributed to the social changes that indirectly promoted honor culture. Among the gentry, he had helped to discredit the traditional Christianity that had discouraged duels in colonial Virginia. After the revolution, most gentlemen favored a tepid, rational Christianity if not outright deism. Neither could inhibit the passion with which the young gentry embraced duels to defend their prickly honor.[27]

Defenders insisted that duels policed polite society, protecting slighter men from bullying by stronger foes—that pistols equalized bodily power while favoring the man of true gentility. Regarding dueling "as a necessary evil," John Randolph argued, "a man may shoot him who invades his character as he may shoot him who breaks into his house." St. George Tucker's cousin, George Tucker, noted the extreme sensitivity that Virginians felt about hostile words. "It is universally admitted that human life is more embittered by insults, than by injuries; that a word, a look, a tone, a gesture . . . are capable of inflicting pains more exquisite than racks, or whips, or chains." Dueling alone could "correct and counteract this fundamental evil" by compelling polite restraint in conversation. He added that, without the formalities of dueling, gentlemen would disgrace themselves "by boxing, cudgeling, and even shooting or stabbing" without restraint or rules, leading to more deaths. Proponents also argued that duels kept the gentry pure, by identifying, shaming, and purging dishonorable liars, cheats, and cowards.[28]

In northern states, duels remained uncommon save for among former military officers, such as Aaron Burr and Alexander Hamilton. Restrained by a more religious culture, most northern gentlemen criticized dueling as a southern folly associated with slavery. That criticism led Virginians to defend dueling as essential to preserving their region from the crass commercialism and religious hypocrisy that they associated with Yankees. Indeed, George Tucker insisted that southern honor best refuted the northern criticism of slavery, asserting that Virginians' "elevated and honourable feelings" went "far to redeem them from the reproach for one of their institutions that has been so lavishly heaped upon them."[29]

Youth

Honor culture reinforced a shift in genteel family life, a shift that began during the 1750s but accelerated after the revolution. Wealthy families forsook the "patriarchal" style of the colonial regime, which had emphasized the father's monarchical authority over wife and children. Genteel families moved toward a more intimate and sentimental style, which cast affection as the shared bond of parents and siblings. Rejecting the traditional notion of children as sinful beings who needed early discipline, genteel parents nurtured them as innately good. Jefferson declared, "The post which a parent may take most advantageous for his child is that of his bosom friend." Parents reduced corporal punishment in favor of offering, or withholding, displays of love depending on a child's conduct. Less physical, discipline became more subtle, manipulative, and psychological.[30]

When boys went off to college, parents insisted that they correspond often. On the one hand, parents wanted letters that shared frank and spontaneous emotions, which renewed family ties despite the distance. Richard Blow exhorted his son George, just starting at William & Mary: "Describe to me all your thoughts upon the passing events. . . . Write with freedom. Be gay, cheerful, or witty. Say whatever your imagination dictates. Write about your frolics, your amusements, your tricks, anything." On the other hand, parents also expected polished letters free of errors in spelling and grammar, to impress their friends and relatives. "It is considered disgraceful & contemptible to spell badly," Blow assured his son.[31]

Young men attended college to claim a place in Virginia's governing class. A celebrated lawyer, William Wirt, exhorted his young brother-in-law, Francis W. Gilmer, to beware "of being buried all your life in obscurity, confounded with the gross and ignorant herd around you—crawling in the kennel of filth and trash with the mass of human maggots and reptiles all your life and then compare with this vile and disgusting condition, the state of the man, who has industriously improved the boon of genius." No longer could young gentlemen rely on birth and connections for easy preeminence. Downward social mobility was a threat, a Virginian explained, "as long as men of education and acquirements continue to have children who are dunces and as long as men of great genius & talents breed sons who are fools." But a young gentleman like Gilmer, with connections like Wirt, could rise above the common "maggots and reptiles," who could not afford higher education. Class distinctions took harder work to maintain in a republic—but they persisted.[32]

Much of that work was social rather than literary. No one, not even Jefferson, rose in Virginia by holing up in his study to the neglect of his social skills, for mastering genteel manners carried more weight than learning from books. David Watson advised his younger brother at college, "Books alone will not do. You must make the best use of the company you keep. . . . I would by no means have you to be a pedant." Genteel parents wanted their sons to gain enough education to seem polished, without absorbing too much to become dull. Sterling Ruffin exhorted his son Thomas to be "attentive to your books, but particularly so to your manners. A man may be better read than his neighbor, and yet not acquire half the respect." Parents worried that overly studious sons became sickly and asocial—too much like their professors.[33]

Young gentlemen attended college to hone social skills and cultivate social networks. A collegian noted, "The students are generally the sons of wealthy men, & are in search of pleasure & anything else but mental improvement." Students valued fashionable attire, elegant posture, polished manners, generosity at buying drinks, witty conversation, and prowess at cards. One student advised a peer to cultivate a "familiar ease of manners & conversation, which in a man's flight to fame is what wings are to birds. The greatest talents & learning can hardly ever succeed in this Republican Country" without polished manners "& with it they as seldom fail of success." A dandy young collegian made a vivid, showy appearance. A critic mocked that the dandy "compresses his thorax and abdomen with corsets" and "draws his cravat with a tightness threatening suffocation" and "booted and spurred, dashes about the country, as he elegantly expresses it, *to see the Gals.*"[34]

To maintain appearances in their competitive society, students spent more money than their parents wished. Sterling Ruffin assured his son: "My wish is to support you genteelly, but not extravagantly." Students replied that they would lose face if compelled to economize. George Blow asserted that he had "not expended more money than was necessary for him to maintain his respectability," for surely his father "would not have penuriousness imputed to him." Blow insisted "that a young man must of necessity be extravagant at this place if he wishes to associate with the best company."[35]

Genteel fathers wanted sons to develop a robust sense of honor. They should avoid conflict with politeness but without submission. David Watson advised his boy, "Be careful of your health and your limbs, but do not be fearful & cowardly, when it is necessary & proper to expose them." Watson preferred that his son duel rather than accept an insult.[36]

Young gentlemen struggled to cooperate, study, and abide authority because their parents trained them to become willful masters of enslaved people. Wirt noted that genteel boys became petty tyrants: "During infancy they are usually committed to the care of *slaves*. . . . Over these teachers they are taught, of course, to exercise sovereign authority—whereby they acquire what the infatuated parent calls a proud, independent spirit—but what is in reality a petulant impatience of all restraint and control." Such boys resented and resisted control by their teachers at academies and colleges.[37]

Going away to college, students left mothers, aunts, and sisters behind, plunging into a masculine environment dominated by fellow adolescents. A Virginian noted, "When multitudes of youth are brought together and for the [first] time [are] separated from all the powerful restraints of virtuous female society, and all the kindly influences of domestic life, ardent, highly excitable, confident in their numbers, and fully united by the *esprit du corps*, they require as much courage and skill to govern them as a mighty army." Eager to prove their manhood and gentility, students bristled at college rules as dishonoring them.[38]

College

Patriots hoped that education would train a new generation of young men better than their elders, who had grown up under British rule. In 1786, the College president assured Jefferson, "Sure I am, and I believe you will rejoice to hear it, that the Spirit of Republicanism is infinitely more pure as well as more ardent in the rising Generation than among any other Class of Citizens." In 1788, Jefferson recommended the College to a parent, "I know no place in the world, while the present professors remain, where I would so soon place a son." Soon enough Jefferson would change his mind.[39]

The College of William & Mary fell short on the republican promise advanced by Jefferson's wartime reforms. For want of money and repairs, buildings deteriorated. The dingy library had only antiquated books, many in French, which few students could read because the professor of modern languages, Carlo Bellini, was too old, sick, and blind to teach. John Randolph recalled him as "an old Frenchman . . . who could neither write nor spell." The medical chair lapsed when Dr. James McClurg deserted the college after attending a single faculty meeting (a perfectly understandable decision for anyone who has been to such meetings). He pursued a more lucrative private practice in booming Richmond. Jefferson's reforms had begun to unravel at the College.[40]

After Jefferson retired as governor, the Board of Visitors became more parochial and conservative. Restoring the grammar school that he had despised and abolished, the Visitors also brought back the Reverend John Bracken to run it. A traveler thought he looked "more like a tavern keeper than a divine." Noting his Federalism and limited support for the revolution, Jefferson disdained Bracken as a "tory" and a "simpleton." The erosion of Jefferson's vision for the College alienated his friend George Wythe, who resigned as law professor in 1789. The president, Bishop James Madison, contained the damage by recruiting another celebrated lawyer, St. George Tucker, to replace Wythe. But Bracken's restoration and Wythe's resignation disgusted Jefferson, who declared, "It is over with the college." Thereafter, he sought a new university to replace, and probably destroy, William & Mary.[41]

During the 1790s, the College students became notorious for drunken disorder. In 1799, Joseph S. Watson assessed his peers: "one fourth are industrious and promising. Most of the rest, devoid of emulation, with a sluggish inactivity of mind, pass their moments away in a total insensibility to the importance of their time, and the advantages which they possess."[42]

Students delighted in playing crude pranks on townsfolk. A friend urged an absent student to return to "the region of that Mirth & jollity which once you so fondly loved. . . . We are as merry & mischievous as ever, & now & then take a trip to the Blue room." In that room faculty held disciplinary hearings, but these had little effect on student conduct. In response to any slight or insult, students rampaged through the town at night. One recalled that they "amuse[d] themselves by putting the town to rights," which meant a raid to knock down garden and yard fences, horse racks, and business signs; break windows; and steal outhouses, carriages, wagons, and carts to build a barricade across the main street. During the Christmas season of December 1797, fifteen students got drunk on eggnog before loudly parading through town with a fiddle to awaken sleeping townspeople and to shatter windows with stones. The locals complained to Bishop Madison, who launched an investigation, summoning groggy students into the Blue Room for questioning. Despite plenty of misconduct, the College expelled no students during the 1790s. Dependent upon tuition for revenue, William & Mary could ill afford to oust paying customers.[43]

Students also battered the statue of Lord Botetourt at the old Capitol. George Tucker recalled that a classmate's "powerful arms had with a brickbat knocked off Lord Botetourt's head." Later, Tucker visited the Raleigh Tavern, where the elderly landlord "took me aside, and opening a desk, took out the head . . . of Lord Botetourt, which the mischievous students had thus mutilated." The landlord acted from respect for the memory of the most popular royal governor in Virginia's fading past. In 1801, Bishop Madison spent $100 in scarce College funds to buy and repair the statue, restoring the head with an iron plug to the body and adding a new nose. Then the Bishop relocated the Lord from the ruined Capitol to the lawn in front of the College.[44]

In addition to harassing the town, students ambushed one another "in the dark passages of a night at the risk of their necks" in the main college building. Stealing cannon balls from the local powder magazine, they rolled them down the hallways, threatening the ankles of the unwary. After one eggnog party, they brought "a horse into college, riding him about the large area below stairs and then endeavouring to carry him up into the upper stories." Then they ventured out to "set the town to rights."[45]

During the 1790s, many students adopted an aggressive deism that mocked organized religion as antiquated stupidity. Isaac A. Coles applauded the "spirit of skepticism, which so much prevailed & which every student acquired as soon as he touched the threshold of the college." Students avidly read an *Enquiry Concerning Political Justice*, written by William Godwin and first published in London in 1793. A former dissenting minister in England, Godwin became a radical critic of church and state, favoring a political minimalism that critics called anarchy. He suggested that people, particularly the young, could perfect themselves by rejecting all forms of traditional authority. This doctrine of human perfectibility outraged pious conservatives, but it appealed to precocious young gentlemen. When Bishop Madison denounced *Political Justice*, the book became a delicious forbidden fruit for the students at William & Mary.[46]

Impious students insulted preachers and damaged churches. In 1791, a Presbyterian minister visited Williamsburg and felt shocked by the "rudeness, infidelity, & ribaldry" of the students, so he denounced the College as a "grand nuisance which ought to be suppressed." Students vandalized the town's parish church to scandalize the minister, John Bracken, deriding his sermons as "the Ravings of an hypocritical Priest." In March 1798, a student reported, "The other evening a large party made an attack upon the sacred property of God; the Communion Table was broken into a thousand pieces, all the prayer Books and Bibles [were] scattered about the Church Yard, one window entirely destroyed, and the pulpit itself bedaubed from one end to the other with human excrement." The Bishop identified culprits but dared expel none because, as one student explained, "the party was so numerous and many of them so respectable." Given the College's tenuous finances, Madison could not afford to alienate parents by expelling their sons.[47]

William & Mary struggled to attract and retain faculty. Joseph C. Cabell reported that the College's professors were "more miserably compensated for the services they render, than any five men in America." The gloomy prospects of the College led even Bishop Madison to despair. In private letters, he lobbied his cousin, the politician James Madison, and Jefferson to found a new university in the Piedmont and appoint him as its first president. Until "such a University be formed, Virginia, will never acquire the Preeminence, which may, & ought to distinguish her," the Bishop noted.[48]

Sunbeams

Americans rarely elect philosophers as their presidents. In the run-up to the pivotal election of 1800, Federalists denounced Jefferson's learning as showy but idiotic. In a July 4, 1799, oration, a Connecticut Federalist satirized Jefferson's science by entitling the speech "Sunbeams May Be Extracted from Cucumbers, but the Process Is Tedious." More than just silly, Jefferson's ideas were menacing, allegedly spreading the anarchic beliefs of French Jacobins who undermined law, order, and religion in the name of bloody revolution. Another Federalist exhorted voters to defend inherited traditions: "Never let us exchange our civil and religious institutions for the wild theories of crazy projectors; or the sober, industrious moral habits of our country, for experiments in atheism, and lawless democracy. *Experience* is a safe pilot; but experiment is a dangerous ocean, full of rocks and shoals."[49]

While Federalists defended the past, Jefferson claimed the future. In rhetoric akin to Godwin's, Jefferson assured a William & Mary student that the human "mind is perfectable to a degree of which we cannot as yet form any conception." Jefferson derided "as cowardly the idea that the human mind is incapable of further advances." Dismissing Federalists as retrograde bigots fond of medieval barbarism, Jefferson insisted that free and wide-ranging inquiry alone could produce new knowledge that would enable humans to make a brighter future. This is what he meant by "science," which included all forms of systematic and experimental inquiry.[50]

Federalists denounced Jefferson for supporting two young Virginians, William A. Burwell and Lewis Harvie, recently ousted from Princeton for leading disturbances and promoting "atheism and infidelity." At Princeton, Republican students from Virginia offended the college president and faculty, who were strict Presbyterians, staunch authoritarians, and firm Federalists. Princeton expelled Burwell and Harvie as ringleaders of protest and vandalism, but they landed on their feet by becoming secretaries for the newly elected President Jefferson. Disgusted Federalists thought the country was going to hell when young men reaped rewards after disrupting a traditional college.[51]

While defending Princeton, Federalist cultural critics blasted William & Mary, whose students so conspicuously supported Jefferson. Critics alleged that Godwin's *Political Justice* served as the College's core text. Worried by those attacks, Bishop Madison responded in an anonymous newspaper essay published in November 1801. He insisted that the College neither taught nor proscribed Godwin, but allowed every student to engage in "free and candid investigation." In the Jeffersonian spirit, Madison asserted that William & Mary offered a "system of rational education, calculated to disseminate truth in morals and politics, and to form wise and virtuous citizens."[52]

A few months later, the students discredited Madison's case for their wisdom and virtue. In February, two students fought a duel, with one suffering a minor wound. The faculty ousted both in the first expulsions of Madison's long presidency. Their outraged peers demanded the restoration of their friends. When the faculty stood firm, students boycotted classes and vandalized College and town, targeting the homes of professors, particularly St. George Tucker. The protestors also broke up a village shop and attacked both the college chapel and the parish church to tear apart Bibles and prayer books. Tucker's son, Henry St. George Tucker, concluded, "The College has been a complete scene of confusion. It has received a blow from which I fear it will never recover."[53]

The Federalist press gleefully seized upon the episode to blame the malign influence of Godwin and Jefferson at the College. Student rioting vindicated the conservative view of human nature as innately depraved—and not remotely perfectible. If unleashed from the restraints of Christianity, Federalists argued, young men produced violent anarchy. The *New York Evening Post* warned, "Thus dies one of the oldest and wealthiest seminaries of learning in the United States of America. These may be considered as some of the blessed effects of the modern, or Jeffersonian, system of religion."[54]

In an anonymous newspaper essay, Bishop Madison correctly reported that the College had not closed, but he misled readers by insisting that the riot involved only five or six students. While he publicly minimized the trouble, the Visitors privately assembled in a crisis session. In March 1802, they threatened to expel any student who failed to adopt studious habits within a month. A good student, they stipulated, "devotes to his studies at least six hours out of every twenty-four, independently of the time spent in the Lecture Rooms."[55]

The Visitors also authorized the faculty to "compel a Student to give Evidence on his honor against any Student accused of an offense." The Visitors sought to redirect honor, so cherished by students, away from protecting one another to accepting a duty to tell the full truth. Students, however, rebuffed that redirection as insulting. In April, nearly half of the College's seventy-one students quit, damaging the school's finances, which depended on tuition. In November 1802, another newspaper essay by the Bishop insisted that all was well thanks to the new rules: "Our college is now the emblem of a well-regulated family. Everyone sees his duty, and knows that a parental authority will enforce that duty."[56]

Student defiance contradicted the Bishop's insistence on a new reign of harmony and order. On March 31, 1803, the faculty expelled four students for staging a duel: two as principles and two as seconds. The expulsions outraged their peers, who again targeted the despised Reverend John Bracken, on April 1. A Norfolk newspaper reported that students "broke into the church, played on the organ for nearly two hours, and then went to the church yard, dug up the body of a female that had been buried for many months, took it from the coffin, and placed it on the floor of an empty house in a situation too shocking to describe!!!"[57]

In an odd and anonymous response published in a newspaper, the Bishop insisted that the stolen corpse was male and came from the insane asylum rather than the parish churchyard. He refused to confirm or deny that the culprits were students but insisted that they had dug up the corpse for medical study, which seems unlikely unless the diggers were students. "Similar cases have frequently occurred in every part of the world, without exciting any extraordinary abhorrence," Madison huffed. The Bishop told less than the full truth, for a student later confirmed, "The Students in their last *insurrection* broke into the Church, beat the windows down, and nearly completed the destruction of the organ. Such frequent behavior has discouraged the inhabitants, and they have abandoned both the Organ and Church."[58]

Madison made matters worse by pushing for another round of tougher rules that mandated bed checks by every professor twice a week to enforce a curfew on students. Then he proclaimed that William & Mary was "in a state of perfect order" because "we will never again permit a student to continue here, a single Day, after he has shewn the least Disposition to Idleness & Irregularity." It must have been hard, however, for students to take seriously the Bishop's new pose as a strict disciplinarian.[59]

Rather than calm the College, the new rules alienated the leading professor, St. George Tucker. He resented the bed checks and a new requirement that he stay at the College throughout the term, rather than leave early to attend to his other job as a judge on the state supreme court. Tucker blasted the new rules as fit only for "the superintendents of the little truants of a country village" and beneath his honor as "a professor of liberal science, honoured with the important trust" of educating young men "destined to fill the most conspicuous stations, and the highest offices of the state." To accept the new regulations "must degrade the professor in the eyes of his pupils, and of the public, & the man in his own eyes." Always proud and increasingly irritable, Tucker resigned in December 1803 (effective March 1804). His successor was an elderly mediocrity, William Nelson, who "danced very merrily though he had silvered locks." Tucker's departure deepened the pervasive gloom over the College's prospects.[60]

The new rules failed to tame the defiant students. In December 1807, the despairing faculty appealed to the state legislature for help. Confessing that they "cannot controul the Conduct of Students under their Care," the professors felt "baffled in almost every attempt to enforce their own Laws. To call upon a Student to give Information, which may [in]criminate the Conduct of a Fellow Student, has been found nugatory. This *Esprit du Corps* exists in every Seminary, & will continue to exist, wherever Youth shall be collected in considerable Numbers." The faculty begged for "legal Authority to compel the Attendance of Witnesses, & of administering an Oath." But legislators declined to endow professors with the powers of magistrates. The faculty would have to muddle on in futility.[61]

William & Mary reached a new low in March 1808, when the faculty tried to suppress drunken parties and balls. Angry students vandalized the College and threatened the Bishop and his home. Ellen Randolph informed her grandfather, Thomas Jefferson: "There has been a terrible riot at Williamsburg. 15 boys were expelled and 5 thrown in Jail and fined 20 dollars a piece." The city militia had to patrol the streets for several nights. A relatively orderly student, Samuel Myers, denounced his riotous peers as having "arrived at a state of depravity and insensibility."[62]

The son of a Norfolk merchant, Myers resolved to study hard and avoid dissipated company, save, he conceded, for two or three times a week. Myers cherished his housemate, William C. Somerville of Richmond: "a better one I believe I could not have possibly chosen. . . .

He is a clever young man and well spoken, but is rendered far more respectable by his fortune, reported to be a hundred thousand pounds." They shared "the same desire and intention of applying closely to our studies and avoiding company as much as possible." But honor disputes could divide the best of friends and cast them on a deadly path.[63]

Three months later, Myers wrote to his father: "Several insults which I had received from Somerville compelled me on Saturday morning to call on him for an explanation." They met at a meadow on the margins of town, where Somerville called Myers a liar, which "drew from me a blow." Myers then offered to fetch two pistols from a friend "that we might decide it on the spot." When Somerville refused, Myers put up a public notice "to post him in the College as a poltroon"—which meant a coward. Although he violated College rules, Myers insisted that "the dictates of honor impelled" his action. A magistrate arrested Myers and Somerville, compelling both to post bond to keep the peace. The faculty held a hearing but merely admonished them.[64]

Leaving college, Myers returned to Norfolk to study law, but he soon ran afoul of it. In May 1811, his father, Moses Myers, visited the city market, where he found Richard Bowden, a former business partner. Resuming an old quarrel, Myers called Bowden "a Rogue, upon which Mr. Bowden gave him several blows with a Cane." Moses staggered home, fainting from the loss of blood just as he met his son. Thinking his father dying, Samuel snatched up a pistol, rushed to Bowden's counting house, and shot him dead. Just twenty-eight years old, Bowden left behind a wife and four children. Thanks to expensive advocates and indulgent judges, Myers escaped trial and later became a leading lawyer in Norfolk.[65]

Meanwhile, in Williamsburg student duels increased. In 1811, St. George Tucker's wife Lelia reported: "Dirks & pistols are carried in the Pockets and Challenges are sent to & from." She urged students to heed an "excellent Sermon" by Reverend Bracken advocating "meek resignation." But few students would ever follow Bracken. Trained to assert their masculine honor, young gentlemen balked at Christian meekness as feminine.[66]

Buried

Enrollment at the College stagnated at about fifty students, two-thirds of its peak in early 1802. In 1804 a student explained, "Parents are afraid to send their children here, lest their morals should be perverted." The College compared poorly to Princeton, Harvard, and Yale, each of which attracted at least 150 students. The College students were also a volatile lot. Few persisted for more than a year or two, and almost none met the requirements to graduate with a degree. From 1800 through 1805, the college granted degrees to only 3 students, during a period when more than 150 attended courses.[67]

One man still thought that he could save the College: Joseph C. Cabell. Born into a wealthy and prestigious family of Amherst County in the Piedmont, Cabell was a sickly but brilliant student who attended the College from 1796 to 1798 and returned in 1800 to study law with St. George Tucker. Jefferson, an old family friend, helped Cabell by providing a reading list on law, politics, religion, math, astronomy, geography, poetry, oratory, philosophy, literary criticism, and chemistry. To strengthen his health, from 1803 to 1805, Cabell toured Europe, where he investigated geology, chemistry, politics, schools, and ancient ruins. Returning to Williamsburg in 1806, he courted Polly Carter Tucker, one of St. George Tucker's stepchildren from his second marriage. Joseph and Polly married in January 1807 and for two years lodged in the rambling Tucker house, while Cabell prepared to launch his political career in Nelson County.[68]

Cabell hoped to rescue William & Mary by rallying support from its distinguished alumni. He sought help from his old friend and classmate Isaac A. Coles, who had become President Jefferson's secretary. Cabell conceded that William & Mary suffered from "the want of an overawing population in the town . . . to suppress the riotous disposition of the students." Still, he concluded, "we ought to make the best of it, as it is all we have." But Coles and Jefferson derided the College as a lost cause and preferred to push for a "great new University" in the Piedmont. Five years later, Cabell considered becoming a professor at William & Mary, but his brother dissuaded him. William H. Cabell insisted that Joseph instead should "keep up the idea that you are still in the world. You would indeed be dead and buried" at the College.[69]

The College's decline accelerated after its longtime president, Bishop James Madison, died in March 1812. The Board of Visitors chose an elderly, unlikely, and unpopular successor: Reverend John Bracken. In December, Cabell tried to force Bracken's resignation by lining up Peter Carr, Jefferson's nephew, as his replacement. But Jefferson wanted the College to fail, so he persuaded Carr to stay home while Bracken remained president. In 1814, William & Mary had only twenty-one students and one professor. Fed up with the decline, the Visitors pressured the decrepit president to resign in October 1814.[70]

They replaced him with Dr. John Augustine Smith, born in Virginia and briefly educated at the College in 1800, but recently a medical professor in New York. Energetic, Smith also taught moral philosophy, law, and political economy. He repaired buildings, upgraded the scientific apparatus, recruited new faculty, and increased enrollment to ninety-two in 1817. In a newspaper piece, Smith boasted, "Contemplate now the great, the rapid, the delightful change, and the heart of every Virginian and of every Republican must exult at the recollection that WILLIAM & MARY IS AGAIN RESTORED."[71]

That bustling energy impressed Cabell, who praised his friend in 1815: "Smith has a happy turn for the Government of young men." A year later, Cabell's nephew Nicholas tested that confidence by becoming a student and tangling with a classmate, Robert Douthat, who threatened him with a humiliating caning. Nicholas obtained a pistol and challenged Douthat to a duel. Douthat refused, so Nicholas posted notices accusing his rival of cowardice. The faculty intervened and suspended both boys for the rest of the term.[72]

The suspension angered Nicholas's father, William H. Cabell, a former governor of the state. Cabell defended Nicholas for seeking a duel to avoid "the degradation of being caned. . . . and so would any other man, whatever professors as such may say to the contrary." Cabell vowed, "I shall never place another son under the guardianship of men who are

capable of such injustice." Cabell preferred to tolerate student disorder
rather than compromise honor:

> The Professors *must* give over the idea of compelling the students
> to give evidence against each other & themselves. I have always
> believed that the disorderly spirit prevailing in our Colleges has
> proceeded from the effort to enforce this regulation. The students
> revolt at it & rush into excesses in order to show their determi-
> nation not to submit. They lose all respect for men who endeavor
> to enforce upon them what they believe to be dishonorable and
> this want of respect & spirit of resistance produce most of the
> disorders which disgrace our Colleges. If the authors of offences
> cannot be discovered, the offences must remain unpunished. The
> remedy, & the only proper one, is to punish very severely the few
> that are detected.

While urging colleges to discipline their students in general, genteel
parents defended their own sons who resisted the rules.[73]

Despite the parental pushback, Smith vowed to reform the students,
rejecting the widespread belief "that young Virginians were absolutely
uncontroulable; that they sucked in with their mother's milk, such high
spirited notions, as to be ever after ungovernable." His crusade provoked defiance. In 1817, Smith complained, "That night after night the
repose of the town had been disturbed by whooping and shouting, by
the ringing of the church-bell, and the firing of cannon." When summoned to testify, no student would confess or implicate others. Smith
sputtered that "these deliberate violations of truth, so far from exciting
the indignation of the virtuous part of the *students*, were becoming matters of mirth." Nothing so enraged the vain Smith as to become the butt
of student mockery. One night, Smith ventured out to catch the culprits,
but he charged into an ambush of hurled plaster and blows from sticks.[74]

In February 1818, students protested when the professor of chemistry charged them fees for a full semester although he had started the
term a month late. When the faculty rejected their petition, students

fired a cannon in the main street and pulled down the gate and broke the windows of a local judge who served on the Board of Visitors. The faculty demanded a written apology from every signer to the petition. A third of the students refused, which led Smith to suspend them. In the *Richmond Enquirer*, they denounced Smith, "Deluded man! Know that Virginians" possess "a spirit of prompt resistance to any encroachment on their just rights."[75]

To break further resistance, Smith required any suspected student to swear under oath to his innocence or guilt. If none confessed to a violation, then in stage two, Smith could demand of any student whether he knew anyone to have lied under oath. The faculty suspended any student who remained silent. Smith explained that no student had to testify "to the disadvantage of a Fellow-Student, until that Fellow-Student has *told a public, deliberate, solemn falsehood*." Smith sought to correct their "abuse of that sacred, but most hackneyed and perverted term HONOR."[76]

Smith's informer policy and expulsions soured many genteel Virginians on the College, reversing his brief revival of William & Mary. One ousted student reported, "The College is in great confusion. They are suspending students every day there." From the peak in 1817 of ninety-two, enrollment plummeted to fifty in the fall of 1818 and to half of that by 1824. Few Virginians would send their sons to a college that compelled them to become informers, thereby imperiling their sacred honor. Smith further alienated Virginians by citing the similar statutes enforced at Harvard, Princeton, and Yale: the bastions of Yankee education.[77]

At his inauguration in 1814, Smith had declared that he "would much prefer" that the faculty "should be ourselves the sole occupants of this venerable pile, than see it crowded with a lawless host of ungovernable students." He nearly succeeded in emptying the College. During his first ten years as president, the College expelled or suspended seventy-seven students, about a fifth of the total attending, and more than twice those ousted during the previous thirty years under Madison and Bracken.[78]

Premature Men

During the early nineteenth century, disorder and riots affected all American colleges, North and South. But the problem was greatest where southern students congregated. The most troubled northern university was Princeton, which had the largest proportion of southern students, usually a third, and they were regarded as the ringleaders of trouble. At Yale, a Virginian denounced northern students who did testify against peers: "If a young man so far violated the laws of propriety as to go and inform against a fellow student, the very fact would blast his every prospect of living, much less of distinction, in the South; it should be so; the name, character, and votaries of Judas Iscariot will ever be condemned and despised, for shame! For shame!"[79]

The student tumult peaked at southern universities. At the University of North Carolina, students shaved the tail of the president's horse, toppled his outhouse, and stole and hid away deep in the woods his cart and garden gate. A student there thought his peers the most drunken, profane, and defiant in the land. His father partially disagreed, "The dissipation you speak of pervades all the States where Slavery abounds. Were you conversant with the habits of So[uth] Carolina or Georgia University, you would find darker traces there than at Chapel Hill." To rile their professors, South Carolina students staged "blackrides," when they blackened their faces, stole the horses of faculty, and galloped about campus while holding flaming torches. After exhausting a horse and drawing a cheering crowd, a "blackrider" dismounted and slipped into the midst of his fellows to hide from investigation. The Carolina students delighted in showing the impotence of frustrated professors.[80]

Most observers regarded southern students as more undisciplined, dissolute, and defiant than their northern peers. Thomas Cooper could compare northern and southern students, for he had taught in Pennsylvania before becoming president of South Carolina College. In February 1822, Cooper reported that students stole his horse for a "blackride," broke his house windows, and even fired guns to startle him. Writing to his friend

Jefferson, Cooper declared, "In my own opinion, the parental indulgence to the south renders young men less fit for college government than the habits of the northern people; and the rigid discipline of the northern seminary must be put in force inexorably in the south."[81]

Southern students built a powerful peer culture that pressured all to seek approval from one another instead of from professors. A South Carolina College graduate recalled that the student "sees his professors for an hour or two only every day. There is no social relation between them. The student herds with the boys alone." He added, "The raw freshman . . . is ambitious to emulate the high spirited example of his senior. He makes rapid advances in smoking, chewing, playing billiards, concocting sherry cobblers, gin slings, and mint juleps." A Virginian at Princeton described the southern-inflected student culture: "There is something wonderfully inflammable in the nature of young men, which is fostered and promoted by the manner of living together. A feeling of resentment or indignation communicates itself like electricity, and what I most wonder at, is that we have not more riots." Peers shunned and insulted the rare student who failed to join them in defying the morality preached by professors. A few painful examples prodded the rest into line with the peer culture.[82]

Southern colleges became trapped in a spiral, where defiant students provoked faculties and Visitors into imposing stricter codes meant to forbid behaviors seen as triggering that defiance. Those rules banned drinking, gaming, dueling, wearing dandy clothes, keeping guns, dogs, and slaves on campus, frequenting prostitutes, staying out late, sleeping in to skip classes, and making a racket to rouse sleeping townspeople. Enforcement fell on the beleaguered faculty. In addition to their full days in the classroom, they had to become the nocturnal monitors of many younger and spryer malcontents. By defying the new rules, students defended their own turf, where they could more readily humiliate professors as ineffectual. Students insisted that the faculty lacked "rightful authority to restrain them in their pleasures and amusements, or interfere at all with their moral conduct."[83]

During the 1810s, college leaders tried to enlist parental support by sending home reports after every term on every student. Instead, parents usually sided with their sons, favoring their stories of innocence persecuted by dishonorable professors. Parents blamed the faculty for failing to set genteel examples that could inspire students without resorting to coercion. Few southern fathers wanted their sons to forfeit the esteem of peers by submitting to rules that compromised honor. In Virginia, the defiant student reflected better on his parents than did the mean fellow who studied in his room and told a professor what he wanted to hear. And family ties were too sentimental and precious to southern parents to ever consider siding with outsiders at the expense of a son's reputation.[84]

Virginia's leaders worried that young men lacked the self-discipline to lead the state after the revolutionary generation passed away. Despite his own youthful follies and duel, even John Randolph felt disgusted. In 1807, Randolph insisted: "A petulant arrogance, or supine, listless indifference, marks the character of too many of our young men. They early assume airs of manhood; and these premature men remain children for the rest of their lives. Upon the credit of a smattering of Latin, drinking grog, and chewing tobacco, these striplings set up for legislators and statesmen."[85]

In 1809, St. George Tucker commiserated with his son-in-law, John Coalter, on the birth of a son, for "unless the manners of our Youth, or the management of their Tutors, shall undergo a most surprising & happy change in this Country, I had rather he should never hear of an *Academy* or a *College* than enter the walls of one." After raising six sons and stepsons, Tucker exulted "that I have no young son to educate."[86]

St. George Tucker's cousin, George Tucker, had attended William & Mary during the 1790s. Twenty years later, he published a satire featuring Harry Whiffler, a Tidewater planter's son who attended "the college of William & Mary, where he soon went thro' the whole circle of *vices* taught in that polite seminary. It is true, he didn't make quite so great a progress in the sciences. He passed, however, for a lad of great genius, principally upon the ground of his laziness." Harry "played cards all night and lay abed all day." Harry had to leave the College after a duel where he "got a slight flesh wound by way of diploma." He returned home to practice law and sought a seat in "the House of Delegates and Congress."[87]

During the 1780s, Jefferson had invested high hopes in the potential of the new generation raised in a free republic. By 1814, however, he felt sadly disillusioned with almost all young gentlemen in Virginia as lazy and arrogant: "Our post-revolutionary youth . . . acquire all learning in their mothers' womb, and bring it into the world ready-made. The information of books is no longer necessary; and all kno[w]lege which is not innate, is [held] in contempt." Pronouncing William & Mary moribund, Jefferson invested his last, desperate hope in founding a new and improved university. Only a fresh start, he believed, could rescue Virginia from the defiant generation spawned by honor culture, the unanticipated fruit of his revolution.[88]

Samuel Myers, c. 1810, by unknown
(Chrysler Museum of Art)

4

MOUNTAIN

ON A LITTLE MOUNTAIN in Virginia, Thomas Jefferson built a mansion fit for "a Sage and a man of taste," a French admirer noted. Visiting in 1782, the Marquis de Chastellux found "a Philosopher, retired from the world and public business, because he loves the world only insofar as he can feel that he is useful." That wary love kept pulling Jefferson down the mountain to hold high political office. In 1779, a friend joked

Anne Cary Randolph Bankhead (1791–1826), by unknown, 1823
(Virginia Museum of History & Culture)

that, by becoming governor, Jefferson had "condescended to come down from above and interest yourself in Human Affairs."[1]

When fed up with public life, Jefferson withdrew to Monticello, where he could meet people on his own terms—or watch them from a comforting distance. At home, he dazzled visitors, particularly close friends. "His manners could never be harsh, but they were reserved towards the world at large," Edmund Randolph recalled. "To his intimate friends he shewed a peculiar sweetness of temper, and by them, was admired and beloved." Jefferson dreaded criticism: "I find the pain of a little censure, even when it is unfounded, is more acute than the pleasure of much praise." And he relished the approval of friends, allies, and voters. "It is a charming thing to be loved by everybody: and the way to obtain it is, never to quarrel or be angry with anybody," he confided. In personal encounters, Jefferson masked his resentments and anger with polite, good temper. His fiery letters to close friends were different.[2]

Jefferson's little mountain rose six hundred feet above the river below. The impractical location multiplied the costs of construction, as Jefferson had to level ten acres on the top and haul up tools, supplies, and materials—some imported at immense cost from Europe. Visitors came by a winding road through a thick forest of twisted, storm-battered trees. "The ascent of this steep, savage hill was as pensive and slow as Satan's ascent to Paradise," a guest recalled. At the final approach, another traveler reported, riders broke into the light to see the mansion, a contrast that rendered the sight "extremely grand & imposing."[3]

The top offered a spectacular view in all directions, of nearby farms, two villages, and the winding Rivanna River. That view stretched for nearly one hundred miles, filled with rising hills, ridges, and mountains in the western distance. A visitor noted the appeal to Jefferson of the "lofty summit, above the contentions and meanness and inconsistencies of his fellow men," where he could "gaze down upon this world which they inhabit, having his mind elevated by its glorious perfection to his Creator and Judge."[4]

Monticello boasted an exuberant garden of ornamental shrubs, flowers, vines, and fruit trees. It also backed onto a long, green lawn, where his grandchildren played, often with Jefferson joining their races and games. Deftly tucked to the sides of the lawn, discreetly out of view, were Jefferson's cisterns, icehouse, cellars, kitchen, work-shops, storerooms, and quarters for enslaved people. Built of brick and designed by Jefferson in a neoclassical style, the central house was an octagon with portals to both east and west and colonnaded porticoes to north and south. On one slope, he kept tame deer and fed them corn by hand.[5]

Stepping through the front door, visitors found an entrance hall devoted to a museum of curiosities. The bones of elk, deer, buffalo, and mammoths filled cabinets while Indian bows, arrows, spears, peace pipes, moccasins, clothing, and hide paintings covered the walls. Between the cabinets rose the busts of great men, including Voltaire, Lafayette, Franklin, Washington, the Russian Czar Alexander, and Jefferson. Pressing into the heart of the building, guests came to the parlor, a place to mingle with the family and admire imported paintings and prints covering the walls. Sometimes a granddaughter played the harpsichord placed in one corner.[6]

Deeper within, Jefferson kept a private sanctuary, a combination library, office, bedroom, and closet, where he spent many hours reading and writing. Devoted to books, Jefferson accumulated 6,500 volumes, including exquisitely bound and finely printed imports from Europe. Rich in classical literature and modern history, philosophy, and fine arts, the library had few novels, which Jefferson disliked as trifles.[7]

Jefferson shared his private space with two trusted slaves, valet Burwell Colbert and maid Sally Hemings. Another Monticello slave recalled, "Mr. Jefferson was on the most intimate terms with her; that, in fact, she was his concubine." After Jefferson's wife died in 1782, he never remarried, keeping a vow to protect the inheritance of their daugh-ters from a legal stepmother and additional white children. Instead, Jefferson relied for intimacy on Hemings, an enslaved woman whose four children (who lived to adulthood) lacked legal standing. As the daughter of an enslaved woman and Jefferson's father-in-law, Hemings was the half-sister of Jefferson's late and beloved wife. Her resemblance and dependence both allured Jefferson.[8]

Jefferson designed Monticello to maximize his control through superior vision and information—while restricting what others could see and know of him. Visitors could enter Jefferson's sanctuary only by invitation and during the day. A nosy guest, Anna Thornton, regretted, "The president's bedchamber is only separated from the library by an arch; he keeps it constantly locked, and I have been disappointed much by not being able to get in today." By nine at night, Jefferson retired into his sanctuary, leaving guests to entertain themselves. Jefferson's private rooms had Venetian blinds that allowed him to see out, while preventing others from looking in. He also had a telescope to peer into Charlottesville and watch over his broad plantation, to the dismay of his enslaved workers.[9]

But Jefferson had less control over appearances than he wished. His second, covert family was well known and much discussed. His friend John Hartwell Cocke reported that Virginia's mixed-race people "would be found by hundreds. Nor is it to be wondered at when Mr. Jefferson's notorious example is considered." In 1811, a Yankee schoolteacher, Elijah Fletcher, visited Monticello to meet Jefferson. "I confess I never had a very exalted opinion of his moral conduct," Fletcher assured his father, "but from the information I gained of his neighbors, who must best know him, I have a much poorer one. The story of black Sal is no farce. That he cohabits with her and has a number of children by her is a sacred truth, and the worst of it is, he keeps the same children slaves, an unnatural crime which is very common in these parts."[10]

Exquisitely designed, Monticello was an expensive gem of artifice. "Monticello is curiosity! Artificial to a high degree," a visitor marveled. Noting the many innovative design touches, Anna Thornton declared, "Everything has a whimsical and droll appearance." A labor of love for Jefferson, Monticello took decades to build, as he kept changing the design. In 1802, Thornton reported, "It is a place you would rather look at now & then than live at. Mr. J has been 27 years engaged in improving the place, but he has pulled down & built up again so often, that nothing is completed, nor do I think ever will be." Every change compounded costs, consuming the revenue from Jefferson's plantation, mill, and shops.[11]

Enslaved labor built and maintained Monticello, and slaves waited on host, family, and guests. A visitor from New England marveled, "I went to my chamber, found there a fire, candle, and a servant in waiting to receive my orders for the morning, and in the morning was waked by his return to build the fire." Jefferson tried to keep his slaves just barely visible, ready to prepare and deliver meals and cleaning before slipping back into the shadows. As was common in Virginia, he favored mixed-race house servants, the lighter the better, to work in the public rooms. A French visitor saw, "especially at Mr. Jefferson's, slaves, who, neither in point of colour nor features, shewed the least trace of their original descent; but their mothers being slaves, they retain, of consequence, the same condition." Darker complexions prevailed among the many enslaved field hands who worked beyond the mansion. The slave quarter saddened Margaret Bayard Smith, a visitor who otherwise admired Jefferson: "They appear poor and their cabins form a most unpleasant contrast with the palace that rises so near them."[12]

Monticello displayed what refined taste, cosmopolitan connections, classical education, and wealth could create—as a haven for Jefferson and an inspiration to others. But by crafting a distinctive place where he could best display himself, Jefferson attracted hordes of admirers. A visitor from Pennsylvania, Richard Rush, noted the irony that Jefferson tried to live "wonderfully lifted above most mortals." But that very distance, the beguiling artifice of his concoction, and his own fame drew the world up to him. Rush added, "as you well know his mountain is made a sort of Mecca."[13]

Jefferson felt "deeply conflicted" about the throngs. On the one hand, he enjoyed holding court, performing for guests how an enlightened leader should appear, act, and talk. On the other hand, too many visitors came, and their numbers wore him out. The strain of entertaining grew greater as his finances withered and his body decayed, but the show went on, and gawkers kept coming. Granddaughter Ellen

Randolph despised the "disagreeable intrusions," "many silly questions," and "giggling impertinence" of so many visitors.[14]

Unwilling to turn admirers away, but unable to host their growing numbers, Jefferson built and retreated to a second, smaller version of Monticello in Bedford County. Known as Poplar Forest, the new home lay three days' travel further west, over bad roads, from Monticello. The extra distance deterred most travelers from following Jefferson. By slipping away for a couple of months at a time, Jefferson bought relaxation and retirement with his beloved granddaughters. But his escapes imposed a greater burden on his daughter Martha, who usually stayed behind to cope with the Monticello household and those visitors who still could not hear no. The sojourns also bore hard upon the enslaved servants taken away to serve Jefferson, leaving their wives and children at Monticello.[15]

His granddaughters relished escaping the visiting throngs to spend cherished time reading, drawing, and talking with their grandfather. "I have often thought that the life of a student must be the most innocent and happy in the world," Ellen wrote from Poplar Forest. But politeness and a relish for *some* company soon led Jefferson to take the girls about in a carriage to call on neighbors and invite them to dinner. The girls hated that extra work and the lost privacy. In September 1819, Cornelia lamented, "In spite of everything, Grandpapa insists upon the lady dinners," which would open the social floodgates, so that "we shall hereafter have more trouble & vexation than we ever had at Monticello."[16]

Sage

For all its charms, beauties, and oddities, the greatest attraction at Monticello was the philosopher. A visitor from New Hampshire, Salma Hale, explained, "Mr. Jefferson I found on the top of his mountain surrounded with curiosities and himself not the least." Hale first glimpsed Jefferson "thro' the window among the trees, a tall, spare man, walking towards the house, throwing his legs about unmindful of his steps, like a man in a reverie." Indeed, Jefferson dwelled in a dream of transcending the contentious world below.[17]

Jefferson was distinctive: a wealthy and learned man with a shambling, easy gait and lounging posture, who carefully wore clothes of apparent carelessness. His attire of shabby, dated gentility conveyed his combination of old money and republican ease. During the 1810s, he was tall, about six feet two, with a freckled face and red hair turning gray, his "figure bony, long and with broad shoulders, a true Virginian," remarked a visitor. "He was like a fine horse—he had no surplus flesh," his plantation manager, Edmund Bacon, recalled. Jefferson wore soft shoes that resembled slippers, "with pointed toes and heels ascending a peak behind" and a blue "coat, of stiff, thick cloth made of the wool of his own merinos and badly manufactured." Observers dwelled on Jefferson's quirky attire, particularly his plush red velvet waistcoat and occasional red breeches, which they associated with his fiery devotion to the French Revolution.[18]

Jefferson's hospitality dazzled visitors. His enslaved staff served tasteful French cuisine and expensive, imported wines, but he ate and drank moderately, never appearing tipsy. Favoring reading, music, and conversation, he discouraged profanity, playing cards, or any gambling in his home. And he was courteous to everyone.[19]

His sprightly conversation ranged widely, touching on politics but dwelling on history, science, diplomacy, philosophy, and religion. One visiting New Englander marveled as Jefferson led an hour-long conversation that danced from Georgia's expansion, the character of Indians and African Americans, federal tariff policy, British diplomacy, and South America to the "Character of Christ and His religion." A lifelong scholar, Jefferson knew a lot about almost everything. By sharing facts and fancies, he enthralled even visiting French intellectuals. Chastellux proclaimed, "It seems, indeed, as though, ever since his youth, he had placed his mind, like his house, on a lofty height, whence he might contemplate the whole universe."[20]

Avoiding disagreement and argument, he nurtured a light, gregarious tone. When clashing opinions emerged, he gently but quickly shifted to a new topic. Francis W. Gilmer praised his conversation, which had "sometimes the agreeable levity of the French, at others the graver instruction of a philosopher, but always . . . simplicity and pleasantry." Another visitor captured Jefferson's virtuosity: "I was delighted with Mr. Jefferson: so much freshness of character; nothing worn out or exhausted; such a magnanimous carelessness in the promulgation of his opinions; such fine talent in almost every matter of human observation; such various knowledge; so easy & cheerful a hospitality."[21]

Visitors noted both the apparent ease and lingering reserve that Jefferson balanced in his manners and talk. The combination expressed, a grandson-in-law recalled, "the persistent control he exercised over his world" at Monticello. Bacon remembered, "His countenance was always mild and pleasant. You never saw it ruffled." The philosopher wanted to put people at ease and win their admiration without conceding initiative to them. George Ticknor recalled the "general conversation, of which Mr. Jefferson was necessarily the leader."[22]

Jefferson's uncanny serenity with people sometimes gave way with animals. His grandson Jeff Randolph recalled, "The only impatience of temper he ever exhibited was with his horse, which he subdued to his will by a fearless application of the whip, on the slightest manifestation of restiveness." Jefferson needed to lead, but did so with humans through a subtlety that he did not waste on horses. Bacon marveled that, even as an elderly man, Jefferson "sat easily upon his horse, and always had him in the most perfect control."[23]

That command weakened after 1815, as Jefferson's health worsened. He suffered from rheumatism and an arthritic wrist that made it painful to write. Yet, he replied to most of the hundreds of letters that poured in from every corner of the nation and Europe, seeking information or endorsements on an array of topics and causes. In 1816, Jefferson complained, "I pass from 4 to 6 hours of every day of my life at my writing table, in the drudgery of answering letters in which I have no personal concern or pleasure. It is weighing and wearing down my life with an oppression of body and mind I am not able to bear up against." He was often in great pain as his prostate and kidneys slowly failed.[24]

As Jefferson aged and grew deaf, more testiness and imperious opinion snuck through his charm. He also became careless in confiding in strangers—and recoiled upon seeing his most pointed comments repeated in print. In 1824, a New Englander met Jefferson at Monticello for the first time. "He is more positive, decided, and passionate than I had expected. . . . His manners are much the most agreeable part of him. They are artificial, he shrugs his shoulders when talking, has much of the Frenchman, is rapid, varying, volatile, eloquent, amusing."[25]

Debt

Keen observers noted frayed edges to Monticello. Spending beyond his means to build, Jefferson struggled to maintain his rambling complex against wear and tear from Virginia's climate, many insects, romping grandchildren, and careless visitors. Cultivating the mountainside invited erosion by pouring rains that gullied the red, clay soil and favored invasive weeds. Within the house, visitors noted the old chairs with bottoms "completely worn through & the hair sticking out in all directions." In 1802, Thornton reported that, although still incomplete, the building "looks like a house going to decay." The deterioration increased as Jefferson grew older and poorer. In 1824, another visitor noted, "His house is rather old and going to decay; appearances about his yard and hill are rather slovenly."[26]

A classic Virginian, Jefferson believed that a run of good crops with high market prices would reduce his massive debts faster than the accumulating interest. In fact, nothing was more predictable than the volatility of seasons, rains, frosts, crop pests, and prices in Virginia. Those variables rarely aligned favorably in a single year and never did so for several years in a row. In 1823, Gilmer declared, "What with the burning heat & polar cold of our climate, the madness & presumption of man, the ravages of the Hessian fly, the devastations of the chinch bug, and the wide wasting desolation of the frost, we are in a woeful case."

Virginians and their farms were, he added, "alternately fried & frozen, roasted & boiled, & devoured by vermin." But planters indulged in the wishful thinking that they stood on the cusp of a prolonged series of bumper crops and good prices. That delusion led them to take on more debt as they bought more consumer goods and improved their plantations, doubling down on their costly way of life.[27]

Fond of expensive books, French wines, and architectural experiments, Jefferson lived beyond his means, and the surge of guests added to his burdens. He also invested $30,000 to build a stone flour mill, four stories tall, with a dam and canal that diverted the Rivanna River. Erratic water levels made that mill unreliable until 1815, when a flood washed away the entire complex. In 1817, Jefferson advised a young man that the primary rule in life was "Never spend your money before you have it." It is always easier to preach than practice thrift.[28]

Jefferson also committed the classic Virginian folly of mixing friendship, business, politics, and family. His primary political lieutenant in state politics was Wilson Cary Nicholas, the largest landowner and slaveholder in southern Albemarle County. As a young legislator during the 1780s, Nicholas helped pass Jefferson's and Madison's Statute for Religious Liberty. As governor from 1814 to 1817, he supported Jefferson's educational schemes. In 1815, Nicholas's daughter Jane married Jefferson's oldest grandson, Jeff Randolph, cementing family bonds.[29]

A charming but reckless wheeler-dealer, Nicholas presided over Richmond's branch of the Bank of the United States. Although Jefferson railed against all banks, especially the federal bank, he turned to it for loans to pay the interest on his mushrooming debts. Nicholas helped him secure $6,000 in 1817–1818, but the other shoe dropped when Nicholas asked Jefferson to cosign two of his loans for a whopping $20,000. Jefferson could hardly say no without rupturing a friendship, political alliance, bank access, and family ties.[30]

In 1819, a severe depression frustrated any hope of making money in Virginia. The price paid for farm produce plummeted and with it the value of farms and slaves. Rather than sell land at half or even a third of its former value, Jefferson and his peers gambled on riding out the depression, waiting in vain for prices to rebound. Meanwhile, interest on their debts mounted, and creditors lost patience, while the depression lingered into the mid-1820s.[31]

In August 1819, Nicholas defaulted on his debts and so informed Jefferson "with the greatest pain & mortification." Two weeks later, he added, "I repeat the assurances before given, that you shall not lose a dollar by me. I say this with the utmost confidence." That false confidence led his friends to ruin. Nicholas placed his assets with trustees to satisfy his debtors, but that proved impossible because he owed a massive $280,000. In 1820, his default made Jefferson responsible for the $20,000 that he had cosigned. At Poplar Forest, Jefferson received Nicholas's shocking letter while suffering from "the severest attack of rheumatism I have ever experienced. My limbs all swelled, their strength prostrate, & pain constant." Jefferson dreaded that he would "close my course by a catastrophe I had never contemplated."[32]

Nicholas's collapse entangled many leading Virginians, including another former governor, William H. Cabell, who had cosigned for $60,000 in loans. Unable to pay, Cabell lost his plantation to foreclosure. Cabell's brother Joseph informed a friend, "I cannot depict to you the misfortunes & afflictions brought on my family by a man whom I once revered as one of the greatest & best of mankind. Alas! What poor blind creatures we are." The losses rippled through the state as Nicholas's cosigners had their own creditors anxious for payment. A Richmond merchant lamented, "The explosion has taken place & is certainly worse than anything of the kind that has yet occurred. . . . We are all looking at each other with despair." In April 1820, Francis W. Gilmer described Nicholas as "broken spirited, broken hearted, haggard & emaciated almost to death. The fiends of blasted hope & tortured pride still gnawed his undevoured liver."[33]

Nicholas moved in with his daughter and her husband, who lived at Tufton, one of the satellite farms of Monticello. Dying there in October 1820, Nicholas landed in the Jefferson family cemetery. Angry creditors suspected a trick by Nicholas to fake his death and complete their ruin, so some came to see the corpse. Two years later, the trustees auctioned Nicholas's plantation for $13,500, a third of its former price. "The negroes, as they always do, sold well," remarked John Hartwell Cocke, who attended and bought some books.[34]

Devoted to mathematics, Jefferson counted everything on his estate and kept meticulous accounts. Yet, he deluded himself over the depth of his financial woes. For more than a decade, his daughter Martha exhorted him to economize. She warned that his misplaced optimism "cast a gloom over my spirits that I cannot shake off. The impossibility of paying serious debts by crops, and living [well] at the same time, has been so often proved, that I am afraid you should trust to it." The Cassandra of her family, Martha would live to see her dire prophecies realized.[35]

Randolphs

After retiring from politics, Jefferson often shared Monticello with the family of his daughter Martha and her husband, Thomas Mann Randolph. In 1784, Randolph went overseas to study for four years at Edinburgh, the premier university for science, which Randolph loved while despising traditional Christianity. By letter, Thomas Jefferson guided the brilliant young man's education, and encouraged his political ambitions.[36]

In 1788, Randolph returned to Virginia and, two years later, married his cousin Martha, the eldest daughter of his mentor. Jefferson encouraged the match and a quick wedding at Monticello in February 1790, although Randolph was just twenty-one and Martha a mere seventeen. They had known each other for only seven weeks. To Jefferson's and Martha's delight, the couple settled on the Edgehill Plantation, a short ride from Monticello.[37]

Too late, Martha discovered Randolph's erratic and volcanic temper. A friend remembered him as "an eccentric man of genius, well educated, wild, visionary," and subject "to the delusions of a vivid imagination. [He was] Brave, generous & romantic." Bacon recalled Randolph as "tall, swarthy, and rawboned—one of the stoutest men I ever saw, and afraid of nothing." He was "very queer anyway. The Randolphs were all strange people."[38]

His plantations lost money, and Randolph lived beyond his means, accumulating debts. He proposed sending most of his field hands to distant Mississippi, where they could raise profitable cotton and thereby provide the means "to give my Son the most complete education by attending institutions of learning and traveling abroad." Slaves endowed the education of elite Virginians. But Jefferson blocked the plan, warning Martha "that it would never do to destroy the goose [that laid the golden eggs], for that nothing could be done without hands." Rather than contradict Jefferson's wishes, Randolph remained with the slaves in Albemarle, where his estate decayed toward bankruptcy even faster than did Jefferson's property.[39]

Jefferson had twelve grandchildren who survived to adulthood; eleven of them were the children of Martha and Thomas Mann Randolph. The old philosopher spent his happiest moments with his grandchildren, romping about the grounds, reading in the library, or playing music in the parlor. "Mr. Jefferson was perfectly devoted to his grandchildren, and they to him," Bacon noted. Granddaughter Ellen recalled that he seemed "to wave the fairy wand, to brighten our lives by his goodness and his gifts." In letters to them, Jefferson cast his love as bait to reward their striving to please him. In 1802, he wrote, "The more I perceive that you are all advancing in your learning and improving in good dispositions, the more I shall love you & the more everybody will love you." Jefferson loomed larger in their lives and affections than did their tormented and erratic father.[40]

Monticello played many educational roles as home, museum, nature observatory, working farm, and manufactory. The lessons provided differed by class and race. While enslaved boys learned to make nails, honored guests enjoyed Native American art collected by the Lewis and Clark expedition. The mansion also had a room set aside as a school, where Martha taught her children. A visitor reported, "She is a very accomplished, sensible woman and takes great pains to instruct them.

She is not handsome." Martha explained, "I never can sit down quietly under the idea of their being blockheads."[41]

Tall, lean, and brilliant, Martha resembled her father. They adored one another, far more than either felt toward her husband. Jefferson referred to Martha as "my dearest daughter and friend." After Jefferson, she was probably the best-educated person in Virginia. In an era when no college or university admitted women, she got the next best thing: training at Paris's prestigious Abbaye Royale de Panthemont, which schooled daughters of the French elite. Martha and her younger sister Maria attended during the 1780s, when Jefferson served as the American minister.[42]

The two oldest grandsons were Thomas Jefferson Randolph (b. 1792) and Francis Eppes (b. 1801), the only son of Maria, who had died young. When they became adolescents, Jefferson took charge of educating the boys, shunting aside their parents. He recommended and provided books, chose subjects to study, and selected boarding schools, often after interviewing the directors.[43]

Large and good-natured, Jeff Randolph struggled as a scholar. Like most gentry sons, he suffered from turnover in tutors and schools, shifting from one to another in rapid and disruptive succession. After one year in college, he returned home to manage Monticello for his grandfather. Bacon noted, "I knew Jeff. Randolph as well as one man can know another. Mr. Jefferson took great pains with his education, but he didn't take after his mother—he wasn't a Jefferson—he wasn't talented." But Jeff proved a better manager than his father or grandfather.[44]

Jefferson wanted his grandsons to avoid any school tainted with conventional piety, particularly if located in the Northeast. In 1820, he assured John Wayles Eppes that his son "Francis's honorable mind, his fine dispositions, and high promise ought not to be exposed to infection from the fanaticism, the hypocrisy, the selfish morals, and crooked politics of the East." Instead, Jefferson sent the boy to South Carolina College, where Francis fit in all too well with the riotous students of South Carolina, leading to his suspension in early 1822. He briefly studied law from his grandfather's daunting reading list. Losing interest, Francis preferred to become a planter, and he married a Randolph cousin of equal gentility but even less money. Jefferson gave Francis a farm and slaves at Poplar Forest—with the promise that he would inherit the rest of that estate.[45]

Jefferson defended conventional gender roles, which restricted free women to marriage and motherhood, assisting husbands who (in theory) alone dealt with the world beyond the household. Martha had pleased her father by accepting domestic subordination. In 1791, Jefferson announced that two letters from her "have given me the greatest pleasure of any I ever received from you. The one announced that you were become a notable housewife, the other a mother." He praised American society for honoring and protecting women in domestic withdrawal from public competition and strife. In turn, nurturing women could regenerate their weary husbands, returning from economic and political conflict to domestic retreats. He believed that genteel daughters should learn a little geography, literature, languages, drawing, and music, so that they could talk intelligently to entertain guests. But Jefferson wanted even more thoroughly to educate his granddaughters.[46]

Jefferson had six granddaughters, all Randolphs: Anne Cary (b. 1791); Ellen Wayles (b. 1796); Cornelia Jefferson (b. 1799); Virginia Jefferson (b. 1801); Mary Jefferson (b. 1803); and Septimia Anne (b. 1814). A visitor admired Martha's "highly polished and highly instructed daughters," who could "write or converse in French, Spanish, Italian, or their mother tongue." Jefferson also helped shape their advanced education. Ellen recalled, "I have known him to lay a course of reading which might have startled a University student." She and her sisters perfected the self-disciplined study that Jefferson preached, largely in vain, to Virginia boys. Jefferson marveled, "Ellen and Cornelia are the severest students I have ever met with. They never leave their rooms but to come to meals." No Virginian ever said the same of a son, or indeed wanted such a studious boy. But the granddaughters' superior learning was a family affectation rather than a career path. They could not venture out into the world or manage plantations, which Jefferson instead entrusted to Jeff Randolph, who had never studied much.[47]

Although overtly resigned to the strict limits that gender placed on their prospects and roles, the granddaughters privately longed to make more of their education. Virginia worried, "I begin to think that my spirits & intellect stagnate from want of change & variety in life, for I am unwilling to consider myself too stupid to improve. Indeed, my occupations at present are not calculated to *sharpen wit*, or raise spirits, for I am so constantly employed at my needle endeavouring to keep two wardrobes in order." Cornelia also felt shrunken "by the life I lead & the functions I perform which are exactly such as a machine might be made to perform with equal success, locking & unlocking doors, pouring out tea & coffee & in the interim plying my needle." She longed to learn Latin but worried that her brothers "would all mutiny" if she neglected feeding them. Despite their superior learning, the girls had to serve the boys.[48]

The granddaughters felt trapped between their family's high social standing and its decaying finances. At Monticello, Cornelia lamented, "I wish I could do something to support myself instead of this unprofitable drudgery of keeping house here, but I suppose, not until we sink entirely, will it do for the grand daughters of Thomas Jefferson to take in work or keep a school." She had to keep pouring tea for his many visiting admirers.[49]

Bankhead

Jefferson longed to gather his daughters, with husbands and children, at Monticello to form a harmonious family, lifted above and beyond the world of strife. In 1797, he assured Martha, "I now see our fireside formed into a group, no one member of which has a fibre in their composition which can ever produce any jarring or jealousies among us." Devoid of "irregular passions," the family would deliver the tranquility that politics never could. Alas, the rancorous world followed Jefferson up the mountain and blossomed within his family.[50]

Jefferson unwittingly invited the serpent into his family Eden by welcoming the marriage of his oldest granddaughter, Anne Cary

Randolph, to Charles Lewis Bankhead, the son of an old friend, Dr.
John Bankhead of Caroline County. Anne was beautiful but immature
at just seventeen. She felt drawn to the handsome Bankhead, and the
adults in her life—parents and grandfather—did little to investigate his
character and slow the courtship, which culminated in a hasty wedding
in September 1808. Jefferson encouraged Bankhead to study law, but he
preferred to become a planter. Jefferson helped him buy a farm a mile
west of Monticello. That situation afforded Jefferson a front row seat for
the miseries that followed.[51]

Bankhead was a drunken, abusive bully who beat his wife and
neglected their farm to haunt taverns and brawl with those who
insulted him. At his drunkest, he rode into barrooms to demand more
whiskey. In August 1810, Elizabeth Trist (a family friend and frequent
guest) noted, "Bankhead has turned out a great sot, always frolicking
and Carousing at the Taverns in the Neighbourhood. Poor Ann[e], I feel
for her." She was then five months pregnant with their first child. Bacon
recalled, "I have seen his wife run from him when he was drunk and
hide in a potato-hole to get out of danger." Writing to Bankhead's father
in October 1815, Jefferson reported that Charles had "committed an
assault on his *wife* of great violence. . . . Nor was this a new thing." The
beatings contributed to her losing eight of twelve pregnancies before or
shortly after birth.[52]

Jefferson counseled abused wives to stand by their men. After his
sister married a violent drunk, Jefferson advised her, "When we see ourselves in a situation which must be endured & gone through, it is best to
make up our minds to it." Rather than take in Anne and kick Bankhead
off the mountain, Jefferson sent them both away to live with Dr. John
Bankhead, declaring that they "would be safe nowhere else."[53]

Charles Bankhead was drunk on masculinity as well as alcohol.
Martha reported that when his father forbade his drinking, Charles told
him "he would be master in his own house and called for a decanter of
whiskey and drank off two draughts to his face." She added, "His Father
is utterly in despair." After a few months, Bankhead returned with his
family to their neglected farm near Monticello and his favorite taverns

in Charlottesville. Martha despaired of redeeming Bankhead: "Sending him to the mad house is but a temporary remedy, for after a few weeks he would be returned with renewed health to torment his family the longer." She favored letting him drink himself to death while a body-guard protected his wife and children from beatings.[54]

Thomas Mann Randolph despised Bankhead. One night at Monti-cello, Bacon overheard a drunken Bankhead bully Jefferson's enslaved valet, Burwell Colbert, for denying him the key to a brandy cabinet. Randolph burst into the dining room and confronted Bankhead, who cursed his father-in-law. In a rage, Randolph seized an iron poker from the nearby fireplace and, in Bacon's words, "knocked him down as quick as I ever saw a bullock fall. The blow pealed the skin off one side of his forehead and face, and he bled terribly. If it had been a square blow, instead of glancing off as it did, it must have killed him."[55]

In January 1819, Bankhead sent an insulting letter to his sister-in-law Jane, wife of Jeff Randolph. Bankhead recycled malicious gossip that went back to that couple's wedding in 1815, when Jane's mother initially had opposed the marriage, citing Jeff's limited means and his mother's homeliness. When the couple married, Anne and Charles resented the new couple for assuming primacy with her parents and grandfather.[56]

On the last day of January, Bankhead and Randolph met in Char-lottesville during a court session that filled the central square with peo-ple. Bearing a horsewhip, Jeff confronted Bankhead, who pulled out a long knife. Jeff got the worst of the clash, taking deep, blood-gushing slashes to hip and arm. Bacon saved Jeff's life by pulling away Bankhead. Carried into a store and laid on a pile of blankets, Jeff got care from four doctors, while a sheriff arrested Bankhead for assault. Informed of the bloody fracas, Jefferson rode down from Monticello to the store, where, according to Elizabeth Trist, he "appeared very much affected as well on Anne's account as Jefferson's [for] he expected that Bankhead would wreak his vengeance on his wife."[57]

Writing to Jefferson, Bankhead offered his side of the story, pitched in the key of wounded honor: "when I cease to respect myself, then I consent that all others may cease to respect me." He cast Jeff as "the aggressor in the most unprovoked manner. He commenced upon me with his loaded horsewhip as I was passing by him & without my having said a word to him." Only after "the third blow to my skull, when I had been knocked upon my knee, did I retaliate by drawing my knife." He concluded, "I can bear bodily pain I suspect with as much fortitude as most men, but the disgrace of having been horse-whipped in the presence of three or four hundred people would have sunk me into the dust and rendered me miserable for life." Rejecting Bankhead's version, Jefferson's circle rallied around Jeff.[58]

Bankhead cleared out, forfeiting his $500 bail and abandoning his farm. Anne went with him, which alarmed her friends. One marveled at the "strange infatuation that she can bear to live in the same house with one who must be the refuse of the earth." His drunkenness "would appear to me enough to disgust any woman of delicacy especially one who has been brought up, as Mrs. B[ankhead] has been, in the most refined circle." Jefferson added, "I have for some time taken for granted that she would fall by his hands, and yet she is so attached to him that no persuasion has ever availed to induce her to separate and come to live with us, with her children."[59]

Sadly resigned to his granddaughter's probable fate, Jefferson faulted her submission rather than himself for supporting her marrying Bankhead. By 1819, she probably could exercise little true choice after years of abuse. Elizabeth Trist thought that Bankhead's father could protect Anne better than Jefferson and the Randolphs had: "I believe upon the whole it is a fortunate thing as he has been obliged to leave this Neighbourhood, for they live now with his Parents who are excessively fond of Ann[e], and he will not behave to her there as he did here."[60]

Jeff Randolph recovered enough to return home and resume riding, but he never fully regained the use of his arm. Disgusted by the indulgent juries of rural Virginia, Jefferson despaired of convicting Bankhead if he returned to Albemarle County. "Our citizens are . . . left in a state of nature to save their own lives by taking that of another." While publicly defending Virginia against Yankee criticism, Jefferson privately mourned the moral erosion of his beloved state. The pervasive code of honor had frustrated Jefferson's efforts to reform the Virginia gentry. And Bankhead had ruined Jefferson's fantasy of a perfect, harmonious family, by bringing violence into the heart of Monticello.[61]

In February 1826, Anne returned to Monticello to give birth—and to die. She was only thirty-five, but her body had suffered twelve pregnancies and uncounted blows. She died embracing the evangelical faith rejected by her family. Attending the deathbed, her pious friend Mary E. Terrell exulted, "I think every Christian will rejoice, at the triumphant testimony our dear friend bore to Christianity in her illness & last moments. She said she had long sought her only consolations in the hopes of the Gospel, & was now ready to depart and be with Christ." The death shocked Jefferson, and his self-control dissolved. One doctor recalled, "It is impossible to imagine more poignant distress than was exhibited by him. He shed tears, and abandoned himself to every evidence of intense grief."[62]

Terrell thought that Anne's death would "either save [Bankhead] or ruin him forever." It did not save him. Seven years later, Anne's younger brother, Benjamin Franklin Randolph, was the doctor summoned to attend Bankhead, who was gravely ill with alcohol poisoning from a prolonged bender. Martha reported that her son "gave him what he thought the case required." The next morning Bankhead died in a final fit. If the doctor gave a fatal dose, he fulfilled Martha's long-standing hope.[63]

Gilmer

Francis Walker Gilmer longed to become a Jefferson-Randolph. Born in 1790, Gilmer grew up at Pen Park, an estate of 4,000 acres on the Rivanna River across from Monticello. His father, Dr. George Gilmer, had joined the Albemarle County elite by marrying the daughter of Dr. Thomas Walker, Peter Jefferson's land-speculating partner. As Thomas Jefferson's dear friend, Dr. Gilmer had ready access to Monticello, where his son Francis learned French from Martha Jefferson Randolph.[64]

Young Gilmer basked in early praise of his brilliance and promise. Jefferson regarded him as a rare intellect in the wasteland of Virginia's fallen standards: "In the vast dearth of scientific education in our state, he presents almost the solitary object, known to me as eminent in genius, in science, in industry & excellent disposition." Mastering botany, rhetoric, and the Greek and Latin classics, Gilmer dazzled the leader of Washington, D.C.'s high society, Margaret Bayard Smith: "He is called the *future hope of Virginia*—its ornament!—its brightest star! I had a long, animated, and interesting conversation with him, really the greatest intellectual feast I have long had. He is the enthusiastic admirer of my dear and revered Mr. Jefferson and a familiar intimate of his family."[65]

Like most young Virginians, however, Gilmer's learning came in fits and starts, often interrupted by erratic teachers and shifting schools, including William & Mary, where he graduated in 1810. A year later, Gilmer moved to Richmond to live and study with the preeminent lawyer William Wirt, who recalled, "His learning is of a curious cast," for often "having no one to direct his studies, he seems to have devoured indiscriminately everything that came his way." Wirt mused, "It was curious to hear a boy of seventeen years speaking with fluency, and even with manly eloquence" while quoting Descartes, Newton, and Locke.[66]

Formerly married to Gilmer's older sister Mildred, who had died, Wirt treated the boy as a prized protégé. Wirt insisted that Gilmer was a "prodigy" and the only Virginian who could match Jefferson's erudition. Wirt wanted "to see what is attainable by man: and I know of no young man so well fitted for the experiment as yourself." He exhorted Gilmer, "I wish you to be much greater than I ever was or can hope to be, [greater] than any other man in Virginia." To become great, Wirt assured Gilmer, "You must read like Jefferson and speak like Henry." Leading Virginians invested excessive hopes in Gilmer because they disdained most of his peers as shallow and lazy coxcombs letting down their state.[67]

Praise fed Gilmer's voracious ego and burning ambition to rise to the top of Virginia's society, but he had to overcome the wreck of the family fortunes. In his last years, Dr. Gilmer lost control of mind, body, and finances thanks to a crippling stroke shortly after Francis's birth.

When he died in 1795, creditors took and sold the family estate, Pen Park. The youngest sons, including Francis, became the wards of Dr. Charles Everette, who had studied with Dr. Gilmer and took over his medical practice.[68]

Slight, sickly, and hypersensitive, Gilmer felt that neighbors mocked his decaying fortune and relished predicting his inevitable failure. He vowed to vindicate his father and "humble the arrogance of those who have set themselves in judgment upon us." Gilmer resented seeing "the seats of our Fathers owned by aliens, the influence of a family once powerful lost even among those who ate the crum[b]s from its table; everything that was sacred trampled on, tarnished & polluted by malevolence & brutality."[69]

Ambitious young Virginians studied the law and pursued politics. Often overlapping, the two careers demanded skilled oratory, a capacity to move voters and jurors with appeals to reason and feeling. By that path Patrick Henry, John Randolph, and William Wirt had risen to fame and fortune, and Gilmer meant to follow their lead. But he sought to do even better, "by introducing a more correct style of speaking." By combining gesture, voice, passion, logic, and learning into a consummate performance, he would sway the uneducated while impressing scholars. "I wish to be a profound reasoner & not a pretty declaimer." But Gilmer worried that he lived in the wrong place for elegant writing and speaking: "In Virginia we must come home to the business of life. The region of sentiment is too ethereal for men fed on bacon & greens."[70]

As Wirt's protégé, Gilmer gained the legal knowledge, rhetorical training, and genteel connections to shine in Virginia society. But studying legal tomes and copying briefs was the tedious lot of a student and clerk. So Gilmer alternated bursts of career optimism with daydreams of pursuing his first love, botany, and writing scientific and political essays. But neither science nor literature paid in Virginia, so he secured his license to practice law. "Since I cannot live as I wish, nay as I deserve, I will reconcile myself to live as I can—a drudge at the bar," he wrote in 1814. Francis fantasized that he could make enough money to retire in a few years, devoting his life thereafter to flowers, essays, and orations.[71]

But law offered diminishing returns during the late 1810s, because the bar was so crowded and the economy so stagnant. Gilmer complained, "I must have wealth & wealth is not to be acquired by the practice of the law in Virginia." He considered moving to Baltimore or Kentucky to seek "a better theatre & a better audience too before whom to act my part in life." But Gilmer could never leave his beloved, if declining, Virginia. He assured his brother Peachy: "Since we resolve not to give up the ship, but to fight for the Old Dominion, let us renew the campaign with double zeal. The first great occasion that offers I shall make another sort of speech to any I have yet attempted. . . . It is time to let off a few sky rockets." A thorough Virginian, Gilmer meant to save his state by giving speeches. He did not consider that Virginia was decaying, in part, because its leaders had fallen in love with the sound of their own voices. The state needed new deeds more than old words.[72]

In 1815, at the age of twenty-five, Gilmer left Richmond to launch his legal career in smaller Winchester, in the lower Shenandoah Valley. Despite taking long breaks for botanical excursions, Gilmer began to shine as a clever and eloquent lawyer. He followed Wirt's advice: "Be patient with your foolish clients and hear all their stupid . . . petitions with calm and kind attention." Gilmer became celebrated for winning acquittals in particularly desperate criminal cases, persuading jurors that witnesses were liars and his clients were insane.[73]

Gilmer returned to Richmond and took over most of Wirt's practice in 1817, when his mentor moved to Washington, D.C., to become the United States Attorney General. "I shall make more money, improve myself more, & be more in the great world," Gilmer assured a friend. But the depression of 1819 lingered into the 1820s, spreading bankruptcies, boarding up shops, and depressing property values in "the fallen & ruined Metropolis." Few clients could pay their lawyers. "I work like a horse for promises. I had hoped to fatten in these days of commercial ruin on the carnage of the field but it is impossible." He added, "My heart grows sick with the repetition of ruin & misery all around me. . . .

God help the poor Old Dominion. She bleeds at every vein. The dismay & horror here are portentous." For distraction, Gilmer attended the performances of "Sind Sam, the Hindoo adventurer or Juggler," who could swallow "a sword 22 inches long" and was "in the highest degree graceful & elegant in his person & manners."[74]

Prickly and hypercompetitive, Gilmer erupted with wounded pride at any perceived slight. Despising his guardian, Gilmer blamed Dr. Everette for allegedly mismanaging his inheritance and interfering with his education: "He knew no more of business or bringing up boys than a horse." When his brothers Harmer and James died young, Gilmer accused Everette of botching their care. Irritated by Gilmer's carping, Everette spread the word that his former ward was a dishonest ingrate. In June 1815, an outraged Gilmer confronted Everette at a tavern in Charlottesville. Rather than back down, Everette loudly repeated his charges, "whereupon," Gilmer noted, "I slapt his cheeks." Everette struck back with a cane, which Gilmer parried. The doctor pulled a sword from within the cane. Seizing that flimsy sword, Gilmer snapped it into three pieces, and tried to stab Everette with the point, but other gentlemen pulled them apart. Crossing Everette risked offending his patron, the powerful James Monroe, then preparing to become president. Attending the Albemarle Court two months after the fight, Monroe convened Everette and Gilmer with other county leaders to broker a cessation to their insults and assaults. Unable to resist Monroe's clout, Gilmer grudgingly made peace.[75]

In June 1821, another lawyer, Robert Stanard, accused Gilmer, in open court, of breaching a professional confidence. During the next recess in the trial, Gilmer accosted Stanard in the lobby and demanded a retraction. When he refused, Gilmer reported, "I struck him in the face." Magistrates separated and arrested both, but they resumed battering one another, Gilmer clubbing with an umbrella while Stanard relied on his fists. Gilmer explained, "I shall bear myself mildly & generously to all the world [but] I will take no insult, nor anything that looks like it, and if any man lay the weight of his finger on me, I will kill

Ellen Wayles Randolph Coolidge (1796–1876),
by Francis Alexander, c. 1830
(©Thomas Jefferson Foundation at Monticello)

Francis W. Gilmer (1790–1826), by unknown
(Courtesy of the Fralin Museum of Art at
the University of Virginia)

him. The matter must be brought to [an] issue in Virginia at once, or honor & courtesy are extinguished forever."[76]

As a short-cut to wealth, Gilmer toyed with marrying an heiress, but he had absurd standards. He dismissed Richmond's belles as too homely and vapid, while they considered him too acerbic, frail, and short. "These city belles want houses & equipages & husbands merely as escorts [for] them in their career of dissipation," he declared. After bursts of social disappointment, Gilmer would resolve again to "become wedded to the profession of Law."[77]

Gilmer blamed his emotional difficulties on an "evil genius," or "evil star," from his youth in Albemarle. No one, he told a friend in 1819, had suffered "a harder & more unmerited fate than that which has by an inexorable destiny kept me a bachelor to this time of life." He "curse[d] from the bottom of my heart, the evil star which has shed a malignant influence on my youth." Gilmer would have married, "but for having been fool enough to believe the cold mountain nymph was [as] sincere & generous as we are." He also described her as "one of these learned ladies who affect dignity & justice by a total disregard of the feelings of other people." His "evil genius," "evil star," and "cold mountain nymph" was Ellen Wayles Randolph, a granddaughter of Thomas Jefferson.[78]

Ellen

Born in 1796, Ellen was the third child of Martha and Thomas Mann Randolph. Brilliant, tall, and thin, with reddish hair and complexion, she resembled her grandfather in body and mind. Home-schooled by her accomplished mother, Ellen became, in the words of a family friend, "one of the best Educated Girls in America, a perfect Mistress of the French, Italian, and Spanish languages." In 1824, a visitor to Monticello added, "Ellen Randolph, is the best talker I have ever heard among women. . . . She is not beautiful but is genteel and good-looking enough."[79]

Ellen was intensely devoted to her mother and grandfather. In 1818, she wrote to Martha: "I bless God for having been born at Monticello, your *daughter* and so much the object of my dear Grandfather's care." And Martha adored her: "Ellen fulfills the promises of her childhood. She is a nurse to me in sickness, a friend and companion in health, and to her grand Father 'the immediate jewel of his Soul.'" But Martha worried that Ellen's keen mind produced a painful sensitivity: "I think sometimes she will never marry and, indeed after her sister's fate, I almost *wish* she never may. Her feelings are too acute for her own happiness. She is very much like her Father but without his temper, and such are not calculated for this selfish world."[80]

Ellen's superior education complicated her adjustment to the ornamental role of a lady. Starting in 1814, at age eighteen, Ellen ventured into high society by visiting friends and relatives in other counties and the cities of Richmond, Washington, D.C., Baltimore, and Philadelphia.

She often felt alone in the fashionable crowd because of her learning. In 1818, Ellen regretted the "folly and frivolity of the beings with whom I associate" in Richmond. Painfully self-aware, she recognized her "timid & anxious disposition, which operated as a perpetual check to the pleasure of being admired, whilst it increased the love of admiration." Both relishing but revolted by praise, she uneasily filled her assigned role as an icon of female brilliance meant for others to watch rather than for her to deploy in the world.[81]

Welcome at Monticello, Gilmer grew up beside Ellen, one of the few Virginians who could match his intellect and education. She also appealed as the special favorite of her mother and grandfather. Gilmer cherished inclusion in Jefferson's circle as validating his worth and easing shame over the declining fortunes of his family. He recalled, "The only persons who began early to make me believe I was born for more than a drudge were the Monticello dynasty." Thomas Mann Randolph encouraged Gilmer's studies, particularly in botany, and Martha Jefferson Randolph treated him as her son, which was his fondest hope. Although Ellen was only twelve and he seventeen in 1807, Gilmer insisted, "She told everyone how devoted she was to me." But her mother's teasing allegedly led Ellen to turn cold and forbidding.[82]

Gilmer never recovered from the shock, cursing Ellen as "cold as a cucumber, hard as a stone, and dry as a Stick; and [she] has no idea that people are made for any other purpose than to be her vassals & to content themselves with admiring her at an awful distance. She holds her head . . . as if she never looked lower than the Milky Way." Working himself up, Gilmer concluded, "Not content with votaries, she must have victims and could her natural propensities be gratified no heathen divinity would have had sacrifices more sanguinary."[83]

Gilmer insisted that the Jefferson-Randolphs rejected him as too poor to marry into their precious family: "It cut me to the core. The wound is healed but the scar remains." He felt enraged that they welcomed the handsome and wealthy Charles Bankhead "as a sort of Messiah," while rejecting him "as an outlaw, a bandit & a pirate & if Miss E[llen] had commanded in chief I should have been hung." He added, "I have no doubt that they would slaver over the face of that slimy reptile Bankhead with more marks of affection than they would me, if I were to save the [lives] of half the family." He felt vindicated in 1819, when Bankhead knifed his brother-in-law in a Charlottesville street.[84]

The rupture mattered to Francis more than to Ellen. In the spring of 1819, she visited Richmond, where they ran into each other in the small circle of local gentility. One night after a dinner party, Ellen needed an escort to take her back to her aunt's home, for genteel women did not walk alone. But only two single men attended the party: Gilmer, whom she knew all too well, and Robert Nicholas, whom she had just met. "In this dilemma," Ellen told her mother, "I chose the least evil, the man whom I had once known to the utter stranger, and accepting his offered arm, we walked after ten o'clock at night in darkness & almost in silence to Aunt R[andolph]'s door, where seeing me safely housed he made his bow & retired." She concluded, "His conduct towards me is marked with such utter indifference that I begin to think that time has removed every feeling even of resentment."[85]

She underestimated the depths of his rancor. Gilmer sarcastically described the encounter to a friend: "Miss E[llen] R[andolph], to whom be all honor & praise, with her accustomed caprice, when she found no one of either sex in all Richmond even civil to her from her unheard of manners betook herself to seeking my favor & patronage with a new & unsuspected enthusiasm. . . . I did her some entirely gratuitous & very unmerited favors. She is past all endurance & so adieu to her." For years, Gilmer kept announcing that he was over Ellen only to launch into another diatribe against her as the source of his miseries.[86]

Gilmer did not recognize that Ellen's social diffidence derived, in part, from the deep pain of rotting teeth. In 1818, she told her mother, "I begin to attribute the decline and fall of my influence to the pale cadaverous face which I carry into company, and the coldness and restraint of manner produced by almost constant indisposition." Between visits to Richmond's dentists, Ellen eased her pain by chewing tobacco. She praised "this admirable plant, which deserves all & more than has ever been said of the poppy."[87]

Gilmer longed to believe that Ellen was even unhappier and less suited for emotional bonds than he was. "She is too self-willed ever to be married, and if married she has neither a temper nor disposition to be happy herself or to permit anyone else to be so." He concluded, "She is destined to misery & I pity her."[88]

His prophecy crumbled when she married Joseph Coolidge of Boston. Coolidge's family had made a fortune through overseas commerce and cotton manufacturing. Bearing a letter of recommendation from his Harvard professor, Coolidge visited Monticello in May 1824, when he befriended Jefferson and wooed Ellen, then twenty-seven years old. Marrying at Monticello a year later, they then moved north to Boston. The family mourned Ellen's departure but felt relieved that she would escape the financial ruin closing in on them. Their cousin Wilson Miles Cary noted, "The family are all delighted with the match as Mr. C[oolidge] is certainly a very desirable Connexion to them. His fortune is ample. . . . He has $30,000 left him by his uncle independent of his expectations from his father, who is worth about $200,000." Money mattered most in a match to the declining Jefferson-Randolphs. Even a Yankee would do, if rich enough.[89]

Gilmer expressed aggressive, predictable, and implausible disinterest at the news: "There is no event whatever on which I am more perfectly indifferent. I would not marry her if she were to solicit me, nor have I any remnant of affection for her." In fact, he ranted on about Ellen, casting her marriage as completing the collapse of the House of Monticello: "The Gov[ernor T. M. Randolph] broke to atoms, in mind, body, & estates; Mrs. R[andolph] melancholy, disappointed & nearly broken; Anne married to a cutthroat & an assassin; Jeff marred & maimed by his brother [in-law]. The proud Miss E[llen] sold off in the decay of her charms to a Yankee-cotton-jenny-man." Her marriage reinforced his prejudice against northerners as wealthy parasites preying on Virginia.[90]

Francis blamed advanced education for Ellen's supposed flaws. When his brother Peachy proposed sending his daughter Emma to a celebrated academy for girls in Richmond, Francis advised keeping her at home in rustic Henry County: "Domestic education for a woman is as necessary as a public one for a man. Abroad they can never learn domestic economy. . . . They acquire tastes & propensies which render them less likely to be happy in the seclusion of the country and the accomplishments they acquire soon cease to be of any advantage to them."[91]

By deriding the Richmond female academy, Gilmer took another shot at Ellen and her family, for that school belonged to Harriett Randolph Hackley, who was Thomas Mann Randolph's sister and Ellen's aunt. Harriet had married a merchant, Richard Hackley, who was charming but dishonest and soon bankrupt. When Hackley lingered in Spain with a mistress, his wife supported herself by opening a fashionable school for young ladies, employing three assistant teachers and attracting fifty-seven students. Harriet Hackley impressed her relatives as, in the words of one niece, "my lady paramount with us all." Ellen praised her aunt's "dignity and self-possession" and "the genius for government which has always distinguished her, since from her sick bed, she maintains an exactness of discipline." Marveling at the school's harmony, Ellen credited Hackley's "presiding power." In the Virginia of 1818, that power was possible for a woman only in a female institution.[92]

Dark Chambers

Gilmer's soured relationship with Ellen complicated his regard for her grandfather. Initially, Gilmer revered Jefferson as an inspirational mentor and a brilliant political thinker. In 1814, Gilmer assured Jefferson: "Nothing will give me more pleasure, than to be able to serve you in any manner whatever. . . . I wish that I may ever be able to add anything to your present happiness, or your future glory." He later added, "I like the originality of his opinions, & the boldness and intelligence with which he defends them."[93]

But as Gilmer matured, he became more reactionary and increasingly (but privately) sniped at Jefferson as recklessly naïve in his democratic confidence in human nature. During the early 1820s, the old philosopher supported the push by western Virginians for a convention

to rewrite the state constitution. By weakening the property requirement to vote, reformers sought to enfranchise almost all white men.
That democratization would shift statewide political power westward,
where more white men of limited means lived. But such a shift horrified
eastern conservatives, who insisted they had to dominate the legislature
to protect their enslaved property from heavier taxes or future abolition.
Of Jefferson's radical propositions, Gilmer insisted, "there is scarcely
one which is true." Gilmer concluded that the philosopher "had some
dark chambers in his apartments—some cloudy spots in his horizon."[94]

Gilmer began to detect Jefferson's deft evasions and manipulation
of appearances and conversation. Writing to Wirt in late 1816, Gilmer
noted, "The old citizen of Monticello is such a *diplomatis* that he has
quite baffled our schemes to obtain his opinion, and when we ask him
one thing he tells us, he 'has reason to believe' something about another."
Gilmer later added, "There is nothing more fascinating about him than
the appearance of perfect candour. He is much more a courtier than
I can ever be, with every aspect of the most unconcerned openness."
Gilmer described the lofty conversation at Monticello as "the music of
the spheres," but he had come to distrust the tune.[95]

While cultivating Jefferson with friendly visits and letters, Gilmer
lampooned his mentor when writing to confidants. He referred to
Jefferson as "the worthy St. Thomas of Canterbury" (because of his
supposed political cant), "Citizen Thomas" (because of his fondness
for the French Revolution), and "Red breeches" (for his antiquated
clothing). A conservative in architecture as well as politics, Gilmer
disdained Jefferson's "octagonal houses, which are a great curse to the
country." Gilmer, however, feared that his doubting words got back
to Thomas: "The next thing I heard was that they said at Monticello I
spoke very unkindly of Mr. J[efferso]n, than which nothing could be
more false."[96]

Gilmer and Jefferson uneasily collaborated in creating a new university for Virginia. By improving higher education, they sought to
halt the state's decline and alleged exploitation by northern moneymen.
In 1822, Gilmer declared, "Virginia is a ruined country. . . . Our pos-

terity will serve an Egyptian bondage to a race of stupid & dishonest Yankeys. V[irgini]a is in the worst condition of any state in the Union." But Gilmer and Jefferson differed on the domestic purpose of that new University. Jefferson hoped that a better-educated new generation of leaders would make the radical reforms of his dreams: democratizing the state constitution and abolishing slavery (while deporting the freed). Gilmer, however, wanted the University to serve as a conservative firewall against radical changes in Virginia. He believed that better-educated leaders would defend the state constitution and resist antislavery proposals.[97]

Gilmer raged against Virginia's most ambitious reformer, Charles Fenton Mercer, a state legislator who would go even further and faster than Jefferson. In addition to constitutional reform, Mercer favored chartering more banks and massive public funding for primary education, transportation improvements, and the overseas colonization of freed slaves. Outraged by this reforming haste, Gilmer declared: "I always knew Mercer, the chief author of the distresses of our state, to be a political *charlatan*. He has no mind, no sense, judgement &c, [and] on banks & colonization he is stark mad, really insane." Gilmer wanted to have Mercer jailed for publicly criticizing slavery, which he considered "inciting the slaves to insurrection." Gilmer concluded, "Such are all the moon-struck dreamers who have been vainly endeavouring to fix the airy visions of their brain into palpable & substantial forms."[98]

Gilmer would support just one major reform in Virginia, a new university, and he did so to stymie more radical changes. Gilmer regarded his countrymen as unsuited to reform: "We Virginians have no sense, Sir. I never yet knew any great work undertaken, that it was not set on foot exactly at the worst time—done in the worst manner, & abandoned before it was half finished." Time would tell whether the University would serve his, or Jefferson's, vision of Virginians and their potential.[99]

5

SLAVERY

I N 1785, THOMAS JEFFERSON finished *Notes on the State of Virginia*, while serving as the American minister to France. The book nudged Virginians to complete his radical reform program, proposed but deferred during the war. He wanted a new state constitution to enfranchise almost

Isaac Granger Jefferson (1775–1850), daguerreotype, c. 1850
(Albert and Shirley Small Special Collections Library, University of Virginia)

all white men and equalize legislative representation throughout the state. He also sought to strengthen the governor to check the overmighty legislature. And he urged Virginians to emancipate and deport their slaves.[1]

Jefferson knew that slavery distorted masters as it exploited enslaved people. Young masters learned tyranny from watching their fathers: "The parent storms, the child looks on, catches the lineaments of wrath, puts on the same airs in the circle of smaller slaves, gives a loose to his worst of passions, and thus nursed, educated, and daily exercised in tyranny, cannot but be stamped by it with odious peculiarities." He marveled that a Virginian could "inflict on his fellow men a bondage, one hour of which is fraught with more misery than ages of that which he rose in rebellion to oppose."[2]

Jefferson worried that enslaved people would revolt and destroy his beloved Virginia. On some hot, dark night, a simmering plot would suddenly erupt into bloody retribution, and Jefferson expected God to help the rebels crush their oppressors. "Indeed, I tremble for my country when I reflect that God is just: that his justice cannot sleep forever. . . . The Almighty has no attribute which can take side with us in such a contest." To avert destruction, Virginia's masters needed to free themselves from slavery.[3]

Jefferson regarded emancipating the slaves as necessary but not sufficient to free whites from danger. He had declared all men created equal, but Jefferson described black people as "inferior to the whites in the endowments both of body and mind." Forsaking his usual optimism about human progress, Jefferson denied that different races could learn to live together as equals. He insisted that former slaves would seek revenge, producing bloody "convulsions," culminating "in the extermination of the one or the other race." He later likened slavery to a dangerous beast: "We have the wolf by the ears and we can neither hold him, nor safely let him go."[4]

Jefferson longed to whiten Virginia by emancipating enslaved people and sending them to a distant colony in Africa or the Caribbean. In 1779, Jefferson drafted a plan to free Virginia's slaves gradually, over the course of two generations, but he would also require their mass deportation. His scheme was prohibitively expensive and economically ruinous for Virginians, who relied on coerced labor. Committed to low taxes and minimal government, they could neither finance nor manage a massive project of overseas colonization. The scheme would annually cost Virginia at least five times its revenue, and a fivefold increase in taxation was unthinkable. Expecting rancor and rejection, Jefferson declined to submit his emancipation plan to the legislature. A French abolitionist visited Monticello and lamented that Jefferson "sees so many difficulties in ... emancipation," and "adds so many conditions to render it practicable, that it is thus reduced to the impossible."[5]

If African Americans could not be deported, Jefferson wanted them to remain slaves. He regarded them as mentally and morally stunted by generations of brutal exploitation: "as incapable as children of taking care of themselves." For want of learning, freed blacks became "pests in society by their idleness, and the depredations to which this leads them."[6]

Rather than educate enslaved people, Jefferson sought to enlighten Virginia's elite young men, counting on them to lead a future effort to emancipate and deport. Black freedom would only come, he argued, "by diffusing light and liberality among their oppressors." Despairing of his generation as too selfish, Jefferson regarded young men as more idealistic: "It is to them I look, to the rising generation, and not to the one now in power for these great reformations." During the 1780s, Jefferson believed that the students at William & Mary had "sucked in the principles of liberty as it were with their mother's milk."[7]

He hoped to catalyze future reform by providing every student with a copy of Notes, but with characteristic caution, Jefferson first wanted to know whether the book "might be displeasing to the country, perhaps to the assembly or to some who lead it. I do not wish to be exposed to their censure." He sent an advance copy to his friend James Madison of Orange County, seeking his opinion on the book's reception in Virginia. If Madison advised against entrusting Notes to every student, Jefferson would "only send over a very few copies to particular friends in confidence and burn the rest . . . and, in no event, do I propose to admit them to go to the public at large."[8]

Madison consulted George Wythe, the law professor at the College, who favored emancipation but worried that "an indiscriminate gift" of the book "might offend some narrow minded parents." Wythe suggested putting a few copies in the College library, where he could discreetly direct the most liberal students. Taking that advice in 1787, Jefferson provided thirty-seven copies for "such young gentlemen of the College as Mr. Wythe from time to time shall think proper, taking one or more for the college library."[9]

At the College, the book moved only a few especially bright and idealistic young men to develop antislavery convictions. Those liberals left William & Mary both inspired and limited by *Notes on the State of Virginia*, for they subscribed to Jefferson's impossible program of requiring mass deportation for any emancipation. That linkage was a poison pill that unwittingly but certainly blocked state-mandated abolition in Virginia. Over the years, the graduates also confronted increasing public resistance to any discussion of black freedom. Indeed, they would discover that Jefferson had grown ambivalent about acting on the antislavery words that he had planted in the College library in 1787.

Reaction

Jefferson had hoped that the passage of time would favor emancipation as young liberals grew up to replace old conservatives among Virginia's leaders. In fact, antislavery sentiment peaked during the revolution, and then declined rapidly. In 1785, the legislature unanimously rejected a proposal pushed by evangelicals to emancipate Virginia's slaves. Sobered by defeat, the Methodists and Baptists retreated from antislavery activity. In 1798, the Methodist bishop, Francis Asbury, sadly observed, "I am brought to conclude [that] slavery will exist in Virginia perhaps for ages; there is not a sufficient sense of religion nor of liberty to destroy it." Among the state's Christian denominations, only Quakers clung to antislavery principles, and they composed a small group despised in Virginia.[10]

In 1782, legislators did enable individual masters voluntarily to free their slaves: a legal process known as "manumission." Manumissions increased the state's free black population from 2,000 in 1782 to 20,000 in 1800 and from 1 percent of all black people in 1782 to 7 percent in 1800. Critics insisted that free blacks lapsed into depraved lives of vicious larceny and drunken indolence: lounging in their cabins or wandering the streets when not preying on the poultry, pigs, orchards, and gardens of their white neighbors. Examples of black freedom also allegedly encouraged slaves to resent and resist their continued enslavement. Worst of all, free blacks might lead a slave revolt to drown Virginia in bloodshed. When depicting free blacks as active subversives, Virginians contradicted the stereotype of them as shiftless. But whether seen as lazy, thieving, or scheming, free blacks were cast as proving the folly of emancipation.[11]

To reduce their supposed danger, legislators restricted the liberty of freedmen, who could not vote, serve on juries, or join the militia, and could only own a gun with the permission of their county court. They had to register with that court and obtain a certificate to display to any suspicious magistrate or slave patroller. No person of color could testify in court against a white man who cheated or struck him or her.[12]

After 1790, cotton cultivation boomed in the Deep South, increasing the demand there for enslaved people bought from Virginia. As the profitable interstate trade in slaves surged, manumissions declined in Virginia. Disliking free blacks, Virginia's leaders preferred to see the enslaved sold out of state rather than freed within their borders. A legislator explained, "I am for opening every outlet to such a destructive species of population and for barring up every avenue by which it may return." Between 1790 and 1810, about 100,000 enslaved people passed from Virginia and Maryland to the Deep South for sale.[13]

Pressured by debts, Virginia masters welcomed the income from selling young slaves to the Deep South. Richard Blow assured his son, "I think it useless to raise up families of them for any other purpose but to sell." Jefferson deemed "a woman who brings a child every two years as more valuable than the best man on the farm. What she produces is an addition to capital, while his labor disappears in mere consumption." While profitable to masters, interstate sales brought misery to the enslaved by separating children from parents and husbands from wives.[14]

During the 1790s, white Virginians felt horrified by a massive slave revolt in Saint-Domingue (now Haiti), a French colony in the West Indies. Virginians dreaded that the successful precedent would inspire their own slaves to rebel. Sympathizing with the planters of Saint-Domingue, Jefferson declared, "Never was so deep a tragedy presented to the feelings of man. . . . It is high time we should foresee the bloody scenes which our children certainly and possibly ourselves (south of the Potomac) will have to wade through and try to avert them." Although Virginians had declared that revolution was a universal right for the oppressed, they shuddered when enslaved people claimed that right. In 1797, Jefferson warned St. George Tucker, "If something is not done & soon done, we shall be the murderers of our own children [for] the revolutionary storm, now sweeping the globe, will be upon us."[15]

Like Jefferson, Tucker regarded slavery as incompatible with republican government, and he too dreaded that a slave revolt would destroy their beloved Virginia. Unlike Jefferson, Tucker thought that whites and freed blacks could coexist within Virginia, if former slaves remained a lower caste denied political and property rights. He expected that inferior status would pressure them gradually but inexorably to migrate westward to the frontier, saving Virginians the cost of colonizing them in Africa.[16]

In November 1796, Tucker had his plan presented to the House of Delegates, something that Jefferson had never dared to do. Tucker naïvely believed that "a large majority of slave-holders among us would cheerfully concur in any feasible plan for the abolition of [slavery]." Instead, the legislators abruptly and angrily rejected the plan. Most feared any public debate of emancipation, no matter how gradual and incomplete, lest slaves learn of the discussion and demand immediate freedom. Virginia's leaders insisted that white silence and black ignorance alone could spare both races from a revolt that would kill thousands of all colors. The rejection of Tucker's plan throttled any further appetite for antislavery reforms in Virginia.[17]

After returning from France in 1789, Jefferson also cooled in his ardor for emancipation as he recognized his economic dependence on slavery. The labor of over 150 enslaved people sustained his genteel standard of living and permitted Jefferson the luxuries of leisure and political leadership. He also wanted to provide generous inheritances to two daughters and a dozen grandchildren (in his legitimate, white lineage). His dependence on enslaved labor intensified as his debts mounted and his family grew. Rather than free slaves, Jefferson sought to ameliorate the slavery practiced at Monticello. To reduce whipping, he tried to motivate enslaved people with small gratuities and favors bestowed on zealous workers. He also reduced the hardest labor on his estates—raising tobacco—by shifting more fields to wheat and more hands to workshops producing cloth and nails. But the work remained plenty hard, and slaves who resisted Jefferson's mastery faced a punitive sale far, far away from family and friends.[18]

To manage farms and slaves, Jefferson relied on white overseers, who received an annual salary and a share in the harvested crop. Overseers freed Jefferson to engage in science and politics, and he could avoid seeing the clubbing and whipping that kept the enslaved producing and reproducing for their master. Overseers had the contradictory assignment to produce large crops while keeping the slaves healthy. Jefferson noted, "My first wish is that labourers may be well treated," but his second was that they work long and hard hours: "The man who can effect both objects is rarely to be found." A former slave, Peter Fossett, recalled, "If you did your task well, you were rewarded; if not, punished."[19]

In 1801, Jefferson became president of the United States, but he did nothing to challenge slavery within the nation. His constitutional principles favored keeping the federal government too weak to interfere in southern slavery. He also owed his election primarily to southern voters, for he won 82 percent of the electoral votes in the South compared to only 27 percent in the North. "I have long since given up the expectation of any early provision for the extinguishment of slavery among us," he explained in 1805. Jefferson preferred to wait for some dramatic shift in public opinion before intervening against slavery, but how that shift would happen without leadership he could not say.[20]

In 1807, President Jefferson did secure a congressional ban on importing more Africans as slaves, effective on January 1, 1808, the earliest date permitted by the Federal Constitution. Most Virginians supported the import ban, reasoning that they had enough slaves, and they feared that African-born slaves were especially prone to revolt. Plus masters could profit from the ban by selling more slaves to meet the voracious demand in the Deep South. The surging profits of that trade discouraged Virginians from freeing more slaves.[21]

In November 1818, on a plantation near Monticello, a young enslaved man hanged himself "30 feet from the ground, in a tree near his Master's door," after receiving a whipping earlier that day. The suicide shocked Jefferson's son-in-law, Thomas Mann Randolph, who had admired the "very sensible, lively, and likely young mulatto man." Randolph also esteemed the master and his overseer as "humane men" of "moral worth," so he blamed slavery in general for distorting their conduct: "What a hideous monster, among the various phaenomena of the social state, is our Southern system!"[22]

Elected Virginia's governor in 1819, Randolph sought to shrink the monstrous system that held masters, as well as their slaves, captive. He dreaded that the growing enslaved population would bring on a race war, where "Barbarian Multitudes" might destroy the state and lead to "a dissolution of the union, and a Civil War in consequence." He urged legislators to appropriate a third of the state's revenues to buy young female slaves and ship them away for their future increase to grow up far from Virginia. Although costly, his program would only reduce the annual increase of the enslaved in that state by about 10 percent. Unwilling to levy higher taxes to lose valuable property, legislators rejected the proposal. To Randolph's dismay, even Jefferson refused to help, deeming the proposal "not ripe to be immediately acted on."[23]

While avoiding public commitment to antislavery, Jefferson tinkered with his emancipation plan in private, occasionally sharing it with a northern correspondent. By 1824, he recognized that Virginians would never pay to free and transport their entire enslaved population. As an alternative, Jefferson proposed to purchase all newborn slaves, for they had the lowest price: just $12.50 each (rather than hundreds of dollars for an adult). The state would work the children for a few years and then ship them to Haiti before they could reproduce. By purchasing 60,000 infants annually, Jefferson calculated that he could launch a death spiral for slavery as "the old stock would die off in the ordinary course of nature . . . until it's final disappearance." Jefferson sought to eliminate slavery without violating the property rights of masters, who would receive compensation for their newborn slaves.[24]

Jefferson regarded ridding Virginia of slavery as worth the sorrow inflicted on enslaved parents and children: "The separation of infants from their mothers too would produce some scruples of humanity. But this would be straining at a gnat, and swallowing a camel." He also ignored the economic folly of saddling masters with the costs of sustaining scores of aging slaves deprived of support from their banished children. Four years before, Jefferson had noted that a planter needed a broad portfolio of ages, so that slaves in their laboring prime could support infants and the aged. With all the precise numeric calculation that he loved as the supposed assurance of rationality, Jefferson concocted a plan that was utterly mad.[25]

By drafting ever more detailed emancipation plans in his study, Jefferson sustained his claim to champion black freedom—provided it was far away from Virginia and he did not have to expend any political capital to push it. While Jefferson withdrew from antislavery activity, his published words had inspired a few of the best and brightest young men studying at William & Mary. They included George Tucker, John Hartwell Cocke, and Edward Coles.

George Tucker

A cousin of St. George Tucker, George Tucker grew up on the island of Bermuda, in the Atlantic about eight hundred miles southeast of Virginia. A house slave was his first teacher: "I was attended by a colored boy several years older than myself. This boy taught me to count, and to multiply as far as 12 by 12. How he acquired this knowledge, I never knew, nor in fact ever enquired." Tucker concluded, "From this incident, together with some others affording similar evidence, I have always had doubts about the inferiority of the intellect of the coloured race."[26]

Later in life, after he moved to Virginia, Tucker saw a slave trader, "a rough looking white man, who sat carelessly lolling in his sulky" while leading a coffle of slaves "loaded with chains to prevent their escape" on the way to South Carolina. Tucker noted "a poor mother, with an infant sucking at her breast as she walked along, while two small children had hold of her apron on either side." They sang "a little wild hymn of sweet and mournful melody." He wondered how Virginians could bear to hear "the shrieks of a mother, torn forever from the bosom of her children . . . and condemned to live long hopeless years of exile, far from all those tender relatives that gladdened life." He concluded that Virginians were hardened "to the daily horrors which pass under their eyes."[27]

Although he owned slaves, Tucker never accepted the canard that black people lacked the capacity for freedom because of their supposed stupidity and cowardice. Tucker had "often witnessed with astonishment, their resolute intrepidity on occasions of fire, in rescuing the property of the whites from the flames. . . . while the timid owners of that very property looked on and trembled." If the enslaved were cowards, he asked, "why this feverish solicitude of the laws to guard against the spirit of insurrection and revenge? And why are . . . the slumbers of wives and mothers disturbed by visions of murder and conflagration?" Tucker knew that masters had to believe in contradictions to maintain slavery.[28]

Tucker faulted Jefferson for promoting racism in *Notes on the State of Virginia*. Tucker regarded as "frivolous" Jefferson's emphasis on the distinctive features of black appearance: "They only prove that the blacks are different, not that they are inferior." Referring to Jefferson's awkward appearance, Tucker insisted that casting blacks as ugly "can prove nothing as to their inferiority of the mind, unless we are to take it for granted that beauty and genius always go together, a proposition for which Mr. J. ought not to contend." Tucker concluded, "There is no excuse for his remarks. I am afraid, indeed, that his opinion is but too popular here, as I have heard several masters ready to justify their severity to these poor wretches, by alleging, that they are an inferior race, created only to be slaves. What a horrible doctrine . . . and what a pity that any gentleman of Mr. J's reputation for talents should lend it the countenance of his name."[29]

In 1795, at age twenty, Tucker enrolled at the College of William & Mary, where his cousin was the law professor. A prankster, Tucker had key talents for impressing other young men: "running slate-pencils up my nose" and chewing glass "without cutting my mouth." He fit right in at the College, where Tucker went to so many parties "that I gave no attention to my studies." In 1797, he married, but his wife died two years later, leaving him bereft. Moving to Richmond, he practiced law with little success. Tucker preferred to write satirical newspaper pieces, which paid little to nothing. He also drank and gambled at cards "with loungers and jesters," which increased his debts. Tucker assured his cousin: "My heart feels sick & uneasy & disgusted with the nothingness of all about me."[30]

In 1800, Tucker received a jolt from the discovery of a plot by enslaved men in and around Richmond to rebel. They rallied to a charismatic, enslaved blacksmith named Gabriel, who planned, on Saturday night, August 30, to assemble five hundred men armed with swords and pikes. Then they would march into town to set fire to the riverside warehouses, seize the state treasury and arsenal, and grab the state's governor, James Monroe. On the appointed day, however, a violent thunderstorm lashed Richmond with sheets of rain, washing away many bridges. Few rebels could make it to their rendezvous, and the confusion spread alarm among those in on the secret. A few saved themselves by revealing the plot to their masters, who alerted militia officers. Called into service, militiamen patrolled the roads and arrested suspects.[31]

Trials commenced on September 11, and executions began the next day, for the injustice inflicted was quick and harsh. Attending the executions, John Minor felt resigned, for he disliked slavery but feared a slave revolt even more: "My heart bleeds for them, and yet this severity is necessary. How dreadful the situation to be obliged to be cruel and unjust, as the only means of self-defense. I am sick of these thoughts." By December 1, twenty-seven men, including Gabriel, paid with their lives for failing at revolution. They met their deaths with a defiance that alarmed John Randolph: "The accused have exhibited a spirit, which, if it becomes general, must deluge the Southern country in blood. They manifested a sense of their rights, and contempt of danger, and a thirst for revenge which portend the most unhappy consequences."[32]

The attempted revolt shook Tucker out of his doldrums and into writing a pamphlet meant to persuade legislators and "the thinking few" to abolish slavery. He warned Virginians to free their slaves or "see our folly [culminate] in one general wreck of property and life." He promised that emancipation would liberate masters, for "the tyrant who lives in fear is himself a slave." Tucker wanted the state to buy adolescent slaves and transport them to the western frontier. Few Virginians, however, would accept increased taxes or the notion that white, wage laborers could replace the deported slaves. Like Jefferson, Tucker was insightful about the problem of slavery but proposed an impossible solution. Capable of searing criticism of slavery, educated Virginians were inept at doing anything to abolish it.[33]

Tucker opposed slavery in principle but clung to it in practice. During the same month that he published his pamphlet, he bought a new slave named Mark. A month later, Tucker complained, "Mark proved to be an arrant scoundrel and, after pilfering me, has gone the Lord knows where." A savvy slave did not wait on the hollow paternalism of a master to gain freedom.[34]

Rejecting Tucker's emancipation plan, legislators instead opted for greater repression meant to intimidate the enslaved. Although free blacks had nothing to do with Gabriel's plot, they became the usual suspects accused of inspiring the rebels. By blaming free blacks for the revolt, Virginians avoided faulting themselves for keeping people in bondage. In the House of Delegates in early 1805, Alexander Smyth led a push to restrict manumissions. Smyth insisted that freeing a slave endangered neighbors, rather like setting fire to one's own house. Casting blacks and whites as perpetual enemies, Smyth concluded, "What should we say of a man, who having his mortal foe bound at his feet, sets him once more at liberty, and plants a stiletto in his hand[?]" The state's leading newspaper, the *Richmond Enquirer*, endorsed the speech, and the House of Delegates passed his bill to outlaw manumission, 77 to 70, but the State Senate refused, for the moment, to concur.[35]

In early 1806, both houses of the legislature agreed to restrict future manumissions. Masters could still manumit, but the freed had to leave the state within one year or face renewed slavery by order of their county court. As intended, this new law had a chilling effect on manumissions. While longing for freedom, enslaved people also wanted to remain among their family and friends. Masters rationalized that they acted humanely by keeping slaves at home in Virginia instead of casting them adrift in the cold uncertainty of the North.[36]

Even George Tucker rallied to the new consensus that slavery was wrong in principle but essential in practice. In his popular novel, *The Valley of Shenandoah*, published in 1825, the young hero, a benevolent master, assures a northern friend: "I freely admit [slavery] to be an evil, both moral and political, [but it] admits of no remedy that is not worse than the disease. No thinking man supposes that we could emancipate them, and safely let them remain in the country; and no good or prudent man would run the risk of renewing the scenes which have made St. Domingo one general scene of waste and butchery." Given the prohibitive cost of deportation, he concluded, Virginians could only "endeavor to *mitigate* a disease which admits of *no cure*."[37]

Cocke

At William & Mary during the late 1790s, John Hartwell Cocke attended Bishop Madison's lectures on moral philosophy, where the student learned that no man had the right to enslave any other. But his father owned three plantations and 130 slaves, whom Cocke inherited in 1801. Eight years later, he moved to Bremo, a 3,100-acre plantation on the upper James River in Fluvanna County in the Piedmont. Cocke decided that he needed slaves to implement labor-intensive agricultural reforms meant to improve soils and crop yields. Their work enabled Cocke to cultivate and fertilize more land and to erect new barns, shops, and mills. He also relished his supposed power to reform the morals and manners of the enslaved. Rigidly self-disciplined and devout, Cocke pressured enslaved people to work hard, pray piously, and renounce gambling, profanity, alcohol, and adultery. He promised someday to free those who reformed, but few could meet Cocke's daunting standards.[38]

Cocke considered slavery "the great Cause of all the Chief evils of our Land," including economic underdevelopment, educational indifference, and the indolence and immorality of so many white people. Admiring northern ingenuity and industry, he disdained Virginia as a "land of Waste & Extravagance." To reform his state, Cocke presided over the Virginia branch of the American Colonization Society, which encouraged masters to free their slaves and ship them to Liberia on the west coast of Africa.[39]

But Cocke never freed himself from needing enslaved workers and subjects for his moral reforms. In December 1816, Cocke's wife died. Nine months later, he suffered a long and nearly fatal illness, so Cocke wrote a new and revealing will that divided his lands and slaves among three daughters and three sons. Because renowned as a critic of slavery, he felt obliged to justify his decision. "It may be asked why have I not emancipated my Negroes? I answer because I believe the mass of human happiness would be diminished by it." Rejecting an "indiscriminant emancipation" as immiserating for blacks, Cocke expected divine approbation: "I have deliberately determined to carry [my deci-sion] before the Tribunal beyond the Grave."[40]

Cocke's will gave priority to the genteel education of his young heirs. "It is my first wish and most earnest desire, in regard to my Children, that the best opportunities for Education which the Country will afford, be given to them." Passed through the generations, enslaved labor enabled the education of gentlemen and ladies trained to manage, increase, and pass on that property within the family line. Elite education and slavery entwined in a state that invested almost no public funds in schools and colleges. Recovering from his illness, Cocke lived for many more years, helping to oversee the new University of Virginia.[41]

In 1817, while Cocke lived, Tadeusz Kosciuszko died far away in Poland. A hero of the American Revolution and the failed Polish struggle for independence from Russia, Kosciuszko had been Jefferson's close friend. In 1798, they were both in Philadelphia, where Jefferson helped Kosciuszko draft his will. That document entrusted Jefferson with a fortune to buy, emancipate, and educate slaves in Virginia, beginning with his own. Twenty years later, how-ever, Jefferson wanted no part of administering the complicated will. In debt and more dependent than ever on his plantations for support, he dared not liberate his slaves and deprive his grandchildren of an inheritance. He also dreaded irritating fellow slaveholders with any public stand against slavery. And he lacked the energy to cope with potential legal challenges to the will from adverse parties in Poland seeking the money.[42]

Rejecting executorship of Kosciuszko's estate, Jefferson enlisted Cocke to replace him in late 1818. But Cocke also had heirs and no desire to buy himself out of mastery. On May 3, 1819, he declined responsi-bility, citing the local prejudices against educating blacks in Fluvanna County "not to mention the effect which might be produced on the minds of my own people." Cocke referred to his other slaves, who would envy those freed and educated. The will became an orphan, and the funds remained entangled in legal controversy. In the end, Kosciuszko's money neither freed nor educated a slave.[43]

Coles

Born in 1786, Edward Coles grew up on an Albemarle County plantation. Nineteen years later, he entered the College of William & Mary,
following in the footsteps of four brothers, including Isaac A. Coles,
who became Jefferson's secretary. An idealistic republican, Edward
Coles believed in the egalitarian words of Jefferson's Declaration of
Independence. Coles also admired Bishop Madison "for the goodness &
purity of his character" and his "extensive learning & profound Knowledge of all subjects." But Coles felt troubled after hearing Madison's lecture on the universal rights of man. Confronting the College president,
Coles asked, "If this be true, how can you hold a slave? How can man
be made the property of man?" Embarrassed, Madison admitted that
slavery "could not be justified on principle, & could only be tolerated
in our Country" by "the difficulty of getting rid of it." Coles responded
that "we could get rid of them with much less difficulty than we did the
King of our forefathers," and if Madison "could not reconcile Slavery
with his principles, . . . he ought not to hold Slaves." Coles vowed to free
any slaves that he inherited.[44]

His father's will put Coles's conscience and brave words to the test,
for he inherited a farm and twenty slaves, and his siblings pressured him
to abandon his vow, lest freedom for his slaves irritate those retained by
the rest of the family. If he acted on his principles, Coles knew that he
would have to forsake "all my relations and friends" by moving with his
freed slaves to a northern state. But, perhaps he could stay in Virginia
if Jefferson would revive his emancipation plan. Writing in July 1814,
Coles insisted that his hero had a duty to crusade against slavery "from
your known philosophical and enlarged view of subjects, and from the
principles you have professed and practiced through a long and useful
life. . . . in establishing on the broadest basis the rights of man."[45]

In a tortured reply written a month later, Jefferson regretted that his
fellow Virginians had failed to free the enslaved. "The love of justice &
the love of country plead equally the cause of these people, and it is a
mortal reproach to us that they should have pleaded it so long in vain."

While he relished Coles's "solitary but welcome voice," Jefferson preferred to wait for some future day to act against slavery. "Yet the hour
of emancipation is advancing in the march of time. It will come; and
whether brought on by the generous energy of our own minds, or by the
bloody process of St. Domingo, . . . is a leaf of our history not yet turned
over." By asserting future inevitability, Jefferson justified present pas-
sivity, insisting that premature action would only delay freedom by irritating slaveholders. Moreover, he was too old to influence anyone: "This
enterprise is for the young; for those who can follow it up, and bear it
through to it's consummation. It shall have all my prayers, and these are
the only weapons of an old man."[46]

Jefferson urged Coles to remain in Virginia as a paternalistic master.
"My opinion has ever been that, until more can be done for them, we
should endeavor, with those whom fortune has thrown on our hands,
to feed & clothe them well, protect them from ill usage, require such
reasonable labor only as is performed voluntarily by freemen, and be
led by no repugnancies to abdicate them, and our duties to them." Eventually, Coles could "come forward in the public councils," to "insinu-
ate & inculcate" emancipation "softly but steadily thro' the medium of
writing & conversation, associate others in your labours, and when the
phalanx is formed, bring on & press the proposition perseveringly until
its accomplishment." In sum, he wanted Coles to adopt Jefferson's ame-
liorating mastery and cautious politics of waiting.[47]

In September, Coles replied, rejecting Jefferson's efforts to shunt
antislavery activism onto a future generation. As a revered statesman,
who had led Virginia through revolution, Jefferson had far greater
sway than any young man ever would. Only clear, moral leadership
at the top could "arouse and enlighten the public sentiment, which in
matters of this kind ought not to be expected to lead but to be led." As
"the first of our aged worthies," Jefferson had "a most solemn obligation" to "awaken our fellow Citizens . . . to a proper sense of Justice."
He should revive his plan for gradual emancipation, and immediately
"form a rallying point for its friends." Coles cited the precedent of

Benjamin Franklin who, as an old man, had helped to abolish slavery in Pennsylvania. Jefferson apparently never responded to this letter.[48]

Discouraged by Jefferson's response, Coles considered emancipation a lost cause in Virginia. In February 1815, he traveled west to buy land beside the Mississippi River in Illinois. Four years later, he moved there, bringing and freeing twenty slaves. He granted 160 acres to each family.[49]

In sending copies of *Notes on the State of Virginia* to William & Mary in 1787, Jefferson encouraged a new generation to seek emancipation. A few students, including John Hartwell Cocke and George Tucker, did criticize slavery, but they were half-hearted reformers who backed down upon encountering opposition. Only Edward Coles persisted in his idealism, sacrificing property and forsaking family to liberate his human property. By doing so, Coles defied rather than pleased Jefferson. Indeed, Coles made more of a difference than Jefferson bargained on. Elected governor of Illinois, Coles helped defeat a powerful effort to legalize slavery there during the early 1820s. By preserving Illinois as a free state, Coles kept slavery from expanding into the Midwest, thereby preserving a balance of power in a Union increasingly divided over slavery. Coles sustained the clear geographic line between free and slave territory that so troubled Jefferson as the irritant that inevitably would bring on a civil war.[50]

Power

In 1808, a former slave wrote anonymously to rebuke Jefferson for keeping people enslaved: "To prove our human-nature, sir, and our rights as citizens of these states, we have only to appeal to the Declaration of Independence, which says . . . all men (not all white men) are created equal." The author exhorted Jefferson to free his slaves and provide them with back pay. Already he had waited too long: "O! Thomas, you have had a long nap, and spent a great number of years in ease & plenty [living] upon our hard earned property, while we have been in the meantime, smarting under the cow hide and sweating in the fields." The author asked, "Is this the fruits of your education, Sir?"[51]

His education taught Jefferson to deny schooling to the enslaved. In 1796, Robert Pleasants, a Virginian Quaker asked Jefferson to contribute to a charity for educating blacks. Pleasants had freed his own slaves, a sacrifice of £3,000 in property, and he established a school for their children. Pleasants regarded "the Instruction of black Children to be a duty we owe to that much degraded part of our fellow Creatures" and "at this enlightened day is generally acknowledged to be their right." But Jefferson declined to contribute, warning that schooling could only deepen the unhappiness of slaves with their lot. "Ignorance and despotism seem made for each other," he concluded. While determined to liberate whites from both, Jefferson accepted ignorance and despotism as necessary for slaves.[52]

Jefferson understood that education could empower and liberate enslaved people to the detriment of their masters. One of his slaves, Israel Gillette, overheard Jefferson talking with the visiting Marquis de Lafayette, who pressed his old friend to do more to educate and emancipate the enslaved. Jefferson replied that he could only favor "teaching the slaves to learn to read print; that to teach them to write would enable them to forge papers, when they could no longer be kept in subjugation." The enslaved faced a contradiction: masters deemed them too ignorant for freedom but balked at educating them as too dangerous.[53]

Jefferson limited education at Monticello to older slaves teaching work techniques to the younger. The closest thing to a school for slaves at Monticello was a workshop for making nails, which employed a dozen boys from ten to sixteen in age. The workshop was supposed to produce better slaves by teaching steadier work habits. Jefferson precisely recorded each worker's daily production of nails and quantity of wasted metal, awarding better food and clothing to the most efficient. The leading historian of slavery at Monticello writes that the "nailery combined the attributes of a school and a prison." One of the former nail workers, Israel Gillette, recalled that he never learned to read and write until he became free and moved to Ohio: "[I] consider what education I have as a legitimate fruit of freedom."[54]

Jefferson did not educate his own enslaved children. Madison

Hemings recalled, "He was not in the habit of showing partiality or fatherly affection to us children. We were the only children of his by a slave woman. He was affectionate toward his white grandchildren." Jefferson lavished attention and money to educate his white grandchildren, but he had Madison Hemings trained as a carpenter by his uncle. Determined to know more, Hemings "learned to read by inducing the white children to teach me the letters and something more; what else I know of books I have picked up here and there till now I can read and write." By naming one of his children after Ellen Wayles Randolph, Madison Hemings revealed the primary teacher of his youth at Monticello.[55]

Jefferson often declared, "knolege is power." His fellow planters agreed, reserving education for the free white families who could pay for it. Masters tried to keep their slaves illiterate, lest they read antislavery literature, write letters to coordinate resistance, or forge passes to assist runaways. A Virginian reasoned, "If taught to read the New Testament, they could read the Bill of Rights, and the history of our revolution, and would think of imitating them." Alexander Smyth favored slavery because it deprived blacks "of the right of locomotion, of the opportunities of combining, and the powers of the mind." Thomas Mann Randolph observed, "Slaves increase much faster than their Masters, and must be kept in a state of barbarous ignorance to insure a submission never to cease." A visitor from New England noted, "The policy is to keep the slaves ignorant of everything but their own work."[56]

Virginians policed those who violated the consensus against keeping blacks in ignorance. In 1799, John Randolph ran for Congress, but a neighbor complained that, earlier in the decade, Randolph had vowed to free his slaves "and provide tutors for them." Reacting quickly and decisively in the press, handbills, and speeches, Randolph became the state's fiercest defender of slavery against federal interference. He won the race and kept to his new word rather than the old vow until his death many years later, when his will freed his slaves and sent them to Ohio.[57]

Masters punished slaves caught reading or writing. A former

Monticello slave, Peter Fossett, covertly learned to read before his sale to Colonel John R. Jones. Finding his new slave reading, Jones grabbed the book, cast it into a fire, and bellowed: "If I ever catch you with a book in your hands, [you will receive] thirty-nine lashes on your bare back." He was right to fear literacy, for Fossett added: "I was teaching all the people around me to read and write, and even venturing to write free passes and sending slaves away from their masters. Of course, they did not know this, or they would not have thought me so valuable." Ostensibly granted by a master, a "free pass" enabled a black person to travel through Virginia.[58]

The lawyer Francis W. Gilmer sought to educate his valet, a young man named James. Spending more time with James than anyone else, Gilmer wanted to enjoy some educated conversation. In 1816, he told a friend, "I am now sending James to school & believe I shall make him a man of learning & perhaps a lawyer."[59]

The lawyer bit was a joke, but James's education did not seem so funny to Gilmer four years later. He "was equally concerned and astonished at the rumour" circulating that James had forged a free pass to help another slave to escape. Gilmer added, "When I had him taught reading and writing, I was perfectly aware of the risk of his doing mischief. . . . I accordingly admonished him, that if he ever used these advantages in an improper manner (which I explained to him) he would suffer severe punishment and that I would sell him to the first negro driver." But Gilmer considered the charge implausible: "His honesty and fidelity have been the most remarkable I have ever seen in a servant. . . . He has had constant opportunities of forging similar certificates for himself, and surely the temptation is stronger than it can be for any other person. Yet he has never given himself a pass for an hour." But Gilmer vowed to act if further evidence convicted James: "I hold no man has a right to keep property which is publicly injurious. . . . I will maintain the laws and enforce subordination in slaves."[60]

In 1821, another master accused James of forging a pass, which weakened Gilmer's defense of his valet. That defense collapsed in June 1823, when Gilmer returned home to Richmond to find "that my servant had neglected half my orders, had several bouts at drinking & has provoked & mortified me [in] every way." This was the last straw for Gilmer: "I accordingly sold him yesterday for half his worth to approve myself a good citizen, a good neighbor, friend, &c. and above all to be as good to James as my word. He is to go to Kentucky. I assure you I had educated him with such pains & had in the main been served by him with such fidelity, that it has distressed me a good deal." No doubt, the sale distressed James far more. For Gilmer, being a good neighbor to fellow whites meant tightly policing the line that kept the enslaved away from literacy and freedom. Gilmer brightly concluded his letter, "I must procure a smart boy of 13 or 15 to clean my shoes, make a fire in winter . . . & bring water. Cast an eye on such an one." But Gilmer would not educate his next valet, preserving him in the greater safety of ignorance.[61]

Virginians also did not want free blacks to gain an education, lest they learn defiance and teach it to the enslaved. In 1807 in Williamsburg, Bishop Madison praised John Wallace De Rozaro, a free black man, twenty years old. Of "so uncommon a Character in Respect to Genius, and good Conduct," De Rozaro had taught himself to read, write, cipher, and even to master some Latin. He also expressed the "strongest Solicitude to attend the Lectures in College." Writing to the state's governor, Madison explained, "I hence thought, that the Mind of such a Man, considering the peculiar Situation of our Country, ought, if possible, to be directed into a safe Channel, & as ardent as he really appears to be, in the Acquisition of Science, I, notwithstanding, advised him to apply himself to those Trades, which he has commenced." His primary trade was gunsmith. Remarkably, Madison insisted that whites were safer when a black man made and repaired guns than when he pursued higher education.[62]

Letters

Virginians tried sharply to distinguish between free and slave, white and black, educated and ignorant. But it proved tough to sustain those polarities in a society in which people of all colors overlapped in experiences. In particular, the children of house slaves interacted with the

young children of planters. George Tucker noted, "But to prove decisively that the inferiority of the negroes is the result of their situation
alone, consider them in their childhood, before they have learnt the
painful lesson that they are slaves, and compare them with the whites
of their own age. They are now the play-fellows of their future masters,
and share the sport with those who will one day refuse to share the toil
with them." Watching black and white children play together, Tucker
saw no difference in "spirit, invention, or genius."[63]

Children learned from one another across the color line in genteel
households. A slave taught Tucker to cipher. As a boy, John Randolph
learned his favorite ballad from an enslaved girl named Patience. Many
visitors noted the influence of African-American words, pronuncia-
tion, and syntax on the speech of the young whites who interacted with
the enslaved.[64]

House slaves could gain literacy with help from white children. In
1819, Jefferson's granddaughter Ellen Wayles Randolph mourned the
death of her beloved nanny Critty, the wife of the philosopher's valet,
Burwell Colbert. Ellen wanted to own "one of her elder children. Mama
promised I should have anyone of them not disposed of . . . for I am
more than ever anxious to have it in my power to befriend and educate as well as I can, one of these children." She especially sought
Martha, "a little, sprightly, black-eyed girl, whom I have often noticed
with pleasure. I think her mother would have liked this disposition of
her." By treating Martha as a favored pet, worthy of some education,
Ellen meant to demonstrate her humane sensibility within the slave system that sustained her family's gentility.[65]

Adolescence transformed the relationship of masters' children to
their enslaved playmates. Masters expected their sons to begin to intimidate and command. Enslaved adolescents quickly had to learn to submit. Psychologically astute, Tucker noted:

  I think there is not in nature a more melancholy picture than that of
  a little black when he first discovers that he is a slave. . . . This is the
  time of transition from happy ignorance to painful knowledge. His

carelessness and neglect of duty must be punished with the whip. With the first stroke, the whole illusion of liberty vanishes never to return. The marks on his body indeed are soon effaced; but what time can obliterate the lashes from his mind? He is now a slave, and he feels that he is one. His mind soon sinks to the level of his condition, from which nothing, not even liberty at a subsequent period, shall ever raise it again. After this, let no man tell me that "it is nature, and not their condition," which has made the blacks inferior to the whites.

Young slaves also got bitter lessons by watching the whipping of friends and observing auctions that ruptured families. Enslaved people learned to treat whites with wary deference while nurturing in private a more effusive and defiant sense of self.[66]

Despite the risk of punishment, African Americans coveted learning. By striving to monopolize literacy, whites rendered it more alluring to blacks as a source of power. A Presbyterian minister explained, "the more anxiety about keeping a secret, the more publicity you give it." In the former slave quarters at Monticello, archaeologists found a piece of slate on which someone had practiced writing letters. In 1794, a French visitor met an enslaved man named Sem, who operated the ferry between Portsmouth and Norfolk: "He had learned to read and write all by himself. . . . His conversation showed clear thinking and an ardent desire for education." It seemed safer for Sem to reveal what he knew to a foreign traveler than to local whites.[67]

Christianity and literacy encouraged pious slaves to preserve a moral identity beyond the master's control. In 1818, Hannah, the enslaved cook at Jefferson's Poplar Forest estate, gently lectured her master, then at Monticello, by letter. Learning of his serious illness, she exhorted Jefferson to find Jesus before it was too late for his soul: "We ought to serve and obey his commandments that you may set to win the prize and after glory run." Hannah felt sure that she knew the most important thing in life and that her master did not. That knowledge gave her the confidence to instruct Jefferson.[68]

Christopher McPherson also understood the power and the peril of education. Born in Louisa County, McPherson was the son of an enslaved woman and a merchant from Scotland. McPherson belonged to another Scot, David Ross, who educated the boy to serve as a clerk and bookkeeper. On the side, McPherson taught a school for white children and worked as a doctor for local slaves. In 1792, Ross formally granted freedom to McPherson in a written deed.[69]

Religious experience empowered McPherson to challenge powerful men. On the night of February 15, 1799, he recalled, a thunderbolt "struck me on the head and ran through me like lightning or an electrical touch, and left a long tinkling sound with me, similar to the dying note of the last touch of a musical instrument. . . . My heart was filled with pure and perfect love." McPherson then saw a flying "Lord Jesus Christ," armed with a sword, who seized "a great red dragon" and chained him to a large pine tree before lopping off his head and casting the body into a "dismal gulph of fire." Christ then cut open McPherson's side to extract his heart and, "as he carried it up to heaven, he washed it thoroughly." Christ restored the improved heart to McPherson, who felt renewed with "Grace, Mercy, Peace, Love, Truth, Justice, Faith, Charity, Courage, Magnanimity, Hope, &c., &c."[70]

McPherson concluded that Christ would soon return to earth to destroy the wicked and save the righteous. He felt compelled to preach to whites and blacks to prepare themselves for the last days. In early 1800, McPherson visited Philadelphia to call on federal leaders for help in converting the nation's many sinners before it was too late. Although rebuffed by the president and senate, McPherson renewed his acquaintance with the vice president, Thomas Jefferson, who entrusted the former slave with sensitive documents to convey to James Madison back in Orange County. Jefferson also arranged protection for McPherson in Charlottesville, where he had brought a lawsuit against a violent white man. Overlooking McPherson's religious zeal, Jefferson respected his character and intellect.[71]

In 1800, McPherson married and moved to Richmond, where he became a clerk in the court of chancery thanks to patronage from George Wythe, the most liberal judge in Virginia. Prospering, McPherson acquired a home, rental properties, and a stake in overseas trade. Proud of his gentility, he rode through Richmond in a carriage until 1810, when the city council barred anyone of color from doing so, unless while driving for a master. He appealed to the legislature, which refused to make a special exception for McPherson. Intelligence and property were not enough to whiten McPherson in the eyes of legislators and city councilors.[72]

In 1811, McPherson founded a night school for freed blacks, employing a white man to teach writing, arithmetic, geography, astronomy, and religion. The school outraged Richmond's leaders, who dreaded any spread of literacy among free blacks, lest they pass it on to the enslaved. Shutting down the school, the city court indicted McPherson for creating a public nuisance. Declaring him insane, the magistrates sent him away to the asylum in Williamsburg. Richmond's leaders insisted that only a madman would found a school for black children. Magistrates also seized his property, which trustees liquidated at half its value to pay his debts. In June, the asylum directors deemed McPherson sane and released him. Returning to Richmond, he sued the city leaders, seeking damages for the ruin inflicted on his reputation and finances. Denied justice in Virginia, he moved north to New York City, where he died in 1817.[73]

A year later in Albemarle County, masters blocked some enslaved people from setting up a school. In late September, Reverend James Robinson, the Presbyterian minister of Cove Meeting House, invited frustrated slaves to attend his services and Sunday school: "You have been disappointed in your school, but do not be dispirited. Come and attend to me. I will instruct you, and I have no doubt but in fifteen or twenty years you will be as free as your masters." This address outraged several masters, who secured a grand jury indictment against Robinson, his son, and six other church leaders "for unlawfully assembling with slaves, and teaching slaves at the Cove Meeting House . . . to the great peril of the peace, harmony, and safety of the good Citizens." The court continued the case for three terms to keep Robinson on notice and in legal peril, before dismissing the indictment, apparently satisfied that he had learned his lesson.[74]

The September 1818 push for education by Albemarle slaves came a month after the celebrated Rockfish Gap Report, written by Jefferson, which favored locating the proposed University of Virginia at Charlottesville. The report generated excited anticipation and animated conversation among the whites of Albemarle. Overhearing that talk, enslaved people sought to claim a share in the power of knowledge. But the Albemarle justices forced Reverend Robinson to eat his words that had fed hope to the enslaved.

The agitation in Albemarle apparently was part of widespread efforts by enslaved Virginians to seek schools in response to the increased statewide discussion by whites of education in 1818–1819. But the legislature acted quickly to suppress aspiration by the enslaved. On March 2, 1819, the state legislators banned the newly "common practice, in many places within this Commonwealth, for slaves to assemble in considerable numbers, at meeting-houses . . . in the night, or at schools for teaching them reading or writing, which, if not restrained, may be productive of considerable evil to the community." Denouncing such schools as unlawful assemblies, the legislators empowered county justices to break them up and inflict twenty lashes on anyone who attended. Together with the bill founding the University of Virginia, which passed earlier in the same session, the ban on schools for slaves linked enlightenment for whites with enforced ignorance for the enslaved.[75]

Jefferson insisted that emancipation required improving both masters and slaves: "Both parties require long and difficult preparation." Masters needed to learn how to override "self-interest to an acquiescence in the rights of others," while enslaved people had to learn "self-government and . . . the honest pursuits of industry and social duty." The reeducation of masters and their slaves, he insisted, "require time, and the former must precede the latter." Giving priority to educating masters, Jefferson created the University of Virginia to train a new class of leaders who could, he hoped, reform and perfect Virginia.[76]

At Monticello, enslaved people watched construction of the new university with alarm. Aware that slaves paid at a master's death for his debts, they worried that the rising university absorbed Jefferson's time and money. One of his slaves, Peter Fossett, claimed that Jefferson intended to free them but could not do so because the "estate was so encumbered by [his] generous gifts to his cherished pet, the University at Charlottesville [so] that all the slaves had to [be] sold" after his death. Fossett exaggerated the scale of Jefferson's gifts to the University, which amounted to less than 5 percent of his total debt. But Fossett perceived a deeper reality. Creating the University absorbed Jefferson's energies, diverting him from managing his imperiled property. His fiscal ruin would cast almost all of his slaves onto the auction block after his death. Nor did the enslaved share Jefferson's optimism that liberal reforms would emerge from students who were the sons of masters. As the university rose beneath Monticello, enslaved people saw a threat to their hopes rather than a platform for their liberation.[77]

6
SCHOOLS

URING THE REVOLUTION, Jefferson hoped radically to reform Virginia through a raft of new laws. In June 1779, he chaired a legislative committee that proposed 126 bills affecting every aspect of public life in Virginia. The package designed, Jefferson explained, "a system by which every fibre would be eradicated of antient or future aristocracy; and a foundation laid for a government truly republican." Above all, he sought to educate every white child.[1]

William Wirt (1772–1834), by Saint-Mémin, 1807 (Library of Congress)

Rejecting monarchy and aristocracy, Patriot leaders wanted the next generation of Americans to master a new culture of republicanism. They insisted that European monarchies might thrive without an educated populace. Indeed, kings and nobles could better dominate and dazzle the ignorant and credulous with the showy ceremonies of monarchy. But republics depended on a broad electorate of common men. To keep their new rights, voters had to protect them with attentive care, lest the republic succumb to a resurgent aristocracy or reckless demagogues who manipulated the ignorant. Jefferson noted, "I have looked on our present state of liberty as a short-lived possession, unless the mass of the people could be informed."[2]

By educating common folk, Jefferson promoted some social mobility. "Worth and genius" should be "sought out from every condition of life and compleately prepared by education for defeating the competition of wealth & birth for public trusts." Rather than rely on private enterprise, he wanted the state to mandate education as a birthright for white children. Jefferson assured George Washington, "It is an axiom in my mind that our liberty can never be safe but in the hands of the people . . . with a certain degree of instruction. This it is the business of the state to effect, and on a general plan."[3]

A republic could only endure, Jefferson insisted, if both voters and leaders gained the information and rationality appropriate to their distinct roles. Common people needed enough learning to cherish and defend their republic. Then an educated electorate could scrutinize ambitious men, voting only for the natural aristocrats of merit and rejecting those who relied on artificial inheritance. Rather than level society, Jefferson regarded an elite as inevitable and necessary, but he wanted to make it more enlightened and responsible to the voters.[4]

Jefferson's plan would subdivide every county into "wards" (or "hundreds"), each the size of a township, about thirty-six square miles. The locals would build schools and hire teachers to educate every white girl and boy to read, write, and cipher over the course of three years. The most promising boys (but no girls) would advance to a district college to study classical languages, geography, mathematics, and natural science.

At those twenty-four colleges, the sons of prosperity would pay tuition, but the best poor boy from each ward school would earn a scholarship. In turn, the finest charity graduate from each college would merit a three-year public scholarship to attend the state university, which capped his system. Jefferson explained that, under his three-tiered system, "the best geniuses will be raked from the rubbish annually." Giving priority to white boys, Jefferson's proposed system provided scant education for girls and none for black people, either free or enslaved. He knew that Virginia's legislators would spend nothing to educate people of color or to advance girls beyond primary schools.[5]

Jefferson's program had three goals, all of them political (rather than economic). First, the colleges and university would train for republican leadership "a few subjects in every state, to whom nature has given minds of the first order." These would come from the wealthier class supplemented by a few charity students. Second, the local schools would enable every common man "to read, to judge & to vote understandingly on what is passing." Third, by creating wards, Jefferson meant to bypass and weaken the county governments dominated by local oligarchies. The wards would train common men in participatory democracy to defend their interests.[6]

Jefferson regarded wards as the fundamental foundation for an elegant four-tier system of government, each tier perfectly distinct yet all mutually dependent and balancing. "The elementary republics of the wards, the county republics, the state republics, and the republic of the Union, would form a gradation of authorities, standing each on the basis of law, holding every one [to] it's delegated share of powers, and constituting truly a system of fundamental balances and checks for the [entire system of] government." By participating in his ward, every free man would feel "that he is a participator in the government of affairs not merely at an election, one day in the year, but every day." In Jefferson's elegant description, such a neat system seemed almost possible.[7]

Jefferson also wanted to secularize primary education, detaching it from traditional ties to religion. He believed that religious dogma stunted the intellectual and moral development of children. By precluding rational and critical inquiry, Jefferson alleged, premature exposure to theology prepared children to submit to arbitrary authority as adults. If kept free from religion in the early classroom, however, children would have time to cultivate a moral sense, which he deemed natural to every person. Only in adolescence could a young person explore religious ideas with the power to discriminate between truth and falsehood.[8]

Jefferson hoped that Virginia's contending denominations would support an educational system that favored none by excluding the doctrines of all. But a leading Presbyterian, Samuel Stanhope Smith, doubted that the schools could be secularized. Where Jefferson imagined that individuals would naturally cooperate in schools, Smith lived in a harsher, real world of contentious groups: "The partialities of sects indeed ought to have no place in a system of liberal education. . . . But such is our misfortune; they exist, and they exist in considerable force."[9]

In 1779, Jefferson's education plan got nowhere in a legislature preoccupied with war and skittish about religious controversy. Most legislators derived from county elites, who feared losing power to Jefferson's democratic system of local wards. The failure of his plan disturbed Jefferson, who considered "the law for educating the common people" as "by far the most important bill in our whole code." He warned, "No other sure foundation can be devised for the preservation of freedom and happiness."[10]

In 1796, legislators passed a watered-down version of Jefferson's system. The new law merely invited every county government to implement primary schools with local, rather than state, taxes to finance it. Only one of Virginia's ninety-two counties did so, and it abandoned the effort after three years. Jefferson blamed county leaders, who balked at a plan that "would throw on wealth the education of the poor; and the justices, being generally of the more wealthy class, were unwilling to incur that burthen." Class divisions precluded the natural sociability and harmony between free people that Jefferson had expected. He blamed elite selfishness for exposing the state to an aristocratic counterrevolution. Jefferson insisted that a local tax for schools was "not more than the thousandth part of what will be paid to [the] kings, priests, and nobles who will rise up among us if we leave the people in ignorance." [11]

Jefferson had hoped that Virginians would invest in education what they had saved by abolishing the church-state establishment. Instead, they preferred to keep the money in their pockets. Consequentially, he saw a great regression in Virginia's schools. In 1820, Jefferson declared, "The mass of education in Virginia, before the revolution, placed her with the foremost of her sister colonies. What is her education now? Where is it? The little we have we import, like beggars, from other states; or import their beggars to bestow on us their miserable crumbs." [12]

While Jefferson faulted county leaders and state legislators, other Virginians regarded common voters as complicit in neglecting education. A reform-minded legislator, David Watson, wrote a satirical essay to insist that common Virginians preferred to buy consumer goods rather than fund education. "This is the way in our country. Boots, bonnets, and brandy must be had at any price; but learning must shift for itself." He doubted that there was "sense enough among the great bulk of the people to prevent a few cunning, ambitious men from taking our houses and land and everything else away from us; and then how shall we get boots, bonnets, and brandy?" [13]

Year after futile year, governors exhorted state legislators to fund public education. The most persistent was John Tyler, Sr., the father of a future president. In 1808, Tyler denounced Virginia's "eternal war declared against the Arts and Sciences and a determination to pay nothing by way of taxes to the support and encouragement of Education—the true and solid foundation of a free Government." In 1809, he assured legislators, "Scarcely a common country school is to be found capable of teaching the mother tongue grammatically." In 1810, Tyler concluded, "He who can go back from the assembly and tell his constituents he has saved a penny secures his popularity against the next Election." The republican revolution bred a contradiction in Virginia: an electorate unwilling to pay for public education. [14]

Because a republic empowered common voters, reformers insisted that no republic could survive without better education for its citizens. Yet most common Virginians would settle for basic literacy and numeracy gained in a couple of years at a private grammar school for their children. These voters wanted gentlemen to pay for educating their own children, and the poor could make do without book learning. In sum, most Virginians felt they could sustain a republic without improving the next generation through public funding for primary schools.[15]

Old Field Schools

Virginia's dispersed population discouraged local schools. The state was huge, rural, and, in the western half, mountainous. In Tidewater and Piedmont Virginia, the employment of slaves enlarged many farms into plantations, which spread white people more thinly over the landscape. In 1820, Virginia's 748,000 whites scattered over 64,284 square miles, compared to compact Massachusetts, where 378,787 whites lived on just 8,327 square miles. In New England, unlike Virginia, enough children lived within walking distance to sustain neighborhood schools.[16]

Slavery also discouraged public education by increasing inequality among white people, as the largest slaveholders held power and opposed paying to educate common whites. In 1810, Elijah Fletcher arrived from Vermont to teach school in Virginia. Fletcher marveled at the hollow republicanism professed by wealthy Virginians: "There is no country, I believe, where property is more unequally distributed than in Virginia. We can see here and there a stately palace or mansion house; while all around for many miles we behold no other but little smoky huts and log cabins of poor, laborious, ignorant tenants." He blamed the lack of public schools: "The poor have no chance at all for an Education. This is their boasted liberty and Equality!!" Fletcher concluded, "Happy, thrice happy are the poor people of New Engl[an]d when compared to that class here."[17]

Common, white Virginians got a smattering of education by spending a few weeks annually at an "old field school" in their neighborhood. These small schools depended upon a cluster of nearby parents who agreed to build or repair a ramshackle log cabin located in an "old field" lying fallow from cultivation and reasonably convenient for their children to walk to. Then the neighbors had to find, hire, and pay a teacher. The compensation included room and board, as well as candles and firewood for the school. In addition, parents had to find and buy schoolbooks, usually a basic speller and pieces of slate for students to write on. The old field schools served only children with parents who could and would pay, which excluded the poorest families. Even children of middling means often could find no nearby school for want of a critical mass of neighbors.[18]

During the 1810s in Bedford County, Jeremiah Jeter attended an old field school "constructed of logs, notched at the corners, daubed with clay, covered with boards, kept in their position by weighty poles laid across them." Lacking glass windows, the cabin admitted scant light through a square hole, covered with a shutter on leather hinges in foul weather. Students sat on crude benches, while the teacher had a chair and table at the front of the room. Barefoot and thinly clad children faced a painful walk of three or four miles over stony roads to get to school.[19]

The teachers relied on rote memorization as students chanted words and phrases with little attention to context and comprehension. A critic noted, "What is learned is learned in *parrot fashion*. It is recited mechanically. . . . Hence most young ones go to school when they *must*; escape from it when they *can*; and finally leave it with a stubborn resolution to have as little to do with books as possible . . . as long as they live."[20]

The teachers were often brutal. Jeter's instructor punished entire benches of students with his rod if anyone made trouble. "Of course, they did not learn much," Jeter concluded. A traveler disagreed, insisting that boys learned violence in Virginia's primary schools: "When they come out of that place of corporal punishment, they tease each other and fight."[21]

In 1801, John Davis, a young immigrant from Britain, met Thomas Jefferson, who helped him land a teaching position on a plantation in Prince William County. But Davis felt like a stranger in the strange land of Virginia. At the end of the school day, the boys "gave loose to the most riotous merriment, and betook themselves to the woods, followed by all the dogs on the plantation." One defiant boy brought two big dogs into school over Davis's protests. To pay that boy back, Davis hired an elderly slave to lure the dogs outside, where he hung them from a pine tree. Because the boy had cost his father the dogs that guarded his farm, "negroes broke open his barn, pilfered his sacks of Indian corn, rode his horses in the night—and thus was I revenged." Davis had adapted to Virginia. But after three months, he wearied of the school and departed, "to the joy of the boys." He wrote up his experiences in a book dedicated to Jefferson.[22]

Teaching at an old field school rarely paid more than $200, half of what a man might make by farming. Most men with able bodies and good minds steered clear of teaching in common schools. A critic declared that rural teachers were "too proud to beg and too lazy to work." Blaming the poor conditions and low pay of teaching, a Virginian noted, "In our country, no man of talents and worth will continue in any calling which is not thought honourable and so treated by the leading men in society."[23]

Theories

In the spring of 1805, Joseph C. Cabell ascended the Alps to visit Yverdun, in Switzerland, accompanied by his friend William Maclure. They went to examine the celebrated and innovative primary school conducted by Johann Heinrich Pestalozzi. In 1806, Cabell returned to Virginia persuaded that Pestalozzi's system offered "a sure cure for the miserable conditions most of our schools have fallen into."[24]

Possessing a deep empathy for children, Pestalozzi pioneered an educational philosophy now called "child-centered." Dispensing with rote and authoritarian teaching, his disciples adapted instruction to individuals, teaching what each could learn and regulating progress by readiness. Viewing children as benign, the methods invited imagination, inspired curiosity, and rendered study more like play. Pestalozzian teachers often took their classes outside to learn from closely observing nature. Working from particulars to general propositions, they broke down each subject into small, graduated steps, of slowly increasing difficulty meant to facilitate confidence and progress. Pestalozzi explained, "Learn to make the simple perfect before going on to the complex." The method promoted engaged and critical thinking rather than memorization.[25]

William Maclure promoted Pestalozian teaching in the United States. A merchant born in Scotland, he emigrated to the United States and, for a time, operated out of the small Virginia village of Milton near Monticello. Moving to Philadelphia, he became rich through overseas trade and used his new money philanthropically. Troubled by inequality and distrusting other rich men, he tried to empower the poor by educating their children. Blaming conventional schools for social miseries, he insisted that reformed teaching could fulfill everyone's true potential. In Pestalozzi's methods, Maclure found a republican mode of teaching: "the total absence of all constraint, every action flowing from free will."[26]

At Yverdun, Maclure befriended one of Pestalozzi's teachers, Joseph Neef, an egalitarian who felt alienated from life in Europe because of Napoleon's despotic rule. Seeking an escape, Neef welcomed Maclure's offer to subsidize his emigration to the United States, where for three years he could study English while preparing a school on the outskirts of Philadelphia. In 1808, Neef published a book that pitched the Pestalozzian system as "Suitable for the Offspring of a Free People, and for all Rational Beings." Opening in 1809, his school attracted great interest and, for a few years, enough students to pay Neef's salary. But Neef's reputation as a deist alarmed many parents, so enrollments declined and the school closed in 1815, when Neef moved to Kentucky to become a farmer.[27]

The Pestalozzian system required especially able and dedicated teachers, who were few in the United States. A supporter praised Pestalozzi's system as "superior to the common one," but he conceded, "I think more depends on the capacity & fitness of the Teacher to render it effective, than in the old system—nor is it so good for a dull or indolent boy as the old method because so much is left" to student initiative. Classes had to be small and intimate, which pushed up the expense of tuition. Maclure conceded that it cost $200 to $300 a year per child, which put a Pestalozian school beyond the reach of the poor: the very people that he wanted to help.[28]

Maclure noted the irony that Pestalozzian pedagogy thrived "amongst the rich, where it probably will be celebrated, but that is not my wish or intention." He insisted that the wealthy had enough "knowledge to cheat the poor. It is the knowledge of the Labourer on which the free Government of this country must depend." Only government support could make Pestalozzian education accessible to poor students, but American leaders balked at taxing the prosperous to promote a more equal society.[29]

Maclure and Cabell shared a passion for education but differed in their social goals. Cabell sought to enhance social order by improving the self-discipline of common whites, but Maclure wanted to transform society by empowering the poor. Maclure considered "an almost equal division of property, knowledge, and power, as the only firm foundation of freedom which includes the happiness of mankind." He also believed that preparing women "to fill all places of honor and profit . . . would be the greatest possible improvement in Society. It would be doubling the mental force of the great mass of mankind." Maclure regarded slavery as poisonous to education and to equality for white people. In 1825, he tried by statistics to persuade Jefferson that free labor was ten times as productive as enslaved labor, but the philosopher did not take the bait. Instead, in reply Jefferson invited Maclure to visit the University of Virginia, without mentioning its construction by enslaved labor.[30]

In 1806, Jefferson had taken an interest in Neef's proposed school in Philadelphia, but he later soured on importing new educational theories into Virginia. In 1816, he declared that Pestalozzi's methods were "calculated for cities or large towns, but not at all for the sparse settlements in the country [that] I inhabit. I have neglected them therefore as useless to us." Pestalozzian education was a poor fit for Virginia, which lacked enough innovative teachers and any public commitment to pay them.[31]

Cabell thought that the solution lay in merging Pestalozzianism with a rival educational theory advanced in England by Joseph Lancaster. Known as "the monitorial system" or "Lancasterian education," this program promised to educate large numbers of poor children cheaply enough to entice taxpayers. The system trained older students as "monitors," each responsible for drilling a dozen younger students. Because monitors cost almost nothing, the system could enable a teacher to superintend hundreds of students in a huge classroom, thereby expanding education at little cost. In a fan letter to Lancaster, Cabell exulted that "one man is competent to teach a thousand pupils more rapidly than the smallest number can be advanced in the ordinary method."[32]

The Quaker son of an artisan, Joseph Lancaster grew up in a poor section of London, where he opened a school in his father's house in 1798. Dispensing with corporal punishment, the system relied on daily competition for small prizes: kites, tops, balls, books, and pictures. Pupils moved up into a higher class as soon as they had mastered a level. A master publicist, Lancaster insisted that his system offered "economy of expense, efficiency of instruction, discipline by routine, motivation by competition, and neutrality in religion." His celebrated school drew curious reformers from Europe and the United States. They felt dazzled by the regimented yet frenetic energy of the classroom, with each corner occupied by a monitor running his students through animated drills.[33]

Lancaster wanted to educate poor children, but to expand his school system he needed financial support from wealthy and powerful men. Pitching his system to suit their conservativism, he promised to remake the poor into disciplined and reliable workers by dissuading them from lives of drink and crime. A supporter said the key question was "whether a boy is to be a stupid animal, or an intelligent animal." By learning to read and cipher, a student became "opposed to the permanent temptation of beer." Lancaster sought a more egalitarian society, but he had to assure contributors that his techniques turned children into coordinating parts of a hierarchical machine.[34]

During the 1810s, Lancaster's system appealed to many Americans, including reform-minded Virginians, by promising mass education at a bargain price. In Richmond, the newspaper editor Thomas Ritchie assured citizens that Lancaster "has made the road so smooth and easy that it may be travelled with very little expense": just $5 per student per year, a sixth of the cost at traditional primary schools.[35]

In Virginia, Lancasterian schools emerged in commercial towns including Alexandria, Fredericksburg, Norfolk, Petersburg, Richmond, and Winchester. The funds came from city governments and private donors. By endowing a female Lancasterian school, a wealthy widow vowed to rescue "from poverty and the sinks of shameless immorality those sweet though wild blossoms," the poor, white girls of Alexandria. In 1819, Lancaster helped the cause by touring Virginia, giving inspirational lectures, including one to the state legislature.[36]

But could Lancaster's system of large schools work in the many rural counties, where most Virginians lived in a dispersion that frustrated even modest-sized neighborhood schools? In his home county, Cabell calculated that only a third of boys and one-eighth of the girls studied arithmetic. He deemed that neglect "the usual state of things in all our schools" throughout the state. "Is it not horrible to think of?—that in the state of Virginia only 1/8 of the female population learn Arithmetic!! Yet such is the fact."[37]

To educate rural people, Cabell designed a model school that applied the Lancasterian system to teaching reading and writing, while deploying Pestalozzian methods for arithmetic. Such a combination defied conventional wisdom that saw the two systems as antithetical: one working best in small groups with an elite teacher, while the other relied on large numbers engaged in mass drills. To implement his plan, Cabell took charge of the Nelson County board of school commissioners and visited the county's eleven schools and wrote to every teacher. He predicted, "I think the Devil himself & all his imps could not now stop the progress of the System." Cabell hoped to impress and sway county leaders throughout the state to adopt his plan. But the experiment proved neither contagious nor sustainable even in Nelson County. As with all educational panaceas, Cabell promised more than any system could fulfill, which bred disdain for other experiments. The old field schools persisted in rural Virginia.[38]

Academies

After a little primary-school education, most Virginians forsook formal education and went to work on farms or in shops. The most ambitious middle-class families sent a few boys to join sons of the elite at an academy, usually in a commercial town, where the students boarded. Between 1790 and 1830, the state authorized seventy academies. Stingy with funds, legislators merely allowed local sponsors to solicit donations or hold a lottery, tapping the Virginian passion for gambling. The organizers had to erect a building and attract instructors. For want of money or teachers only about half the academies operated at any given time.[39]

Jefferson despised these "petty *academies*, as they call themselves, which are starting up in every neighborhood, and where one or two men, possessing Latin, & sometimes Greek, a knolege of the globes, and the first six books of Euclid, imagine & communicate this as the sum of science. They commit their pupils to the theatre of the world with just taste enough of learning to be alienated from industrious pursuits, and not enough to do service in the ranks of science." He even disliked the nearby academy kept by his nephews Peter and Samuel Carr, denouncing their filthy school as "the pest of the neighborhood" for propagating "the itch so general at schools . . . and we are kept in eternal dread of it [spreading] at Monticello."[40]

Dependent on tuition for income, teachers crowded their academies with as many boys as possible. Because the overburdened teachers struggled to keep order, critics insisted that boys learned too much from peers and too little in class. William C. Preston attended an academy "filled with dirty boys of low manners and morals. In six months at this place I unlearned as much as it was possible . . . to unlearn in six months." David Watson exhorted his son to beware of schoolmates lest he "be deceived by villains & disappointed by fools."[41]

Virginia had few teachers qualified to teach at an academy. Because educated Virginians disdained the labor of teaching restless adolescents, academies relied on imported teachers, often from Ireland and Scotland. Academy teachers were unsteady, here today but gone tomorrow in search of better pay and calmer students. Most academies opened and shut quickly, beginning with high hopes but dissolving and staying shuttered until sponsors found new instructors.[42]

Some New Englanders came south to teach, but Virginians distrusted them as the bearers of dangerous ideas on slavery. In fact, Yankees of stiff principles rarely lingered in Virginia, while those who stayed made a profitable peace with slavery. Slavery initially shocked Vermont-born Elijah Fletcher, who noted the slaves' ragged clothes, scant diet, and frequent whipping "for every little offence most cruelly." Fletcher saw an overseer punish an enslaved man and his son for borrowing a horse for an errand. According to Fletcher, the overseer "first tied up the boy and whipt him about a quarter of an hour, and he was begging and praying, yelling to a terrible rate. They then took the man, and I will assure you, they show[ed] him no mercy. The more he cried and begged pardon, the more they whip and, in fact, I thought they would have killed the poor creature." Fletcher added, "They said it would not do to indulge them. They must whip them till they were humble and obedient."[43]

Determined to stay and make money, Fletcher adapted to Virginia. In January 1811, his father wrote to urge his son to help enslaved people become free. Fletcher sadly replied that "to vindicate the rights of that degraded class of human creatures here would render me quite unpopular. There are none the Virginians despise so much as Quakers and those who disapprove of slavery." Instead of criticizing slavery, he told the enslaved that "they are as well off as though free, but I can hardly make them believe this lesson."[44]

In 1813, Fletcher justified slavery in a letter to his father: "To emancipate them at once would be the height of folly and danger. You must not think too badly of slave holders—for your *son* is one." To soften that revelation, Fletcher claimed that he provided decent food and clothing: the sort of amelioration championed by genteel masters who sought to appease their consciences. Marrying the daughter of a wealthy slave owner, Fletcher gave up academy teaching to become a planter in 1814. Within ten years, he acquired fifty slaves. Far from corrupting his students with Yankee notions, Fletcher had become a Virginian. But he reaped what he had sowed, complaining that his sons became true young Virginians: "arrogant, entitled, and beyond parental control." One son would "learn nothing at school and thinks of little but his Gun and amusements." Later, Fletcher's former plantation became the site of Sweet Briar College.[45]

Ogilvie

Jefferson found his ideal teacher in James Ogilvie, a mercurial Scot smitten with the radical Enlightenment championed by the English writer William Godwin. A graduate of King's College in Aberdeen, Scotland, Ogilvie migrated to Virginia in 1793 when twenty years old to teach at academies. An avid self-promoter, Ogilvie published newspaper puff pieces and wrote letters to cultivate patronage from leading men, including Jefferson. Tall, rail-thin, and balding, Ogilvie exulted in his "glorious destiny to be amongst the first instructors who substituted science" and "liberal literature in place of jargon & above [all] an efficient moral order in place of a coercive, barbarous discipline."[46]

By teaching through consent rather than coercion, Ogilvie offered a "scientific" education that reinforced Jefferson's republican vision of politics. Ogilvie insisted "that the happiness of society essentially depends upon a general equality of conditions and opportunities." But to make money he had to teach the paying sons of Virginia's elite rather than the children of common whites. His egalitarianism was a posture rather than a program for action.[47]

Dispensing with corporal punishment, admonishment, and rote memorization, Ogilvie entertained students with flamboyant orations and readings from classical texts. He blended "instruction with amusement . . . to invigorate and inform the understanding, to excite and nourish an active and generous curiosity." Admirers praised his performances as "singularly calculated to awaken and keep alive curiosity: to exercise not only the faculties of the intellect, but the best affections of the heart." His style appealed to young Virginians, who preferred oral performance over studying.[48]

Ogilvie taught government, morality, logic, rhetoric, literary criticism, elocution, philology, English grammar, natural history, Latin, and Greek. He hired an assistant to teach mathematics and French. The term culminated in a public examination during which students gave speeches to demonstrate progress to family, friends, and local notables. Ogilvie capped the day by delivering his own exuberant oration on education. An admirer anticipated "all the patriots, philosophers, and useful citizens, which his unfettered talents would in a long life create."[49]

In the short term, his teaching produced wonders. One student was "an idle, listless boy" until inspired by Ogilvie: "I felt that there was a divine spark in the human mind . . . which might be fanned into a flame." But Ogilvie's methods required immense energy, which wore him down. After teaching a few terms, he shifted to a new academy, moving on from Fredericksburg to Stevensburg, Tappahannock, and Richmond. His pedagogy worked best in short bursts in a new town, where his approach seemed fresh. Familiarity, however, bred suspicion that he was, in fact, superficial. Winfield Scott, a future commander of the American army, recalled his teacher as "a Scotsman rich in physical and intellectual gifts," but "too much was attempted within a limited time by republican short cuts to knowledge."[50]

In early 1806, Jefferson recruited Ogilvie to launch an academy at Milton, a village on the Rivanna River two miles from Monticello. Impressed by his energy, deism, and republicanism, Jefferson sent his grandson, Jeff Randolph, to Ogilvie's academy and gave the teacher free run of the Monticello library, with borrowing privileges. Jefferson even trusted Ogilvie as a confidant charged with dissuading the fiery Thomas Mann Randolph from exchanging pistol shots with his provocative cousin John Randolph.[51]

At Monticello, Jefferson and T. M. Randolph hosted Sunday morning salons for family and friends to hear Ogilvie deliver moral lectures of the deist sort. Dr. Charles Everette attended and marveled, "He seems to step with as much ease from the Earth to the Clouds." Everette concluded, "By Heavens! He is sometimes a most Luminous body of Science & general Intelligence. . . . But he has also times of visions & of Fancy which peep through the soul of his audience and transports & delights beyond measure."[52]

Enrolling the elite sons of Albemarle, Ogilvie promised to develop their future careers as lawyers and statesmen. Francis W. Gilmer's brother, Harmer Gilmer, exulted, "Here no dull monotony fatigues the minds of the pupils. There is a continual variety. . . . Every faculty of the mind is called into action & equally improved." No distant figure of authority, Ogilvie posed as the students' best and brightest friend. Gilmer declared that students felt "as easy in his company as in that of their school fellows; except that his superior information" commanded respect. Basking in their approval, Ogilvie praised his students as "tractable to affectionate admonition."[53]

Ogilvie praised Jefferson's grandson Jeff Randolph for sound morals: "That exuberantly as the seeds of dissipation & vice are at this time scattered thro' Virginia, not one of these noxious atoms has as yet found its way into his mind." The plantation manager at Monticello, Edmund Bacon, remembered it differently. Jeff brought school friends up to Monticello for weekend slumber parties, and while the philosopher was away, the boys would play. The friends included William Cabell Rives, but he broke away to stay with Bacon: "The other boys were too intimate with the negro women to suit him. He was always a very modest boy." While Ogilvie was teaching deist morality at the foot of the mountain, Jeff was promoting white male privilege in a slave society at the top.[54]

Ogilvie's long days began at dawn, when he listened to "the junior classes recite lessons in geography, grammar, geometry, &c." After breakfast, Ogilvie lectured to the senior class "on ethics, rhetoric, natural philosophy, or political economy." In the afternoon, he heard the "junior classes translate passages from the Greek and Latin classics." After a break for dinner, he reassembled his students for "recitation and elocution." He then retired to his chamber for four or five hours to study "the speculations of the deepest thinkers, on the most important subjects." He slept little and took increasing doses of opium.[55]

Exhausted by the long hours of manic activity, Ogilvie lost his early zeal for teaching. He concluded, "There is a disheartening and monotonous drudgery, essentially connected with the business of practical education . . . which, as the instructor advances in life, silently but fatally saps his constitution, benumbs his faculties, and converts the fuel of enthusiasm, into the cold ashes of apathy, or into the lurid smoke of life-loathing melancholy." For a while, he confessed, "the excessive use of opium . . . enabled him to sustain and survive this unremitted and overwhelming drudgery." But he began to fear "insanity and suicide."[56]

In March 1808, Ogilvie closed his Milton school and rode away to launch a new career as a public orator, charging fifty cents for a ticket to attend. Although Ogilvie could not account for all the books he had borrowed, Jefferson wrote letters of introduction to facilitate his speaking tour in distant cities, extolling "the correctness of his morals, the purity of his views, and his high degree of understanding & cultivation."[57]

Ogilvie toured up and down the east coast, visiting major cities and many small towns in between. He dressed in a Roman toga to deliver flamboyant speeches modeled in manner on Cicero but addressing contemporary moral issues, including dueling, gambling, and female education. A young law student praised the performances: "He has fancy, imagination, & a powerful command of language. His action is spirited & graceful. His voice has great compass & is ever well-modulated." Winfield Scott recalled Ogilvie's orations as "magnificent specimens of art; only the art was too conspicuous." He befriended leading cultural figures including John Quincy Adams, Charles Brockden Brown, Thomas Cooper, Washington Irving, and George Ticknor. Irving thought him "quite a visionary but a most interesting one." In the United States Capitol, he addressed President James Madison and both houses of Congress. By vouching for him to their friends, notable men built Ogilvie's celebrity and generated crowds. But he experienced "unaccountable fluctuations of animation, sensibility & energy," with months of depression alternating with bursts of productivity.[58]

Ogilvie noted that Americans most respected writers and orators who were validated by success in London. In 1816, he sailed for England, taking his speaking tour to the great center of English-speaking culture. Success there, he hoped, would redeem a life that he deemed "baffled, embittered & abortive." He also hoped to claim the title and properties of the Earl of Findlater as his due inheritance. Abruptly forsaking his American republicanism, he meant to become an aristocrat in Scotland.[59]

Before departing, Ogilvie published a volume of rambling philosophical essays that renounced his early radical views in favor of conservative positions. He praised Christianity, while denouncing Godwin and other radicals. Having experienced "the *sad* realities of life," Ogilvie no longer was "the youthful day-dreamer of perfectibility." He exhorted people "in the humbler and less envied conditions" to defer to the wealthy and powerful as possessed of superior learning and talents. By turning reactionary, Ogilvie bolstered his bid to join the aristocracy of Scotland. But the incoherence of the essays disgusted Francis W. Gilmer, who denounced his once beloved teacher: "He is utterly incapable of connecting in a natural order any two ideas, and is in every department of knowledge more perfectly a madman & a fool . . . than anyone who ever enjoyed his reputation. I had some idea of putting an extinguisher on the smoke & dim flame of his stinking candle, but perhaps it is better to let him go out in his own feculence."[60]

Ogilvie's return to Britain did not go well. He failed to make good on his flimsy claim to be the true Earl of Findlater. After some early success, his orations fell flat, and audiences shrank. Plunged into depression, Ogilvie shot himself in Perth, Scotland, in September 1820. He had long been prone to "paroxysms of black and blasting melancholy, when a living soul seems to be united to a dead body," and when "every sound is discord, every taste nauseous, every odour fetid." As an orator, he often spoke on the topic of suicide, and he had especially admired a philosopher's essay entitled "On Madness."[61]

In Virginia, Ogilvie left behind an outsized reputation. Admirers recalled him as the consummate teacher, who could inspire youth through entertainment and without coercion. A newspaper writer declared, "The mightiest despot, I ever knew, over the minds of the youths, was the most zealous to improve them—I mean the celebrated Ogilvie." But Ogilvie was unique, and he could thrive only in short bursts. So his example set up false hopes that other teachers could and should make learning easy and pleasant for young Virginians.[62]

Elmwood

During the early nineteenth century, as in the colonial past, most of Virginia's girls received their education from mothers and aunts at home. They learned to milk cows, tend chickens, cultivate a household garden, to make, mend, and clean clothing, prepare meals, tidy houses, wash dishes, and raise children. Some attended an old field school for a time, but only half gained literacy. Change came only for girls at the narrow top of society, where genteel families began to seek education for daughters as well as sons. While boys remained the priority, leading families adopted higher expectations for what girls should learn. Mothers and fathers meant to display their daughters as ornaments, to attest to the high standards of their parents; to attract a husband who valued a wife who could converse intelligently; and to become enlightened mothers able to impart genteel manners and ideas to children. The lawyer William Wirt explained, "Improve the minds of your daughters, and they will make their sons heroes and patriots. They will awaken the curiosity of their infant minds, and inspire them with the love of wisdom and of virtue."[63]

Parents sought to train girls as companionate wives rather than create competitors for sons and husbands. While educating daughters, parents wanted to assure their femininity and marriage. In 1819, a mother noted, "Daughters as well as sons are now thought of by the fond parent. Education is considered equally their due, and in going into company you can often be entertained with sensible remarks on literature and science, issuing from a female mouth, adorned with all that soft sprightliness which is natural to her sex." Although Wirt championed better education for women, he defended their domesticity: "I am aware that nature has established a broad distinction between the sexes; that there are certain spheres of action in which females can never move, and boundaries which they can never with propriety overleap."[64]

Some genteel parents sent their daughters to new boarding schools founded after the revolution and usually located in commercial towns. Fewer than Virginia's academies for boys, the female academies numbered about a dozen by 1820. These schools taught reading and writing in English and French, supplemented by arithmetic, history, geography, and natural science. The teachers also trained girls in ornamental skills that highlighted femininity: drawing, playing a musical instrument, dancing, and making elegant needlework. Wirt complained that the teachers kept girls busy "spoiling paper with colors, producing discord on the Piano, and dancing out of time to the violin." By design, female academies did not teach the classical languages, Greek and Latin. Deemed essential for any young man with professional aspirations, these languages seemed too mentally taxing and masculine for young women to pursue.[65]

During the 1790s, Eliza Parke Custis longed to compete with the boys around her. One day, in the presence of her stepfather, a tutor praised Eliza as "an extraordinary child & would if a *Boy*, make a Brilliant figure." In reply, she "thought it hard [that] they would not teach me Greek & Latin because I was a girl. They laughed & said women ought not to know those things, & mending, writing, Arithmetic, & Music was all I could be permitted to acquire. I thought of this often— with deep regret." Gritting her teeth, Custis engaged in needlework, dancing school, and music lessons.[66]

A few well-educated fathers did tutor daughters privately in Greek and Latin, so that they could share an appreciation for the great writers of antiquity: Cicero, Caesar, Homer, Horace, Ovid, and Virgil. But genteel social circles frowned on displaying this accomplishment in company. Virginia Randolph Cary warned a young woman, "Did you never hear a lady of our acquaintance lament that she had learnt Latin, because it subjected her to such sneers from the gentlemen? She brought this trouble on herself. . . . I know several ladies who understand Latin, but they have contrived to keep this unusual acquisition from the world."[67]

During the 1820s, Virginia's most prestigious female academy was in Essex County on the Elmwood Plantation of James Mercer Garnett and his wife Mary Eleanor Dick Garnett. Mary directed the school, with their daughters as teachers, while James promoted it to genteel friends. The school annually attracted forty to fifty students, drawn from leading families throughout the state. A visiting mother reported, "The house is large & comfortable—handsome walks in every direction—an extensive garden & . . . a Church within a mile of the house and a good Minister where Mrs. G[arnett] goes every Sabbath with all her scholars."[68]

Devout Episcopalians, the Garnetts taught morality and piety as well as academic subjects and ornamental accomplishments. They noted that society expected more conspicuous and consistent religiosity from women than men. James declared that every young lady should "entirely avoid all such subjects as even border on indelicacy, slander, detraction, vulgarity, angry disputation, immorality, and irreligion." Their girls studied academics to make their conversation uplifting and instructive, rather than to change society.[69]

Every girl was supposed to fit in rather than stand out. Young women were on display and closely watched, so the Garnetts preached keeping "always clean, neat, habited according to your circumstances and situations in life, and so far in the fashion, as not to attract notice either for excess, or deficiency in the prevailing mode." The Garnetts prepared girls for marriage, teaching a feminine restraint and softness deemed essential to attract a husband. Garnett insisted that any man would prefer to marry "a frantic bedlamite, or a barrel of gun-powder with a firebrand in it" rather than a "violent tempered woman." The ultimate goal of a female education was to "be praised for your manners, admired for your accomplishments, and loved and esteemed for your powers of conversation."[70]

Cherishing daughters as bonds of family sentiment, genteel parents were often reluctant to send them away to a boarding school among other girls of uncertain values. In September 1825, John Hartwell Cocke warily entrusted his daughter Anne, aged fourteen, to the Elmwood School. Upon arrival, Anne admired Mary Garnett: "I have never seen her in the least angry with any of the Girls, altho' they behave very badly sometimes." But Anne was homesick, informing her parents that she attended church service but could not concentrate: "My eyes would fill with tears. . . . I really feel now [that] if all the world was in my possession I would give it up if I could return home." After less than a year of study, Anne went home.[71]

Mania

In educating their brilliant daughter Laura, William Wirt and his wife, Elizabeth Gamble Wirt, struggled to balance intellectual accomplishment and feminine submission. In 1810, when she was seven, her father declared, "I want her to be something better than common, not a bold unblushing lady of fashion, nor a loquacious & disgusting pedant: but a happy union of female gentleness and delicacy, with masculine learning & genius—simple but elegant—soft and timid, yet dignified & commanding." With Wirt as her tutor, Laura could read Erasmus and Caesar in Latin at age nine. When she entered her teens, however, her parents worried that she was too studious and would put off suitors. Shifting Laura into domestic duties, Wirt warned that a learned woman "may be admired, but she will never be beloved." Depressed by the shift, Laura delayed marrying for five years. Sobered by this experience, the Wirts minimized the classics in educating their two younger daughters.[72]

The Wirts expected too little from their daughters and too much from their only son, Robert. Laura had the ability and equanimity to fulfill her father's hopes for a learned and brilliant heir, but their society barred that. Meanwhile, Robert struggled to match his larger-than-life father, the leading lawyer, wittiest essayist, and most gregarious host in Richmond. To discipline Robert, Wirt sent him to West Point in 1820 to become a cadet, but he bolted in the spring of 1822, to his father's disgust. Risen from the middle class, Wirt recalled that his family could not afford to send him to college, "and here is Robert who has the full cup of science and literature offered to him and he puts it back with his hand." Heading to Virginia, Robert avoided his parents, now in Washington, D.C., where Wirt served as attorney general in the Monroe administration.[73]

In August 1822, Wirt's friend and legal protégé, Francis W. Gilmer, tracked Robert down and brought him to Richmond. Gilmer expressed shock: "No metamorphosis of Ovid was ever more complete or astonishing." Robert had become "mad as the winds" and unrecognizable: "His hair grows over his face. His countenance is dejected yet fierce & sour." Taking in Robert, Gilmer worked "to quiet his disordered mind & soothe his passions." He declared, "It is the phrenzy of inordinate ambition. He talks of nothing short of Caesar & Bonaparte, considers this country as a theatre wholly unworthy [of] his enterprize." Wirt had wanted his son to become a great man, and Robert did so in grand fantasies.[74]

Unwilling to accept insanity as Robert's ailment, Wirt insisted that he merely had a troubled liver that could easily be cured. Indeed, Wirt urged Robert to resume studying to become a doctor. Wirt suggested a stratagem to Gilmer: "Let Robert suppose himself a student, while the Doct[or] will consider him as a patient." Caught between Wirt's delusions and Robert's mania, Gilmer assured a mutual friend, "As to study, it is out of the question, whatever his father may think. . . . He will take into his room 20 (no exaggeration) books at a time, turn over the leaves passionately, confusedly &c., read for twenty minutes—throw down the book—then to another &c, all the while with marks of agony & torture on his mind. His motions are all hurried & artificial, his spirit dark & perturbed." In this manic reading, Robert seemed desperate to fulfill his father's hopes. Gilmer asked a friend, "What strange infatuation is it, that blinds parents toward their children[?]"[75]

By December 1822, Gilmer was at his own wit's end, unable to concentrate on his legal business and fearing for his life. He described the previous two months as "the most painful & anxious of my life." Gilmer could not sleep because Robert threatened to kill him, "not from any hatred, but because he had taken up the notion, that he was destined, fated, &c., to kill me." At any hour of the night, a "wild & frantic" Robert would break into Gilmer's bedroom. Gilmer added that Robert had menacing "eyes glaring like Hamlet's at his father's spectre"—an apt analogy, for his own father haunted Robert's mind.[76]

Gilmer sent Robert to his father, who packed the young man off on a voyage to the Mediterranean for sea air as a cure. He died at sea in December 1824 at the age of nineteen. A tragedy of mania and misunderstanding, Robert's story had played out in Richmond, where a young Edgar Allan Poe grew up and must have taken note. Robert's demise expressed the burden of expectations heaped on young gentlemen, regardless of capacity, while families limited the aspirations of even their most brilliant daughters.[77]

Mercer

In 1809, Jefferson retired from politics and returned to Monticello. He vowed to push two great and interrelated reforms for Virginia: "the public education and the subdivision of the counties into wards. I consider the continuance of republican government as absolutely hanging on these two hooks." He sought to nudge a legislature that had rebuffed his proposals in 1779 and again in 1796.[78]

In 1816, Jefferson sought to revive his educational plan as part of a bid to charter a new institution, Central College, in Charlottesville. As an end run around the county justices, Jefferson wrote into his college bill a power for its Visitors to divide Albemarle into wards and implement a primary school in each. By establishing his system in one county, Jefferson hoped to set a contagious example that would spread throughout the state. But this gambit irritated the county leaders, who defended their control over local taxes. Their opposition compelled Jefferson's legislative lieutenant, Joseph C. Cabell, to drop the local schools provision from the Central College bill.[79]

Jefferson's revived educational plan also faced stiff competition from a rival proposal advanced by Charles Fenton Mercer, a Federalist legislator, lawyer, and planter from Loudon County. Educated at Princeton, Mercer had noted the widening gap between his declining home state and the rapidly growing North. To accelerate Virginia's development, he sought gradually to emancipate and colonize the enslaved; to invest heavily in new roads and canals; and to incorporate many new banks, particularly in the underserved western counties. Above all, Mercer favored a comprehensive system of primary education, funded and supervised by the state government. He privately believed that a better-educated public would see through the Republicans as wealthy frauds who exploited ignorant common voters to retain power.[80]

In 1810, Mercer proposed, and the legislature created, a "Literary Fund" for education. Collecting fines, penalties, and forfeitures to the state government, the Literary Fund did not rely on direct taxes, and that was its political genius. The Literary Fund seemed to conjure money without affecting taxpayers. In 1816, Mercer proposed to augment the fund with a reimbursement of $1,200,000 expected from the federal government for the state's military expenditures during the War of 1812 against the British.

His timing was good, for many state leaders, including the powerful Richmond Junto, felt troubled by Virginia's decline relative to other states and saw a precious opportunity to bolster the state's economy by investing in roads, canals, and education. In December 1815, the *Richmond Enquirer* embraced what had long been heresy, "We say for one, let us have the *taxes* that we may have the *improvements*." A month later, the editor decried the populist legislator who would oppose "taxes, under the miserable hope of currying popularity, while by that single act, he paralyzes the public spirit and arrests the grand destinies of the *Old Dominion*." Following that lead, Governor Wilson Cary Nicholas urged the legislature to apply that enlarged Literary Fund to public education.[81]

But even the new federal funds fell short of fully funding Jefferson's three-tier system of primary schools, academy-colleges, and a university. The legislature would have to choose between them. Mercer favored primary schools as "the greatest public benefit." He explained, "In a republic, it is much more important that the mass of the people should be tolerably well educated, than that a few should be very well educated, because knowledge is power." He would support colleges and a university only if there was any money left after fully funding primary schools for common people. Mercer also wanted to standardize local education through supervision by a state board of education. In February 1817, the House of Delegates approved Mercer's bill by a vote of 66 to 49, but it still had to pass the State Senate.[82]

Jefferson disdained Mercer's plan for its central control and for slighting his priority: building a university. Devoted to decentralizing power, Jefferson doubted that state leaders could manage schools better than would local parents. Why not, he asked sarcastically, "commit to the Governor & Council the management of all our farms, our mills, & merchant stores." The Republican establishment rallied behind Jefferson to discredit Mercer's plan as a Federalist plot to manipulate common people. Thomas Ritchie's *Richmond Enquirer* warned that Mercer would create "a vast and most expensive engine for forming and fashioning the opinions, principles and habits of every future generation." Within "a generation or two" this "*College of Cardinals*" would "blot from our Statute-Book that blessed act for establishing religious freedom." The best way to agitate most Virginians was to detect a threat to their cherished separation of church and state.[83]

The Richmond Junto promoted the now familiar conservative terror that schools could indoctrinate young people with dangerous ideas and "make public opinion what they please." Their disciples would dominate elections, "and he who rules the legislature will rule the people." Ritchie spoke some truth, for his Richmond Junto did rule the legislature and meant to keep it that way rather than see Mercer prevail. In 1815–1816, the Junto had pressed for a new regime of tax-funded improvements in Virginia. They had not bargained on Mercer pushing for an ambitious, centralized program to transform the state in ways that the Republican elite might not control. Recognizing their danger, in 1817 the Junto scuttled back to the old verities of a small-government,

small-tax regime. The *Richmond Enquirer* preached, "The less government has to do with education, the better." Mercer lamented that when-
ever any "friends of philanthropy" proposed reform, the "hunters of
popularity . . . issue forth from their hiding places, and commence the
cry of Innovation! Theory! Philosophy! Tax!"[84]

In the State Senate, Cabell blocked Mercer's system and pushed an
alternative bill written by Jefferson. That bill mandated ward schools
with local control and a reliance on county taxes, thereby saving the
state's Literary Fund entirely for a university. Jefferson's bill also banned
religious readings in the schools and barred ministers from serving as
school superintendents or teachers. He even proposed restricting citizenship to the literate, as an incentive for parents to educate their children. Cabell and his legislative friends had to drop the antireligious and
literacy features as unnecessarily provocative, for they could never pass
a law that offended both the illiterate and the pious in Virginia.[85]

Even without those provisions, the bill faced a fractious legislature.
Cabell assured Jefferson, "There are almost as many opinions as there
are members." But nearly all shared a dread of Jefferson's proposed new
county tax to finance local schools. The few learned legislators disdained most of the others as poorly educated men of petty principles
and minds. In 1817, State Senator John Campbell derided the House
of Delegates as composed of "two hundred & 24 men, nine-tenths of
whom are ignorant & illiterate." Even more vividly, a young gentleman
blamed the state's neglect of education on "the Legislature being composed of ignorant, drunken beasts." According to Cabell, here was the
dilemma: Virginia needed to enhance education to improve its leaders,
but the current "half-witted" legislators lacked the learning to see and
solve the problem. Jefferson sadly agreed that the "first obstacle to science in this country" was the political power "of those who do not know
its value."[86]

Although a well-educated politician, William Branch Giles cyni-
cally appealed to conservative populists by mocking Jefferson's educational proposals as elitist follies. In essays published in January 1818,
Giles derided Jefferson as "a mind long abstracted from the practical

world and delighted with indulging itself in its own delicious contemplations." Giles warned Virginians to beware of "any novel and magnificent scheme" as the path to "a disastrous catastrophe." He insisted that the most "mischievous of the modern notions, for improving the condition of man, is that of obtaining great statesmen . . . by a process of filtration to be practiced upon poor children." Giles appealed to legislators who distrusted social change promoted by government action. They preferred to muddle on in old ways.[87]

Mercer's ambitious proposal had no chance, and on February 11, 1818, the legislature rejected Jefferson's alternative bill. He blamed "ignorance, malice, egoism, fanaticism, religious, political, & local perversities." Instead, the legislature passed a halfway measure, annually committing $45,000 for educating poor boys and $15,000 for a university. A year later, legislators rejected a proposal to expand state support to educate poor girls as well.[88]

Under the 1818 law, commissioners in each county would designate the poor white families eligible for tuition support for their sons. The commissioners could front county funds to pay teachers while applying to the Literary Fund for reimbursement, up to a maximum quota set for their county. While poor boys received state support, families of middle-class means had to pay tuition for their children. The system encouraged more schools by increasing the pool of potential students and paying some state funds to support a teacher, but neighborhood clusters still had to build schools, provide textbooks, and find instructors. The $45,000 annual appropriation also fell far short of the need, educating only about 12,000 of the approximately 27,000 poor boys who qualified in a given year. The system lacked a board of education to provide textbooks and audit the county accounts, and that lack led to financial irregularities.[89]

The system suffered from the class divisions of Virginia. The planter elite served as the unpaid commissioners, who often did little because they resented the drain on their time. The middle class saw scant benefit for their children, who still had to pay for schooling. Many poor parents feared the stigma of accepting charity from the state, or worried that their hungry, ragged, and shoeless children would face ridicule from other boys. In addition, impoverished families often needed the labor of their sons at home.[90]

Over time, most common people warmed to the new system as far better than nothing. In 1822, Madison County's board of commissioners reported, "Several schools have been established in neighbourhoods, which could not have supported them without the assistance of the fund." Hanover County's board noted, "The improvement of the poor children in reading, writing, and arithmetic, has been considerable." James City County's commissioners were "daily more strongly impressed with its great utility in society, and still have to lament the want of more adequate means to carry it into a full and successful operation."[91]

Both Jefferson and Mercer disdained the program to subsidize pauper boys and no others, but they did so for opposite reasons. Mercer mourned the state's failure to educate all white children: girls as well as boys and middle-class as well as poor students. He regretted the "odious distinction between the children of the opulent and the poor" as "calculated to implant in very early life, the feelings of humiliation and dependence in one class of society, and of superiority and pride in another." Taxing the rich to educate everyone would "diminish the evils arising to social order from too great a disparity of wealth." Instead, he complained, Virginia redistributed wealth from the middle class to build a grand university for the sons of wealth.[92]

Jefferson still hoped that the state would implement his entire three-tier educational system, including primary schools. But he adamantly insisted on his model of local control and funding by county (rather than state) taxes. Opposed to spending state funds to educate the poor as a great waste, Jefferson urged legislators to reallocate the $45,000 annual appropriation to the University of Virginia. He concluded, "I believe we had better do one thing at a time: the University first, next the primary schools & lastly the intermediate colleges or academies."[93]

Writing to Cabell in late 1817, William Maclure predicted, "No Legislator ever did or I believe ever will do anything for the education of the mass. They will make colleges and endow them for the education of their own children." Virginia did just that in 1818 and 1819.[94]

By building the state's education from the top down, Jefferson and Cabell would reap the consequences at the University. For want of adequate public schools, almost no poor or middle-class students could qualify to enter the University. Instead, its students would come from the state's richest families, who could afford to send their sons to private academies. And even those boys arrived unprepared for University courses. The faculty chairman later lamented, "There are many students . . . who are incapable of writing a sentence in English correctly." Jefferson conceded that the students consisted of "shameful Latinists . . . such as we will certainly refuse as soon as we can get . . . better schools." But how could Virginia obtain better schools when it would spend so little on them?[95]

7
BUILDINGS

P RESIDENT GEORGE WASHINGTON cherished the national solidarity generated among officers from many different states during the Revolutionary War, but he saw that common sentiment fading during the sectional rivalries and partisan politics of the 1790s. "Prejudices are beginning to revive again," he mourned. As an antidote, he proposed a national university for the capital. By uniting young men from diverse

Joseph Carrington Cabell (1778–1856), by Louis M. D. Guillaume
(Albert and Shirley Small Special Collections Library, University of Virginia)

states for a shared education, he meant to bolster a common American identity. Seeking congressional approval, Washington promised to endow a national university with his shares in two Virginia canal companies.[1]

But his secretary of state, Thomas Jefferson, championed the state-first thinking that so frustrated the first president. Jefferson hoped to capture Washington's canal stock for his own pet project: creating a University of Virginia by moving the faculty of the University of Geneva across the Atlantic. Unsettled by the French Revolution, the faculty sought a new venue in 1794, when Jefferson pitched the scheme to the Virginia state legislature, seeking funds for buildings and salaries. Jefferson also urged Washington to invest his stock in a Genevan university relocated in Virginia. Washington rejected Jefferson's proposal, but Congress failed to approve the university that he did want, and Virginia's legislature rejected investing its own money to buy a faculty.[2]

Once Jefferson became president, a political ally, Joel Barlow of Connecticut, proposed a national university with "a strict adherence to republican principles." Jefferson's support was muted and conditional. While praising the concept to Congress, he stipulated that founding a national university required a constitutional amendment: a daunting prospect that effectively killed Barlow's proposal. Jefferson consoled him: "There is a snail-paced gait for the advance of new ideas on the general mind, under which we must acquiesce.... People generally have more feeling for canals & roads than education."[3]

Jefferson was never keen on a university in the federal capital, deeming it unwanted competition for his primary goal. At a University of Virginia, students would learn his notions of republicanism, rejecting the Federalism of northern schools and George Washington. Jefferson believed that, for a young Virginian, attachments "formed in his own country will be more useful through life than if formed in another state." He assured a friend that a federal university had no chance of passage, but "we consider the institution of our University as supplying its place."[4]

As early as 1792, Jefferson began talking up a new state university out of disgust with William & Mary. Despairing of that College's

malarial location, Jefferson wanted to build a new institution in Albemarle County, which he extolled for having a "delicious climate, good
water, cheap subsistence, an independent yeomanry, many wealthy
persons, good society, and free as air in religion and politics." But he
faced a daunting obstacle: the hostility of Virginians to paying taxes for
education.[5]

In December 1804, a leading lawyer and politician, Littleton W.
Tazewell of Norfolk, proposed to fund a new state university through
a bit of financial sleight-of-hand. He would tap into the revenue from
state-chartered banks and canals, to avoid any new, direct taxes on
individuals. Tazewell cautioned Jefferson to keep this funding plan
strictly confidential "because it is sometimes necessary to conceal the
healing medicine from the patient, lest his sickly appetite may reject
that which alone can bring him health and life." Unless kept in the
dark about the process, common voters and politicians might reject
the prescription.[6]

In January 1805, Tazewell solicited a plan for the university from St.
George Tucker, the law professor at William & Mary. Disgusted by the
College's unruly students, Tucker designed a university meant to control young men. To keep taverns and "other houses of ill-fame" at a distance, Tucker proposed a rural location and a campus of at least 3,000
acres, with college buildings at the center. The surrounding buffer zone
would consist of farms leased out for revenue. At this university, ultimate authority would lie with a chancellor, who had the judicial power
to regulate students and faculty. Tucker wanted the Board of Visitors to
meet every May 15 "in Commemoration of the Declaration of Independence made by the Commonwealth, on the same day in the year 1776."
The state's declaration carried more weight in Virginia than whatever
the Continental Congress had done on July 4.[7]

In an egalitarian move, Tucker sought to make "the acquisition of
a liberal education . . . easy & open to all who are endowed with genius
& virtue sufficient to deserve the public patronage." These "pupils of
the Republic" would receive room, board, tuition, clothing, and books
at public expense. Planning ahead, Tucker hoped that by 1860 three-

fifths of the proposed University's revenue could sustain scholarships for worthy students to "possess the means of acquiring and extending the utmost limits of Science."[8]

Because daring, innovative, and expensive, Tucker's proposal was dead on arrival at a legislature whose members disliked reform and spending money. Tazewell had hoped to milk $15,000 annually from indirect sources, but Tucker estimated that it would cost $40,000 initially to erect buildings and provide a library and scientific apparatus plus another $75,000 endowment to sustain thirty scholarships. He set the total cost over forty years at $170,100. A sympathetic legislator consoled Tucker: "It is truly to be lamented that every improvement attempted in our laws is treated by some members as a dangerous innovation, while others will reject it merely because they will not give themselves time to understand the subject."[9]

In late 1813, Jefferson grumbled, "From the complexion of our popular legislature, and the narrow and niggardly views of ignorance courting the suffrage of ignorance to obtain a seat in it, I see little prospect of such an establishment." He noted a crippling cycle: Virginia needed to improve voters and legislators through education, but they balked at paying to enhance their sons. Rather than despairing, Jefferson came up with a new plan to nudge legislators.[10]

Central College

After retiring from the presidency in 1809, Jefferson sought to make something of the Albemarle Academy, a preparatory school incorporated by the legislature in 1803 but never launched by its indolent trustees. Joining the trustees in March 1814, Jefferson energized them to apply to the legislature for the county's take from two confiscated Anglican glebes. Two years later, the trustees persuaded legislators to elevate the academy as "Central College," a bit of branding meant to advertise the institution as the best site for a state university.[11]

To develop Central College, Jefferson recruited a prestigious new Board of Visitors that included John Hartwell Cocke, Joseph C. Cabell,

President James Madison, and his secretary of state (and successor), James Monroe. In 1817, the Visitors bought a tract one mile west of Charlottesville, employing the money derived from selling the glebes. In October, they launched construction of the first "pavilion" in Jefferson's ambitious design for an "academical village," which wrapped around a central lawn. Each pavilion would house a professor's family and classrooms, while student dorms fronted by a portico would link each pavilion.[12]

Lacking state financing, the Visitors raised private funds by subscription. Jefferson, Madison, Monroe, Cabell, and Cocke each pledged $1,000 to set a good example for others to give generously. To entice subscribers, Jefferson promised to reserve spots for their sons at Central College. By rallying a large subscription, the Visitors hoped to impress state legislators, who might then adopt the college as the state university. But raising private funds went slowly. In Louisa County, a fundraiser lamented: "Persuading people to give away their money, as they call it, is a very dull business & people generally set so much more value on money than on education, that the latter stands a poor chance." By 1818, the Visitors had secured pledges for $35,000, but three-quarters came from Albemarle County. Jefferson complained, "The difficulty I find is to eradicate the idea that it is a local thing, a mere Albemarle academy. I endeavor to convince them [that] it is a general seminary of the sciences meant for the use of the state."[13]

Despite the shortfall in funding, Jefferson felt energized by the new project, throwing himself into rallying statewide support and supervising construction. He confessed to a friend, "Mine, after all, may be an Utopian dream," but he would "indulge in it till I go to the land of dreams, and sleep there with the dreamers of all past and future times." Almost every day, he rode down from his mountain to inspect progress and instruct contractors. In March 1819, an old friend marveled that Jefferson "looked as well as he did 10 years ago, and today, though the wind is blowing a perfect Hurricane, he rode through Charlottesville to visit the College." Between visits, he could watch the progress through his telescope of that "most splendid object and a constant gratification to my sight."[14]

Building the university offered a delicious distraction from his troubled family and finances. He designed the academical village as a constellation of interrelated structures that expressed his concepts of proper order. By giving that complex shape, he gained a sense of control that had become fleeting elsewhere in his life. His friend Peachy Gilmer noted, "He is now engaged in the University project tooth and nail, knee deep in plans, estimates, & conjectures." Gilmer noted, however, that Jefferson had "expected to finish his own house in eighteen months or two years," but it had taken over thirty-five years to complete Monticello. Would he repeat that experience at his university?[15]

While he guided construction in Charlottesville, Jefferson recruited Cabell, a state senator, to manage the legislature at Richmond. Having benefited from Jefferson's educational advice, Cabell revered him as "the most extraordinary" man he had ever met. In the legislature, he had to maneuver through the sectional tensions of Virginia. Western Virginians resented political domination by an eastern elite based in the Piedmont and Tidewater counties. Seeking more banks and improved roads and schools, the westerners felt trapped in underdevelopment because neglected by the state government. Westerners wanted a new state constitution to broaden the vote and equalize representation between the regions. They also pushed to shift the state capital westward from Richmond to the Shenandoah Valley, and they hoped to capture the proposed state university for their region. Easterners clung to Richmond as their capital and wanted no major political reforms and no new state constitution. Because relatively few westerners owned slaves, they seemed untrustworthy to eastern elites, who cherished their own power as essential to protect their property from increased taxes and antislavery measures.[16]

In a divided legislature, Cabell had to perform a great magic trick: persuade eastern conservatives, ordinarily hostile to any innovation, to invest in a new university while inducing westerners to accept its location east of the Blue Ridge. Cabell warned Jefferson, "The liberal

& enlightened views of great statesmen pass over our heads like the spheres above. When we assemble here, an eastern and western feeling supercedes all other considerations."[17]

Cabell also had to reconcile Jefferson's principles, expressed in pointed letters, with the pragmatic compromises needed to build a winning coalition. Jefferson often complicated Cabell's job. To "engage the affections of the coldest members" of the legislature, Cabell proposed that Central College sponsor a school for "the deaf & dumb." Jefferson refused, "The objects of the two institutions are fundamentally distinct. The one is science, the other mere charity. It would be gratuitously taking a boat in tow, which may impede, but cannot aid the motion of the principal institution." To weaken opposition from the state's three colleges, Cabell suggested sharing a state appropriation for education with them. In quick reply, Jefferson demanded it all and derided the colleges as "local interests." Jefferson did not see building the University beneath his mountain as a local interest.[18]

Pained by public controversy, Jefferson preferred to avoid publishing under his name even in support of the University. He peppered Cabell with letters of instruction, but expected him to show them only to trustworthy allies in private meetings. Sometimes, however, Cabell felt compelled to nudge legislators by printing Jefferson's words. Cabell explained, "Everything coming from your pen would have a peculiar weight with many persons here." Before circulating or publishing, Cabell had to edit out the most intemperate sentiments and true estimates of the University's high costs, lest the figures "throw the Assembly into a state of despair."[19]

In fragile health, Cabell paid dearly for the long and tense hours of political lobbying and wrangling. In December 1818, Merit M. Robinson, a Richmond lawyer, worried, "I am afraid, my poor friend, Joe Cabell, will die of a *Central University* . . . as he is tormented day and night with an apprehension" that he could not overcome "the conflicting views and the local prejudices" of other legislators. Passionate for the University, Cabell forged on, saying of his health, "I could not risk it in a better cause." A month later, however, he had "an alarming spitting of blood" from a hemorrhage in his throat strained by too many speeches.[20]

In January 1821, after twelve difficult years in the legislature, Cabell felt worn down. Longing to retire to "domestic, rural & literary leisure," he meant to decline running for reelection in the spring. "Why should I be an eternal slave?" he asked. Informing Jefferson of that decision, Cabell explained that, "to ride from Court House to Court House, making speeches to large crowds, exposed to the rigors of the season, might carry me to the grave."[21]

In prompt reply, Jefferson rebuked Cabell for abandoning, and perhaps destroying, their cherished University: "I perceive that I am not to live to see it opened . . . But the gloomiest of all prospects is in the desertion of the best friends of the institution; for desertion I must call it." He expected Cabell to stay in the legislature until the University opened. "Health, time, labor, on what in the single life which nature has given us, can these be better bestowed than on this immortal boon to our country?" Given his age, Jefferson alone had just grounds to retire from the cause, "but I will die in the last ditch, and so, I hope, you will my friend. . . . Pray then, dear and very dear Sir, do not think of deserting us." Jefferson knew exactly which strings to play in Cabell's mind.[22]

As Jefferson expected, Cabell relented and agreed to run for reelection, declaring, "It is not in my nature to resist such an appeal." Robinson informed Cocke that Jefferson "has produced the unfortunate change. Cabell shewed me, some days ago, a letter to him from that gentleman, whom, I take pleasure in saying, is an ornament to his country, as a gentleman and man of letters, but in whom, as a practical man, either in state affairs or the common concerns of life, I have no confidence." Robinson added, "The letter, like all from his pen, is flattering, plausible, and persuasive; and by art, and not force, has upset poor Cabell." When Cocke expressed similar dismay, Cabell replied, "When I come, I will shew you Mr. Jefferson's letter, which chiefly determined me to offer again for the Senate, and if you can stand such a letter, you must be made of steel." Cabell relished his "destiny so fortunate as to be appointed" with Jefferson "in a course so good & so great."[23]

Jefferson meant to build and run the University with a rigid determination deftly cloaked in attentive charm. One of the first professors, George Tucker, recalled, "No one discharged the offices of hospitality more cordially or with a better grace and, when he was in good health and spirits, there was a suavity, and even elegance in his manners that was irresistibly pleasing." Tucker added that Jefferson "had most winning manners when he chose to exert them, but he was occasionally somewhat dictatorial and impatient of contradiction." Jefferson preferred to guide others with subtlety toward his goals, but he could become abrupt when crossed.[24]

Power

Peter Carr insisted that only a university could save Virginia from declining into poverty and weakness. He warned, "We see our youth flying to foreign countries to obtain that of which they are deprived at home: a liberal education." By foreign countries, he meant northern states, where educators "instill into their young, open, and unsuspecting minds, opinions and sentiments inimical to the interest and happiness of their parent country, for we see that they have too frequently returned back into the bosom of that country with a respect and affection for everything abroad, the effect of which is a contempt and disrespect for everything at home." A dread of northern influence had become the key way to alarm Virginia's legislators into funding a university.[25]

Virginians began to sour on the Union during the War of 1812, when the federal government faltered in defending Chesapeake Bay against British naval attacks that plundered farms and liberated slaves. If the Union could not protect the state's interests with James Madison at the helm, what could Virginia's leaders expect when a future president came from a northern state? The war also increased attacks in the northern, Federalist press against Virginia Republicans as hypocrites who preached democracy while keeping slaves. Seething over these attacks as insults to their honor, Virginians dreaded a federal government that might fall under Yankee control.[26]

Virginia's leaders also feared their state's accelerating decline in relative population, wealth, and influence. In 1800, Virginia had been the most populous and powerful state in the Union. The 1820 census, however, revealed that Virginia had slipped to third behind two more vibrant northern states: New York and Pennsylvania. Attracting few immigrants, Virginia also lost much of its natural increase to outmigration, as so many young people moved south and west to seek larger farms of more fertile land. Virginians obsessed over the published census returns, which shook the longstanding assumption that their primacy in the Union was natural and perpetual.[27]

The demographic decline cost Virginia clout in Washington, D.C., where power shifted in Congress toward the expansive and thriving North. In 1816, Congress passed, and President Madison approved, higher federal tariffs to protect northern industries from foreign imports. That protective tariff hurt southern farmers, who relied on imported consumer goods. Francis W. Gilmer denounced "Yankey manufacturers" and "the union, which has itself spoiled & persecuted us, without ever having done any one act to deserve our gratitude or thanks." Unless they could reverse their decline, Virginians would become "hewers of wood & drawers of water to pamper an insolent & ignorant northern aristocracy."[28]

In 1819, a severe economic depression hit Virginia harder than any other state. From 1818 to 1821, Virginia's exports fell by 56 percent, compared to 42 percent for the nation as a whole. As foreign demand dried up, the prices paid for farm produce declined by 48 percent. Unable to sell their crops at a profit, Virginians struggled to pay their debts, and land values plummeted as bankruptcies and foreclosures surged. Because farms sold by court order at a fraction of their former worth, Jefferson worried that "even small debts will sweep away large masses of property." He concluded, "This state is in a condition of unparalleled distress." From Richmond in early 1820, Gilmer mourned, "Things grow worse & worse—the Merchants all failed—the town ruined—the Banks broke—the Treasury empty—commerce gone, confidence gone, character gone." Rather than fault themselves or market forces, Virginians blamed their economic woes on recent decisions made by federal institutions, particularly the Supreme Court and the Bank of the United States.[29]

Virginians' unease with the Union deepened in 1819 when northern congressmen sought to require gradual emancipation in Missouri for that territory to become a state. Outraged southern leaders denied that Congress could impose restrictions on a new state. They asserted that the push to halt slavery's expansion violated the compromise between the regions made at the 1787 Constitutional Convention in Philadelphia.[30]

Northern "restrictionists" meant to reserve western territories for settlement by free, white farmers, who alone, they argued, could sustain a true republic. Restriction dishonored the southern states as insufficiently republican because tainted by slavery. Virginians felt insulted and marginalized if they could not settle in federal territories with their enslaved property. That limitation seemed especially ominous during the depression, when so many indebted Virginians wanted to migrate to seek new opportunities or to pay debts by selling slaves to western settlers.[31]

Virginians feared becoming entrapped at home with a growing black majority that would erupt in bloody revolt. Most Tidewater and Piedmont counties, including Albemarle, already had black majorities. John Tyler, Sr., warned that restriction would build a "dark cloud" of slavery "over a particular portion of this land until its horrors shall burst." Virginians insisted that the interstate slave trade "diffused" the growing black numbers to the alleged benefit of both races. Jefferson declared that the Missouri Crisis, "like a fire bell in the night, awakened and filled me with terror," for Virginians associated a fire bell's alarm with a slave revolt.[32]

Virginians perceived restriction as a ploy to unite a northern majority in Congress against the South and thereby claim the American future, which emerged through western settlement and the addition of

new states, tilting the regional balance of power in Congress. Northerners could control that future by reserving the West for their way of
life. Virginians dreaded that, if denied a western outlet for their surplus
slaves, their state would become a claustrophobic corner of growing
poverty and weakness in the Union. Then, Jefferson warned, the congressional majority could impose abolition everywhere, "in which case
all the whites South of the Potomac and Ohio must evacuate their states;
and most fortunate [will be] those who can do it first."[33]

In 1820, Congress narrowly adopted a compromise that admitted
Missouri as a slave state but excluded slavery from most of the remaining federal territories. That compromise disgusted Virginians. Jefferson
expected that a civil war between the states would "burst on us as a
tornado, sooner or later. The line of division lately marked out, between
different portions of our confederacy is such as will never, I fear, be oblit-
erated." That impending conflict enhanced the urgency for Virginia to
create a university. Until the state had one, her northern rivals would
win the American struggle for power: "A lamp of light is kindling in
the North which will draw our empire to it; for power attends knolege
as this shadow does its substance, and the ignorant will forever be hewers of wood and drawers of water to the wise." Without a university,
Virginians would suffer "the degradation . . . of falling into the ranks of
our own negroes."[34]

Virginia's leaders considered Congress an adversarial cockpit of
clashing interests threatening to their way of life. Rejecting an American identity, they regarded Virginia as their nation and spoke of the
Union as a confederacy with "foreign states." In 1821, the state's leading
newspaper, the *Richmond Enquirer*, declared that Virginians and New
Englanders belonged to distinct and rival nations: "The internal policy
of Massachusetts or Connecticut is as widely different from that of Virginia or South Carolina as that of England is from that of Prussia." Values changed radically with latitude: "What is sound logic in Virginia is
but . . . sophistry in Pennsylvania." In this view, states uneasily shared a
loose Union that, at its best, could negotiate a coexistence premised on
mutual non-interference.[35]

Fearing the North as alien, the *Richmond Enquirer* concluded, "it is impolitic in the extreme to send our sons into those states" for education. Gilmer warned that northern graduates "returned with foreign manners, habits, &c., to preach up for the edification of their parents and family, the miseries of slavery, to praise pumpkins and laugh at hominy; in short, to like everything foreign and hate everything domestic." A similar fear had fueled the creation of universities at North Carolina in 1795, Georgia in 1801, and South Carolina in 1805. Southern states founded public universities to preserve elite young men from northern ideas and provide able defenders of states' rights.[36]

Virginians wanted better-trained legislators to fend off alleged Yankee subversion and domination. They worried that the rising generation lacked the self-discipline and learning to replace the aging cohort of Jefferson and Madison that had led the revolution. A Norfolk newspaper advised students: "It is the growing and rising generation who must fill up the chasm which death has made in the ranks of our patriots. You are coming to the front of that generation—it is for you to say, whether you will honour or disgrace your country." That country was Virginia.[37]

Northern universities seemed ideologically alien: infected by Federalism and antislavery activism. A Virginia aunt thought it "hazardous to let a boy grow up among the Yankees." She "admire[d] their industry— temperance—economy—enterprise &c, but in other respects I detest the New-England character." Casting that character as "duplicity— low-cunning—roguery—and meanness," she preferred, "with all its faults, the character of the Cavalier to that of the Puritan. A youth from Virginia may act imprudently, but, if he is the Son of a Gentleman, he will seldom act Knavishly. Now, Sir, I prefer folly to knavery." She knew and loved the follies of Virginia.[38]

Virginians exaggerated the dangers of northern influence on southern students. Very few rejected their families and culture after attending a northern school. Occasionally a student expressed a fleeting criticism, but he returned to the fold soon enough. In 1804 at Princeton, Thomas Ruffin wrote home to denounce keeping slaves as cruel. His father patiently replied, "That they are a great civil, political, and moral evil no person will deny, but how to get rid of them ... without endangering the political safety of the State, and perhaps jeopardizing the lives, property, and everything sacred and dear of the Whites" was the great dilemma. Thomas Ruffin soon came home to embrace his inheritance of slaves and plantation.[39]

Most southern students found northern society economically advanced but socially repulsive. They disliked the austere frugality, conspicuous piety, and hard-driving industry of most Yankees. After expulsion from Princeton, William Garnett returned to Virginia to celebrate the state's maxim "Let us eat, drink and be merry for tomorrow we die!" as superior to the northern motto of "A penny saved is a penny got." Virginians were true, generous friends, he concluded, while northerners were greedy misers and religious hypocrites. An unhappy southerner at Princeton found it grim and dull and expected "but few graduates out of those who had to remain here 4 years except those who graduated by Suicide." At northern schools, southerners tended to band together rather than befriend Yankees.[40]

Northern faculty doubted that they could convert southern students. In 1805, Yale's president, Timothy Dwight, wrote to John Taylor of Caroline, a leading Virginia planter and politician, to discourage his sons from coming "to this college. If I may judge from the Virginia youths who have been here during my presidency, I cannot form a rational hope that youths from that country will at all acquire *here* any portion of the New England manners." Indeed, they "despised and hated our manners, morals, industry, and religion. . . . The people of this State are universally industrious; these youths considered industry as the business of slaves and wretches only." Dwight expected that Taylor's sons "would regard their New England companions as plodding drudges, destitute of talents as well as of property. They would esteem their New England life as slavery, unreasonable and useless." Dwight's blunt letter persuaded Taylor that Yale was no place for a Virginia gentleman.[41]

To keep students at home, Virginia needed a university to rival Yale and Harvard. To counter "the overwhelming mass of light & science by which we shall be surrounded," Jefferson wanted to build a great university "worthy of the station of our State in the scale of its confederates and of the nations of the world." Jefferson insisted that 500 young Virginians were studying in the North and "imbibing opinions and principles in discord with those of their own country. This canker is eating on the vitals of our existence." Anticipating a civil war, he concluded, "The signs of the times admonish us to call them home."[42]

By investing in higher education, legislators could reverse Virginia's decline into the bottom ranks of a conflictual Union. Indeed, a university could attract students from throughout the South and West, spreading Virginia's values and restoring her states-rights brand of republicanism to federal leadership. Then Yankees would have to shrink back into their proper place as a feeble minority unable to meddle in western and southern affairs, thereby restoring the glorious situation that had prevailed during Jefferson's presidency. A state legislator proclaimed that a university would "spread the influence of Virginian opinions, habits and manners, which . . . will ultimately silence sectional feelings; abolish party distinctions, and unite us under the common denomination of Americans." Virginians could become Americans once the university's far-flung influence restored the United States as an extension of Virginia.[43]

None of Virginia's three colleges sufficed to train the state's new generation of leaders. Washington College in Lexington and Hampden-Sydney in Prince Edward County were small and underfunded Presbyterian schools. The College of William & Mary had trained Virginia's leading lawyers and legislators, including Jefferson, but most regarded the old College as doomed by its unhealthy climate, declining town, mediocre faculty, and turbulent students. In 1818, when Gilmer toyed with becoming its president, Jefferson warned him to desist because "a more compleat *cul de sac* could not be proposed to you." Gilmer reassured Jefferson: "If I had any hope of being able from the ruins of this decayed corporation to revive the nearly extinguished ardor of Virginia I should be strongly tempted to make the sacrifice which it would cost me. But I fear the old college is too far gone to be resuscitated."[44]

If William & Mary could not compete with northern schools, Virginia needed a university. Legislators calculated that the brain drain cost Virginia $300,000 annually in expenditures by her students attending northern schools. By founding a University of Virginia, legislators sought to repatriate the money and minds of their students in the North. There was no time for Virginians to delay, the *Richmond Enquirer* warned, for "the grave of your former renown is already digging."[45]

Rockfish

In their drive to elevate Central College into the state University, Cabell and Jefferson faced competition from westerners who wanted to locate the institution west of the Blue Ridge at either Lexington or Staunton. In February 1818, the legislature established a commission to select a site. The governor and his council chose one member from each senate district, a formula that favored the east given the skewed representation under the state constitution. Because easterners held fifteen of the twenty-four seats, the westerners had lost the fight before the commission assembled at Rockfish Gap in the Blue Ridge on August 1.[46]

Chosen as a delegate, Jefferson carefully prepared for the meeting, drafting its report in advance and inviting key members to enjoy his hospitality at Monticello during the prior week. Jefferson considered the meeting crucial to "the history of our country because it will determine whether we are to leave this fair inheritance to barbarians or civilized men." He worked to defeat the superior package offered by Lexington's Washington College, where a wealthy donor promised $150,000, three times what Central College could pledge. Jefferson's planning paid off. Twenty-one members attended. Sixteen voted for Charlottesville, and the other five split their votes between Lexington and Staunton. "I have never seen business done with so much order, and harmony, nor in abler nor pleasanter society," Jefferson marveled. The members also approved his report defining the University's structure and purpose.[47]

Many western legislators refused to accept the Rockfish Gap Report as final. When the next legislative session began in December, they reopened the issue of location by casting doubt on Jefferson's calculations that Charlottesville lay closest to the center of Virginia's free population. Critics complained that his count included free blacks, which offended the sensibilities of white men, who regarded all blacks as beyond citizenship. Cabell worried that western legislators might ally with the eastern champions of William & Mary, who wanted no competition from a new university. He also dreaded populist legislators who had other priorities for state funding: "The more ignorant pretend that the Literary Fund has been diverted from its original object, the education of the poor and accuse the friends of the University of an intention to apply all the fund to the benefit of the wealthy."[48]

But the westerners divided in their preference between Staunton and Lexington, while Cabell united the eastern delegates by playing upon their fear of western intent. On January 19, 1819, the House of Delegates located the University at Charlottesville and provided an annual appropriation of $15,000. The State Senate approved six days later. The governor and council appointed a new Board of Visitors that included Cabell, Cocke, Jefferson, Madison, and Monroe. To represent the Tidewater, the governor appointed Robert B. Taylor, who had dueled with John Randolph at William & Mary in 1792. To reconcile the west, Cabell pushed for (and got) the appointment of James Breckinridge and Chapman Johnson, who had lobbied for Staunton as the University site.[49]

The state commitment to build a university seemed momentous. Cocke praised the bill as "the most important act of the legislature since the existence of the Government." An Albemarle County resident celebrated "the triumph obtained over ignorance and narrow mindedness. . . . We are destined to be a great People." He added that town lots in Charlottesville already had doubled in value.[50]

Delay

While pleased by the legislative victory, Jefferson regretted the funding as "miserably short" for executing "the large plan displayed to the world." He grumbled, "In fact it is vain to give us the name of an University without the means of making it so." Jefferson needed a lot of money to fulfill his grand architectural design for "a beautiful Academical village of the finest models of building and of classical architecture in the U.S." He counted on the rising buildings to attract visitors, generate conversation, and pressure legislators to provide more funding.[51]

Before the January 1819 site decision, the Central College Visitors had scrambled to build as much as possible in hopes of swaying the legislators. Once they had secured the University, however, the Visitors decided to delay opening until they had completed all the buildings. Proposed by Cabell and endorsed by Jefferson, the new strategy pressured the legislature to appropriate more money to hasten completion. Jefferson and Cabell calculated that, rather than lose their initial investment, the legislators would grumble but put up extra funds. If, instead, the Visitors opened the University with an incomplete set of buildings, Jefferson feared that the legislature would never pay to finish them. Then the institution "forever would be no more than the paltry academies we now have." Jefferson took a gamble, for disgust at the delay might undermine legislative support, which was already shaky because critics charged that the state was "taxing the poor to educate the rich." Some Visitors wavered during the long delay, but Jefferson remained resolute: "We have only to lie still, to do and say nothing and firmly avoid opening." Knowing the Virginia taste for "a degree of splendor," he wanted to open a complete university as "a brilliant commencement."[52]

By delaying an opening, the Visitors risked alienating parents impatient to send their sons to the University. In 1820, a potential student complained to his brother: "The university no doubt will be ready for our progeny, but not for us." Jefferson urged the impatient to pressure legislators rather than blame him. He warned one father that, unless they became more generous, "the present youths of our country will be old men before" the University opened. Jefferson's resolve was especially bold given his own advanced age and shaky health, for he might die before his cherished institution could commence.[53]

During the early 1820s, Cabell annually returned to the legislature with some new proposal to enhance the University's funding and speed its completion. But the state had scant money to spare after the discovery in January 1820 that the state treasurer, General John Preston, had embezzled $136,000. Unable to secure additional grants from the legislature, Cabell had to settle for three loans of $60,000 each in 1820, 1821, and 1823, for a total of $180,000. The loans sustained construction, but the Visitors had to mortgage their $15,000 annual appropriation from the state to repay the loans at 6 percent annual interest. Unless freed from the debt, the Visitors would lack the money to hire professors and open the University. Paying off the loans might take another sixteen years, a delay that would kill Jefferson. It did not help that so many private subscribers to Central College failed to make their promised payments, leaving that fund $18,503 in arrears in late 1822.[54]

Cabell worried that legislators were losing patience with the delays and growing costs: "These successive applications for money to finish the buildings give grounds of reproach to our enemies & draw our friends into difficulties with their constituents. . . . It is now the fashion to electioneer by crying down the University." In April 1821, several supporters lost bids for reelection because reports "of extravagance in the erection of the buildings . . . had spread far & wide among the mass, and even among a part of the intelligent circle of society." Many Virginians disliked the complex design and refined materials as a waste of taxpayers' money. A critic mocked the architecture as "imitating the example of Greece and Rome in the days of their luxury and extravagance." Gilmer worried: "The plan is the most expensive certainly that can be (and that is wrong) but we must defend the old philosopher. Truly he has imposed a hard task on his friends to defend extravagance in pecuniary disbursements to a Virginia legislature."[55]

Building the University cost far more, and took far longer, than

expected. Virginia lacked the experienced craftsmen needed to realize
Jefferson's complex design, so the Visitors had to recruit tradesmen from
Pennsylvania. Jefferson also underestimated costs in his rosy reports to
Visitors and legislators. In December 1821, Cocke discovered that each
dorm room cost $646 to build, nearly twice the $350 of Jefferson's estimate. Jefferson also hired contractors without binding them with written contracts, and the fiscal accounts submitted to the legislature were
embarrassingly incomplete, arousing suspicions. In April 1821, two Visitors, Chapman Johnson and James Breckinridge, warned: "We should
not again be brought before the legislature with contracts unfulfilled,
with foundations not built upon, with naked walls or useless halls & . . .
threatening to perish as a monument of our want of foresight and our
unprofitable expenditures of public money."[56]

Cocke worried that Jefferson's architectural vision had sacrificed
economy and practicality. A young architect warned Cocke that the
dormitories would broil in summer, when Virginia was "one vast forge
for Vulcan himself. It is ridiculous & fearful." To save money, speed
construction, and cool students, Cocke urged Jefferson to scrap his
sprawling design in favor of one big dorm building of two or three stories topped with a slanted roof to drain the rain. Cocke realized that
such a "roof will be offensive to your cultivated taste." Indeed, Jefferson
rejected Cocke's alternative as offering "a barn for a College and log-
huts for accommodation." Jefferson insisted that only architectural
grandeur could attract many students. "The great object of our aim
from the beginning has been to make this establishment the most eminent in the United States, in order to draw to it the youth of every state,
but especially of the South and West." As for the costly elegance, it was
money well spent to attract "young men of the first respectability" to
study where "the minds of our future politicians, philosophers and
poets are to be cultivated."[57]

Critics on the Board of Visitors lacked the votes to overrule Jefferson,
because Cabell and Madison sided with him. Treating the project as
Jefferson's, supporters dreaded wounding his pride and hurting his reputation. Cabell added that Virginians' love of splendor ultimately would

trump even their frugality: "Altho the dissatisfaction about the style & expenditure has been spread far & wide, yet believe me, our very enemies begin to be awed by the grandeur of the establishment and . . . Virginia is already proud of the noble structure." In April 1823, Cabell declared, "The buildings appear more & more beautiful every time I see them."[58]

In early 1823, the University had 10 pavilions, 6 "hotels" for dining facilities, and 109 dorm rooms completed. But the grandest structure remained unbuilt and unfunded: the Rotunda that would house the library and meeting rooms and provide a lynchpin for the complex. Noting public alarm at the rising costs, Cocke and Johnson wanted to open the University while postponing construction of the Rotunda. Jefferson remained adamant: "If we stop short of the compleat establishment, it will never be completed. . . . And if the legislature shall be disposed to remit the debt, they will swallow a pile of $165,000 with the same effort as one of $120,000."[59]

An optimist when it suited his purposes, Jefferson calculated that the Rotunda would only cost another $45,000 to build. In December 1822, however, a legislative ally, William F. Gordon, showed Cabell a contractor's revised calculation of $70,000. Cabell informed Jefferson, "At my instance, Mr. Gordon threw the letter in the fire . . . to prevent it from being made an improper use of, in the event of its being seen by our enemies." A year later, construction began on the Rotunda.[60]

At the 1823–24 session, Cabell triumphed, persuading the legislators to forgive the University's debt of $180,000 and to advance another $50,000 to buy books and a scientific apparatus. In March 1824, Cabell celebrated that he had secured the University "beyond the reach of vile hypocrites & malignant demons." A month later, the Board of Visitors announced that the University would open, at last, in February 1825. Cabell declared, "Our University will now rise like the pyramids of Egypt to resist the storms of time. . . . [Our] State must & will be great again." Robert B. Taylor predicted that the University would restore proper order to the Union, with Virginia at "the centre of the system, imparting light & heat & motions to the other states."[61]

In February 1826, a traveler published an upbeat account of visiting Jefferson and touring the grand new university. Appearing in the *Richmond Enquirer*, the anonymous account shared an indiscreet conversation: "Mr. Jefferson told me [that] he teased the Legislature for six or seven successive sessions for aid for the University, which, each time, gave him a part or all that he asked for. At length one of the members, a friend of his, asked him why he did not apply for as much at once as was required, so as to give the government no further trouble." Jefferson explained that he had learned how to manage legislators by working incrementally.[62]

By repeating this conversation, the visitor drew back the curtain too far for Jefferson's taste. He knew that legislators would bristle at his boast to have manipulated them. Jefferson complained to Cabell, "I cannot express to you the pain which this unfaithful version & betrayal of private conversation has given me." He lamented that the author "makes me declare that I had intentionally proceeded in a course of dupery of our legislature, teasing them, as he makes me say, for 6 or 7 sessions" while "intentionally concealing the ultimate cost." The lifelong master of words to influence men, Jefferson cringed when his words came back to bite him.[63]

After protesting too much, Jefferson implausibly added, "No man ever heard me speak of the grants of the legislature but with acknolegements of their liberality." Of course many men, and especially Cabell, had heard his many complaints against cheap legislators. Jefferson knew that he and Cabell had drawn legislators along step by halting step, to expend $300,000, more than twice what they had expected in 1819, on a controversial complex of buildings. Jefferson did so shrewdly, persistently, and with an utter conviction that the University offered the cure that Virginians needed. He just did not want them to know how he had done it.[64]

The University of Virginia lacked the egalitarian commitment to scholarships featured in St. George Tucker's plan of 1805. Jefferson spent the state's funds on expensive buildings rather than on financial aid for needy students. The University had none of the charity scholarships common at northern universities. Those scholarships required menial labor, usually serving food and cleaning up in dining halls. No genteel young Virginian would do work associated with slavery in his state.[65]

Because Jefferson had lavished all the state funds on his complex architectural design, the University had to depend on student fees to meet operating costs. The Visitors set such high fees for tuition and board that the University of Virginia was the most expensive college in the country. High fees and no financial aid precluded all but the sons of wealthy families from attending. The institution would suffer from their homogeneity and sense of entitlement. Jefferson also unwittingly undercut his hopes that the university would enlighten the state's next generation of leaders. He wanted them to make the sweeping reforms, including gradual emancipation, that his generation had failed to enact. But these privileged students preferred to conserve, rather than transform, the unequal society that had raised them.[66]

8
PROFESSORS

RICHMOND'S FASHIONABLE THEATER arose on the foundations of an academy never completed for want of money. The city folk preferred to attend plays rather than fund education. On the night of December 26, 1811, six hundred people attended the performance, when a carelessly placed candle ignited a canvas backdrop to the stage. Flames

John Holt Rice (1777–1831), by unknown (Virginia Museum of History & Culture)

shot up to the resinous pine ceiling and spread rapidly over the heads of the stunned audience. Panicking, screaming people scrambled to escape, but the cramped exit became jammed with struggling bodies. "The flame extended with a rapidity scarcely less than the explosion of gun powder— many were suffocated, press[e]d to death, & consumed by the fire. Nothing on earth could surpass the terror & despair. . . . Fathers, mothers, wives, children, perished amidst shrieks of the bitterest anguish & tore their own flesh in the agonies of approaching death," reported Francis W. Gilmer. "The wretched half-burnt females were crawling on their hands & knees in all directions from the smoking ruins in a state of frenzy," added John Coalter.[1]

By morning, the brick theater was a gutted, blackened, crumbling, smoking shell filled with ashes and bones. Coalter saw "wretched survivors" draw "the half-consumed bodies from the ruins," and many of the intermingled corpses defied identification. Workers poured bones into sheets for later burial in a common grave. The seventy-two dead included the state's governor, George William Smith. Most victims belonged to elite families, and many were young women whose fashionable and bulky gowns caught fire as they fled. In distant Bedford County, Jeremiah Jeter later recalled: "No event in all my early years produced such a deep, pervasive, and enduring impression in the State as did the conflagration of the theater and the deplorable sufferings and losses." He added, "The general impression was that the burning of the theatre was a clear manifestation of its divine condemnation."[2]

Despising the theater as profane, evangelicals insisted that God had punished Richmond's gentility for vice and impiety. A center for trade along the James River, Richmond prospered, but the people appeared indifferent to religion, preferring to attend plays and to frequent taverns, brothels, gambling dens, and horse races. After the shocking fire, pious people saw an opportunity to convert the wicked. In January 1812, Richmond's Presbyterians invited a talented, young (thirty-five years old) preacher from the countryside, John Holt Rice, to visit and preach to people shaken by the tragedy. "I am most anxious that so much distress should not be suffered in vain," Rice declared. He warned listeners

immediately to seek salvation "and live as if every year and every day
were to be our last." In the spring, he agreed to return to Richmond
as a resident minister. People flocked to his engaging sermons, and
Rice reported, "A spirit of reading, and of inquiry for religious truth is
spreading rapidly among our town folks."[3]

In 1814, Richmond's Episcopalians hired their own energetic minister, Richard Channing Moore, who also became the church's bishop
in Virginia. Moore took charge of the "Monumental Church" erected
on the site of the fatal theater to honor and entomb the victims. By
acquiring the newest and loveliest church in the city, Episcopalians
gained an edge in enticing the wealthiest class. While appealing to the
gentry with his fine manners, Moore denounced their horse racing,
card playing, heavy drinking, and attending plays. He led an evangelical turn that revived Episcopalian fortunes in Virginia. From just
seven clergymen in 1814, Virginia's old church grew to twenty-three
by 1822.[4]

Evangelical Episcopalians and Presbyterians addressed the growing
concern with bodily health among the gentry. Letters and conversation
dwelled on sickness and death among family and friends, a focus that
bred a longing for salvation in an eternity free from pain and suffering. That hope especially appealed to women, so often anguished by
the loss of children and parents. Sally Cocke Faulcon told her brother,
John Hartwell Cocke: "What happiness it is my beloved Brother to be
able to enjoy the comforts of hope, how consoling is the reflection that
in the hour of death we can lean our heads upon the kind arm of our
Almighty Saviour & trust our souls in his faithful hands."[5]

While professing subordination to men, evangelical women could
display a powerful, pained piety when disappointed by a man's decision or conduct. Soon enough, many husbands sought to please wives
so confident in their spiritual convictions. The feminine power in evangelical gentility disgusted Jefferson: "In our Richmond, there is much
fanaticism, but chiefly among the women. They have their night meetings, and praying-parties, where attended by their priests, and sometimes a hen-pecked husband, they pour forth the effusions of their love

to Jesus in terms as amatory and carnal as their modesty would permit them to use to a more earthly lover."[6]

In turn, genteel evangelicals feared Jefferson as the great infidel of Virginia, the powerful validator of impiety parading as philosophy or as Unitarianism, a rationalized form of Christianity stripped of miracles and the trinity. In July 1813, Reverend Robert Miller visited Albemarle County and concluded, "In my view, an enemy to the religion of Jesus Christ is the worst enemy of his country, . . . and the higher he is in station the more fatal his influence." Bishop Moore longed to convert Jefferson: "Would to God! That his mind was favourably impressed towards Christianity and that by some magnanimous effort, he would restore to the religion of our fathers, the many who have been led into skepticism, through the influence of his opinions." Gilmer feared that Jefferson's friends underestimated the cultural shift: "I have apprehensions. You Albemarle gentlemen do not know what new feelings are growing wild in Virginia." Those wild, new feelings threatened Jefferson's University.[7]

Rivals

Born in 1777, John Holt Rice grew up in a farm family of middling means in Bedford County. With two clergymen for uncles, he voraciously read devotional tracts. His mother died when Rice was twelve, and he suffered from poor health. As a boy, he met Patrick Henry, who advised, "Remember that the best men always make themselves." But they also get timely help, as did Rice, who could attend Liberty Hall Academy and Hampden-Sydney College thanks to scholarships provided by pious and prosperous patrons impressed by his mind and faith. At Hampden-Sydney, dazzled teachers invited him to join the faculty in 1796, when he was nineteen. A colleague recalled, "His appetite for books was rabid. Having access now to the college library, . . . he was like a hungry ox when let into a rich pasture."[8]

Rice also tutored the children of a devout and wealthy couple, whose daughter Anne Morton married him in 1802. Ordained in 1803 as a

Presbyterian clergyman, Rice preached in rotation at three churches in the Southside counties of Charlotte and Prince Edward. Struggling to support his growing family on a salary of $400, Rice ran a farm with slaves provided by his father-in-law. The minister also conducted a boarding school with a genteel curriculum featuring Greek and Latin as well as theology.[9]

Troubled by the low state of education, Rice wanted Virginians to read more—and talk, drink, and sleep much less. He founded a library at the county courthouse and raised scholarship money for "poor and pious youth" to study at Hampden-Sydney for the ministry. Tireless in promoting improvements, he lamented the want of public spirit, blaming the mania for making "money the *alpha and omega, the all in all*, of our existence." Noting Virginians' love for riding, he thought it easier "to endow an Institute for horses" than a seminary to educate youth.[10]

Rice avidly preached to the enslaved, doubling their number in his congregation to one hundred. He praised their impassioned prayers and hymns as superior to those offered by his white congregants. "Many of the black people are anxious to read," he added. Despite local opposition, Rice favored educating them: "a very large proportion can read, and are instructed in religious doctrines and duties, beyond many professors among white people." By professors, he meant not the faculty at a college but people who professed Christianity. "This people have for me a most ardent affection. They appear ready to pluck out their eyes for me, if it were necessary. Ministering to them in the Gospel of Christ is the most delightful service in which I am engaged." But Rice reassured wary masters that his preaching promoted harder work.[11]

A slaveholder but a cautious critic of the system, Rice favored preparing African Americans for freedom in some future generation and overseas colony. Rice worried that pushing for emancipation would inflame reactionaries and thereby "injure religion and retard the march of public feeling in relation to slavery." He also wanted to ban the competition of black preachers, for he felt possessive of his enslaved congregants, described as "my beloved blacks."[12]

In his ministry, Rice gave priority to undermining deism among the gentry, reasoning that common Virginians would follow their lead toward the true faith. As a young man, he had overcome the tempting company and insidious conversation of "gentlemen of sprightly talents and pleasing manners . . . imbued with the principles of infidelity." Combining evangelical fervor with learning and decorum, Rice appealed to genteel people seeking emotion in their faith but "truly disgusted with the rant and the wildness" of Baptists and Methodist preachers. A mentor recalled that young Rice's early sermons "were not, at first, suited to the taste, nor adapted to the edification of the common people; but they were calculated to raise his reputation as a man of learning and abilities, with men of information and discernment."[13]

Writing to a young Virginian at college, Rice explained his crusade to save faith from corruption by rationalist philosophy: "You ought to know that the preachers of Christianity are now divided into two great classes: the rational religionists and the evangelical preachers." The rationalists "affect superior learning, and refinement, and taste; they dwell much on the small moralities of this world; they speculate in a very cool, philosophical manner on virtue . . . and the inconveniences of vice." They were "full of the cant of liberality; [and] as often at places of amusement as at the church, and full of assurance that they are a very good sort of people." As an example, he cited the late Bishop James Madison, long the president of William & Mary.[14]

Rice's lively humor, keen intellect, and fine manners recommended him to genteel circles, where he promoted religious conversation. After Rice moved to Richmond in 1812, a young gentleman concluded, "A more approachable, more genial, more delightful companion could nowhere be found," for he "had no superiors in the art of polite entertainment." To spread his influence statewide, Rice founded and edited the *Virginia Evangelical and Literary Magazine*, which crusaded for education while assailing deist and Unitarian beliefs.[15]

Rice won over William Wirt, Richmond's leading lawyer, who forsook deism and dissipation to join the minister's congregation. In 1816, Wirt helped Rice lobby the legislature to incorporate a theological seminary at Hampden-Sydney to train "*poor* and *pious* youth for

the ministry of the gospel." But the legislators refused, claiming that
any incorporation of a religious body violated the strict separation of
church and state. They saw incorporation as a Presbyterian ploy to seek
a new church establishment as bad as the old Anglican version. Rice's
seminary went ahead without the legal and financial advantages of
state incorporation.[16]

Jefferson and Rice shared important qualities and goals. Genteel
and sociable, both men influenced others through charming conversation and generous hospitality. Unusually self-disciplined, both promoted rigorous and prolonged study by young people. "We are never
more directly in the road to ruin, than when doing just as we please. . . .
Learn, then, habits of self-government," Rice preached. He and Jefferson
cherished books, including the Greek and Latin classics of antiquity.
Seeking to improve Virginia through education, both pushed for a state
university. They questioned slavery but kept slaves to sustain their genteel style and high social status. Both expressed antislavery sentiments
cautiously rather than offend their peers, for they had other priorities
requiring broad support.[17]

Both Jefferson and Rice lived beyond their means, accumulating
debts that dispirited them during the early 1820s. Although Rice disdained money-grubbing by others, he felt entitled to a generous income
sufficient to sustain a genteel household. In 1823, he complained that
his Richmond congregation stinted on his salary: "I have no doubt
that the people here love me. But they have not shown that love in the
most comfortable way. . . . Now if my people had *loved* me every year
two thousand dollars, it would have been a very comfortable display of
love indeed." Pressured by creditors, Rice lamented, "This preys on my
heart, and seems like consuming me."[18]

Like Jefferson, Rice insisted that Virginians needed education at
home to preserve their minds from northern influence. He complained
that when young Virginians returned home from a northern college,
"nothing could be heard from them but censures of the laws, the politics,
the manners and customs, of Virginia." Rice upheld the convention that
Virginians' faults paled compared to "an openheartedness, a generosity,

and a cordiality, which can be found nowhere else. I love Virginia." Living his words, Rice turned down the presidency of Princeton although it paid twice what he made in Virginia.[19]

But he relied on northern benefactors to sustain his seminary. He assured one donor, "Heaven has poured such a tide of wealth unto N[ew] York that if 25,000 dollars could drop from that place into my study, the New Yorkers never would find it out, and our Seminary would get a spring that would make it go forward to the praise of God and the blessing of the Country." To shake money loose, Rice warned that without Presbyterian education "the result would be just this—the Southern nabobs would all be infidels, or the high church Episcopalians; and the common people would be either nothing at all as to religion" or Baptists and Methodists.[20]

Rice and Jefferson came from and spoke for different social classes. Born into the gentry, Jefferson promoted a top-down educational program for Virginia's improvement. Rice came from the middle class and championed hardworking social risers. He despised state support for pauper children at elementary schools as rewarding the "drunken, lazy, and wasteful" at the expense of taxpayers. Instead, he wanted the state to subsidize education for every white child, reducing tuition within the reach of all industrious parents. "The business of the state is, to make education, from its first elements to its highest attainments, *very cheap* so that in our prosperous country suitable exertion may put it within the reach of all."[21]

To reach the poor, Rice favored Sunday schools that relied on pious volunteers as teachers. These schools taught basic literacy and numeracy supplemented with hymns, prayers, and Bible lessons. If provided with $15,000 by the legislature, he claimed that Sunday schools could reach all of the poor, saving the state $30,000 from its $45,000 annual appropriation for pauper education. He would reinvest the savings to fund academies "to the benefit of by far the most valuable part of society, the people in moderate circumstances," who were "the main stay of the republic." But Sunday schools contradicted Jefferson's insistence that young minds should avoid premature exposure to theology. Disdaining academies as well as Sunday schools, Jefferson wanted to capture the entire state appropriation for his University.[22]

Rice countered that Jefferson's University cost too much, thanks to lavish buildings better suited for aristocratic Europe than republican Virginia. That misspending led to high fees, which reserved the state's best education for the wealthy. Rice asked: "Is it not obvious, that, in effect, this is an institution for the rich? Can the *common people* enjoy any direct benefits from it? Let the members of the General Assembly look round on their constituents, and say, who among them can afford to send their sons to the University?"[23]

Above all, Jefferson and Rice clashed over the great issues of life, death, and God. As an evangelical Calvinist, Rice insisted on the universal "depravity of man" derived from the original sin committed by Adam and Eve. Only submission to God could secure atonement and salvation. "My only hope rests upon this doctrine. If it prove[s] false, I know not what is to become of me and of those I love." Rice regarded deism as too rational, too devoid of emotion to provide solace to suffering humanity. Deriding Unitarians like Jefferson as "baptized Deists," Rice accused them of sustaining a heresy that "flatters the pride of human understanding [and] gives license to the depravity of the human heart!"[24]

Jefferson accused his religious critics of "pious whining, hypocritical canting, lying & slandering." Claiming a sunnier view of human nature and divine creation, Jefferson declared, "it is a good world on the whole," so he dismissed Calvinists as "gloomy & hypochondriac minds, inhabitants of diseased bodies, disgusted with the present." Regarding Jesus as a sublime but simple teacher of morality, an exalted man but no God, Jefferson accused traditional clergymen of corrupting Christianity into "mystery & jargon" by "the deliria of crazy imaginations" and "the manic ravings of Calvin, tinctured plentifully with the foggy dreams of Plato" to delude, manipulate, and exploit credulous people.[25]

In private letters to fellow rationalists, Jefferson denounced Presbyterians as bigots bent on destroying freedom and restoring the Middle

Ages, complete with an inquisition. Characterizing them as "the most ambitious, the most intolerant & tyrannical of all our sects," Jefferson insisted that their clergy "dread the advance of science as witches do the approach of day-light." Jefferson charged them with opposing a university that, "by enlightening the minds of the people and encouraging them to appeal to their own comm[o]n sense, is to dispel the fanaticism on which their power is built."[26]

Jefferson expected Unitarianism ultimately to triumph, uniting at least all men in one true faith. Coding reason as masculine, Jefferson predicted that Unitarians "would gather into their fold every *man* under the age of 40. *Female* fanaticism might hold out a while longer." In 1822, Jefferson predicted, "I trust that there is not a *young man* now living in the U.S., who will not die an Unitarian."[27]

Rejecting the traditional Christian emphasis on original sin, Jefferson believed that secular education could advance the progressive improvement of man, converting "what in his nature was vicious and perverse into qualities of virtue and social worth." Echoing William Godwin's notion of human perfectibility, Jefferson concluded that every generation "must advance the knowledge and well-being of mankind . . . *indefinitely*, and to a term which no one can fix and foresee." Instead of a professor of divinity, his University would entrust "the proofs of the being of a God, the creator, preserver, and supreme rule of the universe" to the professor of ethics. Instead of a chapel, his institution would feature a library.[28]

Jefferson's philosophy appalled Rice as murderous to souls. True philosophy, he countered, featured the Christian doctrines of repentance, atonement, and salvation. "The work of education is only half performed, when man's moral powers are uncultivated," Rice noted. Rejecting Jefferson's materialism, Rice cast humans as "immortal beings" tested by a brief time on earth. "Exclude this idea, and we are degraded to reasoning beasts," he concluded. Only religious faith, Rice argued, could restrain the innate violence of human nature. He pointed to the wild youth of Virginia: "They are allowed to live as they list, and their passions, unaccustomed to restraint, are peculiarly violent." Rice concluded "that neither peace, nor order, nor liberty, nor any civil or political institution can be preserved without religion."[29]

In September 1818, Rice visited the new institution under construction and predicted, "This University . . . will be either a fountain of living waters diffusing health and vigour, or a poisoned spring spreading disease and death." Without religious faith, students would curse the University and blight the state. "Will its alumni go out into life with passions inflamed by indulgence, and with hearts hardened, and minds darkened by the pride of philosophy, falsely so called; and thus be prepared to scatter around them arrows, firebrands, and death[?]"[30]

Rather than oppose the University, Rice sought to co-opt it, seeking leverage to alter its mission. In January 1819, with the University bill in peril, Rice explained his legislative strategy: "Now is the time to make a push. The friends of the University are alarmed. They fear a defeat; and dread Presbyterians most of all. I have seized the crisis; gone in among the Monticello-men, and assured them that . . . we rejoice that the state is about to support learning in a style worthy of Virginia." He added, "I gain influence; and if we know how to use it, may make ourselves to be felt in the University." He agreed with Jefferson that it would train Virginia's leaders and shape the state's future, so Rice meant to convert them.[31]

In 1819, Rice's magazine endorsed a vision for the University advanced by Reverend Conrad Speece. An especially fiery Presbyterian, Speece had visited Charlottesville the year before. Trying to preach at the courthouse, he endured heckling from local boys and later overheard tavern blasphemy from "prominent gentlemen." Speece concluded, "When Satan promised all the kingdoms of the world to Christ, *he laid his thumb on Charlottesville*, and whispered, 'Except this place, which I reserve for my own special use.'"[32]

To save the new University from the devil, Speece proposed requiring every professor "solemnly to avow his belief in the existence of one all-perfect God, the Creator and moral Governor of the world" and in the literal scriptures and Holy Trinity. Such professors would fortify "the minds of the young against the assaults of infidelity." Every day would begin and end with prayers attended by all students and professors; and they would devote Sunday to holy worship and reflection. Speece also wanted every student to carry a Bible "ready at all times to be exhibited on demand."[33]

Friends warned Jefferson to beware of the Presbyterian challenge to his university. Joseph C. Cabell noted, "They are an artful, able, aspiring sect" eager "to monopolize in a great degree the education of the country." Francis W. Gilmer worried that Jefferson had lost touch with his neighbors: "While he is indulging the warm reveries of a political *mania*, the neighbourhood is hissing hot with an epidemic [of] religious fanaticism." Gilmer warned his friends: "You gentlemen of the Central College may look out for storms. You have enemies . . . who represent you abroad as a set of gentlemen drilled & disciplined in the school of infidelity."[34]

The storm broke out in 1819, when Jefferson wanted Thomas Cooper to become the University's first professor and "the corner stone of our edifice." A radical émigré from England, Cooper had embraced Jeffersonian republicanism and deism. A brilliant chemist and mineralogist, Cooper also mastered law, political economy, Latin and Greek. Jefferson declared, "Cooper is ackno[w]le[d]ged by every enlightened man who knows him to be the greatest man in America in the powers of mind & in acquired information."[35]

But Cabell warned that Cooper would galvanize opposition to the University from pious Virginians. Rumors also insisted that Cooper drank and quarreled too much. A friend in Philadelphia, William Short, investigated and offered partial reassurance. Cooper had sworn off drink years ago but his temper remained as fiery as ever. On the Board of Visitors, pious John Hartwell Cocke opposed Cooper's appointment, but Cabell reluctantly sided with Jefferson, who prevailed. In March 1819, the Visitors agreed to hire Cooper as "professor of chemistry, mineralogy, and natural philosophy, and as professor of law."[36]

John Holt Rice, however, had the goods on Cooper: a book published in England filled with his unorthodox religious opinions. Rice warned his friend Cocke, "If Cooper should come to the University, he will kindle a flame of opposition which will not soon be extinguished."

Rice lit the blaze by publishing a scathing review of Cooper's "wild doctrine of human perfectibility," equanimity about atheism, and hostility to Trinitarian Christianity.[37]

The review caused a sensation. Cabell's brother William, a former governor, was not particularly pious, but he had enough political sense to avoid alienating evangelicals. William warned his brother to jettison Cooper: "His opinions are damnable. . . . We shall have every religious man in Virginia against us." Taken aback by the firestorm of criticism, Jefferson advised Cooper to relinquish his offer of a professorship. Two months later, Cooper announced that he would accept a permanent post at South Carolina College. Rice claimed victory in exulting letters to friends.[38]

John Augustine Smith (1782–1865), by unknown
(Muscarelle Museum of Art, The College of William & Mary)

After the Cooper debacle, Cabell urged Jefferson to mollify the University's pious critics: "Is it not better to sail a little before the wind, than to risk all by struggling with the tempest?" In 1822, Cabell persuaded the Visitors to invite any denomination to establish an associated theological seminary in Charlottesville. Their students could attend University lectures and use the library, but each seminary would remain "independent of the University." Nice in theory, the offer faltered in practice, because no denomination could afford to build a new seminary. But the overture provided a useful reply for Visitors to deploy when accused of favoring infidelity.[39]

Removal

William & Mary's president, Dr. John Augustine Smith, wanted to revive the old College by embracing the evangelical gentility that Jefferson resisted. To persuade pious parents to send their sons to the College, Smith sought to reverse the school's secularization. As a first step, he added Bishop Moore to the College's Board of Visitors. In 1820, that Board appointed Reverend Reuel Keith, an evangelical Episcopalian, to fill a new professorship of "Humanity and Universal History." In early 1821, Virginia's Episcopal Church agreed to raise funds for a theological seminary associated with the College.[40]

The Episcopal initiative outraged leading Republicans, who jealously guarded the separation of church and state. They insisted that, as a state-sponsored corporation, William & Mary could not favor any one denomination. Denouncing the Episcopalians' new partnership with the College, a critic declared, "Let the ministers attend each to his own duty, and not hunt further for religious establishments."[41]

The Richmond Junto retained power by battling the phantom of a Federalist revival. In 1819, Virginia Republicans were upset over recent decisions by the United States Supreme Court led by the old Federalist John Marshall. Some of those decisions defended corporations as private properties immune to state meddling. In the celebrated case of *Dartmouth v. Woodward*, the Marshall Court rejected efforts by New

Hampshire Republicans to revoke a royal charter held by Dartmouth College. Appalled by that ruling, Virginians vowed to defend state political control over corporations. Otherwise, a Republican argued, "the sages and heroes of our revolution toiled and bled in vain!"[42]

In July 1821, the Richmond Junto's leading ideologue and jurist, Spencer Roane, posed as a "Dissenting Farmer" in the *Richmond Enquirer* to denounce the proposed Episcopal seminary as "unconstitutional and illegal." Reaching for the most provocative analogy, Roane insisted that, with equal justice, William & Mary "might be converted into a college for the instruction of negroes only, to the exclusion of all white people." Race served as a malign trump card played in the polemical exchanges of white Virginians.[43]

The firestorm of criticism staggered the Episcopal alliance with the College. Despairing Episcopalians moved their seminary to Alexandria in 1823, and Professor Keith followed, resigning from the College. Although Cabell did "not approve these unnatural coalitions" of church and corporation, he concluded, "I suppose, however, my friend Smith was hard pressed and I must excuse him." But Smith had another desperate card to play, which would draw Cabell into the game with a vengeance.[44]

Decaying Williamsburg imperiled the survival of William & Mary. In 1823, a student assured his sister, "There is nothing here that would interest you in the least, unless you would be amused with falling walls and decaying houses.... From day to day there revolves one lifeless monotony." A professor mourned "this sad place of solitude and exile," featuring "many half-ruined wooden houses, which afford a tranquil and peaceful asylum to insects of every description." With so many people moving away, the old city was withering. In 1824, a traveler noted, "Thus, Williamsburg may be considered as gradually abandoning the college."[45]

The professors disliked Smith's meddling in their courses and dominating their meetings, while he disdained them as ineffectual. Smith assured state legislators, "Professors ... are a peculiar order of persons. Of all men, they are the most helpless. Absorbed in their abstractions, they know as little of the world when they leave it, as they do when they come into it. Like all animals, which are conscious of wanting the means of resistance, they are timorous." But faculty could resort to the weapons of the weak. The alienated professor of chemistry and natural philosophy, Patrick Kerr Rogers, covertly fed dirt on Smith and the College to Jefferson, who relished discrediting William & Mary. By ingratiating himself to Jefferson, Rogers hoped to land a post at the new university.[46]

But Smith had a daring plan to save the College by moving it from a dying town to Richmond, the state's metropolis of power. There he could cultivate legislators and trump the University, rendering it peripheral in Charlottesville, some eighty miles to the west. As the state capital, Richmond offered the College a precious edge in the fields most celebrated by Virginians: law and politics. More populous than Charlottesville, Richmond also had more cadavers for anatomy classes and sick people for medical students to poke. In Richmond, students could fill the College and, Smith promised, liberate professors "from the intolerable mortification . . . of lecturing to empty benches." As a substantial city, it also had enough magistrates and militiamen to suppress student riots. To promote the move, Richmond's leaders offered a free tract of land and promised to erect buildings. Smith padded the Board of Visitors with new members who approved his plan in July 1824, and the faculty agreed in November.[47]

By publicizing the impending move and neglecting to maintain the College, Smith drove away potential students. In 1824, a traveler reported, "Here I visited the ruins of William & Mary College. . . . The steps are mostly out of their place. Some of the windows are entirely broken out and most or all of them more or less broken, some not having more than three panes of glass in them." That fall, William & Mary had only six students. "Our College," one professor lamented, "is I think completely gone." Smith promoted the decline to demonstrate that William & Mary could never thrive in Williamsburg, but he played a risky hand, for if the move fell through, the College might never recover. In another gamble, Smith sought legislative approval for the move. Thereby, Smith unwittingly rendered the College's charter and endowment vulnerable to the covetous designs of others.[48]

In March 1824, Cabell had regarded the College as doomed: "The downfall of W[illia]m & Mary seems near at hand." His complacency dissolved into shock two months later, when Cabell learned of Smith's daring ploy to move the College. Detecting a grave threat to the University, Cabell alerted Jefferson: "To oppose an Institution struggling to save itself and to thwart the natural endeavors of literary men to advance their fortunes is truly painful. Yet, are we to suffer the labours of so many years to be blasted by an unnecessary & destructive competition? Most assuredly, we must not." Cabell dreaded a revived William & Mary with a vibrant medical school and law school located among the state's leaders.[49]

But Jefferson saw a rich opportunity in Smith's risky submission to the legislature. The canny philosopher meant to ingest the College's money and books while spitting out Smith and the faculty. Jefferson advised Cabell to wait "until the old institution is loosened from its foundation and fairly placed on its wheels" at the start of the legislative session in December. Then they could pounce, seeking legislative dissolution of the royal charter to capture, for the University, "the derelict capital of Wm & Mary, and the large library they uselessly possess." By this coup, Jefferson expected to add $6,000 to the University's annual revenue. He also felt that Smith's gambit saved the University from any moral responsibility to hire or pay severance to the discarded faculty. Professor Rogers had bet on the wrong patron in covertly writing to Jefferson.[50]

Smith had placed an even worse bet by loaning money to Jefferson. For years, Smith had cultivated leading politicians with loans drawn from the College endowment. In January 1823, Jefferson ran out of bank credit and needed thousands of dollars to avoid financial collapse. With Smith's help, Jefferson procured $24,705 from the College. The rescue, however, did nothing to sway Jefferson's low regard for William & Mary. A few weeks later, he assured a friend that the College was "much reduced by ill management of its funds." Although ungrateful, Jefferson was right, and his loan was among the worst decisions that Smith ever made. Jefferson never repaid the principal and, far from helping the College, he worked to block the move to Richmond and strip William & Mary of its endowment. Neither Cabell nor Jefferson felt any loyalty to their alma mater.[51]

By threatening the College's charter and move, Cabell and Jefferson outraged the leading men of Richmond, who insisted that the state would benefit from two first-rate institutions rather than settling for one. These critics included Cabell's older brother, William H. Cabell, a former governor. "For God's sake," William warned Joseph, "reconsider this subject, and do not injure the University & *destroy yourself* by advancing an opinion to which you will never be able to make a single convert among disinterested men." William insisted that seizing the College's funds "would be to abandon all respect for the laws which protect property." He concluded, "I have been much concerned at the *strange* lengths . . . to which your zeal for the University has unknowingly carried you."[52]

But Joseph Cabell clung to his tough politics in service to the University. In December 1824, he assured Jefferson: "I oppose the wishes of my nearest & dearest relatives & friends, and bring upon myself the powerful resentment of the metropolis. . . . I fear the influence of the metropolis, headed by so many able men, will be too strong for us." Richmond's wealthy and fashionable leaders wined and dined rural legislators, adding to Cabell's growing anxiety. "I am worn down. I do not sleep. I hear the clock strike 1, 2, 3, 4, 5 every night. This great work will go on. We have gone too far to recede."[53]

Crossings

To strengthen the University's political position, Jefferson and his fellow Visitors suddenly rushed to hire their own faculty. For years, they had delayed opening in order to extract more money from the legislature, but in 1824 the Visitors sprang into action, proposing to commence in February 1825. They calculated that an operating University would dissuade legislators from allowing the College to become a formidable competitor in Richmond.

Despite that new haste, Jefferson insisted that only "Professors of the first order of science" would do, so that Virginia's "national university" could compete with New England's institutions. Jefferson argued that the Visitors should never "become suitors to Yale and Harvard for their secondary characters. Have we been laboring then merely to get up another Hampden Sydney or [Washington College at] Lexington?" Only a superb faculty could, he explained, "give to our institution splendor and preeminence." Jefferson persuaded his fellow Visitors to seek faculty in Britain, where he expected to find first-rate minds untainted by Yankeeism.[54]

The overseas bid for professors was controversial. Jefferson's northern critics relished the chance to claim superior patriotism. Newspapers in Boston, New Haven, and Philadelphia printed indignation, claiming that Jefferson could have procured perfectly good professors in the United States at half the cost. The Philadelphia paper accused Jefferson of committing one of the "greatest insults which the American people had ever received." On the Board of Visitors, Cocke begged Cabell, "Do save us from this inundation of Foreigners if it is possible." But Cabell balked at irritating Jefferson, and the philosopher stood firm, reserving only the professorships of law and moral philosophy for Americans. Madison lobbied for recruiting an American as medical professor, but Jefferson despised almost all doctors from the United States as deadly hacks or crazy theorists.[55]

In 1824, Gilmer agreed to visit Britain to recruit faculty. Jefferson expected the University to rescue Gilmer from intellectual loneliness in backward Virginia, but Gilmer hoped to save Virginia from Jefferson. Soured on Jefferson's support for democratic reform in Virginia, Gilmer confided, "Mr. J[efferso]n has done & will do more harm in this way than even the overthrow of the tyranny of John Adams did good. God save the Commonwealth from such ruin." By training a conservative elite at the University, Gilmer hoped to defend landholders against "the paupers" and Jefferson. "If I can succeed in this mission," Gilmer boasted, "I shall claim to have done the best service which any son of Virginia (next to Gen. Washington) has ever conferred on his country." That boast elevated Gilmer over Jefferson.[56]

In May, Gilmer sailed for England with $1,500 for his own expenses and $6,000 to buy books and a scientific apparatus. Gilmer could offer each professor a salary of $1,500 plus supplemental fees paid by students. But he had to act fast, for Jefferson wanted to open the University in early 1825, when the state legislators would debate moving the old College. He assured Gilmer: "Your return during the session of the legislature, with the cortege [of professors], so anxiously desired would have a triumphant effect on them." But, Jefferson added, "The greatest of all misfortunes would be your return without any."[57]

Gilmer initially struggled to find British scholars willing to gamble their careers on a new university in a distant country. In London in July, Gilmer scored his first recruit, an émigré named George Wilhelm Blaettermann, a learned scholar of French, German, and Italian. Gilmer had the late James Ogilvie to thank for this first professor, as he had befriended Blaettermann and cultivated his interest in the prospective university five years before. From beyond the grave, Ogilvie kickstarted a faculty for Virginia.[58]

Blaettermann helped Gilmer recruit Thomas Hewett Key, an eager young mathematician with a romantic enthusiasm for the United States. Key enticed his friend George Long to teach Latin and Greek, and they persuaded Charles Bonnycastle to become professor of natural philosophy. Gilmer then signed a promising professor of medicine and anatomy, Robley Dunglison. Gilmer exulted, "They are men of good families, good moral characters, genteel manners, regular education, talents, & from the great Universities." He added, "I have worked wonders. . . . If learning does not raise its drooping head, it shall not be my fault." With his help, Gilmer concluded, "Virginia must still be the great nation." In September, Gilmer prepared to sail home, feeling rejuvenated by his trip: "I shall return to the bar with recruited health and redoubled vigour."[59]

Gilmer sailed for New York in a leaky, overcrowded vessel with an inept captain. It was a voyage from hell for the sickly Gilmer, who nearly died. In mid-November, the ship reached New York after thirty-five days at sea. He reported, "We had tempest after tempest, day & night, so that we could sleep or walk but 3 days." Seasickness had compounded his "raging & devouring fever, aggravated by want of medicine, of food, of rest, of attendance, & the continual tossing of the rude imperious surge.... I am reduced to a shadow & disordered throughout my whole system." He concluded, "Such is the martyrdom I have endured for the old dominion. She will never thank me for it, but I will love & cherish her as if she did." During his convalescence in New York, Gilmer recruited another professor: Irish-born John P. Emmet, who could teach natural history and chemistry.[60]

Only two professors, Blaettermann and Long, had sailed with Gilmer from Britain. Three others—Bonnycastle, Dunglison, and Key—took another ship bound for Norfolk rather than New York. They departed in late October, but had not reached Virginia three months later, more than twice the expected duration of a crossing. Cocke reported, "I fear Mr. J[efferson] & all in that quarter will have to go into Mourning for the loss of our professors." A prospective student (and Jefferson relative), Wilson Miles Cary, confided, "Mr. Jefferson becomes every day more afraid that they have gone to the bottom along with ... the University of V[irgini]a."[61]

The apparently lost professors weakened Cabell's hand in the legislature, where he battled the old College's move to Richmond. In mid-January, he worried that "the party in favor of the removal of the College have gained ground very much." Jefferson had hoped to open the University by February 1, in order to induce legislators "to look more favorably on us," but "to open a university without mathematics or natural philosophy would bring on us ridicule and disgrace." The Visitors published a notice delaying the opening for at least another month. By then, however, the College might defeat the University for priority in Virginia.[62]

To build support in the legislature, Cabell abandoned the unpopular proposal to seize the College's funds for the University. He and Jefferson still meant to plunder the College but now offered to share the loot by funding a statewide system of colleges to serve as feeder schools for the University. The proposal would preserve a shrunken William & Mary in Williamsburg and provide another small college as a sop to Richmond. To buy support elsewhere, Cabell promised colleges to Clarksburg, Fredericksburg, Lewisburg, Lynchburg, Staunton, and Winchester. Cabell depicted a beautiful new system capped by one magnificent University: "There will be one great luminary in the centre, and lesser lights kindled up over the whole extent of our territory." A new convert to the cause of state colleges, Jefferson declared, "This occasion of compleating our system of education is a God-send, which ought not to pass away neglected."[63]

Cabell found partial allies among Tidewater politicians, who sought to save William & Mary for Williamsburg. But they bristled at his effort to divest the College of its charter and endowment. Blaming Smith for William & Mary's decline, the Tidewater legislators despised his push to compel student testimony in discipline cases, which they likened to "a Spanish Inquisition, or the proceedings of a Star Chamber." The leading critic was John Tyler, Jr., a graduate of the college, member of the Board of Visitors, and a future United States president. In 1824, he declared, "To inform against his fellow, is to sever at once the cords of intimacy which have bound them together as one."[64]

As the hearings dragged on, Smith's flamboyant egotism wore on the legislators. In rambling testimony, Smith showed off his broad learning and many opinions. One legislator initially thought him "a very smart, fluent, little fellow" who had "amused in long harangues large crowds of the Legislature on every branch of human knowledge." Soon enough, however, Smith became a pompous know-it-all. He also blundered by introducing a letter from a northern academic endorsing the College's move. An indignant legislator skewered Smith for relying on a letter "from some Yankey, whose name I now forget, and I hope never again to hear, recommending the removal of William & Mary College to

Richmond. . . . Humble as I am, I shall dare to judge for myself, and I shall vote against the removal." Citing a Yankee as an authority was a cardinal sin with Virginia legislators.[65]

On February 7, the legislature defeated removing the College, and Cabell assured Jefferson: "You need not give yourself any further trouble on this subject." In the end, Cabell had not introduced "the bill for dividing the funds of the College. The public mind is not prepared for so bold a measure." Cabell apparently struck a deal to leave the endowment alone provided the College stayed in Williamsburg. Defeated, discredited, and infuriated, Smith left William & Mary to accept a professorship in New York, while the College made a partial recovery by offering Tidewater students a cheaper, local alternative to the University.[66]

Cabell and Jefferson got more good news on February 9, two days after the legislative victory over Smith. Long-awaited and presumed dead, the three missing professors reached Norfolk, after a grim voyage of fourteen weeks through pounding gales in the North Atlantic. With Smith defeated and the professors landed, Cabell celebrated victory and assured Jefferson: "Like a fine steam boat on our noble Chesapeake, cutting her way at the rate of ten knots per hour, and leaving on the horizon all other vessels on the waters, the University will advance with rapid strides, and throw into the rear all the other seminaries of this vast continent."[67]

Faculty

On March 7, 1825, the University of Virginia opened with six professors but with two slots still unfilled: moral philosophy and law. As professor of moral philosophy, James Madison proposed George Tucker, the cousin of St. George Tucker and a member of Congress. Madison noted, "I have never seen him, and can only judge of him by a volume of Miscellaneous Essays published not very long ago. They are written with acuteness & elegance, and indicate a capacity & taste for Philosophical Literature." But those essays included a ringing defense of dueling as essential to civility in public life, which seemed like a poor qualification to teach moral philosophy. Still Jefferson endorsed Madison's nomination: "Altho' not a native, he is considered as thoroughly a Virginian and of good standing." Born in Bermuda, Tucker had attended William & Mary and settled in Virginia. In Congress, he had been a sound Republican of the states' rights school, opposing any restriction on the western expansion of slavery despite his earlier efforts to promote emancipation and colonization. Jefferson did not know of Tucker's blistering criticism, published anonymously, of his racial views in *Notes on the State of Virginia*.[68]

An awkward public speaker, Tucker had floundered in Congress and feared losing his next election. Troubled by gambling debts, he sought a secure salary by accepting the professorship. But he had never taught moral philosophy, so Tucker stayed up late to prepare lectures. He also thought it would help to name his dog "Metaphysics." Deprived of sleep, Tucker suffered "from the grotesque images that floated before my fancy" and worried "that my brain might be seriously affected." Other Virginians considered him intellectually light, for Tucker had written novels, which most men disdained as suited only for women to read. Just fifteen students enrolled to study with him: the fewest for any professor.[69]

In 1825, the most important professorship—of law—remained unfilled because the salary of $1,500 did not appeal to any accomplished lawyer or judge, who could make at least twice as much. Jefferson also imposed a political test on this appointment. Given the interdependence of law and politics in Virginia, he insisted that only a Republican could train the next generation of leaders, lest students learn Federalist "heresies" in government. With Madison's help, Jefferson crafted a list of approved American political writings for the law professor to teach. Featuring the Declaration of Independence, and the 1799 resolutions adopted by the Virginia legislature against the Alien and Sedition Acts, the chosen texts favored states' rights over national consolidation.[70]

Although Jefferson dedicated the University to "the illimitable freedom of the human mind," he assumed that the free pursuit of truth always led to his conclusions. Jefferson cherished his defeat of the Federalists between 1798 and 1801 as the salvation of republican government from threatened monarchy and aristocracy. But the danger had not passed for Jefferson and it never would. During the late 1810s and early 1820s, he viewed every effort to strengthen the nation as an insidious plot to revive Federalism and destroy freedom. Far from alone in this dread, Jefferson spoke for the Republican orthodoxy of Virginia.[71]

Therefore, no Federalist need apply to become professor of law at the University of Virginia. Jefferson rebuffed a proposal to hire James Kent, the brilliant chancellor of the New York judiciary. A northern Federalist like Kent was, Jefferson explained, "out of the question with me. The Federal principle now is consolidation and a prostration of the barrier of the states. An angel from heaven who should inculcate such principles in our school of gov[ernmen]t should be rejected by me." Jefferson even opposed Henry St. George Tucker, a moderate Republican and the son of St. George Tucker. Cocke pushed for young Tucker, but Jefferson despised his support for some nationalizing measures. Declaring "political orthodoxy an essential and indispensable characteristic for our [law] school," Jefferson disdained Tucker's views as "inconsistent with the doctrines of the textbooks we have prescribed for that school."[72]

Jefferson preferred to appoint Gilmer: "I have never heard an unsound opinion on gov[ern]m[en]t uttered by him." In fact, Tucker held political views closer to Jefferson's than did Gilmer, who kept secret from the old philosopher scathing opinions expressed in private letters to friends. Chapman Johnson exhorted Gilmer to accept and "put your shoulder to the wheel and raise old Virginia, poor, feeble old Virginia from the mire." But Gilmer balked, fearing seclusion at the University as an exile from Richmond, the center of law and politics. He also despised Jefferson's architecture, dreading a professor's pavilion as a cramped trap among student dorms: "But to put me down in one of those pavilions is to serve me as an apothecary would a lizard or beetle in a phial of Whiskey, set in a window, & corked tight. I could not for $1500 endure this, even if I had no labour."[73]

In the fall of 1825, however, Gilmer reconsidered, concluding that teaching would suit his decayed health better than practicing law. He also worried that Jefferson was ruining the University. In November, Gilmer assured his friend John Randolph: "The university has been very near its exit in the first few months of its birth. . . . Scarcely a thing has been done which I should approve, and half the utility of my labours in England has been marred by Mr. J[efferson]s self-willed, & misguided mind."[74]

But Gilmer would not live long enough to reshape the University. In mid-January, he sadly informed Jefferson: "I have been so long sick & growing worse, that I have little hope of ever being good for any thing again." Fatally ill with heart and lung diseases, he retreated to the estate of his uncle, George Divers, who lived near Charlottesville. Peachy Gilmer hastened to his brother's bedside and found him "pale, weak, hectick, and worn down to almost nothing." By February 7, he no longer could speak and "converses only with Slate and Pencil."[75]

On his deathbed, Francis embraced Christianity. He assured Peachy: "Mine has been a hard fate, I have known little but misery. There is some bright mansion in the skies for me and for us all, else this world was created by a demon and not by a kind and benevolent deity." This new Christianity did not abate Gilmer's self-pity. Peachy reported, "He complained that the world had done him great injustice, asked me if I had ever known so much injustice done to anyone."[76]

On the morning of February 25, 1826, Gilmer died at the age of thirty-six. Peachy mourned his brother as the last and lost great hope for Virginia, "this sinking and degraded country," which was plunging into a "vortex of ignorance and vice, in which all will soon be overwhelmed in one common and irretrievable ruin." Peachy later declared that Francis was, "I firmly believe, rejoicing in Heaven with angels around the throne of God." His will left money to Peachy and his brother-in-law Peter Minor to educate their children.[77]

Comet

The initial seven professors were all foreign-born, and five had been in the country only a few months. All but Tucker were young men, and none had any teaching experience. Somehow, they were supposed to control southern adolescents, who had frustrated the faculties at every other university. Save for Robley Dunglison, the professors were a quirky lot unlikely to impress Virginia boys. Louisa, Cocke's second wife, described Blaettermann as "the ugliest old man . . . that I ever had seen." Wearing a red cloak and brown fur cap, he "looked like a crazy man" but told "such odd stories, in such an odd, good humoured way, that I laughed till the tears came in my eyes." In November 1825, a drunken Professor Bonnycastle fell off the Rotunda porch, dislocating an arm. Dunglison joked that Bonnycastle would have broken his neck "if it had not been for the vast protuberance of his nose." Cornelia Randolph reported that students disliked Tucker for "eccentricity of character" and inept teaching. She added that Emmet confused students with his rapid-fire Irish brogue: "His words tumble out heels over head." In his pavilion, Emmet kept free-ranging snakes and a white owl, and he had a tame bear in his garden. When he married, his wife eliminated the menagerie. Emmet released the owl in the nearby woods and killed the snakes. The couple then ate the bear.[78]

The professors' secularism delighted Jefferson but dismayed pious folk. A Presbyterian minister described the professors as "of some literary distinction, but of loose religious principles." Critics noted that the University lacked a chapel, offering instead a Rotunda, modeled on a pagan temple and reflecting Enlightenment rationalism. The University held no prayers, offered no Sunday services, and lacked any courses on theology. A visiting New Englander marveled that Virginia provided "the first instance, in the world, of a university without any such provisions." Critics accused the school of breeding infidelity, which misled young minds into lives of dissipation that would culminate in eternal damnation. One student heard a clergyman tell a parent, "Much as I love your son . . . I would, this day, rather follow him to his grave than see him enter the University."[79]

But John Holt Rice still hoped to claim and redeem the University. In 1819, when legislators sited the institution, Rice declared, "Albemarle is now the most important part of our country, as the University of Virginia is located there." In 1824, Virginia's Presbyterian clergy held their annual convention in Charlottesville, the belly of the philosophic beast. Gilmer had predicted that they would "carry the war into the enemy's camp to attack the mountain of infidelity," Monticello. In his keynote sermon of 1824, Rice praised Presbyterianism as the best church for a republican state. "The people did stare at me! The old man of the Mountain was not there, but his family was. The Sermon was reported to him." Rice was baiting Jefferson.[80]

Eight months later, Rice wrote, "Our University has gone into operation with about forty or fifty students. It may be regarded as a comet, which has for the first time just made its appearance; the orbit of which of course is not determined. The aspect, however, is portentous." In that generation, comets alarmed Americans as portents of coming disasters, plagues, wars, and theater fires. The first students would shape the orbit of this comet.[81]

9
STUDENTS

W ILSON MILES CARY grew up entangled in Jeffersons and
Randolphs. His great-grandfather was Thomas Jefferson's college
classmate and best friend, Dabney Carr, who married Jefferson's sister
Martha. Their daughter, Jean Barbara Carr, married Colonel Wilson

Virginia Randolph Cary (1786–1852), by Charles C. Ingham
(Virginia Museum of History & Culture)

Miles Cary, the leading magistrate, planter, and slavemaster in Elizabeth City County. The colonel's children included Wilson Jefferson Cary, who married Virginia Randolph, who was the sister of Thomas Mann Randolph, Jr., and so, the sister-in-law of Martha Jefferson Randolph, daughter of Thomas Jefferson. After her father died in 1793, Virginia lived with her brother and Martha at Edgehill Plantation until marrying Wilson J. Cary a dozen years later at nearby Monticello. Virginia recalled the Jefferson-Randolphs as "the protectors of my orphan childhood."[1]

Wilson J. Cary owned Carysbrook, a large plantation in Fluvanna County, but it came encumbered with debts. A reluctant politician, he sought and won a seat in the House of Delegates in 1821 to satisfy his insistent great-uncle, Thomas Jefferson, who needed a reliable vote from Fluvanna County for funding the University. Attending the winter session of the legislature in Richmond, Cary marveled at the performances of a French acrobat named Godeau, for whom the crowd waited as he rolled a wheel-barrow along a tightrope 150 feet long and 40 feet above the ground. The cat inside the wheelbarrow was not Godeau's first choice. "It is said here," Cary reported, that "he has beaten his wife severely because she would not consent to be rolled by him, up & down the rope in the wheel barrow."[2]

Cary longed to go home: "How gladly would I give up such frivolous gaieties for a quiet evening with my family by our own fireside." Idealizing family as a haven of love in a troublesome world, he assured Virginia, "Experience has long satisfied me, my dear Wife, that we have not much else to look to, besides ourselves and children, in this World of selfishness." Cary hoped that their children would become "an abundant fountain of Happiness & comfort in our old age," but that expected a great deal from their son, Wilson Miles Cary.[3]

Managing his plantation poorly, Wilson J. Cary fell deeper in debt during the long, hard depression that gripped the state after 1819. He began selling off slaves but assured his wife and children that they would weather the crisis "without a sacrifice of any other than some of those whom we can spare with little inconvenience." He ignored the plight, far worse than inconvenience, suffered by enslaved families ruptured by his sales. Cary tended to keep working men, selling away their wives and children. When an enslaved man begged Cary to reunite his scattered family, Cary took offense. He wrote to Virginia, "I really was astonished at Julius's impudent attempt to fasten his wife & children upon us. . . . I wish you to cause her to be removed without delay as I have no idea of supporting other people's negroes, when our own family is so large."[4]

The sales pained Cary as a threat to the family patrimony. "I feel as if daggers were piercing me almost when I am alienating the birth right of my children in this way," he told his wife. But Cary finished that letter with the cheering news that he had bought in Richmond "a Brittania coffee pot as a present for you" and would seek "a set of Dinner knives & forks. Do you want cups and saucers both for tea & coffee[?] . . . I am sure you must want Muslin & Ribbands for Caps & Ruffs." It would not do, he thought, for neighbors to see his children and wife wearing the worn clothes of a decaying estate. He kept selling enslaved people to maintain genteel appearances and fund his son's education.[5]

Virginia Randolph Cary found consolation in devout Presbyterianism. She cooperated with Fluvanna's pious power couple, John Hartwell Cocke and his wife Louisa, in conducting a Sunday school and raising funds for Reverend John Holt Rice's seminary. Virginia's faith demanded submission to her husband, but he did not share her emotional engagement with Jesus. Instead, W. J. Cary held philosophical views of the sort fashionable among educated gentlemen (other than Cocke). In February 1822, the slow and painful death of a nine-year-old daughter exposed the couple's spiritual differences. Virginia exhorted her husband to recognize the fragility of life and the urgency of saving his soul. In reply, he offered the stoicism of philosophy. "We differ, I trust, only in what is not essential, and agree in fact . . . in the doctrine of doing good to all in word and deed as far as our limited means extend." Convinced that a benevolent God would forgive theological differences among good people, W. J. Cary could not comprehend her God, who demanded complete submission as the price of saving human souls otherwise eternally and justly damned by original sin.[6]

Genteel families struggled to educate their sons because good teachers were few and flighty, and their schools short-lived. Wilson Miles Cary compounded that problem with indifference to study and delight in trouble, but the Carys had a trump card to play in educating their son. In 1792, Thomas Jefferson had assured the boy's grandfather: "I should with great zeal do anything I could in aid of the education of your grandsons." Remembering that promise in 1819, Jefferson arranged for young Cary to attend a new academy in Charlottesville.[7]

Stack

The Charlottesville Academy emerged from Jefferson's bid to recruit Thomas Cooper as the University's first professor. While waiting on the slow construction of the institution, Jefferson proposed that Cooper run an academy to prepare adolescents for the University. Cooper preferred to entrust the academy to his protégé, Gerard E. Stack, an accomplished linguist specializing in ancient Greek and Latin. Born in Ireland and educated at Trinity College Dublin, Stack had migrated to the United States and taught at Pennsylvania's Carlisle College, where Cooper became his patron. Visiting Charlottesville in early 1819, Stack impressed Jefferson as "the ablest classical teacher in America and . . . an amiable, modest man." In May, Stack opened the academy with fifteen boys as students. To board them, Jefferson engaged a Frenchman named Peter Laporte, loaning him $500 to improve a leased building. Investing family in this experiment, Jefferson recruited his grandson Francis Eppes as well as Wilson Miles Cary.[8]

Jefferson closely managed the school, applying his pet theories. He directed how Stack should teach Greek and Latin, and mandated French for all conversation in the boardinghouse. He also directed Laporte to provide sparse meals, better suited for an old man than growing boys. No tea, coffee, alcohol, or dessert, and scant meat irritated boys raised on the lavish meals of gentry life. Jefferson also denied any summer vacation, allowing only a holiday in winter, beginning in mid-December and running through January. During the dog days of a Virginia summer, he expected boys to study doggedly. Jefferson often visited the school, a student recalled, "to make some more regulations and to examine us in the different branches of education." Another reported, "That venerable and great man attends to our proceedings very exactly, and often expresses the deepest concern for our welfare."[9]

A sunny optimist about his own ideas put in practice, Jefferson saw what he wanted in the new school. In July 1819, he praised the students: "It suffices to signify a wish as to their diet, conduct and general deportment to secure an immediate and punctual conformity." Jefferson added that Stack's "fatherly demeanor too towards his pupils engages their affections and their obedience." This compliance, he predicted, would carry over into the University, forming "a nucleus of order for assimilation of all new comers to themselves, which I hope will fix the character of the future school." Jefferson was half-right, for the Charlottesville Academy did anticipate the University's future but in ways that defied his hopes.[10]

The boys bristled at the strange rules and scant diet of their new school, especially when the summer of 1819 turned blistering. Writing to Jefferson, Stack lamented a "situation where intense heat and a tainted atmosphere made serious inroads on the mental and bodily powers, which the declining health of myself and boys too seriously prove." Although Jefferson ignored the complaint, he escaped the boys' wrath because of his thick coat of public reverence and mountaintop perch above the village. Students instead vented frustrations on Stack and Laporte, who were lower in status and nearer in altitude.[11]

Stack feared crossing powerful and indulgent parents, who expected an orderly school without physical coercion. So he simply stopped trying. One student noted, "He is the best natured man I ever saw & suffers his boys to do what they please." Another added, "he is so feeble minded that the least thing will discourage him." Intimidated by Jefferson's dogmatic assurance and authoritative meddling, Stack turned down invitations to dine at Monticello from fear that his "quivering nerves" could not handle the stress.[12]

In October 1819, student discontent erupted over bad food served at

Laporte's boardinghouse. Contemptuous of Laporte as a social inferior, Hore Browse Trist complained that he "had the impudence to *invite* me, as he termed it, out of his house because I found a maggot among his dirty victuals. I think I should have kicked him on the spot, had it not been that Mr. J[efferson] patronized him."[13]

Trist organized a party featuring three bottles of wine and three of whiskey consumed with six other students, including Francis Eppes and Wilson Miles Cary. "After making ourselves pretty merry, we agreed to frighten our landlord, who had incurred our displeasure by giving us nothing we could eat," Trist reported. The drunken boys turned their coats "wrong side out, marched around the town 2 or 3 times," hooting and hollering to awaken inhabitants. Gathering around Laporte's house, they hurled stones to smash the windows. "Nothing was talked of the next day but our bad conduct," Trist boasted. But, he added, Laporte "went prancing up to Monticello in his wrath, [and] told fifty lies against me in particular." Trist noted that the riot "displeased the old patriarch very much." Jefferson sent a note to the boys, withdrawing their welcome at Monticello but relented when his daughter Martha intervened on their behalf. In Virginia, the genteel ties of class and kin trumped discipline even for Jefferson.[14]

Word of the riot spread, threatening Jefferson's academy and, by extension, the precious new university. His pious enemies spread riotous tales to demonstrate the folly of Jefferson's educational notions. To deflect blame, Jefferson suddenly distanced himself from the school that he had created and overseen, casting Stack and Laporte as entirely independent. Writing to Cooper, Jefferson derided Stack as "hypochondriac, suspicious, indecisive, and so totally without nerve as to be incapable of keeping up any order or discipline in his school." Stack and Laporte became scapegoats for the troubled school.[15]

Joseph C. Cabell endorsed Jefferson's retreat from public support: "Stack's School has a great reputation for disorder & it was wise in Mr. Jefferson to draw off as he has done." To counteract critics, Cabell added, "I tell them Mr. Jefferson & his friends no longer recommend the school and disapprove of its want of discipline." Belatedly showing some spunk, Stack published a newspaper advertisement, reiterating, Cabell complained, "to the World that he is under the patronage of the Visitors of the University." [16]

In March 1820, Stack sought to bolster his failing school by engaging Thomas Ragland, a young Virginian, to teach math. Alas, Ragland had the wrong background and temper to restrain boys. A close friend to Nicholas P. Trist, Ragland roomed with his brother Hore Browse Trist, who had stirred up the other students. Ragland regretted that Charlottesville celebrated the Fourth of July that year with unusual sobriety. Preferring the more "tumultuous" festivity of past years, when "Bacchus" had reigned in the streets, Ragland lamented that the "sober Multitude . . . retired with long faces. They did not seem to have caught the spirit of the occasion." [17]

Ragland had attended the other university founded by Jefferson: the United States Military Academy at West Point. Designed by the president to counter Federalist dominance in the army, West Point initially nurtured a republican individualism that favored the self-assertion of gentlemen defending honor. The beau ideal of republican gentility, Ragland won favor from the erratic superintendent, Alden Partridge, who promoted him from cadet to instructor of mathematics despite his having hurled a chair at the academy's doctor. Partridge's irregularities and favoritism outraged the secretary of war, who sacked the superintendent in 1817. [18]

The new superintendent, Major Sylvanus Thayer, was a Yankee disciplinarian determined to redefine honor as collective to the corps and requiring the subordination of personal interests to national service. The cadets bristled when investigated for beating a common teamster, whom they regarded as insulting, and they erupted when a new drill instructor manhandled cadets who defied orders. "Officers who are governed by blows must be destitute of all that should characterize a soldier or a man of honor," they complained. Rather than enforce the new rules as an instructor should, Ragland joined four cadets on a committee that wrote an angry protest to Thayer. "Men of honor could not have been otherwise than indignant at such insults as had been offered them," the five declared. In November 1818, Thayer promptly expelled them as mutinous.[19]

Outraged, the militant five appealed to President Monroe, Congress, and, through print, the public. Defending individual pride, they preached, "The sentiments of honor should be cherished; so that . . . the noble soul, jealous of its rights, preserves its purity separate from the sordidness of life." Posing as heirs to the revolution, the five sought to expose "the monarchical ideas of [the academy's] present ruler" bent on "exercising the most galling tyranny." Ragland added that they could "discriminate between the obligations of the American soldier, and the tame submission of the Russian peasant."[20]

In early 1819, Congress and the president vindicated Thayer and faulted the five militants. In disgust, Ragland resigned from the army, bidding "a grateful riddance from the chains of slavery." He returned to Charlottesville to study law with an attorney while teaching math at Stack's academy, where the students lionized his defiance. Leaving the school in August 1820, Ragland moved to Jefferson County to practice law and marry the sister of another of the five militant cadets. Five years later, Nicholas P. Trist learned "of the sudden death of his friend Ragland who died in twenty four hours from the commencement of his illness."[21]

Bremo

At the end of 1819, Ellen Wayles Randolph visited her aunt and uncle, Virginia and Wilson J. Cary, in Fluvanna County for Christmas. Ellen found them irritated with their son Miles for participating in the riotous party against Laporte. Ellen held back from defending the school rather than "involve myself in difficulties with the K.O.K, whose favor is of much importance, and who we thought looked on me with a frowning brow during a ten minute's visit he has paid since my arrival." She invented a grandiose title for him: "Cocke by the grace of God, of Fluvanna, Prince Lord of Cumberland, Defender of the Faith." Ellen and her parents admired his talents, mocked his religious certitude, and feared his resolve. She anticipated that Cocke planned to take over the Charlottesville Academy as Jefferson retreated. By transforming that school, Cocke meant to sway the future university.[22]

Cocke's prototype was the "seminary" he had founded in 1817 at his Bremo Plantation to educate his children and the sons of genteel friends, who admired the general's self-discipline and high moral standards. One father needed help in weaning his son "from effeminacy to hardihood of habit.... For this I am indebted to you. Brought up otherwise, myself, I could not have denied to him, the tenderness and indulgencies that my parents had granted to me."[23]

A demanding man, General Cocke could never keep a teacher for long. His instructors either balked at Cocke's meddling or disappointed his expectations for classical learning, religious piety, and strict discipline. "You will find great difficulty in finding, *in one individual*, a good preacher, a good tutor, and a good man," a friend warned Cocke. One departing teacher assured the general: "From the direction of the studies and the government of the school being entirely in your hands, the discharge of my duty from the first became extremely difficult and finally impossible."[24]

In March 1820, Cocke attended the Albemarle County Court and seized the opportunity to redirect the Charlottesville Academy along the lines of the Bremo Seminary. With magistrates and locals as witnesses, Cocke assembled Stack's students and obliged them to sign their submission to a tough new set of rules, which demanded study rather than dissipation and forbade any gathering of more than two of them in the village streets. A week later, however, Cocke's son reported that his fellow students "pay no more attention to their lessons than they did before the rules were made." Alarmed and angry, Cocke hastened back to Charlottesville to visit the school, where he "saw deplorable evidence of a total want of dignity & authority in Stack with his Pupils, but they are a[s] fine [a] set of boys as I ever saw together." Reserving fault for Stack, Cocke vindicated sons of his own gentry class.[25]

Even the ban on alcohol had collapsed. One student reported sauntering down the Charlottesville streets with a "few Glasses in my hat crown," holding a bottle of rum under his left arm and another of wine under the right. His hands grasped two pitchers for eggnog and punch. Alas, this "very humorous comedy [turned] to a very deep Tragedy" in the morning. "I scarcely ever felt so very unwell in the whole course of my life. . . . My intestines resounded like the distant roaring of Cannon. This dose was very near punching my brains through my Skull."[26]

The Charlottesville Academy unraveled in August 1820, when Stack's students rioted again, lashing out against leading citizens who had prosecuted them for a drunken frolic. The village newspaper complained that the rioters had insulted "our peaceable citizens . . . in the grossest manner" and hurled stones and bricks through house and shop windows. In the morning, a justice tried to arrest three suspects, but they fled. A week later, Stack published a notice, abruptly closing his school. Apparently, he acted under pressure from on high, for he fired a cryptic parting salvo "that he has never stooped to kiss the font of power—he abhors tyranny in any form and despises the mean and malicious." Perhaps he meant Jefferson—or Cocke—or both. Moving to Richmond, Stack opened another academy for young gentlemen, promising "mild and parental" rules.[27]

No such mildness prevailed at "Bremo Seminary," which Cocke revived as the Charlottesville Academy collapsed. His rules required daily attendance at morning and evening prayers "with gravity and reverence during the whole of that service." To discourage dissipation, Cocke limited every boy to just $5 of pocket money per term. The school barred drinking, gambling, card playing, quarreling, cursing, and fighting, while requiring neatness, politeness, and decorum. Challenging the group defiance of Virginia schoolboys, Cocke obliged every student to reveal, when questioned, "all that he may know, as to any particular offence, of which either himself, or any of his fellow pupils, may be suspected." By requiring boys to inform and by inflicting "corporeal punishment" on those who refused, the rules doubly assailed the personal honor cherished by the sons of gentlemen.[28]

The Bremo rules provoked Jefferson's son-in-law, Thomas Mann Randolph, who defended individualism and deism. Randolph insisted that Cocke's school would produce "first Actors, and next Hypocrites," deceptive pretenders to morality and piety. Randolph believed that Cocke, as a "Visitor of the University of Virginia, might have been expected . . . to limit religion to the cultivation of the Moral Faculties and the admiration of the Creator in the study of the immutable Laws by which he governs Nature." Randolph regarded science as the true faith: "To increase our admiration of the Creator by studying the wonders of creation is a sublime Religion in itself." He preferred "Silent admiration" of the cosmos rather than prayer, which he considered a silly and idle attempt to sway the perpetual and perfect design of the Creator.[29]

While dismayed by Cocke's emphasis on faith, Randolph "object[ed] much more as a parent to corporeal punishment, which I deem totally inadmissible in a Republic at this enlightened period. Excite emulation, infuse true taste, and create enthusiasm for learning by rousing and stimulating curiosity." And he denounced compelling students to inform as dishonorable: "Americans are not accustomed to consider systematic, combined resistance to injuries as a crime."[30]

Cocke and Randolph defined a polarity that resurfaced when Jefferson's University opened in 1825. While Jefferson initially shaped the rules, Cocke bided his time, waiting for the right moment to restructure the University and reshape students—just as he had tried to do with Stack's failed school. Jefferson had intended that academy to serve as a test run for the University. So it did by offering a dress rehearsal for the student resistance that would stagger the new institution and for Cocke's bid to control higher education in Virginia.

Mother

After Stack's academy dissolved in 1820, Wilson Miles Cary continued to cycle through the private academies of the Piedmont before heading off to the College of William & Mary: the worst place for an indolent boy. Easily distracted, Miles became more idle and dissolute with every move. Father Cary wrote to his wife, "I hope our son will exert himself and not suffer boys of his own age to outstrip him entirely in the road of improvement." But, Cary quickly added, "I would not wish him to be a mere bookworm, as I expect him to become an active member of society." Ambivalent about learning, gentlemen sought just enough to display their sons in society but not too much, lest they become introverts.[31]

In 1822, Virginia worried that her husband grew thinner and coughed violently. He died a year later, and she had him buried at Monticello, where the couple had married eighteen years before. Long passive as her husband mismanaged their affairs, Virginia Cary felt pleasantly surprised at her new ability to run household and plantation. She confided to Louisa Cocke, "I have been so little accustomed to having my way in such important measures, that I have felt strangely fearful of doing wrong when left to myself. However, to let you into a secret, this feeling wears off daily & I begin to think myself quite discreet enough to be trusted with the government of a family."[32]

Her new self-assurance impressed friends and relatives. In 1825, Martha Jefferson Randolph wrote to her daughter Ellen: "With regard to your Aunt Cary, her affairs are very prosperous, and she [is] in fine spirits, handsomer and more agreeable than I have seen her for years." Ellen's sister Virginia R. Trist marveled that Aunt Cary had become "a perfect hurricane! [with] a voice like thunder & movements as sudden & boisterous as a gale of wind." Mary E. Terrell assured Louisa Cocke, "We have seen a great deal of our dear Mrs. Cary & love her more than ever. I must tell you of a most disastrous dilemma, from which she relieved us all the other day." Cary came with the Monticello family to dine at the Terrell home in Charlottesville, but Anne Randolph Bankhead's drunken and abusive husband rode up as an uninvited and unwanted guest. In vain, Terrell begged Charles Bankhead to leave. Then Cary pretended that she needed a male escort to visit another household, so she obliged him to accompany her—an invitation no would-be gentleman could decline. Virginia Cary knew how to deploy moral authority within gendered conventions to sway men.[33]

Her self-confidence sometimes wavered as the material world brought more suffering and woe. She confessed to longing for death, to find a "peaceful haven." Catching herself, she added, "But these are sinful thoughts, God check them with all my power. Useless & unimportant as I am, my being continued in this state of being so long is a proof that my Heavenly Father has something for me to *do* or to *suffer*." A month later, she was dozing one morning when a commanding voice delivered a divine message: "Awake! Why sleepest thou, when the task is already appointed & the time is short!"[34]

Virginia Cary's piety tested her bonds with her sister-in-law Martha Jefferson Randolph. Each woman felt baffled by the other's convictions after Cary renounced as "infidel" the beliefs of her Randolph childhood and Monticello connections. Awed by Martha's superior education and powerful mind, Virginia added, "The searcher of hearts knows that I feel my immeasurable inferiority to her, in everything but that grace which is His gift. Should this step alienate me from that [be]loved family, as my first public profession of religion did, I shall be nearly alone in the world." When her daughter Louisa neared death, Virginia wrote to Martha exulting in God's will for taking her away to enjoy "endless bliss." Martha denounced "a letter that I think absolutely *monstrous*, in which, true to her character, she acts the heroine over the *death bed* of her child." Martha favored a philosophical resignation "to the bitter dispensations of providence," so she dismissed Virginia's mode of coping as "downright ranting for stage effect." Martha's daughter Mary wryly noted that, during visits to Charlottesville, her Aunt Cary led a "life of religious dissipation" by attending "sermons by day and prayer meetings by night."[35]

Ever persistent, Virginia hoped that a new religious faith could bolster Martha's morale, eroded by the financial woes of her family. In August 1825, Martha wrote a despondent letter that, to Virginia, "unveiled a state of mental distress, the view of which has roused all the sympathies of my nature." The following March, Virginia visited Monticello to console Martha after the death of her daughter Anne Bankhead: "I cannot describe my sorrow at seeing the ravages that grief has made in my beloved sister. She has opened her heart to me & it is plain that even her heroic strength of mind cannot long support her, unless some more potent principle is added to it."[36]

In 1828, Virginia Cary published *Letters on Female Character Addressed to a Young Lady, on the Death of Her Mother*, which advised an imagined young mother on how to manage difficult children and complex households by promoting Christian faith. A pioneering female author in Virginia, she won a wide readership by insisting that women could sway their families while appearing submissive to their husbands. "Let all your actions be *feminine*, not weak and vacillating, but unobtrusive and gentle." A champion of subtlety exercised within the family, she disdained publicly assertive women as "erring spirits, who grasp at more than their allotted portion of power" by seeking an "equality of rights." Cary insisted that woman was "*formed for man*, and therefore must continue in contented subordination to his authority." Apparently recalling her husband's inept management of their plantation, Virginia assured an imagined relative, "I had rather hear you pitied as a submissive wife to a strict husband, than applauded as having usurped the government from the hands of an incompetent person." She regarded the modest, suffering, and enduring woman as a powerful performer of inner authenticity, which ultimately would lead men to do the right things.[37]

At first glance, her message of feminine subordination seems at odds with her success as an independent widow. Hardly passive, Cary was a strong woman seeking a public voice in a culture that insisted on female inferiority. As she saw it, genteel women needed to navigate within social constraints rather than incur the risks of attacking them.

Cary advised young mothers to discipline their children, whom she deemed "young candidates for immortality." Alas, she concluded, most Virginia families preferred immorality. Their sons went away to school with powerful wills encouraged by indulgent parents: "The blame of many an utter failure in education may be traced back to the mismanagement of early childhood." And when adolescent sons came home during school vacations, they enjoyed "such unlimited license" that they returned "to school totally unhinged from every salutary restriction and prompt enough to rebel against efficient discipline." To this she attributed "the insubordination so notorious in Virginia seminaries of learning."[38]

Cary especially dreaded the corrupting power that white boys enjoyed over enslaved girls. "Self-will is fostered from the very cradle," producing relentless exploitation of "the wretched beings who are trained to minister to this over-mastering sin." Casting sons as both predators and prey of immoral servants, she added, "The youth of our state are accustomed from infancy to have their whims gratified, and their irregular desires indulged by the menials who swarm around them." Barely veiling the sexual innuendo, Cary added, "The infant despot enforces his lawless authority over his allotted victim, and thus encourages all the most malignant vices of his nature." She urged mothers to protect the enslaved from sexual predation, while firmly keeping them at work and praising God.[39]

Cary's pointed advice illuminates her relationship with her son Wilson Miles Cary, who grew up selfish, dissipated, lazy, and willful. She explains her own failure by dwelling on reining in the childish will, reinforcing school discipline, and blocking young masters from preying on enslaved girls. In effect, she exhorts her readers: do what I failed to do before it is too late.

After just a year at William & Mary, Miles abruptly left college to prepare for the new university by studying "the *dark* & *dismal* recesses of the Greek Language" with Charlottesville's Episcopal minister. Two family friends, John Hartwell Cocke and Reverend Walter Timberlake, helped finance Miles's higher education by selling some family slaves. Timberlake explained to Cocke, "It is wished by his mama & himself too that I should make sale of some Slaves in Williamsburg & I am told by him you approve of the Plan." Cocke and Timberlake led Fluvanna's chapter of the American Colonization Society, a tepid form of antislavery activity that linked emancipation to deportation. They set aside their vague antislavery convictions to help a young man of their social circle pursue higher education. In Virginia, elite education hinged upon the labor and sale of slaves. Given that the lazy Miles was the beneficiary, the brokered slaves suffered for a bad cause.[40]

Nineteen years old, and superficially educated at nearly a dozen schools and colleges, and expelled from at least two of them, Cary fit in with the first students at the new university. Growing up with slavery, Cary learned mastery by practicing on enslaved children. Mingling with gentlemen, he cultivated their manners and vices, becoming charming and charismatic without developing substance in mind or character. Over the years, he mastered dissimulation by ignoring his mother's pious admonitions while thanking her eloquently for them. A young lawyer considered Miles "a very fine looking fellow & is moreover very clever." Martha Jefferson Randolph knew him better as "*plausible* (they say *clever*), vain, self-conceited, with ungovernable *appetites*." Those appetites would feed on the society of other young men gathered to open the University in 1825.[41]

Design

Virginia's leaders meant to educate a new generation to counter supposed northern cultural and political aggression. But they worried that their way of life bred a great contradiction: young men without the self-discipline needed to defend the South. Writing to his father in 1823, John Hartwell Cocke, Jr., denounced his fellow students as lazy and dissipated: "I[t] would really distress you to see how little emulation, nay how little shame there is among the rising generation of young Virginians. I hope sincerely the Old Dominion has some firmer support . . . than the talents or industry of the present students of William & Mary."[42]

Not even a Cocke could transcend the weaknesses of Virginia youth. In July 1822, the faculty informed his father that young John had "committed an act of indiscretion which has frequently been the source of much disorder in this College." Later that month, General Cocke opened another distressing letter, this one about his younger son Philip St. George Tucker Cocke. His teacher at an academy reported that the boy's "impudence" and "obstinate determination not to learn anything. . . . rendered it absolutely necessary that the rod should be used."[43]

Jefferson and Cabell needed to find a way to govern southern students, or their University would fail. In 1823, Cabell wrote to an expert on European education for advice: "I am particularly anxious to be informed on the best mode of governing a large mass of students, without the use of the bayonet." He wondered "whether any successful cases have occurred, in which the students have been made the instruments of governing themselves," for so Jefferson proposed to do at the University of Virginia.[44]

Jefferson feared student disorder as the greatest threat to the University. In 1822, he listed inadequate state funding as his first challenge "but a second, a greater, and a more desperate one, is the spirit of insubordination and self-will which seizes our youth so early in life as to defeat their education, and the too little control exercised by indulgent parents." Jefferson knew that student turmoil could ruin the new university: "I look to it with dismay in our institution, as a breaker ahead, which I am far from being confident we shall be able to weather." He concluded, "The article of discipline is the most difficult in American education. Premature ideas of independence, too little repressed by parents, beget a spirit of insubordination, which is the great obstacle to science with us, and a principal cause of its decay since the revolution."[45]

It is jarring to read Jefferson write of "premature independence" by the young and of postrevolutionary decay, for we associate him with confidence in people and progress. We also credit him with the national Declaration of Independence. In fact, Jefferson was never entirely comfortable with people as they were. Instead, he sought to improve the next generation through reformed education. He worried, however, that Virginia's adolescents were too spoiled by parental indulgence and bad schools to submit to a proper education.[46]

Jefferson hoped to enlist student consent through a more engaging and less constraining government for the University, just as he had done for citizens as president. In the Rockfish Gap Report, he rejected governing young men by "the degrading motive of fear." Jefferson explained, "Hardening them to disgrace, to corporal punishments, and servile humiliations cannot be the best process for producing erect character." He concluded, "The human character is susceptible of other incitements to correct conduct, more worthy of employ, and of better effect. Pride of character, laudable ambition, and moral dispositions are innate correctives of the indiscretions of that lively age."[47]

Devoted to Enlightenment principles, Jefferson believed that he could arrange buildings and rules gently, but surely, to reshape young men. His architectural design rejected the tradition of one big college building, such as the core structure at William & Mary. "Much observation & reflection on these institutions have long convinced me that the large and crouded buildings in which youths are pent up, are equally unfriendly to health, to study, to manners, morals & order." As an alternative, Jefferson designed an "academical village," which interspersed student rooms and professors' pavilions and arranged them in parallel rows, facing across a lawn, with a grand Rotunda as the head and lynchpin connecting the rows at the north end. Behind each facing row lay a second which featured "hotels" as well as more student rooms; the hotels would provide dining rooms and cleaning services for students. In this precisely calibrated decentralization, the architecture expressed in microcosm his conception of the Union. Equal in size, the pavilions stood in for the states, and the Rotunda served as a central meeting place, a Congress, for those functional equals.[48]

Jefferson claimed that placing faculty pavilions among student dorms would promote "peace & quiet." He predicted, "It would afford that quiet retirement so friendly to study, and lessen the dangers of fire, infection & tumult. Every professor would be the police officer of the students adjacent to his own lodge." He also expected that foreign professors would have a mystique that could command greater respect from students.[49]

In another measure to promote order, Jefferson located his university far from any cities, which he distrusted as crowded dens of strife and vice. Far better, he thought, to isolate students in a rural setting in the heart of the state, and ideally no more than four miles from Monticello and subject to his daily visit and supervision. Such a university would provide "the selected society of a great city separated from the dissipations and levities of its ephemeral insects."[50]

Jefferson also sought to reduce the grievances that led students to riot elsewhere: the wretched meals offered by central dining halls and a mandated curriculum that trapped boys in unwanted classes. He proposed free market solutions to both. The University would sub-contract meal services to hotelkeepers, who had to compete for student customers. If a keeper stinted on bread or served rancid beef, a student could shift to another hotel, sparing the Visitors from his complaints. The institution similarly allowed students to enroll in, and pay for, instruction in only those subjects that interested him. Jefferson assured a potential student: "This will certainly be the fundamental law of our University, to leave every one free to attend whatever branches of instruction he wants, and to decline what he does not want."[51]

Jefferson also rejected the controversial informant rule that had so troubled John Augustine Smith's presidency at the College of William & Mary. University policy declared, "When testimony is required from a student, it shall be voluntary and not on oath, and the obligation to give it shall be left to his own sense of right." But Jefferson proposed to include some students in the discipline of their peers by forming a "board of six Censors, to be named by the Faculty, from among the most discreet of the students." Given jurisdiction over minor infractions, they would "enquire into the facts, propose the minor punishment which they think proportioned to the offence, and to make report thereof to the Professors for their approbation."[52]

Although cast as liberal by public opinion, the university's rules were longer on forbidden behaviors than on concessions to student autonomy. Students could neither possess nor consume any alcohol or tobacco. No student could keep a servant, horse, dog, or gun, or gamble at cards or dice. Anyone who dueled faced immediate and permanent expulsion. Every student must immediately open his door and expose his room to inspection by a professor or risk having the door broken down. Jefferson packaged strict rules within an appearance of indulgence that misled the public more than students. But making rules was easier than enforcing them.[53]

Rascality

The University opened on March 7, 1825, with only forty students, but twenty more arrived during the next two weeks. They were delayed by the deep mud of roads after, Jefferson explained, a "month of almost incessant rain." He praised the students as "a very fine parcel of young men," but conceded that they "come in generally most wretchedly prepared." The University paid a high price for the lack of good preparatory schools in Virginia. The Visitors suspended entrance requirements in mathematics and Latin to accept every paying customer. The Visitors needed all the fees they could capture for operating costs, having spent all of their state subsidy on buildings. The lax admission standards compelled professors to engage in remedial education better suited to an academy. On March 22, Jefferson reported that the students were "half idle, all for want of books," as these had not arrived from a Boston bookseller. "The University has commenced, a little hobblingly," Cocke noted.[54]

The students were young southern gentlemen of the sort that made trouble at every college. Of the 123 students who enrolled by the end of 1825, 108 came from Virginia and 13 more from elsewhere in the South. Only one hailed from a northern state and another sailed from England. The *Richmond Enquirer* celebrated a few young Virginians who left Yale to join a new university that was supposed to repatriate southern minds from northern institutions.[55]

The high fees and cost of living in Charlottesville made the University the most expensive in the Union: $400 a year. One student complained, "There is no college in the United States where the initiation fees are so great and the students so imposed upon as here." His father grumbled that the University cost twice as much as Hampden-Sydney College. That cost, and the lack of scholarships, restricted attendance to sons of wealth.[56]

Tempting fate, Jefferson sought to maximize the number of students in order to make a public splash and ensure a healthy revenue from tuition. Wildly optimistic, he expected to attract at least 500 students drawn from "the whole Southern & Western countries." Five hundred students would make the University seven times as large as William & Mary at its peak. Given that the dorms could only accommodate 218 students, it was unclear where the rest would live. But even 218 was too many for John Holt Rice, who thought it folly "that a very large number of young men, but partially disciplined, should be assembled at any one Seminary." Thanks to high costs and hard times in Virginia, enrollment never reached Jefferson's fantasy in his lifetime.[57]

At first, the students seemed surprisingly tractable. In July, Jefferson declared victory, praising the success of his measures to mollify and motivate students: "We receive and treat our students as gentlemen and friends. They meet us gratefully on that ground and endeavor to merit and to cherish the respect we manifest for them." He added, "We have had no occasion, as yet, even to form our board of Censors, on whom we shall chiefly rely for the preservation of order. It is agreed, by all who judge from their own inspection, and not from the idle tales they hear, that they have never known a more orderly collection of young men." He felt vindicated in his conviction that a little government worked best.[58]

The Harrison brothers, Gessner and Tiffin, knew better. They came east across the Blue Ridge from the Shenandoah Valley, a land of churches and pious people unlike Albemarle. At the University, Gessner noted, "This is to me a strange country." The brothers felt repelled by "the arrogant pride and haughty demeanor" of most students, who came from the state's eastern plantations. Loud, riotous drinking and profanity disturbed every day and night, including on Sundays to the horror of the Harrisons. Gessner lamented, "I see all around me continually examples of vice and an utter want of morals," and contempt for "anything like religion." To avoid trouble, the brothers tried "to live in monkish retirement in the midst of such numbers."[59]

Rather than produce harmony, Jefferson's design and rules increased defiance. During the University's construction, David Watson predicted that the dorms invited disorder. "They are too small & they will be too public for study; for the fine walk in front of them, under the projection of the terrace, will be a thorough fare" and "the student will see &

hear his idle fellow students walking & talking & sporting within arms length of him, every moment in the day."[60]

Instead of controlling students, placing faculty pavilions among the dorms exposed professors to harassment at night. In 1824, a newspaper writer examined the layout and aptly predicted, "The professors will fear the students more than the students fear them." Two years later, faculty faulted Jefferson's dispersed design: "Favoured by the darkness of the arcades, . . . a single Rioter may now pass through the University at night and by shouting, knocking at the doors, ringing Bells or firing gunpowder annoy the whole Establishment for hours. Nor will he be questioned unless a Professor rises from his Bed to go in pursuit," which was futile "for the means of escape are so numerous."[61]

Jefferson also had miscast Charlottesville as a bucolic haven from sin. In fact, it had plenty of raucous taverns to entice students to linger, drink, gamble, and fight. One traveler "got to Charlottesville early enough in the evening to be completely disgusted before bed time with a place, which is denounced by many of its own inhabitants as the most vicious and dissipated even in Virginia." Indeed, Jefferson had advised St. George Tucker to spend a night at Monticello: "It will relieve you from the heats and drunken noise of Charlottesville."[62]

While big enough for sin, the town was too small to offer the cosmopolitan attractions of a city: theaters, art galleries, and museums. A critic declared, "The locality is insulated, and the constant sameness of the company, of fellow-students only, produces the bad results of tedious and too close influence between the students." A student said, "Instead of attending to their Books, they are sauntering about from one day's end to another in all kind of rascality and mischief." Referring to the codifier of card games, a critic blasted the students as "more devoted to *Hoyle* than to *Euclid*," and "equal [to] some of our lawyers and legislators in managing their cards."[63]

Rather than commanding respect, as Jefferson had expected, the foreign professors reaped contempt. Lacking experience as teachers, they struggled to master their subjects while failing to control students. "Our

want of skill in the management of young men was soon but too manifest," George Tucker confessed. One potential student balked at matriculating, reasoning "as the Professors are all Foreigners, they will want
[the] thick sort of Books." Their superior learning offered no offset for
foreign accents and inferior gentility (by Virginia standards). Used to
deferential and diligent British students, the professors rebuked young
Virginians who came ill prepared for class. Sensitive to insult, students
turned against Professor Long because, one noted, he "satirizes their
ignorance and mistakes." Emmet protested when a student prepared
to leave class without permission. With contempt and condescension,
the student responded, "Sir, I think it is sufficient for you to know that
it is my wish to leave the Institution. . . . The abrupt manner in which
you spoke to me does not become you in your present occupation." This
student treated Emmet as his hired hand.[64]

Nor did substituting hotels for a central dining hall avert conflict.
While the competing hotels did avoid clashes over bad food in 1825, they
provided havens for gambling, drinking, and plotting mischief because
the keepers dared not alienate their student clientele. As with interspers-
ing pavilions among dorms, the hotels enhanced student power.[65]

Worse still was Jefferson's board of censors. In July, he deemed that
board unnecessary because the students were so orderly. In fact, none
would serve on it. Professors explained, "Even the best students regard
it with odium as only calculated to make them Spies upon each other."
The student Edmund W. Hubard denounced "Tattlers" as worse than
the many cheating gamblers and boastful brawlers among his peers:
"They pump you of everything you know, when you least expect such a
thing; ask your opinion of various persons, &c., so they continue like a
Fly to glut themselves." Noting this "stigma of the deepest hue to give
testimony against a fellow student," Robley Dunglison concluded that
it was "vain for us to expect any co-operation in the discipline of the
institution from them."[66]

Heat

As at Stack's school, Jefferson denied students a summer vacation, breaking with the practice of other colleges. University rules offered only a single vacation of six weeks in the winter, beginning on December 15. Alas, Jefferson's pretty little dorm rooms baked in the summer sun because of their low roofs and poor ventilation. Writing from Britain in 1824, Gilmer had predicted, "If the heat is insufferable in England, what must it be in our July, August, &c., when there is to be no vacation?" He concluded, "Your short vacation (6 weeks) has done immense mischief and it cannot last a year. Think of 200 boys festering in one of those little rooms in August or July. The very idea is suffocation."[67]

The students resented staying put while friends and kin were relaxing at fashionable spas in the cooler mountains of western Virginia. Trapped at the University, they began to act out. On the morning of June 18, professors condemned the "abandoned miscreants" who had, during the night, "shamefully mutilated" cows belonging to University officials. Ten days later, the faculty received a petition signed by most of the students "praying for a vacation of 10 days or more" starting on July 4. The petitioners cited "the unusual length of the session and the immoderate heat of the weather."[68]

But Jefferson did not budge. After the University's late start, he insisted that students needed to make up for lost time. He worried that dispersion, after just three months, would unravel new habits of study, and Jefferson wanted to score points against William & Mary, which he derided as a malarial hellhole in summer. Keeping students at the University through the summer reinforced his insistence that Charlottesville was the healthiest and happiest place on earth. An open University also could catch and recruit more students as they returned to Virginia for the summer from northern schools. Jefferson vowed "to avoid the common abuse by which two or three months of the year are lost to the Students, under the name of Vacations, the thread of their studies is broken, and more time still to be expended in recovering it. This loss, at their ages from 16 and upwards, is irreparable to them."[69]

The summer of 1825 proved exceptionally hot even by Virginia standards. On July 20, a Charlottesville resident reported, "the heat is more
excessive than was ever felt before." Gessner Harrison complained, "The
heat is almost intolerable, when the whole atmosphere seems fiery. . . .
The nights, the noon, & mornings are all hot!" In August, Harrison
could not study because it was "Hotter than I ever felt in my life."[70]

Student disorder surged as temperatures soared. In Charlottesville,
Mary E. Terrell complained, "O this University!!! What a place it
is—a perfect vortex of pleasure; it seems to attract & engulph everything & everybody." The students were "revolutionizing everything
& the watch word in manners & morals has become *a la mode de
l'Universite*." Jefferson's former secretary, Isaac A. Coles, warned
his friend Cocke, "Swearing, Drinking & Gambling seem to be the
fashionable accomplishments of the day, and a Boy is more distinguished as an *elegant Loo Player*, than for classical attainments. If
half that I hear is true, the place ought spe[e]dily to be burnt down
as a horrible nuisance."[71]

Jefferson, however, could not hear the clamor, assuring a friend
that "the University may be truly said to be as quiet as a Convent."
On September 18, his grandson-in-law, Nicholas P. Trist, shattered
Jefferson's illusions in a detailed letter. Trist reported that the over-
matched professors failed to keep attendance and sometimes skipped
lectures. Only half the students attended class, and few could study at
night because of the drunken noise. Most "did little else but frolic."
Trist's letter shocked Jefferson into action. He compelled the professors
to meet and adopt new measures to enforce discipline. They promptly
scheduled rigorous exams for December and imposed new fines for
drinking, gambling, and nocturnal disturbances.[72]

Irritated by the new pronouncements, students staged raucous protests to demonstrate that the faculty could not control them. At midnight, masked students took over the lawn in front of the pavilions,
loudly "inviting and defying the notice of the Faculty," Tucker noted.
Martha J. Randolph described one rioter as "a rich *fool*," who cursed
"the European professors" and challenged them "to come out that they

George Tucker (1775–1861), by Thomas Sully
(Courtesy of the Fralin Museum of Art at the University of Virginia)

might be taken to the pump" for a dousing. One night, an observer reported, students pushed an ox up the steps of the rotunda and left it at the top "to amuse the students and to awake the Professors by its noisy bellowings." When groggy professors tried to investigate, every student denied knowing anything about the trouble.[73]

On September 30, students hurled a deck of cards and a bottle filled with urine to smash through a window and into the dining room of a faculty pavilion. Professor George Long was serving tea to two matrons and two unusually orderly students, including Gessner Harrison. Evidently, the rioters despised, and sought to intimidate, students who became teachers' pets by studying instead of cavorting.[74]

On the next night, October 1, at least fourteen students donned masks and old clothes and gathered on the central lawn of the University. Some chanted, "Down with the European Professors!" and "Damn the European Professors," while the rest made a racket. Venturing out of their pavilions, Tucker and Emmet confronted the rioters. Trying to unmask the loudest one, Tucker grabbed his shirt. The culprit hollered, "The damn'd rascal has torn my shirt," while his friends hurled sticks, bottles, and a brick at the professors. Tucker got the worst of it. A scandalized Presbyterian remarked, "They gave him a drubbing and sent him off. Well done boys, governed by Virginia honour!"[75]

Servant

Why had Tucker ventured into the fray? Student testimony offers a pivotal detail overlooked in other histories of the riot. Philip Clayton "would not say whether he was concerned in the attack on Mr. Tucker's servant; was within two or three steps of the man at the time; did not know whether they did or did not search his pockets; was not sufficiently near to see." In Virginia, interfering with a master's slave conveyed a pointed insult. By stopping, abusing, and searching Tucker's slave (left unnamed in the records), students dishonored him as an impotent master unable to protect, and thereby truly to own, his human property. No Virginia gentleman could tolerate such an exposure of weakness, which explains why Tucker confronted the rioters.[76]

Enslaved people built the University. They excavated cellars and formed terraces, made and laid bricks, cut and hauled stone, and shaped and painted plaster and wood. Jefferson and his associates, including Edmund Bacon and Charles Bankhead, provided enslaved workers, as did John Hartwell Cocke. The masters received rents of $60 to $70 per slave per year in return. In 1823 a University contractor reported "our workmen are nearly all African."[77]

University rules barred students from bringing their own slaves.

Instead, each hotelkeeper kept an enslaved staff to provide meals, clean student rooms, clothes, and shoes, haul wood, fetch water, and make beds and fires. Every afternoon, an enslaved servant called on his assigned student to take orders for errands around the grounds or in town. The University also rented a few slaves to tend gardens and clean classrooms and outhouses. The professors hired or bought enslaved people, with help from the Visitors. By enhancing faculty comfort, and interesting them in a slave society, Visitors sought to retain professors for the long term. Over one hundred slaves lived in sheds, kitchens, and garrets in and around the hotels or in the soggy basements of pavilions. In effect, the University was an especially complex and crowded plantation where whites and blacks lived side by side but arranged in spaces to maximize white power and black marginality.[78]

Although owned or rented by hotelkeepers, enslaved workers faced commands from over a hundred students, who acted as masters of the University. A student noted that keepers ordinarily commanded slaves within their hotels but "Students control them in Dormitories." Enslaved workers bore the brunt of cruel pranks played by bored students, including setting buckets of cold water atop a door to douse a servant entering to clean. Dependent on students as customers, hotelkeepers could do little to protect their slaves.[79]

By bullying slaves, young masters showed off before their peers. Quick to detect insolence, they struck those who could not strike back. At dinner in Warner Minor's hotel, Thomas Boyd rebuked a slave for serving butter that the student considered watery. The slave (unnamed in the record) muttered surprise "that Mr. B[oyd], having read so many books, should not know the difference between water and butter." Overheard, he suffered a brutal beating with a cane wielded by Boyd in the dining room. Another student noted, "blood was running freely from the servant's head," while Boyd clutched the shattered cane. By beating a slave in a dining room, Boyd expanded the orbit of student control beyond the dorms and into a hotel.[80]

Minor complained to the professors, who held a hearing. Boyd expressed "Astonishment & Indignation at being called before the Faculty for so trifling an affair as that of chastising a servant for his insolence." The professors wanted no part of an honor dispute that pivoted on a slave, so they declined to act. Infuriated by Minor's complaint, Boyd confronted him under the arcade around the lawn: "Told him he had not acted the part of a gentleman—that his conduct had been cowardly" and "if he ever crossed his path, one or the other should be whip[p]ed." Another student, John A. Gretter, called out "Whip him, Boyd—whip him." Gretter explained "that Minor should be whipped, for he had acted in an ungentlemanly way in not suffering Boyd to lead the servant outside to chastise him." Once again, the faculty dithered, merely "expressing their high disapprobation of [Boyd's] conduct."[81]

The faculty balked at intervening when enslaved people belonged to others. In September 1826, several students attacked a young woman owned by a tavern keeper who lived near the University. She had to provide sexual services to his student customers. Accusing her of giving them a venereal disease, students stripped her naked and beat her. The faculty merely reprimanded two ringleaders and wrote to their parents. Professors inflicted "so light a punishment," they explained, because "the parties appeared sorry for the offence ... and had promptly, of their own accord, made a reparation which was accepted by the injured Party." The injured party was the girl's owner, who received $10 from the students for the damage to his human property. She got nothing for her pain and suffering. The faculty punished more severely a student who damaged a library book.[82]

Not even death could end coerced service by enslaved people to the University. At night, medical students exhumed recent graves of slaves to get cadavers for dissection and study. Although a pious Christian, Gessner Harrison thrilled at surreptitious grave-robbing for the medical school. "It is our interest to keep a secret," he told his father, but conceded, "that they all came from this neighborhood." Once, "with much difficulty," he "avoided being detected, the grave being but about 50 or 100 yards from the house."[83]

Miles

On the morning after the riot of October 1, professors suspended lectures and demanded that the students identify culprits. None would cooperate, dreading the odious reputation of informer. Most (65 of 116) instead signed a pointed remonstrance, blaming Tucker and Emmet for provoking the violence by attacking a student guilty only of too much glee. The signers declared, "that it *would* have been truly 'disgraceful' had the student so assaulted not made that resistance which it was incumbent upon him to make as a man of courage and a gentleman."[84]

As young men of honor, students felt insulted when professors demanded cooperation: "That they would be wanting to themselves as students of this Institution, as Virginians and as men, were they to comply with the requisition made by the Faculty. That the Faculty have mistaken their characters in supposing that they will condescend to act the part of informers and that they feel highly indignant at the aspersion which is thus thrown upon them by the Faculty in expressing the belief that they are capable of such baseness." They expected strict confidentiality from "every student of this University and by everyone who boasts himself a *Virginian*." Rather than inform, they threatened to go home.[85]

Students underestimated the Visitors, who convened at Monticello two days after the riot. On October 4, they met in the Rotunda and summoned students to appear. Sitting behind a long table at the center of the room, the Visitors made a formidable impression. They included the great men of Virginia present (Joseph Cabell, John Hartwell Cocke, and Chapman Johnson) and past (James Madison and Thomas Jefferson, who emerged from a sickbed to deal with the crisis). As their rector, Jefferson spoke first, "saying that this was the most painful event of his life." Overcome by emotion and tears, he gave way to Johnson, an eloquent lawyer, who denounced the student riots as dishonorable. Fourteen shaken students came forward to confess and promise testimony, which they gave the next day.[86]

On October 5 and 6, the faculty met and agreed to expel four students and admonish ten others. The expelled included William Eyre, who had enrolled on the day of the riot and had not attended any class. The Visitors endorsed the sentences and adopted new measures to ban masquerading and restrict drinking, swearing, and making disruptive noises at night.[87]

The identity of the primary rioter jolted Jefferson. The young man nabbed by Tucker, provoking the volley of sticks and bricks, was Wilson Miles Cary. For years, Cary had frequented Monticello with his family. Tucker recalled: "The shock which Mr. Jefferson felt when he . . . discovered that the efforts of the last ten years had been foiled and put in jeopardy by one of his family, was more than his own patience could endure," so he erupted in "language of indignation and reproach."[88]

General Cocke rode over to Carysbrook to break the news of Cary's expulsion to his mother, Virginia. "If he is made of penetrable stuff, when he knows the agonies which his conduct has inflicted upon his widowed Mother & Sisters he will surely reform his life. But, alas! I can't but doubt," Cocke added. He persuaded Miles to work as a clerk in the Fluvanna County office while boarding with Reverend Timberlake. Martha Jefferson Randolph expressed "astonishment" at this "most surprising conquest over his pride and love for dissipation, . . . but General Cocke is certainly omnipotent. He is the guardian angel of that family."[89]

Miles faced the demanding love of his dismayed mother, who urged "his weaning himself without delay from habits that were evidently sweeping him to destruction." Her advice did not take. In December 1826, Miles visited Bremo, where Louisa Cocke sadly reported, "Poor Miles has abandoned himself entirely to drinking & says it is now absolutely necessary to his existence." Louisa felt relieved when he abruptly departed on the day before Christmas.[90]

Sinners, however, live to repent, as Miles did a year later as a law student with Henry St. George Tucker. Writing to his mother, Miles announced "a great change in my character" that had shaken his "propensities for wildness and irregularity." Idleness, he confessed, was "the *rock* upon which my early hopes were *wrecked*." He added, "I was early in life left almost entirely to the guidance of a wayward, rash, and fiery disposition which hardly ever anticipated consequences or listened to the voice of prudence."[91]

In 1830, Cary became further entangled in the Jefferson-Randolph clan by proposing to his cousin Jane Margaret Carr, the daughter of Jefferson's nephew Peter Carr. An alarmed relative thought such a marriage "might be feasable for a very industrious, energetic man, but for a man of [Cary's] Indolent temper it would be madness." The couple married in 1831, and, to almost everyone's surprise, Miles made something of himself, practicing law in Charlottesville and editing the local newspaper.[92]

Stories

The riot of October 1, 1825, imperiled the new university. Three days later, Professors Thomas Key and George Long abruptly resigned, deeming the students ungovernable ingrates. Key and Long refused to attend the faculty meetings that confronted the crisis, but the Visitors rejected the resignations and threatened legal action to enforce their five-year contracts. In mid-October, they reluctantly resumed teaching and attending faculty meetings, but Jefferson thought them "somewhat in the pouts as yet."[93]

The riot also threatened to thin out the students, which would reduce the revenue from tuition so essential to the University. Many parents reconsidered sending their boys to such a disorderly institution. One father barred his son's matriculation because "the young men have acted in a manner unworthy of savages." Another parent complained that they "run wild in the mad career of vice, folly, intoxication, blasphemy, gaming, lewdness & what not." He added, "Religion is made a Scoff & butt for Blasphemy & Ridicule, to shoot their poisoned arrows at!" Two Visitors, Cocke and Robert B. Taylor, considered withdrawing their sons in disgust, but they relented to spare the University from a public relations disaster.[94]

Pious critics interpreted the troubles as the inevitable fruits of a godless and anarchic university. Visiting the institution after the riot, a Presbyterian teacher declared, "I regard it as a School in infidelity—a nursery of bad principles, designed in its origin to crush the Institutions of Religion in V[irgini]a." An Albemarle County farmer scoffed at the leeway given to students: "I would as soon turn a parcel of hogs into my potato-patch, and trust to their sense of honor not to root, as I would bring a large number of boys together into one school . . . and trust to their sense of honor not to misbehave."[95]

Supporters had to counter that scathing narrative, or risk losing the University that they relied on to reverse Virginia's decline. On October 11, the *Richmond Enquirer* exhorted students to "look to Thomas Jefferson, whose whole soul is wrapt up in the University—to Virginia, who is sinking in the scale of the nation, & who calls upon them to supply the place of her great sons, who have already left, or are soon destined to leave, the busy scenes of life." But the newspaper also denounced critics for recklessly seeking "to shake the public confidence in its success." In a fuller story published a month later, the *Richmond Enquirer* minimized the riots as "boyish pranks" by a mere dozen students.[96]

Jefferson disliked writing because of the pain to his ailing wrist, but he felt an urgent need to counter the pious critique with an alternative narrative. In mid-October, he wrote and sent long, upbeat letters to far-flung correspondents who could influence public opinion. Jefferson depicted a university briefly ruffled by minor troubles, yet utterly transformed by salutary reforms that quickly had restored order. While keeping up a sunny public façade, however, he seemed worn down by the troubles, according to friends. "Poor old Mr. Jefferson, I fear it will embitter his last days," one confided.[97]

Although in his eighties, Jefferson visited the University almost daily and sought to civilize students by inviting them, in rotating groups of four or five, to Sunday dinners at Monticello. By expressing a warm interest in their families and studies, he made all feel welcome and at ease. But the dinners irritated his granddaughters, who had to wait on the boys. Mary Jefferson Randolph complained, "To our great annoyance, he has resumed the practice of inviting students to dinner on Sunday and we are to have to day a company of school boy guests who . . . are not worth the additional trouble their presence gives, but grandpapa wishes it."[98]

Students felt chastened by the Visitors' dramatic intervention, intimidated by new rules, alarmed by approaching public examinations, and charmed by Jefferson's renewed attention. They ceased their raucous, masked, and nocturnal performances on the lawn, of the sort that had culminated in the riots of September 30 and October 1. In mid-October, a student assured his father, "Everything seems to have changed for the better; the young men are becoming more studious, and have been more punctual in their attendance on lectures than I have ever before known them to be." But that order was the calm before a greater storm generated by Jefferson's financial and physical decline in 1826.[99]

10
ENDS

IN LATE 1825, Jefferson desperately needed money to fend off impatient creditors: "To me it is almost a question of life or death." His daughter recalled that he was "lying awake one night from painful thoughts," when "the idea of the lottery came from the realms of bliss to my father." He

Edgar Allan Poe (1809–1849), by H. Inman, c. 1825
(Albert and Shirley Small Special Collections Library, University of Virginia)

sought authorization from the state legislature to conduct a lottery, with parcels of real estate (excluding Monticello) as prizes. By selling enough tickets, Jefferson could recoup what he considered the land's true value rather than its depressed market value. Jefferson sent his grandson, Jeff Randolph, to Richmond to lobby legislators.[1]

There were obstacles, including Jefferson's prior public statements against lotteries for any purpose. Reversing himself, Jefferson wrote an essay, "Thoughts on Lotteries," which his grandson shared with legislators. It read like a satire on philosophical sophistry: "It is a common idea that games of chance are immoral, but what is Chance? Nothing happens in this world without a cause." He reasoned that everything in life was risky. "If we consider games of chance immoral, then every pursuit of human industry is immoral, for there is not a single one that is not subject to chance." So, he declared, the mariner setting out on the sea or the farmer sowing seed was gambling every bit as much as the man throwing dice or playing cards. John Hartwell Cocke bristled at Jefferson's tortured argument for a lottery, "by which he attempts to prostrate the moral sentiment of the Country which stood between him & his object. Alas, what a commentary upon public life does this winding up of Mr. Jefferson's career afford?" How could the University suppress student gambling when its founder so publicly championed a lottery?[2]

Jefferson's request embarrassed the legislature's Republican leaders, who had taken the lead in discouraging lotteries in Virginia. Noting the "surprise and shock" that met Jefferson's proposal, a leading lawyer assured a friend, "You cannot conceive the sensation which this application and disclosure of his situation created in Richmond & indeed everywhere."[3]

Jefferson despaired as the legislators hesitated. On February 8, he warned his grandson: "I see in the failure of this hope a deadly blast of all peace of mind during my remaining days," for he felt "oppressed with disease, debility, age, and embarrassed affairs." As a patriarch, he was supposed to protect and provide for heirs, so Jefferson dreaded leaving nothing for his "dear & beloved daughter, the cherished companion of my early life and nurse of my age, and her children." Another crushing blow came three days later, when his granddaughter Anne died at Monticello after years of abuse by Charles Bankhead. Jefferson assured Jeff, "Heaven seems to be overwhelming us with every form of misfortune, and I expect your next [letter] will give me the *coup de grace*." A cousin agreed, "If he does not get it, I think it will kill him."[4]

Jeff showed Jefferson's sad letter to key legislators to great effect. One "covered his face with his hands & blubbered like a baby." Endorsing the lottery push, Thomas Ritchie's influential *Richmond Enquirer* declared, "Virginia is mainly indebted to Thomas Jefferson for all that we hold most valuable in her government, her laws, [and] her institutions." On February 20, the lottery bill passed by a margin of 126 to 62 in the House and by near unanimity in the State Senate. But Jeff and Joseph C. Cabell made a painful concession to win approval; they included Monticello among the potential prizes, securing it only for Jefferson's lifetime plus two years for his heirs to relocate elsewhere. When informed of this inclusion, a cousin reported, "Mr. Jefferson turned quite white & set for some time silent."[5]

In the spring, Jeff set out for Baltimore and northern cities to sell lottery tickets to Jefferson's admirers. He sought to convert the lottery into a subscription by encouraging buyers to form associations committed to buy tickets but then to burn them in public ceremonies on July 4, in honor of the author of the Declaration of Independence. If enough tickets sold and burned, then the family could pay Jefferson's debts without losing their home.[6]

The scheme failed as both subscription and lottery, for few tickets sold. Even in Charlottesville, a disgusted cousin reported, "There is nothing doing here, not even talking. Mean wretches." The financial future looked grim for Jefferson's heirs. In April, Martha sadly reported, "He said that he had lived too long, that his death would be an advantage to his family." In fact, only his life fended off creditors, who would close in at the end. In June, Jeff's wife Jane worried, "Heaven only knows what will become of this poor thoughtless family. Mother & Mr. J[efferson] are too much broken in constitution to bear it long, & the younger ones look forward to nothing but misery."[7]

President

By confessing to bankruptcy and seeking a lottery, Jefferson appeared weak, tainting his aura as Virginia's great man. Instead, he became the airy philosopher incapable of managing money, a reputation that hurt the University in early 1826. While legislators granted the lottery, they defeated Cabell's request for extra funding to complete the controversial Rotunda. Jefferson had to hasten to the worksite to suspend construction for want of funds.[8]

The setback emboldened Jefferson's critics on the Board of Visitors. Cocke told Cabell that the defeat "ought to be an admonition to the Old Sachem that the state has [had] enough of his buildings." Robert B. Taylor assured Cocke: "I really fear nothing will ever come to practical good which is under the guidance of Mr. J[efferson]. He has lost the finest opportunity of giving a tone of morality, order, & diligence to the University." Instead of teaching "virtue & intelligence," the institution had "become a sink of Vice," which Taylor blamed on Jefferson's "silly notion that Virginian youths are not to submit to law & control, but to be governed altogether by their own judgment."[9]

In fact, disorder derived from the University's inconsistent rules, which sometimes indulged but more often restricted students arbitrarily. Jefferson wanted them to devote free time to study, or to debating societies and lessons in music, fencing, dancing, and military drills. He rejected other diversions as frivolous distractions. In December 1825, a hotelkeeper sought permission to set up a reading room with newspapers. Surely, such reading would have improved upon the students' usual drunken amusements, but Jefferson insisted that newspapers "would only alienate and entice their minds from their proper studies. The exercises proper and sufficient to occupy all their leisure hours will of course be prescribed to them by their Professors."[10]

Some Visitors blamed student disorders on the weak administration of the university mandated by Jefferson, who had dispensed with the position of president that prevailed at every other university. By Jefferson's design, the faculty selected a chairman, who would rotate annually until every professor had served in that role. Dispersed executive authority suited Jefferson's political tastes, and the lack of a president ensured his own dominance at the institution.[11]

Critics felt that only a president could provide the strong leadership needed to control students and faculty. Taylor complained to Cocke: "While the Sachem continues to retain his influence, I suppose you will continue as heretofore [with] all your professors equal in authority & power & consequently none of them willing to incur either the responsibility or trouble of administration. For some time longer this system, or want of system, may continue but it must ultimately be abandoned & the sooner the better."[12]

In February 1826, several Visitors sought to clip Jefferson's domination by hiring a combination law professor and president. To entice the United States Attorney General, William Wirt, for that dual role, the reformers offered him a double salary of $3,000. While Jefferson's reputation had taken recent hits, Wirt's standing was ascendant, as he had a rare knack in Virginia for making and keeping money. William H. Cabell exulted, "What a splendid Professor he would make! And what numbers he would attract to the University."[13]

On April 3, 1826, at a meeting of the Visitors, Jefferson opposed creating a presidency and filling it with Wirt. Seeking only a new law professor to replace the recently deceased Francis W. Gilmer, Jefferson proposed his own cousin Dabney Carr Terrell, a young lawyer of slender experience and reputation. Appointing Terrell would violate Jefferson's oft-stated strictures against nepotism. The young man also had killed a fellow student in a duel at college in Pennsylvania, but he escaped prosecution by fleeing to Europe, where Jefferson arranged for him to study at the University of Geneva. Returning to the United States, Terrell settled in Kentucky rather than Virginia. His appointment would ill suit a university where the Visitors sought to suppress student duels.[14]

For the first time, the Visitors defeated Jefferson on a key issue. Abandoned even by Cabell, Jefferson retained only the support of James Madison. But Wirt rejected the offer because the $3,000 salary was only a third of his annual income. Lacking confidence in the current professors, the Visitors abandoned their plan for a president. But in another setback for Jefferson, they rejected Terrell and instead appointed John Tayloe Lomax, a Fredericksburg lawyer. Although little more qualified than Terrell, Lomax was at least a Virginia resident and unrelated to Jefferson. Lomax promptly accepted, at last filling the key professorship.[15]

Freed from a president's competing authority, Jefferson resumed managing the professors. They had concentrated on their specialties, but Jefferson demanded that each should teach an array of disparate disciplines. In late April, he directed Professor Emmet to prepare a botanic garden and begin teaching botany on top of his usual chemistry and geology lectures. Emmet rejected "the herculean task" of imparting "Botany, Zoology, Mineralogy, Chemistry, Geology, and Rural Economy." Indeed, he knew of no one on Earth who could teach all six. Unsympathetic, Jefferson responded that the state's limited funding demanded that every professor do more. Madison supported Jefferson's order but cautioned his friend to keep it secret, lest publicity confirm suspicions that the University offered an education "more superficial than comports with the pretensions of the Institution."[16]

Poe

After the riot of October 1825, the Visitors imposed new rules that, Jefferson claimed, brought order to the University. But that order did not last. One student, Gessner Harrison, noted the ebb and flow of collective troublemaking. In March 1826, he reported, "There seems to be a kind of contagious mania that seizes upon the students here every now and then. The faculty suspend or expel a half dozen in such a matter, and everything for a time wears the aspect of calm and quiet, but all at once again the springs of insane revelry are put in motion and nothing but carousing and noise seems to rule. So it is now." After two months of relative quiet, "the tune is changed." Some students bought a hare and released it on the lawn. According to Robert Blow, 150 students came out of their dorms to scramble "in full cry after it. The uproar an[d] noise soon brought out the professors," but "they used all their vociferation to no effect . . . altho' noise upon the lawn is a most flagrant breach of the laws."[17]

Beginning in February 1826, the new term brought a great turnover but little overall growth in the volatile student body. Alienated by the new rules, most of the fall's students did not return. Most of the students were newcomers, and the overall numbers reached only 163, about half the 300 predicted by Jefferson and a disappointing number given that 1826 enrolled two annual classes compared to the 123 of a single class in 1825. As with old William & Mary, the new University attracted a volatile set of students. Of 3,247 students who attended between 1825 and 1842, only 127 stayed for four years. Seeking social connections rather than a degree, most lingered for only a term or two. This instability reduced the influence of professors, Visitors, and rules over students who did not expect to stay for long.[18]

In 1826, the newcomers included a short, wiry, dark-haired boy named Edgar Allan Poe, the son of two traveling actors. Abandoned by Poe's father, his mother died of disease in Richmond in December 1811, when she was twenty-four and her son nearly three. A wealthy, Scots-born tobacco merchant, John Allan, and his wife Frances adopted Poe and paid for his genteel education. Poe disliked mathematics but delighted in classics and poetry, which he began to write with verve. Fast, lithe, and strong, he excelled at running, boxing, jumping, and swimming. But his hard-driving, pragmatic father struggled to understand his moody and artistic son. In November 1824, Allan complained, "He does nothing & seems quite miserable, sulky & ill-tempered to all the Family. . . . The boy possesses not a Spark of affection for us, not a particle of gratitude for all my care and kindness towards him. I have given him a much superior Education than ever I received myself."[19]

In February 1826, Allan sent Poe to the University of Virginia, where he studied literature and languages, ancient and modern. Poe lived in room number 13, in a stretch of dorms known as "Rowdy Row" because of its especially raucous students. A dapper dresser, Poe had dark, expressive eyes, a melodic voice, and mercurial mood swings. A fellow student, Miles George, recalled, "He was very excitable & restless, at times wayward, melancholic & morose, but again in his better moods, frolicksome, full of fun & a most attractive & agreeable companion." George noted Poe's unusual talent at "sketching upon the walls of his dormitory, whimsical, fanciful, & grotesque figures."[20]

Self-absorbed and sensitive, Poe needed praise and became angry and withdrawn when denied. Another student remembered Poe reading aloud a story that he had composed and set "in a mist of impenetrable gloom." When some students mocked the story, Poe angrily cast the pages into a blazing fireplace. Professor George Long later noted, "The beginning of the University of Virginia was very bad. There were some excellent young men, and some of the worst that ever I knew." Struggling to recall Poe, Long concluded, "He could not be among the worst, and perhaps not among the best." Perhaps not.[21]

Poe drank heavily and gambled at cards with his peers. The late-night sessions sometimes culminated in bloody fights with fists, canes, and knives as boys accused one another of cheating and dishonoring. One student described a common type: "If you dispute his word for a moment, he is ready for a fight & talks as big as if he was a Caesar. . . . So he goes on, until at last they all entertain great respect for him, and think him a very fine honorable fellow indeed."[22]

In May 1826, Poe assured Allan that "a common fight is so trifling an occurrence that no notice is taken of it." Robert Blow of Norfolk provoked that spring's primary conflict when he wrote a mocking inscription outside a dorm room, "Jugs for Sale," which insulted the occupants as petty traders lacking gentility. When confronted, Blow blamed another student, Henry Turner Dixon, for the prank. Infuriated, Dixon scuffled with Blow until separated by two professors. Then, Poe noted, "Dixon posted [Blow] in very indecent terms." Soon, feuding students covered every column around the lawn with notes denouncing one another as dishonorable cowards. Dixon next attacked Blow's friend Arthur Smith, striking "him with a large stone on one side of his head—whereupon Smith drew a pistol (which are all the fashion here)." The pistol misfired.[23]

Blow's disgusted grandfather advised the boy to take his pistols and "immediately break them to pieces, or burn them up in the Fire & never to have another." Justifying his actions, Blow replied, "I was abused, trampled upon, insulted and disgraced without any shadow of cause." He obtained a pistol to avoid "being assassinated by the man Dixon whom I believe capable and willing to do so." The conflict and controversy did "sour my disposition and disgust me with human nature. I am weary of this place and almost with the world and shall consider *that* the happiest moment of my life when I leave this institution never to see it again."[24]

The faculty tried Blow, Dixon, and Smith but merely suspended them for two months, and declined to confiscate their weapons: rather light sentences for nearly killing one another. Taking Smith aside, Professor George Tucker apologized for the punishment, adding that the University's "enactments were, in his opinion, too severe about the use of the fire Arms." Such were the fruits of hiring a champion of dueling as professor of moral philosophy. Unreformed, Dixon challenged another student to a duel in November, when the faculty at last expelled him.[25]

In another springtime squabble, Charles Wickliffe and a friend ambushed and whipped a third student suspected of cheating them out of $240 at cards. For this assault, the faculty merely suspended Wickliffe for two months, too light a sentence to chasten him. On September 21, Poe noted, "We have had a great many fights up here lately." In the most sensational, Wickliffe attacked another student. Poe reported, "I saw the whole affair. It took place before my door. Wickliffe was much the strongest, but not content with that, after getting the other completely in his power, he began to bite. I saw the arm afterwards and it was . . . bitten from the shoulder to the elbow and it is likely that pieces of flesh as large as my hand will be obliged to be cut out." Belatedly, the faculty expelled Wickliffe "for general bad conduct."[26]

Tricks

The Visitors believed that drinking, gambling, fighting, and cavorting had bred riots and generated gossip that discredited the University. But gaming and drinking prevailed on the plantations where students grew up, so they resented the suppression of cherished activities. In early 1826, students doubled down on their vices, for dissipation seemed even more alluring when it defied efforts to control them. Venturing into Charlottesville, they haunted taverns and confectionary shops (which served alcohol). A student noted, "Here nothing is more common than to see students so drunk as to be unable to walk." A visitor to Charlottesville reported awakening at 3 A.M. to rowdy students playing "drum, fife, and clarions . . . aided by their Bachanalian clamours of applause." Breaking into the courthouse, students "rang the bell violently for 20 minutes as a solo." Riding back to the University, they tore down a fence and rebuilt it to block the road.[27]

Pious but acerbic, Mary E. Terrell despised the drunken students who infested Charlottesville. In April, she felt "frightened out of my senses by their riotous conduct; but their depravity in another way exceeds all description; we are actually afraid to send a servant into the part of the town they frequent. . . . Happy are those who are not compelled to see or hear what is so shocking." These students relished humiliating and assaulting enslaved people, whom the law kept vulnerable to attack by whites. A few months later, Terrell assured Louisa Cocke: "My dear friend, this place is a sight for Christians & all sober people to weep over. It is a sort of theatre for the wicked & contemptible from every part of the world to assemble at & truly, as Dr. [Conrad] Speece said, 'it is Satan's headquarters.'"[28]

The students relied on hack carriages to come and go to town. Returning late at night, they made a scene, roaring back, the faculty complained, "in a state of intoxication, where they insult everybody on the road and, on their arrival at the University, disturb all the peaceable [people] by their disorderly uproar." In October 1825, a careening hack crashed, hurling two students into the road and smashing the leg of one of them, James Edgar Marshall. The accident alarmed Jefferson's granddaughter, Cornelia Randolph, who had danced with him "one whole evening at a party," and lamented the loss of "one of those beautiful legs." She admired his stoicism during the amputation: "Clasping his hands round the bed post above his head, he submitted to a most dreadful operation without a groan or change of countenance." He died a few days later, and Cornelia mourned: "He was so young, so clever, so handsome & such a favorite among his fellow students, and an idol in his family."[29]

Despite the tragedy, the daredevil driving persisted. In February 1826, in a rollicking carriage, drunken students bellowed insults at a professor's wife. The faculty expelled one student. Professor Tucker sadly informed Joseph C. Cabell that the boy was "your young kinsman [William] Lewis Cabell." Drawn from the small world of Virginia's first families, riotous students had ties of kin and friendship with the University's sober leaders.[30]

The most surprising connection to trouble came from Jane and Mary Cary, the lovely, lively, and fashionable daughters of the state's most conspicuously godly woman, Virginia Randolph Cary. The sisters frequently visited Charlottesville to cultivate genteel students, known as "beaux," and welcomed them to their home in Fluvanna County. Especially beautiful, Mary drew a crowd of admirers. "When she meets with her student beaux, they crowd round her and almost get into a scuffle for her two unfortunate arms are seized & kept close prisoners until she is placed in the carriage or seated in the drawing room," Cornelia Randolph complained. When visiting Charlottesville, the Cary sisters stayed at Monticello, attracting students for nightly dance parties. After more than two weeks of hosting mother Cary and her dancing daughters, Martha Jefferson Randolph declared, "It was extremely annoying to me."[31]

The Cary sisters especially irritated the godly but waspish Mary E. Terrell. In May 1826, Terrell informed her friend Louisa Cocke: "I suppose you have heard what execution your Fluvanna belles have done at the University," for "no Ladies that I have ever seen understand the art of *exhibition* better." Terrell added, "We sober folks have been deeply mortified," because the girls indulged in "one continued round of dissipation with the Students." In June, Terrell welcomed the departure "of our young gallants" to Fluvanna "in search of squirrels & beauties."[32]

Terrell exempted their godly mother from criticism of her flashy daughters: "I am sure our friend Mrs. Cary little knows how imprudent they have been, or she would never have trusted them so near this dreadful place." In fact, mother Cary arranged and often accompanied their visits to Charlottesville, and she welcomed sojourning students to her home, Carysbrook. She sought to facilitate timely and genteel marriages for her daughters, a goal which trumped even religious zeal for Mrs. Cary, an apt character for a Jane Austen novel set in Virginia.[33]

Even the faculty had complicating ties with troublesome students. One Sunday, two drunken students "attempted by force to stop the carriage" of Professor Bonnycastle and his wife returning from church. The culprits included William Emmet, who had become, Cornelia Randolph noted, the "the ring leader of some nightly disturbances at the *University*." He was also the younger brother of Professor Emmet. At the disciplinary hearing, Professor Emmet confronted his brother "with much severity. The young man shewed much contrition & wept bitterly. In this Dr. Emmet joined him." But Cornelia cautioned a sister against repeating sordid tales from the University: "I am so much afraid of prejudices rising against it."[34]

To reduce dissipation (and carriage rides), Visitors sought to limit reasons for students to visit Charlottesville with its tempting taverns. But entrepreneurs moved the town closer by building new, nearby taverns unregulated by any license. The University's hotelkeepers also winked at drinking and gambling on their premises, and students sent enslaved people to fetch alcohol in town. Some cunning students sent along boots for supposed repair; within they included empty bottles. For a fee, the cooperative shoemaker returned the boots with the bottles filled with whiskey. Alcohol fueled a steady succession of parties. When pressed to specify the date for one bacchanalia, a hotelkeeper declared, "They were so numerous he can't mention particularly when or where the playing or drinking took place."[35]

The university bell became a tempting target for student revelers. During the day, it irritated them by issuing faculty commands: to awake or shift to a new class. At night, they reversed the power dynamic, seizing the bell to disturb sleeping professors. Jefferson ordered the proctor to move the bell to atop a pavilion and "contrive how the cord may be protected from the trickish ringings of the students." But resourceful tricksters still broke in to clang the bell. In March, Gessner Harrison reported that, "for several nights it has maintained a continual clatter for half a night." Even Harrison seemed amused, assuring a former student, "You would laugh to hear the bells start most furiously about 11 o'clock, when commonly everything is silent. The professors can't catch them (the bellmen), tho' they try their best."[36]

The drunken racket soon eroded Harrison's good humor. In the spring, he denounced the "headlong, reckless madness" of students engaged in "unchaste reveling" at this "devilish tub of profanity and beastly intoxication." He added, "I am compelled thro' every hour of every day to hear the most revolting deeds avowed by their perpetrators and huzzaed or laughed into countenance by dozens listening in filthy groups about him." Nightly wine parties left the morning ground strewn with broken glasses and bottles. Harrison longed to "abandon this disgusting place" lest he develop "a permanent hatred to the greater part of my species."[37]

Professors resented having to enforce strict rules on restive and violent students. It had become an alluring game for them to bait professors at night and then hide from pursuit with impunity. The faculty regarded no "remuneration sufficient to compensate [them for] the danger of injury to their persons from stones and brickbats or to their feelings as Gentlemen from the coarse abuse of Rioters and Drunkards." They pressed the Visitors to establish a special police force of "six able-bodied white men" to inspect dorms, gather evidence, and arrest culprits. But the Visitors balked at the cost of a professional police. They preferred to rely on the university's janitor and proctor to patrol the university, but they were busy, reluctant, and ineffectual.[38]

On the morning of May 9, the faculty ordered twenty-five students to stay in their dorms, ready to appear before the county grand jury and sheriff investigating gambling and drinking. Instead, Poe reported, the students fled: "The Grand Jury met and put the Students in a terrible fright—so much so that the lectures were unattended—and those whose names were upon the Sheriff's list travelled off into the woods & mountains, taking their beds & provisions along with them." For want of testimony, the grand jury could indict no students.[39]

Burial

Jefferson's health worsened as he brooded over financial collapse and the grim impact on his heirs. Cornelia wrote, "Grandpapa [is] unwell & out of spirits. I cannot bear his pale looks & weak voice." To cope with pain, Jefferson took large doses of laudanum, "88 drops every night," Martha noted. He increased that dose to 100 drops during the stressful October troubles at the University. In February 1826, he lamented that pain rendered "impossible all attention of the mind to anything but exaggerated suffering." Pain and laudanum contributed to the erratic thinking in Jefferson's letters and conversation during his last two years.[40]

In June, Jefferson's final public appearance in Charlottesville had a surreal quality. He attended a traveling circus: a vulgar setting for a learned philosopher. A student marveled, "for a wonder Mr. Jefferson was at it, and several of the Professors." His granddaughter Mary reported, "We braved the rabble . . . to see an exhibition of animals, and, with the assistance of a strong party of gentlemen, actually made good our position in front of the circle of spectators, and I was repaid for my trouble by seeing an elephant for the first time." And the elephant saw Jefferson for the first time, but we do not know what either made of the other.[41]

In the circus scene, we can take the measure of cultural and social changes wrought since the revolution. Colonial Virginia lacked any traveling circus, a phenomenon that emerged in the more diverse and commercial culture of the early republic. Colonial gentry had the dignity and status to claim deference in public settings from common Virginians. Not so in the early republic, when it took some muscle by young gentlemen to nudge aside a more assertive "rabble." But, in the end, the genteel family still claimed pride of place; it had just become less certain and more contested.[42]

In May and June, a prolonged drought dried up wells and halted water wheels at the mills. Albemarle also suffered from "Myriads" of crop-eating and "dark-looking locusts." Then in late June, a week of torrential rain turned the Rivanna River into a raging torrent that wiped out crops in the lowlands and carried away mills. Jane Nicholas Randolph reported that the flood "destroy[ed] all that the drouth left within its reach. . . . I never heard such a frightful storm as we had all night, & today there is a greater fresh[et] than has been known for many years."[43]

As the rains poured down in late June, Jefferson's health collapsed. The only doctor he trusted, Professor Dunglison, told the family that the old philosopher had only a few days left to live. Martha, Jeff, and Nicholas P. Trist (who had married Jeff's sister Virginia) stayed by the bedside, supervising enslaved servants who cared for the dying man. In his last days, Jefferson often spoke about the University "and expressed satisfaction at the progress of the students."[44]

The local Episcopal minister, the Reverend Frederick Hatch, visited, but Jefferson welcomed Hatch only as a good neighbor rather than as a spiritual guide. Jefferson clung to life until he knew it was the Fourth of July, the fiftieth anniversary of his most celebrated achievement. That morning, Trist wrote, "He had been, to the last, the same calm, clear minded amiable *philosopher* . . . with his wonted serenity & inflexibility." By dying at midday as a philosopher, he defied conventional Christians who loved to trumpet deathbed conversions by longtime deists.[45]

On July 5, Jefferson's chaotic burial contradicted his painstaking efforts to depart with dignity. Enslaved people made his coffin and dug a grave in the family plot. Jefferson had wanted a small, quick funeral attended only by family and close friends. But his family was far from the haven of peace and harmony that Jefferson longed for. Self-exiled from Monticello by fury at his son Jeff, Thomas Mann Randolph never visited during Jefferson's last days. Randolph did come to the funeral, where he violently quarreled with Jeff, who denounced his father as "more ferocious than the wolf & more fell than the hyena, hating [Jefferson] in life, neglecting him in death, and insulting his remains when dead." Father and son squabbled over whether to delay the service to accommodate the hundreds of citizens and students ascending the mountain.[46]

Word of Jefferson's death had spread rapidly, drawing a crowd to the courthouse in Charlottesville, where the bell rang and militiamen fired cannon. Mourners donned black crape on the left arm as a sign of grief. They wanted to pay their last respects by attending the funeral, but students and citizens bickered over who should have precedence in processing to Monticello. A student recalled, "Much time was lost, and several of us, becoming tired of the discussion, turned our horses' heads to the mountain." The ascent became a chaotic scramble in a pouring rain. When the throng reached the top, all "were sorely disappointed, and, in some cases, angered" because the service was already over. The students included Edgar Allan Poe, who gained fresh fodder for his dim view of human nature.[47]

The state's newspapers filled their columns with tributes to Jefferson as the greatest Virginian of his generation. By honoring him, Charlottesville's *Central Gazette* sought to shame students into reform. "Who among you, young countrymen, are to be *our future* Jefferson*s*?" On the facing page, that issue offered a "family of valuable negroes for sale, consisting of a likely cooper, his wife, and several children." Another advertisement announced the auction of Jim, wife Lobly, and their child Henrietta on August 1 at the Eagle Hotel. Turning the page, a reader found the local overseer for President James Monroe offering rewards to recover George, aged 30, and Phebe, aged 28, who had escaped with forged papers of freedom. This juxtaposition of slavery with elite education seemed routine to Virginians of 1826.[48]

Five months after viewing Jefferson's fresh grave, Poe's stint at the University came to a double climax. In December 1826, he aced his exams but faced a faculty hearing into drinking and gambling at the hotels. Refusing to inform, Poe insisted that he had "never heard until now of any hotelkeepers playing Cards or drinking with students." Yet, Poe had lost over $2,000 by gambling: enough to buy a good farm. Poe might fool the faculty but not his canny stepfather, John Allan, who refused to pay his son's gambling debts and brought him home. Poe felt dishonored by Allan's refusal to cover his losses. Another student recalled, "He was earnest and emphatic in the declaration, that he was bound by honor to pay . . . every cent of them." At year's end, Poe departed after burning his writing table in a dorm fireplace.[49]

Returning home to Richmond in misery, Poe had to work in Allan's counting house, a despised tedium for the high-strung young man. Moralistic and devoted to the bottom line in business, Allan disdained the notions of honor nurtured by genteel students. Poe confessed to "the infamous conduct of myself & others at that place," but insisted that his stepfather should pay his gambling debts. Allan's refusal left Poe vulnerable to "taunts & abuse . . . even from those who had been my warmest friends." Poe claimed that he took up gambling in a desperate bid to make the money he needed to pay school bills that Allan had been too stingy to cover.[50]

Their tense relationship erupted on March 18, 1827, when Poe accused Allan of depriving him of enough education to achieve "eminence in public life." Poe also felt degraded from his proper position of white privilege: "You suffer me to be subjected to the whims & caprice, not only of your white family, but the complete authority of the blacks—these grievances I could not submit to, and I am gone." Poe felt disgraced when slaves delivered Allan's commands.[51]

Bolting from the house, Poe begged Allan to send him a trunk of clothes and books, while hinting at suicide if refused. Poe added, "I have nowhere to sleep at night, but roam about the Streets. I am nearly exhausted. . . . I have not one cent in the world to provide any food." Allan sent the trunk and enough cash for Poe to sail away to Boston, where he enlisted in the United States Army as a common soldier: a long fall for a son of wealth and a former University student. But Poe published *Tamerlane and Other Poems*, in Boston in 1827, launching his remarkable literary career.[52]

During his eleven months at the University of Virginia, Poe learned about the darker aspects of humanity. He saw drinking, gambling, cheating, insulting, and brawling with fists, whips, knives, pistols, and jaws. Poe became misanthropic by dealing with fellow students, for he

John Hartwell Cocke (1780–1866), daguerreotype, by W. A. Retzer, 1850
(Albert and Shirley Small Special Collections Library, University of Virginia)

considered "their professions of friendship—hollow." At the University, Poe honed a grim sensibility, a fatalism that dwelled on human deception, bodily corruption, and macabre death. He detected a thin, and easily ruptured, line between reason and passion, lucidity and insanity, calm and violence, life and death.[53]

Pessimistic about human nature, Poe derided moralizing and progress as insipid cant. He admired Jefferson's learning but despised as naïve his faith in democracy and Unitarianism. In 1836, Poe concluded, "No respect for the civil services, or the unquestionable mental powers of Jefferson shall blind us to his iniquities." In "Some Words with a Mummy," Poe satirized democracy as a fraud that would culminate in rule by a "usurping tyrant" known as the "Mob."[54]

That Mob killed Poe in October 1849, when Poe arrived in Baltimore during a typically raucous election. Despite his recent temperance pledge,

Poe could not resist the alcohol pressed on him by supporters of rival candidates, bidding for a vote that he could not give. He drank himself into a stupor that led to his death on October 7. After days of battling specters on hospital walls, his last words were, *Lord help my poor Soul.*[55]

Moat

In July 1826, newspaper praise for the departed Jefferson disgusted the conservative planter Otway B. Barraud, who wrote to his friend John Hartwell Cocke: "Mr. Jefferson deserves well of his Country, but 'tis the *fashion* now to deify & worship him, which I never will do as to any man." Casting Jefferson as impractical, Barraud added, "I have not a doubt that his death, at this time, so far from portending [the University's] ruin, as many fear, is most fortuitous for its better government."[56]

The pious Dr. Frank Carr also wasted little time mourning his uncle Thomas Jefferson. Just five days after his death, Carr urged Cocke to transform the University by "endow[ing] it with a Christian Character." Cocke's friend Reverend William Meade endorsed that shift but doubted that legislators would cooperate. Meade distrusted them as "deeply infested still with infidelity" and dependent "upon an ignorant, prejudiced, irreligious & bigotted multitude." Meade thought it better to close the University than to keep one "where God is never worshipped." Cocke urged patience on his pious brethren: "The religious people of our Country ought not to despair because its Corner stone has been laid in infidelity. God is able and doubtless will in his good time, make it contribute to his own glory."[57]

After Jefferson's death, Cocke visited the University more often and lingered longer to exercise greater oversight. As his local residence, he built a nearby brick hotel on the main road to town. Construction began in August 1826, a month after Jefferson died. The hotel provided an orderly alternative to Charlottesville taverns and served as his observation post for watching students coming and going. Locals dubbed the hotel "Mudwall" after the reddish, stucco wall around the two-acre compound.[58]

In a telling move, Cocke attended the auction of Jefferson's furniture at Monticello, where he purchased the great hallway clock. Like so much at that estate, the clock had suffered from neglect during Jefferson's last, ruinous years. Cocke's construction manager reported, "I have gotten the clock from Monticello and indeed it was the most smoke dried thing of the kind I ever saw. . . . The face & inside works of the clock were almost as badly smoked as the case and it is a task to get them in order." By repairing and relocating Jefferson's cherished clock, Cocke posed as the new master of time at the University.[59]

In December 1826, Cocke persuaded the Visitors to adopt strict new rules meant to redress the University's reputation as an expensive den of dissipation. They barred students from entering any tavern or confectionary without written permission from a professor. New rules also restricted student expenditures on fine clothes, food, and drink. Fearful that conspicuous consumption enhanced the influence of flamboyant and idle students, the Visitors meant to abolish "the temptations of parade and pleasure" that undermined "the acquirement of literature & science." They required a new "uniform and plain" dress made of dark grey cloth, at a price of no more than $6 per yard. Students could wear shoes but never the boots that had helped to hide bottles of liquor. In addition to cutting costs for fancy attire, the uniform would enable witnesses to identify students guilty of misdeeds in town.[60]

The new rules also compelled every student to deposit his money with the University proctor at the start of each term. The proctor then had to approve any withdrawal by a student, thereby discouraging bills to taverns and clothiers. Upon matriculating, a student received a copy of the rules and had to swear to honor them. The new regime did offer one concession to student discontent. Starting on July 20, the University would have a summer vacation of six weeks. In mollifying, as in cracking down, the Visitors broke with key policies favored by Jefferson.[61]

The strict rules of December 1826 briefly brought greater order to student life. In February 1827, Cocke's student son, Philip St. George Cocke, reported, "Things are carried on at present quite differently from what they were last year." Every morning at 6:30 A.M., in the predawn darkness, a janitor rang the bell, giving students half an hour before lectures began. Young Cocke added, "I have not heard of [a] single frolick or not even a noise" because the students were so busy "studying and improving their time."[62]

The order of February did not last. In May, the faculty discovered that students hosted two "women of pleasure" in their rooms. The chief culprit, John T. Wormeley, confessed but insisted that he had been "as private as he could be, but several young men rushed into his room, and by this means it became public." Wormeley estimated that, during the preceding three weeks, as "many as 26 students have had the same girls in their rooms." The faculty expelled him as a lone scapegoat rather than evict dozens of tuition-paying students.[63]

A month later, Cocke's son faced a faculty investigation for violating the rule barring students from hosting anyone expelled from the University. In October 1825, the faculty and Visitors had ousted William Eyre for participating in the great riot. Twenty months later, Eyre came back to see his friend Philip Cocke, who assured the faculty (and his father) that he was "in a very delicate situation, that Mr. Eyre had been at my father's house for some time passed, where he had been received and treated as a gentleman [and] that he came from home in company with me to Charlottesville." Philip concluded, "I should esteem a literal compliance with the [University] law as a most unpardonable breach of the sacred laws of hospitality." In Virginia, the social bonds of genteel hospitality trumped all. Rather than evict Philip, the faculty settled for censuring him and informing his father.[64]

Bored students blamed General Cocke for the new austerity. In 1828, the Visitors moved the morning bell to 5 A.M., which outraged the students, as did that year's cancellation of their Christmas vacation. One student complained, "We are all going on here very quietly & studiously and have the same dull routine to go through daily and weekly." Another predicted, "General Cocke, no doubt, with his usual sagacity, will . . . cut a double moat; or construct some kind of a barrier to prevent the students from visiting Charlottesville."[65]

The University paid dearly for its new rules and high costs. The proctor regarded the uniform requirement as "rather a preventative than an inducement to students to come here." Losing popularity, the University fell far short on Jefferson's dream of educating the entire elite of Virginia. The 163 students enrolled in 1826 became a receding peak. Numbers declined to, and then stagnated at, 110 to 120 in 1827 through 1829. A Visitor, James Breckinridge, complained that the institution had dwindled to "an inferior and ordinary Seminary." William Short lamented that many common academies in New England attracted more students than did Virginia's great University: "How different in the Yankee region! . . . Education with them is an indispensable neces-sary, with us it is a luxury only."[66]

Given Virginia's prolonged economic decline, few parents could afford the school's inflated tuition and high boarding costs. Short blamed Jefferson for spending too much on grand buildings, leaving too little for repairs and operating costs. To meet those costs, the University jacked up tuition and board, rendering "the expense oppressive to the parents," which "defeat[s] the great object of the Institution," to edu-cate many Virginians. Declining enrollment then depressed revenue. In 1828, the bursar regretted the expenses as "too high, exceeding much that at other institutions even Yale College." Unless the costs could "be greatly reduced the University must fail." Unwilling to reduce tuition, the Visitors instead lowered the board charged by hotelkeepers.[67]

The hotelkeepers were down-on-their-luck gentlemen out to recoup their fortunes from the hard times of the 1820s. One keeper's wife declared that their "minds have been depressed & kept down by the strong hand of misfortune." They had to crowd large families into just two rooms on the upper story, for the cramped hotels reserved the base-ment for a kitchen and slave quarters and the main floor for a dining hall.[68]

Pinched between high costs and shrinking revenue, the keepers made scant profits. In addition to paying $200 in annual rent to the Vis-itors, a keeper had to buy firewood, candles, and provisions plus rent or buy enslaved people to serve meals and clean rooms, shoes, and cloth-ing. The keepers had additional, unanticipated costs because Jefferson's beautiful, neoclassical plan omitted essential support structures: woodsheds, outhouses, stables, barns, and gardens. These the keepers had to build at their own expense, cluttering the landscape behind the beautiful brick façades. That infill made the place livable but dirtier and more ramshackle. To make money, keepers relied on $150 per term charged to each student, who signed up with that particular hotel. But student enrollment lagged, so there were too few boarders for all six hotels to thrive. In 1826, one keeper, Warner Minor, calculated that he paid $2,086 in costs but reaped only $2,483 in revenue, producing a profit of merely $300, a bare subsistence for his family.[69]

To retain and attract students, hotelkeepers indulged their whims and vices. Minor explained, "Boys enter . . . where they think the greatest liberties can be taken & most endeavours made to humour them." He felt "dependent on the caprice of mostly boys without reflection." To attract boarders, keepers cut into their thin profit margins by offering expensive food. As convivial gentlemen, keepers joined in the fun and games of students. A keeper thought it merely good manners to "treat and be treated by Students." Faculty lamented that the students had "too much power and the Hotel Keepers too little firmness and independence of character." Of the six keepers, only Minor enforced any rules of morality, and he merely discouraged cards and dice, for he considered drinking "impossible to prevent." But even his half measures sufficed to repel most students, rendering his hotel the worst attended and most financially marginal.[70]

When professors investigated, keepers showed solidarity with students, declaring that honor barred them from giving testimony. Otherwise, Minor explained, he would reap "constant insult & a certain loss of business." Professors complained, "The Hotel Keepers become part of the Body of the Students and . . . enter into their School-boy combinations." Cocke demanded, "Can no means be devised of converting these Gentry into policy officers instead of corrupting ministers to the unbridled appetites of indiscreet youth?"[71]

In December 1826, the Visitors sought tighter control by reducing the number of hotels to four, thereby decreasing the competition for scarce boarders and ousting the two most irresponsible keepers: S. B. Chapman and John Gray. But the dismissals proved easier to announce than to implement because the keepers' wives managed most of the work while, Trist reported, their husbands went "off to the springs, to the races, to Richmond, &c." George W. Spotswood confessed that he could never succeed "without a wife, in such an establishment," for "he would have to drag through the year a wretched existence, meeting with nothing but dissatisfaction, losses, & vexation."[72]

Gray's feisty wife, Sarah Carter Gray, worked to save her family by recovering her husband's lease. Writing to the Visitors, she denounced "the cruel sentence which has doomed us to the fate of Vagabonds . . . encumbered with helpless children." The dismissal cost her family a home and her children their best chance for a genteel education. "All these you have destroyed. You have condemned the minds of our Children to remain covered by the strong veil of ignorance & to have their hearts choked up with obnoxious weeds of vice & poison." Claiming the hotel as her responsibility, she blamed her husband's errors on "the galling consciousness of dependence on the exertions of his Wife."[73]

She had influential friends, including six professors, the Visitors' secretary, Trist, and the proctor, who was her relative. Trist attested that "While her husband is a most barefaced rogue," Mrs. Gray was "a most meritorious woman, and has conducted her hotel in the most exemplary manner, working like a slave, while her husband was riding about the country taking his pleasure." Trist warned, "To drive them away *now* would be like . . . tearing out the hearts of their wives & children." In January 1827, the Visitors relented and renewed her husband's lease for another seven months. At the expiration, they dismissed Mr. Gray but allowed his wife to run the establishment with a male relative as the nominal lessee, for the Visitors were too conventional to allow a woman to hold a lease.[74]

During the fall of 1827, Cocke resumed his crusade against "our old offenders, the Hotel keepers." Citing persistent rumors of drinking and gambling, he wanted to sack the lot save for his favorite, Minor. Rather than displace so many families, the Visitors settled for reducing the charge that each keeper could levy on a boarder from $150 to $100. To make ends meet, keepers reduced their services. Renting fewer slaves, the keepers struggled to clean their hotels and the students' rooms. The fare decayed in quality, which angered students.[75]

Spotswood complained that he would have to serve what would "only suit a Yankey who has never been used to any more than Onions, potatoes & Codfish and his coffee sweetened with molasses." Clinging to the Virginia standard of genteel fare, Spotswood lost his original capital of $3,000, replaced by $1,300 in debts. He had come to the university to restore his fortunes and status, but both deteriorated under the new regulations as he reaped insults from students irritated by the declining services. In December 1828, Thomas Hooe assaulted first Spotswood and then his enslaved servant to vent anger over an uncleaned room soiled by the student's dog (in violation of University rules against keeping pets). When the faculty refused to expel Hooe, Spotswood angrily resigned a position that had brought him grief rather than profit.[76]

Rival

Cabell and Cocke understood that one defended and the other challenged Jefferson's legacy at the University. Cabell supported Cocke's efforts to discipline students but balked at overtly Christianizing the institution as contrary to Virginia's separation of church and state. Cocke faulted his friend for defending "the old Sachem in his preposterous schemes." Cabell retorted, "I see you must play the Rival to the old Sachem." Only half in jest, Cocke derided Cabell's secularism as service to Satan: "I must give you up. The arch Fiend has done his work too effectually upon you for me to hope to make any impression now. The new developments of your fidelity in your Master's service lately at the University have blasted my last hopes." For the sake of friendship, Cabell bore Cocke's cajoling with polite patience.[77]

Blocked from Christianizing the institution directly, Cocke sought to correct Jefferson's "original error" by training pious students before they entered the University. At Charlottesville, he proposed founding a

Christian gymnasium as a feeder school. In the early nineteenth century, a gymnasium was a school on a German model that promoted a combination of moral, intellectual, and physical development. Cocke noted glowing reports of new gymnasia in New England at Northampton, Massachusetts and New Haven, Connecticut, which he toured.[78]

Cocke blamed the indolence and dissipation of young Virginians on families and schools that neglected religion and discipline. His gymnasium would train students as early as age six, "before their habits are fixed," by subjecting them to continuous supervision, frequent prayers, and daily Bible lessons—as well as classes in arithmetic, English literature, and ancient and modern languages. Cocke reasoned that "religious instruction will greatly conduce to the maintenance of proper discipline," through a combination of "a gentle, parental manner" with "a little corporal correction." A tall fence around the compound would "secure privacy and facilitate discipline." He concluded, "Boys will be always under the watch & ward of their instructors, . . . for they will not be suffered to go off the ground without special leave & the Professors will always be about or among them." By mandating "constant and unremitted inspection," Cocke's gymnasium would rescue boys from "all the evil communications and insidious influences about them" including "the very imperfect government of their parents." By total and prolonged immersion in a carefully contrived culture, boys would transcend the wayward ways of Virginia, providing a new model student for the University.[79]

To serve as the principal, Cocke recruited Professor Robert B. Patton of Princeton, who had investigated gymnasia in Germany. Visiting Virginia in late 1828 and spring 1829, Patton promoted the scheme with devout lectures. In Charlottesville, Mary E. Terrell gushed, "We are all enchanted with the man and his scheme. He is certainly a most sensible and elegant speaker as well as a most pious and benevolent man. Oh! What a treasure to our state it will be to have him at the head of such an institution as Gen. Cocke contemplates!"[80]

Cocke offered his new hotel for the school, but Patton disliked the building. Never mind, Cocke responded, I have the perfect alternative:

Monticello. The building's fame would advertise the school to Virginia's elite families, and, for Cocke, a Christian gymnasium would exorcize Monticello's infidel origins. He wrote to Jeff Randolph, executor for Jefferson's estate, offering to rent the decaying mansion.[81]

Patton would not commit unless Cocke could recruit at least fifty students, each paying $200, twice the usual tuition and board of a Virginia academy. To line up commitments, Cocke wrote to genteel friends throughout the state. He hoped to open the school in October 1829, but Cocke could procure only a dozen boys. Dismayed by this poor show, Patton opened his own gymnasium at Princeton. Without Patton, most of the parents withdrew the commitment of their sons. Without a principal, students, or Monticello, Cocke had no school.[82]

Virginians declined to pay premium prices to have Cocke take their children and reeducate them to reject the traditional gentry way of life. A friend, Edmund Ruffin, warned Cocke that "any such undertaking in V[irgini]a is utterly hopeless—unless we can *raise* a new generation of teachers as well as *fathers* of scholars." There was the rub. Cocke could not force-feed the Christianization of the gentry and University through an expensive gymnasium. That cultural change would come slowly and primarily through the moral influence of women in genteel families. That transition would get a boost from two epidemics that afflicted the students.[83]

Poor drainage and negligent sanitation bred sickness at the University. An epidemic of measles struck during the summer of 1828 followed by an outbreak of typhus during the winter of 1829. Over the course of nine months, the two epidemics killed at least nine students: more than at the College of William & Mary during any decade. Contrary to Jefferson's insistence, Charlottesville proved deadlier than Williamsburg for young men. Defying orders to remain, most of the students fled to avoid contagion in January and February. To save lives and some face, the faculty suspended classes from February through March 1829.[84]

Alarming reports spread through the state, threatening the University's reputation and survival. In February, Gessner Harrison lamented, "Now melancholy, despondent feelings have usurped the place of joy & chearfulness and are mingled with constant apprehensions." To counter grim reports, the faculty published newspaper essays and sent printed circulars to parents, downplaying death and upheaval at the University. The second epidemic receded in March, and most of the students returned in April.[85]

On May 24, 1829, in the Rotunda of the University, Cocke's friend Reverend William Meade delivered a memorial sermon for the dead students. Despite intense heat, Meade passionately preached to a great crowd that included students, professors, and members of the Monticello family. Asserting a providential view of the world, Meade rejected secular notions of "chance, or some general divine providence which attends only to great things ... but lets the atoms fly at random." He insisted that the dead students demonstrated "that this Institution is an offence unto God, and that he wills its destruction." Taking a swipe at Jefferson, Meade mocked investing hopes in great men: "See how easily the Almighty can blast all their high hopes and dash all their noble schemes to the earth." Meade urged students and professors to save the University by dedicating it to Christianity: "Oh, it is a hazardous experiment to undertake to conduct such an institution, in which the minds of young, immortal, and rational beings are to be instructed, and their passions restrained and their actions regulated, without constantly and earnestly imploring and seeking the aid of God."[86]

By making the dead into witnesses against a sinful university, Meade's sermon generated controversy. In fact, he overlooked a growing minority of pious students who joined with some of the faculty to subscribe funds for a chaplaincy shared by the local Episcopal and Presbyterian ministers who preached at alternate times and days in the Rotunda. In March 1827, Gessner Harrison told his brother Tiffin: "You would be surprised to see so many students attending the Church and generally behaving so well." In April 1829, even Mary E. Terrell, long a fiery critic of the students, praised the trend: "There is something quite new in hearing the sounds of prayer and praise among a set of people in *University uniform*."[87]

Pious students found growing support among the faculty, starting

with the first law professor, John Tayloe Lomax. As the original professors turned over, Visitors replaced them with devout young Virginians.
They included Gessner Harrison, a recent student who had just turned
twenty-one in 1828, when he became professor of ancient languages.
The new faculty lacked intellectual sparkle, but they proved more persistent and pious.[88]

That shift accelerated in 1845, when the Visitors named an ordained
Presbyterian, William Holmes McGuffey, to replace George Tucker as
professor of moral philosophy. McGuffey had published influential and
moralizing primary-school books known as McGuffey Readers. Where
the convivial Tucker favored leniency in discipline, the pious McGuffey
promoted temperance and convened students for morning prayers. One
recalled, "Nothing could have been grander than the continued attack
he made on atheism and infidelity." Every new faculty appointment
moved the university further from Jefferson's vision and toward Cocke's
alternative.[89]

Although Christian students grew in number, they remained too
few to control their rowdy peers, who bristled against enforcement of
the rules. During the 1830s, the University suffered riots far larger and
more violent than the fabled outbursts of 1825. At night, scores of students donned masks and gathered on the lawn to howl and blow tin
horns while others rang the university bell and shot pistols in the air.
They supplemented the ruckus with "corn songs," obscene ditties that
they had heard enslaved field hands sing during harvest. Rioting students also stole and burned barrels filled with tar, clouding the University with toxic smoke. When professors intervened, rioters smashed
pavilion doors and windows. In 1839, students roughed up Professor
Bonnycastle when he tried to stop a brutal beating of his slave named
Fielding. Others horsewhipped Harrison for refusing to apologize
after rebuking two of them. In November 1840, the new law professor,
John A. G. Davis, tried to unmask a rioting student, who pulled out a
pistol and shot Davis. This murder shocked most students into cooperating with an investigation, leading to the arrest of the killer, but he
jumped bail and fled to Texas.[90]

To replace Davis as the law professor, the Visitors hired Henry St. George Tucker fifteen years after Jefferson had rejected him for that post on political grounds. In October 1842, Tucker persuaded students to adopt an honor code, in which they vowed never to cheat on examinations and to identify those who did. University folklore credits the honor code with resolving the long years of violent crisis. In fact, the code was a small part of a larger cultural shift at the University. In July 1842, three months before Tucker's intervention, the faculty and Visitors did more to promote order by abolishing the hated uniform rule and softening enforcement of the despised early rising mandate. By reducing causes for friction, the authorities strengthened the influence of dutiful students. In a third key development of 1842, pious students organized a temperance society committed to abstinence from alcohol.[91]

Christian temperance and self-discipline emerged among the students as Jefferson's philosophy ebbed at the University of Virginia. In 1856 a student attested to a radical change at the University: "I think it is the last place in the world for a lazy man to try to enjoy himself." That shift made the University more attractive to an increasingly evangelical southern gentry. Enrollment surged from the 125 of 1842 to 425 in 1852 and 645 in 1856. In 1845, the Visitors helped that growth by providing, with legislative support, the first scholarships at the university: thirty-two for white boys who could not afford tuition. At last, the University reached the numbers predicted by Jefferson, but did so by embracing a religiosity that he had distrusted. In 1858, the University created the first collegiate chapter of the Young Men's Christian Association (YMCA).[92]

At last, three generations after the revolution, leading Virginians found a culture to modulate and channel the aggressive individualism unleashed by destroying the church establishment of the colonial era. By promoting piety and self-discipline, genteel Christians toned down the violent assertion of personal honor that had disrupted schools for decades.[93]

A fuller accounting of the University's origins would accord John

Hartwell Cocke due credit as a cofounder. He served longer than any Visitor, persisting through hard years of student disorder, while pioneering reforms that eventually stabilized the institution. But Cocke lacks the celebrity of Jefferson, who provides a more alluring and enduring face for the University's origins. During the twentieth century, as the University became more cosmopolitan and resumed a secular identity, Jefferson loomed ever larger, and Cocke receded into the shadows of memory.[94]

By founding the University of Virginia, Jefferson sought to reform the next generation of Virginia leaders in two ways. First, he wanted better legislators able to defend the state's rights in an increasingly contentious and powerful Union manipulated (he thought) by northern interests. Second, he hoped that a more enlightened leadership could reform Virginia, ridding it of social flaws. If properly empowered with the knowledge of "science," the next generation would, he believed, adopt a more democratic state constitution for white men; implement his comprehensive program for education; and both free and deport enslaved people. Despairing of implementing those changes in his own time, Jefferson counted on a new generation to succeed where he had fallen short.

Jefferson did not recognize the contradiction between his two great goals for the students. The University did train able defenders of the states' rights philosophy, but they were conservatives who resisted changing Virginia. They opposed democratizing the state constitution and did nothing more for primary education. Rejecting Jefferson's denunciation of slavery as immoral, they overtly celebrated slavery as a positive good for enslaved people as well as masters. The new generation coated their proslavery ideology in a Christian paternalism that cast masters as benevolent protectors of inferior beings. Rather than uproot slavery, as Jefferson had hoped, the University's students defended it and served the Confederacy in the Civil War.[95]

EPILOGUE

A TOURING COMPANY OF actors entertained Charlottesville in
September 1826, two months after Jefferson's death. The performers
included two dwarves, a brother and sister. The pious Mary E. Terrell saw
only foolish distraction for Charlottesville's many sinners: "This place has
been awfully visited by sickness & death this Summer, but I do not think it
has taught us any lessons of wisdom. The people are more frivolous than I

Martha Jefferson Randolph (1772–1836), by James Westhall Ford, 1823
(©Thomas Jefferson Foundation at Monticello)

ever knew them, wholly given up to pleasures & of the lowest kind—shows & exhibitions of a very groveling nature are all the rage. The Dwarfs have possessed the mind of the public for a fortnight past." She concluded, "The poor Students! These things are one excuse of their excessive dissipation."[1]

But Jefferson's granddaughter Cornelia Randolph enjoyed the show: "They move so quick & are so active & their diminutive size is wonderful. *She* seems good humoured & polite, very gay & coquettish, *he* surly & disposed to maintain his equality among men by airs of importance which only make him appear more ridiculous." Cornelia pitied the woman, "for they say at times her spirits fail her & she laments her fate greatly."[2]

After watching the dwarves perform, Cornelia returned to Monticello and marveled at the beautiful sunset, when "the deep indigo & bold outline of the blue ridge shows against the bright gold coloured or orange western sky." Her family loved the place but knew that they would lose it to pay her grandfather's debts. Where they should go, "whether to Louisiana or Vermont, to the west or the east," Cornelia did not know. Her sister Mary added that they had new schemes "every day, planned, advocated and opposed by the different members of the family."[3]

Jeff Randolph and Francis Eppes wanted to take everyone south and west, where they could rebuild the estate by operating cotton plantations with enslaved labor. Such a move would bolster their masculine self-esteem as patriarchs who provided for dependent women. "I want to go where I can make more money," Eppes explained. Using slang for an enslaved person, he longed to move where "Cuffee hires for one hundred and sixty dollars per annum!!! Here lies the road to wealth! Bundle up, and let us leave our gullies to the Yankee pedlars, who covet them so much." While Jeff lingered in Albemarle, reviving the Edgehill Plantation of his father, Eppes sold Poplar Forest and headed south to Florida. Thriving as a cotton planter, he helped found Florida State University. Building universities ran in the family.[4]

The Randolph women preferred to escape north and east to the land of those Yankees. Martha Jefferson Randolph declared, "The discomfort of slavery I have borne all my life, but its sorrows in all their bitterness

I had never before conceived" until debts compelled her to sell a cherished house servant. "Nothing," she concluded, "can prosper under such a system of injustice." In November 1826, to reduce expenses, Jefferson's granddaughters moved to Jeff's nearby Tufton Farm. Mary reported, "At present we are very homesick."[5]

When the state-authorized lottery failed to rescue Jefferson's estate, gender again divided the family's response. The men blamed the economic influence of Yankees, denounced by Eppes as a "leaden-hearted, copper-souled race of tin pedlars" whose selfish example had turned Virginians into misers. He concluded, "The noxious exhaltations from the eastern states have poisoned our atmosphere. Yankee notions, and Yankee practices have wrought a thorough change in the public mind. The maxim now is to take care of number one; and that too at the expence of every principle of honour, and generosity, and justice." The family's women, however, thought that Virginians needed no lessons in ingratitude from Yankees.[6]

When the lottery failed, the estate had to liquidate assets to satisfy Jefferson's debt of at least $100,000. First the heirs sold personal property—livestock, furniture, and enslaved people—for Virginia law delayed alienating real estate as a last resort. In January 1827, an auctioneer sold 130 enslaved people at Monticello. Jefferson's death was, Israel Gillette recalled, "an affair of great moment and uncertainty to us slaves." Buyers poked and prodded, inspecting muscles and teeth, before making bids. Twelve years old, Peter Fossett was "put upon an auction block and sold to strangers." He later recalled, "Then began our troubles. We were scattered all over the country, never to meet each other again until we meet in another world." In lost family ties and new uncertainties, enslaved people paid the most to satisfy Jefferson's debts.[7]

After the auction of personal property, Monticello remained in limbo for four years before it, too, sold. In September 1827, a visitor found it "dark & much dilapidated with age & neglect." In 1828, Margaret Bayard Smith mourned the contrast wrought by the eighteen years since her last visit, when Jefferson had been alive and vibrant: "No kind friend with his gracious countenance stood in the Portico to welcome us, no train of domestics hastened with smiling alacrity to show us forward. . . . Ruin has already commenced its ravages." Entering the house, she found a "defaced floor" and walls stripped of pictures, "busts, and statues and natural curiosities." Cornelia Randolph added, "I was sad to see the negro cabins lying in little heaps of ruin everywhere." A few years later, a visiting architect noted, "The first thing that strikes you is the utter ruin and desolation of everything. The house is of brick, in the same wretched style as the university."[8]

In his will, Jefferson freed a handful of favored slaves, including his longtime butler, Burwell Colbert, who had tended to the dying philosopher. Living in a cabin on the grounds, Colbert struggled to maintain the fading mansion. "He seems to take pleasure in keeping things as they used to be," Cornelia marveled. But Colbert fought a losing battle against a "vulgar herd" of uninvited tourists, who wrenched away souvenirs, damaging house and gardens. As white people, they laughed at Colbert's protests. Jeff concluded that he needed "to employ some respectable white man to take care of the place."[9]

Weary of living with Jeff at Tufton, his sisters longed to reclaim Monticello if only temporarily. In May 1827, to escape the heat, Cornelia rode up to Monticello, where she indulged in breezes, views, and memories, noting the "mixture of pleasure & pain which I always feel here now." A year later, Martha and her daughters recolonized Monticello, scraping together enough chairs, tables, and beds. The women experienced the mountain more keenly as relative deprivation honed their senses. Cornelia assured a sister, "We never so fully appreciated its beauties & comforts as we do now." She noted, "the indescribable charm that pervades the whole place; the very wind sounds differently from what it does anywhere else; it *rolls*, coming unconfined & uninterrupted from a distance & literally plays with the leaves of the trees & then the birds, the wood robins sing so clearly & feelingly."[10]

But the granddaughters worried that their aunt, Virginia Randolph Cary, would learn of their return and try to join them at Monticello. In November 1826, Cary had lost her home, Carysbrook, to a fire, and then moved to Bremo Recess, a part of Cocke's plantation. But

Cary soon fell out with her longtime friend, Louisa Cocke, while they attended a religious meeting in Lynchburg. Overly possessive of her older brother, Reverend William Maxwell, Louisa suspected her friend of flirting with him. Martha noted, "V[irginia] C[ary]'s conversational powers have always made her a favorite with the Gentlemen." Turning cold and rude, Louisa banished Cary from her carriage and home. Martha concluded that Cary "has lost a friend, whom she certainly loved very much . . . and a very pleasant house, the only genteel one in her immediate neighbourhood to visit at." To discourage her from moving to Monticello, the Randolph women pretended that they would soon return to Tufton Farm.[11]

In June 1828, the death of Martha's husband, Thomas Mann Randolph, came as a relief rather than a blow. In 1826, he had lost his beloved Edgehill to creditors, including his son Jeff, a transition that infuriated his frustrated father. When his son rode through a forest, father ambushed him, hurling stones to kill, but Jeff spurred his horse to safety. Financially ruined and estranged from wife and children, Randolph withdrew to wither in a small cottage at Milton village. In March 1828, he became too sick to live on his own, so he moved to a garden pavilion at Monticello. While Randolph superficially reconciled with his family, he avoided them, eating alone. In June, Randolph's corpse joined Jefferson's in the family plot near Monticello. Martha sighed, "no longer an object of terror or apprehension, he became one of . . . commiseration." She considered his death "for the best," lest he recover and resume his violent fury.[12]

Martha and her daughters had two schemes to recoup their fortunes and save Monticello: publish Jefferson's letters and found a boarding school for girls. Both relied on their genteel, but hitherto underemployed, educations. They spent five to eight hours a day reading and transcribing letters, relying on a magnifying glass to decipher the most difficult handwriting. "We work very hard with the manuscript which . . . leaves us little time to do anything else," Cornelia noted. For this labor of love, they received no pay, as the proceeds went to reduce grandfather's massive debt and to pay tuition at the University for their younger brother Benjamin. Published in 1829, the letters outraged Presbyterians who read Jefferson's rants against them. Obtaining a sneak peek at the Charlottesville printing office, Benjamin Rice (John Holt Rice's brother and fellow preacher) took "great offense." Later that day, he delivered a passionate sermon that assailed Jefferson's religious ideas.[13]

To support themselves, Martha and her daughters proposed founding a boarding school for girls. They would emulate their aunt Hackley's school, recently relocated to Norfolk, and Mrs. Garnett's celebrated Elmwood School. Martha explained that she had no resource left "but an education given in happier days and for very different purposes." She would superintend and teach advanced music, French, and Italian. Cornelia might instruct in drawing, natural history, geography, and Spanish, and her sister Virginia could introduce students to music. But Martha still hoped that state legislatures around the Union would rescue the family financially and "save me from the horrors of keeping a boarding school."[14]

While Martha dreaded the hard work at her age, her daughters relished a chance to prove themselves. Keeping school promised financial independence, which Cornelia considered "infinitely better than dependence, particularly dependence on brother Jeff, for to tell you the truth, he is so possessed with the idea that we do not know how to be economical that nothing would persuade him [to] the contrary if we lived on less than one of his own negroes costs him." He loved to tell people that his silly sisters had spoiled enslaved servants with sugar and coffee (the sisters denied it). Cornelia found inspiration in her grandfather's letters that revealed his resourceful persistence, so she resolved: "We will never despair, we will never be cast down by difficulties, we will bear ourselves bravely & be cheerful in the midst of misfortunes & if we are thrown upon our own resources, we will find them in ourselves." But competition from a similar school in Charlottesville postponed their plans.[15]

In 1829, Martha and her daughters moved away to Washington, D.C., before they had to watch Monticello pass into other hands. She warned that Jefferson's family faced "total ruin" and would feel the "bitter anguish of seeing his abode rendered desolate, the walls dismantled, and the sanctuary of his bed room violated by the auctioneer." Cornelia mourned, "I know not when our afflictions will end & wonder we are not crushed to the earth by the weight of them." She feared that a vulgar entrepreneur would buy Monticello to serve as a tavern. "To me this seems like prophaning a temple & I had rather the weeds & wild animals which are fast taking possession of the grounds, should grow and live in the house itself." In 1831, Monticello sold for $7,000, one-third of the value set on it by Jeff Randolph. That modest return did little to reduce the family's massive debt. The Jefferson-Randolphs retained only the family cemetery on the mountainside.[16]

In 1840, a pious Episcopalian minister visited Monticello and exulted at the decay to Jefferson's grave monument and mansion: "His plans are all defeated. The religion of Jesus triumphs over all his opposition. . . . All his greatness has perished and is forgotten because he was an infidel." That perspective came from his guide, whom he described as a Jefferson relative intimately familiar with Monticello and "a lady well known in the literary world": a combination unique to Virginia Randolph Cary, who loved the Monticello family but hated their beliefs.[17]

While Monticello was lost, the granddaughters had returned with their mother to nearby Edgehill, where she died in 1836. Never marrying, Cornelia and Mary helped Jeff's wife Jane run a school. A pedagogical success, the Edgehill School for Young Ladies had thirty students by 1850, and their tuition helped pay down the family debt.[18]

Then came the Civil War, when Jeff's political choices cost the family dearly. True to his grandfather's politics, Jeff had promoted gradual emancipation and a more democratic constitution as a state legislator during the early 1830s. Unpopular with his Albemarle constituents, those liberal positions cost him reelection. Thereafter, he became more conservative and praised southern slavery for offering the best resolution to "the conflict in all civilized society . . . between capital and labor." During the crisis of 1861, he supported Virginia's secession from the Union and invested heavily in Confederate weapons and bonds, which became worthless when northern forces triumphed in the Civil War. He also lost his slaves to the emancipation forced by the victors.[19]

Once again, the family faced ruin. In 1866, a former Monticello slave, Israel Gillette Jefferson (he added the last name upon gaining his freedom) returned from Ohio on a visit. He found Jeff "surrounded by the evidence of former ease and opulence gone to decay. . . . Except his real estate, the rebellion stripped him of everything, save one old blind mule." No admirer of Jeff, Gillette enjoyed seeing "the proud and haughty Randolph in poverty at Edge Hill."[20]

Jeff's wife and daughters came to the financial rescue a second time, reopening their Edgehill School in 1867. By marketing education for women, the Jefferson-Randolphs stabilized their position in Virginia society. When Jefferson educated his granddaughters, he had no idea that he was preparing them to work as savvy managers and dedicated teachers of a new generation of women. Nor did Jefferson anticipate that they would help save the family from his financial mistakes and those of their brother, to whom the old patriarch had entrusted his estate. Forgiving those mistakes, they revered their grandfather's memory and made the most of Thomas Jefferson's education.[21]

ACKNOWLEDGMENTS

LIKE A VIRGINIAN of the early republic, my debts are many, but mine are far more pleasant to acknowledge. True friends and great scholars, Ari Kelman and Peter Onuf, read the entire manuscript and recommended essential improvements. Brian Balogh, Christa Dierksheide, Carolyn Eastman, Johann Neem, Mark Valeri, and Liz Varon read select chapters and provided invaluable suggestions. Andrew O'Shaughnessy offered many insights, generous support, and the opportunity to present to the conference he organized (with deft assistance from John Ragosta) on education in Jefferson's Virginia. Jeff Looney, the peerless editor of the *Thomas Jefferson Papers, Retirement Series*, provided valuable insights and early access to new volumes. Susan Kern gave a revealing tour of the old campus at the College of William & Mary.

I am also grateful to the Farmington Historical Society, the Library Company of Philadelphia, and the National Humanities Center for opportunities to present early versions of parts of this project. George Gilliam generously arranged my presentation at Farmington: just one of his many kind and thoughtful deeds.

I benefited from generous support at the University of Virginia, particularly from my dean, Ian Baucom, and department chair, Karen Parshall. My morale got a weekly boost from the great friends who convene a seminar at the Biltmore or Michael's Bistro. Sadly, as I finished this book we lost Joseph Miller, a consummate scholar, devoted friend, and adept treasurer. Max Edelson has also been the best of colleagues and friends; an inspirational convener of the Early American Seminar; and, despite affiliating with the Minnesota Twins, a devoted supporter of Mookie Betts. Andy Burstein, Frank Cogliano, Nancy Isenberg, and my aspiring amigo Maurizio Valsania shared their expertise on Jefferson and his world. I learned much about the history of higher education from Steven Brint. All references to pirate culture derive from the boisterous expertise of Kevin R. Convey.

I began writing the book as the Harold Vyvyan Harmsworth Professor at Queens College of the University of Oxford, where many people were exceptionally kind and helpful, including Alexandra and Vyv Harmsworth. I am also grateful to Nicholas Cole, Gareth Davies, Sir John Elliott, Mandy Izadi, Alice Kelly, Margaret MacMillan, Don Ratcliffe, Hamish and Julia Scott, and Bryan Ward-Perkins. At Queens College, I received warm support from the provost, Paul Madden, and his thoroughly competent assistant Elaine Evers. I had an office in the Rothermere American Institute, where Huw David, Hal Jones, Pekka Hämäläinen, Michèle Mendelssohn, and Jane Rawson provided great help. Elsewhere in that green and rainy land, Nicholas Guyatte was the wittiest and best guide through the craggy castles, country pubs, and foggy moors of Yorkshire—as well as the many mysteries of cricket.

Archivists and librarians provided essential support for the research embedded in this book. I am grateful to the staffs at Swem Library of the College of William & Mary, the Library of Virginia, the Historical Society of Virginia, and the Library of Congress, and at Lambeth Palace. In Richmond, Brent Tarter was an indispensable and savvy guide to all things related to Virginia. At William & Mary, Susan Riggs and Martha Howard facilitated my work. I had the good fortune to spend most of my research time at the Albert and Shirley Small Special Collections Library of the University of Virginia, where I received expert guidance from Krystal Appiah, Sara Lee Barnes, Anne P. Causey, Ervin L. Jordan, Regina D. Rush, Penny White, and David Whitesell.

For assistance with illustrations, I am grateful to Camille Worrell of the Library of Congress; Lily Gellman of W. W. Norton; Jeff Looney and John McKee at Monticello/Thomas Jefferson Foundation; Meg Kennedy, Rob Smith, Leah Hildreth Stearns, and David Whitesell of UVA; Laura Fogarty of the Muscarelle Museum of Art at the College of William & Mary; Jamison Davis of the Virginia Historical Society; and Alisa Reynolds of the Chrysler Museum.

As literary representation, Andrew Wylie and his assistants provided expert advocacy and support. Throughout the process of writing and production, I benefited from the sage and supportive guidance of a consummate editor, Steve Forman, and his colleagues at W. W. Norton, including assistant project editor Amy Medeiros.

The book's dedication recognizes the great kindness, good spirits, and inspirational work of two dear and recently deceased friends, Jan E. Lewis and Wilson Smith. In writing about families and cultural change in Jefferson's Virginia, I immensely benefited from Jan's work. A true amigo, her thoughtfulness and wit enriched the lives of all who knew her. A quarter of a century ago, Bill Smith welcomed me to the University of California at Davis and became an unfailing guide to that corner of the world and, with his thoughtful wife Kay, a great benefactor to graduate education in history. I regularly shared lunch and laughter with Bill. His work and conversation about the history of higher education planted seeds that I have tried my best to cultivate. I think of him often and mourn losing him.

The dedication also enables me to pay tribute to my dear friend and spiritual guide, Pablo Ortiz, who, along with Chris Reynolds, provided a memorable road trip across the continent as I started at the University of Virginia. I am helping Pablo to write his autobiography, aptly titled "Born to Be an American," which will offer a truly heroic main text corrected by a running commentary in footnotes written by his wife Ana and daughters Isa and Cami.

Above all, Emily Albu has been the kindest, most selfless person that I will ever know. Plus she is incredibly smart, funny, and blessed with the world's finest penmanship, honed by hours of practice when other children were playing at recess.

NOTES

Collections

BFP	Bryan Family Papers
BLFP	Blow Family Papers
CCFP	Carr-Cary Family Papers
CFP	Campbell Family Papers
CRP&R	Correspondence, Reports, Petitions, and Resolutions Relating to the Construction, Staffing, and Governance of the University
CWBP	Catharine Wistar Bache Papers
DWFP	David Watson Family Papers
DWP	David Watson Papers
ECP	Edward Coles Papers
ELUVA	Early Life at the University of Virginia
EWRCP	Ellen Wayles Randolph Coolidge Papers
FPP	Fulham Palace Papers
FO-NA	Founders Online, National Archives
GFC	Gilmer Family Correspondence
GFN	Gilmer Family Notebooks
GFP	Grinnan Family Papers
HFP	Hubard Family Papers
JBP	Jonathan Boucher Papers
JCCFP	Joseph C. Cabell Family Papers
JFL	Jefferson Family Letters
JHCP	John Hartwell Cocke Papers
JMPM	Journal of the Meetings of the President and Masters, College of William & Mary
JUEL	Jefferson's University, the Early Life (website at UVA)

LPEP	Letters and Papers of Edmund Pendleton
MFP	Maury Family Papers
NPTP	Nicholas P. Trist Papers
PGW-ColS	*Papers of George Washington, Colonial Series*
PGW-ConS	*Papers of George Washington, Confederation Series*
PGW-PS	*Papers of George Washington, Presidential Series*
PGW-RWS	*Papers of George Washington, Revolutionary War Series*
PJM	*Papers of James Madison*
PJM-PS	*Papers of James Madison, Presidential Series*
PJM-RS	*Papers of James Madison, Retirement Series*
PJM-SSS	*Papers of James Madison, Secretary of State Series*
PRGP	Peachy R. Gilmer Papers
PTJ	*Papers of Thomas Jefferson*
PTJ-RS	*Papers of Thomas Jefferson, Retirement Series*
RFEP	Randolph Family of Edgehill Papers
SGAC	Simon Gratz Autograph Collection
SMP	Samuel Myers Papers
TCP	Tucker, Coleman Papers
THSP	Tucker, Harrison, Smith Papers
VMHB	*Virginia Magazine of History and Biography*
WDFP	William Dawson Family Papers
WMQ	*William & Mary Quarterly*

Archives and Libraries

APS	American Philosophical Society (Philadelphia)
ASSCL-UVA	Albert and Shirley Small Special Collections Library, University of Virginia (Charlottesville)
DMRML-DU	David M. Rubenstein Manuscript Library, Duke University (Durham)
HSP	Historical Society of Pennsylvania (Philadelphia)
ICJS	International Center for Jefferson Studies
JDRL-CWF	John D. Rockefeller Library, Colonial Williamsburg Foundation
LPL	Lambeth Palace Library (London, U.K.)
LV	Library of Virginia (Richmond)
MDLC	Manuscript Division, Library of Congress (Washington, D.C.)
SCSL-CWM	Special Collections, Swem Library, College of William & Mary (Williamsburg)
SHC-UNC	Southern Historical Collection, University of North Carolina (Chapel Hill)
VHS	Virginia Historical Society (Richmond)

Introduction

1. Thomas Jefferson to John Harvie, June 14, 1760, in Boyd et al., eds., *PTJ*, vol. 1:3.

2. Thomas Jefferson to Thomas Jefferson Randolph, Nov. 24, 1808, FO-NA, http://founders.archives.gov/documents/Jefferson/99-01-02-9151.

3. "Sketch of a Plan for the Endowment and Establishment of a State University in Virginia," *Richmond Enquirer*, Feb. 1, 1805. For the traditional narrative, see Cremin, *American Education*, 2–8. For Jefferson's limits as an education reformer, see Egerton, "Tombs of the Capulets," 155–74; Kaestle, *Pillars of the Republic*, 8–9, 198–99.

4. Thomas Jefferson to Samuel Knox, Feb. 12, 1810, in Looney et al., eds., *PTJ-RS*, vol. 2:215–16; Glover, "'Let Us Manufacture Men,'" 23–27; Glover, *Southern Sons*, 3–4.

5. Thomas Jefferson to Marquis de Chastellux, June 7, 1785, and Jefferson to James Madison, Sept. 6, 1789, in Boyd et al., eds., *PTJ*, vol. 8:184 ("It is") and vol. 15:392–98; Jefferson to Joseph C. Cabell, Jan. 17, 1814, and Jefferson to Samuel Kercheval, July 12, 1816, in Looney et al., eds., *PTJ-RS*, vol. 7:133–35, and vol. 10:222–28; Grossberg, "Citizens and Families," 3–5.

6. Taylor, *Internal Enemy*, 7–10.

7. Isaac, *Transformation of Virginia*, 181–92.

8. Thomas Jefferson to James Madison, Sept. 6, 1789 Boyd et al., eds., *PTJ*, vol. 15:392–98.

9. Levasseur, *Lafayette in America*, vol. 1:222–23; Gordon-Reed, *Hemingses of Monticello*, 641–45.

10. Glover, *Southern Sons*, 39–41, St. George Tucker quoted on 39; Grossberg, "Citizens and Families," 15–26.

11. St. George Tucker to Theodorick and John Randolph, June 29, 1788, in Kaminski et al., eds., *Documentary History*, vol. 10:1720; Glover, *Southern Sons*, 39–41.

12. Ayers, *Vengeance and Justice*, 3–4, 10–11, 26; D. D. Bruce, *Violence and Culture*, 27; Glover, *Southern Sons*, 22–34, 45–46.

13. Glover, "'Let Us Manufacture Men,'" 36–37; Novak, *Rights of Youth*, 17–23.

14. Koganzon, "Producing a Reconciliation," 428–29; Ravitch, *Left Behind*, 455–59.

1. College

1. Thomas Jefferson to Joseph C. Cabell, Jan. 24, 1816, in Looney et al., eds., *PTJ-RS*, vol. 9:396–98; "Tim Pastime" to William Hunter, 1761, Ms. 1990.4, JDRL-CWF; Morpurgo, *Their Majesties' Royall Colledge*, 125–26; Board of Visitors meetings, Aug. 14, 1760, FPP, vol. 13:284–87, LPL.

2. McColley, *Slavery and Jeffersonian Virginia*, 9–10; R. B. Davis, ed., *Jeffersonian America*, 128–32; Morgan, *Slave Counterpoint*, 29–33.

3. E. C. Carter et al., eds., *Virginia Journals*, vol. 1:78; G. Tucker, *Letters from Virginia*, 18–9; Darrell, "Diary," 147; Morgan, *Slave Counterpoint*, 34; Wyllie, ed., "Observations," 393–96.

4. Jonathan Boucher to John James, Aug. 19, 1759, in Boucher, "Letters," 8; Sobel, *World They Made Together*, 131; Smyth, *Tour*, vol. 1:36–37; John Randolph to James M. Garnett, Aug. 21, 1812, John Randolph Papers, box 3, ASSCL-UVA.

5. John Randolph to James M. Garnett, Aug. 21, 1812, John Randolph Papers, box 3, ASSCL-UVA; Smyth, *Tour*, vol. 1:9, 37 ("perfumes" and "fruits").

6. Kulikoff, *Tobacco and Slaves*, 141–53; Smyth, *Tour*, vol. 1:15.

7. Anbury, *Travels*, vol. 2:322–25, 338–39; E. C. Carter, ed., *Virginia Journals*, vol. 1:102, 127, 140; Darrell, "Diary," 144 ("Now & then"); E. G. Evans, "Topping People," 151–59; Schoepf, *Travels*, vol. 2:31–33, 48; Smyth, *Tour*, vol. 1:15–16, 37, 49–50; Jefferson quoted in Sobel, *World They Made Together*, 117.

8. Slaves quoted in Bayard, *Travels of a Frenchman*, 136; Jonathan Boucher to John James, Aug. 7, 1759, in Boucher, "Letters," 4; Creswell, *Journal*, 268; Gwatkin, "On the Manners," 84.

9. Fithian, *Journal*, 233; Smyth, *Tour*, vol. 1:43, 70–71; G. Tucker, *Letters from Virginia*, 115–18.

10. Boucher, *View of the Causes*, 187–89 ("whilst"); Burnaby, *Travels*, 22–23; Chastellux, *Travels*, vol. 2:438 ("miserable"); Gordon, "Journal of an Officer," 404; Smyth, *Tour*, vol. 2:45–48, 65–68 ("greater distinction").

11. Breen, "Horses and Gentlemen," 246; Bayard, *Travels of a Frenchman*, 20; Peter Collinson quoted in Kern, *Jeffersons at Shadwell*, 19 ("Virginians"); Schoepf, *Travels*, vol. 2:33, 36–37.

12. Boucher, *Reminiscences*, 61–62; Greene, "Foundations," 485–92; E. G. Evans, "Topping People," 121–27; Isaac, *Transformation of Virginia*, 132–33.

13. C. S. Sydnor, *Gentlemen Freeholders*, 28–29, 36–38; G. Wood, *Radicalism*, 49.

14. Bridenbaugh, *Seat of Empire*, 34–39; Tarter, *Grandees of Government*, 87–89.

15. E. G. Evans, "Topping People," 134–39, Nathaniel Burwell quoted on 135; L. Griffith, ed., "English Education for Virginia Youth," 15–16, 19; Isaac, *Transformation of Virginia*, 131.

16. Boucher, "Letters," 12, 339; E. G. Evans, "Topping People," 134–39; Isaac, *Transformation of Virginia*, 131; Zimmer, *Jonathan Boucher*, 38–41, 47–48.

17. Richard Ambler to Edward and John Ambler, Aug. 1, 1748, in L. Griffith, ed., "English Education for Virginia Youth," 14–16; Richard Henry Lee to William Lee, Apr. 13, and July 12, 1772, in Ballagh, ed., *Letters of Richard Henry Lee*, vol. 1:70–71.

18. Bland quoted in Tarter, *Grandees of Government*, 85.

19. Smyth, *Tour*, vol. 1:65.

20. Ayres, "Albemarle County," 36–55; Boucher, "Letters," 163; Du Roi, *Journal*,

155–59 ("seldom"); Gordon-Reed and Onuf, *Most Blessed of the Patriarchs*, 27–28; Majewski, *House Dividing*, 14–16.

21. Gordon-Reed, *Hemingses*, 92–94; Kern, *Jeffersons at Shadwell*, 1–22, 117–20, 127–28, 147–56, 175–79; D. Malone, *Jefferson and His Time*, vol. 1:37–38.

22. Gordon-Reed and Onuf, *Most Blessed of the Patriarchs*, 28; Wagoner, *Jefferson and Education*, 18–19. For the wet nurse, see Kern, *Jeffersons at Shadwell*, 48–49.

23. E. G. Evans, "*Topping People*," 141–44; Kern, *Jeffersons at Shadwell*, 73–77, 114–15.

24. Kern, *Jeffersons at Shadwell*, 2–22, 42–43, 111, 120, 182; Jefferson, "Autobiography," 3; D. Malone, *Jefferson and His Time*, vol. 1:38.

25. Jefferson, "Autobiography," 3–4 ("correct"); Thomas Jefferson to Joseph Priestley, Jan. 27, 1800, in Boyd et al., eds., *PTJ*, vol. 31:339–41 ("I thank him'); Jefferson to James Maury, Jr., Apr. 25, 1812, in Looney et al., eds., *PTJ-RS*, vol. 4:669–71 ("Reviewing"); Jefferson to Thomas Walker Maury, Mar. 3, 1826 ("welcome"), FO-NA, http://founders.archives.gov/documents/Jefferson/98-01-02-5944; Wagoner, *Jefferson and Education*, 19–20.

26. James Maury to John Fontaine, Aug. 9, 1755, in Fontaine and Maury, eds., *Memoirs of a Huguenot Family*, 379; Thomas Jefferson to William Wirt, Aug. 14, 1814, in Looney et al., eds, *PTJ-RS*, vol. 7:544–51 ("I was at").

27. "Philo-Americanus," *Virginia Gazette* (Purdie and Dixon), Nov. 9, 1769, supplement ("brightest gem"); Bridenbaugh, *Seat of Empire*, 35–37; R. B. Davis, *Intellectual Life*, 12–14; Gordon, "Journal of an Officer," 404–5; Gwatkin, "On the Manners," 84 ("The first toasts"); A. Lee, *Essay in Vindication*, 23–24; E. Randolph, "Essay," *VMHB*, vol. 43:117, and vol. 44:43.

28. Fontaine and Maury, eds., *Memoirs of a Huguenot Family*, 392–94; Bridenbaugh, *Seat of Empire*, 1–2. For Botetourt's coach, see Pickering, ed., *Life of Timothy Pickering*, vol. 1:297–98.

29. David Mossom et al. to the House of Burgesses, Aug. n.d., 1751, in Perry, ed., *Historical Collections*, vol. 1:382–83 ("Glory"), 384; James Maury to William Douglass, Nov. 20, 1759 ("such a close"), MFP, box 1, ASSCL-UVA; Boucher, *View of the Causes*, 100–104; Maury, *To Christians of Every Denomination*, 31–32.

30. Buckley, *Church and State*, 11; Burnaby, *Travels*, 17; Morton, *Colonial Virginia*, vol. 2:770–71; Nelson, *Blessed Company*, 43–45, 48–56.

31. Boucher, "Letters," 339; Buckley, *Church and State*, 9–10; Gordon, "Journal of an Officer," 406; Nelson, *Blessed Company*, 6–8; Spangler, *Virginians Reborn*, 33–40.

32. Boucher, "Letters," 9, 16–18; Boucher, *Reminiscences*, 42; Fithian, *Journal*, 262; Gunderson, "Search for Good Men," 457–60; Isaac, "Religion and Authority," 7–12, 32–35, James Maury quoted on 34; Nelson, *Blessed Company*, 30–40, 135–50.

33. Buckley, *Church and State*, 10–11; Burnaby, *Travels*, 17; Gunderson, "Search for Good Men," 453–54; Nelson, *Blessed Company*, 151–56. For John Ramsay, see Francis Fauquier to Bishop of London, Apr. 27, 1767, and St. Anne's Vestry to Fauquier, undated, FPP, vol. 14:109, and 299–300, LPL.

34. Fontaine and Maury, eds., *Memoirs of a Huguenot Family*, 401–2; Burnaby, *Travels*, 18–20; Camm, *Single and Distinct View*, 4; Morpurgo, *Their Majesties' Royall Colledge*, 121; Francis Fauquier to the Board of Trade, Jan. 5, 1759, in Reese, ed., *Official Papers*, vol. 1:144.

35. Burnaby, *Travels*, 19; John Camm et al. to Bishop of London, Nov. 29, 1755, and John Brunskill, Sr., et al. to Bishop of London, Feb. 25, 1756, in Perry, ed., *Historical Collections*, vol. 1:434 ("shall happen"), 443 ("Our being"); Morton, *Colonial Virginia*, vol. 2:787.

36. Morpurgo, *Their Majesties' Royall Colledge*, 121; Francis Fauquier to Board of Trade, Jan. 5, 1759, in Reese, ed., *Official Papers*, vol. 1:145 ("Man of Abilities"); Tate, "Colonial College," 90–96; Lyon G. Tyler, ed., "Sketch of John Camm," *WMQ*, 1st ser., vol. 19 (July 1910): 28–30.

37. James Maury to Jonathan Boucher, Nov. 22, 1763, JBP, box 2, SCSL-CWM; L. Carter, *Letter*, 49; E. G. Evans, *Thomas Nelson*, 30–31; Isaac, "Religion and Authority," 4–6, 17; Morton, *Colonial Virginia*, vol. 2:800, 816–19.

38. Camm, *Critical Remarks*, 19 ("Does the Colonel"), 63 ("*Aegyptian*"); E. Randolph, "Essay," *VMHB*, vol. 43:134; Oast, *Institutional Slavery*, 27–28.

39. William Robinson to Bishop of London, Nov. 20, 1760, and Robinson to the Bishop, c. 1763, in Perry, ed., *Historical Collections*, vol. 1:463–64, 476–78 ("Look at" and "this last"); Francis Fauquier to the Board of Trade, June 30, 1760, in Reese, ed., *Official Papers*, vol. 1:383–85; Tim Pastime to William Hunter, 1761 ("Black sheep"), Ms. 1990–94, JDRL-CWF.

40. James Maury to Jonathan Boucher, Nov. 22, 1763, and Maury, "Narrative of the Determination of a Suit," 1765 ("Enemies"), JBP, box 2, SCSL-CWM; Boucher, *Reminiscences*, 60.

41. Isaac, "Religion and Authority," 19–20; Kukla, *Patrick Henry*, 39–46.

42. Boucher, *View of the Causes*, 100; Buckley, *Church and State*, 12–14; Isaac, "Religion and Authority," 21–23; Jarrett, *Life*, 50–52; Nelson, *Blessed Company*, 285.

43. James Maury to William Douglass, May 31, 1758, MFP, box 1, ASSCL-UVA; Jarrett, *Life*, 21–22, 36–37, 41, 47–49, 83, 87–89; Spangler, *Virginians Reborn*, 36.

44. Fithian, *Journal*, 96 ("destroying"); Isaac, "Rage of Malice," 162; Jarrett, *Life*, 86; Lindman, "Acting the Manly Christian," 393–401.

45. Hildrup, *Edmund Pendleton*, 91–92; Isaac, *Transformation of Virginia*, 192–93; Longmore, "All Matters," 778–81; Ragosta, *Religious Freedom*, 52–55.

46. Boucher, *View of the Causes*, 92–96, 109–12,146; John Camm, "To Samuel Henley and Thomas Gwatkin," and "The Country Gentleman's Answer," *Virginia Gazette* (Purdie and Dixon), May 30, 1771, June 13, 1771; Isaac, *Transformation of Virginia*, 185, 191, 194–96; Longmore, "All Matters," 785–87.

47. Longmore, "All Matters," 791–92.

48. William Short to John Hartwell Cocke, July 8, 1828, JHCP, box 55, ASSCL-UVA;

Jefferson, *Notes on the State of Virginia*, 140 ("rude"); D. Malone, *Jefferson and His Time*, vol. 1:48–54.

49. Burnaby, *Travels*, 4; E. G. Evans, *"Topping People,"* 149; Smyth, *Tour*, vol. 1–20.

50. Dudley Digges to the Bishop of London, July 15, 1767, and James Horrocks to the Bishop, Mar. 29, 1768, FPP, vol. 14:119–26, and 137–40 ("ignorant"), LPL; Tate, "Colonial College," 85–86, 106–7; Thomson, "Reform of the College," 188–90.

51. JMPM, May 4, 1768, *WMQ*, 1st ser., vol. 5 (Oct 1896): 83–85 ("free Corporation," "We presume" and "without further Control"); James Horrocks et al. to Bishop of London, July 22, 1768, FPP, vol. 14:157–60 ("supreme Visitor"), LPL.

52. Axtell, *Invasion Within*, 190–93; Burnaby, *Travels*, 21–22; L. Tyler, "Early Courses and Professors," 74–76; L. Tyler, "Education in Colonial Virginia," 177–78.

53. Stephen Hawtry to Edward Hawtry, Mar. 26, 1765, *VMHB*, vol. 16 (1908): 209–10; Wenger, "Thomas Jefferson," 342–50.

54. JMPM, July 9, 1770, and Aug. 11, 1772, *WMQ*, 2st ser., vol. 13 (Jan. 1905): 154 and (Apr. 1905): 235; Carson, *James Innes*, 18–19; Wenger, "Thomas Jefferson," 342–50.

55. Fithian, *Journal*, 66; Gwatkin, "On the Manners," 82; E. G. Evans, *"Topping People,"* 133.

56. Morpurgo, *Their Majesties' Royal Colledge*, 99, 122–23 (masters quoted, "not only"); Tate, "Colonial College," 92–93.

57. Thomas Robinson to Bishop of London, June 30, 1757, Meeting of the Board of Visitors, Nov. 1, and 4, 1757, in Ganter, ed., "Documents," 538–40, 541–44; JMPM, Feb. 13, and 18, and Mar. 23, 1758, *WMQ*, 2nd ser., vol. 1 (Jan. 1921): 24–26 ("violent measures"); William Robinson to Bishop of London, Nov. 20, 1760, in Perry, ed., *Historical Collections*, vol. 1:468; Morpurgo, *Their Majesties' Royall Colledge*, 123–24; Tate, "Colonial College," 90–94.

58. Board of Visitors meetings, Apr. 26, 30, May 2, and Aug. 14, 1760 ("whom he said"), FPP, vol. 13:284–88, LPL; JMPM, Jan. 20, 1764, *WMQ*, 1st ser., vol. 4 (July 1895): 46; Morpurgo, *Their Majesties' Royall Colledge*, 125–27; Wenger, "Thomas Jefferson," 355.

59. William Robinson to Bishop of London, c. 1761, FPP, vol. 14:281–98 ("private information" and "more properly"), LPL; Robinson to Bishop of London, c. 1763, in Perry, ed., *Historical Collections*, vol. 1:473–74; JMPM, May 2, 1770, *WMQ*, 1st ser., vol. 13 (Jan. 1905): 152–53 ("to enter" and "Would not"); Morpurgo, *Their Majesties' Royall Colledge*, 141–42.

60. JMPM, Apr. 13 and 15, 1769, *WMQ*, 1st ser., vol. 13 (July 1904): 12–13 ("uncommon Waste"), and (Oct. 1904): 133–34 ("that the Youth" and "to maintain").

61. JMPM, Apr. 12, 13, and 15, 1769, *WMQ*, 1st ser., vol. 13 (July 1904): 12–13 ("resolved" and "would never submit"), and (Oct. 1904): 133–34 ("had no Genius" and "out of regard").

62. JMPM, May 3, 1771, and Feb. 26, 1772, *WMQ*, 1st ser., vol. 13 (Jan. 1905): 157, and vol. 14 (July 1905): 27; Meyers, "First Look," 1141–45; Oast, *Institutional Slavery*, 127, 131–38, 158.

63. JMPM, Nov. 16, 1769, *WMQ*, 1st ser., vol. 13 (Oct. 1904): 137.

64. JMPM, May 2, 1770, *WMQ*, 1st ser., vol. 13 (Jan. 1905): 152–53; John Dixon, "To the Country Clergyman," *Virginia Gazette* (Purdie and Dixon), Aug. 1, 1771.

65. JMPM, May 4, 1768, July 22, 1768, and May 2, 1770, *WMQ*, 1st ser., vol. 5 (Oct. 1896): 87–88, vol. 5 (Apr. 1897): 228–29, and vol. 13 (Jan. 1905): 152–54 ("quit"); Tate, "Colonial College," 116–18; Thomson, "Reform of the College," 201–2.

66. James Horrocks to the Bishop of London, Mar. 29, 1768, FPP, vol. 14:137–40, LPL; JMPM, May 4, 1768, *WMQ*, 1st ser., vol. 5 (Oct. 1896): 88 ("forbear").

67. Thomas Jefferson to Louis H. Girardin, Jan. 15, 1815, in Looney et al., eds., *PTJ-RS*, vol. 8:200–201 ("At these dinners"); D. Malone, *Jefferson and His Time*, vol. 1:73–81, 87–88 (Jefferson quoted: "finest school").

68. Thomas Jefferson to Louis H. Girardin, Jan. 15, 1815, in Looney et al., eds., *PTJ-RS*, vol. 8:200–201 ("an extraordinary" and "his enlightened"); Jefferson, "Autobiography," 4 ("fixed"); D. Malone, *Jefferson and His Time*, vol. 1:48–54.

69. Jefferson, "Autobiography," 4 ("From his conversation"); Cohen, *Calculating People*, 112–13.

70. Thomas Jefferson to William Fleming, c. Oct. 1763, in Boyd et al., eds., *PTJ*, vol. 1:13; D. Malone, *Jefferson and His Time*, vol. 1:56–58, 65–70; Page, "Autobiography," 151; L. Tyler, ed., *Letters and Times*, vol. 1:55; Morpurgo, *Their Majesties' Royall Colledge*, 155.

71. Kern, *Jeffersons at Shadwell*, 233; Luebke, "Origins," 344–45; D. Malone, *Jefferson and His Time*, vol. 1:106–9; Neem, "Early Republic," 35–41; Ragosta, *Religious Freedom*, 8–13.

72. E. Randolph, "Essay," *VMHB*, vol. 43:123; Thomas Jefferson to [John Page], July 26, 1764, in Boyd et al., eds., *PTJ*, vol. 27:665.

73. Thomas Jefferson to William Wirt, Aug. 5, 1815, and Sept. 4, 1816, in Looney et al., eds., *PTJ-RS*, vol. 8:641–46 ("His passion") and vol. 10:365–66; Daniel Webster, "Memorandum," in Hayes, ed., *Jefferson in His Own Time*, 95–96 ("preferred"); D. Malone, *Jefferson and His Time*, vol. 1:98–99; E. Randolph, "Essay," *VMHB*, vol. 43:123 ("Mr. Jefferson").

74. Thomas Jefferson, "Advertisement," *Virginia Gazette*, Sept. 14, 1769, in Boyd et al., eds., *PTJ*, vol. 1:33.

75. Jefferson, "Autobiography," 5 ("eminence" and "most agreeable"); Gordon-Reed, *Hemings of Monticello*, 27, 64–76, 97–102; Kern, *Jeffersons at Shadwell*, 211–12; D. Malone, *Jefferson and His Time*, vol. 1:153–59; Sloan, *Principle and Interest*, 14–18.

76. Lee, *Essay in Vindication*, 20; Thomas Jefferson to Jean de Meunier, c. Jan. 1786, Boyd et al., eds., *PTJ*, vol. 10:20–29; E. Randolph, "Essay," *VMHB*, vol. 43:213.

77. Burnaby, *Travels*, 24 ("They are"); Breen, *Tobacco Culture*, 176; Greene, "Intellectual Reconstruction," 226; Isaac, "Religion and Authority," 19–20.

78. Daniel Webster, "Memorandum of Mr. Jefferson's Conversations," 1824, in Hayes, ed., *Jefferson in His Own Time*, 97 ("Our fast"); E. G. Evans, *Thomas Nelson*, 35–41; E. Randolph, "Essay," *VMHB*, vol. 43:214–15.

79. E. G. Evans, *Thomas Nelson*, 35–42; Lord Dunmore to the Earl of Dartmouth, Dec. 24, 1774, in Van Schreeven et al., eds., *Revolutionary Virginia*, vol. 3:66–67.

80. JMPM, May 27, 1775, *WMQ*, 1st ser., vol. 15 (July 1906): 1–2, 6 (Monroe quoted); Morpurgo, *Their Majesties' Royal Colledge*, 172.

81. Carson, *James Innes*, 12–22; Morpurgo, *Their Majesties' Royal Colledge*, 170–72.

82. JMPM, May 27, 1775, *WMQ*, 1st ser., vol. 15 (July 1906): 9–13; Tate, "Colonial College," 123–24.

83. JMPM, May 11, 17, and 27, 1775, *WMQ*, 1st ser., vol. 14 (Apr. 1906): 243, 244–45 ("repeatedly beating," and "the Necessity"), vol. 15 (July 1906): 13–14 ("unseasonable hours"); Morpurgo, *Their Majesties' Royal Colledge*, 172.

84. Van Schreeven et al., eds., *Revolutionary Virginia*, vol. 3:3–6 (Dunmore quoted on 6), 77–78.

85. Carson, *James Innes*, 90n37; David, *Dunmore's New World*, 94–95; Hiner, "Samuel Henley and Thomas Gwatkin," 49; E. A. Jones, "Two Professors," 222–28; Morpurgo, *Their Majesties' Royal Colledge*, 172; Gwatkin quoted in L. Tyler, "Sketch of John Camm," 30 ("rebellious").

86. Thomas Jefferson to John Randolph, Nov. 29, 1775, in Boyd et al., eds., *PTJ*, vol. 1:268–70; *Virginia Gazette*, Nov. 24, 1775; David, *Dunmore's New World*, 100–126; Holton, *Forced Founders*, 153–89; McDonnell, *Politics of War*, 134–44, 152–62.

87. Edmund Pendleton to William Byrd III, Feb. 9, 1776, in Mays, ed., *LPEP*, vol. 1:149; Virginia Convention resolve, June 15, 1776, in Van Schreeven et al., eds., *Revolutionary Virginia*, vol. 7:507; Boucher, *View of the Causes*, 98; W. C. Bruce, *John Randolph*, vol. 1:18.

88. JMPM, Sept. 14, and Nov. 1, 1775, *WMQ*, 1st ser., vol. 15 (Oct. 1906): 135–39.

89. Robert Carter Nicholas quoted in E. Randolph, "Essay," *VMHB*, vol. 44:42; Van Schreeven et al., eds., *Revolutionary Virginia*, vol. 7:1–5.

90. Carson, *James Innes*, 91; Pickering, ed., *Life of Timothy Pickering*, vol. 1:297–98; E. Randolph, "Essay," *VMHB*, vol. 44:109.

91. Jonathan Boucher to John James, Mar. 9, 1767, in Boucher, "Letters," 339 ("very clever"); Boucher, *Reminiscences*, 48 ("pert"); Kern, *Jeffersons at Shadwell*, 164–65; Morpurgo, *Their Majesties' Royall Colledge*, 155; Osborne, *Crisis Years*, 4–5.

92. JMPM, Nov. 29, 1776, *WMQ*, 1st ser., vol. 15 (Oct. 1906): 141–42; Morpurgo, *Their Majesties' Royall Colledge*, 155, 178–80; Osborne, *Crisis Years*, 4–5, 41; Tate "Colonial College," 128.

93. David Meade Randolph, Journal, *WMQ*, 1st ser., vol. 21 (Oct. 1912): 134–35.

94. Maria Digges to Thomas Jefferson, Oct. 25, 1801, in Boyd et al., eds., *PTJ*, vol. 35:502–3.

95. Thomas Jefferson, "Bill for Amending the Constitution of the College of William & Mary," and Jefferson to Samuel Henley, Oct. 14, 1785, in Boyd et al., eds., *PTJ*, vol. 2:535–43, and vol. 8:634–35; Jefferson, "Autobiography," 45; Tate, "Colonial College," 130–36.

96. James Madison to Ezra Stiles, Aug. 27, 1780, *WMQ*. 2nd ser., vol. 7 (Oct. 1927): 293–94 ("Since the Revolution"); James Madison to James Madison, Jan. 18, 1781, in Hutchinson et al., eds., *PJM*, vol. 2:293–95 ("The Law"); Morpurgo, *Their Majesties' Royal Colledge*, 174–83.

97. JMPM, Oct. 23, 1777, Dec. 14, 1780, Sept. 28, 1782, *WMQ*, 1st ser., vol. 15 (Jan. 1907): 165, 174, (Apr. 1907): 268; Oast, *Institutional Slavery*, 145–51.

98. John Brown, Jr., to William Preston, Jan. 26, 1780, in L. Tyler, ed., "Glimpses of Old College Life," 75; Thomson, "Reform of the College," 187.

99. James Madison to Ezra Stiles, Aug. 27, 1780, *WMQ*, 2nd ser., vol. 7 (Oct. 1927): 293–94; Thomson, "Reform of the College," 210–13.

100. Jedediah Morse to Ezra Stiles, Dec. 30, 1786, Chronology File, 1781–1799, SCSL-CWM; Novak, *Rights of Youth*, 96–97.

101. Tate, "Colonial College," 127–28; James Madison to Ezra Stiles, Aug. 27, 1780, *WMQ*, 2nd ser., vol. 7 (Oct. 1927): 294.

2. REVOLUTION

1. Thomas Jefferson to Thomas Nelson, May 16, 1776, Edmund Randolph to Jefferson, June 23, 1776, Jefferson to William Fleming, July 1, 1776, and Jefferson to Richard Henry Lee, July 8, 1776, in Boyd et al., eds., *PTJ*, vol. 1:292–93, 407–8, 411–13, 455–56.

2. John Page to Jefferson, Apr. 26, 1776, in Boyd et al., eds., *PTJ*, vol. 1:288; Beeman, *Old Dominion*, 49–51; Tarter, *Grandees of Government*, 109.

3. Jordan, *Political Leadership*, 9–16, 66, 209–10; Beeman, *Old Dominion*, 28–35, 42–44.

4. Beeman, *Old Dominion*, xi, 39–41; Jordan, *Political Leadership*, 13–14, 23.

5. Beeman, *Old Dominion*, 28, 53; Evans, "Topping People," 192; Jordan, *Political Leadership*, 14; McDonell, *Politics of War*, 519, 524–26.

6. E. Randolph, "Essay," *VMHB*, vol. 44:45; Van Schreeven et al., eds., *Revolutionary Virginia*, vol. 7:13–15 ("that all men").

7. McDonell, *Politics of War*, 490–91; Pybus, "Jefferson's Faulty Math," 243–64.

8. S. G. Tucker, *Dissertation on Slavery*, 1–2; Henry quoted in Kukla, *Patrick Henry*, 123–24.

9. E. G. Evans, "Topping People," 177–94; Lewis, *Pursuit of Happiness*, 1.

10. Samuel Mordecai to R. Mordecai, Sept. 11, 1814 ("miserably poor"), Mss. 2,

M 8114, a2, VHS; E. C. Carter, ed., *Virginia Journals*, vol. 1:127; John Randolph to Josiah Quincy, Mar. 22, 1814, and July 1, 1814, in Quincy, ed., *Life of Josiah Quincy*, 351 ("Nothing"), 354; Evans, *"Topping People,"* 196; Jordan, *Political Leadership*, 6–7; Morgan, *Slave Counterpoint*, 39, 45.

11. Edmund Randolph to Mr. Addison, July 29, 1792, Transcripts, vol. 3, JDRL-CWF.

12. Grossberg, "Citizens and Families," 17–20, 26; G. Wood, *Empire of Liberty*, 551–52; Thomas Jefferson to William G. Munford, June 18, 1799, in Boyd et al., eds., *PTJ*, vol. 31:126–30.

13. Thomas Jefferson to Edmund Pendleton, Aug. 26, 1776, Boyd et al., eds., *PTJ*, vol. 1:504; Walter Jones to James Madison, July 25, 1789, in Hutchinson et al., eds., *PJM*, vol. 12:307–9; Appleby, "Thomas Jefferson," 167; E. Randolph, "Essay," *VMHB*, vol. 44:118.

14. Kulikoff, *Tobacco and Slaves*, 300–311; Lewis, *Pursuit of Happiness*, 48–50.

15. D. Jordan, *Political Leadership*, 22–23; Upton, "Road to Power," 271–73.

16. John Randolph quoted in Dawidoff, *Education of John Randolph*, 88–89 ("old families"); Randolph quoted in Upton, "Road to Power," 272 ("the Nelsons"); Dunn, "Black Society," 67.

17. John Randolph quoted in Kirk, *John Randolph*, 64–65 ("that all men are born"), 80 ("We are governed"); R. B. Davis, *Francis Walker Gilmer*, 185.

18. Buckley, *Church and State*, 17–18; Isaac, "Rage of Malice," 145–46; Jefferson, *Notes on the State of Virginia*, 146–47; Virginia Bill of Rights quoted in Nelson, *Blessed Company*, 295; Ragosta, *Religious Freedom*, 59–61; Spangler, *Virginians Reborn*, 207.

19. Buckley, *Church and State*, ix, 30–36; Buckley, "Evangelicals Triumphant," 36 ("in all time"); Irons, "Believing in America," 397–407, William Woods quoted on 404 ("he knew"); Ragosta, *Religious Freedom*, 40–41, 58–70, 75; Spangler, *Virginians Reborn*, 197–200, 216–22, 229.

20. Brydon, *Virginia's Mother Church*, vol. 2:418–21, 426–27; Rev. Alexander Balmain quoted in Buckley, *Church and State*, 82 ("the revolution" and "every man").

21. Thomas Jefferson, testimonial for Rev. Charles Clay, Aug. 15, 1779, Clay to Jefferson, Aug. 8, 1792, in Boyd et al., eds., *PTJ*, vol. 3:67, vol. 24:367–68; Meade, *Old Churches*, vol. 2:48–50, Charles Clay quoted on 49; Woods, *Albemarle County*, 126 ("immense heap").

22. Buckley, *Church and State*, 43; Jarratt, *Life*, 121–22 ("When I now go"); Nelson, *Blessed Company*, 300; Schoepf, *Travels*, vol. 2:62–63.

23. Jarratt, *Life*, 155; John Buchanan quoted in Brydon, "David Griffith," 213–14 ("thought public"); Buckley, *Church and State*, 84.

24. "A Member of the Established Church," *Virginia Gazette* (Purdie), Nov. 1, 1776 ("harangues"); "Philoepiscopus," *Virginia Gazette* (Dixon), Dec. 13, 1776 ("layman").

25. "An Eastern Layman," and "Social Christian," *Virginia Gazette* (Dixon and

Nicholson), Aug. 14, and Sept. 11, 1779 ("wholly selfish"); Richard Henry Lee to James Madison, Nov. 26, 1784, in Hutchinson et al., eds., *PTJ*, vol. 8:149–52; Eckenrode, *Separation*, 74–76, 84.

26. James Madison to Thomas Jefferson, July 3, 1784, in Boyd et al., eds., *PTJ*, vol. 7:360–61; Buckley, *Church and State*, 38–39, 56–61, 70–78, 86–87, 106–7; Eckenrode, *Separation*, 78–81.

27. The bill quoted in Kukla, *Patrick Henry*, 280.

28. Buckley, *Church and State*, 38–39, 90–91, 113, *Virginia Gazette*, Nov. 8, 1783, quoted on 75 ("The Church"); Eckenrode, *Separation*, 76–77, 84, 95, 97, 107–8.

29. John Blair Smith to James Madison, June 21, 1784, in Hutchinson et al., eds., *PJM*, vol. 8:80–83; Buckley, *Church and State*, 97–98; Eckenrode, *Separation*, 88–89.

30. James Madison, Jr., to James Madison, Sr., Jan. 6, 1785, and Madison, Jr., to Thomas Jefferson, Jan. 9, 1785, in Hutchinson et al., eds., *PJM*, vol. 8:216–18, 222–34; Jefferson to Madison, Jr., Dec. 8, 1784, in Boyd et al., eds., *PTJ*, vol. 7:557–58 ("I am glad"); Buckley, *Church and State*, 109–10; Eckenrode, *Separation*, 83–88, 92–94, 99–102.

31. James Madison to Thomas Jefferson, Apr. 12, 1785, George Nicholas to Madison, Apr. 22, 1785, Madison to James Monroe, Apr. 28, and May 29, 1785, and Madison to Jefferson, Aug. 20, 1785, in Hutchinson et al., eds., *PJM*, vol. 8:260–62, 264–65, 272–74, 285–87, 344–47 ("mutual hatred"); Edmund Pendleton to Richard Henry Lee, Apr. 18, 1785, in Mays, ed., *Letters and Papers*, vol. 2:478; Archibald Stuart quoted in Buckley, *Church and State*, 127–29 ("a set").

32. John Page to Thomas Jefferson, Aug. 23, 1785, and Jefferson to Page, May 4, 1786, in Boyd et al., eds., *PTJ*, vol. 8:428–29, vol. 9:44–46.

33. Thomas Jefferson to James Madison, Dec. 8, 1784, in Hutchinson et al., eds, *PJM*, vol. 8:177–80; Archibald Stuart to Jefferson, Oct. 17, 1785, in Boyd et al., eds., *PTJ*, vol. 8:644–47; Buckley, *Church and State*, 144–49; Kukla, *Patrick Henry*, 280.

34. Edmund Pendleton to Richard Henry Lee, Feb. 28, 1785, and Pendleton to Patrick Henry, in Mays, ed., *Letters and Papers*, vol. 2:474, 483–84; James Madison to Thomas Jefferson, Aug. 20, 1785, in Hutchinson et al., eds., *PJM*, vol. 8:344–47; Archibald Stuart to John Breckinridge, Oct. 21, 1787, in Kaminski et al., eds., *Documentary History*, vol. 8:89 ("We are all contending"); Brydon, "David Griffith," 229n50; Buckley, *Church and State*, 154; Eckenrode, *Separation*, 112–13; Henderson, "Taxation and Political Culture," 104–5.

35. James Madison to Thomas Jefferson, Jan. 22, 1786, in Hutchinson et al., eds., *PJM*, vol. 8:472–82; Madison to Jefferson, Feb. 15, 1787, in Boyd et al., eds., *PTJ*, vol. 11:152–55; Buckley, *Church and State*, 161–69; Ragosta, *Religious Freedom*, 89–90; Eckenrode, *Separation*, 118–29.

36. Buckley, *Church and State*, 130–31, Anne Cary Nicholas quoted on 130.

37. James Currie to Thomas Jefferson, Aug. 5, 1785, in Boyd et al., *PTJ*, vol. 8:342–47; Benjamin Johnson to James Madison, Jan. 19, 1789, in Hutchinson et al., eds.,

PJM, vol. 11:423–25; Brydon, *Virginia's Mother Church*, vol. 2:442–43; Buckley, "Evangelicals Triumphant," 33–40, Baptist petition quoted on 56 ("adulterous connection").

38. Irons, "Spiritual Fruits," 173–74, 186; Buckley, "Evangelicals Triumphant," 42–44; Buckley, *Church and State*, 166; Eckenrode, *Separation*, 125–27, 135–36.

39. Buckley, "Evangelicals Triumphant," 64–67, newspaper article quoted on 65 (*"Republican Bishop"*); Mills, *Bishops by Ballot*, 242–44, 258–59, 284; W. Sydnor, "Doctor Griffith," 14–15.

40. Brydon, *Virginia's Mother Church*, vol. 2:493–97, 501–2; Buckley, "Evangelicals Triumphant," 40–56, law quoted on 54 ("devolved"); Eckenrode, *Separation*, 133–52. In the key vote, the Piedmont-Southside-West combination voted 82 to 18 in favor of confiscation, while the Northern Neck-Tidewater voted against: 34 no votes to 15 in favor.

41. Philip Norborne Nicholas quoted in *Richmond Enquirer*, May 26, 1804 ("all the rights"); Mays, *Edmund Pendleton*, 340–41.

42. Brydon, *Virginia's Mother Church*, vol. 2:504; Eckenrode, *Separation*, 148–49; Mays, *Edmund Pendleton*, 341–45.

43. "On the Press," *Richmond Enquirer*, May 23, 1804; Brydon, *Virginia's Mother Church*, vol. 2:534n6; Eckenrode, *Separation*, 149, 501–2; Reardon, *Edmund Randolph*, 351–53.

44. Brydon, *Virginia's Mother Church*, vol. 2:452, 478; Buckley, "Evangelicals Triumphant," 66–67; John Marshall quoted in Meade, *Old Churches*, vol. 1:30; Osborne, *Crisis Years*, 104–5.

45. R. B. Davis, ed., *Jeffersonian America*, 135; Knight, *Letters*, 60; J. Madison, *An Address*, 9–10; Weld, *Travels*, vol. 1:177 ("with the windows"); Meade, *Old Churches*, vol. 1:301, vol. 2:85.

46. Noah Webster, "Diary, 1785–1786," in E. Ford, ed., *Notes*, vol. 1:143n1 ("Plays"); R. B. Davis, ed., *Jeffersonian America*, 135; Knight, *Letters*, 65–68; Weld, *Travels*, vol. 1:177.

47. Brydon, *Virginia's Mother Church*, vol. 2:493; Buckley, "After Disestablishment," 449; Buckley, "Evangelicals Triumphant," 55.

48. Henderson, "Taxation and Political Culture," 104–11.

49. Buckley, *Church and State*, 6–7, 40–41; Isaac, "Rage of Malice," 161–63; Ragosta, *Religious Freedom*, 34–38; E. Randolph, "Essay," *VMHB*, vol. 44:123; Spangler, *Virginians Reborn*, 3–8.

50. Levasseur, *Lafayette in America*, vol. 1:222–23; Gordon-Reed, *Hemingses*, 641–45.

51. Jefferson to James W. Wallace, May 4, 1823 ("Before"), FO-NA, http://founders .archives.gov/documents/Jefferson/98-01-02-3497.

52. Thomas Jefferson, "Bill to Create Central College," Nov. 18, 1814, in Looney et al., eds., *PTJ-RS*, vol. 8:90–94; Jefferson to Central College Visitors, Jan. 2, 1818, in

Mattern et al., eds, *PJM-RS*, vol. 1:195–97; Cabell, *Early History of the University of Virginia*, 401.

53. O'Shaughnessy, *Men Who Lost America*, 274–76; E. Randolph, "Essay," *VMHB*, vol. 44:318; Selby, *Revolution in Virginia*, 221–25, 271–83.

54. John Tyler to Jefferson, May 16, 1782, and Jefferson to James Monroe, May 20, 1782, in Boyd et al., eds., *PTJ*, vol. 6:183–84, 184–87; Hatzenbuehler, "Growing Weary," 35.

55. Gordon-Reed and Onuf, *Most Blessed of Patriarchs*, 93–94.

56. Schoepf, *Travels*, vol. 2:91–93.

57. John Harvie to Thomas Jefferson, Oct. 18, 1777, Jefferson to Barbe-Marbois, Dec. 5, 1783, and Jefferson to James Madison, May 8, 1784, in Boyd et al., *PTJ*, vol. 2:34–36, vol. 6:373–74, and vol. 7:232–35; E. Randolph, "Essay," *VMHB*, vol. 45:46; Ragsdale, *Planters' Republic*, 265.

58. Matthew Maury to James Maury, Dec. 10, 1787, in Kaminsky et al., eds., *Documentary History*, vol. 8:228; Ragsdale, *Planters' Republic*, 259–62; Sloan, *Principle and Interest*, 22–42.

59. Archibald Stuart to John Breckinridge, Oct. 21, 1787, and William Fleming to Thomas Madison, Feb. 19, 1788, in Kaminski et al., eds., *Documentary History*, vol. 8:89, 383 ("independent Sovereignty"); Ragsdale, *Planters' Republic*, 281.

60. Alexander Donald to Thomas Jefferson, Nov. 12, 1787, in Boyd et al., eds., *PTJ*, vol. 12:345–48 ("the salvation").

61. Col. Grayson quoted in Hugh Williamson to John Gray Blunt, June 3, 1788, in Kaminski et al., eds., *Documentary History*, vol. 9:608–9; E. Randolph, "Essay," *VMHB*, vol. 44:110.

62. Tobias Lear to John Landon, Dec. 3, 1787, Henry Lee to James Madison, Dec. 20, 1787, in Kaminski et al., eds., *Documentary History*, vol. 8:197 ("to divide"), 249 ("other states"); Henry quoted in Beeman, *Old Dominion*, 7–8 ("This government"); Einhorn, "Patrick Henry's Case," 549–73; K. R. Malone, "Fate of Revolutionary Republicanism," 31; Henry quoted in Waldstreicher, *Slavery's Constitution*, 144 ("lay such heavy").

63. Beeman, *Old Dominion*, 3–13; McCoy, "James Madison and Visions," 226–32, 244–47.

64. James Duncanson to James Maury, June 7, 1788, Theodorick Bland to Arthur Lee, June 13, 1788, James Breckinridge to John Breckinridge, June 13, 1788, Diary of William Heth, June 25, 1788, in Kaminski et al., eds., *Documentary History*, vol. 10:1583 ("You never saw"), 1617 ("Half the Crew"), 1621 ("better adapted"), 1677 ("The scene").

65. Thomas Jefferson to Alexander Donald, Feb. 7, 1788, Jefferson to James Madison, Sept. 6, 1789, in Boyd et al., eds., *PTJ*, vol. 12:570–72, vol. 15:392–98; Onuf, *Mind of Thomas Jefferson*, 76, 115–16, 121–22, 131–32; Onuf, *Jefferson's Empire*, 94–97.

66. K. R. Malone, "Fate of Revolutionary Republicanism," 31–33; G. Wood, *Empire of Liberty*, 92–109, 139–44.

67. John Tyler to St. George Tucker, July 10, 1795, *WMQ*, 1st ser., vol. 2 (July 1893): 200–1; Thomas Jefferson to James Monroe, Sept. 6, 1795, Boyd et al., eds., *PTJ*, vol. 28:448–51; E. C. Carter et al., eds., *Virginia Journals*, vol. 2:304–8; Risjord, "Virginia Federalists," 502–3.

68. James Monroe to Thomas Jefferson, July 17, 1792, in Boyd et al., eds., *PTJ*, vol. 24:236–37; Edmund Randolph to George Washington, June 24, 1793, in Abbott et al., eds., *PGW-PS*, vol. 13:137–42; Jordan, *Political Leadership*, 17–18.

69. T. C. Thompson, "Perceptions," 48; G. Wood, *Empire of Liberty*, 197–98.

70. Joseph C. Cabell to David Watson, June 7, 1799, *VMHB*, vol. 29 (July 1921): 263–64; Simon, *What Kind of Nation*, 52–53, 57–62.

71. Ackerman, *Failure of the Founding Fathers*, 97–99, 203–206; Onuf, *Jefferson's Empire*, 100–102.

72. Chapman Johnson to David Watson, Feb. 20, 1801, *VMHB*, vol. 29 (July 1921): 276; Joseph S. Watson to D. Watson, Mar. 2, 1801, *VMHB*, vol. 29 (Apr. 1921): 161–62; Joseph C. Cabell to Nicholas Cabell, Mar. 5, 1801, JCCFP, box 2, ASSCL-UVA.

73. Joseph S. Watson to David Watson, Mar. 2, and Apr. 1, 1801, *VMHB*, vol. 29 (Apr. 1921): 161–62, 165 ("Except"); J. S. Watson to John H. Cocke, Mar. 20, 1801, JHCP, box 1 oversized, ASSCL-UVA; Joseph C. Cabell, to Nicholas Cabell, Mar. 5, 1801 ("Huzza" and "several"), JCCFP, box 2, ASSCL-UVA.

74. Joseph S. Watson to David Watson, Apr. 1, and May 7, 1801, *VMHB*, vol. 29 (Apr. 1921): 166, 167–69; Joseph C. Cabell to Isaac A. Coles, May 16, 1801, JCCFP, box 2, ASSCL-UVA.

75. Thomas Jefferson, "First Inaugural Address," Mar. 4, 1801, in Boyd et al., eds., *PTJ*, vol. 30:645–53; Ackerman, *Failure of the Founding Fathers*, 100–108, 149–50; Onuf, *Jefferson's Empire*, 80–81, 85, 93, 107–8, 117–21; Simon, *What Kind of Nation*, 134–37, 150–51.

76. Beeman, *Old Dominion*, 238–39; D. Jordan, *Political Leadership*, 18–21, 66–70.

77. John Tyler to Thomas Newton, Jan. 20, 1808, *WMQ*, 1st ser., vol. 1 (July 1892): 172–73; Ammon, "Richmond Junto," 395–407; N. Peterson, *Littleton Waller Tazewell*, 61–62.

3. HONOR

1. Thomas Jefferson to Samuel Henley, Oct. 14, 1785, in Boyd et al., eds., *PTJ*, vol. 8:634–35; Carson, *James Innes*, 147–48; Joseph Hadfield quoted in Carson, ed., *We Were There*, 75 ("the ravages").

2. Peter Colt to Mrs. Colt, Mar. 14, 1782 ("This Town"), Letters Collection, JDRL-CW; S. G. Tucker, *Letter to the Rev. Jedediah Morse*, 196n; L. Tyler, "Williamsburg," 57–58; M. Goodwin, *Capitol*, 76; Schoepf, *Travels*, vol. 2:78.

3. John Greenhow to Alexander Galt, Feb. 10, 1793 ("A third"), Galt Papers, ser. 2, box 1, SSCL-CWM; William Brockenbrough to Joseph C. Cabell, June 18, 1801 ("mouldering"), JCCFP, box 2, ASSCL-UVA; William Taylor Barry to unnamed brother, Feb. 15, 1804, *WMQ*, 1st ser., vol. 13 (Oct. 1904): 112–13 ("gloomy"); E. C. Carter et al., eds., *Virginia Journals*, vol. 1:87 ("few old"); S. G. Tucker, *Letter to the Rev. Jedediah Morse*, 188.

4. William Hill, Journal, Jan. 12, 1791 ("Old Capitol"), Transcripts, vol. 3, JDRL-CW; W. A. R. Goodwin, *Brief & True*, 298; E. C. Carter et al., eds., *Virginia Journals*, vol. 1:87–88 ("bedridden"); S. G. Tucker, *Letter to the Rev. Jedediah Morse*, 194n.

5. Joseph S. Watson to David Watson, Dec. 9, 1799, *VMHB*, vol. 29 (Apr. 1921): 150; Chapman Johnson to D. Watson, Dec. 19, 1799, *VMHB*, vol. 29 (July 1921): 266 ("extremely gay"); Kennedy, ed., *Memoirs of the Life of William Wirt*, 122; G. Tucker, *Letters from Virginia*, 122–23; G. Tucker, *Valley of Shenandoah*, vol. 2:215–23.

6. Joseph C. Cabell to D. Watson, Mar. 4, 1798 ("fair sex"), and July 8, 1798, DWP, vol. 1, MDLC; Carter H. Harrison to Watson, Nov. 21, 1798, *VMHB*, vol. 30 (June 1922): 247 ("Gaiety"); Isaac A. Coles to D. Watson, Mar. 21, 1798, Garrett Minor to D. Watson, Apr. 28, 1798, *VMHB*, vol. 30 (June 1922): 241, 244; Joseph S. Watson to D. Watson, Dec. 9, 1799, *VMHB*, vol. 29 (Apr. 1921): 150.

7. Asbury, *Journal*, vol. 1:454 ("desolate"); Gibbs and Rowe, *Public Hospital*, i, 9–13, 28–30, 60, Governor Fauquier quoted on 1; Robert Carter Nicholas to John Norton, Aug. 4, 1772, in Mason, ed., *John Norton & Sons*, 261–62; L. Johnson, "Between the Wars," 185 ("lazy").

8. James Madison to John C. Lettsom, Oct. 26, 1803, Bishop Madison Papers, box 1, SSCL-CWM; Elizabeth Galt to William F. Galt, Apr. 30, 1809, Galt Papers, ser. 2, box 1, SSCL-CWM.

9. Littleton W. Tazewell quoted in Grigsby, *Discourse on the Life*, 12 ("most beautiful") and 13 ("Randolph was"); John Randolph quoted in R. B. Davis, *Francis Walker Gilmer*, 185.

10. St. George Tucker to Theodorick Bland, Jr., Sept. 21, 1781, and May 2, 1782, in Campbell, ed., *Bland Papers*, vol. 2:76, 80; Walker Maury to St. George Tucker, Oct. 6, 1782, TCP, reel M-14, SSCL-CMW; John Randolph to Francis W. Gilmer, July 2, 1825, in R. B. Davis, *Francis Walker Gilmer*, 185.

11. Walker Maury to St. George Tucker, Dec. 29, 1783, TCP, reel M-14, SSCL-CWM; Carson, *James Innes*, 40–44; Walker Maury to St. George Tucker, Jan. 30, Apr. 1, 1783, Aug. 26, 1784, and Aug. 2, 1785 ("I cannot"), TCP, reel M-14, SSCL-CWM; M. Goodwin, *The Capitol*, 71, 76, 78, 82.

12. Walker Maury to St. George Tucker, Jan. 9 ("to curb"), 14 ("the credit"), and 25, 1784, TCP, reel M-14, and Maury to S. G. Tucker, Aug. 2, 1785 ("perfect com-

mand"), and S. G. Tucker to Frances Bland Randolph Tucker, Apr. 23, 1786, TCP, reel M-15, SSCL-CWM.

13. Walker Maury to Col. Theodorick Bland, Aug. 24, 1786, TCP, reel M-15, SSCL-CWM.

14. John Banister to St. George Tucker, Sept. 13, 1786 ("Mr. Maury"), and Walker Maury to Tucker, Sept. 14, 1786 ("with such"), TCP, reel M-15, SSCL-CWM.

15. St. George Tucker to Frances Bland Randolph Tucker, Oct. 23, 1786, and Walker Maury to St. George Tucker, Oct. 24, 1786 ("I never"), Feb. 25, 1787 ("If I have" and "despise"), TCP, reel M-15, SSCL-CWM; M. Goodwin, *The Capitol*, 83; Meade, *Old Churches*, vol. 1:273.

16. St. George Tucker to John and Richard Randolph, June 12, 1787, TCP, reel M-16, SSCL-CWM; W. C. Bruce, *John Randolph*, vol. 1:72–75; John Randolph to Tudor Randolph, Dec. 13, 1813 ("of all things"), GFP, box 3, ASSCL-UVA.

17. John Randolph quoted in W. C. Bruce, *John Randolph*, vol. 1:36–3; Randolph to Tudor Randolph, Dec. 13, 1813, GFP, box 3, ASSCL-UVA.

18. John Greenhow to Alexander Galt, Feb. 10, 1793 ("in the right side"), William C. Galt to A. Galt, May 19, 1793, and Lucretia Craig to A. Galt, June 5, 1793, Galt Papers, ser. 2, box 1, SSCL-CWM; W. C. Bruce, *John Randolph*, vol. 1:65–77, 123–28, Randolph quoted on 126.

19. Archibald Cary to Thomas Jefferson, Oct. 31, 1775, in Boyd et al., eds., *PTJ*, vol. 1:250; Breen, "Horses and Gentlemen," 255n64; E. G. Evans, *"Topping People,"* 154; Morrow, *Williamsburg at Dawn*, 37–50, *Virginia Gazette* quoted on 50.

20. Ayers, *Vengeance and Justice*, 13–15; Freeman, *Affairs of Honor*, xx; Royster, *Revolutionary People*, 207–10.

21. Ayers, *Vengeance and Justice*, 16–17; D. D. Bruce, *Violence and Culture*, 27; Freeman, *Affairs of Honor*, xvii–xx1.

22. M. L. Barraud to Louisa M. H. Cocke, Aug. 4, 1829, JHCP, box 60, ASSCL-UVA.

23. Ayers, *Vengeance and Justice*, 18–19; D. D. Bruce, *Violence and Culture*, 37; Gorn, "Gouge and Bite," 22; Greenberg, *Masters and Statesmen*, 31–37; Greenberg, "The Nose," 68.

24. Ayers, *Vengeance and Justice*, 3–4, 10–11, 26; D. D. Bruce, *Violence and Culture*, 27; Glover, *Southern Sons*, 22–34, 45–46, 64; Greenberg, *Masters and Statesmen*, 23, 40–41; Greenberg, "The Nose," 63–65; Stowe, "Rhetoric of Authority," 933.

25. Ayers, *Vengeance and Justice*, 12–13, William Faux quoted on 16 ("barbarous"); Bruce, *Violence and Culture*, 27; Greenberg, *Masters and Statesmen*, 25–28; Thomas Mann Randolph quoted in Kierner, *Martha Jefferson Randolph*, 134; Wagoner, "Honor and Dishonor," 162–63.

26. Thomas Jefferson, "A Bill for Proportioning Crimes and Punishments in Cases Heretofore Capital," June 18, 1779, in Boyd et al., eds, *PTJ*, vol. 2:492–507; Jefferson to James Ogilvie, June 23, 1806, FO-NA, http://founders.archives

.gov/documents/Jefferson/99-01-02-3892; Kierner, *Martha Jefferson Randolph*, 133–34.

27. D. D. Bruce, *Violence and Culture*, 27.

28. John Randolph quoted in W. C. Bruce, *John Randolph*, vol. 2:382–83; D. D. Bruce, *Violence and Culture*, 29; [G. Tucker], "Eugenius," *Richmond Enquirer*, Aug. 11, 1804 ("universally admitted"); G. Tucker, *Essays on Various Subjects*, 254–60, 264 ("by boxing"), 268–71.

29. G. Tucker, *Essays on Various Subjects*, 270–71.

30. Glover, *Southern Sons*, 12–16, 24–32, 45–46; Grossberg, "Citizens and Families," 15–16; Lewis, *Pursuit of Happiness*, 1–39; D. B. Smith, *Inside the Great House*, 21–22, 26, 40–53, 82–88, 119–20; Stowe, "Private Emotions," 79–80.

31. Richard Blow to George Blow, n.d., c. 1804, BLFP, ser. 2, box 33G, folder 2, item 2, SSCL-CWM; Glover, *Southern Sons*, 92–93; Stowe, "Rhetoric of Authority," 919–24.

32. William Wirt to Francis W. Gilmer, Oct. 9, 1806, GFN, box 1, ASSCL-UVA; David Campbell to unknown, Sept. 27, 1820 ("as long as"), CFP, box 4, DMRML-DU.

33. David Watson to George Watson, June 7, 1799 ("Books alone"), DWFP, box 7, ASSCL-UVA; Sterling Ruffin to Thomas Ruffin, May 5, 1803, and Mar. 14, 1804, in Roulhac Hamilton, ed., *Papers of Thomas Ruffin*, vol. 1:45 ("attentive"), 51; Wagoner, "Honor and Dishonor," 160–61.

34. Merit M. Robinson to John H. Cocke, Aug. 3, 1820, and Otway B. Barraud to John H. Cocke, Jr., Nov. 31, 1823 ("familiar ease"), JHCP, boxes 31, and 39, ASSCL-UVA; J. H. Rice, "An Excursion into the Country," in Rice, ed., *Virginia Evangelical and Literary Magazine*, vol. 1:550; David Swain quoted in "'Let Us Manufacture Men,'" 41 ("The students"); Glover, *Southern Sons*, 72–73, 88–89, 98–110; Stowe, "Rhetoric of Authority," 921–22.

35. Sterling Ruffin to Thomas Ruffin, Dec. 29, 1803, Feb. 3, and Mar. 14, 1804, in Roulhac Hamilton, ed., *Papers of Thomas Ruffin*, vol. 1:47 ("middle course), 50, 52 ("My wish"); George Blow to Richard Blow, Mar. 20, 1804 ("not expended"), and Apr. 9, 1805 ("that a young man"), BLFP, ser 2, box 33G, SSCL-CWM; Glover, *Southern Sons*, 61–64 75–76, 106, 110; Pace, *Halls of Honor*, 83–84, 96–97.

36. David Watson to James Watson, Feb. 10, 1815, DWFP, box 10, ASSCL-UVA; John W. Eppes to Francis Eppes, Jan. 2, 1819, Eppes Family Papers, one box, ASSCL-UVA.

37. Wirt, *Old Bachelor*, 168.

38. "Literary Fund of Virginia," in J. H. Rice, ed., *Evangelical and Literary Magazine*, vol. 5:236; Augustine C. Smith to Samuel Myers, Feb. 11, 1810, SMP, one folder, SCSL-CWM.

39. James Madison to Thomas Jefferson, Dec. 28, 1786, and Jefferson to Ralph Izard, July 17, 1788, in Boyd et al., eds., *PTJ*, vol. 10:642–44, and vol. 13:372–74.

40. L. H. Johnson, "Between the Wars," 166–70; F. B. Evans, "Carlo Bellini," 348–53; Boyd et al., eds, *PTJ*, vol. 31:85–86n; Joseph S. Watson to David Watson, Feb. 9, and Nov. 4, 1799, *VMHB*, vol. 29 (Apr. 1921): 139, 145; Bishop James Madison to Thomas Jefferson, Jan. 17, 1800, in Boyd et al., eds, *PTJ*, vol. 31:316–18; J. Randolph, *Letters*, 13 ("old Frenchman").

41. JMPM, Sept. 1, 1782, *WMQ*, 1st ser., vol. 15 (Apr. 1907): 267; Thomas Jefferson to William Short, Dec. 14, 1789, and James Monroe to Jefferson, July 17, 1792, in Boyd et al., eds., *PTJ*, vol. 16:25, vol. 23:237; Samuel Mordecai to Ellen Mordecai, May 25, 1812 ("more like"), Chronology File, 1802–1819, SCSL-CWM; Thomas Jefferson to William Duane, Jan. 22, 1813, and Jefferson to William Short, Nov. 9, 1813, in Looney et al., eds., *PTJ-RS*, vol. 5:577–79 ("tory"), and vol. 6:604–6 ("simpleton"); Johnson, "Between the Wars," 169–70, 173; W. A. R. Goodwin, "Reverend John Bracken," 380–83.

42. David Yancey to David Watson, June 6, 1795, *VMHB*, vol. 30 (June 1922): 225; Joseph S. Watson to D. Watson, Feb. 9, 1799, *VMHB*, vol. 29 (Apr. 1921): 139–41 ("one fourth").

43. Isaac A. Coles to David Watson, Nov. 29, 1797, *VMHB*, vol. 30 (June 1922): 231 ("the region"); Joseph S. Watson to David Watson, Mar. 2, 1801, *VMHB*, vol. 29 (April 1921): 163 ("amuse[d]"), and 164n29; Garrett H. Minor to D. Watson, Dec. 20, 1797, William Brockenborough to D. Watson, Jan. 14, 1798, and Isaac A. Coles to D. Watson, Mar. 21, 1798, *VMHB*, vol. 30 (June 1922): 234, 237–39, and 240–41; G. Tucker, *Valley of Shenandoah*, vol. 2:220–21; Osborne, *Crisis Years*, 36.

44. G. Tucker, "Autobiography," 101–2; Henry St. George Tucker to St. George Tucker, Aug. 8, 1801, *WMQ*, 2nd ser., vol. 10 (Apr. 1930): 164; H. S. G. Tucker to Joseph C. Cabell, Aug. 8, 1801, JCCFP, box 5, ASSCL-UVA.

45. Joseph S. Watson to John H. Cocke, Feb. 1, 1801, JHCP, box 2, ASSCL-UVA.

46. Joseph C. Cabell to David Watson, Mar. 4, 1798, DWP, vol. 1, MDLC; D. Watson to Cabell, Apr. 21, 1798, JCCFP, box 1, ASSCL-UVA; Isaac A. Coles to Henry St. George Tucker, July 20, 1799, *WMQ*, 1st ser., vol. 4 (Oct. 1895): 107; W. Scott, *Memoirs*, vol. 1:9–10.

47. William Hill, journal, Jan. 14, 1791 ("rudeness"), Transcripts, vol. 3, JDRL-CWF; William Brockenborough to David Watson, Jan. 14, 1798, and Isaac A. Coles to D. Watson, Mar. 21, 1798, *VMHB*, vol. 30 (June 1922): 237–39 ("Ravings"), 240–41 ("The other evening" and "the party").

48. Bishop James Madison to James Madison, Nov. 12, and Dec. 24, 1794, and Jan. 9, 1800, in Hutchinson et al., eds., *PJM*, vol. 15:374–75, 422–23, vol. 17:352–54 ("such a University"); Joseph C. Cabell to Isaac A. Coles, Mar. 1 1807, JCCFP, box 4, ASSCL-UVA.

49. Kerber, *Federalists in Dissent*, 19–22, David Daggett quoted on 19 ("Sunbeams"), Noah Webster quoted on 21 ("Never").

50. Thomas Jefferson to Elbridge Gerry, Jan. 26, 1799, Jefferson to William G. Munford, June 18, 1799 ("mind" and "cowardly"), Jefferson to Joseph Priestley, Jan. 27, 1800, and Mar. 21, 1801, in Boyd et al., eds., *PTJ*, vol. 30:645–53, vol. 31:126–30, 339–41, vol. 33:393–95.

51. Garrett Minor to Joseph C. Cabell, July 8, 1800, Cabell Family Papers, one box, SCSL-CWM; Cutler, *Life, Journals, and Correspondence*, vol. 2:172 ("atheism"); Gawalt, "Strict Truth," 103–4; Noll, *Princeton and the Republic*, 126–51; Wertenbaker, *Princeton*, 134–38.

52. Dwight, *Oration Delivered at New-Haven*, 45; Bishop Madison to James Madison, Oct. 24, 1801, in Stagg et al., eds., *PJM-SSS*, vol. 2:196–97; [Bishop James Madison], "Late a Student of William & Mary," *National Intelligencer*, Nov. 20, 1801; Novak, *Rights of Youth*, 98.

53. Thomas L. Preston to Andrew Reid, Jr., Feb. 22, 1802, in *WMQ*, 1st ser., vol. 8 (Apr. 1900): 216; Charlotte Balfour to Eliza Whiting, Feb. 23, 1802, Blair, Braxton, Horner, Whiting Papers, ser. 1, box 1, SCSL-CWM; Henry St. George Tucker to Joseph C. Cabell, Mar. 28, 1802, JCCFP, box 2, ASSCL-UVA; Osborne, *Crisis Years*, 57–58.

54. *New York Evening Post*, Apr. 3, 1802 ("Thus dies"), and Apr. 16, 1802.

55. Bishop James Madison to Thomas Jefferson, Apr. 15, 1802, in Boyd et al., eds., *PTJ*, vol. 37:241–42; [Bishop Madison], "An Inhabitant of Williamsburg," *Virginia Argus*, May 5, 1802, reprinted in *WMQ*, 2nd ser., vol. 5 (Jan. 1925): 61–62 ("virtue"); Osborne, *Crisis Years*, 59–60 (statute quoted), 64; "A Student," *National Intelligencer*, May 31, 1802.

56. Statute quoted in Osborne, *Crisis Years*, 59–60; Glover, *Southern Sons*, 76; Thomas L. Preston to Andrew Reid, Jr., Apr. 15, 1802, *WMQ*, 1st ser., vol. 8 (Apr. 1900): 217; [Bishop Madison], "Extract of a Letter from a Student at William & Mary," *Virginia Argus*, Nov. 17, 1802, College Chronology File, 1802–1819, SCSL-CWM.

57. "A College Prank," *Norfolk Herald*, Apr. 18, 1803, College Chronology File, 1800–1820, SSCL-CWM; John H. Cocke to Joseph C. Cabell, Apr. 18, 1803, JCCFP, box 2, ASSCL-UVA.

58. [Bishop James Madison], "Gentleman at Williamsburg," *Virginia Argus*, Apr. 30, 1803; Benjamin Crowninshield to B. L. Oliver, May 30, 1804 ("The Students"), Benjamin Crowninshield Papers, one folder, SCSL-CWM; Janson, *Stranger in America*, 304; Osborne, *Crisis Years*, 78; Robert, "William Wirt," 404.

59. Bishop James Madison to James Madison, Dec. 11, 1803, in Stagg et al., eds., *PJM-SSS*, vol. 6:158–59; L. Johnson, "Between the Wars," 184.

60. William Taylor Barry to John Barry, Feb. 15, 1804, *WMQ*, 1st ser., vol. 13 (Oct. 1904): 113; St. George Tucker to John Ambler, Dec. 16, 1801 ("that a professor"), Ambler Family Papers, sec. 2, folder 6, VHS; L. Johnson, "Between the Wars," 174; St. George Tucker quoted in Novak, *Rights of Youth*, 104 ("must degrade"); Osborne, *Crisis Years*, 85–86; Henry St. George Tucker to Joseph C. Cabell, Dec.

27, 1803, JCCFP, box 3, ASSCL-UVA; George Blackburn quoted in L. Johnson, "Between the Wars," 175 ("danced").

61. James Madison et al., petition to the legislature, Dec. n.d., 1807, James City County Petitions, Transcripts, vol. 38, JDRL-CWF.

62. Ellen Randolph to Thomas Jefferson, Mar. 11, 1808, in Betts and Bear, eds., *Family Letters of Thomas Jefferson*, 332, 333n1; James Eyle to Charles S. Todd, March 16, 1808, College Subject File, Chronology, 1800–1820, SCSL-CWM; Samuel Myers to John Myers, Apr. 10, 1808 ("arrived"), SMP, one file, SCSL-CWM.

63. Samuel Myers to John Myers, Apr. 10, and Oct. 26, 1808, SMP, one file, SCSL-CWM.

64. Samuel Myers to Moses Myers, Jan. 30, 1809, and Littleton W. Tazewell to John Myers, Feb. 5, 1809, SMP, one file, SCSL-CWM.

65. St. George Tucker to Frances Coalter, May 31, 1811 ("a Rogue"), Brown, Coalter, Tucker Papers, ser. 1, box 3, SCSL-CWM; *Richmond Enquirer*, June 4, 1811, and Nov. 29, 1811.

66. Lelia Tucker to Francis Coalter, Apr. 12, 1811, Brown, Coalter, Tucker Papers, ser. 1, box 3, SCSL-CWM; Glover, *Southern Sons*, 19–20.

67. William T. Barry to John Barry, Jan. 30, 1804, *WMQ*, 1st ser., vol. 13 (Oct. 1904): 109 ("Parents"); L. H. Johnson, "Between the Wars," 187–88, 300n134; Osborne, *Crisis Years*, 107–8, 117.

68. Lynn A. Nelson, "Joseph Carrington Cabell," in Bearss et al., eds., *Dictionary of Virginia Biography*, vol. 2:488–89; Thomas Jefferson to J. C. Cabell, c. Sept. 1800, in Boyd et al., eds., *PTJ*, vol. 32:176–81; P. Hamilton, *Making and Unmaking*, 130, 140.

69. Joseph C. Cabell to Isaac A. Coles, Feb. 17, Feb. 22, Mar. 1, and Mar. 16, 1807 ("the want" and "we ought"), and Coles to Cabell, May 27, 1807, JCCFP, box 4, ASSCL-UVA; William H. Cabell to J. C. Cabell, June 22, 1812, Joseph Cabell Papers, SCSL-CWM.

70. Thomas Jefferson to James Semple, Oct. 2, 1812, and Jefferson to Thomas Cooper, Jan. 16, and Aug. 25, 1814, in Looney et al., eds., *PTJ-RS*, vol. 5:373–74, and vol. 7:124–31, and 606–7; Osborne, *Crisis Years*, 150–53, 167–72, 181–97.

71. John Augustine Smith, "William & Mary," *Richmond Enquirer*, Aug. 12, 1817; Osborne, *Crisis Years*, 206, 210, 231.

72. William H. Cabell to Joseph C. Cabell, Nov. 12, 1815 ("temptation"), and May 7, 1816, J. C. Cabell to Isaac A. Coles, Dec. 18, 1815, JCCFP, box 11, ASSCL-UVA.

73. "Philodemus," in J. H. Rice, ed., *Evangelical and Literary Magazine*, vol. 9:350–51; William H. Cabell to Joseph C. Cabell, May 7, 14, and 16 ("The Professors"), 1816, and John Augustine Smith to J. C. Cabell, Nov. 10, 1816, JCCFP, box 11, ASSCL-UVA.

74. John Augustine Smith, "Extract from the Address of the President of William & Mary," *Richmond Enquirer*, Nov. 24, 1814 ("that young"); Smith, "William &

Mary College," *Richmond Enquirer*, Aug. 12, 1817; Elizabeth Trist to Catharine Wistar Bache, Sept. 12, 1817, CWBP, box 2, APS; Osborne, *Crisis Years*, 263, 275.

75. John J. Ambler, Jr., to John J. Ambler, Sr., Mar. 9, 1818, Ambler Family Papers, sec. 3, VHS; "William & Mary," and "Williamsburg," *Richmond Enquirer*, Mar. 13, 1818 ("Deluded man!") and Mar. 24, 1818; Margaret Page to Mrs. Lowther, Mar. 18, 1818, Page-Saunders Papers, box 1, folder 3, SCSL-CWM; Osborne, *Crisis Years*, 223, 226.

76. John Augustine Smith, "Commencement Address," *Richmond Enquirer*, July 20, 1816 ("There is no"); Smith, "William & Mary College," *Richmond Enquirer*, Aug. 12, 1817 ("to the disadvantage"); Paulding, *Letters from the South*, 58-62.

77. John J. Ambler, Jr., to John J. Ambler, Sr., Mar. 9, 1818 ("The College"), Ambler Family Papers, sec. 3, VHS; John Augustine Smith, "William & Mary College," *Richmond Enquirer*, Aug. 12, 1817; Smith, "Communication: William & Mary College," *Richmond Enquirer*, July 18, 1823; Smith, "Address to the House of Delegates," *Richmond Enquirer*, Feb. 5, 1825.

78. John Augustine Smith, "Extract from the Address of the President of William & Mary," *Richmond Enquirer*, Nov. 24, 1814 (quotations); Smith, "Commencement Address," *Richmond Enquirer*, July 20, 1816; Ferdinand S. Campbell to John Campbell, July 10, 1818, CFP, folder 2, VHS; Smith, "Address to the House of Delegates," *Richmond Enquirer*, Feb. 5, 1825.

79. Hugh Blair Grigsby quoted in Flournoy, "Hugh Blair Grigsby," 174 ("If a young man"), 178; Geiger, "Introduction," 10; Glover, *Southern Sons*, 77; Noll, *Princeton and the Republic*, 126, 151-58; Novak, *Rights of Youth*, 17-23, 176n1; Wertenbaker, *Princeton*, 134-43. From 1820 to 1860, southerners accounted for 9 percent of Harvard students; 11 percent at Yale; and 36 percent at Princeton. See O'Brien, *Conjectures of Order*, vol. 1:29; Knight, ed., *Documentary History of Education in the South*, vol. 5:279-80.

80. Glover, "Let Us Manufacture Men," 39-42, George Swain quoted on 42 ("dissipation"); Glover, *Southern Sons*, 64-72; Pace, *Halls of Honor*, 65-67; Towles, "Matter of Honor," 6-18.

81. Thomas Cooper to Thomas Jefferson, Feb. 14, 1822, FO-NA, http://founders .archives.gov/documents/Jefferson/98-01-02-2662; Glover, *Southern Sons*, 22–34, 45–46, 64; D. Malone, *Public Life of Thomas Cooper*, 251–58; Towles, "Matter of Honor," 6–18.

82. James W. Alexander to unnamed, Dec. 24, 1824, in Alexander, *Forty Years' Familiar Letters*, vol. 1:71 ("There is"); William J. Grayson quoted in Towles, "Matter of Honor," 12 ("sees his professor"); Glover, *Southern Sons*, 2-3, 64-71, 98-110; Kett, *Rites of Passage*, 58-59.

83. Geiger, "Introduction," 10-12; Glover, *Southern Sons*, 59-60; Novak, *Rights of Youth*, 21-22; Towles, "Matter of Honor," 13-16; Osborne, *Crisis Years*, 203;

"Philodemus," in J. H. Rice, ed., *Evangelical and Literary Magazine*, vol. 9:354 ("rightful authority").

84. Sterling Ruffin to Thomas Ruffin, May 5, 1803, in Roulhac Hamilton, ed., *Papers of Thomas Ruffin*, vol. 1:45; Glover, *Southern Sons*, 12–14, 42, 60–62; Osborne, *Crisis Years*, 203.

85. J. Randolph, *Letters*, 25–26; J. H. Rice, "The University of Virginia," in Rice, ed., *Virginia Evangelical and Literary Magazine*, vol. 3:587.

86. St. George Tucker to John Coalter, June 14, 1809, Brown, Coalter, Tucker Papers, ser. 1, box 3, SCSL-CWM; Joseph C. Cabell to S. G. Tucker, Dec. 30, 1816, TCP, reel M-28, SSCL-CWM.

87. G. Tucker, *Letters from Virginia*, 54–58; Wirt, *Old Bachelor*, 100–101, and 166.

88. Thomas Jefferson to John Adams, July 5, 1814, FO-NA, http://founders.archives.gov/documents/Adams/99-02-02-6314.

4. Mountain

1. Chastellux, *Travels*, vol. 2:390–92; Edward Rutledge to Thomas Jefferson, Feb. 12, 1779 ("condescended"), Boyd et al., eds., *PTJ*, vol. 2:234.

2. Thomas Jefferson to Francis Hopkinson, Mar. 13, 1789, and Jefferson to Anne Cary Randolph, Mar. 7, 1802, in Boyd et al., eds., *PTJ*, vol. 14: 649–51 ("I find"), and vol. 37:20–21 ("charming"); E. Randolph, "Essay," *VMHB*, vol. 43:122; Gordon-Reed and Onuf, *Most Blessed of Patriarchs*, 165–71; Valsania, *Jefferson's Body*, 121–22.

3. Bacon, "Autobiography," 36; Francis C. Gray, Diary, Feb. 4–7, 1815, in Looney et al., eds., *PTJ-RS*, vol. 8:232–38 ("extremely grand"); George Ticknor, *Life*, vol. 1:34 ("The ascent").

4. M. B. Smith, *First Forty Years*, 65; John H. B. Latrobe, in Peterson, ed., *Visitors to Monticello*, 122 ("lofty summit"); Weld, *Travels*, vol. 1:207–8.

5. Bacon, "Autobiography," 36–38; Carrière and Moffatt, eds., "Frenchman Visits Albemarle," 49–50; Chastellux, *Travels*, vol. 2:394.

6. Carrière and Moffatt, eds., "Frenchman Visits Albemarle," 49–51; Ticknor, *Life*, vol. 1:34; Francis C. Gray, Diary, Feb. 4–7, 1815, in Looney et al., eds., *PTJ-RS*, vol. 8:232–38.

7. Wagoner, *Jefferson and Education*, 25–26.

8. Bacon, "Autobiography," 106–7; Madison Hemings, "Memoirs," and Israel Gillette (Jefferson), "Memoirs," in Gordon-Reed, *Thomas Jefferson and Sally Hemings*, 248, 252 ("concubine"); Gordon-Reed, *Hemingses*, 106–8, 254, 288–89, 310; Stanton, *Those Who Labor*, 182–83.

9. Anna Thornton, and Isaac Briggs, in Peterson, ed., *Visitors to Monticello*, 34 ("The president's bedchamber"), 91–92; Addis, *Jefferson's Vision*, 95; Burstein, *Jefferson's Secrets*, 101; R. B. Davis, ed., *Jeffersonian America*, 147; M. B. Smith,

NOTES TO PAGES 104–108

First Forty Years, 68–69; Ticknor, *Life*, vol. 1:37; Stanton, *Those Who Labor*, 84–85, 100; Valsania, *Jefferson's Body*, 123–26.

10. Elijah Fletcher to Jesse Fletcher, May 24, 1811, in Von Briesen, ed., *Letters of Elijah Fletcher*, 35; Cocke quoted in Rothman, "James Callender," 108 ("would number"), see also 113n67; G. Tucker, *Letters from Virginia*, 75.

11. Anna Thornton, and Richard Rush, in Peterson, ed., *Visitors to Monticello*, 33–34, 72–73.

12. La Rochefoucauld-Liancourt, in Hayes, ed., *Jefferson in His Own Time*, 27 ("especially"); M. B. Smith, *First Forty Years*, 68; Ticknor, *Life*, vol. 1:36 ("I went"); Stanton, "Other End of the Telescope," 139–52.

13. Anna Thornton, and Richard Rush, in Peterson, ed., *Visitors to Monticello*, 34, 72–73; Burstein, *Jefferson's Secrets*, 11; E. Randolph, "Essay," *VMHB*, vol. 43:122.

14. Ellen W. Randolph to Martha J. Randolph, Sept. 27, [1816], EWRCP, box 1, ASSCL-UVA; Bacon, "Autobiography," 124–25; Hayes, ed., *Jefferson in His Own Time*, 155, 163–66; Gordon-Reed and Onuf, *Most Blessed of Patriarchs*, 244–48, 262–64. "Deeply conflicted" derives from the immortal words of historian Peter Onuf (who is also immortal).

15. Ellen W. Randolph to Martha J. Randolph, July 28, 1819, and E. W. Randolph to Virginia Randolph, Aug. 4, 1819, EWRCP, box 1, ASSCL-UVA; Burstein, *Jefferson's Secrets*, 101–102.

16. Ellen W. Randolph to Martha J. Randolph, Sept. n.d., 1817 ("entirely ignorant"), July 18, 1819, EWRCP, box 1, ASSCL-UVA; Cornelia J. Randolph to Virginia J. Randolph, Sept. 8, 1819, NPTP, folder 18, SHC-UNC.

17. Salma Hale to Arthur Livermore, May 16, 1818, in Looney et al., eds., *PTJ-RS*, vol. 13:2; Burstein, *Jefferson's Secrets*, 11.

18. Bernhard, *Travels*, vol. 1:197–98; Francis C. Gray, in Peterson, ed., *Visitors to Monticello*, 57 ("figure," "with pointed" and "blue waistcoat"); Ticknor, *Life*, vol. 1:37; Daniel Webster and Edmund Bacon in Hayes, ed., *Jefferson in His Own Time*, 93, 169 ("He was like").

19. Daniel Webster, Thomas Jefferson Randolph, Edmund Bacon, and Peter F. Fossett in Hayes, ed., *Jefferson in His Own Time*, 93, 159–60, 170, 190; M. B. Smith, *First Forty Years*, 68; G. Tucker, *Life of Thomas Jefferson*, vol. 2:487, 502.

20. Chastellux, *Travels*, vol. 2:392; Francis W. Gilmer, "Sketches of American Statesmen," in R. B. Davis, *Francis Walker Gilmer*, 350; La Rochefoucauld and Edmund Bacon, in Hayes, ed., *Jefferson in His Own Time*, 25, 173; Samuel Whitcomb, Jr., in Peterson, ed., *Visitors to Monticello*, 93–95 ("Being" and "the Character").

21. Francis W. Gilmer, "Description of Thomas Jefferson," and Robert Walsh, Jr., to Gilmer, Nov. 4, 1817 ("I was delighted"), in Looney et al., eds., *PTJ-RS*, vol. 8:296–99, vol. 12:101n; Bernhard, *Travels*, vol. 1:197–98; Francis Hall in Peterson, ed., *Visitors to Monticello*, 74–75; Burstein, *Jefferson's Secrets*, 51; Gordon-Reed and Onuf, *Most Blessed of Patriarchs*, 254–57.

22. La Rochefoucauld-Liancourt, and Edmund Bacon, in Hayes, ed., *Jefferson in His Own Time*, 25, 169 ("His countenance"); M. B. Smith, *First Forty Years*, 79–80; Ticknor, *Life*, vol. 1:34–37.

23. Thomas Jefferson Randolph, and Edmund Bacon, in Hayes, ed., *Jefferson in His Own Time*, 164 ("His temper"), 171 ("sat easily").

24. Thomas Jefferson to Joseph C. Cabell, Jan. 24, 1816, to William A. Burwell, Feb. 6, 1817, and to John G. Jackson, Dec. 27, 1818, in Looney et al., eds., *PTJ-RS*, vol. 9:396–98, vol. 11:56, vol. 13:526.

25. Samuel Whitcomb, Jr., in Peterson, ed., *Visitors to Monticello*, 95 ("He is more"); G. Tucker, "Autobiography," 142; Daniel Webster, in Hayes, ed., *Jefferson in His Own Time*, 99; Burstein, *Jefferson's Secrets*, 43.

26. Francis C. Gray, Diary, Feb. 4–7, 1815, Looney et al., eds., *PTJ-RS*, vol. 8:232–38 ("completely"); Anna Thornton, Diary, and Samuel Whitcomb, Jr., May 31, 1824, in Peterson, ed., *Visitors to Monticello*, 34 ("looks"), and 95 ("His house"); Bernhard, *Travels*, vol. 1:198.

27. Thomas Jefferson to David Higginbotham, May 26, 1817, and Jefferson to Wilson Cary Nicholas, Mar. 26, 1818, in Looney et al., eds., *PTJ-RS*, vol. 11:385, vol. 12:556; Francis W. Gilmer to Peter Minor, May 22, 1823 ("What with"), GFC, box 1, ASSCL-UVA; F. W. Gilmer to Peachy Gilmer, May 29, 1823 ("alternately"), PRGP, sec. 2, VHS; D. Malone, *Jefferson and His Time*, vol. 6:301–2, 448; Sloan, *Principle and Interest*, 10–11.

28. Thomas Jefferson to Paul A. Clay, July 12, 1817, in Looney et al., eds., *PTJ-RS*, vol. 11:525 ("Never spend"); D. Malone, *Jefferson and His Time*, vol. 6:289, 308; Sloan, *Principle and Interest*, 10.

29. Kierner, *Martha Jefferson Randolph*, 166–67.

30. Thomas Jefferson to Wilson Cary Nicholas, June 10, 1817, Nicholas to Jefferson, June 16, 1817, Jefferson to Nicholas, Mar. 26, 1818, and Apr. 5, 1818, Nicholas to Jefferson, Apr. 19, 1818, Jefferson to Nicholas, May 1, 1818, Nicholas to Jefferson, June 1, 1819, and Jefferson to Nicholas, July 2, 1819, in Looney et al., eds., *PTJ-RS*, vol. 11:426, 451; vol. 12:556, 572, 649, vol. 13:14, and vol. 14:369, 497; D. Malone, *Jefferson and His Time*, vol. 6:302–4; Sloan, *Principle and Interest*, 209.

31. Thomas Jefferson to James Leitch, June 3, 1819, in Looney et al., eds., *PTJ-RS*, vol. 14:379–80; Jefferson to John Wayles Eppes, June 30, and July 29, 1820, and Jefferson to Thomas Appleton, Aug. 11, 1825, FO-NA, http://founders.archives .gov/documents/Jefferson/98-01-02-1352, -1425, and -5461; Sloan, *Principle and Interest*, 219–21.

32. Wilson Cary Nicholas to Jefferson, Aug. 5, 1819, Jefferson to Nicholas, Aug. 11, 1819, and Jefferson to Nicholas, Aug. 17, 1819, in Looney et al., eds., *PTJ-RS*, vol. 14:586–87 ("greatest pain"), 604, 621 ("I repeat"); Ellen W. Randolph to Martha J. Randolph, Aug. 11, and Aug. 24, 1819, EWRCP, box 1, ASSCL-UVA; D. Malone, *Jefferson and His Time*, vol. 6:310–13.

33. Joseph C. Cabell to John H. Cocke, Oct. 23, 1820 ("I cannot depict"), JCCFP, box 14, ASSCL-UVA; Francis W. Gilmer to Dabney Carr, Sept. 28, 1819, and Apr. 27, 1820 ("broken spirited"), Gilmer-Carr letters, LV; Robert Gamble quoted in K. R. Malone, "Fate of Revolutionary Republicanism," 46 ("The explosion").

34. Elizabeth Trist to Nicholas P. Trist, Nov. 1, 1820, JFL website, ICJS; John H. Cocke to John H. Cocke, Jr., Dec. 23, 1822, JHCP, box 37, ASSCL-UVA; Bacon, "Autobiography," 126; D. Malone, *Jefferson and His Time*, vol. 6:314.

35. Thomas Jefferson to Martha J. Randolph, Jan. 5, 1808, and M. J. Randolph to Jefferson, Jan. 16, 1808, FO-NA, http://founders.archives.gov/documents/Jefferson/99-01-02-7138, and -7217; D. Malone, *Jefferson and His Time*, vol. 6:448–49.

36. Thomas Jefferson to Thomas Mann Randolph, July 6, 1787, in Boyd et al., eds., *PTJ*, vol. 11:556–59; Gaines, *Thomas Mann Randolph*, 3–7, 13–21.

37. Gaines, *Thomas Mann Randolph*, 24–26; Gordon-Reed, *Hemingses*, 414–17; Gordon-Reed and Onuf, *"Most Blessed of Patriarchs,"* 180–81; Kierner, *Martha Jefferson Randolph*, 77–86.

38. Bacon, "Autobiography," 93–96; Gaines, *Thomas Mann Randolph*, 60–63; Peachy R. Gilmer note added at the end of T. M. Randolph to P. R. Gilmer, Mar. 30, 1812 ("eccentric"), T. M. Randolph letters to the Gilmer family, LV.

39. Thomas Mann Randolph to Thomas Jefferson, Mar 6, 1802, and Jefferson to Randolph, Mar. 12, 1802, in Boyd et al., *PTJ*, vol. 37:14–16 ("to give"), 64–67; Jefferson quoted in Elizabeth Trist to Catharine Wistar Bache, Dec. 28, 1810 ("that it would"), JFL website, ICJS; Gordon-Reed, *Hemingses*, 423–24; Kierner, *Martha Jefferson Randolph*, 87–88, 121–22.

40. Thomas Jefferson to Anne C. Randolph et al., Mar. 7, 1802, in Boyd et al., eds., *PTJ*, vol. 37:20–21; T. J. Randolph and Edmund Bacon, in Hayes, ed., *Jefferson in His Own Time*, 161, 174 ("Mr. Jefferson"); Ellen W. R. Coolidge quoted in D. Malone, *Jefferson and His Time*, vol. 6: 298; Burstein, *Jefferson's Secrets*, 11; Lewis, "White Jeffersons," 129–31.

41. Martha J. Randolph to Thomas Jefferson, Apr. 16, 1802, Boyd et al., eds., *PTJ-RS*, vol. 37:246–47; Kierner, *Martha Jefferson Randolph*, 136.

42. Thomas Jefferson to Martha Jefferson, Nov. 28, 1783, Mar. 6, 1786, in Boyd et al., eds., *PTJ*, vol. 6:359–61 ("I have placed"), vol. 9:318; Kierner, *Martha Jefferson Randolph*, 56–65.

43. Thomas Jefferson to John Wayles Eppes, Mar. 30, and Apr. 30, 1816, in Looney et al., eds, *PTJ-RS*, vol. 9:607–9, 712–14; J. W. Eppes to Francis Eppes, Nov. 18, 1818, Eppes Family Papers, folder 8, ASSCL-UVA; Jefferson to Thomas Mann Randolph, July 30, 1821, FO-NA, http://founders.archives.gov/documents/Jefferson/98-01-02-2206.

44. Martha J. Randolph to Jefferson, July 15, 1808, FO-NA, http://founders.archives

.gov/documents/Jefferson/99-01-02-8331; Bacon, "Autobiography," 127; D. Malone, *Jefferson and His Time*, vol. 6:9–11.

45. Thomas Jefferson to John Wayles Eppes, June 30, 1820 ("Francis"), FO-NA, http://founders.archives.gov/documents/Jefferson/98-01-02-1352; F. W. Eppes to Thomas Jefferson, Mar. 22, 1822, Jefferson to F. W. Eppes, Apr. 9, 1822, and F. W. Eppes to Jefferson, May 13, and Oct. 31,1822, in Betts and Bear, eds., *Family Letters*, 442–46; D. Malone, *Jefferson and His Time*, vol. 6:390. Among northern schools, Jefferson could favor only Philadelphia's medical school, which Jeff Randolph briefly attended in 1808.

46. Thomas Jefferson to Martha Jefferson, Feb. 9, 1791, in Boyd et al., eds., *PTJ*, vol. 19:264 ("have given"); Jefferson to Nathaniel Burwell, Mar. 14, 1818, in Looney et al., *PTJ-RS*, vol. 12:532; Burstein, *Jefferson's Secrets*, 87–88, 98–99, 109; Steele, "Thomas Jefferson's Gender Frontier," 21–22, 27–28, 33–35, 40–42; Valsania, *Jefferson's Body*, 175–76.

47. Thomas Jefferson to Martha J. Randolph, Aug. 31, 1817, in Betts and Bear, eds., *Family Letters*, 419 ("Ellen and Cornelia"); Ellen W. Randolph to M. J. Randolph, July 18, 1819, EWRCP, box 1, ASSCL-UVA; Anna Thornton, in Peterson, ed., *Visitors to Monticello*, 34; E. W. Randolph quoted in Burstein, *Jefferson's Secrets*, 88 ("I have known").

48. Cornelia J. Randolph to Virginia J. R. Trist, Dec. 27, 1821 ("by the life"), and Jan. 31, 1822 ("mutiny"), Virginia J. R. Trist to Nicholas P. Trist, Sept. 4, 1825, NPTP, folders 24, 25, and 37, SHC-UNC; V. J. R. Trist to Ellen W. R. Coolidge, Dec. 4, 1825 ("I begin"), EWRCP, box 1, ASSCL-UVA.

49. Cornelia J. Randolph to Ellen W. R. Coolidge, Nov. 24, 1825 ("I wish"), EWRCP, box 1, ASSCL-UVA.

50. Thomas Jefferson to Martha J. Randolph, June 8, 1797, in Boyd et al., eds., *PTJ*, vol. 29:424–25; J. Lewis, "White Jeffersons," 134–41.

51. Cockerham, Keeling, and Parker, "Seeking Refuge," 34; J. Lewis, "White Jeffersons," 132–34; D. Malone, *Jefferson and His Time*, vol. 6:157–59, 299.

52. Elizabeth Trist to Catharine Wistar Bache, Aug. 22, 1810, CWBP, box 1, APS; Thomas Jefferson to John Bankhead, Oct. 28, 1815, and Oct. 14–16, 1816, in Looney et al., eds., *PTJ-RS*, vol. 9:131–32, vol. 10:461–62; Bacon, "Autobiography," 99–101; Kierner, *Martha Jefferson Randolph*, 159, 199.

53. Thomas Jefferson to Mary Jefferson Eppes, Jan. 7, 1798, Boyd et al., eds., *PTJ*, vol. 30:14–16 ("When we see"); Jefferson to John Bankhead, Oct. 28, 1815, Looney et al., eds., *PTJ-RS*, vol. 9:131–32.

54. Thomas Jefferson to John Bankhead, Oct, 14–16, 1816, Martha J. Randolph to Thomas Jefferson, Nov. 20, 1816, Looney et al., eds., *PTJ-RS*, vol. 10:461–62, 536–38.

55. Bacon, "Autobiography," 99–100.

56. Elizabeth Trist to Nicholas P. Trist, Feb. 3, 1819, in Looney et al., eds., *PTJ-RS*, vol. 14:8–19; Crawford, *Twilight at Monticello*, 113–15.

57. Elizabeth Trist to Nicholas P. Trist, Feb. 3, 1819 ("appeared"), and Feb. 7, 1819, in Looney et al., eds., *PTJ-RS*, vol. 14:18–20; Alexander Garrett to John H. Cocke, Feb. 8, 1819, JHCP, box 28, ASSCL-UVA; Hetty Carr to Dabney S. Carr, Feb. 9, 1819, CCFP, box 2, ASSCL-UVA; Bacon, "Autobiography," 99; Vance, "Knives, Whips, and Randolphs," 28–30.

58. Charles Lewis Bankhead to Thomas Jefferson, Feb. 6, 1819, in Looney et al., eds., *PTJ-RS*, vol. 14:16–17.

59. Hetty Carr to Dabney S. Carr, Feb. 9, 1819, CCFP, box 2, ASSCL-UVA; Hore Browse Trist to Nicholas P. Trist, Feb. 19, 1819 ("It seems" and "would appear"), JFL website, ICJS; Thomas Jefferson to Wilson Cary Nicholas, Mar. 8, 1819, Looney et al., eds., *PTJ-RS*, vol. 14:110; D. Malone, *Jefferson and His Time*, vol. 6:300.

60. Elizabeth Trist to Nicholas P. Trist, Feb. 24, 1819, NPTP, folder 17, SHC-UNC.

61. Elizabeth Trist to Nicholas P. Trist, Feb. 24, 1819, NPTP, folder 17, SHC-UNC; Thomas Jefferson to Wilson Cary Nicholas, Mar. 8, 1819, Looney et al., eds., *PTJ-RS*, vol. 14:110; E. Trist to N. P. Trist, June 19, 1819, JFL website, ICJS.

62. Mary E. Terrell to Louisa Cocke, Feb. 15, 1826, JHCP, box 46, ASSCL-UVA; Robley Dunglison quoted in Burstein, *Jefferson's Secrets* 14 ("It is impossible"); Kierner, *Martha Jefferson Randolph*, 199–200. Family members implausibly blamed the doctors for Anne's death. See Cornelia J. Randolph to Ellen W. R. Coolidge, Feb. 23, 1826, and Martha J. Randolph to Joseph Coolidge, Mar. 1, 1826, JFL website, ICJS.

63. Mary E. Terrell to Louisa Cocke, Feb. 15, 1826, JHCP, box 46, ASSCL-UVA; Martha J. Randolph quoted in Vance, "Knives, Whips, and Randolphs," 33.

64. R. B. Davis, *Francis Walker Gilmer*, 8; R. B. Davis, ed., *Correspondence of Jefferson and Gilmer*, 11–12.

65. Thomas Jefferson to Francis W. Gilmer, Nov. 23, 1814, and Jefferson to Caspar Wistar, Nov. 23, 1814 ("In the vast"), in Looney et al., eds., *PTJ-RS*, vol. 8:101, 103; Margaret Bayard Smith quoted in R. B. Davis, *Francis Walker Gilmer*, 136–37.

66. William Wirt quoted in P. A. Bruce, *History of the University*, vol. 1:345; R. B. Davis, ed., *Correspondence of Jefferson and Gilmer*, 11–13; R. B. Davis, *Francis Walker Gilmer*, 21, 51.

67. William Wirt to Francis W. Gilmer, Aug. 26, 1805, and July 23, 1815 ("You must"), GFN, box 1, ASSCL-UVA; R. B. Davis, *Francis Walker Gilmer*, 13 (Wirt quoted: "prodigy"), 51, 54 (Wirt quoted: "to see"), 88 (Wirt quoted: "I wish you").

68. William Wirt to Francis W. Gilmer, Aug. 26, 1805, and Oct. 9, 1806, GFC, box 1, ASSCL-UVA; F. W. Gilmer to Peachy R. Gilmer, Nov. 20, 1812, PRGP, sec. 2, VHS.

69. Francis W. Gilmer to Peachy R. Gilmer, Oct. n.d., 1809, Apr. 17, 1813 ("humble"), Oct. 26, 1813, July 20, 1816, and Mar. 29, 1819 ("the seats"), PRGP, sec. 2, VHS.

70. Francis W. Gilmer to Peachy R. Gilmer, Apr. 30, 1809 ("dry" and "eloquence"), and Nov. 7, 1810, Oct. 24, 1812, Mar. 17, 1813 ("public taste"), May 22, 1813 ("I wish"), PRGP, sec. 2., VHS; F. W. Gilmer to Dabney Carr, Nov. 5, 1820 ("In Virginia"), Gilmer-Carr letters, LV.

71. Francis W. Gilmer to Peachy R. Gilmer, Apr. 16, 1811 ("There is"), Apr. 17, 1813, Dec. 21, 1813 ("O that I had"), Jan. 25, 1814, and Apr. 29, 1814 ("Since I cannot"), PRGP, sec. 2, VHS.

72. Francis W. Gilmer to Peachy R. Gilmer, Feb. 23, 1812, Oct. 14, 1813 ("I must have"), Jan. 6, 1814, Apr. 29, 1814 ("a better theatre"), Oct. 25, 1816, Dec. 14, 1818, Mar. 14, 1819, and Mar. 29, 1819 ("Since we resolve"), PRGP, sec. 2, VHS.

73. Francis W. Gilmer to Peachy R. Gilmer, Aug. 18, 1815, Mar. 8, 1816, May 25, 1816, PRGP, sec. 2, VHS; F. W. Gilmer to William Wirt, May 4, 1816, Gilmer-Wirt letters, LV; F. W. Gilmer to Peter Minor, Mar. 4, and May 12, 1816, GFC, box 1, ASSCL-UVA; R. B. Davis, ed., *Correspondence of Jefferson and Gilmer*, 16–17.

74. Francis W. Gilmer to Peter Minor, May 10, 1818 ("I shall make"), GFC, box 1, ASSCL-UVA; F. W. Gilmer to Dabney Carr, May 25, 1818 ("Sind Sam"), and June 22, 1819 ("the fallen"), Gilmer-Carr letters, LV; F. W. Gilmer to Peachy R. Gilmer, Feb. 19, 1820 ("I work" and "My heart"), PRGP, sec. 2, VHS.

75. R. B. Davis, *Francis Walker Gilmer*, 57–58, 360–61; Francis W. Gilmer to Peachy R. Gilmer, Jan. 6, 1814, June 25 (description of the fight), and Aug. 18, 1815, and June 9, 1819 ("He knew"), PRGP, sec. 2, VHS; unsigned anonymous statement re F. W. Gilmer and Dr. Charles Everette, William Douglas Papers, sec. 5, VHS; Boyd et al., eds., *PTJ*, vol. 24, 733n and 742; L. G. Tyler, ed., "Letters of James Monroe," 96.

76. Francis W. Gilmer to Dabney Carr, June 13, 1821 ("I struck"), and June 27, 1821 ("I shall bear"), Gilmer-Carr letters, LV; John Campbell to David Campbell, June 16, 1821, CFP, box 4, DMRML-DU; R. B. Davis, *Francis Walker Gilmer*, 149.

77. Francis W. Gilmer to Peachy R. Gilmer, Nov. 20, 1812, Dec. 24, 1812 ("become wedded"), Oct. 14, 1813, Dec. 8, 1813, Feb. 8, 1814, Mar. 4, 1814, and Feb. 22, 1818 ("These city belles"), Sept. 7, 1818, and Feb. 27, 1822, PRGP, sec. 2, VHS.

78. Francis W. Gilmer to Peachy R. Gilmer, Feb. 25, Mar. 4, and Apr. 4, 1814 ("one of these"), PRGP, sec. 2, VHS; F. W. Gilmer to Peter Minor, Mar. 12, and Oct. 20, 1819 ("a harder"), GFC, box 1, ASSCL-UVA; F. W. Gilmer to Dabney Carr, Sept. 30, 1820 ("but for having"), Gilmer-Carr correspondence, LV.

79. Elizabeth Trist to Catharine W. Bache, Aug. 22, 1814 ("one of the best"), CWBP, box 1, APS; Horace Holley to Orville L. Holley, Sept. 6, 1824 ("Ellen"), Misc. Mss. 11896, University Archives, ASSCL-UVA; Burstein, *Jefferson's Secrets*, 72–76.

80. Ellen W. Randolph to Martha J. Randolph, Mar. 30, 1814, and Jan. 28 ("I bless"),

and Sept. 27, 1818, EWRCP, box 1, ASSCL-UVA; M. J. Randolph to Elizabeth Trist, May 31, 1815 ("Ellen fulfills" and "I think"), JFL website, ICJS.

81. Ellen W. Randolph to Martha J. Randolph, Apr. 24, 1814, Jan. 28 ("folly"), and Sept. 27, 1818, July 28, 1819, and May 31, 1820, and autobiographical note, June 15, 1828 ("timid"), EWRCP, boxes 1 and 2, ASSCL-UVA.

82. Elizabeth Trist to Catharine Wistar Bache, Aug. 22, 1814, CWBP, box 1, APS; Francis W. Gilmer to Peachy R. Gilmer, Sept. 17, 1818 ("Her decided"), and June 9, 1819 ("only persons"), PRGP, sec. 2, VHS; Burstein, *Jefferson's Secrets*, 72–76.

83. Francis W. Gilmer to Dabney Carr, Mar. 4, and 25, 1821 (quotations), Gilmer-Carr letters, LV.

84. Francis W. Gilmer to Peachy R. Gilmer, Sept. 17, and Sept. 27, 1818 ("I have no doubt"), and May 15, 1820 ("It cut me"), PRGP, sec. 2, VHS; F. W. Gilmer to Dabney Carr, Mar. 16, 1819 ("Messiah" and "outlaw"), Gilmer-Carr letters, LV.

85. Ellen W. Randolph to Martha J. Randolph, Mar. 29, [1819], EWRCP, box 1, ASSCL-UVA.

86. Francis W. Gilmer to Peachy R. Gilmer, Mar. 29, 1819, PRGP, sec. 2, VHS; F. W. Gilmer to Dabney Carr, May 31, 1819 ("Miss E[llen]"), Gilmer-Carr correspondence, LV.

87. Ellen W. Randolph to Martha J. Randolph, Jan. 28, 1818 ("I begin"), Mar. 18, 1819, and Jan. 9, 1820 ("admirable plant"), EWRCP, box 1, ASSCL-UVA.

88. Francis W. Gilmer to Peachy R. Gilmer, Nov. 29, 1816 ("She is too"), and Mar. 29, 1819 ("She is destined"), PRGP, sec. 2, VHS.

89. Wilson Miles Cary to Virginia Cary, n.d., c. Feb. 1825, CCFP, box 2, ASSCL-UVA; Burstein, *Jefferson's Secrets*, 73; D. Malone, *Jefferson and His Time*, vol. 6:456–59.

90. Francis W. Gilmer to Peachy R. Gilmer Papers, Dec. 22, 1824 ("There is no event"), and June 19, 1825 ("broke to atoms"), PRGP, sec. 2, VHS.

91. Francis W. Gilmer to Peachy R. Gilmer, Jan. 1, 1817, Sept. 27, 1818 ("Domestic education"), and Oct. 25, 1818, PRGP, sec. 2, VHS.

92. Francis W. Gilmer to Peachy R. Gilmer, Sept. 27, 1818, PRGP, sec. 2, VHS; Boyd et al., eds., *PTJ*, vol. 38:419n, vol. 42:324n; Looney et al., eds. *PTJ-RS*, vol. 8:296n, and vol. 9:57n; Harriet Hackley to Catharine Wistar Bache, Mar. 24, 1811, and Feb. 17, 1813, Martha J. Randolph to Elizabeth Trist, May 31, 1815, Mary E. Randolph to Jane Nicholas Randolph, Jan. 13, 1822 ("my lady paramount"), JFL website, ICJS; Ellen W. Randolph to M. J. Randolph, Mar. 29, 1819 ("presiding"), EWRCP, box 1, ASSCL-UVA.

93. Francis W. Gilmer to Thomas Jefferson, Nov. 13, 1814, and Gilmer, "Description of Thomas Jefferson and Monticello," Feb. 1815, Looney et al., eds., *TJ-RS*, vol. 8:78, 296–99; Gilmer to Peter Minor, June 29, 1818 ("I like"), GFC, box 1, ASSCL-UVA.

94. Francis W. Gilmer to Peter Minor, June 24, 1816, and June 29, 1818 ("scarcely one"), GFC, box 1, ASSCL-UVA; F. W. Gilmer to Peachy R. Gilmer, Sept. 20, 1816, and Nov. 12, 1818, PRGP, sec. 2. VHS; F. W. Gilmer to William Wirt, Dec. 20, 1816 ("dark chambers"), Gilmer-Wirt letters, LV; D. P. Jordan, *Political Leadership*, 10–14.

95. Francis Walker Gilmer to William Wirt, Dec. 20, 1816, and Mar. 28, 1817, Gilmer-Wirt letters, LV; F W. Gilmer to Dabney Carr, Sept. 24, 1821 ("music"), Gilmer-Carr letters, LV.

96. Francis Walker Gilmer to William Wirt, Jan. n.d., 1816 ("St. Thomas"), Gilmer-Wirt letters, LV; F. W. Gilmer to Dabney Carr, Oct. 12, 1818 ("Citizen Thomas"), and Dec. 19, 1819 ("The next thing"), Gilmer-Carr letters, LV; F. W. Gilmer to Peachy R. Gilmer, Mar. 30, 1823 ("Red breeches" and "octagonal houses"), PRGP, sec. 2, VHS.

97. Francis W. Gilmer to Thomas Jefferson, Mar. 18, 1818, in R. B. Davis, ed., *Correspondence of Jefferson and Gilmer*, 58; F. W. Gilmer to Peachy R. Gilmer, Feb. 22, and Apr. 23, 1821, and May 30, 1822 ("Virginia is a ruined country"), PRGP, sec. 2, VHS.

98. Francis W. Gilmer to Peachy R. Gilmer, June 29, 1819, PRGP, sec. 2, VHS.

99. Francis W. Gilmer to Peter Minor, May 22, 1823, GFC, box one, ASSCL-UVA.

5. Slavery

1. Jefferson, *Notes*, 103–20; Gordon-Reed and Onuf, *Most Blessed of Patriarchs*, 83–90.

2. Jefferson, *Notes*, 150–51 ("the parent"); Jefferson to Marquis de Chastellux, Sept. 2, 1785, and Jefferson to Jean Nicholas Demeunier, June 26, 1786, in Boyd et al., eds., *PTJ*, vol. 8:467–70, and vol. 10:61–64 ("inflict").

3. Jefferson, *Notes*, 150–51; Gordon-Reed and Onuf, *Most Blessed of Patriarchs*, 91–93.

4. Thomas Jefferson to John Holmes, Apr. 22, 1820 ("We have a wolf"), FO-NA, http://founders.archives.gov/documents/Jefferson/98-01-02-1234; Jefferson, "Autobiography," 44; Jefferson, *Notes*, 128 ("convulsions") and 133 ("inferior").

5. Gordon-Reed and Onuf, *Most Blessed of Patriarchs*, 143–49; Sidbury, "Saint Domingue in Virginia," 531–52; La Rochefoucauld-Liancourt quoted in Stanton, *Those Who Labor*, 306–7n24; S. G. Tucker, *Dissertation on Slavery*, 49–51.

6. Thomas Jefferson to Edward Bancroft, Jan. 26, 1789, in Boyd et al., eds., *PTJ*, vol. 14:492–93; Jefferson to Edward Coles, Aug. 25, 1814, in Looney et al., eds., *PTJ-RS*, vol. 7:603–5 ("as incapable" and "pests"); Onuf, *Mind of Thomas Jefferson*, 260.

7. Thomas Jefferson to Marquis de Chastellux, June 7, 1785, Jefferson to Richard Price, Aug. 7, 1785, and Jefferson to Jean Nicholas Demeunier, Jan. 24, and June

26, 1786, in Boyd et al., eds., *PTJ*, vol. 8:184 ("It is to them"), 356 ("sucked in"), vol. 10:18, 61–64 ("by diffusing").

8. Thomas Jefferson to James Madison, May 11, 1785, and Jefferson to Marquis de Chastellux, June 7, 1785, in Boyd et al., eds., *PTJ*, vol. 8:147 ("might be" and "only send"), 184.

9. James Madison to Thomas Jefferson, Nov. 15, 1785, and Jefferson to George Wythe, Sept. 16, 1787, Boyd et al., eds., *PTJ*, vol. 9:38 ("an indiscriminate"), and 12:130 ("such young").

10. Wolf, *Race and Liberty*, 93–95, 129 (Francis Asbury quoted).

11. St. George Tucker to Jeremy Belknap, June 29, 1795, in Belknap, "Queries," 407; Wolf, *Race and Liberty*, xi–xii, 6, 21–27, 143.

12. Ely, *Israel on the Appomattox*, 8–11; S. G. Tucker, *Dissertation on Slavery*, 9.

13. L. K. Ford, *Deliver Us from Evil*, 4; Deyle, *Carry Me Back*, 24–26; Richard D. Bayly to John Cropper, Jan. 6, 1805 ("I am"), John Cropper Papers, sec. 1, VHS.

14. Thomas Jefferson to John Wayles Eppes, June 30, 1820, FO-NA, http://founders .archives.gov/documents/Jefferson/98-01-02-1352; Deyle, *Carry Me Back*, 28; Richard Blow quoted in J. Lewis, *Pursuit of Happiness*, 142–43 ("I think it").

15. Thomas Jefferson to James Monroe, July 14, 1793, and Jefferson to St. George Tucker, Aug. 28, 1797, in Boyd et al., eds., *PTJ*, vol. 26:501–3 ("never"), and vol. 29:519–20 ("If something").

16. S. G. Tucker, *Dissertation on Slavery*, 2, 27–28, 54–60.

17. St. George Tucker to Jeremy Belknap, June 29, 1795 ("large majority"), Apr. 3, 1797, and Aug. 13, 1797, in Belknap, ed., "Queries," 407, 426, and 427–28; Tucker to Robert Pleasants, June 29, 1797, in "St. George Tucker Notes," 38, TCP, box 63, SCSL-CWM; P. Hamilton, *Making and Unmaking*, 81–82; Egerton, *Gabriel's Rebellion*, 15.

18. Dierksheide, *Amelioration*, 20, 27–29, 46; D. Malone, *Jefferson and His Time*, vol. 6:316–18; Stanton, *Those Who Labor for My Happiness*, 79–83.

19. Thomas Jefferson to Thomas Mann Randolph, Apr. 19, 1792, in Boyd et al., eds., *PTJ*, vol. 23:435–36; Peter Fossett in Hayes, ed., *Jefferson in His Own Time*, 191.

20. Jefferson to Burwell, Jan. 28, 1805 ("I have long since"), FO-NA, http://founders .archives.gov/documents/Jefferson/99-01-02-1057; McColley, *Slavery and Jeffersonian Virginia*, 130–31; Onuf, *Mind of Thomas Jefferson*, 252–55.

21. Fehrenbacher and McAfee, *Slaveholding Republic*, 136–47; Deyle, *Carry Me Back*, 24.

22. Thomas Mann Randolph, Jr., to Nicholas P. Trist, Nov. 22, 1818, Trist Family Papers, ASSCL-UVA; Gaines, *Thomas Mann Randolph*, 76.

23. Thomas Mann Randolph to Nicholas P. Trist, June 5, 1820, NPTP, folder 20, SHC-UNC; Gaines, *Thomas Mann Randolph*, 124–28; Thomas Jefferson to David Bailie Warden, Dec. 26, 1820, FO-NA, http://founders.archives.gov/documents/ Jefferson/98-01-02-1709.

24. Thomas Jefferson to Jared Sparks, Feb. 4, 1824, FO-NA, http://founders.archives
    .gov/documents/Jefferson/98-01-02-4020.

25. Thomas Jefferson to John Wayles Eppes, July 29, 1820, and Jefferson to Jared Sparks,
    Feb. 4, 1824 ("separation"), FO-NA, http://founders.archives.gov/documents/
    Jefferson/98-01-02-1425 and -4020; Onuf, *Mind of Thomas Jefferson*, 213–15, 221–28.

26. G. Tucker, "Autobiography," 85–86; McLean, *George Tucker*, 3–4.

27. G. Tucker, *Letters from Virginia*, 29–33.

28. G. Tucker, *Letters from Virginia*, 81–83.

29. G. Tucker, *Letters from Virginia*, 73–77; R. B. Davis, ed., *Jeffersonian America*,
    148–49.

30. George Tucker to St. George Tucker, Aug. 12, 1799, and Mar. 3, 1801 ("I feel"),
    TCP, reel M-19, and M-20, SCSL-CWM; G. Tucker, "Autobiography," 84–85, 99–
    102, 111 ("with loungers"); McLean, *George Tucker*, 5–13.

31. George Tucker to St. George Tucker, Sept. 1, 1800, TCP, reel M-20, SCSL-CWM;
    Egerton, *Gabriel's Rebellion*, 20–33, 48–49, 50–53, 64–65, 69–79; Nicholls, *Whis-
    pers of Rebellion*, 25–29, 57–70; Sidbury, *Ploughshares into Swords*, 6–7.

32. John Minor to Lucy Minor, Sept. 16, 1800, Minor and Wilson Family Papers, box 1,
    ASSCL-UVA; Egerton, *Gabriel's Rebellion*, 83–112; John Randolph quoted in Bruce,
    John Randolph, vol. 2:250 ("The accused"); Sidbury, *Ploughshares into Swords*, 7.

33. George Tucker to St. George Tucker, Nov. 2, 1800, and Jan. 18, 1801 ("think-
    ing few") [misfiled as 1800], TCP, reel M-20, SCSL-CWM; G. Tucker, *Letter to
    a Member*, 3–4, 7, 14, 18–21, 22 ("the tyrant"), and 23 ("see our folly"); Egerton,
    Gabriel's Rebellion, 151–53.

34. George Tucker to St. George Tucker, Nov. 2, 1800, Jan. 18, 1801 [misfiled as 1800],
    and Feb. 24, 1801 ("Mark proved"), TCP, reel M-20, SCSL-CWM.

35. Smyth, *Speeches*, 22, 24 ("There is" and "may be"); L. K, Ford, *Deliver Us from
    Evil*, 65.

36. L. K. Ford, *Deliver Us from Evil*, 65; Jeter, *Recollections*, 67–69; Nicholls, *Whis-
    pers of Rebellion*, 146; Wolf, *Race and Liberty*, 101, 121–23, 130–32.

37. G. Tucker, *Valley of the Shenandoah*, vol. 1:84–85.

38. John H. Cocke, "Notes on Lectures at William & Mary College," JHCP, box 1,
    ASSCL-UVA; Jennifer R. Loux, "John Hartwell Cocke," in Bearss, ed., *Dictio-
    nary of Virginia Biography*, vol. 3:330–31; Dierksheide, *Amelioration*, 58, 65–67.

39. Dierksheide, *Amelioration*, 58–67, Cocke quoted on 66 ("the great Cause"); John
    H. Cocke to Joseph C. Cabell, Apr. 3, 1825, JHCP, box 17, ASSCL-UVA; Cocke to
    John H. Cocke, Jr., Feb. 21, 1825 ("land of"), JHCP, box 42, ASSCL-UVA.

40. John H. Cocke, Last Will and Testament, Sept. 4, 1817, JHCP, box 25, ASSCL-UVA.

41. John H. Cocke, Last Will and Testament, Sept. 4, 1817, JHCP, box 25, ASSCL-UVA.

42. Nash and Hodges, *Friends of Liberty*, 213–24, 258–59.

43. John H. Cocke to Thomas Jefferson, May 3, 1819, in Looney et al., eds., *PTJ-RS*,
    vol. 14:261–65.

44. Leichtle and Carveth, *Crusade*, 10–13; Meyers, "Thinking About Slavery," 1246–47; Ketcham, "Dictates of Conscience," 47–48 (quotations).

45. Edward Coles to John Coles, Jr., May 6, 1812, ECP, box 2, HSP; Ketcham, "Dictates of Conscience," 49–50; Leichtle and Carveth, *Crusade*, 16–29; Edward Coles to Thomas Jefferson, July 31, 1814, Looney et al., eds., *PTJ-RS*, vol. 7:503–4 ("all my relations").

46. Thomas Jefferson to Edward Coles, Aug. 25, 1814, in Looney et al., eds., *PTJ-RS*, vol. 7:603–5.

47. Thomas Jefferson to Edward Coles, Aug. 25, 1814, and Jefferson to Thomas Humphreys, Feb. 8, 1817, in Looney et al., eds., *PTJ-RS*, vol. 7:603–5 (all quotations), vol. 11:60–61.

48. Edward Coles to Thomas Jefferson, Sept. 26, 1814, in Looney et al., eds., *PTJ-RS*, vol. 7:702.

49. Ketcham, "Dictates of Conscience," 53–62; Leichtle and Carveth, *Crusade*, 49–59.

50. Hatzenbuehler, "Growing Weary," 34; Schwarz, *Migrants Against Slavery*, 777–78.

51. T. Baker, "'A Slave,'" 141–45. Baker persuasively argues that the author had experienced slavery.

52. Robert Pleasants to Jefferson, June 1, 1796, and Jefferson to Pleasants, Aug. 27 1796, in Boyd et al., eds, *PTJ*, vol. 29:120, 177–78; Neem, "To Diffuse Knowledge," 65–66; Oakes, "Why Slaves Can't Read," 180–81, 190–92.

53. Israel Gillette (Jefferson), "Life Among the Lowly, No. III," *Pike County (Ohio) Republican*, Dec. 25, 1873; Stanton, *Those Who Labor*, 23.

54. Burstein, *Jefferson's Secrets*, 120, 134; Dierksheide, *Amelioration*, 20–29, 36–39, 44–46, 49–53; Israel Gillette (Jefferson), "Memoirs," in Gordon-Reed, *Thomas Jefferson and Sally Hemings*, 251 ("I consider"); La Rochefoucauld-Liancourt, in Hayes, ed., *Jefferson in His Own Time*, 25; Stanton, *Those Who Labor*, 79–83, quotation on 79 ("nailery combined").

55. Madison Hemings, "Memoirs," in Gordon-Reed, *Thomas Jefferson and Sally Hemings*, 247–48; Stanton, *Those Who Labor*, 164–65; Burstein, *Jefferson's Secrets*, 182–85.

56. Thomas Jefferson to Samuel Knox, Dec. 11, 1818, in Looney et al., eds., *PTJ-RS*, vol. 13:484 ("knolege"); Smyth, *Speeches*, 18–19; Thomas Mann Randolph to Nicholas P. Trist, June 5, 1820, NPTP, folder 20, SHC-UNC; Cornelius, *When I Can Read My Title Clear*, 27; H. C. Knight, *Letters from the South*, 74–75 ("The policy"); "Thoughts on Slavery," in J. H. Rice, ed., *Virginia Evangelical and Literary Magazine*, vol. 2:296 ("if taught").

57. N. Wood, "John Randolph," 110–12, William Hopkins quoted on 111 ("and provide").

58. Joseph Fossett in Hayes, ed., *Jefferson in His Own Time*, 191–93.

59. Francis W. Gilmer to Peter Minor, Feb. 6, 1816 ("I am now"), GFC, box 1, ASSCL-UVA.

60. Francis W. Gilmer to Peter Minor, Nov. 10, 1820, GFC, box 1, ASSCL-UVA.

61. Francis W. Gilmer to Peter Minor, Nov. 10, 1820 ("I hold"), Dec. 22, 1821, and June 18, 1823 (all quotations), GFC, box 1, ASSCL-UVA.

62. James Madison to William H. Cabell, July 30, 1807, Digitalarchive.wm.edu; Meyers, "Thinking About Slavery," 1248n174.

63. D. B. Smith, *Inside the Great House*, 83; G. Tucker, *Letters from Virginia*, 98–99.

64. John Randolph to Elizabeth Tucker Coalter, Feb. 20, 1822, in W. C. Bruce, *John Randolph*, vol. 1:38; H. C. Knight, *Letters from the South*, 69, 82.

65. Ellen W. Randolph to Virginia Randolph, Aug. 31, 1819, EWRCP, box 1, ASSCL-UVA.

66. G. Tucker, *Letters from Virginia*, 99–101; D. B. Smith, *Inside the Great House*, 83.

67. Cornelius, *When I Can Read My Title Clear*, 1–5; "Thoughts on Slavery," in J. H. Rice, ed., *Virginia Evangelical and Literary Magazine*, vol. 2:297 ("the more anxiety"); K. and A. M. Roberts, eds, *Moreau de St. Méry's American Journey*, 66; Stanton, *Those Who Labor*, 165–66.

68. Hannah to Thomas Jefferson, Nov. 15, 1818, in Looney et al., eds., *PTJ-RS*, vol. 13:393.

69. Berkeley, "Prophet Without Honor," 180–86; McPherson, *Short History*, 5–6.

70. McPherson, *Short History*, 24–27.

71. Thomas Jefferson to James Madison, Apr. 4, 1800, in Hutchinson et al., eds., *PJM*, vol. 17:378–79; Jefferson to Peter Carr, Apr. 4, 1800, in Boyd et al., eds., *PTJ*, vol. 31:475–77; Berkeley, "Prophet Without Honor," 180–86.

72. Berkeley, "Prophet Without Honor," 180–86; McPherson, *Short History*, 5–6.

73. Berkeley, "Prophet Without Honor," 186–89; Tyler-McGraw and Kimball, *In Bondage and Freedom*, 63–64; McPherson, *Short History*, 8–10.

74. The quotations come from Law Orders Book, 1809–1821, 337 (Oct. 13, 1818), Record Vault, Clerk's Office, Albemarle County Courthouse, Charlottesville; Alexander, *The Life of Archibald Alexander*, 432–33; Dabney, "Jefferson's Albemarle," 172–73.

75. Leigh, ed., *Revised Code*, vol. 1:424–25.

76. Thomas Jefferson to David Barrow, May 1, 1815, in Looney et al., eds., *PTJ-RS*, vol. 8:454–55; Hatzenbuehler, "Growing Weary," 32–36; Onuf, *Mind of Thomas Jefferson*, 252–55.

77. Stanton, *Those Who Labor*, 98–99, Peter Fossett quoted on 98.

6. Schools

1. Jefferson, "Autobiography," 44–45.

2. Thomas Jefferson to James Madison, Dec. 20, 1786, in Boyd et al., eds., *PTJ*, vol.

12:438–43; Jefferson to Littleton W. Tazewell, Jan. 5, 1805 ("I have looked"), FO-NA, http://founders.archives.gov/documents/Jefferson/99-01-02-0958; R. Brown, "Bulwark of Revolutionary Liberty," 100–102.

3. Thomas Jefferson to George Washington, Jan. 4, 1786, in Boyd et al., eds., *PTJ*, vol. 9:150–52 ("an axiom"); Jefferson to John Adams, Oct. 28, 1813, in Looney et al., eds., *PTJ-RS*, vol. 6:562–68 ("Worth and genius"); Neem, "Diffuse Knowledge," 47–48.

4. Jefferson, "Autobiography," 44–45; Brewer, "Beyond Education," 48–58; Hatzenbuehler, "Growing Weary," 27.

5. Thomas Jefferson, "Bill for the More General Diffusion of Knowledge," in Boyd et al., eds., *PTJ*, vol. 2:526–35; Jefferson, "Autobiography," 42–43; Jefferson, *Notes on the State of Virginia*, 135 ("the best"); Brewer, "Beyond Education," 61; Neem, "Diffuse Knowledge," 60–64.

6. Thomas Jefferson, "Bill for the More General Diffusion of Knowledge," and Jefferson to Mann Page, Aug. 30, 1795, in Boyd et al., eds., *PTJ*, vol. 2:526–35, and vol. 28:440–41; Jefferson to Littleton W. Tazewell, Jan. 5, 1805 ("a few subjects"), FO-NA, http://founders.archives.gov/documents/Jefferson/99-01-02 -0958; Brown, "Bulwark of Revolutionary Liberty," 96–97; R. B. Davis, *Intellectual Life*, 30–31.

7. Thomas Jefferson to Joseph C. Cabell, Feb. 2, 1816, in Looney et al., eds., *PTJ-RS*, vol. 9:435–39; Swift, "Thomas Jefferson," 36.

8. Addis, *Jefferson's Vision*, 10–11; Neem, "Diffuse Knowledge," 50–51, 63.

9. Samuel Stanhope Smith to Thomas Jefferson, n.d., c. Mar. 1779, and Jefferson to Joseph Priestley, Jan. 27, 1800, in Boyd et al., eds., *PTJ*, vol. 2:246, and vol. 31:339–41; Addis, *Jefferson's Vision*, 19.

10. Thomas Jefferson to George Washington, Jan. 4, 1786, and Jefferson to George Wythe, Aug. 13, 1786, in Boyd et al., eds., *PTJ*, vol. 9:150–52, 10:243–45 ("the law" and "No other").

11. Thomas Jefferson to George Wythe, Aug. 13, 1786, in Boyd et al., eds., *PTJ*, vol. 10:243–45 ("not more than"); Jefferson, "Autobiography," 43 ("would throw"); Jefferson to John Adams, Oct. 28, 1813, in Looney et al., eds., *PTJ*, vol. 6:562–68; Wagoner, *Jefferson and Education*, 42.

12. Thomas Jefferson to Joseph C. Cabell, Nov. 28, 1820, FO-NA, http://founders .archives.gov/documents/Jefferson/98-01-02-1660.

13. [David Watson], "John Truename," in Wirt, *Old Bachelor*, 160–62.

14. John Tyler, Sr., to William H. Cabell, Feb. 10, 1808, in Flournoy, ed., *Calendar of Virginia State Papers*, vol. 10:3 ("eternal war"); John Tyler, Sr., messages of Dec. 4, 1809, and Dec. 13, 1810, in Joseph C. Cabell, "Extracts from Gubernatorial Messages Regarding Education," JCCFP, box 1, ASSCL; John Tyler, Sr., to Thomas Jefferson, May 12, 1810, in Looney et al., eds., *PTJ-RS*, vol. 2:384–88 ("He who can"); Kaestle, *Pillars of the Republic*, 9–10.

15. R. D. Brown, *Strength of a People*, 146–47; G. Wood, *Empire of Liberty*, 472.

16. "On Public Schools," *Richmond Enquirer*, Mar. 23, 1805; Joseph C. Cabell to Thomas Jefferson, Dec. 3, 1817, in Looney et al., eds., *PTJ-RS*, vol. 12:232; Swift, "Thomas Jefferson," 34. For calculations of population and scale, see Maddox, *Free School Idea*, 16.

17. Elijah Fletcher to Jesse Fletcher, Oct. 1, 1810, and Jan. 11, 1811, in Von Briesen, ed., *Letters of Elijah Fletcher*, 16 ("They may boast" and "the poor"), and 25 ("Happy").

18. James Murphy to Joseph C. Cabell, Nov. 11, 1819, JCCFP, box 13, ASSCL-UVA; "Schools," in J. H. Rice, ed., *Virginia Evangelical and Literary Magazine*, vol. 8:373; Jeter, *Recollections*, 3.

19. Jeter, *Recollections*, 3–6.

20. "Philodemus," in J. H. Rice, ed., *Virginia Evangelical and Literary Magazine*, vol. 9:136; John Augustine Smith to Wilson Cary Nicholas, Nov. 7, 1816, in E. W. Knight, ed., *Documentary History of Education in the South*, 548–49.

21. Bayard, *Travels*, 56 ("When"); Jeter, *Recollections*, 4–5; Wirt, *British Spy*, 71; Maddox, *Free School Idea*, 108–9, 114.

22. J. Davis, *Travels*, vol. 1:362–64, 373 ("gave loose"), 392–93 ("negroes," and "the joy").

23. American Education Society, "Education in Virginia," *Quarterly Register*, vol. 5 (1833), 322; "Objections to the Present Plan of Education," "Reply to 'A Friend to the Poor,'" and "Philodemus," in J. H. Rice, ed., *Virginia Evangelical and Literary Magazine*, vol. 2:180, vol. 6:430 ("too proud"), and vol. 9:136–37 ("In our country"); Speece, *Mountaineer*, 166–67.

24. Washington Irving to William Irving, Jr., Apr. 4, and May 31, 1805, in Aderman et al., eds., *Washington Irving Letters*, vol. 1:176, 190; Joseph C. Cabell to George Sullivan, Apr. 13, 1825, JCCFP, box 17, ASSCL-UVA; Heafford, *Pestalozzi*, vii; Cabell quoted in E. W. Knight, *Documentary History of Education*, vol. 5:326n4 ("a sure cure").

25. William Maclure to Joseph C. Cabell, Nov. 4, 1817, JCCFP, box 12, ASSCL-UVA; Neef, *Sketch of a Plan*, 6–7, 16–19, 26–27, 30–43; Cohen, *Calculating People*, 134–37; Gutek, *Joseph Neef*, 6–34, Pestalozzi quoted on 14; Neem, *Democracy's Schools*, 51–53.

26. William Maclure to Jefferson, July 30, 1825 ("total absence"), FO-NA, http://founders.archives.gov/documents/Jefferson/98-01-02-5422; Gutek, *Joseph Neef*, 16–20.

27. Isaac Cox Barnet to Thomas Jefferson, Feb. 20, 1806, FO-NA, http://founders.archives.gov/documents/Jefferson/99-01-02-3260; Gutek, *Joseph Neef*, 3–12, 16–17, 21 (Neef quoted: "Suitable").

28. William Maclure to Joseph C. Cabell, Nov. 4, 1817, and W. W. Seaton to James Pleasants, Apr. 11, 1822 ("superior" and "I think"), JCCFP, boxes 12 and 15, ASSCL-UVA.

29. William Maclure to Joseph C. Cabell, Nov. 4, 1817, JCCFP, box 12, ASSCL-UVA.

30. William Maclure to Benjamin Silliman, Oct. 19, 1822, and Maclure to Marie Duclos Fretageot, Aug. 25, 1824, in Bestor, ed., *Education and Reform*, 294, 306 ("to fill" and "almost equal"); Maclure to Thomas Jefferson, July 30, 1825, and Jefferson to Maclure, Aug. 8, 1825, FO-NA, http://founders.archives.gov/documents/Jefferson/98-01-02-5422 and -5452.

31. Thomas Jefferson to Joseph Neef, June 23, 1806, FO-NA, http://founders.archives .gov/documents/Jefferson/99-01-02-3891; Jefferson to Nicholas G. Dufief, Sept. 16, 1816, and Jefferson to William Maclure, Nov. 2, 1817, in Looney et al., eds., *PTJ-RS*, vol. 10:390–91 ("calculated"), and vol. 12:165–66.

32. Joseph C. Cabell to Joseph Lancaster, July 1, 1819, in E. W. Knight, ed., *Documentary History of Education*, vol. 5:325 ("one man"); Cabell to George Sullivan, Apr. 13, 1825, JCCFP, box 17, ASSCL-UVA; Cabell to Mr. White, June 13, 1826, JHCP, box 47, ASSCL-UVA.

33. "Outlines," *Richmond Enquirer*, May 23, 1809; Kaestle, *Joseph Lancaster*, 3–18, Lancaster quoted on 4 ("economy").

34. "Outlines," *Richmond Enquirer*, May 23, 1809 (quotations); Kaestle, *Joseph Lancaster*, 8–16.

35. "An Appeal to the Citizens of Richmond," and "To the Citizens of Richmond," *Richmond Enquirer*, Oct. 14, 1815, Oct. 18, 1815 ("now roving" and "has made the road"); Griffin, "Thomas Ritchie," 447–49; Wirt, *Old Bachelor*, 182–83.

36. "To My Friends in the Country," and "To the Editor of the Enquirer," *Richmond Enquirer*, Nov. 5, and 23, 1819; Griffin, "Thomas Ritchie," 447–56; McGroarty, "Alexandria's Lancasterian Schools," 111–17, Mrs. Washington quoted on 117 ("from poverty").

37. Joseph C. Cabell to John H. Cocke, Oct. 22, 1825 (quotations), JCCFP, box 18, ASSCL-UVA; Cabell, "Nelson County School Commissioners Report," in "Extracts from the Reports of School Commissioners," 1825, JHCP, box 35, ASSCL-UVA.

38. Joseph C. Cabell to George Sullivan, Apr. 13, 1825, Cabell to John H. Cocke, Aug. 24, 1825 ("I think"), and Oct. 22, 1825 ("to banish"), JCCFP, boxes 13, 17, and 18, ASSCL-UVA; Cabell, "Extracts from the Reports of School Commissioners," 1825, JHCP, box 35, ASSCL-UVA; Dabney, *Universal Education*, 119–20.

39. "Education in Virginia," American Education Society, *Quarterly Register*, vol. 5:322; R. B. Davis, *Intellectual Life in Jefferson's Virginia*, 35–38.

40. Thomas Jefferson to John Adams, July 5, 1814, and Jefferson to John Wayles Eppes, May 3, 1818, in Looney et al., eds., *PTJ-RS*, vol. 7:451–55 ("petty"), and vol. 13:17 ("pest" and "itch").

41. David Watson to James Watson, May 12, [1815], Oct. 30, 1815 ("deceived"), DWFP, box 10, ASSCL-UVA; Yarborough, ed., *Reminiscences of William C. Preston*, 4.

42. [Francis W. Gilmer], "Necessity of a Better System of Instruction," in J. H. Rice, ed., *Virginia Evangelical and Literary Magazine*, vol. 1:317.

43. Elijah Fletcher to Jesse Fletcher, Aug. 4, and Aug. 29, Oct. 31, 1810, in Von Briesen, *Letters of Elijah Fletcher*, 8, 14–15 (all quotations), 21.

44. Elijah Fletcher to Jesse Fletcher, Jan. 11, 1811, in Von Briesen, ed., *Letters of Elijah Fletcher*, 25–26.

45. Elijah Fletcher to Jesse Fletcher, Mar. n.d., 1811, Sept. 5, 1813, May 2, 1814, and July 23, 1825, in Von Briesen, ed., *Letters of Elijah Fletcher*, xv-xvii, 32, 77 ("To emancipate"), 79–80, 96; D. B. Smith, *Our Family Dreams*, 19–28, 72, 99 ("arrogant" and "learn nothing").

46. James Ogilvie to Thomas Jefferson, c. July 3, 1795, and Mann Page to Jefferson, July 3, 1795, in Boyd et al., eds, *PTJ*, vol. 28:401–4; Ogilvie, "Stevensburg Academy," *National Intelligencer*, Mar. 8, 1802; "Extract of a Letter," [Baltimore] *Democratic Republican*, May 8, 1802; Ogilvie to Francis W. Gilmer, May 23, 1812 ("glorious destiny"), GFN, box 1, ASSCL-UVA.

47. Ogilvie, *Cursory Reflexions*, 17–20, 37 ("the happiness"); Ogilvie, *Philosophical Essays*, x.

48. Ogilvie, "Stevensburg Academy," *National Intelligencer*, Feb. 18, 1802 ("instruction"); Ogilvie, *Cursory Reflexions*, 34 ("an almost"); Ogilvie, *Philosophical Essays*, ix ("the precious"); [Anonymous], "Recollections of James Ogilvie," 534–35; R. B. Davis, "James Ogilvie," 293–96, Trustees of the University of South Carolina quoted on 296 ("singularly").

49. James Ogilvie to Thomas Jefferson, c. July 3, 1795, and Mann Page to Jefferson, July 3, 1795, in Boyd et al., eds, *PTJ*, vol. 28:401–5; John Taylor to Peter Carr, Sept. 18, 1806 ("all the patriots"), Gabriella Page Coll., one folder, VHS; Ogilvie, *Philosophical Essays*, i-iii.

50. [Anonymous], "Recollections of James Ogilvie," 534–35 ("an idle" and "I felt"); James Ogilvie, "Stevensburg Academy," *National Intelligencer*, Feb. 18, 1802; W. Scott, *Memoirs*, vol. 1:8; Ogilvie to James Madison, Mar. 9, 1804, in Stagg et al., eds., *PJM-SSS*, vol. 6:575.

51. Thomas Jefferson to James Ogilvie, Jan. 31, May 31, and June 23, 1806, FO-NA, http://founders.archives.gov/documents/Jefferson/99-01-02-3156, -3785, -3892; Ogilvie, "Education," *Richmond Enquirer*, Jan. 29, 1807; Boyd et al., eds., *PTJ*, vol. 28:404n.

52. Ogilvie, *Philosophical Essays*, v-viii; Charles Everette to Peachy R. Gilmer, undated fragment, PRGP, sec. 2, VHS. The fragment does not name the orator, but the content fits Ogilvie.

53. Harmer Gilmer to Peachy R. Gilmer, Oct. 12, 1806 ("Here is no"), and Mar. 3, 1807 ("as easy"), Francis W. Gilmer to P. R. Gilmer, Nov. 3, 1807, PRGP, sec. 2, VHS; Ogilvie, *Philosophical Essays*, v ("tractable").

54. Bacon, "Autobiography," 92; James Ogilvie to Thomas Jefferson, Aug. 12, 1807, FO-NA, http://founders.archives.gov/documents/Jefferson/99-01-02-6161.

55. Ogilvie, *Philosophical Essays*, vii.

56. Ogilvie, *Philosophical Essays*, vii–viii.

57. Ellen W. Randolph to Jefferson, Mar. 18, 1808, and Jefferson to John Glendy, June 21, 1808 ("the correctness"), FO-NA, http://founders.archives.gov/documents/Jefferson/99-01-02-7656, and -8186; Ogilvie, *Philosophical Essays*, vi, xii–xiii.

58. Ogilvie, "The Citizens of Baltimore," [Baltimore], *Federal Republican*, Aug. 26, 1808; Washington Irving to Henry Brevoort, Sept. 27, 1818, Aderman et al., eds., *Washington Irving Letters*, vol. 1:534 ("quite"); Ogilvie, *Philosophical Essays*, xxxvii ("unaccountable"); W. Scott, *Memoirs*, vol 1:9; R. B. Davis, "James Ogilvie," 292–95; John Gallison quoted in Eastman, *Nation of Speechifiers*, 37 ("He has fancy"); Eastman, "Transatlantic Celebrity," 1–7.

59. James Ogilvie to Francis W. Gilmer, Feb. 4, 1814 ("baffled"), GFN, box 1, ASSCL-UVA; Thomas Cooper to Thomas Jefferson, Mar. 20, and Aug. 17, 1814, in Looney et al., eds., *PTJ-RS*, vol. 7:257–59; R. B. Davis, "James Ogilvie," 295; Eastman, "Transatlantic Celebrity," 8.

60. Ogilvie, *Philosophical Essays*, 159–60 ("*sad* realities"), 172 ("in the humbler"); Francis W. Gilmer to William Wirt, Feb. 4, 1817, Gilmer-Wirt letters, LV.

61. Washington Irving, Aug. 28, 1817, and Irving to Henry Brevoort, Sept. 27, 1818, Aderman et al., eds., *Washington Irving Letters*, vol. 1:496, 534; Ogilvie, *Philosophical Essays*, xvii ("On Madness"), xxxvi ("paroxysms"); Eastman, "Transatlantic Celebrity," 8–12.

62. "William & Mary College," *Richmond Enquirer*, Nov. 24, 1814.

63. John Tyler to James Monroe, Jan. 1, 1804, *WMQ*, 1st ser., vol. 26:22; Wirt, *Rainbow*, 63; J. Lewis, *Pursuit of Happiness*, 149–50; D. B. Smith, *Inside the Great House*, 62–63, 76–80.

64. Mary H. Campbell to Mary Humes, Sept. 21, 1819 ("Daughters"), CFP, box 4, DMRML-DU; Wirt, *Rainbow*, 61; J. Lewis, *Pursuit of Happiness*, 150–51.

65. "Polite Accomplishments," "Interesting to Parents," "Williamsburg Female Academy," *Richmond Enquirer*, July 9, 1805, Sept. 19, 1806, and Nov. 29, 1808; Wirt, *Old Bachelor*, 190; D. B. Smith, *Inside the Great House*, 62–67.

66. W. D. Hoyt, ed., "Self-Portrait: Eliza Custis, 1808," *VMHB*, vol. 53:97–98.

67. Dabney Carr to Dabney Carr Terrell, Dec. 11, 1818, Terrell Family Papers, box 1, ASSCL-UVA; Cary, *Letters on Female Character*, 197.

68. Anne B. Cocke to John H. Cocke, n.d., c. Sept. 1825, and Sally Faulcon to Louisa Cocke, Oct. 1, 1825 ("The house"), JHCP, boxes 44 and 45, ASSCL-UVA; J. M. Garnett, *Seven Lectures on Female Education*, 79–80; Jabour, "Grown Girls," 42–44; Maddox, *Free School Idea*, 35.

69. James Mercer Garnett to John H. Cocke, Aug. 30, 1825, JHCP, box 44, ASSCL-

UVA; J. M. Garnett, *Seven Lectures on Female Education*, 19, 79–80, 87 ("entirely avoid"), 88, 101–2.

70. J. M. Garnett, *Seven Lectures on Female Education*, 19, 48, 60 ("frantic bedlamite"), 79–80 ("always clean"), 89 ("be praised"), 103–5.

71. Anne B. Cocke to John H. Cocke, n.d., c. Sept. 1825 ("I have never"), and Oct. 1, 1825 ("we have), and A. B. Cocke to Louisa Cocke, Oct. 8, 1825 ("My eyes"), and to J. H. Cocke, Jan. 27, 1826, and May 1, 1826, JHCP, boxes 40, 43, 44, 45, 46, and 47, ASSCL-UVA.

72. Wirt, *Old Bachelor*, 190–93; William Wirt quoted in Jabour "Grown Girls," 30 ("I want"), 35 ("may be admired"); Jabour, *Marriage in the Early Republic*, 12.

73. Francis W. Gilmer to William Wirt, Nov. 21, 1812, Gilmer-Wirt letters, LV; Jabour, "Grown Girls," 31; William Wirt to Francis W. Gilmer, Nov. 22, 1822, GFN, box 3, ASSCL-UVA; Jabour, *Marriage in the Early Republic*, 74, 79, 117.

74. Francis W. Gilmer to Dabney Carr, Aug. 7, 1822 ("No metamorphosis," "His hair," and "the phrenzy"), Sept. 7 ("to quiet"), and 27, and Nov. 1, 1822 ("mad as"), Gilmer-Carr letters, LV.

75. Francis W. Gilmer to Dabney Carr, Aug. 7, and Nov. 1, 1822 ("As to study" and "What strange"), Gilmer-Carr letters, LV; F. W. Gilmer to Peter Minor, Oct. 22, 1822, GFP, box 1, ASSCL-UVA; William Wirt to F. W. Gilmer, Nov. 22, 1822 ("Let Robert"), and Dec. 19, 1822, GFN, box 3, ASSCL-UVA.

76. Francis W. Gilmer to Dabney Carr, Nov. 25, 1822 ("eyes glaring"), Gilmer-Carr letters, LV; F. W. Gilmer to Peachy Gilmer, Dec. 5, 1822 ("not from any" and "wild"), PRGP, sec. 2, VHS.

77. William Wirt to Francis W. Gilmer, Dec. 4, and Dec. 19, 1822, GFN, box 3, ASSCL-UVA; F. W. Gilmer to Dabney Carr, Nov. 25, 1822 ("prescribed"), Gilmer-Carr letters, one box, LV; R. B. Davis, *Francis Walker Gilmer*, 148–49; Jabour, *Marriage*, 118–19.

78. Thomas Jefferson to Joseph C. Cabell, Jan. 31, 1814, and Jefferson to Peter Carr, Sept. 7, 1814, in Looney et al., eds., *PTJ-RS*, vol. 7:176–77 ("the public education"), 636–42.

79. Thomas Jefferson, "Bill to Create Central College," Nov. 18, 1814, Joseph C. Cabell to Jefferson, Jan. 16, and 23, 1816, and Jefferson to Cabell, Jan. 24, and Feb. 2, 1816, in Looney et al., eds., *PTJ-RS*, vol. 8:90–94, vol. 9:360–62, 394–95 ("would place"), 396–98, 435–39.

80. Charles F. Mercer to John H. Cocke, Sept. 16, 1825, JHCP, box 44, ASSCL-UVA; Egerton, *Charles Fenton Mercer*, 13–16; Egerton, "To the Tombs," 168–70.

81. [Literary Fund], *Sundry Documents*, 20 ("funds"); "Virginia Legislature," *Richmond Enquirer*, Dec. 5, 1815 ("We say"), and Jan. 13, 1816 ("We are" and "taxes"); Egerton, "To the Tombs," 157–160, 170n50; Wagoner, *Jefferson and Education*, 75.

82. [Charles F. Mercer], "A Virginian," *Richmond Enquirer*, Mar. 20, 1818 ("In

a republic"); [Literary Fund], *Sundry Documents*, 20–21, 33 ("the greatest"); Egerton, *Charles Fenton Mercer*, 119–20; Egerton, "To the Tombs," 155–56, 168–70.

83. Thomas Jefferson to Joseph C. Cabell, Feb. 2, 1816, in Looney et al., eds., *PTJ-RS*, vol. 9:435; "Public Education," and "To the Senate of Virginia," *Richmond Enquirer*, Feb. 18, 1817 ("a vast," and "College of Cardinals"), Feb. 20, 1817; Neem, *Democracy's Schools*, 79.

84. "To the Senate of Virginia," *Richmond Enquirer*, Feb. 20, 1817; [Charles F. Mercer], "A Virginian," *Richmond Enquirer*, Mar. 20, 1818.

85. Thomas Jefferson, "Bill for Establishing Elementary Schools," Sept. 9, 1817, Jefferson to Joseph C. Cabell, Sept. 9, and 10, and Dec. 3, and 29, 1817, in Looney et al., eds., *PTJ-RS*, vol. 12:10–14 ("by the disfranchisement"), 15, 18, 232 ("There are"), 285–87; Egerton, "To the Tombs," 161, 168–72; D. Malone, *Jefferson and His Time*, vol. 6: 267–68.

86. John Campbell to David Campbell, Feb. 20, 1817, CFP, box 3, DMRML-DU; Joseph C. Cabell to Thomas Jefferson, Jan. 5, and Feb. 6, 1818, in Looney et al., eds., *PTJ-RS*, vol. 12:318, and 432 ("half-witted"); Hore Browse Trist to Nicholas P. Trist, Jan. 1, 1819 ("The Legislature"), JFL website, ICJS; Jefferson to Thomas Cooper, Mar. 9, 1822, FO-NA, http://founders.archives.gov/documents/Jefferson/98-01-02-2705.

87. [William Branch Giles], "A Constituent," *Richmond Enquirer*, Jan. 1, ("fascinating" "a mind," and "any novel"), Jan. 15, and 31, 1818, and Feb. 12, 1818 ("mischievous"); Joseph C. Cabell to Thomas Jefferson, Jan. 5, 1818, in Looney et al., eds., *PTJ-RS*, vol. 12:318–19.

88. Joseph C. Cabell to Thomas Jefferson, Feb. 13, 1818, and Jefferson to Albert Gallatin, Feb. 15, 1818, in Looney et al., eds., *PTJ-RS*, vol. 12:457–58, 467–68 ("ignorance"); Egerton, *Charles Fenton Mercer*, 128; Maddox, *Free School Idea*, 73–74, 79.

89. [Virginia], *Journal of the House of Delegates . . . 1823*, Appendix B; P. A. Bruce, *History of the University*, vol. 1:92; Maddox, *Free School Idea*, 74–86.

90. Robert S. Garnett to Thomas Jefferson, July 13, 1819, in Looney et al., eds., *PTJ-RS*, vol. 14:530; "Iota," in J. H. Rice, ed., *Virginia Evangelical and Literary Magazine*, vol. 6:426–27; Maddox, *Free School Idea*, 90–92.

91. "Friend to the Poor," and "Primary Schools," in J. H. Rice, ed., *Virginia Evangelical and Literary Magazine*, vol. 6:281–83 and vol. 8:370–72; [Virginia], *Journal of the House of Delegates . . . 1823*, Appendix B; "Extracts from the Reports of School Commissioners Relating to the Progress and State of the Primary Schools," 1825, JHCP, box 35, ASSCL-UVA.

92. Charles F. Mercer to John H. Cocke, Aug. 29, 1825, JHCP, box 44, ASSCL-UVA; quotations from Mercer, *Discourse on Public Education*, 57–58; Maddox, *Free School Idea*, 74n28, 95.

93. Thomas Jefferson to William Taylor Barry, July 2, 1822, FO-NA, http://founders
.archives.gov/documents/Jefferson/99-01-02-2919); Jefferson to Cabell, Jan. 28,
1823, and Jefferson to William Cabell Rives, Jan. 28, 1823 ("I believe"), FO-NA,
http://founders.archives.gov/documents/Jefferson/98-01-02-3290, and -3292;
Addis, *Jefferson's Vision for Education*, 97–99.

94. William Maclure to Joseph C. Cabell, Nov. 4, 1817, JCCFP, box 12, ASSCL-UVA.

95. Thomas Jefferson to William Branch Giles, Dec. 26, 1825, FO-NA, http://
founders.archives.gov/documents/Jefferson/98-01-02-5771; Robley Dunglison
to the Board of Visitors, July 10, 1829 ("There are many"), Misc. Mss. 11957, University Archives, ASSCL-UVA. Virginia did not create a public education system
until the Reconstruction that followed the Civil War.

7. BUILDINGS

1. George Washington to Alexander Hamilton, Sept. 1, 1796, in Syrett et al., eds,
Papers of Alexander Hamilton, vol. 20:311–14; G. Thomas, *Founders and the
Idea*, 2–7.

2. Thomas Jefferson to Wilson Cary Nicholas, Nov. 23, 1794, Jefferson to François
D'Ivernois, Feb. 6, 1795, George Washington to Jefferson, Mar. 15, 1795, in Boyd
et al., eds., *PTJ*, vol. 28:208–9, 262–64, 306–9; Shawen, "Thomas Jefferson and a
'National' University," 316–21.

3. Joel Barlow to Thomas Jefferson, Sept. 15, 1800, in Boyd et al., eds., *PTJ*, vol.
32:141–44 ("strict"); Barlow to Jefferson, Jan. 17, 1806, Albert Gallatin to
Jefferson, Nov. 16, 1806, Jefferson to Congress, Dec. 2, 1806, and Jefferson to
Barlow, Dec. 10, 1807 ("snail-paced"), FO-NA, http://founders.archives.gov/
documents/Jefferson/99-01-02-3027, -4551, -4615, and -6952; Kerber, *Federalists
in Dissent*, 107; Wagoner, *Jefferson and Education*, 66–68.

4. Thomas Jefferson to Littleton W. Tazewell, Jan. 5, 1805, and Jefferson to Robert Patterson, Oct. 13, 1808 ("formed"), FO-NA, http://founders.archives.gov/
documents/Jefferson/99-01-02-0958 and -8851; Jefferson to George Ticknor,
Oct. 25, 1818, in Looney et al., eds., *PTJ-RS*, vol. 13:338 ("we consider").

5. Bishop James Madison to James Madison, Nov. 12, 1794, in Hutchinson et al.,
eds., PJM, vol. 15:374–75; Thomas Jefferson to Joseph Priestley, Jan. 18, 1800, in
Boyd et al., eds., PTJ, vol. 31:319–23; Jefferson to Peter Carr, Sept. 7, 1814, and Jefferson to Thomas Cooper, Sept. 1, 1817, in Looney et al., eds., *PTJ-RS*, vol. 7:636–
42, and vol. 12:3 ("delicious").

6. Littleton W. Tazewell to Thomas Jefferson, Dec. 24, 1804, and Jefferson to Tazewell, Jan. 5, 1805, FO-NA, http://founders.archives.gov/documents/Jefferson/99
-01-02-0891, and -0958.

7. St. George Tucker, "Sketch of a Plan," Jan. 4, 1805, TCP, reel M-22, SCSL-
CWM; R. B. Davis, *Intellectual Life*, 61.

8. St. George Tucker, "Sketch of a Plan," Jan. 4, 1805, TCP, reel M-22, SCSL-CWM.

9. St. George Tucker, "Sketch of a Plan," Jan. 4, 1805, and William Henning to St. George Tucker, Jan. 8, 1805, TCP, reel M-22, SCSL-CWM.

10. Thomas Jefferson to Pierre Samuel Du Pont de Nemours, Nov. 29, 1813, in Looney et al., eds., *PTJ-RS*, vol. 7:6–9; Addis, *Jefferson's Vision for Education*, 30, 174n181.

11. Thomas Jefferson to Caspar Wistar, Aug. 25, 1814, Jefferson, "Bill to Create Central College," Nov. 18, 1814, and Joseph C. Cabell to Jefferson, Feb. 21, 1816, in Looney et al., eds., *PTJ-RS*, vol. 7:607–8, vol. 8:90–94, and vol. 9:495–98, see also vol. 7:264–66.

12. Joseph C. Cabell to Thomas Jefferson, Jan. 12, 1817, John H. Cocke, "Description of Central College Board of Visitors Meeting," May 5, 1817, in Looney et al., eds., *PTJ-RS*, vol. 10:659–60, vol. 11:319; D. Malone, *Jefferson and His Time*, vol. 6:255–65.

13. Jefferson to Joseph C. Cabell, Sept. 10, 1817, Cabell to Jefferson, Dec. 3, 1817, and Archibald Thweatt to Jefferson, Feb. 17, 1818, in Looney et al., eds., *PTJ-RS*, vol. 12:18 ("The difficulty"), 232, 472; D. Malone, *Jefferson and His Time*, vol. 6:255–65. Albemarle residents subscribed for $27,443 of the $35,000 total. See Thomas Jefferson, "Report of Central College Visitors," Jan. 6, 1818, in N. F. Cabell, *Early History*, 404–12.

14. Jefferson to José Correa da Serra, Nov. 25, 1817, in Looney et al., eds., *PTJ-RS*, vol. 12:200–2 ("Utopian dream"); Elizabeth Trist to Nicholas P. Trist, Mar. 9, 1819 ("looked as well"), NPTP, folder 17, SHC-UNC; Thomas Jefferson to Maria Hadfield Cosway, Oct. 24, 1822 ("most splendid"), FO-NA, http://founders.archives .gov/documents/Jefferson/98-01-02-3111.

15. Peachy Gilmer to Francis W. Gilmer, Mar. 18, 1819, GFC, box 1, ASSCL-UVA; G. Tucker, *Life of Thomas Jefferson*, vol. 2:430–31; Sloan, *Principle and Interest*, 221.

16. Thomas Jefferson to Joseph C. Cabell, Jan. 5, 1815, and Cabell to Jefferson, Mar. 5, 1815, and Feb. 26, 1816, in Looney et al., eds., *PTJ-RS*, vol. 7:182–84, vol. 8:316–18, vol. 9:506–507; Cabell to Isaac A. Coles, Dec. 18, 1815 ("extraordinary" and "I shall do"), Cabell Family Papers, box 1, SCSL-CWM; S. Dunn, *Dominion of Memories*, 153–69; Wolf, *Race and Liberty*, 182–96; Tarter, *Grandees of Government*, 175–79.

17. Joseph C. Cabell to Thomas Jefferson, Jan. 7, 1819, in Looney et al., eds., *PTJ-RS*, vol. 13:560.

18. Joseph C. Cabell to Thomas Jefferson, Jan. 23, 1816, Jefferson to Cabell, Jan. 24, 1816, Cabell to Jefferson, Oct. 14, 1817, Jefferson to Cabell, Oct. 24, 1817, and Cabell to Jefferson, Feb. 1, 1818, in Looney et al., eds., *PTJ-RS*, vol. 9:394–95 ("to engage"), 396–98 ("The objects"), vol. 12:98–99, 133–34 ("I have always"), 413–14.

19. Joseph C. Cabell to Thomas Jefferson, Dec. 3, and 29, 1817, Jefferson to Cabell, Jan. 6, 1818, and Cabell to Jefferson, Feb. 1, 1818, and Feb. 10, 1818, in Looney et al., eds., *PTJ-RS*, vol. 12:232, 284, 324–25, 413–14 ("Everything"), 448–49 ("throw").

20. Joseph C. Cabell to Thomas Jefferson, Nov. 18, 1818, Dec. 8, and 17, 1818, Jan. 18, 21, and 25, 1819, in Looney et al., eds., *PTJ-RS*, vol. 13:398, 472–73, 498 ("I could not risk"), 583–84 ("an alarming"), 592–93, 600–601; Merit M. Robinson to John H. Cocke, Dec. 24, 1818 ("I am afraid"), JHCP, box 27, ASSCL-UVA.

21. Joseph C. Cabell to St. George Tucker, Jan. 21, 1821 ("Why should"), TCP, reel M-30, SCSL-CWM; Cabell to Thomas Jefferson, Jan. 25, 1821 ("to ride"), FO-NA, http://founders.archives.gov/documents/Jefferson/98-01-02-1791.

22. Thomas Jefferson to Joseph C. Cabell, Jan. 31, 1821, FO-NA, http://founders.archives.gov/documents/Jefferson/98-01-02-1814.

23. Joseph C. Cabell to Thomas Jefferson, Feb. 8, 1822, FO-NA, http://founders.archives.gov/documents/Jefferson/98-01-02-1822; John H. Cocke to Cabell, Feb. 19, 1821, Cabell to Cocke, Mar. 10 ("When I come"), and Nov. 21, 1821 ("destiny" and "in a course"), JCCFP, box 14, ASSCL-UVA; Merit M. Robinson to Cocke, Feb. 22, 1821 ("Mr. Jefferson"), JHCP, box 33, ASSCL-UVA.

24. G. Tucker, "Autobiography," 142–43 ("most winning"); G. Tucker, *Life of Thomas Jefferson*, vol. 2: 477, 487 ("No one"), 489, 502, 504, and 506.

25. Peter Carr's petition for Albemarle Academy, 1814, quoted in P. A. Bruce, *History of the University*, vol. 1:128–29.

26. Schoen, "Calculating the Price," 177, 184, 194–200; A. Taylor, *Internal Enemy*, 389–98.

27. Haulman, *Virginia and the Panic of 1819*, 23; D. Jordan, *Political Leadership*, 205–24; D. Malone, *Jefferson and His Time*, vol. 6:387; Van Cleve, *Slaveholders' Union*, 228.

28. Francis W. Gilmer to Peter Minor, Jan. 29, 1821, GFC, one box, ASSCL-UVA.

29. Thomas Jefferson to Wilson Cary Nicholas, July 2, 1819 ("even small debts"), and Jefferson to Hugh Nelson, Mar. 12, 1820 ("This state"), in Looney et al., eds., *PTJ-RS*, vol. 14:497–98, vol. 15:463–64; Francis W. Gilmer to Peachy R. Gilmer, Jan. 16, 1820 ("Things grow"), PRGP, sec. 2, VHS; S. Dunn, *Dominion of Memories*, 7–8; Haulman, *Virginia and the Panic of 1819*, 3–4, 8–11, 18–19, 57–61.

30. Ammon, "Richmond Junto," 411–12; Freehling, *Road to Disunion*, 145–46; D. Jordan, *Political Leadership*, 19–20; M. Mason, *Slavery and Politics*, 195.

31. M. Mason, *Slavery and Politics*, 193, 199; Thomas Jefferson to Charles Pinckney, Sept. 30, 1820, FO-NA, http://founders.archives.gov/documents/Jefferson/98-01-02-1544; Onuf, *Mind of Thomas Jefferson*, 214; Wolf, *Race and Liberty*, 175–78.

32. Thomas Jefferson to John Holmes, Apr. 22, 1820 ("fire bell"), in Looney et al., eds., *PTJ-RS*, vol. 15:550–51; Jefferson to Albert Gallatin, Dec. 26, 1820, FO-NA, http://founders.archives.gov/documents/Jefferson/98-01-02-1705; John Tyler quoted in Freehling, *Road to Disunion*, 151 ("dark cloud").

33. Thomas Jefferson to Albert Gallatin, Dec. 26, 1820, FO-NA, http://founders

.archives.gov/documents/Jefferson/98-01-02-1705; Van Cleve, *Slaveholders' Union*, 232–34.

34. Thomas Jefferson to Joseph C. Cabell, Nov. 28, 1820 ("the degradation"), Jefferson to James Breckinridge, Feb. 15, 1821 ("burst on us"), and Jefferson to Thomas Cooper, Mar. 9, 1822 ("A lamp"), FO-NA, http://founders.archives.gov/documents/Jefferson/98-01-02-1660, -1836, -1839, and -2705.

35. "Academus," *Richmond Enquirer*, Jan. 25, 1821; Francis W. Gilmer to Peter Minor, Mar. 25, 1821, GFC, one box, ASSCL-UVA.

36. [Francis W. Gilmer], "Necessity of a Better System of Instruction," in J. H. Rice, ed., *Virginia Evangelical and Literary Magazine*, vol. 1:315; Borrowman, "False Dawn," 10–12; Glover, *Southern Sons*, 52–58; Sugrue, "We Desired," 91–114.

37. [Norfolk] *American Beacon and Commercial Diary*, Nov. 22, 1815 ("growing"); "Academus," and "What Shall be Done for the University?" *Richmond Enquirer*, Jan. 25, 1821, and Dec. 12, 1822; Glover, "Let Us Manufacture Men," 24–27; Glover, *Southern Sons*, 3–4.

38. Beverley Kennon to John H. Cocke, July 3, 1828, JHCP, box 55, ASSCL-UVA.

39. Sterling Ruffin to Thomas Ruffin, June n.d., 1804, in Roulhac Hamilton, ed., *Papers of Thomas Ruffin*, vol. 1:54–55.

40. William Garnett to Thomas Ruffin, Jan. 21, 1805, in Roulhac Hamilton, ed., *Papers of Thomas Ruffin*, vol. 1:66 ("let us eat"); William D. Lowther to Maria L. Skinner, Feb. 25, 1812 ("but few"), Skinner Family Collection, box 1, SHC-UNC; Flournoy, "Hugh Blair Grigsby," 174–75; Glover, "Let us Manufacture Men," 24–26, 37; O'Brien, *Conjectures of Order*, vol. 1:27, 38.

41. Timothy Dwight to John Taylor, Sept. 3, 1805, and Taylor to Dwight, n.d., in Barbee, ed., "Sheaf of Old Letters," 82–85.

42. Thomas Jefferson to Joseph C. Cabell, Jan. 22, 1820 ("overwhelming mass"), in Looney et al., eds., *PTJ-RS*, vol. 15:344–45; Jefferson to Col. John Taylor, Feb. 14, 1821 ("the signs"), and Jefferson to James Breckinridge, Feb. 15, 1821 ("imbibing"), FO-NA, http://founders.archives.gov/documents/Jefferson/98-01-02-1836 and -1839); "University of Virginia," *Richmond Enquirer*, Jan. 3, 1822; Jefferson, "Report of the Central College Visitors," Jan. 6, 1818, in N. F. Cabell, *Early History*, 401 ("worthy").

43. Thomas Jefferson to James Breckinridge, Apr. 9, 1822, FO-NA, http://founders.archives.gov/documents/Jefferson/98-01-02-2756; "Gen. Blackburn's Speech, in the House of Delegates," and "What Shall be Done for the University?" *Richmond Enquirer*, Apr. 24, 1821 ("imperceptibly"), and Dec. 10, 1822.

44. Francis W. Gilmer to Thomas Jefferson, Mar. 18, 1818, and Jefferson to Gilmer, Apr. 10, 1818, in R. B. Davis, ed., *Correspondence of Jefferson and Gilmer*, 58, 60; R. B. Davis, *Intellectual Life*, 54–57; Osborne, *Crisis Years*, 194.

45. "Academus," "What Shall Be Done for the University?" and "Brindley," *Rich-

mond Enquirer, Jan. 25, 1821, Dec. 21, 1822 ("the grave"), and Dec. 27, 1822; Glover, *Southern Sons*, 53–58.

46. Joseph C. Cabell to Jefferson, Feb. 1, 20, 22, 1818, in Looney et al., eds., *PTJ-RS*, vol. 12:413–14, 488–90, 500–501; Cabell to James Madison, Feb. 16, 1818, in Mattern et al., eds., *PJM-RS*, vol. 1:220–22; D. Malone, *Jefferson and His Time*, vol. 6:275–76.

47. Thomas Jefferson to Spencer Roane, June 28, 1818, and Jefferson to Littleton W. Tazewell, June 28, 1818, in Looney et al., eds., *PTJ-RS*, vol. 13:110 ("the history"), 111; Jefferson to James Madison, June 28, 1818, in Mattern et al., eds., *PJM-RS*, vol. 1:295–97; Jefferson to Martha J. Randolph, Aug. 4, 1818, in Betts and Bear, eds., *Family Letters of Thomas Jefferson*, 423 ("I have never seen"); Jefferson, "Rockfish Gap Report," Aug. 4, 1818, in N. F. Cabell, *Early History*, 432–35, 441; D. Malone, *Jefferson and His Time*, vol. 6:276–77.

48. Joseph C. Cabell to Thomas Jefferson, Dec. 14, 17, and 24, 1818, and Jan. 18, 1819, in Looney et al., eds., *PTJ-RS*, vol. 13:490–91, 497–98, 514–15, 583–84, see also 401n.

49. Joseph C. Cabell to Thomas Jefferson, Jan. 7, Jan. 21, Feb. 4, and 15, 1819, in Looney et al., eds., *PTJ-RS*, vol. 13:558–60, 592–93, vol. 14:12–14, 34–36.

50. William C. Rives to John H. Cocke, Jan. 20, 1819, JHCP, box 27, ASSCL-UVA; James O. Carr to Dabney S. Carr, Feb. 7, 1819 ("the triumph"), CCFP, box 2, ASSCL-UVA; Cocke to Cabell, Feb. 8, 1819, JCCFP, box 12, ASSCL-UVA.

51. Thomas Jefferson to Joseph C. Cabell, Jan. 28, 1819, Jefferson to Wilson Cary Nicholas, Jan. 28, 1819, and Cabell to Jefferson, Feb. 22, 1819, Looney et al., eds., *PTJ-RS*, vol. 13:607–8 ("miserably short" and "give us"), 613, and vol. 14:55–56.

52. Joseph C. Cabell to Thomas Jefferson, Feb. 22, 1818, Feb. 15, 1819, Jefferson to Cabell, Feb. 19, 1819, Board of Visitors Minutes, Feb. 26, 1819, and Jefferson to James Breckinridge, Dec. 19, 1819 ("taxing"), in Looney et al., eds., *PTJ-RS*, vol. 12:501, vol. 14:34–36, 45, 71, vol. 15:295–96; Jefferson to John W. Eppes, June 30, 1820 ("a beautiful"), Jefferson to Cabell, Jan. 31, 1821 ("forever"), and Jefferson to Breckinridge, Apr. 9, 1822 ("We have only"), FO-NA, http://founders.archives.gov/documents/Jefferson/98-01-02-1352, -1814, and -2756.

53. Thomas Jefferson to Thomas Fairfax, Oct. 16, 1821 ("present youths"), FO-NA, http://founders.archives.gov/documents/Jefferson/98-01-02-2376; Hore Browse Trist to Nicholas P. Trist, Jan. 30, 1820 ("progeny"), NPTP, folder 19, SHC-UNC.

54. C. W. Gooch to David Campbell, Jan. 20, 1820, and Thomas Mann Randolph to David Campbell, Aug. 23, 1820, CFP, box 4, DMRML-DU; Joseph C. Cabell to Thomas Jefferson, Feb. 3, and 24, 1820, in Looney et al., eds., *PTJ-RS*, vol. 15:366, 415; Cabell to Jefferson, Feb. 3, 1823, FO-NA, http://founders.archives.gov/documents/Jefferson/98-01-02-3303; D. Malone, *Jefferson and His Time*, vol. 6:375. For arrears on the subscription in 1820, see N. F. Cabell, *Early History*, 463.

55. Joseph C. Cabell to Thomas Jefferson, Jan. 4, 18, and 25, and Feb. 25, 1821
     ("These successive"), and Apr. 28, 1821, Jan. 7, Feb. 25, and Mar. 6, 1822 ("of
     extravagance"), FO-NA, http://founders.archives.gov/documents/Jefferson/98
     -01-02-1747, -1775, -1791, -1863, -2030, -2569, -2681, and -2697; Francis W. Gilmer
     to Dabney Carr, Sept. 30, 1820 ("The plan"), Gilmer-Carr letters, LV; "Applica-
     tion of the Literary Fund," in J. H. Rice, ed., *Virginia Evangelical and Literary
     Magazine*, vol. 5:284–85 ("imitating").

56. John H. Cocke to Thomas Jefferson, May 2, 1819, and Chapman Johnson and
     James Breckinridge to Cocke, Apr. 5, 1821, JHCP, boxes 28 and 33, ASSCL-UVA.

57. Thomas Jefferson to James Madison, July 7, 1819, in Mattern et al., eds., *PJM-RS*,
     vol. 1:480–83; Otway B. Barraud to Cocke, Aug. 4, 1822 ("forge"), and Cocke to
     Jefferson, Feb. 22, 1823, JHCP, boxes 37, and 38, ASSCL-UVA; Cocke to Joseph
     C. Cabell, Mar. 20, 1820, Apr. 11, Dec. 8, 1821, and Feb. 15, 1823, JCCFP, boxes
     13, 14, and 15, ASSCL-UVA.

58. Joseph C. Cabell to John H. Cocke, Apr. 15, 1819, JCCFP, box 13, ASSCL-UVA;
     Cabell to Thomas Jefferson, Apr. 17, 1819, and Robert B. Taylor to Jefferson, July
     27, 1819, in Looney et al., eds., *PTJ-RS*, vol. 14:233, 560; Cabell to Louisa Cocke,
     Apr. 8, 1823 ("The buildings"), JHCP, box 38, ASSCL-UVA.

59. Thomas Jefferson to James Madison, Oct. 30, 1821, and Apr. 7, 1822, in Mattern
     et al., eds., *PJM-RS*, vol. 2:413–14 ("If we stop"), 501–2.

60. Joseph C. Cabell to Jefferson, Dec. 23, 1822 ("At my instance"), and Jefferson
     to Cabell, Dec. 28, 1822 ("great object"), FO-NA, http://founders.archives.gov/
     documents/Jefferson/98-01-02-3230, and -3238.

61. Robert B. Taylor to John H. Cocke, Mar. 3, 1823, JHCP, box 38, ASSCL-UVA;
     Joseph C. Cabell to Cocke, Mar. 17, 1824 ("Our University"), JCCFP, box 16,
     ASSCL-UVA; Cabell to Jefferson, Jan. 26, and 29, Feb. 19, and Mar. 7, 1824
     ("beyond"), FO-NA, http://founders.archives.gov/documents/Jefferson/98-01
     -02-4009, -4014, -4064, and -4091; "The University of Virginia," *Richmond
     Enquirer*, June 4, 1824.

62. "Original Correspondence," *Richmond Enquirer*, Feb. 4, 1826.

63. Thomas Jefferson to Joseph C. Cabell, Feb. 7, 1826, FO-NA, http://founders
     .archives.gov/documents/Jefferson/98-01-02-5882.

64. Thomas Jefferson to Joseph C. Cabell, Feb. 7, 1826, FO-NA, http://founders
     .archives.gov/documents/Jefferson/98-01-02-5882. For Jefferson's mastery at
     guiding legislators, see G. Tucker, *Life of Thomas Jefferson*, vol. 2:506–7.

65. "Philodemus," in J. H. Rice, ed., *Virginia Evangelical and Literary Magazine*, vol.
     9:198–99; Wall, "Students and Student Life," 60. In 1828, the state treasurer con-
     cluded that the state had spent $294,427 to build the University. See Wagoner,
     Jefferson and Education, 126.

66. Wall, "Students and Student Life," 66.

8. PROFESSORS

1. Francis W. Gilmer to Peachy R. Gilmer, Dec. 27, 1811, PRGP, sec. 2, VHS; John Coalter to St. George Tucker, Dec. 29, 1811, TCP, box 31, SCSL-CWM; Baker, *Richmond Theater Fire*, 24–39; Maxwell, *Memoir*, 70–73.

2. John Coalter to St. George Tucker, Dec. 29, 1811, TCP, box 31, SCSL-CWM; Jeter, *Recollections*, 214–15 (quotation); Baker, *Richmond Theater Fire*, 47–57, 64–74.

3. John Holt Rice to Judith Randolph, Jan. 17, 1812 ("and live"), and Rice to Archibald Alexander, May 14, 1812, in Maxwell, *Memoir*, 75 ("I am"), 79 ("A spirit"); Baker, *Richmond Theater Fire*, 23–24; A. D. Thomas, "Reasonable Revivalism," 327.

4. Henshaw, *Memoir*, 144, 149, 159–60, 172–75; "Episcopal Convention," *Richmond Enquirer*, May 24, 1822; Baker, *Richmond Theater Fire*, 177–78; Meade, *Old Churches*, vol. 1:50.

5. Mary Chandler to John H. Cocke, Jan. 22, 1821, and Sally Faulcon to Cocke, Apr. 3, 1821, JHCP, box 33, ASSCL-UVA.

6. Thomas Jefferson to Thomas Cooper, Nov. 2, 1822, FO-NA, http://founders .archives.gov/documents/Jefferson/98-01-02-3137.

7. Wight and Miller, eds., "Journals of Reverend Robert J. Miller," 163; Bishop Moore quoted in Henshaw, *Memoir*, 173 ("Would to God!"); Francis W. Gilmer to Peter Minor, May 31, 1818, GFC, one box, ASSCL-UVA.

8. Foote, *Sketches of Virginia*, 241–43, 251–55; Maxwell, *Memoir*, 1–16, Patrick Henry quoted on 9; A. Alexander quoted in J. W. Alexander, *Life of Archibald Alexander*, 195–96 ("His appetite").

9. Maxwell, *Memoir*, 16–37, 109, 111.

10. Maxwell, *Memoir*, 37–38 ("poor"); Rice, "An Excursion into the Country," in J. H. Rice, ed., *Virginia Evangelical and Literary Magazine*, vol. 1:511 ("money"), 515 ("to endow"), 551.

11. John Holt Rice to Ashbel Greene, n.d. 1810 ("This people" and "Many"), SGAC, box 233, folder 17, HSP; Foote, *Sketches of Virginia*, 302–3; Maxwell, *Memoir*, 30–36, Rice quoted on 36 ("a very large"); Weeks, "John Holt Rice," 31.

12. John Holt Rice to Ashbel Greene, n.d. 1810 and May 1, 1811, SGAC, box 233, folder 17, HSP; Rice to unknown, May 11, 1812 ("my beloved"), SGAC, box 39, folder 2, HSP; Weeks, "John Holt Rice," 28–30, Rice quoted on 29 ("injure").

13. John H. Rice to Ashbel Green, May 1, 1811 ("truly disgusted"), SGAC, box 233, folder 17, HSP; Maxwell, *Memoir*, 10 ("gentlemen"), 20, 32 (Archibald Alexander quoted: "were not").

14. John Holt Rice to Theodorick T. Randolph, Sept. 23, 1812, in Maxwell, *Memoir*, 86.

15. John Holt Rice to William Maxwell, Apr. 10, 1816, in Maxwell, *Memoir*, 127; White, *Rev. William S. White*, 35–36 ("delightful parlor"); A. D. Thomas, "Reasonable Revivalism," 328.

16. John Holt Rice to Thomas Chalmers, July 25, 1817, in Moore, ed., "Letters of John Holt Rice," 311; William Wirt to Rice, Sept. 6, 1818, Wirt Letters, VHS; Rice, *Illustration of the Character*, 5, 45 ("*poor* and *pious*"), 48–52; Addis, *Jefferson's Vision*, 78–80; Buckley, "After Disestablishment," 448–55; Foote, *Sketches of Virginia*, 239–40; Maxwell, *Memoir*, 121–22.

17. "Objections to the Present Plan of Education," in J. H. Rice, ed., *Virginia Evangelical and Literary Magazine*, vol. 2:183–84; J. H. Rice, *Sermon to Young Women*, 12 ("We are never"); Addis, *Jefferson's Vision*, 74–78; Swift, "Thomas Jefferson," 33, 44.

18. John Holt Rice to Micah Baldwin, June 14, 1823 ("I have no doubt"), July 31, 1824, Dec. 11, 1824 ("This preys"), Dec. 24, 1825, and Feb. 18, 1826, SGAC, box 233, folder 17, HSP.

19. John Holt Rice, *Illustration of the Character*, 45; Rice to Theodorick Randolph, May 19, 1813, and Rice to Archibald Alexander, Mar. 5, 1823, in Maxwell, *Memoir*, 93–95 ("nothing" and "an openheartedness"), 232–33; Swift, "Thomas Jefferson," 33–34.

20. John Holt Rice to Micah Baldwin, June 14, Oct. 4, and Dec. 9, 1823, Apr. 17, 1824, June 25, 1825 ("Heaven" and "The result"), and Nov. 15, 1826 ("spring up"), SGAC, box 233, folder 17, HSP.

21. John Holt Rice, "Crito," *Richmond Enquirer*, Jan. 9, 1819 ("drunken"); "Literature and Science," "Iota," and "Literary Fund," in Rice, ed., *Virginia Evangelical and Literary Magazine*, vol. 2:47 ("The business"), vol. 5:92,184–86.

22. "Iota," "Literary Fund," and "Philodemus," in J. H. Rice, ed., *Virginia Evangelical and Literary Magazine*, vol. 5:94–96 ("to the benefit"), 240, and vol. 9:84–85 ("main stay").

23. "Literary Fund of the State of Virginia," and "To the President and Directors of the Literary Fund," in J. H. Rice, ed., *Virginia Evangelical and Literary Magazine*, vol. 5:187–89, and vol. 9:198–99 ("Is it not obvious"); Swift, "Thomas Jefferson," 48–49.

24. John Holt Rice to Theodorick T. Randolph, Oct. 19, 1814, Rice to Archibald Alexander, Sept. 3, 1818, and Rice to William S. White, Aug. 6, 1821, in Maxwell, *Memoir*, 105–6 ("My only hope"), 150–51, and 193 ("flatters"); Rice to Thomas Chalmers, Apr. 30, 1819, in Moore, ed., "Letters of John Holt Rice," 314 ("baptized").

25. Thomas Jefferson to Horatio G. Spafford, Mar. 17, 1814, Jefferson, "Essay on New England Religious Intolerance," c. Jan. 1816, Jefferson to John Adams, Apr. 8, 1816, in Looney et al., eds., *PTJ-RS*, vol. 7:248–49 ("mystery"), vol. 9:380–81 ("pious whining"), and 649–52 ("it is good" and "gloomy"); Jefferson

to Benjamin Waterhouse, June 26, 1822 ("the deliria"), and Jefferson to John Davis, Jan. 18, 1824 ("manic ravings"), FO-NA, http://founders.archives.gov/documents/Jefferson/98-01-02-2905, and -3994; Neem, "Early Republic," 35–37; Ragosta, *Religious Freedom*, 14–28.

26. Thomas Jefferson to José Correa da Serra, Apr. 11, 1820 ("dread the advance"), in Looney et al., eds., *PTJ-RS*, vol. 15:525–26; Jefferson to William Short, Oct. 19, 1822 ("most ambitious"), and Jefferson to Thomas Cooper, Apr. 12, 1823 ("by enlightening"), FO-NA, http://founders.archives.gov/documents/Jefferson/98-01-02-3103 and -3454.

27. Thomas Jefferson to Benjamin Waterhouse, June 26, 1822 ("I trust"), and Jefferson to William Short, Oct. 19, 1822 ("would gather"), FO-NA, http://founders.archives.gov/documents/Jefferson/98-01-02-2905, and -3103.

28. Thomas Jefferson, "Rockfish Gap Report," Aug. 4, 1818, in N. F. Cabell, *Early History*, 436 ("what in his nature"), 441 ("the proofs"); Jefferson to Joseph C. Cabell, Nov. 20, 1818, in Looney et al., eds., *PTJ-RS*, vol. 13:407; D. Malone, *Jefferson and His Time*, vol. 6:280.

29. John H. Rice, ed., *Virginia Evangelical and Literary Magazine*, vol. 3:120–22 ("They are"), and vol. 9: 351 ("The morality"), and 352 ("The work"); Rice to Thomas Chalmers, July 25, 1817, in Moore, ed., "Letters of John Holt Rice," 310 ("that neither peace"); Rice, *Sermon to Young Women*, 15 ("Exclude").

30. John Holt Rice to Archibald Alexander, Sept. 3, 1818, in Maxwell, *Memoir*, 150–51.

31. John Holt Rice to William Maxwell, Jan. 10, 1819, in Maxwell, *Memoir*, 154–55 ("Now" and "I gain"); Addis, *Jefferson's Vision*, 74–78; Swift, "Thomas Jefferson," 35.

32. John Holt Rice, "Review, The Mountaineer," in Rice, ed., *Virginia Evangelical and Literary Magazine*, vol. 2:363–75; Speece quoted in W. S. White, *Rev. William S. White*, 111.

33. John Holt Rice, "Review, The Mountaineer," in Rice, ed., *Virginia Evangelical and Literary Magazine*, vol. 2:363–75; Speece, *The Mountaineer*, 188–90 (all quotations).

34. Francis W. Gilmer to Peachy R. Gilmer, Sept. 20, 1816 ("while he is indulging"), PRGP, sec. 2, VHS; F. W. Gilmer to Peter Minor, Oct. 18, 1817 ("You gentlemen"), GFC, one box, ASSCL-UVA; Joseph C. Cabell to Jefferson, Dec. 29, 1817, in Looney et al., eds., *PTJ-RS*, vol. 12:284–85 ("They are").

35. Thomas Jefferson to Joseph C. Cabell, June 27, 1810, Cooper to Jefferson, Sept. 15, 1814, Jefferson to Cooper, Aug. 7, 1818, Cooper to Jefferson, Apr. 19, 1818, and Jefferson to Cabell, Mar. 1, 1819, in Looney et al., eds., *PTJ-RS*, vol. 2:489–90, vol. 7:657–66, vol. 12:3, 647, vol. 14:79–80 ("Cooper is"); Jefferson to Robert B. Taylor and Chapman Johnson, May 16, 1820 ("the corner stone"), in Looney et al., eds., PTJ-RS, vol. 15:602–4.

36. Joseph C. Cabell to Thomas Jefferson, Feb. 22, 1819, and William Short to Jefferson, May 25, 1819, Looney et al., eds., *PTJ-RS*, vol. 14:55–56, 321–

24; John H. Cocke to Cabell, Mar. 1, 1819, and Cabell to Cocke, Mar. 6, 1819, JCCFP, box 13, ASSCL-UVA; Short to Cocke, Mar. 16, 1819 ("kind of"), JHCP, box 28, ASSCL-UVA; Board of Visitors Meeting, Mar. 29, 1819, in Looney et al., eds., *PTJ-RS*, vol. 14:176–78 ("professor").

37.   John Holt Rice to John H. Cocke, Jan. 6, 1820, JHCP, box 30, ASSCL-UVA; "Miscellaneous Articles," and "Review," in Rice, ed., *Virginia Evangelical and Literary Magazine*, vol. 3:49, 63–74, quote on 69 ("wild doctrine").

38.   William H. Cabell to Joseph C. Cabell, Mar. 21, 1820, and J. C. Cabell to John H. Cocke, Apr. 14, 1820, JCCFP, boxes 13 and 14, ASSCL-UVA; Jefferson to Thomas Cooper, Apr. 8, 1820, Cooper to Jefferson, May 3, 1820, and Jefferson to Robert B. Taylor and Chapman Johnson, May 16, 1820, in Looney et al., eds., *PTJ-RS*, vol. 15:515–17, 565–66, 602–4; John Holt Rice to Ashbel Green, Oct. 11, 1820, SGAC, box 233, folder 17, HSP.

39.   Joseph C. Cabell to Thomas Jefferson, Jan. 14, 1822 ("Is it not") and Jan. 21, 1822, FO-NA, http://founders.archives.gov/documents/Jefferson/98-01-02-2585, and -2602; N. F. Cabell, *Early History*, 474–75 ("independent").

40.   Richard Channing Moore to John H. Cocke, July 15, 1819, JHCP, box 29, ASSCL-UVA; Joseph C. Cabell to Cocke, Nov. 21, 1821, JCCFP, box 14, ASSCL-UVA; Henshaw, *Memoir*, 166–70; O'Brien, *Conjectures of Order*, vol. 2:622; Osborne, *Crisis Years*, 231–40.

41.   "A Visitor of William & Mary," *Richmond Enquirer*, Aug. 21, 1821 ("Let the public"); Joseph C. Cabell to Thomas Jefferson, Dec. 22, 1820, and James Madison to Jefferson, Dec. 31, 1824, FO-NA, http://founders.archives.gov/documents/Jefferson/98-01-02-1696, and -4824.

42.   "Charters," and Mr. Bryce, "Speech," *Richmond Enquirer*, Feb. 1, 1825 ("the sages"), Feb. 15, 1825; Joseph C. Cabell to Thomas Jefferson, Jan. 30, 1825, FO-NA, http://founders.archives.gov/documents/Jefferson/98-01-02-4920.

43.   [Spencer Roane] "A Dissenting Farmer," "Caius," and "Visitor of William and Mary," *Richmond Enquirer*, July 27, 1821 ("might be") Aug. 7, and 17, 1821.

44.   Joseph C. Cabell to John H. Cocke, Nov. 21, 1821, JCCF, box 14, ASSCL-UVA; Henshaw, *Memoir*, 167–70.

45.   William H. Garland to Sarah A. Garland, Nov. 6, 1823, *WMQ*, 2nd ser., vol. 11 (Apr. 1931): 136–37 ("There is nothing"); C. De La Pena to John A. Smith, Nov. 3, 1827, in Carson, ed., *We Were There*, 102 ("this sad place" and "many half-ruined"); "Another Friend of William & Mary," *Richmond Enquirer*, Nov. 23, 1824 ("Thus").

46.   Patrick Kerr Rogers to Thomas Jefferson, Jan. 14, 1824, FO-NA, http://founders.archives.gov/documents/Jefferson/98-01-02-3990; John Tyler, "William & Mary College," *Richmond Enquirer*, July 13, 1824; John A. Smith, address, Jan. 31, 1825, *Richmond Enquirer*, Feb. 5, 1825 ("Professors"); Osborne, *Crisis Years*, 244.

47.   Joseph C. Cabell to Thomas Jefferson, May 5, 1824, and James Madison to

Jefferson, Dec. 31, 1824, FO-NA, http://founders.archives.gov/documents/Jefferson/98-01-02-4245, and -4824); City of Richmond Common Council, report, July 1, 1824, College Papers Collection, folder 15 (1821–1830), SCSL-CWM; "College of William & Mary," "A Friend to Education," and John A. Smith, address, *Richmond Enquirer*, July 2, 1824, Dec. 21, 1824, and Feb. 5, 1825 ("intolerable").

48. "William & Mary," "College of William & Mary," "Another Friend of William & Mary," and "William & Mary College," *Richmond Enquirer*, May 4, 1824 ("falling rapidly"), July 2, Nov. 23, 1824 ("Here I visited"), and Nov. 30, 1824; City of Richmond Common Council, report, July 1, 1824, College Papers Collection, folder 15, SCSL-CWM; Ferdinand S. Campbell to John Campbell, Oct. 30, 1824 ("Our College"), CFP, folder 2, VHS; "William & Mary College," *New York Observer*, Nov. 13, 1824; Osborne, *Crisis Years*, 278.

49. Joseph C. Cabell to Thomas Jefferson, Mar. 17, and May 5, 1824, FO-NA, http://founders.archives.gov/documents/Jefferson/98-01-02-4122, and -4245; Cabell to John H. Cocke, May 5, 1824, JCCFP, box 16, ASSCL-UVA.

50. Thomas Jefferson to Joseph C. Cabell, May 16, 1824 ("until the old" and "the derelict"), FO-NA, http://founders.archives.gov/documents/Jefferson/98-01-02-4271; Jefferson to Francis W. Gilmer, June 5, 1824, in R. B. Davis, ed., *Correspondence of Jefferson and Gilmer*, 84.

51. Thomas Jefferson et al., indenture with the College of William & Mary, Jan. 22, 1823, and Jefferson to Sydney Edwards Morse, Mar. 9, 1823 ("much reduced"), FO-NA, http://founders.archives.gov/documents/Jefferson/98-01-02-3281, and -3380; L. H. Johnson, "Sharper than a Serpent's Tooth," 145–62.

52. William H. Cabell to Joseph C. Cabell, Oct. 28, 1824, and John Coalter to J. C. Cabell, Dec. 27, 1824, JCCFP, boxes 16 and 17, ASSCL-UVA.

53. Joseph C. Cabell to Thomas Jefferson, Dec. 21, 1824 ("I oppose"), and Jan. 16, 1825, FO-NA, http://founders.archives.gov/documents/Jefferson/98-01-02-4798, and -4875; Cabell to John H. Cocke, Jan. 2, 1825 ("I am worn down"), JCCFP, box 17, ASSCL-UVA.

54. Thomas Jefferson to Alexander Keech, Jan. 26, 1822 ("Professors of the first order"), Jefferson to Joseph C. Cabell, Dec. 28, 1822 ("become suitors"), Feb. 3, 1824 ("give to our"), and Jefferson to James Madison, Oct. 6, 1824, FO-NA, http://founders.archives.gov/documents/Jefferson/98-01-02-2616, -3238, -4018, and -4601. Jefferson had tried to recruit a pair of bright young scholars from New England—Nathaniel Bowditch and George Ticknor—in a move that would weaken Harvard while boosting Virginia. When both turned him down, Jefferson refused to consider anyone of lower standing from the distrusted north.

55. John H. Cocke to Joseph C. Cabell, Apr. 10, 1824, JCCFP, box 16, ASSCL-UVA; Cabell to Thomas Jefferson, Apr. 16, 1824, James Madison to Jefferson, Apr. 16, 1824, and Jefferson to Madison, Oct. 11, 1824, FO-NA, http://founders.archives

.gov/documents/Jefferson/98-01-02-4194, -4195, and -4613; "Importation of Professors," *Richmond Enquirer*, Dec. 21, 1824; P. A. Bruce, *History of the University*, vol. 2:1-2, *Philadelphia Gazette* quoted on 2.

56. Francis W. Gilmer to Peachy R. Gilmer, Apr. 9, 1824, and Apr. 28, 1824 ("do more harm"), PRGP, sec. 2, VHS; F. W. Gilmer to John Randolph, Apr. 29, 1824, in L. G. Tyler, ed., "Letters of Gilmer to Randolph," 194 ("paupers"); F. W. Gilmer to David Watson, July 26, 1824, *VMHB*, vol. 29 (July 1921): 285 ("If I can succeed"); R. B. Davis, *Francis Walker Gilmer*, 196-97.

57. Thomas Jefferson to Francis W. Gilmer, Oct. 12, 1824, in R. B. Davis, ed., *Correspondence of Jefferson and Gilmer*, 108-9, see also 17-20.

58. George W. Blaettermann to Thomas Jefferson, Apr. 27, 1819, and George Ticknor to Jefferson, May 27, 1819, Looney et al., eds., *PTJ-RS*, vol. 14:252-53 and 344-46; Francis W. Gilmer to Peachy R. Gilmer, July 31, 1824, PRGP, sec. 2, VHS.

59. Francis W. Gilmer to Thomas Jefferson, Aug. 13, 27, Sept. 15, and Nov. 12, 1824, in R. B. Davis, ed., *Correspondence of Jefferson and Gilmer*, 95-97, 98, 101-3, 113; Gilmer to Dabney Carr, Sept. 17, 1824 ("I have worked," "Virginia must," and "I shall return"), Gilmer-Carr Letters, LV; Gilmer to John Randolph, Sept. 25, 1824, in L. G. Tyler, ed., "Letters of Gilmer to Randolph," 196 ("They are men").

60. Francis W. Gilmer to Dabney Carr, Nov. 14, 1824 (all quotations), Gilmer-Carr Letters, one folder, LV; Gilmer to Thomas Jefferson, Nov. 12, 1824, and Dec. 3, 1824, in R. B. Davis, ed., *Correspondence of Jefferson and Gilmer*, 113 and 123.

61. Joseph C. Cabell to Thomas Jefferson, Jan. 16, 1825, FO-NA, http://founders .archives.gov/documents/Jefferson/98-01-02-4875; Wilson Miles Cary to Virginia Cary, n.d., c. Jan. 1825, CCFP, box 2, ASSCL-UVA; John H. Cocke to John H. Cocke, Jr., Jan. 24, 1825, JHCP, box 42, ASSCL-UVA.

62. Thomas Jefferson to Joseph C. Cabell, Jan. 11, 1825, and Cabell to Jefferson, Jan. 16, 1825, FO-NA, http://founders.archives.gov/documents/Jefferson/98-01-02 -4856, and -4875.

63. [Joseph C. Cabell], "Friend to Science," *Richmond Enquirer*, Feb. 3, 1825 ("great luminary"); Cabell to Thomas Jefferson, Dec. 17, 1824, Jefferson to Cabell, Dec. 22, 1824, and Cabell to Jefferson, Jan. 28, 1825, FO-NA, http://founders.archives .gov/documents/Jefferson/98-01-02-4785, -4834, and -4917.

64. "William & Mary College," "To the Alumni of William & Mary College," and John Tyler, speech, *Richmond Enquirer*, July 13, 1824 ("To inform"), July 27, 1824 ("Spanish"), Feb. 10, 1825; Joseph C. Cabell to Thomas Jefferson, Feb. 3, 1825, FO-NA, http://founders.archives.gov/documents/Jefferson/98-01-02-4931; Osborne, *Crisis Years*, 283.

65. John Campbell quoted in Osborne, *Crisis Years*, 299-300 ("very smart" and "amused"); John A. Smith, address, *Richmond Enquirer*, Feb. 3, and 5, 1825; Mr. Jones, speech, *Richmond Enquirer*, Feb. 22, 1825 ("from some Yankey").

66. Joseph C. Cabell to Thomas Jefferson, Feb. 7, 1825, FO-NA, http://founders .archives.gov/documents/Jefferson/98-01-02-4945; "Virginia Legislature," *Richmond Enquirer*, Feb. 19, 1825; John A. Smith to Cabell, Mar. 7, 1825, and John H. Cocke to Cabell, Apr. 3, 1825, JCCFP, box 17, ASSCL-UVA. For historical criticism of Jefferson and Cabell for trying to destroy their *alma mater*, see L. Johnson, "Sharper than a Serpent's Tooth," 148–49, and P. A. Bruce, *History of the University*, vol. 1:310, 312, 319. For a defense, see D. Malone, *Jefferson and His Time*, vol. 6:413n9.

67. Robley Dunglison to Thomas Jefferson, Feb. 10, 1825, and Joseph C. Cabell to Jefferson, May 25, 1825 ("Like a fine"), FO-NA, http://founders.archives.gov/ documents/Jefferson/98-01-02-4947, and -5255; Joseph C. Cabell to Isaac A. Coles, Feb. 20, 1825 ("How pleasing"), JCCFP, box 17, ASSCL-UVA; Dunglison, "Autobiographical Ana," 18–21.

68. James Madison to Thomas Jefferson, Dec. 3, 1824, and Thomas Jefferson to Madison, Dec. 10, 1824, FO-NA, http://founders.archives.gov/documents/ Jefferson/98-01-02-4732, and -4771; McLean, *George Tucker*, 22–23.

69. George Tucker to Thomas Jefferson, Feb. 23, 1825, and Apr. 23, 1825, FO-NA, http://founders.archives.gov/documents/Jefferson/98-01-02-4994, and -5167; Dunglison, "Autobiographical Ana," 24; G. Tucker, "Autobiography," 130, 136 ("grotesque images" and "that my brain"); Hore Browse Trist to Nicholas P. Trist, May 18, 1825, NPTP, folder 36, SHC-UNC; David Watson, "Miscellaneous Memoranda," June 1825 (p. 39), DWP, box 3, LC; McLean, *George Tucker*, 21–28, 31, 99; Shackelford, *George Wythe Randolph*, 19.

70. Thomas Jefferson to James Madison, Feb. 1, 1825, Jefferson to Joseph C. Cabell, Feb. 3, 1825, James Madison to Jefferson, Feb. 8, 1825, and Jefferson to Madison, Feb. 17, 1826, FO-NA, http://founders.archives.gov/documents/Jefferson/98 -01-02-4929, -4932, -4946, and -5912; Gordon-Reed and Onuf, *Most Blessed of Patriarchs*, 277–78.

71. Thomas Jefferson to William Roscoe, Dec. 27, 1820 ("illimitable"), and Jefferson to James Madison, Feb. 17, 1826, FO-NA, http://founders.archives.gov/documents/ Jefferson/98-01-02-1712, and -5912.

72. Thomas Jefferson to Francis Walker Gilmer, Jan. 20, 1825, FO-NA, http:// founders.archives.gov/documents/Jefferson/98-01-02-4890; Jefferson to James Madison, Jan. 20, 1826, in Mattern et al., eds., *PJM-RS*, vol. 3:668–70.

73. Thomas Jefferson to James Madison, Feb. 1, 1825, in Mattern et al., eds., *PJM-RS*, vol. 3:470–71; Chapman Johnson to Francis W. Gilmer, Dec. 6, 1824, and Gilmer to Johnson, Aug. 7, 1824 ("But to put"), GFN, box 3, ASSCL-UVA.

74. Francis W. Gilmer to John Randolph, Nov. 3, 1825, in L. G. Tyler, ed., "Letters of Francis Walker Gilmer," 197.

75. Francis W. Gilmer to Thomas Jefferson, Jan. 14, 1826 ("I have been"), in R. B. Davis, ed., *Correspondence of Jefferson and Gilmer*, 153; Sally Minor Watson to James

Watson, Jr., Feb. 7, 1826 [but misfiled as 1825] ("converses"), DWFP, box 14, ASSCL-UVA; Peachy R. Gilmer, "Death Scenes," GFN, box 4, ASSCL-UVA.

76. P. R. Gilmer, "Particulars of the Last Days and Death of Francis Gilmer," in R. B. Davis, *Francis Walker Gilmer*, 337–40.

77. Jane Margaret Carr to Dabney S. Carr, Feb. 27, 1826, CCFP, box 2, ASSCL-UVA; Peachy R. Gilmer note of Aug. 15, 1833, PRGP, sec. 2, VHS; Peachy R. Gilmer, "Death Scenes," GFN, box 4, ASSCL-UVA; R. B. Davis, *Francis Walker Gilmer*, 340–41.

78. Cornelia J. Randolph to Ellen W. R. Coolidge, Aug. 3, 1825, EWRCP, box 1, ASSCL-UVA; Robley Dunglison quoted in Edmund W. Hubard to Robert T. Hubard, Nov. 8, 1825, HFP, subseries 1.5, folder 42, SHC-UNC; Louisa M. H. Cocke to John H. Cocke, Jan. 10, 1826, JHCP, box 46, ASSCL-UVA. For the menagerie, see John P. Emmett to Arthur S. Brockenbrough, Jan. 5, 1826, THSP, box 2, ASSCL-UVA; P. A. Bruce, *History of the University*, vol. 2:17.

79. [Anon.], "Proceedings and Report of the Commissioners for the University of Virginia," *North American Review*, vol. 10 (1820): 118, 130 ("first instance"); Tutwiler, *Address*, 6 ("Much as I love"); Addis, *Jefferson's Vision for Education*, 103–4; Wagoner, *Jefferson and Education*, 139.

80. Francis W. Gilmer to Dabney Carr, June 13, 1818 ("to carry"), Gilmer-Carr Letters, LV; John Holt Rice to Archibald Alexander, Apr. 13, 1819, in Maxwell, *Memoir*, 164 ("Albemarle"); Rice to Micah Baldwin, July 31, 1824 ("The people"), SGAC, box 233, folder 17, HSP.

81. John Holt Rice to Archibald Alexander, Mar. 18, 1825, in Maxwell, *Memoir*, 266.

9. STUDENTS

1. Virginia R. Cary to Louisa Cocke, Aug. 17, 1825, JHCP, box 44, ASSCL-UVA; V. C. Hall, *Portraits*, 46; F. Harrison, *The Virginia Carys*, 108–13; Kierner, "Dark and Dense," 185–217.

2. Joseph C. Cabell to Thomas Jefferson, Mar. 15, 1818, in Looney et al., eds, *PTJ-RS*, vol. 12:539; Wilson J. Cary to Virginia R. Cary, Dec. n.d., ("It is said"), Jan. 16, Feb. 21, and Dec. 9, 1822 ("celebrated"), CCFP, box 2, ASSCL-UVA; F. Harrison, *The Virginia Carys*, 112–13.

3. Wilson J. Cary to Virginia R. Cary, Jan. 16, 1822 (quotations), and Jan. 6, 1823, CCFP, box 2, ASSCL-UVA.

4. Wilson J. Cary to Virginia R. Cary, Jan. 9, 1822 ("good," "promising," and "without a sacrifice"), and Jan. 16, 1822 ("I really was"), CCFP, box 2, ASSCL-UVA.

5. Wilson J. Cary to Virginia R. Cary, Jan. 16, 1822, and Jan. 6, 1823 (quotations), CCFP, box 2, ASSCL-UVA.

6. Virginia R. Cary to Louisa Cocke, Jan. n.d., 1822, and Louisiana B. Cocke to Louisa Cocke, May 3, 1825, Wilson J. Cary to John H. Cocke, Feb. 3, 1822, JHCP, boxes 35, 36, and 43, ASSCL-UVA; W. J. Cary to Virginia R. Cary, Feb. 11, 1822, CCFP, box 2, ASSCL-UVA.

7. Wilson J. Cary to John H. Cocke, Jan. 29, 1818 ("Poor fellow"), and John H. Cocke, Jr., to J. H. Cocke, Jan. 22, 1819, JHCP, boxes 25 and 27, ASSCL-UVA; Wilson Miles Cary, Sr. to Thomas Jefferson, Oct. 10, 1792, and Jefferson to W. M. Cary, Sr., Nov. 4, 1792, in Boyd et al., eds., PTJ, vol. 24: 458-59, 574; Wilson J. Cary to Wilson M. Cary, Apr. 20, 1819, CCFP, box 2, ASSCL-UVA; Jefferson to W. J. Cary, May 4, 1819, in Looney et al., eds., PTJ-RS, vol. 14:267.

8. Thomas Cooper to Thomas Jefferson, Apr. 19, 1818, Jefferson to Cooper, Aug. 7, 1818, and Apr. 2, 1819, Jefferson to Francis Eppes, Jan. 1, 1819, Gerard E. Stack to Jefferson, Apr. 12, 1819, Jefferson to John H. Cocke, May 3, 1819, Cocke to Jefferson, May 4, 1819, Jefferson to Wilson J. Cary, May 4, 1819, Jefferson to Peter Laporte, May 6, 1819, in Looney et al., eds., PTJ-RS, vol. 12:648, vol. 13:233, vol. 14: 191-92, 223, 261 ("ablest"), 267, 268-69, 272-73, 274.

9. Thomas Jefferson to Peter Laporte, June 4, 1819, and Jefferson to Robert S. Garnett, June 18, 1819, in Looney et al., eds., PTJ-RS, vol. 14:382, 438; John B. Preston to John Preston, Oct. 4, 1819 ("to make some"), Preston and Radford Families Papers, box 2, ASSCL-UVA; Thomas W. Gilmer to Francis W. Gilmer, Nov. 23, 1819 ("That venerable"), GFN, box 2, ASSCL-UVA.

10. Thomas Jefferson to John H. Cocke, July 7, 1819, and Jefferson to John Wayles Eppes, July 9, 1819, in Looney et al., eds., PTJ-RS, vol. 14:511-12 ("a nucleus"), 525-26 ("It suffices" and "fatherly").

11. Gerard E. Stack to Thomas Jefferson, Aug. 13, 1819 ("situation"), and Jefferson to Stack, Aug. 29, 1819, in Looney et al., eds., PTJ-RS, vol. 14:606-7, 643-44.

12. John H. Cocke, Jr., to John H. Cocke, Aug. 27 ("feeble minded"), Sept. 10, and Sept. 25, 1819, JHCP, box 29, ASSCL-UVA; Hore B. Trist to Nicholas P. Trist, Sept. 24, 1819 ("best natured"), JFL website, ICJS; Gerard E. Stack to Thomas Jefferson, Nov. 21, 1819 ("quivering"), and Apr. 16, 1820, in Looney et al., eds., PTJ-RS, vol. 15:230-31, 546.

13. Hore B. Trist to Nicholas P. Trist, Oct. 19, 1819, NPTP, reel 1, MDLC.

14. Hore B. Trist to Nicholas P. Trist, Oct. 19, 1819 (quotations), NPTP, reel 1, MDLC; Alexander Garrett to John H. Cocke, Oct. 24, 1819, and J. H. Cocke to John H. Cocke, Jr., Nov. 5, 1819 [misfiled in 1829], JHCP, boxes 29 and 61, ASSCL-UVA.

15. Thomas Jefferson to Gerard E. Stack, Nov. 25, 1819, in Looney et al., eds., PTJ-RS, vol. 15:241-42; Jefferson to Thomas Cooper, July 4, 1820, FO-NA, http://founders .archives.gov/documents/Jefferson/98-01-02-1359.

16. Joseph C. Cabell to John H. Cocke, May 2, 1820 ("Stack's School," and "I tell"), and May 29, 1820 ("to the World"), JCCFP, box 14, ASSCL-UVA.

17. Thomas Ragland to Nicholas P. Trist, Mar. 18, 1820, Hore B. Trist to N. P. Trist, Mar. 23, 1820, and Ragland to N. P. Trist, July 15, 1820 (quotations), NPTP, folders 19 and 20, SHC-UNC; [Charlottesville] *Central Gazette*, Apr. 1, 1820.

18. Crackel, "Military Academy," 99–100; Pappas, *To the Point*, 79–95; Ragland, *Defence*, 8; Wagoner and McDonald, "Mr. Jefferson's Academy," 118–53; Watson, "Developing Republican Machines," 165–70.

19. [U.S. Congress], *American State Papers, Military Affairs*, vol. 2:6–7 ("Men of honor"), 12–13 ("Officers"), 20, 138; Dupuy, "Mutiny at West Point," 257–71; Pappas, *To the Point*, 113–24.

20. [U.S. Congress], *American State Papers: Military Affairs*, vol. 2: 6–8 ("monarchical," and "exercising"), 12; Pappas, *To the Point*, 125–26; Ragland, *Defence*, 8 ("discriminate").

21. Ragland, *Defence*, 2–8, ("grateful" on 2); W. M. C. Fairfax to Nicholas Trist, May 17, 1821, and Abram P. Maury to Trist, Aug. 12, 1821, NPTP, folders 23 and 24, SHC-UNC; Trist quoted in Mary J. Randolph to Ellen W. R. Coolidge, Oct. 2, 1825, EWRCP, box 1, ASSCL-UVA.

22. Ellen W. Randolph to Martha J. Randolph, Dec. 29, [1819], EWRCP, box 1, ASSCL-UVA.

23. Robert Saunders to Cocke, Apr. 9, 1819, and Merit M. Robinson to Cocke, July 29, 1819 ("from effeminacy"), JHCP, boxes 26 and 29, ASSCL-UVA.

24. Benjamin Payne to Cocke, Nov. 23, 1818 ("From the direction"), and Merit M. Robinson to Cocke, Jan. 17, 1820 ("You will find"), JHCP, boxes 27 and 30, ASSCL-UVA.

25. Joseph C. Cabell to John H. Cocke, Mar. 11, 1820, and Cocke to Cabell, Mar. 20, 1820 ("deplorable"), JCCFP, box 13, ASSCL-UVA; John Faulcon to Cocke, Mar. 21, 1820, John H. Cocke, Jr., to John H. Cocke, Mar. 17, 1820 ("pay no more"), JHCP, box 31, ASSCL-UVA.

26. Howard S. Poole to John B. Preston, July 12, 1820, Preston and Radford Families Papers, box 2, ASSCL-UVA.

27. Thomas Jefferson to Thomas Cooper, Aug. 14, 1820, FO-NA, http://founders .archives.gov/documents/Jefferson/98-01-02-1453; Hore B. Trist to Nicholas P. Trist, Aug. 17, 1820, NPTP, folder 20, SHC-UNC; [Charlottesville], *Central Gazette*, Aug. 25, 1820 ("peaceable"), Sept. 1, 1820 (Stack's notice), and Sept. 15, 1820; Stack, "Education," *Richmond Enquirer*, Aug. 21, 1821.

28. John H. Cocke, "Rules and Regulations of the Bremo Seminary," July 10, 1820, JHCP, box 30, ASSCL-UVA.

29. Thomas Mann Randolph to Joseph C. Cabell, Aug. 11, 1820, Thomas Mann Randolph Papers, one folder, DMRML-DU.

30. Thomas Mann Randolph to Joseph C. Cabell, Aug. 5, 1820, Thomas Mann Randolph Papers, one folder, DMRML-DU.

31. Wilson J. Cary to Virginia R. Cary, Dec. 25, 1821, CCFP, box 2, ASSCL-UVA.

32. Virginia R. Cary to Louisa Cocke, Mar. 15, May 28, and Aug. 30, 1822 ("I have been"), and May 13, 1823, JHCP, boxes 36, 37, and 38, ASSCL-UVA; Thomas Jefferson to Francis Bowman, Sept. 6, 1823, FO-NA, http://founders.archives.gov/documents/Jefferson/98-01-02-3743; F. Harrison, *The Virginia Carys*, 112–13.

33. Virginia J. R. Trist to Ellen W. R. Coolidge, Sept. 3, 1825, Martha J. Randolph to E. W. R. Coolidge, Sept. 18, 1825, and Mary Jefferson Randolph to E. W. R. Coolidge, Oct. 2, 1825, EWRCP, box 1, ASSCL-UVA; Mary E. Terrell to Louisa M. H. Cocke, Sept. 21, 1825, JHCP, box 44, ASSCL-UVA.

34. Virginia R. Cary to Louisa M. H. Cocke, Feb. n.d., 1826 ("sinful"), and Mar. 9, 1826 ("Awake"), JHCP, box 46, ASSCL-UVA.

35. Martha J. Randolph to Virginia J. R. Trist, Jan. 27, 1822, NPTP, folder 25, SHC-UNC; Virginia R. Cary to Louisa M. H. Cocke, Nov. 24, 1825 ("The searcher"), and Feb. 25, 1829 ("infidel"), JHCP, box 58, ASSCL-UVA; Mary Jefferson Randolph to Ellen W. R. Coolidge, Oct. 2, 1825, EWRCP, box 1, ASSCL-UVA; Kierner, *Martha Jefferson Randolph*, 164.

36. Virginia R. Cary to Louisa M. H. Cocke, Aug. 17, 1825 ("unveiled"), and Mar. 14, 1826 ("I cannot describe"), JHCP, boxes 44 and 46, ASSCL-UVA.

37. Cary, *Letters on Female Character*, v ("erring" and "*formed*"), 20–21, 49–50 ("I confess"), 197 ("Let all"); Varon, *We Mean to Be Counted*, 14–15, 41.

38. Cary, *Christian Parent's Assistant*, iii–iv ("young candidates"); Cary, *Letters on Female Character*, 133–34 (all other quotations).

39. Cary, *Letters on Female Character*, 172–74; Varon, *We Mean to Be Counted*, 41–42.

40. Walker Timberlake to John H. Cocke, May 31, 1824, JHCP, box 40, ASSCL-UVA; Wilson Miles Cary to Virginia R. Cary, c. Jan. 1825 ("the *dark*"), CCFP, box 2, ASSCL-UVA.

41. Martha J. Randolph to Ellen W. R. Coolidge, Oct. 13, 1825, EWRCP, box 1, ASSCL-UVA; John A. G. Davis to Dabney Carr Terrell, May 31, 1826 ("a very fine"), Terrell-Carr Papers, box 2, ASSCL-UVA.

42. John H. Cocke, Jr., to John H. Cocke, Jan. 26, 1823, JHCP, box 37, ASSCL-UVA.

43. Ferdinand S. Campbell to John H. Cocke, July 6, 1822 ("committed"), Thomas P. Hunt to J. H. Cocke, July 22, 1822 ("impudence"), and John H. Cocke, Jr., to J. H. Cocke. Jan. 26, 1823, JHCP, boxes 36 and 37, ASSCL-UVA.

44. Joseph C. Cabell to David Baillie Warden, Apr. 1, 1823, in Hoyt, ed., "Mr. Cabell, Mr. Warden, and the University," 1823," 352–53.

45. Thomas Jefferson to Thomas Cooper, Mar. 9, 1822 ("but a second"), and Jefferson to Cooper, Nov. 2, 1822 ("I look" and "article of"), and Jefferson to George Ticknor, July 16, 1823, FO-NA, http://founders.archives.gov/documents/Jefferson/98-01-02-2705, -3137, and -3639.

46. Brewer, "Beyond Education," 48–58

47. Thomas Jefferson, "Rockfish Gap Report," Aug. 4, 1818, in Looney et al., eds., *PTJ-RS*, vol. 13:209–22.

48. Thomas Jefferson to Trustees of the Lottery for East Tennessee College, May 6, 1810, in Looney et al., eds., *PTJ-RS*, vol. 2:365–66 ("Much observation" and "academical village"); Jefferson, "Report of Central College Visitors," Jan. 6, 1818, in Looney et al., eds., *PTJ-RS*, vol. 12:326–29; Wenger, "Thomas Jefferson," 366–68.

49. Thomas Jefferson to Trustees of the Lottery for East Tennessee College, May 6, 1810, and Jefferson to Wilson Cary Nicholas, Apr. 2, 1816, in Looney et al., eds., *PTJ-RS*, vol. 2:365–66 ("It would afford"), vol. 9:623–29 ("peace & quiet").

50. Thomas Jefferson to William Short, Oct. 31, 1819 ("selected society"), in Looney et al., eds., *PTJ-RS*, vol. 15:162–65; Jefferson to Maria Cosway, Oct. 24, 1822, FO-NA, http://founders.archives.gov/documents/Jefferson/98-01-02-3111; Wenger, "Thomas Jefferson," 371.

51. Thomas Jefferson, "Rockfish Gap Report," Aug. 4, 1818, in Looney et al., eds., *PTJ-RS*, vol. 13:209–22; Jefferson to Francis Eppes, Dec. 13, 1820 ("This will"), and Jefferson to George Ticknor, Apr. 7, 1825, FO-NA, http://founders.archives.gov/documents/Jefferson/98-01-02-1687, and -5119; D. Malone, Jefferson and His Time, vol. 6:418.

52. University of Virginia, *Enactments* (1825), 8–10; Jefferson to George Ticknor, Apr. 7, 1825, FO-NA, http://founders.archives.gov/documents/Jefferson/98-01-02-5119; Dunglison, "Autobiographical Ana," 29–30; Wall, "Students," 31–40; Wenger, "Thomas Jefferson," 369–70.

53. D. Malone, *Jefferson and His Time*, vol. 6:425.

54. [Charlottesville] *Central Gazette*, Mar. 7, 1825; Thomas Jefferson to Littleton W. Tazewell, Mar. 13, 1825 ("month" and "a very fine"), Jefferson to James Madison, Mar. 22, 1825, and Jefferson to George Ticknor, Apr. 7, 1825 ("come in"), FO-NA, http://founders.archives.gov/documents/Jefferson/98-01-02-5047, -5067, and -5119; John H. Cocke to J. H. Cocke, Jr., Mar. 21, 1825 ("University"), JHCP, box 43, ASSCL-UVA.

55. University of Virginia, *Catalogue*, 9; "A Student of the University of Virginia," and "A Professor of the University of Virginia," *Richmond Enquirer*, May 27, and 30, 1825; P. A. Bruce, *History of the University*, vol. 2:60–61, 68; Wagoner, "Honor and Dishonor," 167.

56. David Watson, "Miscellaneous Memoranda," 39–40, Mar. 1, 1825, DWP, box 3, MDLC; Robert Blow to George Blow, Nov. 9, 1826 ("There is no college"), and G. Blow to Richard Blow, Dec. 5, 1826, BLFP, ser. 2, box 21, SCSL-CWM; Wall, "Students," 43–45, 48–49.

57. Thomas Jefferson to Joseph C. Cabell, Jan. 25, 1822, and Jan. 23, 1824 ("the whole"), FO-NA, http://founders.archives.gov/documents/Jefferson/98-01-02-2614, and -4005; Henry St. George Tucker to Joseph C. Cabell, Mar. 22, 1825, JCCFP, box 17, ASSCL-UVA.

58. Thomas Jefferson to Robert Greenhow, July 24, 1825 (quotations), and Jefferson to Ellen W. R. Coolidge, Aug. 27, 1825, FO-NA, http://founders.archives.gov/documents/Jefferson/98-01-02-5403, and -5493.

59. Gessner Harrison to Peachey Harrison, Mar. 20, 1825, Apr. 18, 1825, May 26, 1825 ("I see") and May 30, 1825 ("the enmity"), and E. Tiffin Harrison to P. Harrison, Mar. 21, Apr. 9, and Apr. 30, 1825, THSP, box 1, ASSCL-UVA; G. Harrison to Ann Moore, n.d., c. Aug. 1825 ("This is to me"), and G. Harrison to Thomas Jones, n.d., c. 1826 ("to live"), and G. Harrison to E. T. Harrison, Nov. 28, 1827 ("arrogant pride"), THSP, box 2, ASSCL-UVA.

60. David Watson to John H. Cocke, Mar. 8, 1819, JHCP, box 28, ASSCL-UVA.

61. *The Virginian*, Jan. 30, 1824, quoted in Cameron, *Jefferson's Vision*, 118 ("The professors"); Report of Charles Bonnycastle et al., Apr. 3, 1826, CRP&R, ASSCL-UVA; P. A. Bruce, *History of the University*, vol. 1:182n; Wall, "Students," 125–28.

62. Thomas Jefferson to St. George Tucker, Sept. 15, 1795, in Boyd et al., eds., *PTJ*, vol. 28:468 ("It will relieve you"); N. Beverley Tucker to Frances Coalter, Oct. 16, 1804 ("got to"), BFP, box 1, ASSCL-UVA.

63. Edmund W. Hubard to Robert T. Hubard, n.d., c. Nov. 1825 ("Instead of"), HFP, ser. 1.4, folder 42, SHC-UNC; J. H. Rice, "Philodemus," in Rice, ed., *Virginia Evangelical and Literary Magazine*, vol. 9:203 ("more devoted to"); Mr. Hasler quoted in Dunglison, "College Instruction," 297 ("The locality").

64. Edmund W. Hubard to Robert T. Hubard, Mar. 5, 1825 ("as the Professors"), HFP, ser. 1.4, folder 41, SHC-UNC; Gessner Harrison to Peachey Harrison, Apr. 18, 1825 ("satirizes"), THSP, box 1, ASSCL-UVA; W. N. Shriver quoted in Faculty Minutes, Oct. 14, 1826 ("Sir"), JUEL website, UVA; G. Tucker, "Autobiography," 137; Wagoner, "Honor and Dishonor," 165.

65. G. Tucker, "Autobiography," 137.

66. Nicholas P. Trist to Thomas Jefferson, Sept. 18, 1825, FO-NA, http://founders.archives.gov/documents/Jefferson/98-01-02-5543; Report of Bonnycastle, Tucker, and Emmet, Apr. 3, 1826, CRP&R, box 1, ASSCL-UVA; Dunglison, "College Instruction," 294; Edmund W. Hubard to Robert T. Hubard, Nov. 8, 1825, HFP, ser. 1.5, folder 42, SHC-UNC.

67. Francis W. Gilmer to Chapman Johnson, Aug. 7, 1824 ("If the heat"), GFN, box 3, ASSCL-UVA; Gilmer to Thomas Jefferson, July 20, 1824, and Jefferson to Gilmer, Oct. 12, 1824, in R. B. Davis, ed., *Correspondence of Jefferson and Gilmer*, 93, and 106.

68. Faculty Minutes, June 18, ("abandoned" and "shamefully"), June 23, June 28 ("praying" and "unusual length"), and Aug. 6, 1825, JUEL website UVA. Seventy-eight students signed the June 28 petition.

69. Wilson Cary Nicholas to Thomas Jefferson, Jan. 25, 1819, in Looney et al., eds., *PTJ-RS*, vol. 13:602; Jefferson to George Ticknor, Apr. 7, 1825, and Jefferson to Robley Dunglison, June 29, 1825, FO-NA, http://founders.archives.gov/documents/Jefferson/98-01-02-5119 and -5343; P. A. Bruce, *History of the University*, vol. 2:65.

70. Thomas Watkins Leigh to Francis W. Gilmer, July 11, 1825, GFN, box 3, ASSCL-UVA; Maria J. Carr to Dabney S. Carr, July 20, 1825 ("the heat is more exces-

sive"), CCFP, box 2, ASSCL-UVA; Gessner Harrison to Ann Moore, n.d., c. Aug. 1825, THSP, box 2, ASSCL-UVA.

71. Edmund W. Hubard, "On the Manners and Customs of the Students of the University," Oct. 17, 1825, HFP, ser. 1.5, folder 42, SHC-UNC; Isaac A. Coles to John H. Cocke, Aug. 30, 1825, and Mary E. Terrell to Louisa M. H. Cocke, Sept. 21, 1825, JHCP, box 44, ASSCL-UVA.

72. Thomas Jefferson to William Short, Aug. 9, 1825, and Nicholas P. Trist to Jefferson, Sept. 18, 1825, FO-NA, http://founders.archives.gov/documents/Jefferson/98-01 -02-5455 and -5543; Faculty Minutes, Sept. 26, 1825, JUEL website, UVA.

73. G. Tucker, "Autobiography," 137–38 ("inviting"); Faculty Minutes, Sept. 20, 22, and 26, 1825, JUEL website, UVA; Martha J. Randolph to Ellen W. Randolph, Oct. 13, 1825, EWRCP, box 1, ASSCL-UVA; George Pierson to Albert Pierson, Nov. 2, 1825 ("to amuse"), Misc. Mss. 11898, University Archives, ASSCL-UVA; Tutwiler, *Address*, 10.

74. Faculty Minutes, Oct. 6, and 14, 1825, JUEL website, UVA; Martha J. Randolph to Ellen W. Randolph, Oct. 13, 1825, EWRCP, box 1, ASSCL-UVA; Gessner Harrison to Peachey Harrison, Oct. 28, 1825, THSP, box 1, ASSCL-UVA.

75. G. Tucker, "Autobiography," 137–38; Faculty Minutes, Oct. 5, 1825, JUEL website, UVA; George Pierson to Albert Pierson, Nov. 2, 1825 ("They gave"), Misc. Mss. 11897, University Archives, ASSCL-UVA.

76. Testimony of Philip Clayton, John George, and Philip Slaughter in Faculty Minutes, Oct. 5, 1825, JUEL website UVA. For standard accounts that omit the servant, see Bowman and Santos, *Rot, Riot, and Rebellion*, 33–38; D. Malone, *Jefferson and His Time*, vol. 6:465–66; Pace, *Halls of Honor*, 87; Wall, "Students," 156.

77. Bacon, "Autobiography," in Pierson, ed., *Jefferson at Monticello*, 105; Martin and Von Daacke, *President's Commission on Slavery*, 16–28, John Neilson quoted on 17 ("our workmen"); Oast, *Institutional Slavery*, 175–76; Stanton, *Those Who Labor*, 140.

78. Alexander Garrett to John H. Cocke, Apr. 7, and 8, 1825, JHCP, box 43, ASSCL-UVA; Addis, *Jefferson's Vision*, 121–23; Martin and Von Daacke, *President's Commission on Slavery*, 18–19, 25; Oast, *Institutional Slavery*, 142, 174, 184–86; Wall, "Students," 69.

79. Student quoted in Faculty Minutes, June 26, 1828, JUEL website, UVA; Martin and Von Daacke, *President's Commission on Slavery*, 24–26; Oast, *Institutional Slavery*, 182–89.

80. Faculty Minutes, June 26, 1828, JUEL website, UVA.

81. Faculty Minutes, June 26, and 28, 1828, JUEL website, UVA.

82. Faculty Minutes, Sept. 20, 1826, JUEL website, UVA.

83. Gessner Harrison to Peachey Harrison, Nov. 28, 1827 ("our interest"), and G. Harrison to Edward Tiffin Harrison, Dec. 24, 1827 ("much difficulty"), THSP,

box 2, ASSCL-UVA; P. A. Bruce, *History of the University*, vol. 2:111; Oast, *Institutional Slavery*, 188–89.

84. Edgar Mason et al. to the Faculty of the University, n.d., c. Oct. 3, 1825 (quotation), CRP&R, ASSCL-UVA; Faculty Minutes, Oct. 3, and 5, 1825, JUEL website, UVA; Gessner Harrison to Peachey Harrison, Oct. 28, 1825, THSP, box 1, ASSCL-UVA.

85. Edgar Mason et al., to the Faculty of the University, n.d., c. Oct. 3, 1825 (quotations), CRP&R, ASSCL-UVA.

86. Board of Visitors Minutes, Oct. 4, 1825, FO-NA, http://founders.archives.gov/documents/Jefferson/98-01-02-5569; M. B. Smith, *First Forty Years*, 229–30; G. Tucker, *Life of Thomas Jefferson*, vol. 2:480; Tutwiler, *Address*, 10 ("saying").

87. Faculty Minutes, Oct. 5–6, 1825, JUEL website, UVA; Board of Visitors Minutes, Oct. 6–7, 1825, and Thomas Jefferson to Joseph Coolidge, Oct. 13, 1825, FO-NA, http://founders.archives.gov/documents/Jefferson/98-01-02-5569, and -5596; Edmund W. Hubard to Robert T. Hubard, Oct. 17, 1825, HFP, ser. 1.5, folder 42, SHC-UNC.

88. Faculty Minutes, Oct. 5, 1825, JUEL website, UVA; Martha J. Randolph to Ellen W. R. Coolidge, Oct. 13, 1825, EWRCP, box 1, ASSCL-UVA; D. Malone, *Jefferson and His Time*, vol. 6:468; G. Tucker, *Life of Thomas Jefferson*, vol. 2:481 ("The shock").

89. John H. Cocke to Joseph C. Cabell, Oct. 13, 1825, JCCFP, box 18, ASSCL-UVA; Martha J. Randolph to Ellen W. R. Coolidge, Nov. 26, 1826, EWRCP, box 1, ASSCL-UVA.

90. Virginia R. Cary to Louisa M. H. Cocke, Mar. 9, 1826, and L. M. H. Cocke to John H. Cocke, Dec. 28, 1826, JHCP, box 46, ASSCL-UVA.

91. Wilson Miles Cary to Virginia R. Cary, Jan. 1, 1828, CCFP, box 2, ASSCL-UVA.

92. F. Harrison, *The Virginia Carys*, 115–16; J. Lewis, *Pursuit of Happiness*, 125–26, Peggy Nicholas quoted on 126 ("might be").

93. Board of Visitor Minutes, Oct. 4, and 6, 1825, and Thomas Jefferson to James Madison, Oct. 18, 1825 ("somewhat"), FO-NA, http://founders.archives.gov/documents/Jefferson/98-01-02-5569, and -5602; Faculty Minutes, Oct. 5, and 14, 1825, JUEL website, UVA; Thomas H. Key and George Long to James Madison, Oct. 6, 1825, in Mattern et al., eds., *PJM-RS*, vol. 3:612; *Martha Jefferson Randolph* to Ellen W. R. Coolidge, Oct. 13, 1825, EWRCP, box 1, ASSCL-UVA.

94. St. George Tucker Coalter to St. George Tucker, Oct. 14, 1825 ("the young men"), BFP, box 1, ASSCL-UVA; George Blow to Richard Blow, Dec. 5, 1826 ("run wild"), BLFP, ser. 2, box 33G, SCSL-CWM; Robert B. Taylor to John H. Cocke, Oct. 16, 1825 and Mar. 10, 1826, J. H. Cocke to Louisa M. H. Cocke, Jan. 18, 1826, J. H. Cocke to Charles Cocke, Jan. 23, 1826, JHCP, boxes 45 and 46, ASSCL-UVA.

95. John Holt Rice, "University of Virginia," and "Literary Fund of Virginia," in

Rice, ed., *Virginia Evangelical and Literary Magazine*, vol. 3:388, 5:239; Tutwiler, *Address*, 6; W. S. White, *Rev. William S. White*, 105, 122 (farmer quoted); George Pierson to Albert Pierson, Nov. 2, 1825 ("I regard"), Misc. Mss. 11897, University Archives, ASSCL-UVA.

96. "University," and "Citizen of Virginia," *Richmond Enquirer*, Oct. 11, and Nov. 15, 1825.

97. Thomas Jefferson to Joseph Coolidge, Oct. 13, 1825, Jefferson to William Short, Oct. 14, 1825, Jefferson to James W. Wallace, Oct. 26, 1825, and Jefferson to Short, Nov. 15, 1825, FO-NA, http://founders.archives.gov/documents/Jefferson/98-01 -02-5596, -5598, -5620, and -5662; Randolph Harrison to John H. Cocke, Oct. 20, 1825 ("Poor old"), JHCP, box 45, ASSCL-UVA.

98. Mary J. Randolph to Ellen W. R. Coolidge, Apr. 16, 1826, EWRCP, box 2, ASSCL-UVA; G. Tucker, *Life of Thomas Jefferson*, vol. 2:477; Tutwiler, *Address*, 8-9.

99. Philip St. George Cocke to John H. Cocke, Oct. 12, 1825 ("Everything"), JHCP, box 45, ASSCL-UVA.

10. ENDS

1. Sloan, *Principle and Interest*, 221; Thomas Jefferson to Joseph C. Cabell, Jan. 20, 1826, FO-NA, http://founders.archives.gov/documents/Jefferson/98-01-02 -5843; Martha J. Randolph to Ellen W. R. Coolidge, Apr. 5, 1826, EWRCP, box 2, ASSCL-UVA.

2. Thomas Jefferson to Trustees for East Tennessee College, May 6, 1810, *PTJ-RS*, vol. 2:365-66; Jefferson, "Thoughts on Lotteries," Jan. 20, 1826, FO-NA, http:// founders.archives.gov/documents/Jefferson/98-01-02-5845; John H. Cocke to Joseph C. Cabell, Feb. 15, 1826, JCCFP, box 18, ASSCL-UVA.

3. Joseph C. Cabell to Thomas Jefferson, Jan. 30, 1826, and Thomas J. Randolph to Thomas Jefferson, Feb. 3, 1826, FO-NA, http://founders.archives.gov/ documents/Jefferson/98-01-02-5866, and -5875; John A. G. Davis to Dabney Carr Terrell, Feb. 13, 1826 ("surprise" and "You cannot"), Terrell-Carr Papers, box 2, ASSCL-UVA.

4. Hetty Carr to Dabney S Carr, Feb. 1, 1826 ("If he does not"), CCFP, box 2, ASSCL-UVA; Thomas Jefferson to T. J. Randolph, Feb. 8, 1826 ("I see," and "dear & beloved"), and Feb. 11, 1826 ("Heaven seems"), FO-NA, http://founders.archives .gov/documents/Jefferson/98-01-02-5893, and -5900; D. Malone, *Jefferson and His Time*, vol. 6:476.

5. "Mr. Jefferson," *Richmond Enquirer*, Feb. 11, 1826; Jane Margaret Carr to Dabney S. Carr, Feb. 27, 1826 ("covered his face"), and Hetty Carr to D. S. Carr, Mar. 13, 1826 ("Mr. Jefferson"), CCFP, box 2, ASSCL-UVA; D. Malone, *Jefferson and His Time*, vol. 6:475-76, 479.

6. T. Jefferson Randolph to Thomas Jefferson, Apr. 3, 1826, FO-NA, http://founders

.archives.gov/documents/Jefferson/98-01-02-6010; Joseph C. Cabell to John H. Cocke, Apr. 6, and July 1, 1826, JCCFP, box 18, ASSCL-UVA.

7. Hetty Carr to Dabney S. Carr, Apr. 4, and Apr. 11, 1826 ("nothing doing"), CCFP, box 2, ASSCL-UVA; Martha J. Randolph to E. W. R. Coolidge, Apr. 5, 1826, ("He said") EWRCP, box 2, ASSCL-UVA; Gordon-Reed and Onuf, *Most Blessed of Patriarchs,* 19–20.

8. Thomas Jefferson to Joseph C. Cabell, Feb. 4, 1826, and Jefferson to James Madison, Feb. 17, 1826, FO-NA, http://founders.archives.gov/documents/ Jefferson/98-01-02-5876, and -5912.

9. John H. Cocke to Cabell, Feb. 6, 1826, JCCFP, box 18, ASSCL-UVA; Robert B. Taylor to Cocke, Feb. 8, 1825, JHCP, box 46, ASSCL-UVA.

10. John B. Richeson to Thomas Jefferson, Dec. 10, 1825, and Jefferson to Richeson, Dec. 14, 1825, FO-NA, http://founders.archives.gov/documents/Jefferson/98-01 -02-5738, and -5744.

11. Chapman Johnson to John H. Cocke, Oct. 3, 1824, JHCP, box 42, ASSCL-UVA; Johnson to Thomas Jefferson, Apr. 23, 1825, FO-NA, http://founders.archives .gov/documents/Jefferson/98-01-02-5162; G. Tucker, "Autobiography," 141–43.

12. Robert B. Taylor to Cocke, n.d. but filed as June 1825, JHCP, box 43, ASSCL-UVA.

13. John H. Cocke to Joseph C. Cabell, Feb. 15, 1826, and William H. Cabell to J. C. Cabell, Apr. 1, 1826, JCCFP, box 18, ASSCL-UVA; John A. G. Davis to Dabney Carr Terrell, Apr. 6, 1826, Terrell-Carr Papers, box 2, ASSCL-UVA.

14. Thomas Jefferson to Henry Jackson, Jan. 31, 1816, Looney et al., eds., *PTJ-RS,* vol. 9:417; Jefferson to James Madison, Apr. 3, 1826, FO-NA, http://founders.archives .gov/documents/Madison/99-02-02-0651; Hetty Carr to Dabney S. Carr, Apr. 4, 1826, CCFP, box 2, ASSCL-UVA; John A. G. Davis to Dabney Carr Terrell, Apr. 6, 1826, Terrell-Carr Papers, box 2, ASSCL-UVA; Looney et al., eds., *PTJ-RS,* vol. 9:482n.

15. Board of Visitors, minutes, Apr. 3–7, 1826, and Thomas Jefferson to John Tayloe Lomax, Apr. 12, 1826, FO-NA, http://founders.archives.gov/documents/ Jefferson/98-01-02-6013, and -6040; John A. G. Davis to Dabney Carr Terrell, Apr. 6, 1826, Terrell-Carr Papers, box 2, ASSCL-UVA; Lomax to Cabell, Apr. 22, 1826, JCCFP, box 18, ASSCL-UVA.

16. Thomas Jefferson to John P. Emmet, Apr. 27, 1826, Emmet to Jefferson, Apr. 28, 1826, Jefferson to Emmet, May 2, 1826, Jefferson to James Madison, May 3, 1826, and Madison to Jefferson, May 6, 1826, FO-NA, http://founders.archives.gov/ documents/Jefferson/98-01-02-6075, -6077, -6087, -6091, and -6100.

17. Robert Blow to George Blow, Mar. 4, 1826, BLFP, ser. 2, box 26, folder 5, SCSL-CWM; Gessner Harrison to Thomas Jones, n.d., c. Mar. 1826, THSP, box 2, ASSCL-UVA.

18. Thomas Jefferson to James Madison, Feb. 17, 1826, FO-NA, http://founders .archives.gov/documents/Jefferson/98-01-02-5912; P. A. Bruce, *History of the*

University, vol. 2:71–73; Wagoner, "Honor and Dishonor," 170; Wall, "Students," 58–59.

19. Baker, *Richmond Theater Fire*, 6–7, 29; Bondurant, *Poe's Richmond*, 17–19; Silverman, *Edgar A. Poe*, 1–28; Thomas and Jackson, eds., *Poe Log*, 3–16, 47–62, John Allan quoted on 61.

20. Bondurant, *Poe's Richmond*, 20; Silverman, *Edgar A. Poe*, 29–31; Stovall, "Edgar Poe," 299, 305–6 ("Rowdy"), 310; Thomas and Jackson, eds., *Poe Log*, 67–69, 79–80, Miles George quoted on 69; Wilson, "Personality of Poe," 136–37.

21. Thomas and Jackson, eds., *Poe Log*, 68 (George Long quoted), 75–76.

22. Edmund W. Hubard to Robert T. Hubard, Nov. 8, 1825 ("If you dispute"), HFP, ser. 1.5, folder 42, SHC-UNC; Wall, "Students," 90–94.

23. Faculty Minutes, May 24, 1826, JUEL website, UVA; Edgar Allan Poe to John Allan, May 25, 1826, in Ostrom, ed., *Letters of Edgar Allan Poe*, vol. 1:5; William Cunningham to his mother, May 29, 1826 ("Jugs"), BFP, box 30, SCSL-CWM.

24. Richard Blow to Robert Blow, June 3, 1826 ("immediately"), and Robert Blow to George Blow, June 19, 1826, BFP, box 26, SCSL-CWM.

25. Faculty Minutes, May 24–25, and Nov. 10, 13, 1826, JUEL website, UVA; William Cunningham to his mother, May 29, 1826 (Tucker quoted), BFP, box 30, SCSL-CWM.

26. Faculty Minutes, May 27, and Sept. 19, 1826, JUEL website, UVA; Edgar Allan Poe to John Allan, Sept. 21, 1826 (all quotations), in Ostrom, *Letters of Edgar Allan Poe*, vol. 1:6; Thomas and Jackson, eds., *Poe Log*, 71–73.

27. William Goodaire to Wirt Robinson, Aug. 13, 1826 ("drum" and "rang"), Misc. Mss. 11912, University Archive, ASSCL-UVA; P. A. Bruce, *History of the University*, vol. 2:274–75, 290; Wall, "Students," 2, 75–78, John Armistead Carter quoted on 76 ("Here nothing").

28. Mary E. Terrell to Louisa Cocke, Apr. 3, 1826 ("generally" and "frightened"), and Sept. 22, 1826 ("My dear friend"), JHCP, boxes 47 and 48, ASSCL-UVA.

29. Report by Professors Key, Long, and Blaetterman, Apr. 3, 1826 ("in a state"), in CRP&R, box 1, ASSCL-UVA; Faculty Minutes, Oct. 30, 1826, JUEL website, UVA; Cornelia J. Randolph to Ellen W. R. Coolidge, Oct. 31, 1825, and Nov. 24, 1825, EWRCP, box 1, ASSCL-UVA; *Richmond Enquirer*, Nov. 8, 1825.

30. Faculty Minutes, Feb. 14, 1826, JUEL website, UVA; John H. Cocke to Joseph C. Cabell, Feb. 15, 1826, and George Tucker to Cabell, Feb. 25, 1826, JCCFP, box 18, ASSCL-UVA.

31. Virginia J. R. Trist to Ellen W. R. Coolidge, Sept. 3, 1825, Martha J. Randolph to Coolidge, Sept. 18, 1825 ("extremely annoying"), and Cornelia J. Randolph to Coolidge, Oct. 31, 1825 ("When she"), EWRCP, box 1, ASSCL-UVA.

32. Mary E. Terrell to Louisa Cocke, May 29, and June 20, 1826, JHCP, box 47, ASSCL-UVA.

33. Mary E. Terrell to Louisa Cocke, May 29, 1826, JHCP, box 47, ASSCL-UVA.

34. Faculty Minutes, Feb. 28, and Mar. 15, 1826 ("attempted"), JUEL website, UVA; Cornelia J. Randolph to Ellen W. R. Coolidge, Mar. 18, 1826, EWRCP, box 2, ASSCL-UVA.

35. Report of Professors Key, Long, and Blaetterman, Apr. 3, 1826, CRP&R, box 1, ASSCL-UVA; Testimony of George W. Spotswood, Dec. 21, 1826 ("They were so numerous"), and Edwin Conway in Faculty Minutes, Dec. 22, 1826, JUEL website, UVA; Dunglison, "College Instruction," 301; Martin and Von Daacke, *President's Commission on Slavery*, 26–27.

36. Thomas Jefferson to Arthur S. Brockenbrough, Jan. 3, 1826, and Board of Visitors Minutes, Apr. 3–7, 1826, FO-NA, http://founders.archives.gov/documents/Jefferson/98-01-02-5801, and -6013; Gessner Harrison to Thomas Jones, n.d., c. Mar. 1826, THSP, box 2, ASSCL-UVA.

37. Gessner Harrison to Thomas Jones, n.d., c. June 1826 ("headlong," "devilish," and "abandon"), and G. Harrison to Peachey Harrison, n.d., c. July 1826 ("unchaste"), THSP, box 2, ASSCL-UVA.

38. Faculty Minutes, Feb. 28, 1826, JUEL website UVA; Report of Professors Bonnycastle, Tucker, and Emmet, Apr. 3, 1826 (quotations), CRP&R, box 1, ASSCL-UVA.

39. Board of Visitors Minutes, Apr. 3–7, 1826, Thomas Jefferson to Arthur S. Brockenbrough, Apr. 7, 1826, and Brockenbrough to Jefferson, Apr. 12, 1826, FO-NA, http://founders.archives.gov/documents/Jefferson/98-01-02-6013, -6019, and -6037; Faculty Minutes, May 9–11, 13, 1826, JUEL website, UVA; Law Orders Book, 1822–1831, 212 (May 11, 1826), Record Vault, Clerk's Office, Albemarle County Courthouse, Charlottesville; Alexander Garrett to John H. Cocke, May 20, 1826, JHCP, box 47, ASSCL-UVA; Edgar Allan Poe to John Allan, May 25, 1826, Ostrom, ed., *Letters of Edgar Allan Poe*, vol. 1:4; Wall, "Students," 162–63.

40. Cornelia J. Randolph to Ellen W. R. Coolidge, July 13, 1825, and Martha J. Randolph to Joseph Coolidge, Jr., Sept. 16 (88 drops), Oct. 13 (100 drops), and Nov. 26, 1825, and Apr. 5, 1826, EWRCP, box 2, ASSCL-UVA; Thomas Jefferson to Joseph C. Cabell, Feb. 14, 1826, FO-NA, http://founders.archives.gov/documents/Jefferson/98-01-02-5904; Gordon-Reed and Onuf, *Most Blessed of Patriarchs*, 23–24.

41. Mary J. Randolph to Ellen W. Randolph, June 6, 1826, EWRCP, box 2, ASSCL-UVA; Edmund W. Hubard to Robert T. Hubard, June 16, 1826, HFP, ser. 1.5, folder 42, SHC-UNC.

42. Eastman, "Transatlantic Celebrity," 3; J. Ellis, *After the Revolution*, 8–12, 19–21, 24–30.

43. Alexander Garrett to John H. Cocke, May 20, 1826, JHCP, box 47, ASSCL-UVA; Arthur S. Brockenbrough to Thomas Jefferson, May 20, 1826, FO-NA, http://founders.archives.gov/documents/Jefferson/98-01-02-6123; *Richmond Enquirer,*

May 26, 1826 ("Myriads"); Jane N. Randolph to Cary Ann N. Smith, June 27, 1826, JFP website, ICJS.

44. T. Jefferson Randolph, in Hayes, ed., *Jefferson in His Own Time*, 166–68; Henry Lee, in M. D. Peterson, ed., *Visitors to Monticello*, 109–10 ("expressed"); Burstein, *Jefferson's Secrets*, 23, 28; Dunglison, "Autobiographical Ana," 32–33; D. Malone, *Jefferson and His Time*, vol. 6:496–97.

45. Nicholas P. Trist to Joseph Coolidge, Jr., July 4, 1826, EWRCP, box 2, ASSCL-UVA; T. Jefferson Randolph to Dabney S. Carr, July 11, 1826, CCFP, box 2, ASSCL-UVA; T. J. Randolph, in Hayes, ed., *Jefferson in His Own Time*, 166–68; Dunglison, "Autobiographical Ana," 32–33; D. Malone, *Jefferson and His Time*, vol. 6:496–97.

46. Alexander Garrett to Evelina Bolling Garrett, July 4, 1826, T. Jefferson Randolph to Dabney S. Carr, July 11, 1826 ("more ferocious"), and Andrew K. Smith, memoir, Oct. 15, 1875, JFP website, ICJS; Louise McIntire to Jane Margaret Carr, July 6, 1826, CCFP, box 2, ASSCL-UVA; D. Crawford, *Twilight at Monticello*, 242–45; D. Malone, *Jefferson and His Time*, vol. 6:498.

47. Henry H. Worthington to Reuben B. Hicks, July 5, 1826, and Andrew K. Smith, memoir, Oct. 15, 1875 ("Much time" and "were sorely"), JFP website, ICJS; Juliet Minor Gilmer to Emma W. Gilmer, July 19, 1819, GFN, box 4, ASSCL-UVA; "From the Central Gazette," *Richmond Enquirer*, July 14, 1826; G. Tucker, *Life of Jefferson*, vol. 2:496.

48. "Virginius," [Charlottesville] *Central Gazette*, July 15, 1826.

49. "Notes on Student Examinations," Dec. 20–27 ("never heard"), 1826; Thomas and Jackson, *Poe Log*, 73–76, William Wertenbaker quoted on 76 ("He was earnest").

50. Edward G. Crump to Edgar A. Poe, Mar. 25, 1827, in Thomas and Jackson, eds., *Poe Log*, 78; Poe to John Allan, Feb. 4, 1829, and Jan. 3, 1831, in Ostrom, ed., *Letters of Edgar Allan Poe*, vol. 1:14 ("taunts" and "infamous conduct"), 39–41; Silverman, *Edgar A. Poe*, 33–34.

51. Edgar A. Poe to John Allan, Mar. 19, 1827, in Ostrom, ed., *Letters of Edgar Allan Poe*, vol. 1:7–8; Silverman, *Edgar A. Poe*, 34–36; Thomas and Jackson, eds., *Poe Log*, 77.

52. Edgar A. Poe to John Allan, Mar. 19, and Mar. 20, 1827, and Jan. 3, 1831, in Ostrom, ed., *Letters of Edgar Allan Poe*, vol. 1:7–8 ("I have"), 39–42; Silverman, *Edgar A. Poe*, 38–42.

53. Edgar A. Poe to John Allan, Jan. 3, 1831, in Ostrom, ed., *Letters of Edgar Allan Poe*, vol. 1:41 ("their professions"); Bruce, *Violence and Culture*, 232–39; Hubert, "Southern Element," 200–210; O'Brien, *Conjectures of Order*, vol. 2:713–18; Silverman, *Edgar A. Poe*, 31–32, 204–7.

54. Edgar A. Poe, "Review," in Thompson, ed., *Edgar Allan Poe*, 565 ("No respect"); P. A. Bruce, *History of the University*, vol. 3:208–9; Stovall, "Edgar Poe,"

312–13; Whalen, *Edgar Allan Poe and the Masses*, 29–30; Wilson, "Personality of Poe," 133, 139.

55. Thomas and Jackson, eds., *Poe Log*, 843–46, Poe quoted on 846 ("*Lord help*").

56. Ottway B. Barraud to John H. Cocke, July 25, 1826, JHCP, box 47, ASSCL-UVA.

57. Frank Carr to John H. Cocke, July 9, 1826, J. H. Cocke to Louisa Cocke, Oct. 4, 1826, and William Meade to J. H. Cocke, May 29, 1827, JHCP, boxes 47, 48, and 51, ASSCL-UVA.

58. Mary Rawlings, ed., *Early Charlottesville*, 102–3; Woods, *History of Albemarle County*, 170.

59. Robert S. Jones to John H. Cocke, Jan. 27, 1827 ("I have gotten"), and Feb. 27, 1827, JHCP, box 49, ASSCL-UVA.

60. Warner W. Minor to John H. Cocke, Oct. n.d., 1826, JHCP, box 48, ASSCL-UVA; Board of Visitor Minutes, Dec. 16, 1826 (quotations), JUEL website, UVA; P. A. Bruce, *History of the University*, vol. 2:246–50; Dunglison, "College Instruction," 300–301.

61. Board of Visitor Minutes, Dec. 16, 1826, JUEL website, UVA; Dunglison, "College Instruction," 298–300; Silverman, *Edgar A. Poe*, 32–33.

62. Faculty Minutes, Feb. 3, 1827, JUEL website, UVA; Philip St. George Cocke to John H. Cocke, Feb. 5 ("Things" and "I have not"), and Feb. 18, 1827, and Alexander Garrett to J. H. Cocke, Mar. 14, 1827, JHCP, box 50, ASSCL-UVA; Wall, "Students," 165.

63. Faculty Minutes, May 10, 1827, JUEL website, UVA; Gessner Harrison to E. Tiffin Harrison, n.d., c. 1827, THSP, box 2, ASSCL-UVA.

64. Philip St. George Cocke to John H. Cocke, June 26, 1827, JHCP, box 51, ASSCL-UVA; Faculty Minutes, June 15, 1827, JUEL website, UVA.

65. Robert Blow to Richard Blow, Mar. 5, 1828 ("We are all"), BLFP, ser. 2, box 26, SCSL-CWM; W. H Mayall to William M. Radford, June 1, 1828 ("General Cocke"), Preston and Radford Family Papers, box 2, ASSCL-UVA; Wall, "Students," 73–74, 116, 165–66.

66. James Breckinridge to the Board of Visitors, n.d., c. 1828, Misc. Mss. 11952, University Archives, ASSCL-UVA; Nicholas P. Trist to John H. Cocke, Sept. 24, 1828, and William Short to Cocke, July 1, 1829 ("How different"), JHCP, boxes 56 and 60, ASSCL-UVA; Arthur Brockenbrough, "Subjects for Consideration," June 4, 1829 [misdated as Dec. 1828] ("rather"), JHCP, box 57, ASSCL-UVA; P. A. Bruce, *History of the University*, vol. 2:71–73.

67. James Breckinridge to the Board of Visitors, n.d., c. 1828, Misc. Mss. 11952, University Archives, ASSCL-UVA; Alexander Garrett to John H. Cocke, July 1, 1828 (quotations), and William Short to Cocke, Sept. 12, 1828), JHCP, boxes 55 and 56, ASSCL-UVA.

68. George W. Spotswood to James Madison, Nov. 29, 1825, Stagg et al., eds., *PJM-RS*, vol. 3:640–42; Sarah Carter Gray to Joseph C. Cabell, Dec. 2, 1826 ("minds"),

JCCFP, box 18, ASSCL-UVA; John B. Richeson to John H. Cocke, Jan. 9, 1827, JHCP, box 49, ASSCL-UVA; P. A. Bruce, *History of the University*, vol. 2:221–23; Frank, "Academical Village," 34–35.

69. Warner W. Minor to John H. Cocke, Oct. n.d., 1826, JHCP, box 48, ASSCL-UVA; P. A. Bruce, *History of the University*, vol. 2:79; Frank, "Academical Village," 31–56.

70. Warner W. Minor and Edwin Conway to Board of Visitors, Oct. 1, 1826, FO-NA, http://founders.archives.gov/documents/Madison/99-02-02-0750; George W. Spotswood testimony, Dec. 21, 1826 ("treat"), JUEL website, UVA; Report of Professors Key, Long, and Blaetterman, Apr. 3, 1826, CRP&R, box 1, ASSCL-UVA; Minor to John Hartwell Cocke, Oct. n.d., 1826, JHCP, box 48, ASSCL-UVA; Faculty Minutes, Feb. 5, 1827, JUEL website, UVA.

71. John H. Cocke to Joseph C. Cabell, Feb. 15, 1826, JCCFP, box 18, ASSCL-UVA; Report of Professors Key, Long, and Blaetterman, Apr. 3, 1826, CRP&R, box 1, ASSCL-UVA; Warner W. Minor to Cocke, Oct. n.d., 1826, JHCP, box 48, ASSCL-UVA.

72. George W. Spotswood to James Madison, Nov. 29, 1825, in Stagg et al., eds., *PJM-RS*, vol. 3:640–42; Board of Visitors, enactments, Dec. 16, 1826, and Nicholas P. Trist to James Madison, Jan. 8, 1827, FO-NA, http://founders.archives.gov/documents/Madison/99-02-02-0837, and -0862.

73. Sarah Carter Gray to James Madison, Nov. 15, 1825 ("galling consciousness"), and Gray to John H. Cocke, Dec. 20, 1826, JHCP, boxes 45 and 49, ASSCL-UVA; Gray to Joseph C. Cabell, Dec. 2, 1826 ("cruel sentence" and "All these"), JCCFP, box 18, ASSCL-UVA.

74. John Tayloe Lomax to John H. Cocke, Dec. 18, 1826, and Nicholas P. Trist to Cocke, Nov. 26, 1827 ("To drive"), JHCP, boxes 49 and 53, ASSCL-UVA; Trist to James Madison, Jan. 8, 1827 ("While"), FO-NA, http://founders.archives.gov/documents/Madison/99-02-02-0862.

75. John H. Cocke to Joseph C. Cabell, May 24 ("old offenders"), and Nov. 8, 1827, and John B. Richeson to Cabell, June 9, 1827, JCCFP, box 19, ASSCL-UVA; Faculty Minutes, Sept. 15, and 16, and Dec. 31, 1828, and Journal of the Chairman, Oct. 8, 1828, JUEL website, UVA; W. W. Minor, "Estimate of Expenses," n.d., c. Dec. 1828, JHCP, box 57, ASSCL-UVA.

76. Journal of the Chairman, Dec. 19–23, 1828, and Faculty Meetings, Dec. 19–20, and 23, 1828, JUEL website, ASSCL-UVA; Arthur S. Brockenbrough to John H. Cocke, Dec. 22, 1828, JHCP, box 57, ASSCL-UVA; Frank, "It Took an Academical Village," 40 (Spotswood quoted).

77. Chapman Johnson to John H. Cocke, Oct. 5, 1827, JHCP, box 52, ASSCL-UVA; Cocke to Joseph C. Cabell, July 27, 1827 ("I must"), July 29 ("preposterous"), and Sept. 19, 1828, and Cabell to Cocke, Aug. 1, and Nov. 4, 1828 ("I see"), JHCFP, boxes 19 and 20, ASSCL-UVA.

78. John H. Cocke to Nicholas Cobbs, Apr. 5, 1828 ("original error"), J. H. Cocke to Louisa M. H. Cocke, Apr. 29, 1828, J. H. Cocke to James M. Garnett, Oct. 16, 1828, and J. H. Cocke, "Proposals of a New School for Boys," n.d., but c. Dec. 1828, JHCP, box 57, ASSCL-UVA.

79. John H. Cocke to James M. Garnett, Oct. 16, 1828 ("secure privacy"), and Cocke, "Proposals of a New School for Boys," undated, but c. Dec. 1828 ("religious instruction," "in a gentle," and "Boys will be"), JHCP, boxes 56 and 57, ASSCL-UVA; [Cocke and William Maxwell], "A Friend of Boys," *Norfolk Herald*, Mar. 25, 1829 ("before," "constant," and "very imperfect").

80. John H. Cocke, "Proposals of a New School for Boys," n.d., c. Dec. 1828, and Mary E. Terrell to Louisa M. H. Cocke, Apr. 30, 1829, JHCP, boxes 57 and 59, ASSCL-UVA.

81. John H. Cocke to T. Jefferson Randolph, Nov. 1, and Dec. 20, 1828, JHCP, box 57, ASSCL-UVA; Cocke and William Maxwell to Joseph C. Cabell, Mar. 30, 1829, JCCFP, box 21, ASSCL-UVA.

82. John H. Cocke, "Proposals of a New School for Boys," n.d., c. Dec. 1828, Joseph Nimmo to Cocke, May 7, 1829, Jesse Armistead to Louisa M. H. Cocke, May 29, 1829, and Robert B. Patton to Cocke, May 7, and July 10, 1829, JHCP, boxes 57, 59, and 60, ASSCL-UVA; Cocke and William Maxwell to Joseph C. Cabell, Mar. 30, 1829, JCCP, box 21, ASSCL-UVA.

83. Chapman Johnson to John H. Cocke, Mar 1, 1829, and Edmund Ruffin to Cocke, June 20, 1829, Robert P. Patton to Cocke, July 10, 1829, and Ruffin to Cocke, Nov. 1, 1829 ("any such undertaking"), JHCP, boxes 58, 59, and 60, ASSCL-UVA.

84. Martha J. Randolph to Ellen W. R. Coolidge, Aug. 15, 1828, EWRCP, box 2, ASSCL-UVA; Faculty Minutes, July 5, and 9, 1828, Feb. 6, 20, 25, and 26, 1829, JUEL website, UVA; Journal of the Chairman, Jan. 21–30, Feb. 7, and 10, Mar. 4, 6, 15, and 16–17,1829, JUEL website, UVA; P. A. Bruce, *History of the University*, vol. 2:237–44; W. Meade, *Sermon Delivered at the Rotunda*, 11.

85. Robley Dunglison to Madison, Feb. 19, 1829, FO-NA, http://founders.archives.gov/documents/Madison/99-02-02-1704; Gessner Harrison to Peachey Harrison, Feb. 19, 1829, THSP, box 2, ASSCL-UVA; Faculty Minutes, Feb. 6, 20, 25, and 26, and Mar. 14, 1829, JUEL website, UVA; Faculty Resolution, Mar. 12, 1829, and Dunglison to the Board of Visitors, July 10, 1829, Misc. Mss., 11956 and 11957, University Archives, ASSCL-UVA; Dunglison to John H. Cocke, Feb. 18, 1829, JHCP, box 58, ASSCL-UVA.

86. Gessner Harrison to Peachey Harrison, May 24, 1829, THSP, box 2, ASSCL-UVA; Martha J. Randolph to Ellen W. R. Coolidge, May 28, 1829, EWRCP, box 2, ASSCL-UVA; W. Meade, *Sermon Delivered at the Rotunda*, iv, 11–12, 22–25 ("offence to God" on 23, "hazardous experiment" on 25); P. A. Bruce, *History of the University*, vol. 2:370–71; Meade, *Old Churches*, vol. 2:53–55; M. B. Smith, *First Forty Years*, 229.

NOTES TO PAGES 304–310

87. Gessner Harrison to E. Tiffin Harrison, Mar. 31, 1827, and Jan. 10, 1828, and John Temple to E. T. Harrison, Jan. 31, 1828, THSP, box 2, ASSCL-UVA; Mary E. Terrell to Louisa Cocke, May 13, 1828, and Apr. 30, 1829 ("There is something"), JHCP, box 55 and 59, ASSCL-UVA; Journal of the Chairman, May 3, 1829, JUEL website, ASSCL-UVA.

88. P. A. Bruce, *History of the University*, vol. 2:144–57, 171–74, 371–73, 379–80.

89. Bowman and Santos, *Rot, Riot, and Rebellion*, 130, 147; P. A. Bruce, *History of the University*, vol. 3:70–71, 90–92, R. T. W. Duke, Jr., quoted on 92 ("Nothing"); Wagoner, "Honor and Dishonor," 178.

90. Bowman and Santos, *Rot, Riot, and Rebellion*, 84–92, 121–27; P. A. Bruce, *History of the University*, vol. 2:169–71, 266–74, 292–94, 301–13; Martin and Von Daacke, *President's Commission on Slavery*, 22; Wagoner, "Honor and Dishonor," 175–78.

91. Bowman and Santos, *Rot, Riot, and Rebellion*, 133–35; P. A. Bruce, *History of the University*, vol. 2:213–16, 253–54, vol. 3:1–2, 53–56, 128–36; Wagoner, "Honor and Dishonor," 178.

92. P. A. Bruce, *History of the University*, vol. 3:2–7, 128–30; Wagoner, "Honor and Dishonor," 170 (Albert H. Snead quoted: "I think"), 178–79.

93. Wagoner, "Honor and Dishonor," 178–79.

94. P. A. Bruce, *History of the University*, vol. 3:143–44.

95. Martin and Von Daacke, *President's Commission on Slavery*, 35, 37–38.

Epilogue

1. Mary E. Terrell to Louisa Cocke, Sept. 22, 1826, JHCP, box 48, ASSCL-UVA.

2. Cornelia J. Randolph to Ellen W. R. Coolidge, Sept. 11, 1826, EWRCP, box 2, ASSCL-UVA.

3. Cornelia J. Randolph to Ellen W. R. Coolidge, Sept. 11, 1826, and Mary J. Randolph to E. W. R. Coolidge, Mar. 18, 1827, box 2, ASSCL-UVA.

4. Francis Eppes to Nicholas P. Trist, Nov. 7, 1826, JFL website, ICJS; Shackelford, ed., *Collected Papers*, vol. 1:175.

5. Martha J. Randolph to Ellen W. R. Coolidge, Aug. 2, 1825, Mary J. Randolph to E. W. R. Coolidge, Nov. 26, 1826, and Cornelia J. Randolph to E. W. R. Coolidge, Dec. 11, 1826, EWRCP, boxes 1 and 2, ASSCL-UVA.

6. Francis Eppes to Nicholas P. Trist, Nov. 7, 1826, JFL website, ICJS; Cornelia Jefferson Randolph to Ellen W. R. Coolidge, Feb. 4, and Apr. 10, 1827, EWRCP, box 2, ASSCL-UVA.

7. Mary J. Randolph to Ellen W. R. Coolidge, Jan. 25, 1827, EWRCP, box 2, ASSCL-UVA; Burstein, *Jefferson's Secrets*, 113; Israel Gillette (Jefferson), "Memoirs," in Gordon-Reed, *Thomas Jefferson and Sally Hemmings*, 250; Peter Fossett in Hayes, ed., *Jefferson in His Own Time*, 191; Crawford, *Twilight at Monticello*, 247–49; Stanton, *Those Who Labor*, 24.

8. Henry D. Gilpin, and John H. B. Latrobe, in Peterson, ed., *Visitors to Monticello*, 111 ("dark"), 120 ("first thing"); M. B. Smith, *First Forty Years*, 229–31; Cornelia J. Randolph to Ellen W. R. Coolidge, July 6, 1828, EWRCP, box 2, ASSCL-UVA.

9. Virginia R. Trist to Ellen W. R. Coolidge, Mar. 23, and May 1, 1827 ("vulgar herd" and "to employ"), and Cornelia J. Randolph to E. W. R. Coolidge, May 18, 1827 ("He seems"), EWRCP, box 2, ASSCL-UVA; Stanton, *Those Who Labor*, 181–84.

10. Cornelia J. Randolph to Ellen W. R. Coolidge, May 18, 1827 ("mixture"), and Aug. 12, 1829 ("We never"), and Martha J. Randolph to E. W. R. Coolidge, May 28, 1829, EWRCP, box 2, ASSCL-UVA.

11. Cornelia J. Randolph to E. W. R. Coolidge, Apr. 22, 1827, EWRCP, box 2, ASSCL-UVA; Martha J. Randolph to Ann C. Morris, Jan. 24, 1828, and Virginia J. R. Trist to Virginia R. Cary, May 2, 1828, JFL website, ICJS.

12. Martha J. Randolph to Ellen W. R. Coolidge, July 21, 1828, EWRCP, box 2, ASSCL-UVA; Crawford, *Twilight at Monticello*, 250–51; Gaines, *Thomas Mann Randolph*, 157–65, 184–86.

13. Cornelia J. Randolph to Ellen W. R. Coolidge, May 18, 1827, Martha J. Randolph to Joseph Coolidge, Jr., May 12, 1829, and Mary J. Randolph to E. W. R. Coolidge, Aug. 23, 1829 ("great offence"), EWRCP, box 2, ASSCL-UVA; Shackelford, ed., *Collected Papers*, vol. 1:81–82.

14. Martha J. Randolph to Ann C. Morris, Mar. 22, 1827, JFL website, ICJS; Mary J. Randolph to E. W. R. Coolidge, Jan. 25, 1827, and Virginia J. R. Trist to E. W. R. Coolidge, Feb. 11, 1827, EWRCP, box 2, ASSCL-UVA; Kierner, *Martha Jefferson Randolph*, 205–6.

15. Cornelia J. Randolph to Ellen W. R. Coolidge, Dec. 11, 1826, EWRCP, box 2, ASSCL-UVA.

16. Martha J. Randolph to Ellen W. R. Coolidge, Oct. 22, 1826 ("total ruin" and "bitter anguish"), and May 28, 1829, EWRCP, box 2, ASSCL-UVA; Cornelia J. Randolph to Ellen W. R. Coolidge, July 6, 1828 ("I know not"), and Aug. 12, 1829 ("To me"), EWRCP, box 2, ASSCL-UVA; Shackelford, ed., *Collected Papers*, vol. 1:81; Sloan, *Principle and Interest*, 272n176.

17. Stephen Higginson Tyng, in Peterson, ed., *Visitors to Monticello*, 124–28.

18. Mead, *Historic Homes*, 69; Shackelford, ed., *Collected Papers*, vol. 1:85–86, 152.

19. Crawford, *Twilight at Monticello*, 261–63; Kierner, *Martha Jefferson Randolph*, 270–72, 279; E. Mead, *Historic Homes*, 70–71; Shackelford, ed., *Collected Papers*, vol. 1:82–85 (Jeff Randolph quoted on 84).

20. Israel Gillette (Jefferson), "Memoirs," in Gordon-Reed, *Thomas Jefferson and Sally Hemings*, 251; Shackelford, ed., *Collected Papers*, vol. 1:85–86.

21. E. Mead, *Historic Homes*, 69–71.

BIBLIOGRAPHY

Abbott, William W., et al., eds., *The Papers of George Washington, Presidential Series*, 20 vols. to date (Charlottesville: University Press of Virginia, 1987–).

Ackerman, Bruce, *The Failure of the Founding Fathers: Jefferson, Marshall, and the Rise of Presidential Democracy* (Cambridge: Harvard University Press, 2005).

Addis, Cameron, "Jefferson and Education," in Francis D. Cogliano, ed., *A Companion to Thomas Jefferson* (Chichester, U.K.: Wiley-Blackwell, 2012): 457–73.

Addis, Cameron, *Jefferson's Vision for Education, 1760–1845* (New York: Peter Lang, 2003).

Aderman, Ralph M., et al., eds., *Letters of Washington Irving*, vol. 1: 1802–1823 (Boston: Twayne Publishers, 1978).

Alexander, James W., *Forty Years' Familiar Letters of James W. Alexander, D.D.*, 2 vols. (New York: Charles Scribner, 1860).

Alexander, James W., *The Life of Archibald Alexander* (New York: Charles Scribner, 1856).

Allmendinger, David F., Jr., "The Dangers of Ante-Bellum Student Life," *Journal of Social History*, vol. 7 (Fall 1973): 75–85.

Ammon, Harry, "The Richmond Junto, 1800–1824," *Virginia Magazine of History and Biography*, vol. 61 (Oct. 1953): 395–418.

Anbury, Thomas, *Travels Through the Interior Parts of America, in a Series of Letters*, 2 vols. (London: William Lane, 1789).

[Anonymous], "Article VII: Proceedings and Report of the Commissioners for the University of Virginia," *North American Review*, vol. 10 (1820): 115–37.

[Anonymous], "Education in Virginia," American Education Society, *Quarterly Register*, vol. 5 (May 1833): 321–24.

[Anonymous], *The Freeman's Remonstrance Against an Ecclesiastical Establishment: Being Some Remarks on a Late Pamphlet Entitled The Necessity of an Established Church in Any State* (Williamsburg: John Dixon & William Hunter, 1777).

[Anonymous], "Letters from William & Mary College, 1798–1801," *Virginia Magazine of History and Biography*, vol. 29 (Apr. 1921): 120–79.

[Anonymous], "Letters to David Watson," *Virginia Magazine of History and Biography*, vol. 29 (July 1921): 257–86.

[Anonymous], "Recollections of James Ogilvie, Earl of Findlater, by One of His Pupils," *Southern Literary Messenger*, vol. 14 (Sept. 1848): 534–37.

Appleby, Joyce, "Thomas Jefferson and the Psychology of Democracy," in James Horn, Jan Ellen Lewis, and Peter S. Onuf, eds., *The Revolution of 1800: Democracy, Race, and the New Republic* (Charlottesville: University of Virginia Press, 2002): 155–72.

Asbury, Francis, *The Journal of the Rev. Francis Asbury, Bishop of the Methodist Episcopal Church, from August 7, 1771 to December 7, 1815*, 3 vols. (New York: N. Bangs & T. Mason, 1821).

Axtell, James, *The Invasion Within: The Context of Cultures in Colonial North America* (New York: Oxford University Press, 1985).

Ayers, Edward L., *Vengeance and Justice: Crime and Punishment in the 19th-Century American South* (New York: Oxford University Press, 1984).

Ayres, S. Edward, "Albemarle County, 1744–1770: An Economic, Political, and Social Analysis," *Magazine of Albemarle County History*, vol. 25 (1966–67): 36–55.

Bacon, Edmund, "Autobiography," in Hamilton W. Pierson, ed., *Jefferson at Monticello: The Private Life of Thomas Jefferson* (New York: C. Scribner, 1862).

Baker, Meredith Henne, *The Richmond Theater Fire: Early America's First Great Disaster* (Baton Rouge: Louisiana State University Press, 2012).

Baker, Thomas N., "'A Slave' Writes Thomas Jefferson," *William & Mary Quarterly*, 3rd ser., vol. 68 (Jan. 2011): 127–54.

Ballagh, James Curtis, ed., *The Letters of Richard Henry Lee, 1732–1794*, 2 vols. (New York: Macmillan Co., 1911–14).

Barbee, David Rankin, ed., "A Sheaf of Old Letters," *Tyler's Quarterly Historical and Genealogical Magazine*, vol. 32 (Oct. 1950): 77–102.

Bayard, Ferdinand-Marie, *Travels of a Frenchman in Maryland and Virginia, with a Description of Philadelphia and Baltimore in 1791* (Ann Arbor, Mich.: Edwards Brothers, 1950).

Bearss, Sara B., et al., eds., *Dictionary of Virginia Biography*, 3 vols. (Richmond: Library of Virginia, 2001).

Beeman, Richard R., *The Evolution of the Southern Backcountry: A Case Study of Lunenburg County, Virginia, 1746–1832* (Philadelphia: University of Pennsylvania Press, 1984).

Beeman, Richard R., *The Old Dominion and the New Nation, 1788–1801* (Lexington: University Press of Kentucky, 1972).

Beeman, Richard R., *Patrick Henry: A Biography* (New York: McGraw-Hill, 1974).

Belknap, Jeremy, ed., "Queries Relating to Slavery in Massachusetts," *Massachusetts Historical Society, Collections*, 5th ser., vol. 3 (1877): 378–431.

Berkeley, Edmund, Jr., "Prophet Without Honor: Christopher McPherson, Free Person of Color," *Virginia Magazine of History and Biography*, vol. 77 (Apr. 1969): 179–90.

Bernhard, Duke of Saxe-Weimar-Eisenach, *Travels in North America in 1825 and 1826*, 2 vols. (Philadelphia, Carey, Lea & Carey, 1828).

Bestor, Arthur E., Jr., ed., *Education and Reform at New Harmony: Correspondence of William Maclure and Marie Duclos Fretageot, 1820–1833* (Indianapolis: Indiana Historical Society, 1948).

Betts, Edwin Morris, and James Adam Bear, Jr., eds., *The Family Letters of Thomas Jefferson* (Columbia: University of Missouri Press, 1966).

Bly, Antonio T., "In Pursuit of Letters: A History of the Bray Schools for Enslaved Children in Colonial Virginia," *History of Education Quarterly*, vol. 51 (Nov. 2011): 429–59.

Bondurant, Agnes M., *Poe's Richmond* (Richmond: Garrett & Massie, 1942).

Borrowman, Merle, "The False Dawn of the State University," *History of Education Quarterly*, vol. 1 (June 1961): 6–22.

Boucher, Jonathan, "Letters of Rev. Jonathan Boucher," *Maryland Historical Magazine*, vol. 7 (1912): 3–26, 150–164, 286–304, 337–56; vol. 8 (1913): 34–50, 168–86, 235–56, 338–52.

Boucher, Jonathan, *Reminiscences of an American Loyalist, 1738–1789* (Boston: Houghton Mifflin Co., 1925).

Boucher, Jonathan, *A View of the Causes and Consequences of the American Revolution; in Thirteen Discourses, Preached in North America Between the Years 1763 and 1775* (London: G. G. and J. Robinson, 1797).

Bowman, Rex, and Carlos Santos, *Rot, Riot, and Rebellion: Mr. Jefferson's Struggle to Save the University that Changed America* (Charlottesville: University of Virginia Press, 2013).

Boyd, Julian P., et al., eds., *The Papers of Thomas Jefferson*, 43 vols. to date (Princeton: Princeton University Press, 1950–).

Breen, T. H., "Horses and Gentlemen: The Cultural Significance of Gambling Among the Gentry of Virginia," *William & Mary Quarterly*, 3rd ser., vol. 34 (Apr. 1977): 239–57.

Breen, T. H., *Tobacco Culture: The Mentality of the Great Tidewater Planters on the Eve of Revolution* (Princeton: Princeton University Press, 1985).

Brewer, Holly, "Beyond Education: Thomas Jefferson's 'Republican' Revision of the Laws Regarding Children," in James Gilreath, ed., *Thomas Jefferson and the Education of a Citizen* (Washington, D.C.: Library of Congress, 1999): 48–62.

Brewer, Holly, "Entailing Aristocracy in Colonial Virginia: 'Ancient Feudal Restraints' and Revolutionary Reform," *William & Mary Quarterly*, 3rd. ser., vol. 54 (Apr. 1997): 307–46.

Bridenbaugh, Carl, *Seat of Empire: The Political Role of Eighteenth-Century Williamsburg* (Williamsburg: Colonial Williamsburg, 1958).

Brock, R. A., ed., *The Official Records of Robert Dinwiddie, Lieutenant-Governor of the Colony of Virginia, 1751–1758,* 2 vols. (Richmond: Virginia Historical Society, 1883–84).

Brown, Ralph H., "St. George Tucker versus Jedidiah Morse on the Subject of Williamsburg," *William & Mary Quarterly,* 2nd ser., vol. 20 (Oct. 1940): 487–91.

Brown, Richard D., "Bulwark of Revolutionary Liberty: Thomas Jefferson and John Adams's Programs for an Informed Citizenry," in James Gilreath, ed., *Thomas Jefferson and the Education of a Citizen* (Washington, D.C.: Library of Congress, 1999): 91–102.

Brown, Richard D., *Knowledge Is Power: The Diffusion of Information in Early America, 1700–1865* (New York: Oxford University Press, 1989).

Brown, Richard D., *The Strength of a People: The Idea of an Informed Citizenry in America, 1650–1870* (Chapel Hill: University of North Carolina Press, 1996).

Bruce, Dickson D., Jr., *Violence and Culture in the Antebellum South* (Austin: University of Texas Press, 1979).

Bruce, Philip Alexander, *The History of the University of Virginia, 1819–1919: The Lengthened Shadow of One Man,* 5 vols. (New York: Macmillan Co., 1920–22).

Bruce, William Cabell, *John Randolph of Roanoke, 1773–1833,* 2 vols. (New York: G. P. Putnam's Sons, 1922).

Brydon, George MacLaren, "The Clergy of the Established Church in Virginia and the Revolution," *Virginia Magazine of History and Biography,* vol. 41 (Jan. 1933): 11–23, (Apr. 1933): 123–43, (July 1933): 231–43, and (Oct. 1933): 297–309.

Brydon, George MacLaren, "David Griffith, 1742–1789: First Bishop Elect of Virginia," *Historical Magazine of the Protestant Episcopal Church,* vol. 9 (Sept. 1940): 194–230.

Brydon, George MacLaren, *Virginia's Mother Church and the Political Conditions Under Which It Grew,* 2 vols. (Philadelphia: Church Historical Society, 1947–52).

Buckley, Thomas E., "After Disestablishment: Thomas Jefferson's Wall of Separation in Antebellum Virginia," *Journal of Southern History,* vol. 61 (Aug. 1995): 445–80.

Buckley, Thomas E., *Church and State in Revolutionary Virginia, 1776–1787* (Charlottesville: University Press of Virginia, 1977).

Buckley, Thomas E., "Evangelicals Triumphant: The Baptists' Assault on the Virginia Glebes, 1786–1801," *William & Mary Quarterly,* 3rd ser., vol. 45 (Jan. 1988): 33–69.

Burnaby, Andrew, *Travels Through the Middle Settlements in North-America in the Years 1759 and 1760* (Ithaca: Cornell University Press, 1960, reprint of London, 1775).

Burstein, Andrew, *The Inner Jefferson: Portrait of a Grieving Optimist* (Charlottesville: University of Virginia Press, 1995).

Burstein, Andrew, *Jefferson's Secrets: Death and Desire at Monticello* (New York: Basic Books, 2005).

Cabell, Nathaniel Francis, ed., *Early History of the University of Virginia as Con-*

tained in the Letters of Thomas Jefferson and Joseph C. Cabell (Richmond: J. W. Randolph, 1856).

Camm, John, *Critical Remarks on a Letter Ascribed to Common Sense Containing an Attempt to Prove that the Said Letter Is an Imposition on Common Sense* (Williamsburg: Joseph Royle, 1765).

Camm, John, *A Single and Distinct View of an Act Vulgarly Called the Two-Penny Act* (Annapolis, Md.: Jonas Green, 1763).

Campbell, Charles, ed., *The Bland Papers: Being a Selection from the Manuscripts of Colonel Theodorick Bland, Jr.*, 2 vols. (Petersburg: Edmund & Julian C. Ruffin, 1840).

Canby, Courtland, "A Note on the Influence of Oxford upon William & Mary College in the Eighteenth Century," *William & Mary Quarterly*, 2nd ser., vol. 21 (July 1941): 243–47.

Carrière, J. M., and L. G. Moffatt, eds., "A Frenchman Visits Albemarle, 1816," *Papers of the Albemarle County Historical Society*, vol. 4 (1943–44): 39–55.

Carson, Jane, ed., *We Were There: Descriptions of Williamsburg, 1699–1859, Compiled from Contemporary Sources and Arranged Chronologically* (Charlottesville: University Press of Virginia, 1965).

Carter, Edward C., II, et al., eds., *The Virginia Journals of Benjamin Henry Latrobe, 1795–1798*, 2 vols. (New Haven: Yale University Press, 1977).

Carter, Landon, *A Letter to the Right Reverend Father in God, the Lord B[isho]p of L[ondo]n* (Williamsburg: William Hunter, 1760).

Cary, Virginia Randolph, *Christian Parent's Assistant, or Tales for the Moral and Religious Instruction of Youth* (Richmond: Ariel Works, 1829).

Cary, Virginia Randolph, *Letters on Female Character Addressed to a Young Lady, on the Death of Her Mother* (Richmond: Ariel Works, 1828).

Chastellux, François-Jean, Marquis de, *Travels in North America, in the Years 1780, 1781, and 1782*, 2 vols. (Chapel Hill: University of North Carolina Press, 1963).

Cockerham, Anne Z., Arlene W. Keeling, and Barbara Parker, "Seeking Refuge at Monticello: Domestic Violence in Thomas Jefferson's Family," *Magazine of Albemarle County History*, vol. 64 (2006): 29–52.

Cohen, Patricia Cline, *A Calculating People: The Spread of Numeracy in Early America* (Chicago: University of Chicago Press, 1982).

Cornelius, Janet Duitsman, *"When I Can Read My Title Clear": Literacy, Slavery, and Religion in the Antebellum South* (Columbia: University of South Carolina Press, 1991).

Crackel, Theodore J., "The Military Academy in the Context of Jeffersonian Reform," in Robert M. S. McDonald, ed., *Thomas Jefferson's Military Academy: Founding West Point* (Charlottesville: University of Virginia Press, 2004): 99–117.

Crawford, Alan Pell, *Twilight at Monticello: The Final Years of Thomas Jefferson* (New York: Random House, 2008).

Cremin, Lawrence A., *American Education: The National Experience, 1783–1876* (New York: Harper & Row, 1980)

Cresswell, Nicholas, *The Journal of Nicholas Creswell, 1774–1777* (New York: Dial Press, 1924).

Crowe, Charles, "Bishop James Madison and the Republic of Virtue," *Journal of Southern History*, vol. 30 (Feb. 1964): 58–70.

Cutler, William Parker, and Julia Perkins Cutler, eds., *Life, Journals, and Correspondence of Rev. Manasseh Cutler, LL.D.*, 2 vols. (Cincinnati: Robert Clarke & Co., 1888).

Dabney, Charles William, *Universal Education in the South: A Story of Great Men and Great Movements*, 2 vols. (Chapel Hill: University of North Carolina Press, 1936).

Dabney, William Minor, "Jefferson's Albemarle: History of Albemarle County, Virginia, 1728–1819" (Ph.D. diss.: University of Virginia, 1951).

Darrell, John Harvey, "Diary of John Harvey Darrell: Voyage to America," *Bermuda Historical Quarterly*, vol. 5 (1948): 142–49.

David, James Corbett, *Dunmore's New World: The Extraordinary Life of a Royal Governor in Revolutionary America* (Charlottesville: University of Virginia Press, 2013).

Davis, John, *Travels of Four Years and a Half in the United States of America During 1798, 1799, 1800, 1801, and 1802*, 2 vols. (New York: H. Caritat, 1803).

Davis, Richard Beale, ed., *Correspondence of Thomas Jefferson and Francis Walker Gilmer, 1814–1826* (Columbia: University of South Carolina Press, 1946).

Davis, Richard Beale, *Francis Walker Gilmer: Life and Learning in Jefferson's Virginia* (Richmond: Dietz Press, 1939).

Davis, Richard Beale, *Intellectual Life in Jefferson's Virginia, 1790–1830* (Knoxville: University of Tennessee Press, 1972).

Davis, Richard Beale, "James Ogilvie, an Early American Teacher of Rhetoric," *Quarterly Journal of Speech*, vol. 28 (Oct. 1942): 289–97.

Davis, Richard Beale, ed., *Jeffersonian America: Notes on the United States of America Collected in the Years 1805–6–7 and 11–12 by Sir Augustus John Foster, Bart.* (San Marino, Calif.: Huntington Library, 1954).

Deyle, Steven, *Carry Me Back: The Domestic Slave Trade in American Life* (New York: Oxford University Press, 2005).

Dierksheide, Christa, *Amelioration and Empire: Progress and Slavery in the Plantation Americas* (Charlottesville: University of Virginia Press, 2014).

Dreisbach, Donald L., "Church-State Debate in the Virginia Legislature: From the Declaration of Rights to the Statute for Establishing Religious Freedom," in Garrett W. Sheldon and Dreisbach, eds., *Religion and Political Culture in Jefferson's Virginia* (Lanham, Md.: Rowman & Littlefield, 2000): 135–65.

Dunglison, Robley, "The Autobiographical Ana of Robley Dunglison, M.D.," *American Philosophical Society, Transactions*, vol. 53 (1963): 1–212.

Dunglison, Robley, "College Instruction and Discipline," *American Quarterly Review*, vol. 18 (June 1831): 283–314.

Dunn, Richard S., "After Tobacco: The Slave Labor Pattern on a Large Chesapeake Grain-and-Livestock Plantation in the Early Nineteenth Century," in John J. McCusker and Kenneth Morgan, eds., *The Early Modern Atlantic Economy* (New York: Cambridge University Press, 2000): 344–63.

Dunn, Susan, *Dominion of Memories: Jefferson, Madison & the Decline of Virginia* (New York: Basic Books, 2007).

Dupuy, R. Ernest, "Mutiny at West Point," *American Heritage*, vol. 7 (Dec. 1955): 257–70.

Du Roi, August Wilhelm, *Journal of Du Roi the Elder, Lieutenant and Adjutant in the Service of the Duke of Brunswick, 1776–1778* (New York: D. Appleton & Co., 1911).

Dwight, Theodore, *An Oration Delivered at New-Haven on the 7th of July, A.D. 1801, Before the Society of the Cincinnati, for the State of Connecticut* (Suffield, Conn.: Edward Gray, 1801).

Eastman, Carolyn, *A Nation of Speechifiers: Making an American Public After the Revolution* (Chicago: University of Chicago Press, 2009).

Eastman, Carolyn, "The Transatlantic Celebrity of Mr. O: Oratory and the Networks of Reputation in Early Nineteenth-Century Britain and America," *Comparative American Studies: An International Journal*, vol. 14 (Mar. 2016): 1–14.

Eckenrode, H. J., *Separation of Church and State in Virginia: A Study in the Development of the Revolution* (New York: Da Capo Press, 1971).

Egerton, Douglas R., *Charles Fenton Mercer and the Trial of National Conservatism* (Jackson: University Press of Mississippi, 1989).

Egerton, Douglas R., *Gabriel's Rebellion: The Virginia Slave Conspiracies of 1800 and 1802* (Chapel Hill: University of North Carolina Press, 1993).

Egerton, Douglas R., "'To the Tombs of the Capulets': Charles Fenton Mercer and Public Education in Virginia, 1816–1817," *Virginia Magazine of History and Biography*, vol. 93 (Apr. 1985): 155–74.

Einhorn, Robin L., "Patrick Henry's Case Against the Constitution: The Structural Problem with Slavery," *Journal of the Early Republic*, vol. 22 (Winter 2002): 549–73.

Ellis, Joseph J., *After the Revolution: Profiles of Early American Culture* (New York: W. W. Norton, 1979).

Ely, Melvin P., *Israel on the Appomattox: A Southern Experiment in Black Freedom from the 1790s through the Civil War* (New York: Alfred A. Knopf, 2004).

Evans, Emory G., *Thomas Nelson of Yorktown: Revolutionary Virginian* (Charlottesville: University Press of Virginia, 1975).

Evans, Emory G., *A "Topping People": The Rise and Decline of Virginia's Old Political Elite, 1680–1790* (Charlottesville: University of Virginia Press, 2009).

Evans, Frank B., "Carlo Bellini and His Russian Friend Fedor Karzhavin," *Virginia Magazine of History and Biography*, vol. 88 (July 1980): 338–54.

Fehrenbacher, Don E., and Ward M. McAfee, *The Slaveholding Republic: An Account of the United States Government's Relations to Slavery* (New York: Oxford University Press, 2001).

Fithian, Philip Vickers, *Journal & Letters, 1773–1774: A Plantation Tutor of the Old Dominion* (Williamsburg: Colonial Williamsburg, Inc., 1943).

Flournoy, Fitzgerald, "Hugh Blair Grigsby at Yale," *Virginia Magazine of History and Biography*, vol. 62 (Apr. 1954): 166–90.

Flournoy, H. W., ed., *Calendar of Virginia State Papers and Other Manuscripts*, 12 vols. (New York: Kraus Reprint, 1968, of Richmond, 1890).

Fontaine, James, and Ann Maury, *Memoirs of a Huguenot Family* (New York: G. P. Putnam & Sons, 1872).

Foote, William Henry, *Sketches of Virginia, Second Series* (Philadelphia: J. B. Lippincott Co., 1856).

Ford, Lacy K., *Deliver Us from Evil: The Slavery Question in the Old South* (New York: Oxford University Press, 2009).

Frank, Marie, "It Took an Academical Village: Jefferson's Hotels at the University of Virginia," *Magazine of Albemarle County History*, vol. 59 (2001): 31–56.

Freehling, William W., *The Road to Disunion: Secessionists at Bay, 1776–1854* (New York: Oxford University Press, 1990).

Freeman, Joanne B., *Affairs of Honor: National Politics in the New Republic* (New Haven: Yale University Press, 2001).

Friend, Craig Thompson, and Lorri Glover, "Rethinking Southern Masculinity: An Introduction," in Friend and Glover, eds., *Southern Manhood: Perspectives on Masculinity in the Old South* (Athens: University of Georgia Press, 2004): viii–xvii.

Gaines, William H., Jr., *Thomas Mann Randolph: Jefferson's Son-in-Law* (Baton Rouge: Louisiana State University Press, 1966).

Ganter, Herbert L., "Documents Relating to the Early History of the College of William & Mary and to the History of the Church in Virginia," *William & Mary Quarterly*, 2nd ser., vol. 20 (Oct. 1940): 524–44.

Ganter, Herbert L, "William Small, Jefferson's Beloved Teacher," *William & Mary Quarterly*, 3rd ser., vol. 4 (Oct. 1947): 505–11.

Garnett, James Mercer, *Seven Lectures on Female Education Inscribed to Mrs. Garnett's Pupils at Elm-Wood, Essex County, Virginia* (Richmond: T. W. White, 1824).

Geiger, Roger L., "Introduction: New Themes in the History of Nineteenth-Century Colleges," in Geiger, ed., *The American College in the Nineteenth Century* (Nashville: Vanderbilt University Press, 2000): 1–36.

Gibbs, Patricia A., and Linda H. Rowe, *The Public Hospital, 1766–1885* (Williamsburg: Colonial Williamsburg Foundation Library Research Report, 1974).

Gilmer, George, "Papers Military and Political, 1775–1778, of George Gilmer, M.D., of 'Pen Park' Albemarle County, VA," *Collections of the Virginia Historical Society*, vol. 6 (1887): 71–140.

Glover, Lorri, "'Let Us Manufacture Men': Educating Elite Boys in the Early National South," in Craig Thompson Friend and Lorri Glover, eds., *Southern Manhood: Perspectives on Masculinity in the Old South* (Athens: University of Georgia Press, 2004): 22–48.

Glover, Lorri, *Southern Sons: Becoming Men in the New Nation* (Baltimore: Johns Hopkins University Press, 2007).

Goodwin, Mary, *The Capitol: Second Building, 1747–1832* (Williamsburg: Colonial Williamsburg Research Report, 1934).

Goodwin, Mary, *The College of William & Mary* (Williamsburg: Colonial Williamsburg Research Report, 1967).

Goodwin, W. A. Rutherford, *A Brief & True Report Concerning Williamsburg in Virginia* (Williamsburg: Colonial Williamsburg Foundation, 1941).

Goodwin, W. A. Rutherford, "The Reverend John Bracken (1745–1818), Rector of Bruton Parish and President of William & Mary College in Virginia," *Historical Magazine of the Protestant Episcopal Church*, vol. 10 (Dec. 1941): 354–89.

Gordon, Lord Adam, "Journal of an Officer in the West Indies Who Travelled over a Part of the West Indies, and of North America, in the Course of 1764 and 1765," in Newton D. Mereness, ed., *Travels in the American Colonies* (New York: Macmillan Co., 1916): 369–453.

Gordon-Reed, Annette, *The Hemingses of Monticello: An American Family* (New York: W. W. Norton, 2008).

Gordon-Reed, Annette, *Thomas Jefferson and Sally Hemings: An American Controversy* (Charlottesville: University of Virginia Press, 1997).

Gordon-Reed, Annette, and Peter S. Onuf, *"Most Blessed of the Patriarchs": Thomas Jefferson and the Empire of the Imagination* (New York: W. W. Norton, 2016).

Gorn, Elliott J., "'Gouge and Bite, Pull Hair and Scratch': The Social Significance of Fighting in the Southern Backcountry," *American Historical Review*, vol. 90 (Feb. 1985): 18–43.

Greenberg, Kenneth S., *Masters and Statesmen: The Political Culture of American Slavery* (Baltimore: Johns Hopkins University Press, 1985).

Greenberg, Kenneth S., "The Nose, the Lie, and the Duel in the Antebellum South," *American Historical Review*, vol. 95 (Feb. 1990): 57–74.

Greene, Jack P., ed., *The Diary of Colonel Landon Carter of Sabine Hall, 1752–1778*, 2 vols. (Charlottesville: University Press of Virginia, 1965).

Greene, Jack P., "Foundations of Political Power in the Virginia House of Burgesses, 1720–1776," *William & Mary Quarterly*, 3rd ser., vol. 16 (Oct. 1959): 485–506.

Greene, Jack P., "The Intellectual Reconstruction of Virginia in the Age of Jefferson," in Peter S. Onuf, ed., *Jeffersonian Legacies* (Charlottesville: University Press of Virginia, 1993): 225–53.

Griffin, Barbara J., "Thomas Ritchie and the Founding of the Richmond Lancastrian School," *Virginia Magazine of History and Biography*, vol. 86 (Oct. 1978): 447–60.

Griffith, Lucille, ed., "English Education for Virginia Youth: Some Eighteenth-Century Ambler Family Letters," *Virginia Magazine of History and Biography*, vol. 69 (Jan. 1961): 7–27.

Grigsby, Hugh Blair, *Discourse on the Life and Character of the Hon. Littleton Waller Tazewell* (Norfolk: J. D. Ghiselin, Jr., 1860).

Grossberg, Michael, "Citizens and Families: A Jeffersonian Vision of Domestic Relations and Generational Change," in James Gilreath, ed., *Thomas Jefferson and the Education of a Citizen* (Washington, D. C.: Library of Congress, 1999): 3–27.

Gundersen, Joan, "The Search for Good Men: Recruiting Ministers in Colonial Virginia," *Historical Magazine of the Protestant Episcopal Church*, vol. 48 (Dec. 1979): 453–64.

Gutek, Gerald Lee, *Joseph Neef and the Americanization of Pestalozzianism* (Tuscaloosa: University of Alabama, 1978).

Gwatkin, Thomas, "On the Manners of Virginians, c. 1770," *William & Mary Quarterly*, 3rd ser., vol. 9 (Jan. 1952): 81–85.

Hamilton, Phillip, *The Making and Unmaking of a Revolutionary Family: The Tuckers of Virginia, 1752–1830* (Charlottesville: University of Virginia Press, 2003).

Harrison, Fairfax, *The Virginia Carys: An Essay in Genealogy* (New York: DeVinne Press, 1919).

Hatzenbuehler, Ronald L, "Growing Weary in Well-Doing: Thomas Jefferson's Life Among the Virginia Gentry," *Virginia Magazine of History and Biography*, vol. 101 (Jan. 1993): 5–36.

Haulman, Clyde A., *Virginia and the Panic of 1819: The First Great Depression and the Commonwealth* (London: Pickering & Chatto, 2008).

Hayes, Kevin J., ed., *Jefferson in His Own Time: A Biographical Chronicle of His Life, Drawn from Recollections, Interviews, and Memoirs by Family, Friends, and Associates* (Iowa City: University of Iowa Press, 2012).

Heafford, Michael, *Pestalozzi: His Thought and Its Relevance Today* (London: Methuen & Co., 1967).

Henderson, H. James, "Taxation and Political Culture: Massachusetts and Virginia, 1750–1800," *William & Mary Quarterly*, 3rd ser., vol. 47 (Jan. 1990): 90–114.

Henshaw, J. P. K. *Memoir of the Life of the Rt. Rev. Richard Channing Moore, D.D.* (Philadelphia: William Stanley & Co., 1843).

Hogan, David, "The Market Revolution and Disciplinary Power: Joseph Lancaster and the Psychology of the Early Classroom System," *History of Education Quarterly*, vol. 29 (Autumn 1989): 381–417.

Holton, Woody, *Forced Founders: Indians, Debtors, Slaves, and the Making of the*

American Revolution in Virginia (Chapel Hill: University of North Carolina Press, 1999).

Horner, Frederick, *The History of the Blair, Banister, and Braxton Families* (Philadelphia: J. B. Lippincott Co., 1898).

Hoyt, William D., Jr., ed., "Mr. Cabell, Mr. Warden, and the University, 1823," *Virginia Magazine of History and Biography*, vol. 49 (Oct. 1941): 351–53.

Hoyt, William D., Jr., ed., "Self-Portrait: Eliza Custis, 1808," *Virginia Magazine of History and Biography*, vol. 53 (Apr. 1945): 89–100.

Hubert, Thomas, "The Southern Element in Poe's Fiction," *Georgia Review*, vol. 28 (Summer 1974): 200–212.

Hutchinson, William T., et al., eds, *The Papers of James Madison, Congressional Series*, 17 vols. to date (Charlottesville: University Press of Virginia, 1962–).

Irons, Charles F., "Believing in America: Faith and Politics in Early National Virginia," *American Baptist Quarterly*, vol. 21 (2002): 396–412.

Irons, Charles F., *The Origins of Proslavery Christianity: White and Black Evangelicals in Colonial and Antebellum Virginia* (Chapel Hill: University of North Carolina Press, 2008).

Irons, Charles F., "The Spiritual Fruits of Revolution: Disestablishment and the Rise of the Virginia Baptists," *Virginia Magazine of History and Biography*, vol. 109 (2001): 159–86.

Isaac, Rhys, *Landon Carter's Uneasy Kingdom: Revolution and Rebellion on a Virginia Plantation* (New York: Oxford University Press, 2005).

Isaac, Rhys, "'The Rage of Malice of the Old Serpent Devil': The Dissenters and the Making and Remaking of the Virginia Statute for Religious Freedom," in Merrill D. Peterson and Robert C. Vaughan, eds., *The Virginia Statute for Religious Freedom: Its Evolution and Consequences in American History* (New York: Cambridge University Press, 1988), 139–69.

Isaac, Rhys, "Religion and Authority: Problems of the Anglican Establishment in Virginia in the Era of the Great Awakening and the Parsons' Cause," *William & Mary Quarterly*, 3rd. ser., vol. 30 (Jan. 1973): 3–36.

Isaac, Rhys, *The Transformation of Virginia, 1740–1790* (Chapel Hill: University of North Carolina Press, 1982).

Jabour, Anya, "'Grown Girls, Highly Cultivated': Female Education in an Antebellum Southern Family," *Journal of Southern History*, vol. 64 (Feb. 1998): 23–64.

Jabour, Anya, "Male Friendship and Masculinity in the Early National South: William Wirt and His Friends," *Journal of the Early Republic*, vol. 20 (Spring 2000): 83–111.

Jabour, Anya, *Marriage in the Early Republic: Elizabeth and William Wirt and the Companionate Ideal* (Baltimore: Johns Hopkins University Press, 1998).

Janson, Charles William, *The Stranger in America, 1793–1806* (New York: Press of the Pioneers, 1935).

Jarratt, Devereux, *The Life of Devereux Jarratt, Rector of Bath Parish, Dinwiddie County, Virginia, Written by Himself, in a Series of Letters Addressed to the Rev. John Coleman, One of the Ministers of the Protestant Episcopal Church in Maryland* (Baltimore: Warner & Hanna, 1806).

Jefferson, Thomas, "Autobiography," in Merrill D. Peterson, ed., *Thomas Jefferson, Writings* (New York: Library of America, 1984): 3–103.

Jefferson, Thomas, *Notes on the State of Virginia*, edited by Peter S. Onuf (New York: Barnes & Noble, 2010, reprint of 1785).

Jeter, Jeremiah Bell, *The Recollections of a Long Life* (Richmond: Religious Herald Co., 1891).

Johnson, Ludwell H., "Between the Wars, 1782–1862," in Susan H. Godson et al., eds., *The College of William & Mary: A History*, 2 vols. (Williamsburg: King and Queen Press, 1993), vol. 1:165–291.

Johnson, Ludwell H., "Sharper than a Serpent's Tooth: Thomas Jefferson and His Alma Mater," *Virginia Magazine of History and Biography*, vol. 99 (Apr. 1991): 145–62.

Jones, E. Alfred, "Two Professors of William & Mary College," *William & Mary Quarterly*, 1st. ser., vol. 26 (Jan. 1918): 221–31.

Jordan, Daniel P., *Political Leadership in Jefferson's Virginia* (Charlottesville: University Press of Virginia, 1983).

Jordan, Ervin, "'Chastising a Servant for his Insolence': The Case of the Butter Bully," Ervin Jordan, in John A. Ragosta, Peter S. Onuf, and Andrew J. O'Shaughnessy, eds., *The Founding of Mr. Jefferson's University* (Charlottesville: University of Virginia Press, 2019): 76–91.

Kaestle, Carl F., *Joseph Lancaster and the Monitorial School Movement: A Documentary History* (New York: Teachers College Press, 1973).

Kaestle, Carl F., *Pillars of the Republic: Common Schools and American Society, 1780–1860* (New York: Hill & Wang, 1983).

Kaminski, John P., et al., eds., *The Documentary History of the Ratification of the Constitution*, 6 vols. (Madison: State Historical Society of Wisconsin, 1988).

Kennedy, John P., *Memoirs of the Life of William Wirt*, 2 vols. (Philadelphia: Lee & Blanchard, 1850).

Kerber, Linda K., *Federalists in Dissent: Imagery and Ideology in Jeffersonian America* (Ithaca: Cornell University Press, 1970).

Kern, Susan, *The Jeffersons at Shadwell* (New Haven: Yale University Press, 2010).

Ketcham, Ralph, "The Dictates of Conscience: Edward Coles and Slavery," *Virginia Quarterly Review*, vol. 36 (Winter 1960): 46–62.

Kett, Joseph F., *Rites of Passages: Adolescence in America, 1790 to the Present* (New York: Basic Books, 1977).

Kierner, Cynthia A., "'The Dark and Dense Cloud Perpetually Lowering over Us': Gender and the Decline of the Gentry in Post-Revolutionary Virginia," *Journal of the Early Republic*, vol. 20 (Summer 2000): 185–217.

Kierner, Cynthia A., *Martha Jefferson Randolph, Daughter of Monticello: Her Life and Times* (Chapel Hill: University of North Carolina Press, 2012).

Knight, Edgar W., ed., *A Documentary History of Education in the South Before 1860*, 5 vols. (Chapel Hill: University of North Carolina Press, 1945–53).

Knight, Henry C., *Letters from the South and West* (Boston: Richardson & Lord, 1824).

Koganzon, Rita, "'Producing a Reconciliation of Disinterestedness and Commerce': The Political Rhetoric of Education in the Early Republic," *History of Education Quarterly*, vol. 52 (Aug. 2012): 414–29.

Kukla, Jon, *Patrick Henry: Champion of Liberty* (New York: Simon & Schuster, 2017).

Kulikoff, Allan, *Tobacco and Slaves: The Development of Southern Cultures in the Chesapeake, 1660–1800* (Chapel Hill: University of North Carolina Press, 1986).

La Rochefoucauld-Liancourt, François Alexandre Frederic, Duc de, *Travels Through the United States of North America . . . in the Years, 1795, 1796, and 1797*, 4 vols. (London: R. Phillips, 1800).

Lee, Arthur, *An Essay in Vindication of the Continental Colonies of America, from a Censure of Mr. Adam Smith, in his Theory of Moral Sentiments, with some Reflections on Slavery in General, by an American* (London: T. Becket & P. Hondt, 1764).

Leichtle, Kurt E., and Bruce G. Carveth, *Crusade Against Slavery: Edward Coles, Pioneer of Freedom* (Carbondale: Southern Illinois University Press, 2011).

Levasseur, Auguste, *Lafayette in America in 1824 and 1825: Journal of a Voyage to the United States*, 2 vols. (New York: White, Gallaher & White, 1829).

Lewis, Jan, "Jefferson, the Family, and Civic Education," in James Gilreath, ed., *Thomas Jefferson and the Education of a Citizen* (Washington, D.C.: Library of Congress, 1999): 63–75.

Lewis, Jan, *The Pursuit of Happiness: Family and Values in Jefferson's Virginia* (New York: Cambridge University Press, 1983).

Lewis, Jan, "The White Jeffersons," in Lewis and Peter S. Onuf, eds., *Sally Hemings & Thomas Jefferson: History, Memory, and Civic Culture* (Charlottesville: University of Virginia Press, 1999), 127–60.

Lindman, Janet Moore, "Acting the Manly Christian: White Evangelical Masculinity in Revolutionary Virginia," *William & Mary Quarterly*, 3rd ser., vol. 57 (Jan. 2000): 393–416.

[Literary Fund], *Sundry Documents on the Subject of a System of Public Education for the State of Virginia* (Richmond: Ritchie, Trueheart & Duval, 1817).

Lohrenz, Otto, "The Reverend Alexander White of Colonial Virginia: His Career and Status," *Fides et Historia*, vol. 24 (Summer 1992): 56–75.

Long, George, *Letters of George Long*, edited by Thomas Fitzhugh (Charlottesville: University of Virginia Library, 1917).

Longmore, Paul K, "'All Matters and Things Relating to Religion and Morality': The Virginia Burgesses' Committee for Religion, 1769 to 1775," *Journal of Church and State*, vol. 38 (Autumn 1996): 775–97.

Looney, J. Jefferson, et al., eds., *The Papers of Thomas Jefferson, Retirement Series*, 15 vols. to date (Princeton: Princeton University Press, 2005–).

Luebke, Fred G., "The Origins of Thomas Jefferson's Anti-Clericalism," *Church History*, vol. 32 (Sept. 1963): 344–56.

Maddox, William Arthur, *The Free School Idea in Virginia Before the Civil War: A Phase of Political and Social Evolution* (New York: Teachers College, Columbia University, 1918).

Madison, [Bishop] James, *An Address, to the Members of the Protestant Episcopal Church, in Virginia* (Richmond: T. Nicolson, 1799).

Majewski, John, *A House Dividing: Economic Development in Pennsylvania and Virginia Before the Civil War* (New York: Cambridge University Press, 2000).

Malone, Dumas, *Jefferson and His Time*, 6 vols. (Boston: Little, Brown, & Co., 1948–1977).

Malone, Dumas, *The Public Life of Thomas Cooper, 1783–1839* (New Haven: Yale University Press, 1926).

Malone, Kathryn R., "The Fate of Revolutionary Republicanism in Early National Virginia," *Journal of the Early Republic*, vol. 7 (Spring 1987): 27–51.

Martin, Marcus L., and Kirt von Daacke, *President's Commission on Slavery and the University: Report to President Teresa A. Sullivan* (Charlottesville: University of Virginia Press, 2018).

Mason, Francis Norton, *John Norton & Sons: Merchants of London and Virginia* (Richmond: Dietz Press, 1937).

Mason, Matthew, *Slavery and Politics in the Early American Republic* (Chapel Hill: University of North Carolina Press, 2006).

Mattern, David B., et al., eds., *Papers of James Madison, Retirement Series*, 4 vols. to date (Charlottesville: University of Virginia Press, 2009–).

Maury, James, *To Christians of Every Denomination Among Us, Especially Those of the Established Church, an Address Enforcing an Inquiry into the Grounds of the Pretensions of the Preachers, Called Anabaptists, to an Extraordinary Mission from Heaven to Preach the Gospel* (Annapolis: Anne Catharine Green, 1771).

Maxwell, William, *Memoir of the Rev. John H. Rice, D.D., First Professor of Christian Theology in Union Theological Seminary, Virginia* (Philadelphia: J. Whetham, 1835).

Mays, David John, *Edmund Pendleton, A Biography, 1721–1803*, 2 vols. (Cambridge: Harvard University Press, 1952).

Mays, David John, ed., *The Letters and Papers of Edmund Pendleton, 1734–1803*, 2 vols. (Charlottesville: University of Virginia Press, 1967).

McColley, Robert, *Slavery and Jeffersonian Virginia* (Urbana: University of Illinois Press, 1964).

McCoy, Drew R., "James Madison and Visions of American Nationality in the Confederation Period: A Regional Perspective," in Richard Beeman, Stephen Botein, and Edward C. Carter II, eds., *Beyond Confederation: Origins of the Constitution and American National Identity* (Chapel Hill: University of North Carolina Press, 1987): 226–58.

McDonnell, Michael A., *The Politics of War: Race, Class, and Conflict in Revolutionary Virginia* (Chapel Hill: University of North Carolina Press, 2007).

McGroarty, William Buckner, "Alexandria's Lancasterian Schools," *William & Mary Quarterly*, 2nd ser., vol. 21 (Apr. 1941): 111–18.

McLean, Robert Colin, *George Tucker: Moral Philosopher and Man of Letters* (Chapel Hill: University of North Carolina Press, 1961).

McPherson, Christopher, *A Short History of the Life of Christopher McPherson* (Lynchburg: Virginian Job Office, 1855).

Mead, Edward C., *Historic Homes of the South-West Mountains, Virginia* (Philadelphia: J. B. Lippincott Co., 1899).

Meade, William, *Old Churches, Ministers, and Families of Virginia*, 2 vols. (Philadelphia: J. B. Lippincott Co., 1857).

Mercer, Charles Fenton, *A Discourse on Public Education Delivered in the Church at Princeton* (Princeton: D. A. Borrenstein, 1826).

Meyers, Terry L, "A First Look at the Worst: Slavery and Race Relations at the College of William & Mary," *William & Mary Bill of Rights Journal*, vol. 16 (2008): 1141–68.

Meyers, Terry L., "Thinking About Slavery at the College of William & Mary," *William & Mary Bill of Rights*, vol. 21 (2013): 1215–57.

Mills, Frederick V., *Bishops by Ballot: An Eighteenth-Century Ecclesiastical Revolution* (New York: Oxford University Press, 1978).

Moore, Margaret DesChamps, ed., "Letters of John Holt Rice to Thomas Chalmers, 1817–1819," *Virginia Magazine of History and Biography*, vol. 67 (July 1959): 307–17.

Morgan, Philip D., *Slave Counterpoint: Black Culture in the Eighteenth-Century Chesapeake and Lowcountry* (Chapel Hill: University of North Carolina Press, 1998).

Morpurgo, Jack E., *Their Majesties' Royall Colledge: William & Mary in the Seventeenth and Eighteenth Centuries* (Washington, D.C.: Hennage Creative Printers, 1976).

Morrow, George T., *Williamsburg at Dawn: The Duel That Touched Off a Revolution in Arthur Lee* (Williamsburg: Telford Publications, 2011).

Morton, Richard L., *Colonial Virginia*, 2 vols. (Chapel Hill: University of North Carolina Press, 1960).

Nash, Gary, and Graham R. G. Hodges, *Friends of Liberty: Thomas Jefferson, Tadeusz Kosciuszko, and Agrippa Hull* (New York: Basic Books, 2008).

Neef, Joseph, *Sketch of a Plan and Method of Education, Founded on an Analysis of Human Faculties, and Natural Reason, Suitable for the Offspring of a Free People and for All Rational Beings* (Philadelphia: Neef, 1808).

Neem, Johann N., *Democracy's Schools: The Rise of Public Education in America* (Baltimore: Johns Hopkins University Press, 2017).

Neem, Johann N., "The Early Republic: Thomas Jefferson's Philosophy of History and the Future of American Christianity," in Charles Mathewes and Christopher McNight Nichols, eds., *Prophesies of Godlessness: Predictions of America's Imminent Secularization, from the Puritans to the Present Day* (New York: Oxford University Press, 2008): 35–52.

Neem, Johann N., "'To Diffuse Knowledge More Generally Through the Mass of the People': Thomas Jefferson on Individual Freedom and the Distribution of Knowledge," in Robert M. S. McDonald, ed., *Light & Liberty: Thomas Jefferson and the Power of Knowledge* (Charlottesville: University of Virginia Press, 2012): 47–74.

Nelson, John K., *A Blessed Company: Parishes, Parsons, and Parishioners in Anglican Virginia, 1690–1776* (Chapel Hill: University of North Carolina Press, 2001).

Nicholls, Michael L., *Whispers of Rebellion: Narrating Gabriel's Conspiracy* (Charlottesville: University of Virginia Press, 2012).

Noll, Mark A., *Princeton and the Republic, 1768–1822: The Search for a Christian Enlightenment in the Era of Samuel Stanhope Smith* (Princeton: Princeton University Press, 1989).

Novak, Steven J., *The Rights of Youth: American Colleges and Student Revolt, 1798–1815* (Cambridge: Harvard University Press, 1977).

Oakes, James, "Why Slaves Can't Read: The Political Significance of Jefferson's Racism," in James Gilreath, ed., *Thomas Jefferson and the Education of a Citizen* (Washington, D.C.: Library of Congress, 1999): 177–92.

Oast, Jennifer, *Institutional Slavery: Slaveholding Churches, Schools, Colleges, and Businesses in Virginia, 1680–1860* (New York: Cambridge University Press, 2016).

O'Brien, Michael, *Conjectures of Order: Intellectual Life and the American South, 1810–1860*, 2 vols. (Chapel Hill: University of North Carolina Press, 2004).

Ogilvie, James, *Cursory Reflexions on Government, Philosophy, and Education* (Alexandria: J. & J. D. Westcott, 1802).

Ogilvie, James, *Philosophical Essays, to Which Are Subjoined Copious Notes, Critical and Explanatory, and a Supplementary Narrative* (Philadelphia: John Conrad, 1816).

Onuf, Peter S., *Jefferson's Empire: The Language of American Nationhood* (Charlottesville: University of Virginia Press, 2000).

Onuf, Peter S., *The Mind of Thomas Jefferson* (Charlottesville: University of Virginia Press, 2007).

Onuf, Peter S., and Jane Ellen Lewis, eds., *Sally Hemings and Thomas Jefferson: History, Memory, and Civic Culture* (Charlottesville: University Press of Virginia, 1999).

Osborne, Ruby Orders, *The Crisis Years: The College of William & Mary in Virginia, 1800–1827* (Richmond: Dietz Press, 1989).

O'Shaughnessy, Andrew Jackson, *The Men Who Lost America: British Leadership, the American Revolution, and the Fate of the Empire* (New Haven: Yale University Press, 2013).

Ostrom, John Ward, ed., *The Letters of Edgar Allan Poe*, 2 vols. (Cambridge: Harvard University Press, 1948).

Pace, Robert, *Halls of Honor: College Men in the Old South* (Baton Rouge: Louisiana State University Press, 2004).

Page, John, "Autobiography," *Virginia Historical Register and Literary Note Book*, vol. 3 (Richmond: MacFarlane & Fergusson, 1850): 142–51.

Pappas, George S., *To the Point: The United States Military Academy, 1802–1902* (Westport, Conn.: Praeger, 1993).

Paulding, James Kirke, *Letters from the South by a Northern Man*, 2 vols. (New York: Harper & Brothers, 1835).

Perry, William Stevens, *Historical Collections Relating to the American Colonial Church*, 2 vols. (New York: AMS Press, 1969, reprint of Hartford, 1870–78).

Peterson, Merrill D., ed., *Visitors to Monticello* (Charlottesville: University Press of Virginia, 1989).

Peterson, Norma Lois, *Littleton Waller Tazewell* (Charlottesville: University Press of Virginia, 1983).

Pickering, Octavius, ed., *The Life of Timothy Pickering*, 4 vols. (Boston: Little, Brown & Co., 1867).

Pollin, Burton R., "Godwin's Letter to Ogilvie, Friend of Jefferson, and the Federalist Propaganda," *Journal of the History of Ideas*, vol. 28 (July–Sept. 1967): 432–44.

Pybus, Cassandra, "Jefferson's Faulty Math: The Question of Slave Defections in the American Revolution," *William & Mary Quarterly*, 3rd. ser., vol. 62 (Apr. 2005): 243–64.

Ragland, Thomas, *Defence Before a General Court-Martial Held at West-Point, in the State of New-York, in the Month of May, Eighteen Hundred and Nineteen* (Newburgh, N.Y.: Uriah C. Lewis, 1819).

Ragsdale, Bruce, *A Planters' Republic: The Search for Economic Independence in Revolutionary Virginia* (Madison, Wis.: Madison House, 1996).

Randolph, Edmund, "Essay on the Revolutionary History of Virginia, 1774–1782," *Virginia Magazine of History and Biography*, vol. 43 (Apr. 1935): 113–38; (July 1935): 209–32; (Oct. 1935): 294–315; vol. 44 (Jan. 1936): 35–50; (Apr. 1936): 105–15; (July 1936): 223–31; (Oct. 1936): 312–22; vol. 45 (Jan. 1937): 46–47.

Randolph, John, *Letters of John Randolph, to a Young Relative: Embracing a Series of Years, from Early Youth, to Mature Manhood* (Philadelphia: Carey, Lea & Blanchard, 1834).

Ravitch, Diane, *Left Back: A Century of Failed School Reforms* (New York: Simon & Schuster, 2000).

Reardon, John J., *Edmund Randolph: A Biography* (New York: Macmillan, 1974).

Reese, George, ed., *The Official Papers of Francis Fauquier, Lieutenant Governor of Virginia, 1758–1768*, 3 vols. (Charlottesville: University Press of Virginia, 1983).

Rice, John Holt, *An Illustration of the Character & Conduct of the Presbyterian Church in Virginia* (Richmond: DuVal & Burke, 1816).

Rice, John Holt. *A Sermon to Young Women* (Richmond: W. W. Gray, 1819).

Rice, John Holt, ed., *The Virginia Evangelical and Literary Magazine*, 10 vols. (Richmond: N. Pollard, 1816–27).

Risjord, Norman K., "The Virginia Federalists," *Journal of Southern History*, vol. 33 (Nov. 1967): 486–517.

Robert, Joseph C., "William Wirt, Virginian," *Virginia Magazine of History and Biography*, vol. 80 (Oct. 1972): 387–41.

Roberts, Kenneth, and Anna M. Roberts, eds., *Moreau de St. Méry's American Journey, 1793–1798* (Garden City, N.Y.: Doubleday & Co., 1947).

Robson, David W., *The College in the Era of the American Revolution, 1750–1800* (Westport, Conn.: Greenwood Press, 1985).

Rothman, Joshua, D., "James Callender and Social Knowledge of Interracial Sex in Antebellum Virginia," in Peter S. Onuf, and Jane Ellen Lewis, eds., *Sally Hemings and Thomas Jefferson: History, Memory, and Civic Culture* (Charlottesville: University of Virginia Press, 1999): 87–113.

Roulhac Hamilton, J. G. de, ed., *The Papers of Thomas Ruffin*, 3 vols. (Raleigh: Edwards & Broughton Printing Co., 1918–20).

Royster, Charles, *A Revolutionary People at War: The Continental Army and American Character, 1775–1783* (Chapel Hill: University of North Carolina Press, 1979).

Schoen, Brian, "Calculating the Price of Union: Republican Economic Nationalism and the Origins of Southern Sectionalism, 1790–1828," *Journal of the Early Republic*, vol. 23 (Summer 2003): 173–206.

Schoepf, Johann David, *Travels in the Confederation, 1783–1784*, 2 vols. (Philadelphia: W. J. Campbell, 1911).

Schwarz, Philip J., *Migrants Against Slavery: Virginians & the Nation* (Charlottesville: University of Virginia Press, 2001).

Scott, Diana, *Louisa Maxwell Holmes Cocke, 1788–1843* (Palmyra: Fluvanna County Historical Society, 1992).

Scott, Winfield, *Memoirs of Lieut.-Genl. Scott, LL.D., Written by Himself*, 2 vols. (New York: Sheldon & Co., 1864).

Schwarz, Philip J., "Gabriel's Challenge: Slaves and Crime in Late Eighteenth-Century Virginia," *Virginia Magazine of History and Biography*, vol. 90 (1982): 283–309.

Selby, John, *The Revolution in Virginia, 1775–1783* (Williamsburg: Colonial Williamsburg Foundation, 1988).

Shackelford, George Green, ed., *Collected Papers to Commemorate Fifty Years of the Monticello Association of the Descendants of Thomas Jefferson*, 2 vols. (Princeton: Princeton University Press, 1965).

Shackelford, George Green, *George Wythe Randolph and the Confederate Elite* (Athens: University of Georgia Press, 1988).

Shawen, Neil McDowell, "Thomas Jefferson and a 'National' University: The Hidden Agenda for Virginia," *Virginia Magazine of History and Biography*, vol. 92 (July 1984): 309–35.

Sidbury, James, *Ploughshares into Swords: Race, Rebellion, and Identity in Gabriel's Virginia, 1730–1810* (New York: Cambridge University Press, 1997).

Sidbury, James, "Saint Domingue in Virginia: Ideology, Local Meanings, and Resistance to Slavery, 1790–1800," *Journal of Southern History*, vol. 63 (1997): 531–52.

Silber, Kate, *Pestalozzi: The Man and his Work* (London: Routledge & Kegan Paul, 1973).

Silverman, Kenneth, *Edgar A. Poe: Mournful and Never-Ending Remembrance* (New York: HarperCollins, 1991).

Simon, James F., *What Kind of Nation: Thomas Jefferson, John Marshall, and the Epic Struggle to Create a United States* (New York: Simon & Schuster, 2002).

Sloan, Herbert E., *Principle and Interest: Thomas Jefferson and the Problem of Debt* (New York: Oxford University Press, 1995).

Smith, Daniel Blake, *Inside the Great House: Planter Family Life in Eighteenth-Century Chesapeake Society* (Ithaca: Cornell University Press, 1980).

Smith, Daniel Blake, *Our Family Dreams: The Fletchers' Adventures in Nineteenth-Century America* (New York: St. Martin's Press, 2016).

Smith, John Augustine, *A Syllabus of the Lectures Delivered to the Senior Students in the College of William & Mary on Government* (Philadelphia: Thomas Debson & Son, 1817).

Smith, Margaret Bayard, *The First Forty Years of Washington Society: Portrayed by the Family Letters of Mrs. Samuel Harrison Smith* (New York: Charles Scribner's Sons, 1906).

Smyth, J. F. D, *A Tour in the United States of America: Containing An Account of the Present Situation of That Country*, 2 vols. (London: G. Robinson, 1784).

Sobel, Mechal, *The World They Made Together: Black and White Values in Eighteenth-Century Virginia* (Princeton: Princeton University Press, 1987).

Spangler, Jewel L, *Virginians Reborn: Anglican Monopoly, Evangelical Dissent, and the Rise of the Baptists in the Late Eighteenth Century* (Charlottesville: University of Virginia Press, 2008).

Speece, Conrad, *The Mountaineer* (Staunton: Isaac Collett, 1823).

Stagg, J. C. A., et al., eds., *Papers of James Madison, Presidential Series*, 12 vols. to date (Charlottesville: University Press of Virginia, 1984–)

Stagg, J. C. A., et al., eds., *Papers of James Madison, Secretary of State Series*, 13 vols. to date (Charlottesville: University of Virginia Press, 1986–).

Stanton, Lucia C., "The Other End of the Telescope: Jefferson Through the Eyes of His Slaves," *William & Mary Quarterly*, 3rd ser., vol. 57 (Jan. 2000): 139–52.

Stanton, Lucia C., *"Those Who Labor for My Happiness": Slavery at Thomas Jefferson's Monticello* (Charlottesville: University of Virginia Press, 2012).

Stanton, Lucia C., and James A. Bear, Jr., eds., *Jefferson's Memorandum Books: Accounts, with Legal Records and Miscellany, 1767-1826*, vol. 1 (Princeton: Princeton University Press, 1997).

Steele, Brian, "Thomas Jefferson's Gender Frontier," *Journal of American History*, vol. 95 (June 2008): 17-42.

Stovall, Floyd, "Edgar Poe and the University of Virginia," *Virginia Quarterly Review*, vol. 43 (Spring 1967): 297-317.

Stowe, Steven M., "Private Emotions and Public Man in Early Nineteenth-Century Virginia," *History of Education Quarterly*, vol. 27 (Spring 1987): 75-81.

Stowe, Steven M. "Rhetoric of Authority: The Making of Social Values in Planter Family Correspondence," *Journal of American History*, vol. 73 (Mar. 1987): 916-33.

Sugrue, Michael, "'We Desired Our Future Leaders to be Educated Men': South Carolina College, the Defense of Slavery, and the Declaration of Secessionist Politics," in Roger L. Geiger, ed., *The American College in the Nineteenth Century* (Nashville: Vanderbilt University Press, 2000): 91-114.

Swem, Earl G., ed., "Notes Relating to Some of the Students Who Attended the College of William & Mary, 1753-1770," *William & Mary Quarterly*, 2nd ser., vol. 1 (Jan. 1921): 27-41.

Swem, Earl G., "Notes Relative to Some of the Students Who Attended the College of William & Mary, 1770-1778," *William & Mary Quarterly*, 2nd ser., vol. 1 (Apr. 1921): 116-30.

Swem, Earl G. ed., "Some Notes on the Four Forms of the Oldest Building of William & Mary College," *William & Mary Quarterly*, 2nd ser., vol. 8 (Oct. 1928): 217-307.

Swift, David E., "Thomas Jefferson, John Holt Rice, and Education in Virginia, 1815-1825," *Journal of Presbyterian History*, vol. 49 (Spring 1971): 32-58.

Sydnor, Charles S., *Gentlemen Freeholders: Political Practices in Washington's Virginia* (Chapel Hill: University of North Carolina Press, 1952).

Sydnor, William, "David Griffith—Chaplain, Surgeon, Patriot," *Historical Magazine of the Protestant Episcopal Church*, vol. 44 (Sept. 1975): 247-56.

Sydnor, William, "Doctor Griffith of Virginia: The Breaking of a Church Leader, September 1786—August 3, 1789," *Historical Magazine of the Protestant Episcopal Church*, vol. 45 (June 1976): 113-32.

Sydnor, William, "Doctor Griffith of Virginia: Emergence of a Church Leader, May 1779—June, 3, 1786," *Historical Magazine of the Protestant Episcopal Church*, vol. 45 (Mar. 1976): 5-24.

Syrett, Harold C., et al., eds., *The Papers of Alexander Hamilton*, 27 vols. (New York: Columbia University Press, 1961-87).

Tarter, Brent, *The Grandees of Government: The Origins and Persistence of Undemocratic Politics in Virginia* (Charlottesville: University of Virginia Press, 2013).

Tate, Thad W., "The Colonial College, 1693–1782," in Susan H. Godson et al., eds., *The College of William & Mary: A History*, 2 vols. (Williamsburg: King and Queen Press, 1993), vol. 1:1–162.

Tate, Thad W., "The Coming of the Revolution in Virginia: Britain's Challenge to Virginia's Ruling Class, 1763–1776," *William & Mary Quarterly*, 3rd ser., vol. 19 (July 1962): 323–43.

Tate, Thad W., *The Negro in Eighteenth-Century Williamsburg* (Williamsburg: Colonial Williamsburg, 1965).

Taylor, Alan, *The Internal Enemy: Slavery and War in Virginia, 1772–1832* (New York: W. W. Norton, 2013).

Thomas, Arthur Dicken, Jr., "Reasonable Revivalism: Presbyterian Evangelization of Educated Virginians, 1787–1837," *Journal of Presbyterian History*, vol. 61 (Fall 1983): 316–34.

Thomas, Dwight, and David K. Jackson, eds., *The Poe Log: A Documentary Life of Edgar Allan Poe, 1809–1849* (Boston: G. K. Hall & Co., 1987).

Thomas, George, *The Founders and the Idea of a National University: Constituting the American Mind* (New York: Cambridge University Press, 2015).

Thompson, Gary R., ed., *Edgar Allan Poe, 1809–1849: Essays and Reviews* (New York: Library of America, 1984).

Thompson, Thomas C., "Perceptions of a 'Deist Church' in Early National Virginia," in Garrett Ward Sheldon and Daniel L. Dreisbach, eds., *Religion and Political Culture in Jefferson's Virginia* (New York: Bowman & Littlefield, 2000): 41–58.

Thomson, Robert Polk, "The Reform of the College of William & Mary, 1763–1800," *Proceedings of the American Philosophical Society*, vol. 115 (June 1971): 187–213.

Ticknor, George, *Life, Letters, and Journals of George Ticknor*, 2 vols. (Boston: Houghton Mifflin Co., 1909).

Towles, Louis P., "A Matter of Honor at South Carolina College, 1822," *South Carolina Historical Magazine*, vol. 94 (Jan. 1993): 6–18.

Tucker, George, "Autobiography of George Tucker," *Bermuda Historical Quarterly*, vol. 18 (Autumn and Winter 1961): 73–159.

Tucker, George, *Essays on Various Subjects of Taste, Morals, and National Policy* (Georgetown, D.C.: Joseph Milligan, 1822).

Tucker, George, *Letter to a Member of the General Assembly of Virginia, on the Subject of the Late Conspiracy of the Slaves; with a Proposal for their Colonization* (Baltimore: Bonsal and Niles, 1801).

Tucker, George, *Letters from Virginia Translated from the French* (Baltimore: Fielding Lucas, Jr., 1816).

Tucker, George, *The Life of Thomas Jefferson, Third President of the United States*, 2 vols. (Philadelphia: Carey, Lea & Blanchard, 1837).

Tucker, George, *The Valley of the Shenandoah: or, Memoirs of the Graysons*, 3 vols. (New York: C. Wiley, 1825).

Tucker, St. George, *A Dissertation on Slavery: With a Proposal for the Gradual Aboli-tion of It in the State of Virginia* (Philadelphia: Mathew Carey, 1796).

Tucker, St. George, *A Letter to the Rev. Jedediah Morse, A.M., Author of the American Universal Geography* (Richmond: Thomas Nicolson, 1795), reprinted in *William & Mary Quarterly*, 1st. ser., vol. 2 (July 1893): 181–97.

Tutwiler, Henry, *Address of H. Tutwiller, A.M., LL.D., of Alabama Before the Alumni Society of the University of Virginia, Thursday, June 29th, 1882* (Charlottesville: Charlottesville Chronicle Book & Job Office, 1882).

Tyler, Lyon G., "Early Courses and Professors at William & Mary College," *William & Mary Quarterly*, 1st ser., vol. 14 (Oct 1905): 71–83.

Tyler, Lyon G., "Education in Colonial Virginia, Part IV: The Higher Education," *William & Mary Quarterly*, 1st ser., vol. 6 (Jan. 1898): 171–87.

Tyler, Lyon G., ed., "Glimpses of Old College Life," *William & Mary Quarterly*, 1st ser., vol. 8 (Apr. 1900): 213–27, and vol. 9 (July 1900): 18–23, and vol. 9 (Oct. 1900): 75–83.

Tyler, Lyon G., ed., "Letters of Francis Walker Gilmer," *Tyler's Quarterly Historical and Genealogical Magazine*, vol. 6 (July 1924): 16–21.

Tyler, Lyon G., ed., "Letters of Francis Walker Gilmer to John Randolph," *Tyler's Quarterly Historical and Genealogical Magazine*, vol. 6 (Jan 1925): 187–98.

Tyler, Lyon G., ed., "Letters of Francis Walker Gilmer to Thomas Walker Gilmer," *Tyler's Quarterly Historical and Genealogical Magazine*, vol. 6 (Apr. 1925): 240–49.

Tyler, Lyon G., ed., "Letters of James Monroe," *Tyler's Quarterly Historical and Gene-alogical Magazine*, vol. 4 (1923): 96–108, 405–11.

Tyler, Lyon G., ed., "Letters of Judge Thomas Todd of Kentucky to his Son at College," *William & Mary Quarterly*, 1st ser., vol. 22 (July 1913): 20–29.

Tyler, Lyon G., ed., *The Letters and Times of the Tylers*, 3 vols. (Richmond: Whittet & Shepperson, 1884–96).

Tyler, Lyon G., "Williamsburg—the Old Colonial Capital," *William & Mary Quar-terly*, 1st ser., vol. 16 (July 1907): 1–65.

Tyler-McGraw, Marie, *An African Republic: Black and White Virginians in the Mak-ing of Liberia* (Chapel Hill: University of North Carolina Press, 2007).

Tyler-McGraw, Marie, and Gregg D. Kimball, *In Bondage and Freedom: Antebel-lum Black Life in Richmond, Virginia* (Chapel Hill: University of North Carolina Press, 1988).

United States Congress, *American State Papers: Military Affairs*, vol. 2 (16th Con-gress, 1st Session) (Washington, D.C.: Gales & Seaton, 1834).

University of Virginia, *Enactments by the Rector and Visitors of the Univer-sity of Virginia for Constituting, Governing, and Conducting That Institution* (Charlottesville: C. P. McKennie, 1825).

Upton, Anthony F., "The Road to Power in Virginia in the Early Nineteenth Century," *Virginia Magazine of History and Biography*, vol. 62 (July 1954): 259–80.

Valsania, Maurizio, *Nature's Man: Thomas Jefferson's Philosophical Anthropology* (Charlottesville: University of Virginia Press, 2013).

Van Cleve, George William, *A Slaveholders' Union: Slavery, Politics, and the Constitution in the Early Republic* (Chicago: University of Chicago Press, 2010).

Van Schreeven, William J., Brent Tarter, and Robert L. Scribner, eds., *Revolutionary Virginia: The Road to Independence*, 7 vols. (Charlottesville: University Press of Virginia, 1973).

Vance, Joseph C., "Knives, Whips, and Randolphs on the Court House Lawn," *Magazine of Albemarle County History*, vol. 15 (1955–56): 28–35.

Varon, Elizabeth R., *We Mean to Be Counted: White Women and Politics in Antebellum Virginia* (Chapel Hill: University of North Carolina Press, 1998).

Von Briesen, Martha, ed., *The Letters of Elijah Fletcher* (Charlottesville: University Press of Virginia, 1965).

Von Daacke, Kirt, *Freedom Has a Face: Race, Identity, and Community in Jefferson's Virginia* (Charlottesville: University of Virginia Press, 2012).

Wagoner, Jennings L., Jr., "Honor and Dishonor at Mr. Jefferson's University: The Antebellum Years," *History of Education Quarterly*, vol. 26 (Summer 1986): 155–79.

Wagoner, Jennings L., Jr., *Jefferson and Education* (Charlottesville: Thomas Jefferson Foundation, 2004).

Wagoner, Jennings L., Jr., and Christine Coalwell McDonald, "Mr. Jefferson's Academy: An Educational Interpretation," in Robert M. S. McDonald, ed., *Thomas Jefferson's Military Academy: Founding West Point* (Charlottesville: University of Virginia Press, 2004): 118–53.

Waldstreicher, David, *Slavery's Constitution: From Revolution to Ratification* (New York: Hill & Wang, 2009).

Wall, Charles Coleman, Jr., "Students and Student Life at the University of Virginia, 1825–1861" (Ph.D. diss.: University of Virginia, 1978).

Watson, Samuel J., "Developing Republican Machines: West Point and the Struggle to Render the Officer Corps Safe for America, 1802–33," in Robert M. S. McDonald, ed., *Thomas Jefferson's Military Academy: Founding West Point* (Charlottesville: University of Virginia Press, 2004): 154–81.

Webster, Noah, "Diary, 1785–1786," in Emily Ellsworth Fowler Ford, ed., *Notes on the Life of Noah Webster*, 2 vols. (New York: privately printed, 1912).

Weld, Isaac, Jr., *Travels Through the States of North America and the Provinces of Upper and Lower Canada, During the Years 1795, 1796, and 1797*, 2 vols. (London: John Stockdale, 1800).

Wenger, Mark R., "Thomas Jefferson, the College of William & Mary, and the University of Virginia," *Virginia Magazine of History and Biography*, vol. 103 (July 1995): 339–74.

Wertenbaker, Thomas Jefferson, *Princeton, 1746–1896* (Princeton: Princeton University Press, 1946).

Whalen, Terence, *Edgar Allan Poe and the Masses: The Political Economy of Literature in Antebellum America* (Princeton: Princeton University Press, 1999).

White, William S., *Rev. William S. White, D.D., and His Times, 1800–1873, An Autobiography* (Richmond: Presbyterian Committee of Publications, 1891).

Wight, Willard E., and Robert J. Miller, eds., "The Journals of the Reverend Robert J. Miller, Lutheran Missionary in Virginia, 1811 and 1813," *Virginia Magazine of History and Biography*, vol. 61 (Apr. 1953): 141–66.

Wilson, Douglas L, "Jefferson and Literacy," in James Gilreath, ed., *Thomas Jefferson and the Education of a Citizen* (Washington, D.C.: Library of Congress, 1999): 79–90.

Wilson, James Southall, "The Personality of Poe," *Virginia Magazine of History and Biography*, vol. 67 (Apr. 1959): 131–42.

Wirt, William, *The British Spy, or Letters to a Member of the British Parliament* (Newburyport, Mass.: Repertory Office, 1804).

Wirt, William, *The Old Bachelor* (Richmond: Thomas Ritchie & Fielding Lucas, 1814).

Wirt, William, ed., *The Rainbow* (Richmond: Ritchie & Worsley, 1804).

Wolf, Eva Sheppard, *Race and Liberty in the New Nation: Emancipation in Virginia from the Revolution to Nat Turner's Rebellion* (Baton Rouge: Louisiana State University Press, 2006).

Wood, Gordon S., *Empire of Liberty: A History of the Early Republic, 1789–1815* (New York: Oxford University Press, 2009).

Wood, Gordon S., *The Radicalism of the American Revolution* (New York: Alfred A. Knopf, 1992).

Wood, Nicholas, "John Randolph of Roanoke and the Politics of Slavery in the Early Republic," *Virginia Magazine of History and Biography*, vol. 120 (April 2012): 106–43.

Woods, Edgar, *Albemarle County in Virginia* (Charlottesville: Michie Co., 1901).

Wright, Natalia, ed., *Washington Irving: Journals and Notebooks, Volume I, 1803–1806* (Madison: University of Wisconsin Press, 1969).

Wyllie, John Cooke, ed., "Observations Made During a Short Residence in Virginia: In a Letter from Thomas H. Palmer, May 30, 1814," *Virginia Magazine of History and Biography*, vol. 76 (Oct. 1968): 387–414.

Yarborough, Minnie Clare, ed., *The Reminiscences of William C. Preston* (Chapel Hill: University of North Carolina Press, 1933).

Zimmer, Anne Y., *Jonathan Boucher: Loyalist in Exile* (Detroit: Wayne State University Press, 1978).

INDEX

Page references in *italics* refer to figures.